S0-BAH-653

ATLA BIBLIOGRAPHY SERIES
edited by Dr. Kenneth E. Rowe

1. *A Guide to the Study of the Holiness Movement,* by Charles Edwin Jones. 1974.
2. *Thomas Merton: A Bibliography,* by Marquita E. Breit. 1974.
3. *The Sermon on the Mount: A History of Interpretation and Bibliography,* by Warren S. Kissinger. 1975.
4. *The Parables of Jesus: A History of Interpretation and Bibliography,* by Warren S. Kissinger. 1979.
5. *Homosexuality and the Judeo-Christian: An Annotated Bibliography,* by Thom Horner. 1981.
6. *A Guide to the Study of the Pentecostal Movement,* by Charles Edwin Jones. 1983.
7. *The Genesis of Modern Process Thought: A Historical Outline with Bibliography,* by George R. Lucas, Jr. 1983.
8. *A Presbyterian Bibliography,* by Harold B. Prince. 1983.
9. *Paul Tillich: A Comprehensive Bibliography...,* by Richard C. Crossman. 1983.
10. *A Bibliography of the Samaritans,* by Alan David Crown. 1984 (see no. 32).
11. *An Annotated and Classified Bibliography of English Literature Pertaining to the Ethiopian Orthodox Church,* by Jon Bonk. 1984.
12. *International Meditation Bibliography, 1950 to 1982,* by Howard R. Jarrell. 1984.
13. *Rabindranath Tagore: A Bibliography,* by Katherine Henn. 1985.
14. *Research in Ritual Studies: A Programmatic Essay and Bibliography,* by Ronald L. Grimes. 1985.
15. *Protestant Theological Education in America,* by Heather F. Day. 1985.
16. *Unconscious: A Guide to Sources,* by Natalino Caputi. 1985.
17. *The New Testament Apocrypha and Pseudepigrapha,* by James H. Charlesworth. 1987.
18. *Black Holiness,* by Charles Edwin Jones. 1987.
19. *A Bibliography on Ancient Ephesus,* by Richard Oster. 1987.
20. *Jerusalem, the Holy City: A Bibliography,* by James D. Purvis. Vol. I, 1988; vol. II, 1991.
21. *An Index to English Periodical Literature on the Old Testament and Ancient Near East Studies,* by William G. Hupper. Vol. I, 1987; vol. II, 1988; vol. III, 1990; vol. IV, 1990; vol. V, 1992; vol. VI, 1994. Vol. VII, 1998.
22. *John and Charles Wesley: A Bibliography,* by Betty M. Jarboe. 1987.
23. *A Scholar's Guide to Academic Journals in Religion,* by James Dawsey. 1988.
24. *An Oxford Movement and Its Leaders: A Bibliography of Secondary and Lesser Primary Sources,* by Lawrence N. Crumb. 1988; Supplement, 1993.

25. *A Bibliography of Christian Worship*, by Bard Thompson. 1989.

26. *The Disciples and American Culture: A Bibliography of Works by Disciples of Christ Members, 1866–1984*, by Leslie R. Galbraith and Heather F. Day. 1990.

27. *The Yogacara School of Buddhism: A Bibliography*, by John Powers. 1991.

28. *The Doctrine of the Holy Spirit: A Bibliography Showing Its Chronological Development* (2 vols.), by Esther Dech Schandorff. 1995.

29. *Rediscovery of Creation: A Bibliographical Study of the Church's Response to the Environmental Crisis*, by Joseph K. Sheldon. 1992.

30. *The Charismatic Movement: A Guide to the Study of Neo-Pentecostalism with Emphasis on Anglo-American Sources*, by Charles Edwin Jones. 1995.

31. *Cities and Churches: An International Bibliography* (3 vols.), by Loyde H. Hartley. 1992.

32. *A Bibliography of the Samaritans*, 2nd ed., by Alan David Crown. 1993.

33. *The Early Church: An Annotated Bibliography of Literature in English*, by Thomas A. Robinson. 1993.

34. *Holiness Manuscripts: A Guide to Sources Documenting the Wesleyan Holiness Movement in the United States and Canada*, by William Kostlevy. 1994.

35. *Of Spirituality: A Feminist Perspective*, by Clare B. Fischer. 1995.

36. *Evangelical Sectarianism in the Russian Empire and the USSR: A Bibliographic Guide*, by Albert Wardin, Jr. 1995.

37. *Hermann Sasse: A Bibliography*, by Ronald R. Feuerhahn. 1995.

38. *Women in the Biblical World: A Study Guide. Vol. I: Women in the World of Hebrew Scripture*, by Mayer I. Gruber, 1995.

39. *Women and Religion in Britain and Ireland: An Annotated Bibliography from the Reformation to 1993*, by Dale A. Johnson, 1995.

40. *Emil Brunner: A Bibliography*, by Mark G. McKim, 1996.

41. *The Book of Jeremiah: An Annotated Bibliography*, by Henry O. Thompson, 1996.

42. *The Book of Amos: An Annotated Bibliography*, by Henry O. Thompson, 1997.

An Index to
English Periodical Literature
on the Old Testament
and
Ancient Near Eastern Studies

Volume VII

Compiled and Edited by

William G. Hupper

ATLA Bibliography Series, No. 21

Research is the process of going up alleys to see if they are blind.
... *Marston Bates*

The American Theological Library Association, and
The Scarecrow Press, Inc.
Lanham MD, & London 1998

NORTH PARK UNIVERSITY
LIBRARY
3225 W. FOSTER AVE.
CHICAGO, IL 60625

Cover illustration is of a bronze lion cub from the Persian period excavated at Mizpeh Yamim by Rafael Frankel on behalf of Haifa University. Used by permission.

British Library Cataloguing-in-Publication data available

Library of Congress Cataloging-in-Publication Data
(Revised for volume 7)

Hupper, William G.
  An index to English periodical literature on the Old
Testament and ancient Near Eastern studies.

  (ATLA bibliography series no. 21)
  1. Bible. O.T.—Periodicals—Indexes. 2. Middle
East—Periodicals—Indexes. I. American Theological
Library Association. II. Title. III. Series.
Z 7772.A1H86 1987 [BS1171.2]   016.221   86-31448
  ISBN 0-8108-1984-8 (v. 1)
  ISBN 0-8108-2126-5 (v. 2)
  ISBN 0-8108-2319-5 (v. 3)
  ISBN 0-8108-2393-4 (v. 4)
  ISBN 0-8108-2618-6 (v. 5)
  ISBN 0-8108-2822-7 (v. 6)
  ISBN 0-8108-3493-6 (v. 7)

Copyright © 1998 by William G. Hupper
Manufactured in the United States of America
Printed on acid-free paper

Sem.
Ref.
Z
7772
H86
1987
v.7

Table of Contents

Table of Contents

Table of Contents

Table of Contents

Table of Contents

Table of Contents

---

1.   Listed here as a matter of convenience due to geographical distribution. Actual
linguistic family has not been determined.

Table of Contents

Table of Contents

Preface

After nearly a four-year hiatus in publication, Volume VII is now complete. Volume VIII, covering theological studies and Qumran literature, has already been transferred from file cards into the computer and should follow shortly. Volume IX, an author and subject index, which includes additions and corrections, is partially finished, and will complete the project.

Since it is more than ten years since the publication of the first volume in this series, it was felt advisable to reiterate a few remarks made in the original preface. "Articles may not necessarily follow all the present library conventions, as more attention has been given to listing entries as near as possible to the exact title shown in the periodical from which they were derived. This includes variant spellings, italics, and underscores as they actually appear. Subdivisions of articles are listed in brackets at the end of a particular title, sometimes with page numbers, especially for lengthy articles.[1] Occasionally an editorial remark has been made indicating an outstanding bibliography or to show that an article was not continued. These remarks will be found at the end of a particular entry in brackets and italics."[2]

A word of explanation regarding the breakdown of this volume is necessary. While standard convention divides Cuneiform languages into categories such as Neo-, Late, Old, Standard, etc., no attempt at such a narrow classification has been made here. Rather, using the basic language as a main division, further subdivision is by literary genre where possible. In some cases where it was very difficult to conclude on a specific Cuneiform language, articles were placed under Akkadian - General Studies.

The completion of this volume could not have been accomplished without the assistance of several people who, though previously mentioned in connection with Volume V, have helped with the section on Ancient Near Eastern Literature: Dr. James K. Hoffmeier, Wheaton College, for reading the sections on Egyptian Literature; Jay Ellison, Ph.D. candidate, Harvard University; and Dr. James C. Moyer, Southwestern Missouri State University for checking many of the articles on Cuneiform early in the project. Assistance in the final stages of this volume was made possible by Scobie P. Smith, Ph.D. candidate, Harvard University. As always, thanks to Mrs. Florence Hall for her continued aid in proofreading the first draft of the entire manuscript and checking it against the original file cards.

---

1.   cf. Volume I, p. xxiii.
2.   cf. Volume I, p. xxi.

Additional thanks go to McAlister Library at Fuller Theological Seminary, Pasadena, California, and the library of Southern California School of Theology at Claremont, Claremont, California, for use of their facilities during the final phase of this volume.

Thanksgiving eve, 1997
Torrance, CA

Periodical Abbreviations*

A

A&A   *Art and Archaeology; the arts throughout the ages*
(Washington, DC, Baltimore, MD, 1914-1934)

A/R   *Action/Reaction* (San Anselmo, CA, 1967ff.)

A&S   *Antiquity and Survival* (The Hague, 1955-1962)

A(A)   *Anadolu (Anatolia)* (Ankara, 1956ff.) [Subtitle varies;
Volume 1-7 as: *Anatolia: Revue Annuelle
d'Archeologie*]

AA   *Acta Archaeologica* (Copenhagen, 1930ff.)

AAA   *Annals of Archaeology and Anthropology* (Liverpool,
1908-1948; Suspended, 1916-1920)

AAAS   *Annales archéologiques arabes Syriennes. Revue
d'Archéologie et d'Histoire* (Damascus, 1951ff.)
[Volumes 1-15 as: *Les Annales archéologiques de Syrie*
- Title Varies]

AAASH   *Acta Antiqua Academiae Scientiarum Hungaricae*
(Budapest, 1951ff.)

AAB   *Acta Archaeologica* (Budapest, 1951ff.)

AAI   *Anadolu Araştirmalari Istanbul Üniversitesi Edebiyat Fakültesi
eski Önasya Dilleri ve Kültürleri Kürsüsü Tarafindan
Čikarilir* (Istanbul, 1955ff.) [Supersedes: *Jahrbuch für
Kleinasiatische Forschungen*]

AAOJ   *American Antiquarian and Oriental Journal* (Cleveland,
Chicago 1878-1914)

AASCS   *Antichthon. The Australian Society for Classical Studies*
(Sydney, 1967ff.)

ABBTS   *The Alumni Bulletin [of] Bangor Theological Seminary*
(Bangor, ME; 1926ff.)

ABenR   *The American Benedictine Review* (St. Paul, 1950ff.)

ABR   *Australian Biblical Review* (Melbourne, 1951ff.)

Abr-N   *Abr-Nahrain, An Annual Published by the Department of
Middle Eastern Studies, University of Melbourne*
(Melbourne, 1959ff.)

ACM   *The American Church Monthly* (New York, 1917-1939)
[Volumes 43-45 as: *The New American Church Monthly*]

*All the journals indexed are listed in the Periodical Abbreviations even though no
specific citation may appear in the present volume. Although the titles of many foreign
language journals have been listed, only English language articles are included in this
index (except as noted). Articles from modern Hebrew language journals are referred to
by their English summary page.

Periodical Abbreviations

ACQ *American Church Quarterly* (New York, 1961ff.)
  [Volume 7 on as: *Church Theological Review*]

ACQR *The American Catholic Quarterly Review* (Philadelphia, 1876-1929)

ACR *The Australasian Catholic Record* (Sydney, 1924ff.)

ACSR *American Catholic Sociological Review* (Chicago, 1940ff.)
  [From Volume 25 on as: *Sociological Analysis*]

ADAJ *Annual of the Department of Antiquities of Jordan* (Amman, 1957ff.) [Volume 14 not published—destroyed by fire at the publishers]

AE *Annales d'Ethiopie* (Paris, 1955ff.)

AEE *Ancient Egypt and the East* (New York, London, Chicago, 1914-1935; Suspended, 1918-1919)

Aeg *Aegyptus: Rivista Italiana di Egittologia e di Papirologia* (Milan,1920ff.)

AER *American Ecclesiastical Review* (Philadelphia, New York, Cincinnati, Baltimore, 1889ff.) [Volumes 11-19 as: *Ecclesiastical Review*]

AfER *African Ecclesiastical Review: A Quarterly for Priests in Africa* (Masaka, Uganda, 1959ff.)

Aff *Affirmation* (Richmond, VA, 1966ff.) [Volume 1 runs from 1966 to 1980 inclusive]

AfO *Archiv für Orientforschung; Internationale Zeitschrift für Wissenschaft vom Vorderen Orient* (Berlin, 1923ff.)

AfRW *Archiv für Religionswissenschaft* (Leipzig, 1898-1941)

AHDO *Archives d'histoire du droit oriental et Revue internationale des droits de l'antiquité* (Brussels, 1937-38, 1947-1951, N.S., 1952-53)

AHR See *AmHR*

AIPHOS *Annuaire de l'institut de philologie et d'histoire orientales et slaves* (Brussels, 1932ff.)

AJ *The Antiquaries Journal. Being the Journal of the Society of Antiquaries of London* (London, 1921ff.)

AJA *The American Journal of Archaeology* (Baltimore, 1885ff.) [Original Series, 1885-1896 shown with *O. S;* Second Series shown without notation]

AJBA *The Australian Journal of Biblical Archaeology* (Sydney, 1968ff.) [Volume 1 runs from 1968 to 1971 inclusive]

AJP *The American Journal of Philology* (Baltimore, 1880ff.)

AJRPE *The American Journal of Religious Psychology and Education* (Worcester, MA, 1904-1915)

AJSL *The American Journal of Semitic Languages and Literatures* (Chicago, 1884-1941) [Volumes 1-11 as: *Hebraica*]

AJT *American Journal of Theology* (Chicago, 1897-1920)

Periodical Abbreviations

AL	*Archivum Linguisticum: A Review of Comparative Philology and General Linguistics* (Glasgow, 1949-1962)
ALUOS	*The Annual of the Leeds University Oriental Society* (Leiden,1958ff.)
Amb	*The Ambassador* (Wartburg Theological Seminary, Dubuque, IA, 1952ff.)
AmHR	*American Historical Review* (New York, Lancaster, PA, 1895ff.)
AmSR	*American Sociological Review* (Washington, DC, 1936ff.)
Anat	*Anatolica: Annuaire International pour les Civilisations de l'Asie Anterieure* (Leiden, 1967ff.)
ANQ	*Newton Theological Institute Bulletin* (Newton, MA, 1906ff.) [Title varies as: *Andover-Newton Theological Bulletin; Andover-Newton Quarterly, New Series,* beginning 1960ff.]
Anthro	*Anthropos; ephemeris internationalis ethnologica et linguistica* (Salzburg, Vienna, 1906ff.)
Antiq	*Antiquity: A Quarterly Review of Archaeology* (Gloucester, England, 1927ff.)
Anton	*Antonianum. Periodicum Philosophico-Theologicum Trimestre* (Rome, 1926ff.)
AO	*Acta Orientalia ediderunt Societates Orientales Bœtava Donica, Norvegica* (Lugundi Batavorum, Havniæ, 1922ff.)
AOASH	*Acta Orientalia Academiae Scientiarum Hungaricae* (Budapest, 1950ff.)
AOL	*Annals of Oriental Literature* (London, 1820-21)
APST	*Aberdeen Philosophical Society, Transactions* (Aberdeen, Scotland, 1840-1931)
AQ	*Augustana Quarterly* (Rock Island, IL, 1922-1948)
AQW	*Anthropological Quarterly* (Washington, DC, 1928ff.) [Volumes1-25 as: *Primitive Man*]
AR	*The Andover Review* (Boston, 1884-1893)
Arch	*Archaeology* (Cambridge, MA, 1948ff.)
Archm	*Archaeometry. Bulletin of the Research Laboratory for Archaeology and the History of Art, Oxford University* (Oxford, 1958ff.)
ARL	*The Archæological Review* (London, 1888-1890)
ArOr	*Archiv Orientální. Journal of the Czechoslovak Oriental Institute, Prague* (Vlašska, Czechoslovakia, 1929ff.)
AS	*Anatolian Studies: Journal of the British Institute of Archaeology at Ankara* (London, 1951ff.)
ASAE	*Annales du service des antiquités de l'Égypte* (Cairo, 1899ff.)

ASBFE   *Austin Seminary Bulletin. Faculty Edition* (Austin, TX; begins
           with volume 71*[sic]*, 1955ff.)
ASR   *Augustana Seminary Review* (Rock Island, IL, 1949-1967)
           [From volume 12 on as: *The Seminary Review*]
ASRB   *Advent Shield and Review* (Boston, 1844-45)
ASRec   *Auburn Seminary Record* (Auburn, NY, 1905-1932)
ASSF   *Acta Societatis Scientiarum Fennicae* (Helsinki, 1842-1926)
           [Suomen tideseura]
ASTI   *Annual of the Swedish Theological Institute (in Jerusalem)*
           (Jerusalem, 1962ff.)
ASW   *The Asbury Seminarian* (Wilmore, KY, 1946ff.)
AT   *Ancient Times: A Quarterly Review of Biblical Archaeology*
           (Melbourne, 1956-1961)
ATB   *Ashland Theological Bulletin* (Ashland, OH, 1968ff.)
ATG   *Advocate for the Testimony of God* (Richmond, VA, 1834-
           1839)
AThR   *The American Theological Review* (New York, 1859-1868)
           [*New Series* as: *American Presbyterian and Theological
           Review,* 1863-1868]
'Atiqot *'Atiqot: Journal of the Israel Department of Antiquities*
           (Jerusalem, 1955ff.)
ATJ   *Africa Theological Journal* (Usa River, Tanzania, 1968ff.)
ATR   *Anglican Theological Review* (New York, Lancaster, PA;
           1918ff.)
AubSRev *Auburn Seminary Review* (Auburn, NY, 1897-1904)
Aug   *Augustinianum* (Rome, 1961ff.)
AULLUÅ   *Acta Universitatis Lundensis. Lunds Universitets Årsskrift.
           Första Avdelningen. Teologi, Juridik och Humanistika
           Ämnen* (Lund, 1864-1904; *N.S.,* 1905-1964)
AUSS   *Andrews University Seminary Studies* (Berrien Springs, MI,
           1963ff.)
AusTR   *The Australasian Theological Review* (Highgate, South
           Australia, 1930-1966)

B

B   *Biblica* (Rome, 1920ff.)
BA   *The Biblical Archaeologist* (New Haven; Cambridge, MA;
           1938ff.)
Baby   *Babyloniaca Etudes de Philologie Assyro-Babylonienne* (Paris,
           1906-1937)

BASOR	*Bulletin of the American Schools of Oriental Research* (So. Hadley, MA; Baltimore, New Haven, Philadelphia, Cambridge, MA;1919ff.)
BASP	*Bulletin of the American Society of Papyrologists* (New Haven, 1963ff.)
BAVSS	*Beiträge zur Assyriologie und vergleichenden semitischen Sprachwissenschaft* (Leipzig, 1889-1927)
BBC	*Bulletin of the Bezan Club* (Oxford, 1925-1936)
BC	*Bellamine Commentary* (Oxon., England; 1956-1968)
BCQTR	*British Critic, Quarterly Theological Review and Ecclesiastical Record* (London, 1793-1843) [Superseded by: *English Review*]
BCTS	*Bulletin of the Crozer Theological Seminary* (Upland, PA, 1908-1934)
Bery	*Berytus. Archaeological Studies* (Copenhagen, 1934ff.)
BETS	*Bulletin of the Evangelical Theological Society* (Wheaton, IL, 1958ff.)
BFER	*British and Foreign Evangelical Review, and Quarterly Record of Christian Literature* (Edinburgh, London, 1852-1888)
BH	*Buried History. Quarterly Journal of the Australian Institute of Archaeology* (Melbourne, 1964-65; 1967ff.)
BibR	*Biblical Repertory* (Princeton, NJ; New York, 1825-1828)
BibT	*The Bible Today* (Collegeville, MN, 1962ff.)
BIES	*Bulletin of the Israel Exploration Society* (Jerusalem, 1937-1967) [*Yediot-* ידיעות בחקידת ארץ־ישראל ועתיקותיה-Begun as: *Bulletin of the Jewish Palestine Exploration Society* through volume 15. English summaries discontinued from volume 27 on as translations published in: *Israel Exploration Journal*]
BIFAO	*Bulletin de l'institut français d'archéologie orientale au Caire* (Cairo, 1901ff.)
BJ	*Biblical Journal* (Boston, 1842-1843)
BJRL	*Bulletin of the John Rylands Library* (Manchester, 1903ff.)
BM	*Bible Magazine* (New York, 1913-1915)
BMB	*Bulletin du Musée de Byrouth* (Paris, 1937ff.)
BN	*Bible Numerics: a Periodical Devoted to the Numerical Study of the Scriptures* (Grafton, MA; 1904)
BO	*Bibliotheca Orientalis* (Leiden, 1944ff.)
BofT	*Banner of Truth* (London, 1955ff.)
BOR	*The Babylonian and Oriental Record: A Monthly Magazine of the Antiquities of the East* (London, 1886-1901)
BQ	*Baptist Quarterly* (Philadelphia, 1867-1877)
BQL	*Baptist Quarterly* (London, 1922ff.)

BQR	*Baptist Quarterly Review* (Cincinnati, New York, Philadelphia, 1879-1892)
BQRL	*The British Quarterly Review* (London, 1845-1886)
BR	*Biblical Review* (New York, 1916-1932)
BRCM	*The Biblical Review and Congregational Magazine* (London, 1846-1850)
BRCR	*The Biblical Repository and Classical Review* (Andover, MA, 1831-1850) [Title varies as: *Biblical Repository; The Biblical Repository and Quarterly Observer; The American Biblical Repository*]
BRec	*Bible Record* (New York, 1903-1912) [Volume 1, #1-4 as: *Bible Teachers Training School, New York City, Bulletin*]
BRes	*Biblical Research: Papers of the Chicago Society of Biblical Research* (Amsterdam, Chicago, 1956ff.)
BS	*Bibliotheca Sacra* (New York, Andover, Oberlin, OH; St. Louis, Dallas, 1843, 1844ff.)
BSAJB	*British School of Archaeology in Jerusalem, Bulletin* (Jerusalem, 1922-1925)
BSOAS	*Bulletin of the School of Oriental and African Studies. University of London* (London, 1917ff.)
BSQ	*Bethel Seminary Quarterly* (St. Paul, MN; 1952ff.) [From Volume 13 on as: *Bethel Seminary Journal*]
BT	*Biblical Theology* (Belfast, 1950ff.)
BTF	*Bangalore Theological Forum* (Bangalore, India, 1967ff.)
BTPT	*Bijdragen Tijdschrift voor philosophie en theologie* (Maastricht, 1938ff.) [Title varies as: *Bijdragen. Tijdschrift voor filosofie en theologie*]
BTr	*Bible Translator* (London, 1950ff.)
BUS	*Bucknell University Studies* (Lewisburg, PA; 1941ff.) [From Volume 5 on as: *Bucknell Review*]
BVp	*Biblical Viewpoint* (Greenville, SC, 1967ff.)
BW	*Biblical World* (Chicago, 1893-1920)
BWR	*Bible Witness and Review* (London, 1877-1881)
BWTS	*The Bulletin of the Western Theological Seminary* (Pittsburgh, 1908-1931)
BZ	*Biblische Zeitschrift* (Paderborn, 1903-1939; *New Series,* 1957ff.) [*N.S.* shown without notation]

C

C&C	*Cross and Crown. A Thomistic Quarterly of Spiritual Theology* (St. Louis, 1949ff.)
CAAMA	*Cahiers archéologiques fin de l'antiquité et moyen age* (Paris, 1961ff.)

CAAST	*Connecticut Academy of Arts and Sciences, Transactions* (New Haven, 1866ff.)
Carm	*Carmelus. Commentarii ab instituto carmelitano editi* (Rome, 1954ff.)
CBQ	*Catholic Biblical Quarterly* (Washington, DC; 1939ff.)
CC	*Cross Currents* (West Nyack, NY; 1950ff.)
CCARJ	*Central Conference of American Rabbis Journal* (New York,1953ff.)
CCBQ	*Central Conservative Baptist Quarterly* (Minneapolis, 1958ff.) [From volume 9, #2 on as: *Central Bible Quarterly*]
CCQ	*Crisis Christology Quarterly* (Dubuque, IA; 1943-1949) [Volume 6 as: *Trinitarian Theology*]
CD	*Christian Disciple* (Boston, 1813-1823) [Superseded by: *Christian Examiner*]
CdÉ	*Chronique d'Égypte* (Brussels, 1925ff.)
CE	*Christian Examiner* (Boston, New York, 1824-1869)
Cent	*Centaurus. International Magazine of the History of Science and Medicine* (Copenhagen, 1950ff.)
Center	*The Center* (Atlanta, 1960-1965)
CFL	*Christian Faith and Life* (Columbia, SC, 1897-1939) [Title varies: Original Series as: *The Bible Student and Religious Outlook,* volumes 1 & 2 as: *The Religious Outlook;* New Series as: *The Bible Student;* Third Series as: *The Bible Student and Teacher;* several volumes as: *Bible Champion*]
ChgoS	*Chicago Studies* (Mundelein, IL; 1962ff.)
CJ	*Conservative Judaism* (New York, 1945ff.)
CJL	*Canadian Journal of Linguistics* (Montreal, 1954ff.)
CJRT	*The Canadian Journal of Religious Thought* (Toronto, 1924-1932)
CJT	*Canadian Journal of Theology* (Toronto, 1955ff.)
ClR	*Clergy Review* (London, 1931ff.)
CM	*The Clergyman's Magazine* (London, 1875-1897)
CMR	*Canadian Methodist Review* (Toronto, 1889-1895) [Volumes 1-5 as: *Canadian Methodist Quarterly*]
CNI	*Christian News from Israel* (Jerusalem, 1949ff.)
CO	*Christian Opinion* (New York, 1943-1948)
Coll	*Colloquium. The Australian and New Zealand Theological Review* (Auckland, 1964ff.) [Volume 1 through Volume 2, #1 as: *The New Zealand Theological Review*]
CollBQ	*The College of the Bible Quarterly* (Lexington, KY, 1909-1965) [Break in sequence between 1927 and 1937, resumes in 1938 with volume 15 duplicated in number]
ColTM	*Columbus Theological Magazine* (Columbus, OH; 1881-1910)
CongL	*The Congregationalist* (London, 1872-1886)

CongML	*The Congregational Magazine* (London, 1818-1845)
CongQB	*The Congregational Quarterly* (Boston, 1859-1878)
CongQL	*The Congregational Quarterly* (London, 1923-1958)
CongR	*The Congregational Review* (Boston, Chicago, 1861-1871) [Volumes 1-6 as: *The Boston Review*]
CongRL	*The Congregational Review* (London, 1887-1891)
ConstrQ	*The Constructive Quarterly. A Journal of the Faith, Work, and Thought of Christendom* (New York, London, 1913-1922)
Cont	*Continuum* (St. Paul, 1963-1970)
ContextC	*Context (Journal of the Lutheran School of Theology at Chicago)* (Chicago, 1967-1968)
ContR	*Contemporary Review* (London, New York, 1866ff.)
CovQ	*The Covenant Quarterly* (Chicago, 1941ff.) [Volume 1, #1 as: *Covenant Minister's Quarterly*]
CQ	*Crozer Quarterly* (Chester, PA; 1924-1952)
CQR	*Church Quarterly Review* (London, 1875-1968)
CR	*The Church Review* (New Haven, 1848-1891) [Title varies; Volume 62 not published]
CraneR	*The Crane Review* (Medford, MA; 1958-1968)
CRB	*The Christian Review* (Boston, Rochester; 1836-1863)
CRDSB	*Colgate-Rochester Divinity School Bulletin* (Rochester, NY; 1928-1967)
Crit	*Criterion* (Chicago, 1962ff.)
CRP	*The Christian Review: A Quarterly Magazine* (Philadelphia, 1932-1941)
CS	*The Cumberland Seminarian* (McKenzie, TN; Memphis; 1953-1970)
CSQ	*Chicago Seminary Quarterly* (Chicago, 1901-1907)
CSQC	*The Culver-Stockton Quarterly* (Canton, MO; 1925-1931)
CSSH	*Comparative Studies in Society and History: An International Quarterly* (The Hague, 1958ff.)
CT	*Christian Thought* (New York, 1883-1894)
CTJ	*Calvin Theological Journal* (Grand Rapids, 1966ff.)
CTM	*Concordia Theological Monthly* (St. Louis, 1930ff.)
CTPR	*The Christian Teacher [and Chronicle]* (London, 1835-1838; N.S., 1838-1844 as: *A Theological and Literary Journal*) [Continues as: *The Prospective Review; A Quarterly Journal of Theology and Literature*]
CTSB	*Columbia Theological Seminary Bulletin* (Columbia, SC; Decatur, GA; 1907ff.) [Title varies]
CTSP	*Catholic Theological Society, Proceedings* (Washington, DC; Yonkers, NY; 1948ff.)
CTSQ	*Central Theological Seminary Quarterly* (Dayton, OH; 1923-1931)

CUB   *Catholic University Bulletin* (Washington, DC; 1895-1914)
           [Volumes 1-20 only]

D

DDSR   *Duke Divinity School Review* (Durham, NC; 1936ff.)
            [Volumes 1-20 as: *The Duke School of Religion Bulletin;*
            Volumes 21-29 as: *Duke Divinity School Bulletin*]
DG   *The Drew Gateway* (Madison, NJ; 1930ff.)
DI   *Diné Israel. An Annual of Jewish Law and Israeli Family*
            Law דיני ישראל, שנתון למשפט עברי ולדיני
            משפחה בישראל (Jerusalem, 1969ff.)
DJT   *Dialogue: A Journal of Theology* (Minneapolis, 1962ff.)
DownsR   *Downside Review* (Bath, 1880ff.)
DQR   *Danville Quarterly Review* (Danville, KY; Cincinnati;
            1861-1864)
DR   *Dublin Review* (London, 1836-1968) [Between 1961 and 1964
            as: *Wiseman Review*]
DS   *Dominican Studies. A Quarterly Review of Theology and
            Philosophy* (Oxford, 1948-1954)
DSJ   *The Dubuque Seminary Journal* (Dubuque, IA; 1966-1967)
DSQ   *Dubuque Seminary Quarterly* (Dubuque, IA; 1947-1949)
            [Volume 3, #3 not published]
DTCW   *Dimension: Theology in Church and World* (Princeton, NJ;
            1964-1969) [Volumes 1 & 2 as: *Dimension* ; New
            format beginning in 1966 with full title, beginning again
            with Volume 1]
DTQ   *Dickinson's Theological Quarterly* (London, 1875-1883)
            [Superseded by *John Lobb's Theological Quarterly*]
DUJ   *The Durham University Journal* (Durham, 1876ff.; *N.S.,*
            1940ff.) [Volume 32 of *O.S.* = Volume 1 of *N.S.*]
DUM   *Dublin University Magazine* (Dublin, London, 1833-1880)
DunR   *The Dunwoodie Review* (Yonkers, NY; 1961ff.)

E

EgR   *Egyptian Religion* (New York, 1933-1936)
EI   *Eretz-Israel. Archaeological, Historical and Geographical
            Studies* (Jerusalem, 1951ff.) ארץ-ישראל,

            מחקרים בידיעת הארץ ועתיקותיה
            [English Summaries from Volume 3 on]

EJS	*Archives européennes de Sociologie / European Journal of Sociology / Europäisches Archiv für Soziologie* (Paris, 1960ff.)
EN	*The Everlasting Nation* (London, 1889-1892)
EQ	*Evangelical Quarterly* (London, 1929ff.)
ER	*Evangelical Review* (Gettysburg, PA; 1849-1870) [From Volume 14 on as: *Evangelical Quarterly Review*]
ERCJ	*Edinburgh Review, or Critical Journal* (Edinburgh, London, 1802-1929)
ERG	*The Evangelical Repository: A Quarterly Magazine of Theological Literature* (Glasgow, 1854-1888)
ERL	*The English Review, or Quarterly Journal of Ecclesiastical and General Literature* (London, 1844-1853) [Continues *British Critic*]
ESS	*Ecumenical Study Series* (Indianapolis, 1955-1960)
ET	*The Expository Times* (Aberdeen, Edinburgh, 1889ff.)
ETL	*Ephemerides Theologicae Lovanienses* (Notre Dame, 1924ff.)
Eud	*Eudemus. An International Journal Devoted to the History of Mathematics and Astronomy* (Copenhagen, 1941)
Exp	*The Expositor* (London, 1875-1925)
Exped	*Expedition* (Philadelphia, 1958ff.) [Continues: *The University Museum Bulletin*]

F

F&T	*Faith and Thought* (London, 1958ff.) [Supersedes: *Journal of the Transactions of the Victoria Institute, or Philosophical Society of Great Britain*]
FBQ	*The Freewill Baptist Quarterly* (Providence, London, Dover, 1853-1869)
FDWL	*Friends of Dr.Williams's Library (Lectures)* (Cambridge, Oxford, 1948ff.)
FLB	*Fuller Library Bulletin* (Pasadena, CA; 1949ff.)
FO	*Folia Orientalia* (Kraków, 1960ff.)
Focus	*Focus. A Theological Journal* (Willowdale, Ontario, 1964-1968)
Folk	*Folk-Lore: A Quarterly Review of Myth, Tradition, Institution & Custom being The Transactions of the Folk-Lore Society And Incorporating the Archæological Review and the Folk-Lore Journal* (London, 1890ff.)
Found	*Foundations (A Baptist Journal of History and Theology)* (Rochester, NY; 1958ff.)
FUQ	*Free University Quarterly* (Amsterdam-Centrum, 1950-1965)

G

GBT	*Ghana Bulletin of Theology* (Legon, Ghana; 1957ff.)
GJ	*Grace Journal* (Winona Lake, IN; 1960ff.)
GOTR	*Greek Orthodox Theological Review* (Brookline, MA; 1954ff.)
GR	*Gordon Review* (Boston; Beverly Farms, MA; Wenham, MA; 1955ff.)
GRBS	*Greek, Roman and Byzantine Studies* (San Antonio; Cambridge, MA; University, MS; Durham, NC; 1958ff.) [Volume1 as: *Greek and Byzantine Studies*]
Greg	*Gregorianum; Commentarii de re theologica et philosophica* (Rome, 1920ff.) [Volume 1 as: *Gregorianum; rivista trimestrale di studi teologici e filosofici*]
GUOST	*Glasgow University Oriental Society, Transactions* (Glasgow, 1901ff.)

H

H&T	*History and Theory: Studies in the Philosophy of History* (The Hague, 1960ff.)
HA	*Hebrew Abstracts* (New York, 1954ff.)
HDSB	*Harvard Divinity School Bulletin* (Cambridge, MA; 1935-1969)
Herm	*Hermathena; a Series of Papers on Literature, Science and Philosophy by Members of Trinity College, Dublin* (Dublin, 1873ff.) [Volumes 1-20; changes to issue number from #46 on]
HeyJ	*The Heythrop Journal* (New York, 1960ff.)
HJ	*Hibbert Journal* (London, Boston, 1902-1968)
HJAH	*Historia. Zeitschrift für alte Geschichte / Revue d'Histoire Ancienne / Journal of Ancient History / Rivista di Storia Antica* (Baden, 1950ff.)
HJud	*Historia Judaica. A Journal of Studies in Jewish History Especially in the Legal and Economic History of the Jews* (New York, 1938-1961)
HQ	*The Hartford Quarterly* (Hartford, CT; 1960-1968)
HR	*Homiletic Review* (New York, 1876-1934)
HRel	*History of Religions* (Chicago, 1961ff.)
HS	*Ha Sifrut. Quarterly for the Study of Literature* הספרות, רבעון למדע הספרות) Tel-Aviv, 1968ff.)
HSR	*Hartford Seminary Record* (Hartford, CT; 1890-1913)
HT	*History Today* (London, 1951ff.)

Periodical Abbreviations

HTR   *Harvard Theological Review* (Cambridge, MA; 1908ff.)
HTS   *Hervormde Teologiese Studien* (Pretoria, 1943ff.)
HUCA   *Hebrew Union College Annual* (Cincinnati, 1904, 1924ff.)

I

IA   *Iranica Antiqua* (Leiden, 1961ff.)
IALR   *International Anthropological and Linguistic Review*
            (Miami, 1953-1957)
IAQR   *Asiatic Quarterly Review* (London, 1886-1966) [1st Series as:
            Asiatic Quarterly Review, (1886-1890); 2nd Series as:
            The Imperial and Asiatic Quarterly and Oriental and
            Colonial Record, (1891-1895); 3rd Series, (1896-1912);
            New Series, Volumes 1 & 2 as: *The Asiatic Quarterly*
            Review (1913); Volumes 3-48 (1914-1952) as: *Asiatic*
            Review, New Series; Volumes 49-59 (1953-1964) as:
            Asian Review, New Series; continued as: *Asian Review,*
            Incorporating Art and Letters [and] the Asiatic Review,
            New Series, Volumes 1-3 (1964-1966)]
ICHR   *Indian Church History Review* (Serampore, West Bengal,
            1967ff.)
ICMM   *The Interpreter. A Church Monthly Magazine* (London,
            1905-1924)
IEJ   *Israel Exploration Journal* (Jerusalem, 1950ff.)
IER   *Irish Ecclesiastical Record (A Monthly Journal under*
            Episcopal Sanction) (Dublin, 1864-1968)
IES   *Indian Ecclesiastical Studies* (Bangalore, India, 1962ff.)
IJA   *International Journal of Apocrypha* (London, 1905-1917)
            [Issues #1-7 as: *Deutero-Canonica,* pages unnumbered]
IJT   *Indian Journal of Theology* (Serampore, West Bengal,
            1952ff.)
ILR   *Israel Law Review* (Jerusalem, 1966ff.)
Inter   *Interchange: Papers on Biblical and Current Questions*
            (Sydney, 1967ff.)
Interp   *Interpretation; a Journal of Bible and Theology* (Richmond,
            1947ff.)
IPQ   *International Philosophical Quarterly* (New York, 1961ff.)
IR   *The Iliff Review* (Denver, 1944ff.)
Iran   *Iran: Journal of the British Institute of Persian Studies*
            (London, 1963ff.)
Iraq   *Iraq. British School of Archaeology in Iraq* (London, 1934ff.)
IRB   *International Reformed Bulletin* (London, 1958ff.)

IRM	*International Review of Missions* (Edinburgh, London, Geneva, 1912ff.)
Isis	*Isis. An International Review devoted to the History of Science and Civilization* (Brussels; Cambridge, MA; 1913ff.)
ITQ	*Irish Theological Quarterly* (Dublin, Maynooth, 1906ff.)

J

JAAR	*Journal of the American Academy of Religion* (Wolcott, NY; Somerville, NJ; Baltimore; Brattleboro, VT) [Volumes 1-4 as: *Journal of the National Association of Biblical Instructors;* Volumes 5-34 as: *Journal of Bible and Religion*]
JANES	*Journal of the Ancient Near Eastern Society of Columbia University* (New York, 1968ff.)
Janus	*Janus; Archives internationales pour l'Histoire de la Médecine et pour la Géographie Médicale* (Amsterdam; Haarlem; Leiden; 1896ff.)
JAOS	*Journal of the American Oriental Society* (Baltimore, New Haven, 1843ff.)
JAOSS	*Journal of the American Oriental Society, Supplements* (Baltimore, New Haven, 1935-1954)
JARCE	*Journal of the American Research Center in Egypt* (Gluckstadt, Germany; Cambridge, MA; 1962ff.)
JASA	*Journal of the American Scientific Affiliation* (Wheaton, IL, 1949ff.)
JBL	*Journal of Biblical Literature* (Middletown, CT; New Haven; Boston; Philadelphia; Missoula, MT; 1881ff.)
JC&S	*The Journal of Church and State* (Fresno, CA; 1965ff.)
JCE	*Journal of Christian Education* (Sydney, 1958ff.)
JCP	*Christian Philosophy Quarterly* (New York, 1881-1884) [From Volume 2 on as: *The Journal of Christian Philosophy*]
JCS	*Journal of Cuneiform Studies* (New Haven; Cambridge, MA;1947ff.)
JCSP	*Journal of Classical and Sacred Philology* (Cambridge, England, 1854-1857)
JEA	*Journal of Egyptian Archaeology* (London, 1914ff.)
JEBH	*Journal of Economic and Business History* (Cambridge, MA;1928-1932)
JEOL	*Jaarbericht van het Vooraziatisch-Egyptisch Gezelschap Ex Oriente Lux* (Leiden, 1933ff.)
JES	*Journal of Ethiopian Studies* (Addis Ababa, 1963ff.)

Periodical Abbreviations

JESHO	*Journal of the Economic and Social History of the Orient* (Leiden, 1958ff.)
JHI	*Journal of the History of Ideas. A Quarterly Devoted to Intellectual History* (Lancaster, PA; New York;1940ff.
JHS	*The Journal of Hebraic Studies* (New York; 1969ff.)
JIQ	*Jewish Institute Quarterly* (New York, 1924-1930)
JJLP	*Journal of Jewish Lore and Philosophy* (Cincinnati, 1919)
JJP	*Rocznik Papirologii Prawniczej-Journal of Juristic Papyrology* (New York, Warsaw, 1946ff.) [Suspended 1947 & 1959-60]
JJS	*Journal of Jewish Studies* (London, 1948ff.)
JKF	*Jahrbuch für Kleinasiatische Forschungen* (Heidelberg, 1950-1953) [Superseded by *Anadolu Araştirmalari Istanbul Üniversitesi Edebiyat Fakültesi eski Önasya Dilleri ve Kültürleri Kürsüsü Tarafindan Čikarilir*]
JLTQ	*John Lobb's Theological Quarterly* (London, 1884)
JMTSO	*Journal of the Methodist Theological School in Ohio* (Delaware, OH; 1962ff.)
JMUEOS	*Journal of the Manchester Egyptian and Oriental Society* (Manchester, 1911-1953) [Issue #1 as: *Journal of the Manchester Oriental Society*]
JNES	*Journal of Near Eastern Studies* (Chicago, 1942ff.)
JP	*The Journal of Philology* (Cambridge, England; 1868-1920)
JPOS	*Journal of the Palestine Oriental Society* (Jerusalem, 1920-1948) [Volume 20 consists of only one fascicle]
JQR	*Jewish Quarterly Review* (London, 1888-1908; *N.S.*, Philadelphia, 1908ff.) [Includes 75th Anniversary Volume as: *JQR, 75th*]
JR	*Journal of Religion* (Chicago, 1921ff.)
JRAI	*Journal of the Royal Anthropological Institute of Great Britain and Ireland* (London, 1872-1965) [Volumes 1-69 as: *Journal of the Anthropological Institute* Continued as: *Man, N.S.*]
JRAS	*Journal of the Royal Asiatic Society of Great Britain and Ireland* (London, 1827ff.) [*Transactions,* 1827-1835 as *TRAS; Journal* from 1834 on: (Shown without volume numbers)]
JRASCS	*Centenary Supplement of the Journal of the Royal Asiatic Society, being a Selection of papers read to the society during the celebrations of July, 1923* (London, 1924)
JRelH	*Journal of Religious History* (Sydney, 1960ff.)
JRH	*Journal of Religion and Health* (Richmond, 1961ff.)
JRT	*Journal of Religious Thought* (Washington, DC; 1943ff.)
JSL	*Journal of Sacred Literature and Biblical Record* (London,1848-1868)

Periodical Abbreviations

JSOR	*Journal of the Society of Oriental Research* (Chicago, 1917-1932)
JSP	*The Journal of Speculative Philosophy* (St. Louis, 1868-1893)
JSS	*Journal of Semitic Studies* (Manchester, 1956ff.)
JTALC	*Journal of Theology of the American Lutheran Conference* (Minneapolis, 1936-1943) [Volumes 1-5 as: *American Lutheran Conference Journal;* continued from volume 8, #3 as: *Lutheran Outlook* (not included)]
JTC	*Journal for Theology and the Church* (New York, 1965ff.)
JTLC	*Journal of Theology: Church of the Lutheran Confession* (Eau Claire, WI; 1961ff.)
JTS	*Journal of Theological Studies* (Oxford, 1899-1949; *N.S.,* 1950ff.)
JTVI	*Journal of the Transactions of the Victoria Institute, or Philosophical Society of Great Britain* (London, 1866-1957) [Superseded by *Faith & Thought*]
Jud	*Judaism. A Quarterly Journal of Jewish Life and Thought* (New York, 1952ff.)
JWCI	*Journal of the Warburg and Courtauld Institutes* (London,1937ff.)
JWH	*Journal of World History-Cahiers d'Histoire Mondiale -Cuadernos de Historia Mundial* (Paris, 1953ff.)

K

Kêmi	*Kêmi. Revue de philologie et d'archéologie égyptiennes et coptes* (Paris, 1928ff.)
Klio	*Klio. Beiträge zur alten Geschichte* (Leipzig, 1901ff.)
Kobez	*Kobez (Qobeṣ);* קובץ החברה העברית לחקירת ארץ־ישראל ועתיקתיה (Jerusalem, 1921-1945)
KSJA	*Kedem; Studies in Jewish Archaeology* (Jerusalem, 1942, 1945)
Kuml	*Kuml. Årbog for Jysk Arkæologisk Selskab* (Århus, 1951ff.)
Kush	*Kush. Journal of the Sudan Antiquities Service* (Khartoum, Sudan, 1953-1968)
KZ	*Kirchliche Zeitschrift* (St. Louis; Waverly, IA; Chicago; Columbus; 1876-1943)
KZFE	*Kadmos. Zeitschrift für vor-und frühgriechische Epigraphik* (Berlin, 1962ff.)

L

L	*Levant (Journal of the British School of Archaeology in Jerusalem)* (London, 1969ff.)
Lang	*Language. Journal of the Linguistic Society of America* (Baltimore, 1925ff.)
LCQ	*Lutheran Church Quarterly* (Gettysburg, PA; 1928-1949)
LCR	*Lutheran Church Review* (Philadelphia, 1882-1927)
Lĕš	*Lĕšonénu. Quarterly for the Study of the Hebrew Language and Cognate Subjects* לשוננו (Jerusalem, 1925ff.) [English Summaries from Volume 30 onward]
LIST	*Lown Institute. Studies and Texts* (Brandeis University. Lown School of Near Eastern and Judaic Studies. Cambridge, MA; 1963ff.)
Listen	*Listening* (Dubuque, IA; 1965ff.) [Volume numbers start with "zero"]
LofS	*Life of the Spirit* (London, 1946-1964)
LQ	*The Quarterly Review of the Evangelical Lutheran Church* (Gettysburg, PA; 1871-1927; revived in 1949ff.) [From 1878 on as: *The Lutheran Quarterly*]
LQHR	*London Quarterly and Holborn Review* (London, 1853-1968)
LS	*Louvain Studies* (Louvain, 1966ff.)
LSQ	*Lutheran Synod Quarterly* (Mankato, MN, 1960ff.) [Formerly *Clergy Bulletin* (Volume 1 of *LSQ* as *Clergy Bulletin,* Volume 20, #1 & #2)]
LTJ	*Lutheran Theological Journal* (North Adelaide, South Australia, 1967ff.)
LTP	*Laval Theologique et Philosophique* (Quebec, 1945ff.)
LTQ	*Lexington Theological Quarterly* (Lexington, KY; 1966ff.)
LTR	*Literary and Theological Review* (New York; Boston, 1834-1839)
LTSB	*Lutheran Theological Seminary Bulletin* (Gettysburg, PA; 1921ff.)
LTSR	*Luther Theological Seminary Review* (St. Paul, MN; 1962ff.)
LWR	*The Lutheran World Review* (Philadelphia, 1948-1950)

M

Man	*Man. A Monthly Record of Anthropological Science* (London,1901-1965; *N. S.,* 1966ff.) [Articles in original series referred to by *article* number not by *page* number - New Series subtitled: *The Journal of the Royal Anthropological Institute*]
ManSL	*Manuscripta* (St. Louis, 1957ff.)
MB	*Medelhavsmuseet Bulletin* (Stockholm, 1961ff.)
MC	*The Modern Churchman* (Ludlow, England; 1911ff.)
McQ	*McCormick Quarterly* (Chicago, 1947ff.) [Volumes 1-13 as: *McCormick Speaking*]
MCS	*Manchester Cuneiform Studies* (Manchester, 1951-1964)
MDIÄA	*Mitteilungen des deutsches Instituts für ägyptische Altertumskunde in Kairo* (Cairo, 1930ff.)
Mesop	*Mesopotamia* (Torino, Italy, 1966ff.)
MH	*The Modern Humanist* (Weston, MA; 1944-1962)
MHSB	*The Mission House Seminary Bulletin* (Plymouth, WI; 1954-1962)
MI	*Monthly Interpreter* (Edinburgh, 1884-1886)
MidS	*Midstream (Council on Christian Unity)* (Indianapolis, 1961ff.)
Min	*Ministry. A Quarterly Theological Review for South Africa* (Morija, Basutolan, 1960ff.)
Minos	*Minos. Investigaciones y Materiales Para el Estudio de los Textos Paleocretenses Publicados Bajo la Dirección de Antonio Tovar y Emilio Peruzzi* (Salamanca, 1951ff.) [From Volume 4 on as: *Minos Revista de Filología Egea*]
MIO	*Mitteilungen des Instituts für Orientforschung [Deutsche Akademie der Wissenschaften zu Berlin Institut für Orientforschung]* (Berlin, 1953ff.)
Miz	*Mizraim. Journal of Papyrology, Egyptology, History of Ancient Laws, and their Relations to the Civilizations of Bible Lands* (New York, 1933-1938)
MJ	*The Museum Journal. Pennsylvania University* (Philadelphia,1910-1935)
MMBR	*The Monthly Magazine and British Register* (London, 1796-1843) [*1st Ser.,* 1796-1826, Volumes 1-60; *N.S.,* 1826-1838, Volumes 1-26; *3rd Ser.,* 1839-1843, Volumes 1-9, however, Volumes 7-9 are marked 95-97[sic]]

ModR   *The Modern Review* (London, 1880-1884)

Monist   *The Monist. An International Quarterly Journal of General Philosophical Inquiry* (Chicago; La Salle, IL; 1891ff.)

Mosaic   *Mosaic* (Cambridge, MA; 1960ff.)

MQ   *The Minister's Quarterly* (New York, 1945-1966)

MQR   *Methodist Quarterly Review (South)* (Louisville, Nashville, 1847-1861; 1879-1886; 1886-1930) [*3rd Ser.* as: *Southern Methodist Review;* Volume 52 (1926) misnumbered as 53; Volume 53 (1927) misnumbered as 54; and the volume for 1928 is also marked as 54]

MR   *Methodist Review* (New York, 1818-1931) [Volume 100 not published]

MTSB   *Moravian Theological Seminary Bulletin* (Bethlehem, PA; 1959-1970) [Volume for 1969 apparently not published]

MTSQB   *Meadville Theological School Quarterly Bulletin* (Meadville, PA;1906-1933) [From Volume 25 on as: *Meadville Journal*]

Muséon   *Le Muséon. Revue d'Études Orientales* (Louvain, 1882-1915;1930/32ff.)

MUSJ   *Mélanges de l'Université Saint-Joseph. Faculté orientale* (Beirut, 1906ff.) [Title varies]

Mwa-M   *Milla wa-Milla. The Australian Bulletin of Comparative Religion* (Parkville, Victoria, 1961ff.)

N

NB   *Blackfriars. A Monthly Magazine* (Oxford, 1920ff.) [From Volume 46 on as: *New Blackfriars*]

NBR   *North British Review* (Edinburgh, 1844-1871)

NCB   *New College Bulletin* (Edinburgh, 1964ff.)

NEAJT   *Northeast Asia Journal of Theology* (Kyoto, Japan, 1968ff.)

NEST   *The Near East School of Theology Quarterly* (Beirut, 1952ff.)

Nexus   *Nexus* (Boston, 1957ff.)

NGTT   *Nederduitse gereformeerde teologiese tydskrif* (Kaapstad, N.G., Kerk-Uitgewers, 1959ff.)

NOGG   *Nihon Orient Gakkai geppo* (Tokyo, 1955-1959) [Being the *Bulletin of the Society for Near Eastern Studies in Japan*-Continued as: *Oriento*]

NOP   *New Orient* (Prague, 1960-1968)

NPR	*The New Princeton Review* (New York, 1886-1888)
NQR	*Nashotah Quarterly Review* (Nashotah, WI; 1960ff.)
NT	*Novum Testamentum* (Leiden, 1955ff.)
NTS	*New Testament Studies* (Cambridge, England; 1954ff.)
NTT	*Nederlandsch Theologisch Tijdschrift* (Wageningen, 1946ff.)
NTTO	*Norsk Teologisk Tidsskrift* (Oslo, 1900ff.)
Numen	*Numen; International Review for the History of Religions* (Leiden, 1954ff.)
NW	*The New World. A Quarterly Review of Religion, Ethics and Theology* (Boston, 1892-1900)
NYR	*The New York Review. A Journal of The Ancient Faith and Modern Thought (St. John's Seminary)* (New York, 1905-1908)
NZJT	*New Zealand Journal of Theology* (Christchurch, 1931-1935)

O

OA	*Oriens Antiquus* (Rome, 1962ff.)
OBJ	*The Oriental and Biblical Journal* (Chicago, 1880-1881)
OC	*Open Court* (Chicago, 1887-1936)
ONTS	*The Hebrew Student* (Morgan Park, IL; New Haven; Hartford; 1881-1892) [Volumes 3-8 as: *The Old Testament Student;* Volume 9 onwards as: *The Old and New Testament Student*]
OOR	*Oriens: The Oriental Review* (Paris, 1926)
OQR	*The Oberlin Quarterly Review* (Oberlin, OH; 1845-1849)
Or	*Orientalia commentarii de rebus Assyri-Babylonicis, Arabicis, and Aegyptiacis, etc.* (Rome 1920-1930)
Or, N.S.	*Orientalia: commentarii, periodici de rebus orientis antiqui* (Rome, 1932ff.)
Oriens	*Oriens. Journal of the International Society of Oriental Research* (Leiden, 1948ff.)
Orient	*Orient. The Reports of the Society for Near Eastern Studies in Japan* (Tokyo, 1960ff.)
Orita	*Orita. Ibadan Journal of Religious Studies* (Ibadan, Nigeria, 1967ff.)
OrS	*Orientalia Suecana* (Uppsala, 1952ff.)
OSHTP	*Oxford Society of Historical Theology, Abstract of Proceedings* (Oxford, 1891-1968) [Through 1919 as: *Society of Historical Theology, Proceedings*]
Osiris	*Osiris* (Bruges, Belgium; 1936-1968) *[Subtitle varies]*
OTS	*Oudtestamentische Studiën* (Leiden, 1942ff.)

OTW   *Ou-Testamentiese Werkgemeenskap in Suid-Afrika,*
              Proceedings of die (Pretoria, 1958ff.) [Volume 1
              in Volume 14 of: *Hervormde Teologiese Studies*]

P

P   *Preaching: A Journal of Homiletics* (Dubuque, IA; 1965ff.)

P&P   *Past and Present* (London, 1952ff.) *[Subtitle varies]*

PA   *Practical Anthropology* (Wheaton, IL; Eugene, OR;
              Tarrytown, NY; 1954ff.)

PAAJR   *Proceedings of the American Academy for Jewish
              Research* (Philadelphia, 1928ff.)

PAOS   *Proceedings of the American Oriental Society*
              (Baltimore, New Haven; 1842, 1846-50,
              1852-1860) [After 1860 all proceedings
              are bound with *Journal*]

PAPA   *American Philological Association, Proceedings*
              (Hartford, Boston, 1896ff.) [*Transactions* as:
              TAPA. Transactions and *Proceedings* combine
              page numbers from volume 77 on]

PAPS   *Proceedings of the American Philosophical Society*
              (Philadelphia, 1838ff.)

PBA   *Proceedings of the British Academy* (London, 1903ff.)

PEFQS   *Palestine Exploration Fund Quarterly Statement*
              (London, 1869ff.) [From Volume 69 (1937) on as:
              Palestine Exploration Quarterly]

PEQ   *Palestine Exploration Quarterly* [See: *PEFQS*]

PER   *The Protestant Episcopal Review* (Fairfax, Co., VA;
              1886-1900) [Volumes 1-5 as: *The Virginian
              Seminary Magazine*]

Person   *Personalist. An International Review of Philosophy,
              Religion and Literature* (Los Angeles, 1920ff.)

PF   *Philosophical Forum* (Boston, 1943-1957; *N.S.*, 1968ff.)

PHDS   *Perspectives. Harvard Divinity School* (Cambridge, MA;
              1965-1967)

PIASH   *Proceedings of the Israel Academy of Sciences and
              Humanities* (Jerusalem, 1967ff.)

PICSS   *Proceedings of the International Conference on Semitic
              Studies held in Jerusalem, 19-23 July 1965*
              (Jerusalem, 1969)

PIJSL   *Papers of the Institute of Jewish Studies, London*
              (Jerusalem,1964)

PJT   *Pacific Journal of Theology* (Western Samoa, 1961ff.)

Periodical Abbreviations

PJTSA	*Jewish Theological Seminary Association, Proceedings* (New York, 1888-1902)
PP	*Perspective* (Pittsburgh, 1960ff.) [Volumes 1-8 as: *Pittsburgh Perspective*]
PQ	*The Presbyterian Quarterly* (New York, 1887-1904)
PQL	*The Preacher's Quarterly* (London, 1954-1969)
PQPR	*The Presbyterian Quarterly and Princeton Review* (New York, 1872-1877)
PQR	*Presbyterian Quarterly Review* (Philadelphia, 1852-1862)
PR	*Presbyterian Review* (New York, 1880-1889)
PRev	*The Biblical Repertory and Princeton Review* (Princeton, Philadelphia, New York, 1829-1884) [Volume 1 as: *The Biblical Repertory, New Series;* Volumes 2-8 as: *The Biblical Repertory and Theological Review*]
PRR	*Presbyterian and Reformed Review* (New York, Philadelphia, 1890-1902)
PSB	*The Princeton Seminary Bulletin* (Princeton, 1907ff.)
PSTJ	*Perkins School of Theology Journal* (Dallas, 1947ff.)
PTR	*Princeton Theological Review* (Princeton, 1903-1929)
PUNTPS	*Proceedings of the University of Newcastle upon Tyne Philosophical Society* (Newcastle upon Tyne, 1964-70)

Q

QCS	*Quarterly Christian Spectator* (New Haven, 1819-1838) [*1st Series* and *New Series* as: *Christian Spectator*]
QDAP	*The Quarterly of the Department of Antiquities in Palestine* (Jerusalem, 1931-1950)
QRL	*Quarterly Review* (London, 1809-1967)
QTMRP	*The Quarterly Theological Magazine, and Religious Repository* (Philadelphia, 1813-1814)

R

R&E	*[Baptist] Review and Expositor* (Louisville, 1904ff.)
R&S	*Religion and Society* (Bangalore, India, 1953ff.)
RAAO	*Revue d'Assyriologie et d'Archéologie Orientale* (Paris, 1886ff.)

Periodical Abbreviations

RChR   *The Reformed Church Review* (Mercersburg, PA;
           Chambersburg, PA; Philadelphia; 1849-1926)
           [Volumes 1-25 as: *Mercersburg Review;*
           Volumes 26-40 as: *Reformed Quarterly Review;*
           4th Series on as: *Reformed Church Review*]

RCM   *Reformed Church Magazine* (Reading, PA; 1893-1896)
           [Volume 3 as: *Reformed Church Historical Magazine*]

RdQ   *Revue de Qumran* (Paris, 1958ff.)

RDSO   *Rivista degli Studi Orientali* (Rome, 1907ff.)

RÉ   *Revue Égyptologique* (Paris, 1880-1896; *N.S.,*
           1919-1924)

RefmR   *The Reformation Review* (Amsterdam, 1953ff.)

RefR   *The Reformed Review. A Quarterly Journal of the*
           Seminaries of the Reformed Church in America
           (Holland, MI; New Brunswick, NJ; 1947ff.)
           [Volumes 1-9 as: *Western Seminary Bulletin*]

RÉg   *Revue d'Égyptologie* (Paris, 1933ff.)

RelM   *Religion in the Making* (Lakeland, FL; 1940-1943)

Resp   *Response—in worship—Music—The arts* (St. Paul, 1959ff.)

RestQ   *Restoration Quarterly* (Austin, TX; Abilene, TX; 1957ff.)

RFEASB   *The Hebrew University / Jerusalem: Department of*
           Archaeology. Louis M. Rabinowitz Fund for the
           Exploration of Ancient Synagogues, Bulletin
           (Jerusalem, 1949-1960)

RHA   *Revue Hittite et Asianique* (Paris, 1930ff.)

RIDA   *Revue internationale des droits de l'antiquité* (Brussels,
           1948ff.)

RJ   *Res Judicatae. The Journal of the Law Students' Society*
           of Victoria (Melbourne, 1935-1957)

RL   *Religion in Life* (New York, 1932ff.)

RO   *Rocznik Orjentalistyczny. (Wydaje Polskie towarzystwo*
           orjentalisyczne) (Kraków, Warsaw, 1914ff.)

RP   *Records of the Past* (Washington, DC; 1902-1914)

RR   *Review of Religion* (New York, 1936-1958)

RS   *Religious Studies* (London, 1965ff.)

RTP   *Review of Theology and Philosophy* (Edinburgh,
           1905-1915)

RTR   *Recueil de travaux relatifs à la philologie et à*
           l'archéologie egyptiennes et assyriennes (Paris,
           1870-1923)

RTRM   *The Reformed Theological Review* (Melbourne, 1941ff.)

S

SAENJ	*Seminar. An Annual Extraordinary Number of the Jurist* (Washington, DC; 1943-1956)
SBAP	*Society of Biblical Archæology, Proceedings* (London, 1878-1918)
SBAT	*Society of Biblical Archæology, Transactions* (London, 1872-1893)
SBE	*Studia Biblica et Ecclesiastica* (Oxford, 1885-1903) [Volume 1 as: *Studia Biblica*]
SBFLA	*Studii (Studium) Biblici Franciscani. Liber Annuus* (Jerusalem, 1950ff.)
SBLP	*Society of Biblical Literature & Exegesis, Proceedings* (Baltimore, 1880)
SBO	*Studia Biblica et Orientalia* (Rome 1959) [Being Volumes 10-12 respectively of *Analecta Biblica. Investigationes Scientificae in Res Biblicas*]
SBSB	*Society for Biblical Studies Bulletin* (Madras, India, 1964ff.)
SCO	*Studi Classici e Orientali* (Pisa, 1951ff.)
Scotist	*The Scotist* (Teutopolis, IL; 1939-1967)
SCR	*Studies in Comparative Religion* (Bedfont, Middlesex, England, 1967ff.)
Scrip	*Scripture. The Quarterly of the Catholic Biblical Association* (London, 1944-1968)
SE	*Study Encounter* (Geneva, 1965ff.)
SEÅ	*Svensk Exegetisk Årsbok* (Uppsala-Lund, 1936ff.)
SEAJT	*South East Journal of Theology* (Singapore, 1959ff.)
Sefunim	*Sefunim (Bulletin)* [היפה] ספונים (Haifa, 1966-1968)
SGEI	*Studies in the Geography of Eretz-Israel* מחקרים בגיאוגרפיה של ארץ־ישראל (Jerusalem, 1959ff.) [English summaries in Volumes 1-3 only; continuing the *Bulletin of the Israel Exploration Society (Yediot)*]
SH	*Scripta Hierosolymitana* (Jerusalem, 1954ff.)
Shekel	*The Shekel* (New York, 1968ff.)
SIR	*Smithsonian Institute Annual Report of the Board of Regents* (Washington, DC; 1846-1964; becomes: *Smithsonian Year* from 1965 on]
SJH	*Seminary Journal* (Hamilton, NY; 1892)
SJT	*Scottish Journal of Theology* (Edinburgh, 1947ff.)
SL	*Studia Liturgica. An International Ecumenical Quarterly for Liturgical Research and Renewal* (Rotterdam, 1962ff.)

SLBR	*Sierra Leone Bulletin of Religion* (Freetown, Sierra Leone; 1959-1966)
SMR	*Studia Montes Regii* (Montréal, 1958-1967)
SMSDR	*Studi e Materiali di Storia Delle Religioni* (Rome, Bologna, 1925ff.
SO	*Studia Orientalia* (Helsinki, 1925ff.)
SOOG	*Studi Orientalistici in Onore di Giorgio Levi Della Vida* (Rome, 1956)
Sophia	*Sophia. A Journal for Discussion in Philosophical Theology* (Parkville, N.S.W., Australia, 1962ff.)
SP	*Spirit of the Pilgrims* (Boston, 1828-1833)
SPR	*Southern Presbyterian Review* (Columbia, SC; 1847-1885)
SQ/E	*The Shane Quarterly* (Indianapolis, 1940ff.) [From Volume 17 on as: *Encounter*]
SR	*The Seminary Review* (Cincinnati, 1954ff.)
SRL	*The Scottish Review* (London, Edinburgh, 1882-1900; 1914-1920)
SS	*Seminary Studies of the Athenaeum of Ohio* (Cincinnati, 1926-1968) [Volumes 1-15 as: *Seminary Studies*]
SSO	*Studia Semitica et Orientalia* (Glasgow, 1920, 1945)
SSR	*Studi Semitici* (Rome, 1958ff.)
ST	*Studia Theologica* (Lund, 1947ff.)
StEv	*Studia Evangelica* (Berlin, 1959ff.) [Being miscellaneous volumes of: *Text und Untersuchungen zur Geschichte der altchristlichen Literatur,* beginning with Volume 73]
StLJ	*The Saint Luke's Journal* (Sewanee, TN; 1957ff.) [Volume 1, #1 as: *St. Luke's Journal of Theology*]
StMR	*St. Marks Review: An Anglican Quarterly* (Canberra, A.C.T., Australia, 1955ff.)
StP	*Studia Patristica* (Berlin, 1957ff.) [Being miscellaneous volumes of: *Text und Untersuchungen zur Geschichte der altchristlichen Literatur,* beginning with Volume 63]
StVTQ	*St. Vladimir's Theological Quarterly* (Crestwood, NY; 1952ff.) [Volumes 1-4 as: *St. Vladimir's Seminary Quarterly*]
Sumer	*Sumer. A Journal of Archaeology in Iraq* (Baghdad, 1945ff.)
SWJT	*Southwestern Journal of Theology* (Fort Worth, 1917-1924; N.S., 1950ff.)
Syria	*Syria, revue d'art oriental et d'archéologie* (Paris, 1920ff.)

T

T&C	*Theology and the Church / SÎN-HÁK kap kàu-Hōe (Tainan Theological College)* (Tainan, Formosa, 1957ff.)
T&L	*Theology and Life* (Lancaster, PA; 1958-1966)
TAD	*Türk tarih, arkeologya ve etnoğrafya dergisi* (Istanbul, 1933-1949; continued as: *Türk arkeoloji Dergisi,* Ankara, 1956ff.)
TAPA	*American Philological Society, Transactions* (See: *PAPA*)
TAPS	*Transactions of the American Philosophical Society* (Philadelphia, 1789-1804; *N.S.,* 1818ff.)
Tarbiz	*Tarbiz. A quarterly review of the humanities;* תרביץ, רבעון למדעי היהדות (Jerusalem, 1929ff.) [English Summaries from Volume 24 on only]
TB	*Tyndale Bulletin* (London, 1956ff.) [Numbers 1-16 as: *Tyndale House Bulletin*]
TBMDC	*Theological Bulletin: McMaster Divinity College* (Hamilton, Ontario, 1967ff.)
TD	*Theology Digest* (St. Mary, KS, 1953ff.)
TE	*Theological Education* (Dayton, 1964ff.)
Tem	*Temenos. Studies in Comparative Religion* (Helsinki, 1965ff.)
TEP	*Theologica Evangelica. Journal of the Faculty of Theology, University of South Africa* (Pretoria, 1968ff.)
Text	*Textus. Annual of the Hebrew University Bible Project* (Jerusalem, 1960ff.)
TF	*Theological Forum* (Minneapolis, 1929-1935)
TFUQ	*Thought. A Quarterly of the Sciences and Letters* (New York, 1926ff.) [From Volume 15 on as: *Thought. Fordham University Quarterly*]
ThE	*Theological Eclectic* (Cincinnati; New York, 1864-1871)
Them	*Themelios, International Fellowship of Evangelical Students* (Fresno, CA; 1962ff.)
Theo	*Theology; A Journal of Historic Christianity* (London, 1920ff.)
ThSt	*Theological Studies* (New York; Woodstock, MD; 1940ff.)
TLJ	*Theological and Literary Journal* (New York, 1848-1861)
TM	*Theological Monthly* (St. Louis, 1921-1929)
TML	*The Theological Monthly* (London, 1889-1891)
TPS	*Transactions of the Philological Society* (London, 1842ff.) [Volumes 1-6 as: *Proceedings*]
TQ	*Theological Quarterly* (St. Louis, 1897-1920)

Tr	*Traditio. Studies in Ancient and Medieval History, Thought and Religion* (New York, 1943ff.)
Trad	*Tradition, A Journal of Orthodox Jewish Thought* (New York, 1958ff.)
TRep	*Theological Repository* (London, 1769-1788)
TRFCCQ	*Theological Review and Free Church College Quarterly* (Edinburgh, 1886-1890)
TRGR	*The Theological Review and General Repository of Religious and Moral Information, Published Quarterly* (Baltimore, 1822)
TRL	*Theological Review: A Quarterly Journal of Religious Thought and Life* (London, 1864-1879)
TT	*Theology Today* (Lansdowne, PA; Princeton, NJ; 1944ff.)
TTCA	*Trinity Theological College Annual* (Singapore, 1964-1969) [Volume 5 apparently never published]
TTD	*Teologisk Tidsskrift* (Decorah, IA; 1899-1907)
TTKB	*Türk Tarih Kurumu Belleten* (Ankara, 1937ff.)
TTKF	*Tidskrift för teologi och kyrkiga frågor (The Augustana Theological Quarterly)* (Rock Island, IL; 1899-1917)
TTL	*Theologisch Tijdschrift* (Leiden, 1867-1919) [English articles from Volume 45 on only]
TTM	*Teologisk Tidsskrift* (Minneapolis, 1917-1928)
TUSR	*Trinity University Studies in Religion* (San Antonio, 1950ff.)
TZ	*Theologische Zeitschrift* (Basel, 1945ff.)
TZDES	*Theologische Zeitschrift (Deutsche Evangelische Synode des Westens, North America)* (St. Louis, 1873-1934) [Continued from Volumes 22 through 26 as: *Magazin für Evangel. Theologie und Kirche;* and from Volume 27 on as: *Theological Magazine*]
TZTM	*Theologische Zeitblätter, Theological Magazine* (Columbus,1911-1919)

U

UC	*The Unitarian Christian* (Boston, 1947ff.) [Volumes 1-4 as: *Our Faith*]
UCPSP	*University of California Publications in Semitic Philology* (Berkeley, 1907ff.)
UF	*Ugarit-Forschungen. Internationales Jahrbuch für die Altertumskunde Syrien-Palästinas* (Neukirchen, West Germany; 1969ff.)
ULBIA	*University of London. Bulletin of the Institute of Archaeology* (London, 1958ff.)

UMB   *The University Museum Bulletin (University of Pennsylvania)* (Philadelphia, 1930-1958)

UMMAAP   *University of Michigan. Museum of Anthropology. Anthropological Papers* (Ann Arbor, 1949ff.)

UnionR   *The Union Review* (New York, 1939-1945)

UPQR   *The United Presbyterian Quarterly Review* (Pittsburgh, 1860-1861)

UQGR   *Universalist Quarterly and General Review* (Boston, 1844-1891)

URRM   *The Unitarian Review and Religious Magazine* (Boston, 1873-1891)

USQR   *Union Seminary Quarterly Review* (New York, 1945ff.)

USR   *Union Seminary Review* (Hampden-Sydney, VA; Richmond; 1890-1946) [Volumes 1-23 as: *Union Seminary Magazine*]

UTSB   *United Theological Seminary Bulletin* (Dayton, 1905ff.) [Including: *The Bulletin of the Evangelical School of Theology; Bulletin of the Union Biblical Seminary,* later, *Bonebrake Theological Bulletin*]

UUÅ   *Uppsala Universitets Årsskrift* (Uppsala, 1861-1960)

V

VC   *Virgiliae Christianae: A Review of Early Christian Life and Language* (Amsterdam, 1947ff.)

VDETF   *Deutsche Vierteljahrsschrift für englisch-theologische Forschung und Kritik / herausgegeben von M. Heidenheim* (Leipzig, Zurich, 1861-1865) [Continued as: *Vierteljahrsschrift für deutsch – englisch- theologische Forschung und Kritik...* 1866-1873]

VDI   *Vestnik Drevnei Istoriĭ. Journal of Ancient History* (Moscow, 1946ff.) [English summaries from 1967 on only]

VDR   *Koinonia* (Nashville, 1957-1968) [Continued as: *Vanderbilt Divinity Review,* 1969-1971]

VE   *Vox Evangelica. Biblical and Historical Essays by the Members of the Faculty of the London Bible College* (London, 1962ff.)

Voice   *The Voice* (St. Paul, 1958-1960) [Subtitle varies]

VR   *Vox Reformata* (Geelong, Victoria, Australia, 1962ff.)

VT   *Vetus Testamentum* (Leiden, 1951ff.)

VTS   *Vetus Testamentum, Supplements* (Leiden, 1953ff.)

W

Way	*The Way. A Quarterly Review of Christian Spirituality* (London, 1961ff.)
WBHDN	*The Wittenberg Bulletin (Hamma Digest Number)* (Springfield, OH; 1903ff.) [Volumes 40-60 (1943-1963) only contain *Hamma Digest Numbers*]
WesTJ	*Wesleyan Theological Journal. Bulletin of the Wesleyan Theological Society* (Lakeville, IN; 1966ff.)
WLQ	*Wisconsin Lutheran Quarterly* (Wauwatosa, WI; Milwaukee;1904ff.) [Also entitled: *Theologische Quartalschrift*]
WO	*Die Welt des Orients . Wissenschaftliche Beiträge zur Kunde des Morgenlandes* (Göttingen, 1947ff.)
Word	*Word: Journal of the Linguistic Circle of New York* (New York, 1945ff.)
WR	*The Westminster Review* (London, New York, 1824-1914)
WSQ	*Wartburg Seminary Quarterly* (Dubuque, IA; 1937-1960) [Volumes 1-9, #1 as: *Quarterly of the Wartburg Seminary Association*]
WSR	*Wesleyan Studies in Religion* (Buckhannon,WV; 1960-1970) [Volumes 53-62 only*[sic]*]
WTJ	*Westminster Theological Journal* (Philadelphia, 1938ff.)
WW	*Western Watch* (Pittsburgh, 1950-1959) [Superseded by: *Pittsburgh Perspective*]
WZKM	*Wiener Zeitschrift für die Kunde des Morgenlandes* (Vienna, 1886ff.)

Y

YCCAR	*Yearbook of the Central Conference of American Rabbis* (Cincinnati, 1890ff.)
YCS	*Yale Classical Studies* (New Haven, 1928ff.)
YDQ	*Yale Divinity Quarterly* (New Haven, 1904ff.) [Volumes 30-62 as: *Yale Divinity News,* continued as: *Reflections*]
YR	*The Yavneh Review. A Religious Jewish Collegiate Magazine* (New York, 1961ff.) [Volume 2 never published]

Z

Z   *Zygon. Journal of Religion and Science* (Chicago, 1966ff.)

ZA   *Zeitschrift für Assyriologie und verwandte Gebiete*
        [Volumes 45 on as: *Zeitschrift für Assyriologie
        und vorderasiatische Archäologie]* (Leipzig, Strassburg,
        Berlin, 1886ff.)

ZÄS   *Zeitschrift für ägyptische Sprache und Altertumskunde*
        (Leipzig, Berlin, 1863ff.)

ZAW   *Zeitschrift für die alttestamentliche Wissenschaft*
        (Giessen, Berlin, 1881ff.)

ZDMG   *Zeitschrift der Deutschen Morgenländischen
        Gesellschaft* (Leipzig, Wiesbaden, 1847ff.)

ZDPV   *Zeitschrift des Deutschen Palästina-Vereins* (Leipzig,
        Wiesbaden, 1878ff.) [English articles from
        Volume 82 on only]

Zion   *Zion. A Quarterly for Research in Jewish History,
        New Series* ציון, רבעין לחורתולדוה ישראל
        (Jerusalem, 1935ff.)
        [English summaries from Volume 3 on only]

ZK   *Zeitschrift für Keilschriftforschung*
        (Leipzig, 1884-1885)

ZNW   *Zeitschrift für die neutestamentliche Wissenschaft und
        die Kunde des Urchristentums (...Kunde der
        älteren Kirche, 1921—)* (Giessen, Berlin,
        1900ff.)

ZS   *Zeitschrift für Semitistik und verwandte Gebiete*
        (Leipzig, 1922-1935)

Sigla[1]

*   Indicates article is additionally listed in other sections of the index.

†   Indicates that title is from the table of contents; from the header; or a composite if title is completely lacking as in early journals.

‡   Indicates a bibliographical article on a specific subject.

(§###)   Section numbers in parentheses in the Table of Contents and in the headers are included for sake of outline continuity, but no articles are referenced in that section.

---

1.   Complete information may be found in Volume I, page xxiii.

§820 *4. Ancient Near Eastern Literature - General Studies*

*†Anonymous, "The Connection between the Sacred Writings and the Literature of Jewish and Heathen Authors," *BCQTR, N.S.,* 12 (1819) 638-652; 13 (1820) 309-316. *(Review)*

*E. F. Rockwell, "Superiority of the Greeks in Literature and the Fine Arts," *SPR* 15 (1862-63) 198-204.

Lewis R. Packard, "The Beginning of a Written Literature in Greece," *TAPA* 11 (1880) 34-51.

Justin A. Smith, "Primitive Literatures," *ONTS* 1 (1882) #1, 5-8.

*Justin A. Smith, "Studies in Archaeology and Comparative Religion: Pagan Literature in Relation to Pagan Faith," *ONTS* 5 (1885-86) 75-82.

Francis Brown, "The Resurrection of Buried Languages," *NPR* 2 (1886) 338-354.

*A. Gudeman, "The Knowledge of the Latin Language and Literature among Greek Writers," *PAPA* 22 (1890) vii-x.

William Simpson, "Potsherds," *PEFQS* 24 (1892) 41-42.

J. F. McCurdy, "Greece, Rome and Israel [Sixth Reinicker Lecture for 1898-'99]," *PER* 12 (1898-99) 471-486. *[Comparison of literatures]*

William Ridgeway, "The Origin of Tragedy," *QRL* 209 (1908) 504-523. *(Review)*

‡Anonymous, "A Library of Ancient Inscriptions,"*JAOS* 39 (1919) 283-284.

(Miss) Marion E. Blake, "A Suggestion to Teachers of Epigraphy," *AJA* 24 (1920) 79-80.

*Cornelia Catlin Coulter, "The 'Great Fish' in Ancient and Medieval Story," *TAPA* 57 (1926) 32-50.

Theodor [H.] Gaster, "The Chronology of Palestinian Epigraphy," *PEQ* 67 (1935) 128-140.

Theodor [H.] Gaster, "The Chronology of Palestinian Epigraphy II. The Chronology of the Earlier Scripts," *PEQ* 69 (1937) 43-58.

T[heodor] H. Gaster, "A Note on Palestinian Epigraphy," *PEQ* 69 (1937) 260-262.

*Solomon Gandz, "The Dawn of Literature: Prolegomena to a history of unwritten literature," *Osiris* 7 (1939) 261-522.

*J. W. Jack, "Recent Biblical Archaeology. Value of Tablets," *ET* 51 (1939-40) 546-547.

*L. P. Kirwan, "An Inscribed Block at 'Aṭbara, Sudan," *JEA* 26 (1940) 83.

Pentti Aalto, "Notes on Methods of Decipherment of Unknown Writings and Languages," *SO* 11 (1945) #4, 1-26.

James Robson, "Catalogue of the Oriental MSS. in the Library of the University of Glasgow," *SSO* 2 (1945) 116-137. [I. Arabic; II. Persian; III. Urdu; IV. Hebrew; V. Syriac; VI. Miscellaneous MSS]

Ralph Marcus, "Alphabetic Acrostics in the Hellenistic and Roman Periods," *JNES* 6 (1947) 109-115.

Anonymous, "What is it?" *Arch* 4 (1951) 115. *[Unknown inscription]*

*Helen North, "The Use of Poetry in the Training of the Ancient Orator," *Tr* 8 (1952) 1-33.

R. T. O'Callaghan, "Ritual, Myth and Drama in Ancient Literature," *Or, N.S.,* 22 (1953) 418-425. *(Review)*

*Charles F. Fensham, "Widow, Orphan and the Poor in Ancient Near Eastern Legal and Wisdom Literature," *JNES* 21 (1962) 129-139.

*Samuel Noah Kramer, "Cuneiform Studies and the History of Literature: The Sumerian Marriage Texts," *PAPS* 107 (1963) 485-527.

J. Gwyn Griffiths, "Allegory in Greece and Egypt," *JEA* 53 (1967) 79-102.

*Carroll Mizicko, "Wisdom Literature in Israel and the Ancient Near East," *Scotist* 23 (1967) 47-73.

*I. V. Kuklina, "Ἄβιοι in Ancient Literary Tradition," *VDI* (1969) #3, 130.

§821 *4.1 The Development of Literature - General Studies
[See also: The Development of the Art of
Writing & Book Production ←§82]*

*T. H. Weir, "Arab and Hebrew Prose Writers," *ContR* 92 (1907) 375-380.

Clarence Eugene Boyd, "The Art of Authorship Among the Ancients,"
MQR, 3rd Ser., 54 (1927) 99-118.

Edward F. D'Arms, "The Influence of Aristotle on Ancient Biography,"
PAPA 66 (1935) xxvii.

*H. L. Lorimer, "Homer and the Art of Writing: A Sketch of Opinion
between 1713 and 1939," *AJA* 52 (1948) 11-23. [Corrections, *AJA* 54
(1950) p. 203]

*Cyrus H. Gordon, "Homer and the Bible. The Origin and Character of East
Mediterranean Literature," *HUCA* 26 (1955) 43-108.

*F. W. Walbank, "History and Tragedy," *HJAH* 9 (1960) 216-234.

*James William Johnson, "Chronological Writing: Its Concepts and
Development," *H&T* 2 (1962-63) 124-145.

G. P. Gooch, "The Evolution of Historical Writing: I," *ContR* 203 (1963)
192-194. *[Part II not applicable]*

*T. Donald, "The Semantic Field of Rich and Poor in the Wisdom Literature
of Hebrew and Accadian," *OA* 3 (1964) 27-41.

*W. G. Lambert, "Literary Style in First Millennium Mesopotamia," *JAOS*
88 (1968) 123-132.

*Moshe Held, "Rhetorical Questions in Ugaritic and Biblical Hebrew," *EI* 9
(1969) 71-79. *[Non-Hebrew Section]*

*S. L. Utchenko, "Some Tendencies in the Development of Roman
Historical Writing (third to first centuries B.C.)," *VDI* (1969) #2, 74.

§822 *4.2 Papyrology - General Studies [See also: Egyptian Papyri -*
Unclassified §847; Demotic Papyri - Unclassfied
§848; and Greek Papyri §948→]

A. S. Hunt, "Papyri and Papyrology," *JEA* 1 (1914) 81-92.

‡Idris H. Bell, "Bibliography of 1912-13: Graeco-Roman Egypt," *JEA* 1 (1914) 129-139.

‡Idris H. Bell, "Bibliography: Graeco-Roman Egypt: A. Papyri (1913-14)," *JEA* 2 (1915) 95-107.

‡Idris H. Bell, "Bibliography: Graeco-Roman Egypt. A. Papyri," *JEA* 3 (1914-15) 129-138.

‡Idris H. Bell, "Bibliography: Graeco-Roman Egypt. A. Papyri (1915-1919)," *JEA* 6 (1920) 119-146.

‡Idris H. Bell, "Bibliography: Graeco-Roman Egypt: A. Papyri (1919-1920)," *JEA* 7 (1921) 87-104.

‡Idris H. Bell, "Bibliography: Graeco-Roman Egypt: A. Papyri (1920-1921)," *JEA* 8 (1922) 83-101.

A. S. Hunt, "Twenty-five Years of Papyrology," *JEA* 8 (1922) 121-128.

‡Idris H. Bell, "Bibliography: Graeco-Roman Egypt: A. Papyri (1921-1922)," *JEA* 9 (1923) 96-113.

‡Idris H. Bell, "Bibliography: Graeco-Roman Egypt: A. Papyri (1922-1923)," *JEA* 10 (1924) 147-171.

‡Idris H. Bell, "Bibliography: Graeco-Roman Egypt: A. Papyri (1923-1924)," *JEA* 11 (1925) 84-106.

‡I[dris] H. Bell, A. D. Nock, and H. J. M. Milne, "Bibliography: Graeco-Roman Egypt: A. Papyri (1924-1926) *JEA* 13 (1927) 84-121.

‡H. J. M. Milne, A. D. Nock, I. H. Bell, J. G. Milne, N. H. Baynes, F. de Zulueta, M. E. Dicker, and R. McKenzie, "Bibliography: Graeco-Roman Egypt. A. Papyri (1926-1927)," *JEA* 14 (1928) 131-158.

*H. J. M. Milne, "A New Speech of Lysias," *JEA* 15 (1929) 75-77.

‡H. J. M. Milne, A. D. Nock, I. H. Bell, J. G. Milne, N. H. Baynes, F. de Zulueta, M. E. Dicker, and R. McKenzie, "Bibliography: Graeco-Roman Egypt. A. Papyri (1927-1928)," *JEA* 15 (1929) 110-136.

‡H. J. M. Milne, A. D. Nock, I. H. Bell, J. G. Milne, N. H. Baynes, F. de Zulueta, M. E. Dicker, and R. McKenzie, "Bibliography: Graeco-Roman Egypt. A. Papyri (1928-1929)," *JEA* 16 (1930) 120-140.

Henry-Bartlett Van Hoesen, "Papyrus Studies in the United States," *CdÉ* 6 (1931) 383-391.

A. E. R. Boak and Campbell Bonner, "The Papyrological Work at the University of Michigan," *CdÉ* 6 (1931) 392-395.

Arthur S. Hunt, "Papyrology in England," *CdÉ* 6 (1931) 396-397.

‡H. J. M. Milne, A. D. Nock, I. H. Bell, J. G. Milne, N. H. Baynes, F. de Zulueta, M. E. Dicker, and R. McKenzie, "Bibliography: Graeco-Roman Egypt. A. Papyri (1929-1930)," *JEA* 17 (1931) 117-142.

I. H. Bell, "Papyrology in Egypt," *CdÉ* 7 (1932) 134-136.

I. H. Bell, "Note on Methods of Publication," *CdÉ* 7 (1932) 270-271.

Arthur S. Hunt, "A Note on the Transliteration of Papyri," *CdÉ* 7 (1932) 272-274.

‡H. J. M. Milne, A. D. Nock, I. H. Bell, J. G. Milne, N. H. Baynes, F. de Zulueta, M. E. Dicker, and R. McKenzie, "Bibliography: Graeco-Roman Egypt. A. Papyri (1930-1931)," *JEA* 18 (1932) 77-104.

‡H. J. M. Milne, A. D. Nock, I. H. Bell, J. G. Milne, N. H. Baynes, F. de Zulueta, M. E. Dicker, and R. McKenzie, "Bibliography: Graeco-Roman Egypt. A. Papyri (1931-1932)," *JEA* 19 (1933) 67-93.

‡H. J. M. Milne, A. D. Nock, C. C. Edgar, J. G. Milne, N. H. Baynes, F. de Zulueta, M. E. Dicker, and R. McKenzie, "Bibliography: Graeco-Roman Egypt. A. Papyri (1932-1933)," *JEA* 20 (1934) 78-128.

‡H. J. M. Milne, A. D. Nock, T. C. Skeat, J. G. Milne, N. H. Baynes, F. de Zulueta, and R. McKenzie, "Bibliography: Graeco-Roman Egypt. I: Papyrology (1934)," *JEA* 21 (1935) 71-104.

‡H. J. M. Milne, A. D. Nock, T. C. Skeat, J. G. Milne, N. H. Baynes, H. F. Jolowicz, and R. McKenzie, "Bibliography: Graeco-Roman Egypt: Papyrology (1935)," *JEA* 22 (1936) 55-99.

‡E. A. Barber, H. J. Rose, T. C. Skeat, E. G. Turner, J. G. Milne, H. F. Jolowicz, and R. McKenzie, "Bibliography: Graeco-Roman Egypt. Part I: Papyrology (1936)," *JEA* 23 (1937) 83-106.

Anonymous, "Progress of the Science of Papyrology," *BJRL* 21 (1937) 297-299.

Anonymous, "The Rylands Papyri," *BJRL* 21 (1937) 298-302.

‡E. A. Barber, H. J. Rose, T. C. Skeat, E. G. Turner, J. G. Milne, and L. R. Palmer, "Bibliography: Graeco-Roman Egypt. Papyrology (1937)," *JEA* 24 (1938) 92-123.

‡E. A. Barber, H. J. Rose, T. C. Skeat, E. G. Turner, J. G. Milne, and L. R. Palmer, "Bibliography: Graeco-Roman Egypt. Part I: Papyrology (1938)," *JEA* 25 (1939) 70-89.

Fr. Pringsheim, "Bibliography: Graeco-Roman Egypt Papyrology (1939) 6. Law," *JEA* 26 (1940) 139-147.

I. H. Bell, "British Papyrology during the War," *Aeg* 25 (1945) 1-10.

A. E. R. Boak, "Papyrological Studies in the United States: 1940-1944," *Aeg* 25 (1945) 11-15.

Bror Olsson, "The papyrological work in Sweden (and Finland) 1940-45," *Aeg* 25 (1945) 26-27.

Warren R. Dawson, "Anastasi, Sallier, and Harris and their Papyri," *JEA* 35 (1949) 158-166.

Rafael*[sic]* Taubenschlag, "Survey of the literature from 1939 until 1945," *JJP* 1 (1946) 80-98.

Rafael*[sic]* Taubenschlag, "Survey of papyri published 1939-1945," *JJP* 1 (1946) 99-119.

‡A. Berger and R[aphael] Taubenschlag, "Bibliography," *JJP* 1 (1946) 152-155.

Raphael Taubenschlag, "Survey of Literature chiefly from 1945 until 1949," *JJP* 3 (1949) 147-169.

Raphael Taubenschlag, "Survey of Papyri published from 1944-1949," *JJP* 3 (1949) 170-194.

‡Jerzy Falenciak, "Survey of Soviet Juristic Papyrology 1946—1948," *JJP* 3 (1949) 195-197.

Abd el-Mohsen Bakir, "The approach to papyrology through Egyptian Hieratic," *ASAE* 50 (1950) 411-419.

Raphael Taubenschlag, "Survey of the Literature chiefly from 1949 until 1950," *JJP* 4 (1950) 349-374.

Raphael Taubenschlag, "Survey of the Papyri published chiefly from 1949 until 1950," *JJP* 4 (1950) 375-388.

Raphael Taubenschlag, "Survey of Literature chiefly 1950 till 1951," *JJP* 5 (1951) 239-252.

Raphael Taubenschlag, "Survey of Papyri chiefly from 1950 till 1951," *JJP* 5 (1951) 253-275.

Raphael Taubenschlag, "Survey of the Literature chiefly 1951 till 1952," *JJP* 6 (1952) 269-293.

Raphael Taubenschlag, "Survey of the Papyri and other publications chiefly from 1951 till 1952," *JJP* 6 (1952) 295-322.

Raphael Taubenschlag, "Survey of the Literature chiefly from 1952 till 1953," *JJP* 7&8 (1953-54) 357-393.

Raphael Taubenschlag, "Survey of the Papyri chiefly from 1952 till 1953," *JJP* 7&8 (1953-54) 395-412.

Raphael Taubenschlag, "Survey of the Literature chiefly from 1953 till 1955," *JJP* 9&10 (1955-56) 477-526.

Raphael Taubenschlag, "Survey of the Papyri chiefly from 1953 till 1955," *JJP* 9&10 (1955-56) 527-580.

Raphael Taubenschlag, "Survey of Literature chiefly from 1955 till 1957," *JJP* 11&12 (1957-58) 293-346.

Raphael Taubenschlag, "Survey of the Papyri chiefly from 1955 till 1957," *JJP* 11&12 (1957-58) 347-380.

Cezary Kunderewicz, Henryk Kupiszewski and Anna Świderek, "Survey of Papyri," *JJP* 14 (1962) 151-183.

Cezary Kunderewicz, Henryk Kupiszewski and Anna Świderek, "Survey of Literature," *JJP* 14 (1962) 185-206.

Herbert C. Youtie, "The Papyrologist: Artificer of Fact," *GRBS* 4 (1963) 19-32.

Anna Świderek, "Survey of Papyri," *JJP* 15 (1965) 397-416.

I. F. Fikhman, "Survey of Soviet Papyrology," *JJP* 15 (1965) 417-427.

Herbert C. Youtie, "Text and Context in Transcribing Papyri," *GRBS* 7 (1966) 251-258.

(§823) *4.3 Afroasiatic - General Studies*

§824 *4.3.1 Hamitic - General Studies*

*Justin A. Smith, "Studies in Archaeology and Comparative Religion," *ONTS* 5 (1885-86) 17-24. [IX. The Literature of Paganism]

§825 *4.3.1.1 Egyptian - General Studies*

*Anonymous, "Ancient Egypt, its Literature and People," *ER* 4 (1852-53) 35-57.

*J. Estlin Carpenter, "Art and Literature in Egypt at the Time of the Exodus," *URRM* 4 (1875) 441-470.

John Robert Towers, "Are Ancient Egyptian Texts Metrical?" *JMUEOS* #20 (1936) 41-44.

Keith C. Seele, "The Epigraphical Survey of the Oriental Society," *AJA* 41 (1937) 111.

George R. Hughes, "Recording Egypt's Ancient Documents," *Arch* 5 (1952) 201-204.

§826 *4.3.1.1.1 Egyptian Correspondence*

Daniel Hy. Haigh, "The Story of Saneha," *ZÄS* 13 (1875) 98-105.

W. St. C[had] Boscawen, "Some Letters to Amenophis III," *BOR* 5 (1891) 174-179.

*Percy E. Newberry, "Extracts from my Notebook. (I). ," *SBAP* 21 (1899) 303-308. [The Story of Sanehat, and the Inscription of Amenemheb: a correction, p. 303]

Alan H. Gardiner, "A Late-Egyptian Letter," *SBAP* 31 (1909) 5-13.

Anonymous, "The Oldest Love Letter in the World," *AAOJ* 33 (1911) #2, 40-41.

Battiscombe Gunn, "A Sixth Dynasty letter from Saqqara," *ASAE* 25 (1925) 242-255.

T. Eric Peet, "Two Eighteenth Dynasty Letters. Papyrus Louvre 3230," *JEA* 12 (1926) 70-74.

T. Eric Peet, "Two Letters from Akhetaten," *AAA* 17 (1930) 82-97.

Alan H.Gardiner, "An Administrative Letter of Protest,"*JEA* 13(1927)75-78.

S. R. K. Glanville, "The Letters of Aaḥmōse of Peniati," *JEA* 14 (1928) 294-312.

Paul C. Smither, "An Old Kingdom Letter Concerning the Crimes of Count Sabni," *JEA* 28 (1942) 16-19.

Paul C. Smither, "The Semnah Despatches," *JEA* 31 (1945) 3-10.

William C. Hayes, "A Much-Copied Letter of the Early Middle Kingdom," *JNES* 7 (1948) 1-10.

Edward F. Wente, "A Letter of Complaint to the Vizier To," *JNES* 20 (1961) 252-257.

*Raphael Giveon, "A Ramesside 'Semitic' Letter,"*RDSO* 37 (1962) 167-173.

Klaus Baer, "An Eleventh Dynasty Farmer's Letters to his Family," *JAOS* 83 (1963) 1-19.

§827 *4.3.1.1.2 Egyptian Didactic and Wisdom Literature*

M. Philippe Virey and M. François Chabas, "'The Oldest Book in the World.' Society, Ethics, Religion, in Egypt before 2000 B.C. The French Version of the Papyrus Prisse, by M. Philippe Virey, and of the Maxims of Ani, by M. François Chabas," *BS* 45 (1888) 629-668. *(Trans. by Howard Osgood)*

F. L. Griffith, "The Proverbs of Ptah-Hotep; The Tomb of Rekmara at Thebes; The Qnbt," *SBAP* 13 (1890-91) 145-149.

W. Max Muller, "The Story of a Peasant," *SBAP* 15 (1892-93) 343-344.

J. N. Fradenburgh, "The Wisdom of the Egyptians," *MR* 78 (1896) 229-241.

*F. Ll. Griffith, "The Millingen Papyrus (teaching of Amenemhet). With note on the compounds formed with substantivised *n*," *ZÄS* 34 (1896) 35-51.

*Howard Osgood, "Morals before Moses," *PRR* 8 (1897) 267-278. *[Precepts of Ani]*

*James Henry Breasted, "The Philosophy of a Memphite Priest," *ZÄS* 39 (1901) 39-54.

Percy E. Newberry, "King of the story of the Eloquent Peasant," *ZÄS* 50 (1912) 123.

Alan H. Gardiner, "Notes on the Story of the Eloquent Peasant," *SBAP* 35 (1913) 264-276; 36 (1914) 15-23, 69-74.

Warren R. Dawson, "Schoolboy Scribe and Sage in Ancient Egypt," *IAQR* 19 (1923) 668-674.

Alan H. Gardiner, "The Eloquent Peasant," *JEA* 9 (1923) 5-25.

G. D. Hornblower, "The Story of the Eloquent Peasant—A suggestion," *JEA* 10 (1924) 44-45.

Anonymous, "The Egyptian Book of Proverbs," *Exp, 9th Ser.,* 3 (1925) 223-225.

*Aylward M. Blackman, "Philological Notes," *JEA* 11 (1925) 210-215. [3. A Note on Three Passages in the *Admonitions of an Egyptian Sage,* pp. 213-215]

*Samuel A. B. Mercer, "A New-Found Book of Proverbs," *ATR* 8 (1925-26) 237-244. *[Precepts of Amen-en-ope]*

F. Ll. Griffith, "The Teaching of Amenophis the Son of Kanakht. Papyrus B.M. 10474," *JEA* 12 (1926) 191-231.

*D. C. Simpson, "The Hebrew Book of Proverbs and the Teaching of Amenophis," *JEA* 12 (1926) 232-239

Battiscombe Gunn, "Some Middle-Egyptian Proverbs," *JEA* 12 (1926) 282-284.

*Anonymous, "Egyptian and Hebrew Prophets," *MR* 109 (1926) 462-464.

*W. O. E. Oesterley, "The 'Teaching of Amen-em-ope' and the Old Testament," *ZAW* 45 (1927) 9-23.

*Robert Oliver Kevin, "The Wisdom of Amen-em-apt and its possible dependence upon the Hebrew Book of Proverbs," *JSOR* 14 (1930) 115-157.

P. A. A. Boeser, "Some Observations on a Moral Text in Demotic," *EgR* 2 (1934) 1-5.

*Samuel A. B. Mercer, "The Wisdom of Amenemope and Monotheism," *EgR* 2 (1934) 18-20.

*G. A. Wainwright, "Zeberged: The Shipwrecked Sailor's Island," *JEA* 32 (1946) 31-38.

Alan H. Gardiner, "The Instruction addressed to Kagemni and his Brethren," *JEA* 32 (1946) 71-74.

*G. A. Wainwright, "Zeberged: A Correction," *JEA* 34 (1948) 119.

*Oliver H. Myers, "Zeberged," *JEA* 34 (1948) 119-120.

Walter Federn, "Notes on the Instruction to Kegemni and His Brethren," *JEA* 36 (1950) 48-50.

Alan [H.] Gardiner, "Kagemni once again," *JEA* 37 (1951) 109-110.

R. O. Faulkner, "The Man Who was Tired of Life," *JEA* 42 (1956) 21-40.

Alan H. Gardiner, "A New Moralizing Text," *WZKM* 54 (1957) 43-45.

H. S. Smith, "A Cairo text of part of 'Instructions of 'Onchsheshonqy'," *JEA* 44 (1958) 121-122.

*Rudolf Anthes, "The Legal Aspect of the Instruction of Amenemhet," *JNES* 16 (1957) 176-191.

Rudolf Anthes, "A Further Remark on the Introduction to the Instruction of Amenemhet," *JNES* 17 (1958) 208-209.

Alan [H.] Gardiner, "A Didactic Passage Re-examined," *JEA* 45 (1959) 12-15.

*B. Gemser, "The instructions of 'Onchsheshonqy and Biblical wisdom literature," *VTS* 7 (1960) 102-128.

Ronald J. Williams, "The Alleged Semitic Origin of the *Wisdom of Amenemope*," *JEA* 47 (1961) 100-106.

Alexander Badawy, "Two passages from ancient Egyptian literary texts reinterpreted," *ZÄS* 86 (1961) 144-145. *[Instruction of Parahhotep; "Man who is tired of Life"]*

Hans Goedicke, "A Neglected Wisdom Text," *JEA* 48 (1962) 25-35.

*P. Walcot, "Hesiod and the Instruction of 'Onchsheshonqy," *JNES* 21 (1962) 215-219.

John Van Seters, "A Date for the 'Admonitions' in the Second Intermediate Period," *JEA* 50 (1964) 13-23.

R. O. Faulkner, "Notes on 'The Admonitions of an Egyptian Sage'," *JEA* 50 (1964) 24-36.

R. O. Faulkner, "The Admonitions of an Egyptian Sage," *JEA* 51 (1965) 53-62.

Edward F. Wente, "A Note on 'The Eloquent Peasant,' B I, 13-15," *JNES* 24 (1965) 105-109.

B. J. Peterson, "A New Fragment of *THE WISDOM OF AMENEMOPE*," *JEA* 52 (1966) 120-128.

Hans Goedicke, "Admonitions 3, 6-10," *JARCE* 6 (1967) 93-95.

Hans Goedicke, "The Beginning of the Instruction of King Amenamhet," *JARCE* 7 (1968) 15-21.

John Barns, "A New Wisdom Text from a Writing-board in Oxford," *JEA* 54 (1968) 71-76.

K. A. Kitchen, "Studies in Egyptian Wisdom Literature," *OA* 8 (1969) 189-208.

§828   **4.3.1.1.3 *Egyptian Graffiti***

A. H. Sayce, "Gleanings from the land of Egypt," *RTR* 17 (1895) 160-164.
[VI. Graffiti in the Southern Temple, opposite Wadi-Helfa]

*G. Legrain, "The Inscriptions in the Quarries of El Hosh," *SBAP* 28 (1906)
17-26.

E. J. Pilcher, "The Scribings at Sinai," *SBAP* 31 (1909) 38-41. (Note by A.
H. Sayce, p. 132)

Alan H.Gardiner,"The Graffito from the Tomb of Pere,"*JEA* 14 (1928)10-11.

Anonymous, "Notes and Comments. 'Graffito No. 5'," *A&A* 30 (1930) 48.

William F. Edgerton, "Preliminary Report on the Ancient Graffiti at Medinet
Habu," *AJSL* 50 (1933-34) 116-127.

H. E. Winlock, "Graffiti of the Priesthood of the Eleventh Dynasty Temples
at Thebes," *AJSL* 58 (1941) 146-168.

Jaroslav Černý, "Graffiti at the Wādi el 'Allāḳi," *JEA* 33 (1947) 52-57.

L[abib] Habachi, "Graffito of the Chamberlain and the Controller of Works
Antef at Sehēl," *JEA* 39 (1953) 50-59.

P. de Bruyn, "A graffito of the scribe Ḏḥutḥotpe, reckoner of gold, in the
south-eastern desert," *JEA* 42 (1956) 121-122.

Labib Habachi, "Two Graffiti at Sehel from the Reign of Queen Hatshepsut," *JNES* 16 (1957) 88-104.

*Labib Habachi, "The Graffiti and Work of the Viceroys of Kush in the
Region of Aswan," *Kush* 5 (1957) 13-36.

Labib Habachi, "A Group of Unpublished Old and Middle Kingdom Graffiti
on Elephantine," *WZKM* 54 (1957) 55-71.

P. de Bruyn, "Falcon Graffiti in the Eastern Desert," *JEA* 44 (1958) 97-98.

§829   **4.3.1.1.4 *Egyptian Historical Texts***

*J. P. Lesley, "Notes on Some of the Historical and Mythological Features
of the D'Obriney Papyrus," *PAPS* 10 (1865-69) 543-560.

*Joseph P. Thompson, "Notes on Egyptology," *BS* 26 (1869) 184-191; 577-585. [Data for the Hyksos Period, pp. 581-585] *(Review)*

S. Birch, "On an Hieroglyphic Tablet of Alexander, son of Alexander the Great, recently discovered at Cairo," *SBAT* 1 (1872) 20-27.

[E. L.] Lushington, "The Third Sallier Papyrus, containing the Wars of Ramses II against the Cheta," *SBAT* 3 (1874) 83-103.

C. W. Goodwin, "Translation of a Fragment of an Historical Narrative relating to the Reign of Tothmes III. *From a Papyrus in the British Museum,*" *SBAT* 3 (1874) 340-348.

S. Birch, "The Inscription of Darius at the Temple of El-Khargeh," *SBAT* 5 (1876-77) 293-302.

E. L. Lushington, "The Victories of Seti I recorded in the Great Temple at Karnak," *SBAT* 6 (1878-79) 509-534.

E. L. Lushington, "The Historical Inscriptions of Seti I. in the Temple at Karnak," *SBAP* 1 (1878-79) 32-33.

*P. Thomson, "Nebuchadnezzar's Conquest of Egypt. [confirmed from a contemporary Hieroglyphic inscription]," *Exp, 1st Ser.,* 10 (1879) 397-403.

A. Eisenlohr, "An Egyptian Historical Monument," *SBAP* 3 (1880-81) 97-102. [Fyoom, No. 7798]

*†Henry George Tomkins, "A Paper on the Topography of Northern Syria, with special reference to the Karnak Lists of Thothmes III," *SBAP* 7 (1884-85) 160-163.

Henry George Tomkins, "The Karnak Tribute Lists of Thothmes III," *SBAP* 9 (1886-87) 162-167.

*Max Müller, "Notes on the 'Peoples of the Sea' of Merenptaḥ," *SBAP* 10 (1887-88) 147-154.

*Max Müller, "Supplementary Notes to 'Notes on the "Peoples of the Sea",' etc.," *SBAP* 10 (1887-88) 287-289.

A. Wiedemann, "A forgotten Prince," *SBAP* 12 (1889-90) 258-261.

F. Ll. Griffith, "James Burton's copy of the inscription of Thothmes campaigns," *ZÄS* 33 (1895) 125-126.

*Percy E. Newberry, "Extracts from my Notebook. (I).," *SBAP* 21 (1899) 303-308. [The Story of Sanehat, and the Inscription of Amenemheb: a correction, p. 303]

*James Henry Breasted, "The Annals of Thuthmose III, and the Location of Megiddo," *SBAP* 22 (1900) 96-98.

W. Spiegelberg, "The Hieratic Text in Mariette's *Karnak,* Pl. 46: A Contribution to the History of the Veziers of the New Empire," *SBAP* 24 (1902) 320-324.

*Percy E. Newberry, "Extracts from my Notebooks. VIII.," *SBAP* 27 (1905) 101-105. [60. Pyramidion of an Official of Queen Sensenb, p. 102]

*A. H. Sayce, "An Inscription of S-ankh-ka-Ra; Karian and other Inscriptions," *SBAP* 28 (1906) 171-177.

*Arthur E. P. Weigall, "A Report on some Objects recently found in Sebekh and other diggings," *ASAE* 8 (1907) 39-50. [Inscriptions of Nekhti, an official from Kom-Ombo, p. 43]

*P. Scott-Moncrieff, "Some Notes on the XVIIIth Dynasty Temple at Wady Ḥalfa," *SBAP* 29 (1907) 39-46.

*Arthur E. P. Weigall, "Upper-Egyptian Notes," *ASAE* 9 (1908) 105-112. [3. An Inscription of Senmut at Eduf, p. 106; 7. An Inscription of Thoutmosis III at El Kab, p. 108; 13. An Inscription of Hatshepsut and Thoutmosis III, p. 110]

*M. G. Kyle, "Some Geographic and Ethnic Lists of Rameses II at the Temple of Luxor," *RTR* 30 (1908) 219-223.

J[ames] H[enry] B[reasted], "The Royal Feud in the Wadi Halfa Temple," *SBAP* 31 (1909) 269-279.

P. Scott-Moncrieff, "'The Royal Feud in the Wadi Halfa Temple.' A Reply," *SBAP* 31 (1909) 333-338.

James Henry B[reasted], "The Royal Feud in the Wadi Halfa Temple: A Rejoinder," *AJSL* 26 (1909-10) 162-168.

*A. H. Sayce, "Karian, Egyptian and Nubian-Greek Inscriptions from the Sudan," *SBAP* 32 (1910) 261-268. [Record of Egyptian Conquest of the Second Cataract, pp. 262-263]

P. D. Scott-Moncrieff, "The Royal Feud in the Wady Halfa Temple," *AJSL* 27 (1910-11) 90-91.

*Max W. Müller, "An Egyptian Document for the History of Palestine," *JQR, N.S.,* 4 (1913-14) 651-656.

Alan H. Gardiner, "The Defeat of the Hyksos by Kamōse: The Carnarvon Tablet, No. I," *JEA* 3 (1915) 95-110.

Alan H. Gardiner, "An Ancient List of the Fortresses of Nubia," *JEA* 3 (1915) 184-192.

*Stanley A. Cook, "An Egyptian List of Palestinian Ambassadors," *PEFQS* 47 (1915) 43-44.

*Battiscombe Gunn and Alan H. Gardiner, "New Renderings of Egyptian Texts," *JEA* 5 (1918) 36-56. [II. The Expulsion of the Hyksos]

*S[tephen] Langdon and Alan H. Gardiner, "The Treaty of Alliance between Ḫattušili, King of the Hittites, and the Pharaoh Ramesses II of Egypt," *JEA* 6 (1920) 179-205.

T. G. Allen, "The Story of an Egyptian Politician," *AJSL* 38 (1921-22) 55-62. [Stela of _DMY_]

T. Eric Peet, "A Historical Document of Ramesside Age," *JEA* 10 (1924) 116-127.

Alan H. Gardiner, "The Autobiography of Rekhmereʿ," *ZÄS* 60 (1925) 62-76.

T. Eric Peet, "The supposed Revolution of the High-priest Amenḥotpe under Ramesses IX," *JEA* 12 (1926) 254-259. [B.M. Papyrus 10052(13.24)]

John A. Wilson, "The Texts of the Battle of Kadesh," *AJSL* 43 (1926-27) 266-287.

*S. R. K. Glanville, "Some Notes on Material for the Reign of Ameophis III," *JEA* 15 (1929) 2-8.

*S. R. K. Glanville, "Records of a Royal Dockyard of the Time of Thutmosis III.: Papyrus British Museum 10056," *ZÄS* 66 (1931) 105-121; 68 (1932) 7-41. [The Writing; Origin of the Pap. B. M. 10056; Translation; Commentary; Conclusion; Index of words discussed in the notes and of proper names; Appendix: I. Pap. Anastasi IV 7, 9-8, 7; II. Stela B. M. 1332; III. Comparative table of measurements (in cubits) of timber, etc.]

W. C. Hayes Jr.[sic], "A statue of the herald Yamu-Nedjeḥ in the Egyptian Museum, Cairo, and some biographical notes on its owner," *ASAE* 33 (1933) 6-16.

S. R. K. Glanville, "The Admission of a Priest of Soknebtynis in the Second Century B.C. Merton Demotic Papyri I," *JEA* 19 (1933) 34-41.

Alan W. Shorter, "Reliefs showing the Coronation of Ramesses II," *JEA* 20 (1934) 18-19.

*S. Yeivin, "A New Egyptian Source for the History of Palestine and Syria," *JPOS* 14 (1934) 194-239.

Alan Rowe, "Preliminary Report on Excavations of the Institute of Archaeology, Liverpool, at Athribis," *AAA* 25 (1938) 123-137. (Note by A. M. Blackman, pp. 132.) *[Translation of an Inscription of Ramesses II, pp. 132-137]*

*Alan Rowe, "Provisional notes on the Old Kingdom inscriptions from the diorite quarries," *ASAE* 38 (1938) 391-396. [I. The Chisel Inscription, pp. 391-393]

Dows Dunham, "The Biographical Inscriptions of Nekhebu in Boston and Cairo," *JEA* 24 (1938) 1-8.

Harold H. Nelson, "The Naval Battle Pictured at Medinet Habu," *JNES* 2 (1943) 40-55.

William C. Hayes, "Royal Decrees from the Temple of Min at Coptus," *JEA* 32 (1946) 3-23.

*William S. Smith, "Inscriptional Evidence for the History of the Fourth Dynasty," *JNES* 11 (1952) 113-128.

*Alan [H.] Gardiner, "The Coronation of King Ḥaremḥab," *JEA* 39 (1953) 13-31.

*Kurt Pfluger, "The Edict of King Haremhab," *JNES* 5 (1946) 260-276.

*W[illiam] F[oxwell] Albright, "Northwest-Semitic Names in a List of Egyptian Slaves from the Eighteenth Century B.C.," *JAOS* 74 (1954) 222-233.

*Giuseppe Botti, "A Fragment of the Story of a Military Expedition of Tuthmosis III to Syria (P. Turin 1940-1941)," *JEA* 41 (1955) 64-66.

*S. Yeivin, "Topographic and Ethnic Notes," *'Atiqot* 2 (1959) 155-164. [B. The Relief in Iny's tomb at Deshashe and the Date of the Execration Texts, pp. 159-163]

Hans Goedicke, "A Fragment of a Biographical Inscription of the Old Kingdom," *JEA* 45 (1959) 8-11.

*K. A. Kitchen, "Some New Light on the Asiatic Wars of Ramesses II," *JEA* 50 (1964) 47-70.

*Edouard B. Ghazouli, "The palace and magazines attached to the Temple of Sety I at Abydos and the facade of this Temple," *ASAE* 58 (1964) 99-186.

Ahmad Abd-El-Hamid Yousseff, "Mereaptah's fourth year Text at Amada," *ASAE* 58 (1964) 273-280.

§830 *4.3.1.1.4.1 Egyptian Stelae and Obelisks (with Texts)*

Joseph Bonomi, "On the Cylindrical Monument of Nechtharhebes in the Museum of Turin," *SBAT* 3 (1874) 422-424.

S[amuel] Birch, "Steles of the XII dynasty," *ZÄS* 12 (1874) 65-67.

G. Maspero, "On the Stele C 14 in the Museum of the Louvre," *SBAT* 5 (1876-77) 555-562.

†E. L. Lushington, "On the Stele of Mentuhotep," *SBAP* 3 (1880-81) 116.

E. L. Lushington, "The Stele of Mentuhotep," *SBAT* 7 (1880-82) 353-369.

E. A. W. Budge, "Notes on Egyptian Stelae, principally of the Eighteenth Dynasty," *SBAT* 8 (1883-84) 299-346.

Aug. C. Merriam, "Translation of the Obelisk in New York," *AAOJ* 6 (1884) 167-173.

†E. A. Wallis Budge, "Notes on Egyptian Stelae, principally of the Eighteenth Dynasty," *SBAP* 7 (1884-85) 7-10.

†E. A. Wallis Budge, "Some Egyptian Stelae in the Collection of Queen's College, Oxford," *SBAP* 7 (1884-85) 122-123.

Hugh Macmillan, "Egyptian Obelisks," *BFER* 34 (1885) 261-304.

*†E. A. Wallis Budge, "On an Egyptian Stele in the Museum at Bath," *SBAP* 8 (1885-86) 213-214.

A. Wiedemann, "Stelae of Libyan Origin," *SBAP* 11 (1888-89) 227.

A. Wiedemann, "Stela at Frieburg in Baden," *SBAP* 13 (1890-91) 31-39.

W. E. Crum, "Stelae from Wady Halfa," *SBAP* 16 (1893-94) 16-19.

F. Ll. Griffith, "Stela of Mentuhetep, Son of Hepy," *SBAP* 18 (1896) 195-204.

W. E. Crum, "A Stele of the XIIIth Dynasty," *SBAP* 18 (1896) 272-274.

Alan H. Gardiner, "Notes on Some Stelæ," *RTR* 19 (1897) 83-86.

(Miss) M. Murray, "The Stela of Duȧ-er-neheh," *SBAP* 19 (1897) 77.

F. Ll. Griffith, "The Aberdeen Reshep Stela," *SBAP* 22 (1900) 271.

James Henry Breasted, "The Wadi Halfa Stela of Senwosret I," *SBAP* 23 (1901) 230-235.

James Henry Breasted, "The Obelisks of Thutmose III. and his Building Season in Egypt," *ZÄS* 39 (1901) 55-61.

E. [J.] Quibell, "Statue and Steles given by Professor Sayce to the Museum," *ASAE* 3 (1902) 240-242.

*Percy E. Newberry, "Extracts from my Notebooks. V.," *SBAP* 24 (1902) 244-252. [30. A Stela of Teta, p. 246]

*Howard Carter, "Report of Work Done in Upper Egypt," *ASAE* 4 (1903) 171-180. [IV. Stela of Taharka, pp. 178-180]

*Percy E. Newberry, "Extracts from my Notebooks. VI.," *SBAP* 25 (1903) 130-138. [41. A Stela dated in the reign of Ab-aa, pp. 130-134; 44. An Early Thirteenth Dynasty Stela, pp. 135-136]

Garrett Chatfield Pier, "A New Historical Stela of the Intefs," *AJSL* 21 (1904-05) 159-162

*Arthur E. P. Weigall, "A Report on some Objects recently found in Sebekh and other diggings," *ASAE* 8 (1907) 39-50. [Stele of Psammetekh II from Shellah, pp. 39-42]

*Arthur E. P. Weigall, "Upper-Egyptian Notes," *ASAE* 9 (1908) 105-112. [10. A Stela from Dehmîd, p. 109; 16. Six Stelae of the New Empire from Binban, pp. 111-112; 17. New Empire Stela from Koptos, p. 112]

*H. R. Hall, "The *Di-hetep-suten* Formula. A Funerary Stela of a Man from Gabelen; and other notes," *SBAP* 30 (1908) 5-12. [From Gebelen: "Kharakein and Kharazieu(?)"; Mōḥōn - Mehendi; A Greek Mummy Ticket]

Alan H. Gardiner, "The Stele of Bilgai," *ZÄS* 50 (1912) 49-57.

A. F. R. Platt, "Notes on the Stele of Sekhmet-mer," *SBAP* 35 (1913) 129-132.

Fr. W. von Bissing, "Three Stelae at Graz," *AEE* 1 (1914) 14-15.

Alan H. Gardiner, "A Stele of the Early Eighteenth Dynasty from Thebes," *JEA* 3 (1915) 256.

Alan H. Gardiner, "A Stele in the MacGregor Collection," *JEA* 4 (1916) 188-189.

*M. A. Murray, "Some Fresh Inscriptions," *AEE* 4 (1917) 62-68. [I. False door of Ni-kau-Ptah; Round Topped Stele of Tehuti-hetep and Kayay]

A. H. Sayce, "A Stela found on the Site of Meroe," *SBAP* 39 (1917) 183.

Samuel A. B. Mercer, "The Junkin Stela," *JSOR* 2 (1918) 88.

T. E. Peet, "A Stela of the Reign of Sheshonk IV," *JEA* 6 (1920) 56-57.

H. Winlock, "Stela of Pernesbastet from Hassaïa," *JEA* 6 (1920) 209-211.

*A. Rowe, "An Egypto-Karian Bilingual Stele in the Nicholson Museum of the University of Sydney," *JRAS* (1920) 85-95.

R. Engelbach, "Steles and tables of offerings of the late Middle Kingdom from Tell Edfû," *ASAE* 22 (1922) 113-138.

Alan H. Gardiner, "A Stela of the Earlier Intermediate Period," *JEA* 8 (1922) 191-192.

R. Engelbach, "The Obelisks of Pylon VII at Karnak," *AEE* 8 (1923) 60-62. (Note by [W.M.] F[linders] P[etrie], p. 62)

R. Engelbach, "Small obelisk of Amenophis II from Aswan," *ASAE* 23 (1923) 163-164.

R. Engelbach, "Two steles of the late Middle Kingdom from Tell Edfû," *ASAE* 23 (1923) 183-186.

Anonymous, "The Palestine Expedition: An Historical Inscription," *MJ* 14 (1923) 5-7. *[Egyptian Stele of Seti I in Beth-Shean]*

M. A. Murray, "The Stele of the Artist. C 14 of the Louvre," *AEE* 10 (1925) 33-35.

G. A. Wainwright, "Three stelae from Nag' ed Deir," *ASAE* 25 (1925) 163-166.

*M. A. Murray, "Egyptian Objects Found in Malta," *AEE* 13 (1928) 45-51. [Stele of Onkhef; Stele of Thuy; Stele of Tetaty; Stele of Har-em-Hesit]

H[enri] Frankfort, "The Cemeteries of Abydos: Work of the Season 1925-26," *JEA* 14 (1928) 235-245. [I. Stelae]

W[illiam] F[oxwell] Albright and Alan Rowe, "A Royal Stele of the New Empire from Galilee," *JEA* 14 (1928) 281-287.

Battiscombe Gunn, "A Middle Kingdom Stela from Edfu," *ASAE* 29 (1929) 5-14.

Alan Rowe, "The Two Royal Stalæ of Beth-Shan," *MJ* 20 (1929) 89-98.

Hans Jakob Polotsky, "The Stela of Ḥeḳa-yeb," *JEA* 16 (1930) 194-199.

H. W. Fairman, "Notes on the Date of Some Buchis Stelae," *JEA* 16 (1930) 240-241.

Aylward M. Blackman, "The Stele of Thethi, Brit. Mus. No. 614," *JEA* 17 (1931) 55-61.

G. A. Reisner, "Inscribed Monuments from Gebel Barkal," *ZÄS* 66 (1931) 77-100. [The More Important Inscriptions. The Sandstone Stela of Piankhy, No. 26, pp. 89-100]

Alan H. Gardiner, "The Dakhleah Stela," *JEA* 19 (1933) 19-30.

Alan W. Shorter, "A Stela of Seti I in the British Museum," *JEA* 19 (1933) 60-61.

Nathaniel Julius Reich, "A Hieroglyphic Stela from Mt. Serabit of the Sinai Peninsula," *Miz* 1 (1933) 144-146. *[Introduction by Romain Butin]*

G. A. Reisner and M. B. Reisner, "Inscribed Monuments from Gebel Barkal," *ZÄS* 69 (1933) 24-39 73-78. [Part 2. The granite Stela of Thutmosis III., pp. 24-39; Part 3. The Stela of Sety I., pp. 73-78]

M. B. Reisner, "Inscribed monuments from Gebel Barkal," *ZÄS* 70 (1934) 35-46. [Part 4: The Stela of Prince Khaliut]

A. M. Blackman, "The Stela of Nebipusenwosret: British Museum No. 101," *JEA* 21 (1935) 1-9.

M[ary] L[ouise] M[orton], "The Stela of Mery," *UMB* 6 (1935-37) #2, 43-45.

P[hilippus] M[iller], "Stela of Sisopduyenhab and His Relatives," *UMB* 6 (1935-37) #5, 7-10.

*Ahmed Fakury, "Miscellanea," *ASAE* 37 (1937) 25-38. [1. Two New Staelae of Tiberus from Luxor Temple; 3. A note on the Zernikh Stele, pp. 30-33]

Pahor Cl. Labib, "The Stela of Nefer-ronpet," *ASAE* 36 (1936) 194-196.

Selim bey Hassan, "The great limestone stela of Amenhotep II," *ASAE* 37 (1937) 129-134.

Philippus Miller, "A Family Stela in the University Museum, Philadelphia," *JEA* 23 (1937) 1-6.

I. E. S. Edwards, "A Toilet Scene on a Funerary Stela of the Middle Kingdom," *JEA* 23 (1937) 165. [B.M. 1658]

*Alan Rowe, "Provisional notes on the Old Kingdom inscriptions from the diorite quarries," *ASAE* 38 (1938) 391-396. [I. The Chisel Inscription; II. The Cheops Stela Inscription; III. The Sahurēʿ Stela Inscription]

Ahmed Fakhry, "Stela of the boat-captain Inikaf," *ASAE* 38 (1938) 35-46.

A. N. Dakin, "The Stela of the Sculptor Sirēʿ at Oxford," *JEA* 24 (1938) 190-197.

A. Hamada, "A stela from Manshîyet eṣ-Ṣadr," *ASAE* 38 (1938) 217-230.

Moharram Kamal, "The stela of ⊙ 𓈖𓏺𓂋𓏲 in the Egyptian Museum," *ASAE* 38 (1938) 265-284.

Alan Rowe, "Additional references to the article: 'Provisional notes on the Old Kingdom inscriptions from the diorite Quarries' *in Annales du Service,* XXXVIII," *ASAE* 38 (1938) 678-688.

Guy Brunton, "A monument of Àmenemhet IV," *ASAE* 39 (1939) 177-181.

Alan Rowe, "Three new stelæ from the south-eastern desert," *ASAE* 39 (1939) 187-194. [I. Stela of Horus; II. Stela of Henenew; III. Stela of 'Meṭew-Ḥotep's Son Ḥenenew']

A. Hamada, "Stela of Putiphar," *ASAE* 39 (1939) 273-276.

*J. Gwyn Griffiths, "P. Oslo. 1, 105-9 and Metternich Stela 85-6," *JEA* 25 (1939) 101.

Paul C. Smither and Alec N. Dakin, "Stelae in the Queen's College, Oxford," *JEA* 25 (1939) 157-165.

*G. Lefebvre, "A Note on Brit. Mus. 828 (Stela of Simontu)," *JEA* 25 (1939) 218. (Note by Battiscombe Gunn, pp. 218-219)

*Sidney Smith, "Late Eighteenth Dynasty or Nineteenth?" *JEA* 25 (1939) 219-220.

Moharram Kamal, "The stela of ⊙⎮⎯⎮⎮ ⎮ in the Egyptian Museum (verso)," *ASAE* 40 (1940-41) 209-229.

Battiscombe Gunn, "Notes on the Naukratis Stela," *JEA* 29 (1943) 55-59.

Abd el-Moḥsen Bakir, "A donation stela of the twenty-second dynasty," *ASAE* 43 (1943) 75-81.

*Kurt Pfluger, "The Private Funerary Stelae of the Middle Kingdom and Their Importance for the Study of Ancient Egyptian History," *JAOS* 67 (1947) 127-135.

T. Säve-Söderberg, "A Behen Stela from the Second Intermediate Period (Kharṭūm No. 18)," *JEA* 35 (1949) 50-58.

Jean Saint Fare Garnot, "Notes on the Inscriptions of Suty and Ḥor. (British Museum Stela No. 826)," *JEA* 35 (1949) 63-68.

*H. H. Rowley, "Recent Foreign Theology. A Beth-shan Stele of Seti I," *ET* 61 (1949-50) 381. *(Review)*

L. Habachi, "An Inscription at Aswān referring to Six Obelisks," *JEA* 36 (1950) 13-18.

M. F. Laming Macadam, "Four Meroitic Inscriptions," *JEA* 36 (1950) 43-47. [1. Stela Kharṭūm 5162; 2. Stela Kharṭūm 5261; 3. Stela Kharṭūm 3725; 4. Stela Kharṭūm 3732]

R. O. Faulkner, "The Stela of Rudj'aḫua," *JEA* 37 (1951) 47-52.

W[illiam] F[oxwell] Albright, "The Smaller Beth-Shan stele of Sethos I (1309-1290 B.C.)," *BASOR* #125 (1952) 24-32.

R. O. Faulkner, "The Stela of the Master-Sculptor Shen," *JEA* 38 (1952) 3-5.

Manfred Cassirer, "A *ḥb-sd* Stela of Amenophis III," *JEA* 38 (1952) 128-130.

Jozef M. A. Janssen, "The Stela (Khartoum Museum No. 3) from Uronarti," *JNES* 12 (1953) 51-55.

S. Yeivin, "A Fragmentary Stele of Tuthmosis III from Armant," *BIES* 18 (1953-54) #3/4, III.

*Labib Habachi, "Preliminary report on Komose Stela and other inscribed blocks found reused in the foundations of two statues at Karnak," *ASAE* 53 (1955) 195-202.

Kate Bosse-Griffiths, "The Memphite Stela of Merptaḥ and Ptaḥmosĕ," *JEA* 41 (1955) 56-63.

Charles F. Nims, "A Stele of Penre Builder of Ramesseum," *MDIÄA* 14 (1956) 146-149.

Henry George Fischer, "A God and a General of the Oasis of a Stela of the Late Middle Kingdom," *JNES* 16 (1957) 223-235.

Jean Vercoutter, "Upper Egyptian Settlers in Middle Kingdom Nubia (Stela Khartoum Mus. 11778, 372A and 247, Statue Khartoum Mus. 5516)," *Kush* 5 (1957) 61-69.

E. P. Uphill, "The Stela of 'Ankhefenmut," *JEA* 43 (1957) 1-2.

H. S. K. Bakry, "The Stela of Dedu ⸗ *Ddw*," *ASAE* 55 (1958) 63-65.

H. S. K. Bakry, "The Stela of 𓇋𓂝𓊪 ⫶ 𓏏𓏤 *Nfr-Šḥrw,* Artisan of Ptaḥ, at Saqqarah," *ASAE* 55 (1958) 67-71.

J[aroslav] Černý, "Stela of Ramsses II from Beisan," *EI* 5 (1958) 75*-82*.

Alan R. Schulman, "A Faience Stela from the New Kingdom," *Exped* 2 (1959-60) #4, 32-33.

K. A. Kitchen, "Four Stelae in Leicester City Museum," *Or, N.S.,* 29 (1960) 75-97.

Alexander Badawy, "The Stela of Irtysen," *CdÉ* 36 (1961) 269-275.

Jaroslav Černý, "The Stela of Merer in Cracow," *JEA* 47 (1961) 5-9.

K. A. Kitchen, "An Unusual Stela from Abydos," *JEA* 47 (1961) 10-18.

William K. Simpson, "An Additional Fragment of a 'Hatnub' Stela," *JNES* 20 (1961) 25-30.

H. S. K. Bakry, "The Stela of *pꜣ-ḥꜣty* the follower of Seth," *ASAE* 57 (1962) 7-8.

H. S. K. Bakry, "Two New-Kingdom Stela," *ASAE* 57 (1962) 9-14.

*John Bennett, "A new interpretation of B.M. stela 1203," *JEA* 48 (1962) 158-159.

*William Stevenson Smith, "The Stela of Prince Wepemnofret," *Arch* 16 (1963) 2--13.

Jac. J. Janssen, "An Unusual Donation Stela," *JEA* 49 (1963) 64-70.

Edward F. Wente, "Two Ramesside Stelas Pertaining to the Cult of Amenophis I," *JNES* 22 (1963) 30-36.

Henry George Fischer, "A Stela of the Heracleopolitan Period at Saqqara: The Osiris *'Iti,*" *ZÄS* 90 (1963) 35-41.

*W[illiam] A. Ward and M. F. Martin, "The Balu'a Stele: A New Transcription with Palaeological and Historical Notes," *ADAJ* 8&9 (1964) 5-29.

Ricardo A. Caminos, "The Nitocris Adoption Stela," *JEA* 50 (1964) 71-101.

Abd el-Hamid Zayed, "A Free-standing Stela of the XIXth Dynasty," *RÉg* 16 (1964) 193-208.

William Kelly Simpson, "The Stela of Amun-wosre, Governor of Upper Egypt in the Reign of Ammenemes I or II," *JEA* 51 (1965) 63-68.

*Raphael Giveon, "Two Egyptian Documents Concerning Bashan from the Time of Ramses II," *RDSO* 40 (1965) 197-202. [1. The Job Stone, pp. 197-200; 2. The Stela of Benanzan, pp. 200-202]

Bengt Julius Peterson, "Two Egyptian Stelae," *OrS* 14&15 (1965-66) 3-8.

Ibrahim Kamel, "A stela from Mendes," *ASAE* 59 (1966) 27-31.

Hans Goedicke, "Some Remarks on the 400-Year Stela," *CdÉ* 41 (1966) 23-39.

W[illiam] K[elly] Simpson, "Provenance and date of the stela of Amun-wosre (*JEA* 51, 63-68)," *JEA* 52 (1966) 174.

Jaroslav Černý, "Stela of Emḥab from Tell Edfu," *MDIÄA* 24 (1969) 87-92.

*H. S. K. Bakry, "Psammĕtichus II and his Newly-Found Stela at Shellâl," *OA* 6 (1967) 225-244.

Ḥ[assan] S. K. Bakry, "A stela of Horus standing on crocodiles from the Middle Delta," *RDSO* 42 (1967) 15-18.

Dia' Abou-Ghazi, "Two New Monuments inscribed in Hieroglyphics from Ptolemaic Egypt," *BIFAO* 66 (1968) 165-169.

G. A. Gaballa and K. A. Kitchen, "Ramesside Varia I," *CdÉ* 43 (1968) 259-270. [3. Fragment of a Stela of Sethos II]

Cyril Aldred, "Two Monuments of the Reign of Horemḥeb," *JEA* 54 (1968) 100-106.

Jac. J. Janssen, "The Smaller Dâkhla Stela (Ashmolean Museum no. 1894. 107b)," *JEA* 54 (1968) 165-172.

Abd el Hamid Zayed, "Painted Wooden Stelae in the Cairo Museum," *RÉg* 20 (1968) 149-170.

R. Holthoer, "An Egyptian Late Middle Kingdom stela in the Finnish National Museum at Helsinki," *SO* 37 (1968) #1, 1-122.

*Richardo A. Caminos, "An Ancient Egyptian Donation Stela in the Archae-ological Museum of Florence (Inv. No. 7207)," *Cent* 14 (1969) 42-46.

Hans Goedicke, "Some Notes on the Nitocris Adoption Stela," *JARCE* 8 (1969-70) 69-71.

§831 *4.3.1.1.4.2 Merenptah Inscription*

Ronald G. Macintyre, "The New Discovery in Egypt," *ET* 7 (1895-96) 445-446.

Alfred Colbeck, "The New Discovery in Egypt II," *ET* 7 (1895-96) 446.

J. J. Lias, "The New Discovery in Egypt III," *ET* 7 (1895-96) 446-447.

J. T. Marshall, "The New Discovery in Egypt IV," *ET* 7 (1895-96) 447.

J. A. Selbie, "Israel in the Newly-Discovered Egyptian Inscription," *ET* 7 (1895-96) 548-549. *[Merenptah Inscription]*

*A. A. Berle, "Semitic and Oriental Note. Israel in Egypt," *BS* 53 (1896) 745-747. *[Merenptah Inscription]*

*W. M. Flinders Petrie, "Israel and Egypt," *ContR* 69 (1896) 617-627. [The Merenptah Tablet, pp. 620-622]

F. Hommel, "Merenptah and the Israelites I.," *ET* 8 (1896-97) 15-17.

J. William Dawson, "Merenptah and the Israelites II.," *ET* 8 (1896-97) 17-18.

J. A. Selbie, "The Merenptah Inscription," *ET* 8 (1896-97) 76.

A. H. Sayce, "The Israelites on the Stela of Merenptah," *ET* 8 (1896-97) 89-90.

Josiah Mullens, "Merenptah and Israel," *ET* 8 (1896-97) 286-287.

*W. W. Moore, "The Latest Light from Egypt," *USR* 8 (1896-97) 30-38. [The Merenptah Inscription, pp. 31-34]

*[George H. Schodde], "Biblical Research Notes," *ColTM* 17 (1897) 117-121. [Mer-en-ptah and His Inscriptions, p. 121]

*Joseph Offord, "Two Texts Referred to in Report to the Oriental Congress," *SBAP* 20 (1898) 53-55. *[Merenptah Inscription]*

Anonymous, "'The Israel Tablet'," *CFL, O.S.,* 1 (1897) 46-47.

*F. Ll. Griffith, "The Israel Stela," *SBAP* 19 (1897) 298-299.

W. W. Moore, "The Israel Tablet of Merenptah," *PQ* 12 (1898) 1-23.

*Joseph Offord, "Two Texts Referred to in Report of the Oriental Congress," *SBAP* 20 (1898) 53-55. [Meneptah Inscription, pp. 54-55]

Anonymous, "The Stele of Merenptah," *MQR, 3rd Ser.,* 32 (1906) 183-184.

*Hanbury Brown, "The Exodus Mentioned on the Stele of Merephtah[sic]," *JEA* 4 (1916) 16-20.

J. W. Jack, "The Israel Stele of Merenptah," *ET* 36 (1924-25) 40-44.

J. Murtagh, "The Stela of Merenptah," *Scrip* 20 (1968) 20-23.

§832   **4.3.1.1.5 Egyptian Legal Texts including Contracts and Marriage Documents**

*Joseph P. Thompson, "Notes on Egyptology," *BS* 26 (1869) 184-191; 577-585. [A State Trial in Ancient Egypt, pp. 577-581] *(Review)*

*E. Revillout and V. Revillout, "*Sword Obligations* in Egyptian and Babylonian Law," *BOR* 1 (1886-87) 101-104.

F. Ll. Griffith, "The account papyrus No. 18 of Bulaq," *ZÄS* 29 (1891)102-116.

Claude R. Conder, "Tadukhepa's Dowry," *PEFQS* 25 (1893) 321-322.

F. Ll. Griffith, "A Sale of Land in the reign of Philopator," *SBAP* 23 (1901) 294-302.

Anonymous, "An Ancient Egyptian Lawsuit," *RP* 4 (1905) 351. *[The Inscription of Mes]*

F. Ll. Griffith, "A Contract of the Fifth Year of Amenhotp IV," *SBAP* 30 (1908) 272-275.

*F. Ll. Griffith, "A Demotic Marriage Contract of the Earlier Ptolemaic Type," *SBAP* 31 (1909) 47-56.

*F. Ll. Griffith, "The Earliest Egyptian Marriage Contracts," *SBAP* 31 (1909) 212-220.

F. Ll. Griffith, "An Early Contract Papyrus in the Vatican," *SBAP* 32 (1910) 5-10.

Herbert Thompson, "Demotic Tax-Receipts," *SBAP* 35 (1913) 114-117, 150-153, 187-188, 227-228, 261-263.

T. E. Peet, "A Mortuary Contract of the XIth Egyptian Dynasty," *AAA* 7 (1914-16) 81-88.

*Nathaniel Reich, "A Notary of Ancient Thebes," *MJ* 14 (1923) 22-25.

*Nathaniel Reich, "Marriage and Divorce in Ancient Egypt: Papyrus Documents discovered at Thebes by the Eckley B. Coxe Jr. Expedition to Egypt," *MJ* 15 (1924) 50-57.

J[aroslav] Černý and T. Eric Peet, "A Marriage Settlement of the Twentieth Dynasty. An Unpublished Document from Turin,"*JEA* 13 (1927) 30-39.

S. R. K. Glanville, "Book-keeping for a Cult of Rameses II," *JRAS* (1929) 19-26. [B.M. Pap. 10447]

Nathaniel Julius Reich, "A Demotic Divorce," *Miz* 1 (1933) 135-139.

*Nathaniel Julius Reich, "The Codification of the Egyptian Laws by Darius and the Origin of the 'Demotic Chronicle'," *Miz* 1 (1933) 178-185.

Alan H. Gardiner, "A Lawsuit arising from the Purchase of Two Slaves," *JEA* 21 (1935) 140-146.

*J. Capart, A. H. Gardiner, and B. van de Walle, "New Light on the Ramesside Tomb-Robberies," *JEA* 22 (1936) 169-193. [Papyrus Leopold II]

N[athaniel] J[ulius] Reich, "The Legal Transactions of a Family: Preserved in the University Museum at Philadelphia. (The Demotic Papyri from Drah Abu 'l-Negga Covering a Century of Early Ptolemaic Period)," *Miz* 2 (1936) 13-29.

N[athaniel] J[ulius] Reich, "The Field Museum Papyrus. (A Promissory Note of the Year 109/8 B.C.)," *Miz* 2 (1936) 36-51.

N[athaniel] J[ulius] Reich, "A Deed of Gift in 317 B.C. (Papyrus University Museum, Philadelphia, Jar 2; 800 d; 888; 29-86-523B = Document I)," *Miz* 2 (1936) 57-69.

N[athaniel] J[ulius] Reich, "Barter for Annuity and Perpetual Provision of the Body (Papyrus University Museum, Philadelphia, 873; Jar 1; 29-86-508 = Document II)," *Miz* 3 (1936) 9-17.

N[athaniel] J[ulius] Reich, "Terms for Repayment of a Seed-Loan. Preserved in Turin," *Miz* 3 (1936) 26-30.

N[athaniel] J[ulius] Reich, "Witness-Contract-Copies in the University Museum at Philadelphia (and Other Documents Written on the Same Papyrus-Sheet as the Original Text)," *Miz* 3 (1936) 31-50.

A. de Buck, "The Judicial Papyrus of Turin," *JEA* 23 (1937) 152-164.

*Jaroslav Černy, "Restitution of, and Penalty attaching to, Stolen Property in Ramesside Times," *JEA* 23 (1937) 186-189.

N[athaniel] J[ulius] Reich, "The Greek Deposit-Notes of the Record-Office on the Demotic Contracts of the Papyrus-Archive in the University Museum," *Miz* 9 (1938) 19-32.

*Alan H. Gardiner, "Adoption Extraordinary," *JEA* 26 (1940) 23-29.

*Richard A. Parker, "A Late Demotic Gardening Agreement. Medinet Habu Ostracon 4038," *JEA* 26 (1940) 84-113.

*Alan H. Gardiner, "Ramesside Texts relating to the Taxation and Transport of Corn," *JEA* 27 (1941) 19-73.

Paul C. Smither, "A Tax-Assessor's Journal of the Middle Kingdom," *JEA* 27 (1941) 74-76.

*Jaroslav Černý, "The Will of Naunakhte and the Related Documents," *JEA* 31 (1945) 29-53.

*Kurt Pfluger, "The Edict of King Haremhab," *JNES* 5 (1946) 260-276.

Girgis Mattha, "An Early Ptolemaic bank-reciept from Elephantine," *BIFAO* 45 (1947) 57-58.

William F. Edgerton, "The Nauri Decree of Seti I: A translation and Analysis of the Legal Portion," *JNES* 6 (1947) 219-230.

Paul C. Smither, "The Report concerning the Slave-girl Senbet," *JEA* 34 (1948) 31-34. [P. Berlin 10470]

Alan [H.] Gardiner, "A protest against unjustified tax-demands," *RÉg* 6 (1951) 115-133.

*J[acob] J. Rabinowitz, "A Legal Formula in the Susa Tablets, in an Egyptian Document of the Twelfth Dynasty, in the Aramaic Papyri, and in the Book of Daniel [4, 14]," *B* 36 (1955) 223-226.

*Jacob J. Rabinowitz, "A Legal Formula in Egyptian, Egyptian-Aramaic, and Murabba'at Documents," *BASOR* #145 (1957) 33-34.

E. A. E. Jelínková, "Sale of Inherited Property in the First Century B.C. (P. Brit. Mus. 10075, Ex Salt Coll. No. 418)," *JEA* 43 (1957) 45-55; 45 (1959) 61-74.

*Rudolf Anthes, "The Legal Aspect of the Instruction of Amenemhet," *JNES* 16 (1957) 176-191.

H. S. Smith, "Another Witness-Copy Document from the Fayyūm," *JEA* 44 (1958) 86-96. [P.B.M. 10750]

Jacob J. Rabinowitz, "Semitic Elements in the Egyptian Adoption Papyrus Published by Gardiner," *JNES* 17 (1958) 145-146.

W. Erichsen and C. F. Nims, "A Further Category of Demotic Marriage Settlements," *AO* 23 (1958-59) 119-133.

A. F. Shore and H. S. Smith, "A Demotic Embalmers' Agreement (Pap. dem. B.M. 10561)," *AO* 25 (1960) 277-294.

Henry G. Fischer, "Land Records on Stelae of the Twelfth Dynasty," *RÉg* 13 (1961) 107-109.

Richard A. Parker, "A Demotic Marriage Document from Deir el Ballas," *JARCE* 2 (1963) 113-116.

*Hans Goedicke, "Was Magic used in the Harem Conspiracy against Ramesses III (P. Rollin and P. Lee)?" *JEA* 49 (1963) 71-92.

*Richard H. Pierce, "A Note on Some Alleged Certificates of Registration from Ptolemaic Egypt," *Aeg* 44 (1964) 170-173.

Bryan G. Haycock, "A New Kingdom royal funerary estate mentioned in the Twenty-sixth Dynasty," *JEA* 50 (1964) 180-181.

J. J. Janssen, "A Twentieth-Dynasty Account Papyrus (Pap. Turin no. Cat. 1907/8)," *JEA* 52 (1966) 81-94.

A. F. Shore, "The Sale of the House of Senkhonsis Daughter of Phibis," *JEA* 54 (1968) 193-198.

Mustafa el-Amir, "Further Notes on the Demotic Papyri in the Turin Museum (Topographical and Legal Studies)," *BIFAO* 68 (1969) 85-120.

§833 *4.3.1.1.6 Egyptian Literary Texts*

C. W. Goodwin, "Translation of a Fragment of an Egyptian Fabulous Tale. *From an Egyptian Papyrus in the British Museum,*" *SBAT* 3 (1874) 349-356. *[The Doomed Prince]*

Anonymous, "The Testimony of the Monuments," *OBJ* 1 (1880) 24-25. *[The Tale of the Two Brothers]*

P. le Page Renouf, "Parallels in Folk Lore," *SBAP* 11 (1888-89) 177-189. *[The Tale of the Two Brothers]*

F. L. Griffith, "Fragments of Old Egyptian Stories," *SBAP* 14 (1891-92) 451-472.

*Percy E. Newberry, "Extracts from my Notebooks (I).," *SBAP* 21 (1899) 303-308. [1. The Story of Sanehat and the Inscription of Amenemheb: a correction, p. 303]

Wilhelm Spiegelberg, "Contributions to the Second Tale of Khamuas," *SBAP* 23 (1901) 252-254.

Alan H. Gardiner, "Notes on the Tale of the Shipwrecked Sailor," *ZÄS* 45 (1908) 60-66.

Alan H. Gardiner, "Notes on the Story of Sinuhe," *RTR* 32 (1910) 1-28, 214-230; 33 (1911) 67-94, 221-230; 34 (1912) 52-77, 193-206; 36 (1914) 17-50, 192-209.

Alan H. Gardiner, "New Literary Works from Ancient Egypt," *JEA* 1 (1914) 20-36, 100-106. [Pap. Petersburg 1116A, *recto;* 1116B *recto*]

Warren R. Dawson, "New Literary Works from Ancient Egypt," *IAQR* 21 (1926) 305-312.

A. Rosenvasser, "A New Duplicate Text of the Story of Sinuhe," *JEA* 20 (1934) 47-50.

*A. M. Blackman, "Some Notes on the Story of Sinuhe and other Egyptian Texts," *JEA* 22 (1936) 35-44.

J. J. Clère, "Three New Ostraca of the Story of Sinuhe," *JEA* 25 (1939) 16-29.

A. de Buck, "A Note on Sinuhe B, 71-72," *JEA* 25 (1939) 100.

*J[aroslav] Černý, "Philological and Etymological Notes. I," *ASAE* 41 (1942) 335-338. [2. The opening words of the tales of the Doomed Prince and the Two Brothers, pp. 336-338]

Girgis Mattha, "Notes and Remarks on the Tale of the Doomed Prince, from pap. Harris 500, verso," *ASAE* 51 (1951) 269-272.

G. Posener, "On the Tale of the Doomed Prince," *JEA* 39 (1953) 107.

*Hans Goedicke, "The Route of Sinuhe's Flight," *JEA* 43 (1957) 77-85.

Werner Vycichl, "Notes on the Story of the Shipwrecked Sailor," *Kush* 5 (1957) 70-72.

W. K. Simpson, "Papyrus Lythgoe: A Fragment of a Literary Text of the Middle Kingdom from El-Lisht," *JEA* 46 (1960) 65-70.

Hans Goedicke, "Sinuhe's Reply to the King's Letter," *JEA* 51 (1965) 29-47.

J. W. B. Barns, " Sinuhe's Message to the King: A Reply to a Recent Article," *JEA* 53 (1967) 6-14.

§834 *4.3.1.1.7 Egyptian Mathematical, Astronomical, Medical and "Scientific" Texts*

*G. Seyffarth, "Three Lectures on Egyptian Antiquities, &c., delivered at the Stuyvesant Institute, New York, May 1856," *ER* 8 (1856-57) 34-104. [IX. The Zodiac of Dendera, pp. 78-79; X. The Isis-table (*Tabula Bembina*), p. 79]

*S[amuel] Birch, "Geometric Papyrus," *ZÄS* 6 (1868) 108-110.

Samuel Birch, "An Egyptian Tablet in the British Museum.   On Two Architects of the XIXth Dynasty," *SBAP* 3 (1880-81) 56-58.

*S[amuel] Birch, "On a Tablet in the British Museum relating to two Architects," *SBAT* 8 (1883-84) 143-163.

*S[amuel] Birch, "Medical Papyrus with the name of Cheops," *ZÄS* 9 (1871) 61-64. [Brit. Mus. 10059]

*P. le Page Renouf, "Note on the Medical Papyrus of Berlin," *ZÄS* 11 (1873) 123-125.

*P. le Page Renouf, "Calendar of Astronomical Observations found in Royal Tombs of the XXth Dynasty," *SBAT* 3 (1874) 400-421.

*P. le Page Renouf, "The Eclipse in Egyptian Texts," *SBAP* 7 (1884-85) 163-170.

F. Ll. Griffith, "The Rhind Mathematical Papyrus," *SBAP* 13 (1890-91) 328-332. [B.M. Pap. 10,057 + 10,058]

*F. L. Griffith, "The Metrology of the Medical Papyrus Ebers," *SBAP* 13 (1890-91) 392-406, 526-538.

*A. Eisenlohr, "Extract from a Letter," *SBAP* 13 (1890-91) 596-598. [Rhind Mathematical Papyrus & Ebers Medical Papyrus]

*F. L. Griffith, "The Rhind Mathematical Papyrus," *SBAP* 14 (1891-92) 26-31; 16 (1893-94) 164-173, 201-208, 230-248.

*†August Eisenlohr, "Letter to Mr. Rylands referring to the Mathematical Papyrus," *SBAP* 21 (1899) 49-50.

*Charles Warren, "Egyptian Weights and Measures Since the Eighteenth Dynasty and of the Rhind Mathematical Papyrus," *PEFQS* 32 (1900) 149-150.

*F. M. Barber, "An Ancient Egyptian Mechanical Problem. Papyrus Anastasi I. About 1300. B.C.," *OC* 26 (1912) 705-716.

*Howard Carter and Alan H. Gardiner, "The Tomb of Ramesses IV and the Turin Plain of a Royal Tomb," *JEA* 4 (1916) 130-158.

*B. Touraeff, "The Volume of the Truncated Pyramid in Egyptian Mathematics," *AEE* 4 (1917) 100-102.

*[W. M.] Flinders Petrie, "Egyptian Working Papyrus," *AEE* 11 (1926) 24-27. *[Architectural Blueprint]*

S. R. K. Glanville, "The Mathematical Leather Roll in the British Museum," *JEA* 13 (1927) 232-239. [B.M. 10250]

*Battiscombe Gunn and T. Eric Peet, "Four Geometrical Problems from the Moscow Mathematical Papyrus," *JEA* 15 (1929) 167-185.

*W. R. Thomas, "Moscow Mathematical Papyrus, No. 14," *JEA* 17 (1931) 50-52.

*Vladimir Vikentiev, "Nâr-Ba-Thai," *JEA* 17 (1931) 67-80. [I. Nâr-Mertha or Nâr-Ba-Thai? pp. 67-71; II. The hero of Papyrus d'Orbiney and his relation to *nʿr*-fish, pp. 71-74; II. The Valley and the Trea of Ba-Ta, pp. 74-78; Conclusions, pp. 78-80]

*T. Eric Peet, "A Problem in Egyptian Geometry," *JEA* 17 (1931) 100-106.

*A[lexander] Pogo, "The Astronomical Inscriptions on the Coffins of Heny (XIth dynasty?)," *Isis* 18 (1932) 7-13.

*O. Neugebauer, "Egyptian Planetary Texts," *TAPS, N.S.,* 32 (1941-43) 209-250.

John A. Wilson, "A Note on the Edwin Smith Surgical Papyrus," *JNES* 11 (1952) 76-80.

*Richard A. Parker, "Two Demotic Astronomical Papyri in the Carlsberg Collection," *AO* 26 (1961-62) 143-147.

§835 *4.3.1.1.8 Egyptian Ostraca*

C. W. Goodwin, "On a hieratic inscription upon a stone in the British Museum," *ZÄS* 10 (1872) 20-24. [Sinuhe-Ostrakon B.M. 5629]

†Samuel Birch, "Remarks on the Ostraka at Queen's College, Oxford," *SBAP* 5 (1882-83) 119-120.

W. Max Müller, "An Ostracon in the Museum of New York," *RTR* 22 (1900) 103-105.

Anonymous, "Ostraca from the Valley of the Kings," *RP* 11 (1912) 148.

Herbert Thompson, "A Demotic Ostracon," *SBAP* 35 (1913) 95-96.

W. Spiegelberg, "Hieratic Ostraka from Thebes," *AEE* 1 (1914) 106-111.

*W. M. F[linders] P[etrie], "Boat Names in Egypt," *AEE* 2 (1915) 136-137.

Warren R. Dawson, "Note on some Ostraca from El-'Amarnah," *JEA* 10 (1924) 133..

*Alan W. Shorter, "A Magical Ostracon," *JEA* 22 (1936) 165-168.

F. M. Heichelheim, "On Medīnet Habu Ostracon 4038," *JEA* 27 (1941) 161.

J[aroslav] Černý, "A Hieroglyphic Ostracon in the Museum of Fine Arts at Boston," *JEA* 44 (1958) 23-25.

W. C. Hayes, "A Selection of Tuthmoside Ostraca from Dēr El Baḥri," *JEA* 46 (1960) 29-52.

S. Yeiven, "A Hieratic Ostracon from Tel Arad," *IEJ* 16 (1966) 153-159.

Hans Goedicke, "Four Hieratic Ostraca of the Old Kingdom," *JEA* 54 (1968) 23-30. [Ostracon Leiden J 426; J 427; J 428; J 429]

§836 *4.3.1.1.9 Palettes*

*E. Towry Whyte, "An Egyptian Painter's Palette,"*SBAP* 23 (1901) 130-131.

*William C. Hayes, "A Writing-Palette of the Chief Steward Amenḥotpe and Some Notes on its Owner," *JEA* 24 (1938) 9-24.

*Ruth Amiran, "Note on One Sign in the Narmer Palette," *JARCE* 7 (1968) 127.

Bernard V. Bothmer, "A New Fragment of an Old Palette," *JARCE* 8 (1969-70) 5-8.

§837 *4.3.1.1.10 Egyptian Religious Texts including Rituals and Incantations*

†Anonymous, "The Book of Fate," *BCQTR, N.S.,* 20 (1823) 138-143. *(Review)*

P. le Page Renouf, "On some Religious Texts of the Early Egyptian Period preserved in Hieratic Papyri in the British Museum," *SBAP* 7 (1884-85) 6.

P. le Page Renouf, "On some Religious Texts of the Early Egyptian Period. Preserved in Hieratic Papyri in the British Museum," *SBAT* 9 (1886-93) 295-306.

Aug. Eisenlohr, "A Phoenician Monument at the Frontier of Palestine," *SBAP* 14 (1891-92) 364-370. *[Egyptian Text]*

*Alan H. Gardiner, "The goddess Ningal in an Egyptian text," *ZÄS* 43 (1906) 97.

*Anonymous, "The Pyramid Texts and the Future Life," *AAOJ* 30 (1908) 346-348.

*F. Ll. Griffith and U. Wilcken, "A bilingual sale of liturgies in 136 B.C.," *ZÄS* 45 (1908) 103-110.

Aylward M. Blackman, "Some Middle Kingdom Religious Texts," *ZÄS* 47 (1910) 116-132.

*I. Sneguireff, "Some Unpublished Egyptian Objects from Kertch, Olbia and Tiflis," *AEE* 14 (1929) 101-103.

Alan H. Gardiner, "A New Letter to the Dead," *JEA* 16 (1930) 19-22.

George S. Duncan, "The Oldest Immortality Inscriptions—2600 B.C.," *AJA* 36 (1932) 38.

A. Lucas and Alan Rowe, "The Ancient Egyptian *Bekhen-* stone," *ASAE* 38 (1938) 127-156.

A. Lucas and Alan Rowe, "Additional references to the article: 'The ancient Egyptian *Bekhen-* Stone'," *ASAE* 38 (1938) 677.

A. M. Blackman, "A Further Note on the Sacred Heart at Athribis," *AAA* 26 (1939-40) 10.

*A[lan] Rowe, "Newly-Identified monuments in the Egyptian Museum showing the deification of the dead together with brief details of similar objects elsewhere," *ASAE* 40 (1940-41) 1-50.

Guy Burton, "Bekhen-stone," *ASAE* 40 (1940-41) 617-618.

*N. Shiah, "Some remarks on the *Bekhen-* stone," *ASAE* 41 (1942) 189-205.

A. Lucas and Alan Rowe, "Additions and corrections to *The Ancient Egyptian* Bekhen-Stone (in *Annales du Service,* XXXVIII)," *ASAE* 41 (1942) 347.

Harold H. Nelson, "The Identity of Amon-Re of United-With-Eternity," *JNES* 1 (1942) 127-155.

Harold H. Nelson, "The Rite of 'Bringing the Foot' as portrayed in Temple Reliefs," *JEA* 35 (1949) 82-86.

*A. M. Blackman and H. W. Fairman, "The Significance of the Ceremony Ḥwt Bḥsw in the Temple of Horus at Edfu," *JEA* 35 (1949) 98-112; 36 (1950) 63-81.

George R. Hughes, "A Demotic Astrological Text," *JNES* 10 (1951) 256-264.

Labib Habachi and Banoub Habachi, "The Naos with the Decades (Louvre D37) and the Discovery of another Fragment," *JNES* 11 (1952) 251-263.

R. O. Faulkner, "An Ancient Egyptian 'Book of Hours'," *JEA* 40 (1954) 34-39.

William Kelly Simpson, "Two Middle Kingdom Personifications of Seasons," *JNES* 13 (1954) 265-268.

*Manfred Cassirer, "A Ushabti with an unusual formula," *JEA* 42 (1956) 120.

George R. Hughes, "A Demotic Letter to Thoth," *JNES* 17 (1958) 1-12.

H. W. Fairman, "A Scene of the Offering of Truth in the Temple of Edfu," *MDIÄA* 16 (1958) 86-92.

Titia Stolk-Coops, "Miscellanea. Note on Two Keftiu Incantations," *Minos* 6 (1958-60) 66.

*J. Gwyn Griffiths, "Some Remarks on the Enneads of Gods," *Or, N.S.,* 28 (1959) 34-56.

*J. Vercoutter, "The Napatan Kings and Apis Worship (*Serapeum Burials of the Napathan Period*)," *Kush* 8 (1960) 62-76.

George R. Hughes, "A Demotic Plea to Thoth in the Library of G. Michaelides," *JEA* 54 (1968) 176-182.

§838 *4.3.1.1.10.1 Egyptian Rituals, Myths and Legends*

*J. P. Lesley, "Notes on Some of the Historical and Mythological Features of the D'Orbiney Papyrus," *PAPS* 10 (1865-69) 543-560.

*W. R. Cooper, "On the Myth of Ra (the Supreme Sun-God of Egypt), with copious Citations from the Solar and Pantheistic Litanies," *JTVI* 11 (1877-78) 339-343-345. (Discussion, pp. 339-343)

E. Lefébure, "The Book of Hades. Being a Translation of the Egyptian Text, engraved upon the Belzoni Sarcophagus, preserved in the Soane Museum," *SBAP* 3 (1880-81) 20.

*Fritz Hommel, "A Second Ancient Egyptian Parallel to the Creation Narrative," *ET* 9 (1897-98) 480.

*Fritz Hommel, "Miscellanea," *ET* 9 (1897-98) 524-526. [1. The Egyptian Creation Narrative, pp. 524-525]

A. Wiedemann, "A Mythological-Geographical Text," *SBAP* 22 (1900) 155-160.

F. W. Read and A. C. Bryant, "A Mythological Text from Memphis," *SBAP* 23 (1901) 160-187.

*James Henry Breasted, "The Philosophy of a Memphite Priest," *ZÄS* 39 (1901) 39-54.

F. W. Read and A. C. Bryant, "A Mythological Text from Memphis: a reply to criticism," *SBAP* 24 (1902) 206-216.

J[ames] H. Breasted, "The Mythological Text from Memphis again," *SBAP* 24 (1902) 300.

*M. G. Kyle, "Egyptological Notes," *RP* 4 (1905) 32. *[Flood Story in Egypt]*

*A. H. Sayce, "The Astarte Papyrus and the Legend of the Sea," *JEA* 19 (1933) 56-59.

*H. W. Fairman, "The Myth of Horus at Edfu—I," *JEA* 21 (1935) 26-36. [A. The Legend of the Winged Disk; B. *Not published*]

*A. M. Blackman and H. W. Fairman, "The Myth of Horus at Edfu—II," *JEA* 28 (1942) 32-38. [C. The Triumph of Horus over his Enemies: A Sacred Drama]

*A. M. Blackman and H. W. Fairman, "The Myth of Horus at Edfu—II," *JEA* 29 (1943) 2-36. [C. The Triumph of Horus over his Enemies: A Sacred Drama *(Continued)*]

*A. M. Blackman and H. W. Fairman, "The Myth of Horus at Edfu—II," *JEA* 30 (1944) 5-22. [C. The Triumph of Horus over his Enemies: A Sacred Drama *(Concluded)*]

*A. M. Blackman and H. W. Fairman, "Additions and Corrections to A. M. Blackman and H. W. Fairman, 'The Myth of Horus at Edfu—II,' in *JEA* XXIX-XXX," *JEA* 30 (1944) 79-80.

*Theodor [Herzl] Gaster, "The Egyptian 'Story of Astarte' and the Ugaritic Poem of Baal," *BO* 9 (1952) 82-85.

*John A. Wilson, "The Royal Myth in Ancient Egypt," *PAPS* 100 (1956) 439-442.

§839 *4.3.1.1.10.2 Egyptian Oracles, Prophecies and Magical Texts*

*S[amuel] Birch, "The Amulet of the Tie," *ZÄS* 9 (1871) 13-15.

Edouard Naville, "Inscription of the Destruction of Mankind in the Tomb of Rameses III," *SBAP* 7 (1884-85) 93-95.

W. Pleyte, "Oracle of Amon: Papyrus in the British Museum, No. 10335," *SBAP* 10 (1887-88) 41-55.

Warren R. Dawson, "An Oracle Papyrus. B.M. 10335," *JEA* 11 (1925) 247-248.

Aylward M. Blackman, "Oracles in Ancient Egypt," *JEA* 11 (1925) 249-255. [B.M. 10335]

Aylward M. Blackman, "Oracles in Ancient Egypt," *JEA* 12 (1926) 176-185. [B.M. Ostracon, 5624; 5625; 5637; B.M. Papyrus 10417]

*Battiscombe Gunn, "A Pectoral Amulet," *ASAE* 29 (1929) 130-132.

*Alan W. Shorter, "The Amulets for the Steward Iy and of the Vizier Iuti," *AAA* 17 (1930) 73-76.

Warren R. Dawson, "Notes on Egyptian Magic," *Aeg* 11 (1930-31) 23-28. [I. - A Spell for Averting Death; II. - Protection of Parts of the Body by the Gods; III. - The Power of the Name]

Alan W. Shorter, "A magical ivory," *JEA* 18 (1932) 1-2.

*F. G. Gordon, "The Keftiu spell," *JEA* 18 (1932) 67-68.

Alan W. Shorter, "A Magical Ostracon," *JEA* 22 (1936) 165-168.

Paul Smither, "A Ramesside Love Charm," *JEA* 27 (1941) 131-132.

*Keith C. Seele, "Oriental Institute Museum Notes. Horus on the Crocodiles," *JNES* 6 (1947) 43-52. *[Amulet]*

Charles F. Nims, "An Oracle Date in 'the Repeating of Births'," *JNES* 7 (1948) 157-162.

John Barns, "The Nevill Papyrus: A Late Ramesidde Letter to an Oracle," *JEA* 35 (1949) 69-71.

M. Heerma von Voss, "An Egyptian magical brick," *JEOL* #18 (1964) 314-316.

Boleslaw Marczuk, "Messages from Beyond the Grave," *BibT* #26 (1966) 1843-1847.

I. E. S. Edwards, "Ḳenḥikhopshef's Prophylactic Charm," *JEA* 54 (1968) 155-160.

§840 *4.3.1.1.10.3 Egyptian Prayers and Hymns*

C. W. Goodwin, "Translation of an Egyptian Hymn to Amen," *SBAT* 2 (1873) 250-263.

C. W. Goodwin, "Hymns to Amen," *SBAT* 2 (1873) 353-359.

*Paul Pierret, "Libation Vase of Osor-ur, preserved in the Museum of the Louvre (No. 908)," *SBAP* 2 (1879-80) 57-60.

E. A. Wallis Budge, "Remarks on a Papyrus containing Formulae for Recitation in the Temple of Amen, and the service of the Slaughter of Apepi," *SBAP* 9 (1886-87) 11-26.

A. Wiedemann, "Two Monuments with a Votive Formula for a Living Person," *SBAP* 17 (1895) 195-198.

Alan H. Gardiner, "Hymns to Amon from a Leiden Papyrus," *ZÄS* 42 (1905) 12-42. (Correction, p. 145)

*Garrett Chatfield Pier, "An Egyptian Statue with Sun Hymn," *AJSL* 22 (1905-06) 43-44.

*Arthur E. P. Weigall, "Miscellaneous Notes," *ASAE* 11 (1911) 170-176. [6. An inscription from the Fayum, p. 172] *[Hymn]*

(Miss) M. Mogensen, "A Stele of the XVIIIth or XIXth dynasty, with a Hymn to Ptah and Sekhmet," *SBAP* 35 (1913) 37-40.

Alan H. Gardiner, "In Praise of Death: A Song from a Theban Tomb," *SBAP* 35 (1913) 165-170.

*R. O. Faulkner, "The 'Cannibal Hymn' from the Pyramid Texts," *JEA* 10 (1924) 97-103.

William Wallace Martin, "A Prevailing Prayer of an Egyptian Queen," *MQR, 3rd Ser.,* 51 (1925) 494-504.

A. Piankoff and J. J. Clère, "A Letter to the Dead on a Bowl in the Louvre," *JEA* 20 (1934) 157-169.

Abd el-Moḥsen Bakir, "A hymn to Amon-Rē' at Ṭura," *ASAE* 42 (1943) 83-91.

A[ylward] M. Blackman, "The King of Egypt's Grace before Meat," *JEA* 31 (1945) 57-73.

*Jean Sainte Fare Garnot, "A Hymn to Osiris in the Pyramid Texts," *JNES* 8 (1949) 98-103.

T. George Allen, "Some Egyptian Sun Hymns," *JNES* 8 (1949) 349-355.

Alan [H.] Gardiner, "Tuthmosis III returns Thanks to Amūn," *JEA* 38 (1952) 6-23.

Alan [H.] Gardiner, "Hymns to Sobk in a Ramesseum Papyrus," *RÉg* 11 (1957) 43-56.

Ricardo A. Caminos, "A Prayer to Osiris," *MDIÄA* 16 (1958) 20-24.

Helen Wall-Gordon, "A New Kingdom Libation Basin Dedicated to Ptah. Second Part: The Inscriptions," *MDIÄA* 16 (1958) 168-175.

J. Zandee, "Prayers to the Sun-god from Theban Tombs," *JEOL* #16 (1959-62) 48-71.

*H. M. Stewart, "Some Pre-'Amārnah Sun Hymns," *JEA* 46 (1960) 83-90.

J. Zandee, "Hymnical Sayings, Addressed to the Sun-god by the High-priest of Amūn Nebwenenef, from his tomb in Thebes," *JEOL* #18 (1964) 253-265.

William K. Simpson, "The Letter to the Dead from the Tomb of Meru (N 3737) at Nag 'ed-Deir," *JEA* 52 (1966) 39-52.

H. M. Stewart, "Traditional Egyptian Sun Hymns of the New Kingdom," *ULBIA* 6 (1966) 29-74.

Hans Goedicke, "Remarks on the Hymns to Sesostris III," *JARCE* 7 (1968) 23-26.

§841 *4.3.1.1.10.4 Egyptian Mortuary and Coffin Texts*

*S[amuel] Birch, "On sepulchral figures," *ZÄS* 2 (1864) 89-96, 103-105; 3 (1865) 4-8, 20-22. *[Texts]*

S[amuel] Birch,"On the formulas of three royal Coffins,"*ZÄS* 7 (1869) 49-53.

C. W. Goodwin, "On the enigmatic writing on the coffin of Seti I," *ZÄS* 11 (1873) 138-144.

Eugene L. Roy, "Egyptian Funeral Tablet in the Soane Museum," *SBAT* 6 (1878-79) 418-419.

†Samuel Birch, "Remarks on a Board with an Hieratic Inscription, and four Sepulchral Vases," *SBAP* 5 (1882-83) 76-80.

*Samuel Birch, "Observations on Canopic Vases from Tel-Basta, exhibited by F. G. Hilton-Price," *SBAP* 5 (1882-83) 98-100.

†S[amuel] Birch, "The Inscriptions on Sepulchral Objects in the British Museum," *SBAP* 7 (1884-85) 52-54.

*[Heinrich] Brugsch, "An Inscription from a Tomb in El-Kab," *ONTS* 4 (1884-85) 226-227.

†E. A. Wallis Budge, "On a Sepulchral Stèle in the British Museum," *SBAP* 9 (1886-87) 358-365.

*A. H. Sayce, "Gleanings from the land of Egypt," *RTR* 13 (1890) 62-67, 181-191. [§II.—An Inscription from the tombs of Beni-Mohammed el-Kufûr, pp. 65-67]

*A. H. Sayce, "Gleanings from the land of Egypt," *RTR* 13 (1890) 62-67,

181-191. [§III. —The Tomb of at Bersheh, pp. 187-191]

Arthur E. Weigall, "The Funeral Tablets in the Brighton Museum," *SBAP* 22 (1900) 272-273.

Howard Carter, "Report on Tomb-pit opened on the 26th January 1901, in the Valley of the Tombs of the Kings between n° 4 and N° 28," *ASAE* 2 (1901) 144-145. *[Coffin Text]*

F. Ll. Griffith, "A Meroitic funerary text in hieroglyphic," *ZÄS* 48 (1910) 67-68.

*Percy E. Newberry, "Egyptian Historical Notes. I," *SBAP* 35 (1913) 156-158. [w. The Funeral Papyrus of the Vezier User, p. 156]

Samuel A. B. Mercer, "The Gorringe Collection of Egyptian antiquities," *RTR* 36 (1914) 176-178. *[The Mortuary Stela of Ptaḥmes]*

Aylward M. Blackman, "The Funerary Papyrus of 'Enkhefenkhons," *JEA* 4 (1916) 122-129.

*Howard Carter and Alan H. Gardiner, "The Tomb of Ramesses IV and the Turin Plan of a Royal Tomb," *JEA* 4 (1916) 130-158.

Aylward M. Blackman, "The Funerary Papyrus of Nespeḥer'an (*Pap. Skrine, no. 2*)," *JEA* 5 (1918) 24-35.

*N. de Garis Davies, "The Tomb of Tetaky and Thebes (No. 15)," *JEA* 11 (1925) 10-18.

Battiscombe Gunn, "The Coffins of Ḥeny," *ASAE* 26 (1926) 166-170.

*R.Engelbach, "The so-called Coffin of Akhenaten," *ASAE* 31(1931) 98-114.

Dows Dunham, "A Fragment from the Mummy Wrappings of Thuthmosis III," *JEA* 17 (1931) 209-210.

*W. Stevenson Smith, "The Coffin of Prince Min-Khar," *JEA* 19 (1933) 150-159.

*N. de G. Davies, "Foreigners in the Tomb of Amenemḥab (No. 85)," *JEA* 20 (1934) 189-192.

A. Piankoff, "The Funerary Papyrus of the Shieldbearer Amon-m-Saf in the Louve Museum," *EgR* 3 (1935) 139-157.

A. Piankoff, "The Funerary Papyrus of Tent-Amon," *EgR* 4 (1936) 49-70.

*Ahmed Fakury, "Miscellanea," *ASAE* 37 (1937) 25-38. [5. Six Funerary Cones, pp. 33-35]

Moharram Kamal, "Two unpublished coffins in the Egyptian Museum," *ASAE* 37 (1937) 125-128.

*Moharram Kamal, "An unpublished Middle Empire Coffin in the Egyptian Museum," *ASAE* 38 (1938) 29-34.

Alan Rowe, "Inscriptions on the model coffin containing the lock of hair of Queen Tyi," *ASAE* 40 (1940-41) 623-627.

H[ermann] R[anke], "An Egyptian Tombstone of the New Kingdom," *UMB* 9 (1941-42) #1, 20-24.

Alan Rowe, "Corrections and additions to *Report on Tomb-Pit opened on the 26th January, 1901, in the Valley of the Tombs of the Kings between N° 4 and N° 28* by Howard Carter (in *Annales du Service,* II, pp. 144ff)," *ASAE* 41 (1942) 346-347.

H[ermann] Ranke, "An Egyptian Tombstone from a Period of Transition," *UMB* 13 (1947-48) #3, 25-29.

Cyril Aldred, "The Funerary Papyrus of Woseramūn," *JEA* 36 (1950) 112.

John Barns, "A Demotic Coffin Inscription in Edinburgh," *ArOr* 20 (1952) 69-71.

M. Cassirer, "An Egyptian Funerary Stele with a rare title," *ASAE* 52 (1952-54) 41-44.

*Manfred Cassirer, "A Ushabti with an unusual formula," *JEA* 42 (1956) 120.

Walter Federn, "The 'Transformations' in the Coffin Texts. A New Approach," *JNES* 19 (1960) 241-257.

R. O. Faulkner, "Spells 38-40 of the Coffin Texts," *JEA* 48 (1962) 36-44.

*John Ruffle, "Four Egyptian Pieces in the Birmingham City Museum," *JEA* 53 (1967) 39-46. [1. Part of a New-kingdom funerary group (69'96); 2. A New-kingdom funerary stela (70'96)]

§842 *4.3.1.1.10.5 Pyramid Texts*

Samuel A. B. Mercer, "The 'Eye of Horus' in the Pyramid Texts," *JSOR* 4 (1920) 29-32.

*Battiscombe Gunn, "'Finger-Numbering' in the Pyramid Texts," *ZÄS* 57 (1922) 71-72.

Warren R. Dawson, "The Oldest Religious Book in the World," *IAQR* 20 (1924) 663-668.

*R. O. Faulkner, "The 'Cannibal Hymn' from the Pyramid Texts," *JEA* 10 (1924) 97-103.

*M. A. Murray, "The Dying God," *AEE* 13 (1928) 8-11. [Speech No. 570 of the Pyramid Texts]

*Jean Sainte Fare Garnot, "A Hymn to Osiris in the Pyramid Texts," *JNES* 8 (1949) 98-103.

Alan [H.] Gardiner, "Spell 413 of the Pyramid Texts," *JEA* 38 (1952) 127.

*Rudolf Anthes, "Remarks on the Pyramid Texts and the Early Egyptian Dogma," *JAOS* 74 (1954) 35-39.

Dia' Abou-Ghazi, "Bewailing the King in the Pyramid Texts," *BIAFO* 66 (1968) 157-164.

§843 *4.3.1.1.10.6 The Egyptian Book of the Dead and Hypocephalus*

C. Nicholson, "Translations of the Hieroglyphic Writing on an Inscribed Linen Cloth brought from Egypt," *JRAS* (1863) 323-325. *[Book of the Dead, chap. 129]*

Charles W. Goodwin, "On a Text of the Book of the Dead belonging to the old kingdom," *ZÄS* 4 (1866) 53-56.

C[harles] W. Goodwin, "On the 112th chapter of the Ritual," *ZÄS* 9 (1871) 144-147.

C[harles] W. Goodwin, "On chap. 115 of the Book of the Dead," *ZÄS* 11 (1873) 104-107.

†Anonymous, "The Egyptian Book of the Dead," *LQHR* 43 (1874-75) 1-31. *(Review)*

R. O. Williams, "Egyptian Book of the Dead," *UQGR, N.S.,* 13 (1876) 398-415.

†Samuel Birch, "Hypocephalus in the possession of Sir Henry B. Meux, Bart.," *SBAP* 6 (1883-84) 37-40.

†Samuel Birch, "Description of Hypocephalus, No. 8445*c,* in the British Museum," *SBAP* 6 (1883-84) 52.

†W. H. Rylands, "Hypocephali in the British Museum," *SBAP* 6 (1883-84) 52.

†Samuel Birch, "Description of Hypocephalus, No. 8445*a,* in the British Museum," *SBAP* 6 (1883-84) 106-107.

†Theo. G. Pinches, "Letter from G. Bertin, on the Communications of Dr. Oppert and M. J. Menant," *SBAP* 6 (1883-84) 115-116. (Remarks by Theo. G. Pinches, W. H. Rylands, and D. Marshall, p. 116)

†Samuel Birch, "Description of Hypocephali, No. 8445*a,* and 8445*e,* in the British Museum," *SBAP* 6 (1883-84) 129-131.

†M. P. J. de Horrack, "Hypocephalus in the Louvre," *SBAP* 6 (1883-84) 126-129.

†Samuel Birch, "The Hypocephalus of Harnetatf, No. 8446, in the British Museum," *SBAP* 6 (1883-84) 170-173.

*P. le Page Renouf, "The Horse in the Book of the Dead," *SBAP* 7 (1884-85) 41-42.

J. Lieblein, "The Title of the Book of the Dead," *SBAP* 7 (1884-85) 187-193.

P. le Page Renouf, "The Title of the Book of the Dead," *SBAP* 7 (1884-85) 210-213.

*S[amuel] Birch, "Hypocephalus in the Collection of Walter Myers, Esq., F.S.A.," *SBAP* 7 (1884-85) 213-214. *[Egyptian Amulet containing Chap. 162 of the Book of the Dead]*

T. O. Paine, "Pre-historic Revelations among the Nile-dwellers," *JAOS* 11 (1885) ix-x. *[Book of the Dead]*

P. le Page Renouf, "Two Vignettes of the Book of the Dead," *SBAP* 11 (1888-89) 26-28.

W. C. Winslow, "On Naville's Book of the Dead," *JAOS* 13 (1889) xlvii-clviii.

*†P. le Page Renouf, "The Egyptian Book of the Dead. Meanings of certain Primitive Words," *SBAP* 14 (1891-92) 349-351.

*†P. le Page Renouf, "The Egyptian Book of the Dead—Introductory," *SBAP* 14 (1891-92) 37-38.

P. le Page Renouf, "The Book of the Dead. Chapter I," *SBAP* 14 (1891-92) 213-222.

P. le Page Renouf, "The Book of the Dead. Chapters II-XIV," *SBAP* 14 (1891-92) 270-279.

P. le Page Renouf, "The Book of the Dead. Chapters XV, and XVI," *SBAP* 14 (1891-92) 352-363. *[Title on cover of part 7 erroneously reads "Chapters XIV, XV, and XVI"]*

P. le Page Renouf, "The Book of the Dead. Chapter XVII," *SBAP* 14 (1891-92) 377-395.

[J. Offord], "The Mythology and Psychology of the Egyptians as Exhibited in their sacred literature, with especial reference to the so-called *Book of the Dead*," *IAQR, 2nd Ser.,*4 (1892) 377-413.

P. le Page Renouf, "The Book of the Dead. Chapters XVIII-XX," *SBAP* 15 (1892-93) 4-12.

P. le Page Renouf, "The Book of the Dead. Chapters XXI-XXV," *SBAP* 15 (1892-93) 63-69.

P. le Page Renouf, "The Book of the Dead. Chapters XXVI-XXXB," *SBAP* 15 (1892-93) 98-107.

P. le Page Renouf, "The Book of the Dead. Chapters XXXI-XXXVII," *SBAP* 15 (1892-93) 155-163.

P. le Page Renouf, "The Book of the Dead. Chapters XXXVIII-XLI," *SBAP* 15 (1892-93) 219-228.

P. le Page Renouf, "The Book of the Dead. Chapters XLII-LVI," *SBAP* 15 (1892-93) 276-290.

P. le Page Renouf, "The Book of the Dead. Chapters LVII-LXIIIB," *SBAP* 15 (1892-93) 377-384.

*Alfred C. Bryant, "The Great Pyramid and the Book of the Dead," *BOR* 7 (1893-94) 134-144.

†P. le Page Renouf, "The Book of the Dead. Chapter LXIV," *SBAP* 16 (1893-94) 3-12.

†P. le Page Renouf, "The Book of the Dead. Chapters LXV-LXX," *SBAP* 16 (1893-94) 27-32.

†P. le Page Renouf, "The Book of the Dead. Chapters LXXI-LXXVI," *SBAP* 16 (1893-94) 64-72.

†P. le Page Renouf, "The Book of the Dead. Chapters LXXVII-LXXVIII," *SBAP* 16 (1893-94) 100-103.

†P. le Page Renouf, "The Book of the Dead. Chapters LXXVIII-LXXXII," *SBAP* 16 (1893-94) 123-130.

†P. le Page Renouf, "The Book of the Dead. Chapters LXXXIII-XCI," *SBAP* 16 (1893-94) 179-187.

†P. le Page Renouf, "The Book of the Dead. Chapters XCII-XCVIII," *SBAP* 16 (1893-94) 218-224.

†P. le Page Renouf, "The Book of the Dead. Chapters XCIX-CVII," *SBAP* 16 (1893-94) 263-273.

†P. le Page Renouf, "The Book of the Dead. Chapters CVIII-CIX," *SBAP* 16 (1893-94) 293-298.

Camden M. Cobern, "The Sacred Scriptures of the Egyptians," *HR* 28 (1894) 483-489.

Anonymous, "The Book of the Dead," *MR* 77 (1895) 311-314.

Sara Y. Stevenson, "The Book of the Dead," *NW* 4 (1895) 321-345.

†P. le Page Renouf, "The Book of the Dead. Additional Notes to Chapter 109; also Chapters CXI-CXVI," *SBAP* 17 (1895) 6-15.

P. le Page Renouf, "The Book of the Dead. Chapter CX," *SBAP* 17 (1895) 51-56.

P. le Page Renouf, "The Book of the Dead. *Continuation of Notes on Chapter* 110," *SBAP* 17 (1895) 97-102.

P. le Page Renouf, "The Book of the Dead. Chapters CXVII-CXXIII," *SBAP* 17 (1895) 123-129.

P. le Page Renouf, "The Book of the Dead. Chapter CXXIV," *SBAP* 17 (1895) 192-194.

P. le Page Renouf, "The Book of the Dead. Chapter CXXV. Parts I and II," *SBAP* 17 (1895) 216-219.

P. le Page Renouf, "The Book of the Dead. Chapter CXXV. Part III," *SBAP* 17 (1895) 273-277.

W. St. C[had] Boscawen, "The Book of the Dead," *BOR* 8 (1895-1900) 14-17.

P. le Page Renouf, "The Book of the Dead. Chapter CXXV, Part IV," *SBAP* 18 (1896) 7-16.

P. le Page Renouf, "The Book of the Dead, Notes to Chapter CXXV *(continued),*" *SBAP* 18 (1896) 47-53, 81-85, 113-117.

P. le Page Renouf, "The Book of the Dead. Chapters CXXVI and CXXVII," *SBAP* 18 (1896) 149-155.

P. le Page Renouf, "The Book of the Dead. Notes to Chapter CXXVIII," *SBAP* 18 (1896) 165-169.

P. le Page Renouf, "The Book of the Dead. Chapters CXXIX, CXXX," *SBAP* 19 (1897) 65-67.

P. le Page Renouf, "The Book of the Dead. Chapters CXXX to CXXXII," *SBAP* 19 (1897) 107-112.

†P. le Page Renouf, "The Book of the Dead. Chapters CXXXIII to CXXXV," *SBAP* 19 (1897) 125-131.

Walter L. Nash and P. le Page Renouf, "Hypocephalus from Luxor," *SBAP* 19 (1897) 145-146.

†P. le Page Renouf, "The Book of the Dead. Chapters CXXXVIA and CXXXVIB," *SBAP* 19 (1897) 160-164.

†P. le Page Renouf, "The Book of the Dead. Chapters CXXXVIIA-CXXXIX," *SBAP* 19 (1897) 225-228.

Rudolph Buti, "On an Interesting Fragment of the 'Book of the Dead'," *PAPS* 38 (1899) 79-81.

W. St. Chad Boscawen, "Egyptian Eschatology. *The Rubric of Chap. XXXVIa* of the Book of the Dead," *BOR* 9 (1901) 11-16.

E. Naville, "The Book of the Dead. Introductory Note," *SBAP* 24 (1902) 135-136.

†E. Naville, "The Book of the Dead. Chapters CXL-CXLIII," *SBAP* 24 (1902) 136-143.

†E. Naville, "The Book of the Dead. Chapters CXLIV-CXLVI," *SBAP* 24 (1902) 195-204.

E. Naville, "The Book of the Dead. Chapter CXLVII," *SBAP* 24 (1902) 268-271.

†E. Naville, "The Book of the Dead. Chapters CXLVIII, CXLIX," *SBAP* 24 (1902) 313-316.

Walter L. Nash, "The Book of the Dead," *ET* 14 (1902-03) 286.

Francis R. Beattie, "'The Egyptian Book of the Dead'," *PQ* 16 (1902-03) 30-44.

Anonymous, "The Book of the Dead," *MR* 85 (1903) 139-142.

†E. Naville, "The Book of the Dead. Chapter CXLIX *(continued),*" *SBAP* 25 (1903) 11-14.

†E. Naville, "The Book of the Dead. Chapters CXLIX *(continued)* and CL," *SBAP* 25 (1903) 67-70.

†E. Naville, "The Book of the Dead *(continued).* Chapters CLI, CLIA *bis,* CLII," *SBAP* 25 (1903) 105-110.

E. Naville, "The Book of the Dead. Chapter CLIIIA," *SBAP* 25 (1903) 167-172.

†E. Naville, "The Book of the Dead. Chapters CLIIIB and CLIV," *SBAP* 25 (1903) 237-242.

†E. Naville, "The Book of the Dead *(continued).* Chapters CLV-CLXI," *SBAP* 25 (1903) 299-304.

†E. Naville, "The Book of the Dead *(continued)*. Chapters CLXII-CLXIV," *SBAP* 25 (1903) 339-346.

†E. Naville, "The Book of the Dead *(continued)*. Chapters CLXV-CLXXI," *SBAP* 26 (1904) 6-16.

†E. Naville, "The Book of the Dead *(continued)*. Chapters CLXXII-CLXXIII," *SBAP* 26 (1904) 45-50.

†E. Naville, "The Book of the Dead *(continued)*. Chapters CLXXIV-CLXXIX," *SBAP* 26 (1904) 79-89.

†E. Naville, "The Book of the Dead *(continued)*. Chapters CLXXX-CLXXXII," *SBAP* 26 (1904) 117-124.

†E. Naville, "The Book of the Dead *(continued)*. Chapters CLXXXIII-CLXXXVI," *SBAP* 26 (1904) 181-184.

*E. Naville, "The Mention of a Flood in the Book of the Dead," *SBAP* 26 (1904) 251-257, 287-294.

*Joseph Offord, "Book of the Dead compared with the Bible," *AAOJ* 30 (1908) 276-278.

Clarence Waterer, "The Book of the Resurrection," *WR* 173 (1910) 520-528, 689-699; 174 (1910) 79-94. *[The Book of the Dead]*

Henry Proctor, "The Egyptian Bible," *AAOJ* 31 (1909) 230-233; 33 (1911) 220-223.

Anonymous, "Copy of the Book of the Dead," *RP* 10 (1911) 184.

*George W. Gilmore, "The Ethnic Scriptures. I. Egypt - Pyramid Texts and the Book of the Dead (The Future Life)," *HR* 67 (1914) 100-109.

Warren R. Dawson, "A Rare Vignette from the Book of the Dead," *JEA* 10 (1924) 40.

[W. M.] Flinders Petrie, "The Origins of the Book of the Dead," *AEE* 11 (1926) 41-45.

Samuel A. B. Mercer, "Some Religious Ideas in the Seventeenth Chapter of the Book of the Dead," *JSOR* 11 (1927) 217-221.

F. S. Thompson, "The Book of the Dead. Recent Discoveries and Translations of Ancient Egyptian Writings," *BS* 87 (1930) 89-106.

Nathaniel Julius Reich, "An Abbreviated Demotic Book of the Dead. A Palaeographical Study of Papyrus British Museum 10072," *JEA* 17 (1931) 85-97.

T. George Allen, "The Late Book of the Dead in the Oriental Institute Collections," *AJSL* 49 (1932-33) 141-149.

Alan W. Shorter, "A Leather Manuscript of the Book of the Dead in the British Museum," *JEA* 20 (1934) 33-40.

*E. E. Boughey, "An Ancient Egyptian Flood-Legend?" *JMUEOS* #19 (1935) 27-31. *[Book of the Dead, Chapter 175]*

T. George Allen, "Types of Rubrics in the Egyptian Book of the Dead," *JAOS* 56 (1936) 145-154.

A. de Buck, "The Earliest Version of the Book of the Dead 78," *JEA* 35 (1949) 87-97.

T. George Allen, "Additions to the Egyptian Book of the Dead," *JNES* 11 (1952) 177-186.

C. de Wit, "A new version of Spell 181 of the Book of the Dead," *BO* 10 (1953) 90-94.

Louis V. Žabkar, "Some Observations on T. G. Allen's Edition of the Book of the Dead," *JNES* 24 (1965) 75-87.*(Review)*

*J. Murtagh, "The Book of Job and the Book of the Dead," *ITQ* 35 (1968) 166-173.

Ḥassan Bakry, "A Stela from Hēliopolis Dedicated to Edjō," *RDSO* 44 (1969) 177-180.

§844 *4.3.1.1.11 The Rosetta Stone*

Anonymous, "An Account of the celebrated Inscription, in Three Languages, lately discovered near Rosetta, in Egypt and now deposited in the British Museum," *MMBR* 17 (1804) 409-410. *[Rosetta Stone]*

William Aikman, "The Rosetta Stone," *AThR* 2 (1860) 655-662.

*J. D. Baldwin, "Remarks on the Discovery of a second 'Rosetta Stone' at Tanis in Lower Egypt," *JAOS* 9 (1871) lxxviii-lxxix.

J. P. Mahaffy, "The Rosetta Stone," *RP* 1 (1902) 89-95.

Paul Carus, "The Rosetta Stone," *OC* 18 (1904) 531-536.

Paul Carus, "The History and Significance of the Rosetta Stone," *OC* 19 (1905) 89-91.

Roy Beaman, "The Sesquicentennial of the Discovery of the Rosetta Stone," *JBL* 68 (1949) v.

Warren R. Dawson, "The Discoverer of the Rosetta Stone,"*JEA* 43 (1957) 117.

Warren R. Dawson, "The Discoverer of the Rosetta Stone: a Correction," *JEA* 44 (1958) 123.

§845 *4.3.1.1.12 Egyptian Secular Songs and Poems*

C. W. Goodwin, "On Four Songs contained in an Egyptian Papyrus in the British Museum," *SBAT* 3 (1874) 380-388.

W. R. Dawson and T. E. Peet, "The so-called Poem of the King's Chariot," *JEA* 19 (1933) 167-174.

*Miriam Lichtheim, "The Songs of the Harpers," *JNES* 4 (1945) 178-212.

Walter Federn, "The Opening Lines of the Antef Song," *JNES* 5 (1946) 259.

Paul C. Smither, "Prince Meḥy of the Love Songs," *JEA* 34 (1948) 116.

*Edward F. Wente, "Egyptian 'Make Merry' Songs Reconsidered," *JNES* 21 (1962) 118-128.

William Kelly Simpson, "A Short Harper's Song of the Late New Kingdom in the Yale University Art Gallery," *JARCE* 8 (1969-70) 49-50.

§846 *4.3.1.1.13 Miscellaneous Egyptian Texts - Unclassified*

†Anonymous, "The New Pharaonic Tablets of Memphis and Abydos," *BQRL* 41 (1865) 169-190. *(Review)*

C. W. Goodwin, "On an Egyptian text in Greek characters," *ZÄS* 6 (1868) 18-24.

C. W. Goodwin, "On an inscription of Takelut II," *ZÄS* 6 (1868) 25-29.

S[amuel] Birch, "The chapter of the Pillow," *ZÄS* 6 (1868) 52-54. [B.M. 8308a; 9900; 6680]

*J. D. Baldwin, "Remarks on the Discovery of a second 'Rosetta Stone,' at Tanis in Lower Egypt," *JAOS* 9 (1871) lxxviii-lxxix.

S[amuel] Birch, "On some leather rolls," *ZÄS* 9 (1871) 103-104, 117-118.

Samuel Sharpe, "Account of an Egyptian Altar in the Museum at Turin," *SBAT* 3 (1874) 110-112. *(Drawn by Joseph Bonomi)*

S[amuel] Birch, "Translation of the Hieroglyphic Inscription on the Granite Altar at Turin," *SBAT* 3 (1874) 113-117.

S[amuel] Birch, "Translation of the Hieroglyphic Inscription upon the Altar of Nechtarhebes," *SBAT* 3 (1874) 425-429.

S[amuel] Birch, "Inscription of Haremhebi on a Statue at Turin," *SBAT* 3 (1874) 486-495.

P. le Page Renouf, "The royal tombs at Biban-el-Moluk and 'Enigmatical' writing," *ZÄS* 12 (1874) 101-105.

S[amuel] Birch, "Tablets of the twelfth dynasty," *ZÄS* 12 (1874) 111-114.

S[amuel] Birch, "Tablets of the XIIth Dynasty," *ZÄS* 13 (1875) 50-51.

S[amuel] Birch, "The Tablet of Antefaa II," *SBAT* 4 (1875) 172-194.

G. Maspero, "Inscription of King Nastosenen," *SBAT* 4 (1875) 203-225.

S[amuel] Birch, "Tablet of the reign of Thothmes III," *ZÄS* 14 (1876) 4-7.

*G. Maspero, "The Egyptian Documents relating to the Statues of the Dead," *SBAP* 1 (1878-79) 44.

(Miss) Gertrude Austin, "On a Fragmentary Inscription of Psametik I, in the Museum at Palermo," *SBAT* 6 (1878-79) 287-288.

Daniel Hy. Haigh, "Ramses, Messen, Horus Horemheb," *ZÄS* 17 (1879) 154-160.

*†W. St. C[had] Boscawen, "The Monuments and Inscriptions on the Rocks on the Nahr-el-Kelb, Syria," *SBAP* 2 (1879-80) 27-28.

S[amuel] Birch, "Inscription of Tahraka," *ZÄS* 18 (1880) 22-24.

Thomas Tyler, "The Inscription of Tarkutimme, and the Monuments from Jerablus in the British Museum," *SBAP* 3 (1880-81) 6-8, 12-13. (Remarks by Hyde Clarke, p. 9; William Wright, pp. 9-10; W. Harry Rylands, pp. 10-11; Richard Cull; pp. 11-12; Chas. Jas. Bell, pp. 12-13; and W. F. Birch, p. 13)

†George Dennis, "Letter sent to C. T. Newton, C.B., from Consul George Dennis, Smyrna, on the Hieroglyphics carved upon the Niobe of Cybele at Magnesia," *SBAP* 3 (1880-81) 49.

Amelia B. Edwards, "Relics from the tomb of the priest-kings at Dayr-el-Baharee," *RTR* 4 (1883) 79-87.

E[dward] Y[orke] McCauley, "Inscription on a Mummy Case at the XIXth Dynasty in the Memorial Hall, in Philadelphia," *PAPS* 21 (1883-84) 488-489.

S[amuel] Birch, "The Tablet of Amenhotep in the British Museum," *SBAT* 8 (1883-84) 421.

†S[amuel] Birch, "Hieroglyphic Inscription near the Cataract of Tangur," *SBAT* 7 (1884-85) 121.

A. Wiedemann, "Two Dated Monuments of the Museum Meermanno-Westreenianum at the Haag," *SBAP* 7 (1884-85) 179-184.

*A. H. Sayce, "Hieroglyphic Inscription at How, containing the Name of a New King," *SBAP* 7 (1884-85) 185-187. *[Hathor-nofer-hotep]*

*A. Wiedemann, "On a Monument of the Time of King Chu-en-iten," *SBAP* 7 (1884-85) 200-203.

Aug. Eisenlohr, "On the How Inscriptions," *SBAP* 8 (1885-86) 77-79.

A. Wiedemann, "The Egyptian Monuments at Venice," *SBAP* 8 (1885-86) 87-92.

A. Wiedemann, "The Monuments of the Ancient and of the Middle Empire in the Museum at Karlsruhe," *SBAP* 8 (1885-86) 95-101.

*G. Maspero, "Egyptian Documents relating to Statues of the Dead," *SBAT* 7 (1880-82) 6-36.

*Samuel Birch, "Monuments of the Reign of Tirhakah," *SBAT* 7 (1880-82) 193-203.

A. Macalaster, "An Inscription of Aahmes in the Fitzwilliam Museum," *SBAP* 9 (1886-87) 98-100.

A. Macalaster, "An Inscription of the XIIIth Dynasty in the Dublin National Museum," *SBAP* 9 (1886-87) 125-127.

A. Wiedemann, "A Monument of the first Dynasties of Egypt," *SBAP* 9 (1886-87) 180-184.

A. H. Sayce, "A dated Inscription of Amenophis III," *SBAP* 9 (1886-87) 195-197.

P. le Page Renouf, "Note on the Inscription of Amenophis III," *SBAP* 9 (1886-87) 206.

F. Ll. Griffith, "Two Egyptian Monuments," *BOR* 2 (1887-88) 55-56.

W. M. Flinders Petrie, "The Rock Inscriptions of Upper Egypt," *BOR* 2 (1887-88) 166-169.

P. le Page Renouf, "Inscription at Kūm-el-aḥmar," *SBAP* 10 (1887-88) 73-78, 132.

F. G. Hilton Price, "An Inscribed Fragment of Wood from Thebes," *SBAP* 10 (1887-88) 130-133.

(Miss) Amelia B. Edwards, "The provincial and private collections of egyptian antiquities in Great Britain," *RTR* 10 (1888) 121-133.

F. Ll. Griffith, "The Inscriptions of Siût and Dêr Rîfeh," *BOR* 3 (1888-89) 121-129, 164-168, 174-184.

F. Ll. Griffith, "Inscriptions of Siût and Dêr Rifeh: Bibliography. (Siût)," *BOR* 3 (1888-89) 244-252.

A. Wiedemann, "Some Monuments of Mont at Thebes," *SBAP* 11 (1888-89) 69-75.

P. le Page Renouf, "Errata. Inscription at Kūm-el-aḥmar," *SBAP* 11 (1888-89) 76.

A. Wiedemann, "Texts of the Collection of Mr. Lee," *SBAP* 11 (1888-89) 417-421.

A. Wiedemann, "Texts of the Second Part of the Eighteenth Dynasty," *SBAP* 11 (1888-89) 422-425.

F. L. Griffith, "Notes on Egyptian Inscriptions of the Middle Kingdom," *SBAP* 12 (1889-90) 85-88.

F. L. Griffith, "Notes on Egyptian Texts of the Middle Kingdom. Part II," *SBAP* 12 (1889-90) 263-268.

*A. H. Sayce, "Gleanings from the land of Egypt," *RTR* 13 (1890) 62-67. 187-191. [§I. Inscriptions from the neighbourhood of Girgeh, pp. 62-65]

F. L. Griffith, "Notes on Egyptian Texts of the Middle Kingdom.— III," *SBAP* 13 (1890-91) 65-76.

A. Wiedemann, "Miscellanea," *SBAP* 13 (1890-91) 272-279. [Egyptian Inscriptions, Nos. 1-7]

P. le Page Renouf, "Remarks," *SBAP* 13 (1890-91) 316. *[Ref: "Notes au Jour le Jour]*

H.W. Mengedoht, "The Tablet of Mentusa (Dyn. XII)," *BOR* 5 (1891) 13-17.

[W. M.] Flinders Petrie, "Epigraphy in Egyptian Research," *IAQR, 2nd Ser.,* 2 (1891) 315-323.

F. L. Griffith, "A Cup with Hieratic Inscription," *SBAP* 14 (1891-92) 328-330.

A. Wiedemann, "On some Egyptian Inscriptions in the Musée Guimet at Paris," *SBAP* 14 (1891-92) 331-339.

*†A. Wiedemann, "Note on Dr. Young's Interpretation," *SBAP* 14 (1891-92) 483-484.

P. le Page Renouf, "Note on an Alabaster Vase," *PEFQS* 24 (1892) 251-252.

A. C. Bryant and F. W. Read, "An Inscription of Khuenaten," *SBAP* 15 (1892-93) 206-215.

*A. H. Sayce, "Gleanings from the land of Egypt," *RTR* 15 (1893) 147-148. [§IV. Near the Cataract of Assouân]

*F. L. Griffith, "A detail of Geography in the Inscription of Herkhuf," *SBAP* 16 (1893-94) 50-52.

*F. L. Griffith, "A Relic of Pharaoh Necho from Phoenicia," *SBAP* 16 (1893-94) 90-91.

A. Wiedemann, "Egyptian Monuments at Dorpat," *SBAP* 16 (1893-94) 150-155.

A. H. Sayce, "Gleanings from the land of Egypt," *RTR* 16 (1894) 169-176. [§V. Between the First and Second Cataract]

H. W. Mengedoht, "The Shrine of the Scribe Pa-suten-se (Dyn. XII.) B.C. 2266, British Museum, 1135.," *BOR* 7 (1893-94) 190-192.

W. Max Muller, "An Egyptian Inscription from Phoenicia," *SBAP* 16 (1893-94) 298-299.

A. Wiedemann, "Inscription of the Time of Amenophis IV," *SBAP* 17 (1895) 152-158.

D. Kaufmann, "Egyptian Sutta-Megilla," *JQR* 9 (1896-97) 170-172.

*A. H. Sayce, "Gleanings from the land of Egypt," *RTR* 20 (1898) 111-112. *[§VII; §VIII]*

*A. H. Sayce, "Gleanings from the land of Egypt," *RTR* 20 (1898) 169-176. [§X. The tombs of Beni-Mohammed el Kufur; §XI. *(untitled);* §XII. *(untitled)*]

A. H. Sayce, "Some Old Empire Inscriptions from El-Kab," *SBAP* 21 (1899) 111-114.

*Percy E. Newberry, "Extracts from my Notebook. (I). ," *SBAP* 21 (1899) 303-308. [The Inscription of Amenemheb: a correction, p. 303]

*Percy E. Newberry, "Extracts from my Notebook. 4. A Statue of User, Vezîr of Upper Egypt under Thotmes III," *SBAP* 21 (1899) 306-308.

*James Henry Breasted, "Ramses II. and the Princes in the Karnak Reliefs of Seti I," *ZÄS* 37 (1899) 130-139.

Percy E. Newberry, "A Statue of Hapu-Senb: Vezir of Tothmes II," *SBAP* 22 (1900) 31-36.

James Henry Breasted, "The Monuments in the Inscriptions," *SBAP* 22 (1900) 88-95.

*George Adam Smith, "Notes on a Journey Through Hauran, with Inscriptions Found by the Way," *PEFQS* 33 (1901) 340-361. (Note by R. A. S. Macalister, *PEFQS* 34 (1902), p. 79)

*Percy E. Newberry, "Extracts from my Notebooks (IV)," *SBAP* 23 (1901) 218-224. [23. A Priest of Astarte, pp. 219-220; 25. Handle of a Model Dagger(?), and a Plaque inscribed with the name of Bak-en-Khensu, p. 225]

A. Wiedemann, "Egyptian Notes," *SBAP* 23 (1901) 248-251.

Arthur E. Weigall, "An Inscribed Disc of the XXIInd Dynasty," *SBAP* 23 (1901) 259-260.

Alan H. Gardiner, "A Monument of Antef V, from Coptos," *SBAP* 24 (1902) 205.

*Percy E. Newberry, "Extracts from my Note-books. V," *SBAP* 24 (1902) 244-252. [28. A Statuette of Renï, Mayor of El Kab, pp. 244-245; 29. A Statuette of Min-nekht, pp. 245-246; 30. A Stela of Teta, p. 246.; 32. Some inscribed Pendants, Beads, etc., pp. 248-249]

Alan H. Gardiner, "Imhotep and the Scribe's Libation," *ZÄS* 40 (1902-03) 146.

*Percy E. Newberry, "Extracts from my Notebooks. VI.," *SBAP* 25 (1903) 130-138. [46. Some Small Inscribed Objects, pp. 137]

F. W. Green, "Notes on an Inscription at el-Kab," *SBAP* 25 (1903) 215-216.

Percy E. Newberry, "The Sekhemet Statues of the Temple of Mut, at Karnak," *SBAP* 25 (1903) 217-221.

A. H. Sayce, "Note on the Inscriptions at el-Kab," *SBAP* 25 (1903) 249.

W. M. Flinders Petrie, "The inscriptions of Sobah Rigaleh," *ASAE* 5 (1904) 144.

Anonymous, "Fragment of the Tablet of Negadah," *RP* 3 (1904) 254. *[Tablet of Menes]*

Alan H. Gardiner, "The Installation of a Vizier," *RTR* 26 (1904) 1-19.

W. Max Müller, "Some small Egyptian Monuments dispersed in America," *RTR* 26 (1904) 32-34.

James Henry Breasted, "The Report of Wenamon," *AJSL* 21 (1904-05) 100-109.

*Percy E. Newberry, "Extracts from my Notebooks. VIII.," *SBAP* 27 (1905) 101-105. [60. Pyramidion of an Official of Queen Sensenb, p. 102; 61. Hieratic Inscriptions in the Pyramid at Medum, pp. 102-103; 63. Some Small Inscribed Objects, pp. 103-105]

John Garstang, "The Tablet of Mena," *ZÄS* 42 (1905) 61-64.

J. E. Quibell, "Report on Work done in Upper Egypt during the Winter of 1904-1905," *ASAE* 7 (1906) 8-10.

F. Legge, "The Tablets of Negadah and Abydos," *SBAP* 28 (1906) 252-263; 29 (1907) 18-24, 70-73, 101-106, 150-154, 243-250.

J. E. Quibell, "Lintel of Merenptah at Mitrahineh," *ASAE* 8 (1907) 120-121.

Arthur E. P. Weigall, "Some Inscriptions in Prof. Petrie's Collection of Egyptian Antiquities," *RTR* 29 (1907) 216-222.

*Arthur E. P. Weigall, "Upper-Egyptian Notes," *ASAE* 9 (1908) 105-112. [1. A Rock Inscription of Taharqu, pp. 105-106; 15, An Inscribed Copper Chisel, p. 111]

*F. Ll. Griffith and U. Wilcken, "A bilingual sale of liturgies in 136 B.C.," *ZÄS* 45 (1908) 103-110.

Alan H. Gardiner, "Inscriptions from the tomb of Si-renpowet I prince of Elephantine," *ZÄS* 45 (1908) 123-140.

Anonymous, "Manuscripts Found with a Mummy," *RP* 8 (1909) 319-320.

*A. H. Sayce, "Meroitic Inscriptions," *SBAP* 31 (1909) 189-203. [The Meroitic Hieroglyphic Inscriptions; Unpublished Inscription of Ra-khnum-ab; The Decipherment of the Meroitic Hieroglyphs; The Temple of Basa; The Age of the Meroitic Inscriptions; Table of Offerings of Usertesen I]

*F. W. Green, "Notes on Some Inscriptions in the Etbai District. I.," *SBAP* 31 (1909) 247-254.

*F. W. Green, "Notes on Some Inscriptions in the Etabi District. II.," *SBAP* 31 (1909) 319-323.

*Alan H. Gardiner, "The tomb of Amenemhet, high-priest of Amon," *ZÄS* 47 (1910) 87-99.

George Reisner, "A Scribe's Tablet found by the Hearst Expedition at Giza," *ZÄS* 48 (1910) 113-114.

*C. C. Edgar, "Notes from the Delta," *ASAE* 11 (1911) 87-96. [I. Bouto and Chemmis]

*Arthur E. P. Weigall, "Miscellaneous Notes," *ASAE* 11 (1911) 170-176. [4. The Cartouches of Sety II at Abu Fouda, p. 171; 5. The name of Khufu at Sehel, p. 171]

C. C. Edgar, "Inscribed stones at Kom Frin and Kom Barnougi," *ASAE* 11 (1911) 277-278.

Aylward M. Blackman, "Some Chapters of the Totenbuch and other Texts on the Middle Kingdom," *ZÄS* 49 (1911) 54-66.

Percy E. Newberry, "The Inscribed Tombs of Ekhmim," *AAA* 4 (1911-12) 99-120.

*W. Max Müller, "The Doomed Island of Philae," *AJA* 17 (1913) 83-84.

Percy E. Newberry, "Notes on the Carnarvon Tablet No. I," *SBAP* 35 (1913) 117-122.

W. M. Finders Petrie, "The Earliest Inscriptions," *AEE* 1 (1914) 61-77.

*Percy E. Newberry and G. A. Wainwright, "King Udy-mu (Den) and the Palermo Stone," *AEE* 1 (1914) 148-155.

C. C. Edgar, "Notes from my Inspectorate," *ASAE* 13 (1914) 277-284.

A. H. Sayce, "Egyptian Notes," *SBAP* 36 (1914) 47. *[Cartouches]*

W.M. F[linders] P[etrie], "More of the Earliest Inscriptions," *AEE* 2 (1915) 78-82.

F. Ll. Griffith, "A New Monument from Coptos," *JEA* 2 (1915) 5-7.

F. Ll. Griffith, "Meroitic Studies," *JEA* 3 (1915) 22-30, 111-124. *[Parts I & II]*

*Alan H. Gardiner, "The Tomb of a much travelled Theban Official," *JEA* 4 (1916) 28-38.

*Aylward M. Blackman, "The Buren and Haggard Collections of Ancient Egyptian Antiquities," *JEA* 4 (1916) 39-46.

B[oris] Touraeff, "The Inscriptions upon the Lower Part of a Naophorous Statue in my Collection," *JEA* 4 (1916) 119-121.

W. M. Flinders Petrie, "New Portions of the Annals," *AEE* 3 (1916) 114-120.

F. Ll. Griffith, "Meroitic Studies, III," *JEA* 4 (1916) 21-27.

F. Ll. Griffith, "Meroitic Studies, IV," *JEA* 4 (1916) 159-173.

Battiscombe Gunn and Alan H. Gardiner, "New Renderings of Egyptian Texts," *JEA* 4 (1916) 241-252. [I. The Temple of Wâdy Abbâd]

*M. A. Murray, "Some Fresh Inscriptions," *AEE* 4 (1917) 62-68. [I. False door of Ni-kau-Ptah; Round Topped Stele of Tehuti-hetep and Kayay]

*George A. Reisner, "The Tomb of Hepzefa, Nomarch of Siût," *JEA* 5 (1918) 79-98.

Battiscombe Gunn, "The Naophorus Statue belonging to Professor Touraeff," *JEA* 5 (1918) 125-126.

*H. E. Winlock, "Statue of Steward Roy singing the Psalm to Rē'," *JEA* 6 (1920) 1-3.

*R. Engelbach, "Report on the inspectorate of Upper Egypt from April 1920 to March 1921," *ASAE* 21 (1921) 61-76.

*R. Engelbach, "Notes of inspection, April 1921," *ASAE* 21 (1921) 188-196.

C. C. Edgar, "Some hieroglyphic inscriptions from Naukratis," *ASAE* 22 (1922) 1-6.

R. Engelbach, "A monument of Senusret Ist," *ASAE* 23 (1923) 161-162.

*R. Engelbach, "Seizure of bronzes from Buto (Tell Far'aîn)," *ASAE* 24 (1924) 169-177.

*H. E. Winlock, "A Statue of Horemhab before his Accession," *JEA* 10 (1924) 1-5.

*Nathaniel Reich, "A Grammatical Exercise of an Egyptian Schoolboy," *JEA* 10 (1924) 285-288.

Percy E. Newberry, "A Duplicate Text of Horemheb's Coronation Inscription," *AEE* 10 (1925) 4.

Alan H. Gardiner, "The Secret Chambers of the Sanctuary of Thoth," *JEA* 11 (1925) 2-5.

G. A. Wainwright, "Statue of Horus, son of Kharu and Mer-n-Neith-it-s," *ASAE* 25 (1925) 259-261.

Battiscombe Gunn, "The inscribed Sarcophagi in the Serapeum," *ASAE* 26 (1926) 82-91.

Battiscombe Gunn, "Two misunderstood Serapeum Inscriptions," *ASAE* 26 (1926) 92-94.

*Battiscombe Gunn, "Inscriptions from the Step Pyramid site," *ASAE* 26 (1926) 177-202. [I. An inscribed Statue of King Zoser, pp. 177-196]

*H. R. Hall, "An Egyptian Royal Bookplate: The *Ex Libris* of Amenophis III and Teie," *JEA* 12 (1926) 30-33.

*Warren R. Dawson, "The number 'Seven' in Egyptian Texts," *Aeg* 8 (1927) 97-107.

Kirsopp Lake, Robert P. Blake and Arthur W. Johnson, "The Serabit Inscriptions," *ASAE* 27 (1927) 238-240.

F. Ll. Griffith, "The Abydos Decree of Seti I at Nauri," *JEA* 13 (1927) 193-208.

P[ercy] E. Newberry, "An unpublished monument of a 𓏏� 'Priest of the Double Axe' named 𓊵𓏏𓊪, Hetep-heren-Ptah," *ASAE* 28 (1928) 138-140.

P[ercy] E. Newberry, "A statue of the King's Scribe Amenhotep son of Hapu," *ASAE* 28 (1928) 141-143.

Battiscombe Gunn, "Inscriptions from the Step Pyramid site.—III. Fragments of inscribed Vessels," *ASAE* 28 (1928) 153-174.

H. R. Hall, "The Statues of Sennemut and Menkheperrē'senb in the British Museum," *JEA* 14 (1928) 1-2.

*I. Sneguireff, "Some Unpublished Egyptian Objects from Kertch, Olbia and Tiflis," *AEE* 14 (1929) 101-103.

Percy E. Newberry, "The Base of a Statuette of the Lady Duat-nefret, mother of Queen Nubkhaes," *ASAE* 29 (1929) 76.

*S. R. K. Glanville, "Some Notes on Material for the Reign of Amenophis III," *JEA* 15 (1929) 2-8. I. Fragment of a statue of Amenophis, son of Hapu, pp. 2-5; II. Inscribed panel from a box, pp. 5-6]

Dows Dunham, "Three Inscribed Statues in Boston," *JEA* 15 (1929) 164-166.

H. R. Hall, "An Unknown Script from Egypt," *AAA* 17 (1930) 81.

R. Engelbach, "A Monument of Prince Meneptaḥ from Athribis (Benha)," *ASAE* 30 (1930) 197-202.

F. W. Green, "The Secret Chambers of the Sanctuary of Thoth," *JEA* 16 (1930) 33-35.

*Alan W. Shorter, "The Tomb of Aaḥmose, Supervisor of the Mysteries in the House of the Morning," *JEA* 16 (1930) 54-62.

Aylward M. Blackman, "A New Translation of the Inscription of Ḥerwerrē' at Serâbît el-Khâdim," *BIFAO* 30 (1931) 97-101.

*F. Ll. Griffith, "Four Granite Stands at Philæ," *BIFAO* 30 (1931) 127-130.

*T. Eric Peet, "An Ancient Egyptian Ship's Log," *BIFAO* 30 (1931) 481-490.

*H. R. Hall, "Three Royal Shabtis in the British Museum," *JEA* 17 (1931) 10-12.

*John A. Wilson, "Ceremonial Games of the New Kingdom," *JEA* 17 (1931) 211-220.

*John A. Wilson, "Ancient text corrections in Madient Habu," *ZÄS* 68 (1932) 48-56.

T. C. Townsend, "A XIIth Dynasty inscription near the Cairo-Suez road," *ASAE* 33 (1933) 1-5. (with notes by R. Engelbach)

*Percy E. Newberry, "A Statue and a Scarab," *JEA* 19 (1933) 53-54.

F. Lexa, "Oriental Institute in Praha: Research Department. Ancient Egyptian Texts Bearing on Prehistorical Burials," *ArOr* 6 (1934) 408-409.

*Battiscombe Gunn, "The Berlin statue of Ḥarwa and some notes on other Ḥarwa statues," *BIFAO* 34 (1934) 135-142.

*R. O. Faulkner, "A Statue of a Serpent-Worshipper," *JEA* 20 (1934) 154-156.

Battiscombe Gunn, "Inscriptions from the Step Pyramid site," *ASAE* 35 (1935) 62-65. [IV. The inscriptions of the Funerary Chamber]

*A. Hamada, "A Sarcophagus from Mit-Rahîna," *ASAE* 35 (1935) 122-131.

*R. Englebach, "Statuette-Group, from Kîmân Faris, of Sebekḥotpe and his womenfolk," *ASAE* 35 (1935) 203-205.

Dows Dunham, "Four New Kingdom Monuments in the Museum of Fine Arts, Boston," *JEA* 21 (1935) 147-151.

Alan H. Gardiner, "Piankhi's Instructions to His Army," *JEA* 21 (1935) 219-223.

*Wm. Stevenson Smith, "The Old Kingdom Linen List," *ZÄS* 71 (1935) 134-149.

Dows Dunham, "Notes on Some Old Squeezes from Egyptian Monuments," *JAOS* 56 (1936) 173-177.

Harold H. Nelson, "Three Decrees of Ramses III from Karnak," *JAOS* 56 (1936) 232-241.

William F. Edgerton, "Wood Tablet from Qâw," *ZÄS* 72 (1936) 77-79.

R. Engelbach, "Statuette of Yi from Elephantine," *ASAE* 37 (1937) 1-2.

Mahmud Hamaz, "The statue of Menephtaḥ I, found at Athar en-Nabi and the route of Piʿankhi from Memphis to Heliopolis," *ASAE* 37 (1937) 233-242.

*Alan Rowe, "Interesting New Finds in Egypt," *ET* 49 (1937-38) 323-325. ["Letter" about Canaanite Well; Discovery of Alphabetic Writing in Scarab Texts]

*Jaroslav Černý, "Two Puzzles of Ramesside Hieratic," *JEA* 23 (1937) 60-62.

P[hilippus] M[iller], "Conversations and Calls Recorded on the Walls of the Tomb of Kaipurē," *UMB* 7 (1937-39) #3, 26-30.

*Alan Rowe, "Provisional notes on the Old Kingdom inscriptions from the diorite quarries," *ASAE* 38 (1938) 391-396. [I. The Chisel Inscription; II. The Cheops Stela Inscription; III. The Saḥurēʿ Stela Inscription]

*Ahmed Fakhry, "Baḥria and Farafra oases. A preliminary note on the new discoveries," *ASAE* 38 (1938) 397-434.

*Alan Rowe, Additional references to the article: 'Provisional notes on the Old Kingdom inscriptions from the diorite Quarries' *in Annales du Service,* XXXVIII," *ASAE* 38 (1938) 876-688.

Alan H. Gardiner, "A Later Allusion to Akhenaten," *JEA* 24 (1938) 124. [B.M. 3040A]

Percy E. Newberry. "Three Old-Kingdom Travellers to Byblos and Pwenet," *JEA* 24 (1938) 182-184.

Battiscombe Gunn, "A note on 'Eine Bleitafel mit hieroglyphisher Inschrift'," *ZÄS* 74 (1938) 147.

*Ahmed Fakhry, "Baḥria and Farafra oases. Second preliminary note on the new discoveries," *ASAE* 39 (1939) 627-642.

John Bennett, "The Restoration Inscription of Tutʿankhamūn," *JEA* 25 (1939) 8-15.

*Sidney Smith, "Late Eighteenth Dynasty or Nineteenth?" *JEA* 25 (1939) 219-220.

*Georg Steindorff, "The Statuette of an Egyptian Commissioner in Syria," *JEA* 25 (1930) 30-33.

*Paul C. Smither, "A Postal Register of the Ramesside Age," *JEA* 25 (1939) 103.

I. E. S. Edwards, "The Prudhoe Lions," *AAA* 36 (1939-40) 3-9.

*Ahmed Fakhry, "Baḥria and Farafra oases. Third preliminary note on the new discoveries," *ASAE* 40 (1940-41) 855-871.

*L. P. Kirwan, "An Inscribed Block at 'Aṭbara, Sudah," *JEA* 26 (1940) 83.

Dows Dunham, "A Statue formerly at Uriage," *JEA* 26 (1940) 138.

Alan Rowe, "Newly-identified monuments in the Egyptian Museum showing the deification of the dead together with brief details of similar objects elsewhere," *ASAE* 40 (1940-41) 1-67.

Alan Rowe, "Additions to *Newly-identified Monuments in the Egyptian Museum,* by Alan Rowe (in *Annales du Service,* XL, pp. 1-ff.)," *ASAE* 40 (1940-41) 291-296. (Note by W. G. Waddell, p. 297)

R. Engelbach, "Two monuments of the Chief Prophet of Amūn, Bekenkhons, with some remarks on other monuments similarly inscribed," *ASAE* 40 (1940-41) 507-516.

*Battiscombe Gunn, "Notes on Ammenemes I," *JEA* 27 (1941) 2-6.

Rosalind Moss, "Some Rubbings of Egyptian Monuments made a Hundred Years ago," *JEA* 27 (1941) 7-11.

Paul Smither, "A Ramesside Love Charm," *JEA* 27 (1941) 131-132.

W. E. Crum, "An Egyptian Text in Greek Characters," *JEA* 28 (1942) 20-31.

*Marcus N. Tod, "A Bilingual Dedication from Alexandria," *JEA* 28 (1942) 53-56.

Hermann Ranke, "A Late Ptolemaic Statue of Hathor from Her Temple at Dendereh," *JAOS* 65 (1945) 238-248.

Alan H. Gardiner, "Davies's Copy of the Great Speos Artemidos Inscription," *JEA* 32 (1946) 43-56.

*M. F. Laming Macadam, "Gleanings from the Bankes MSS," *JEA* 32 (1946) 57-64.

A. M. Blackman and H. W. Fairman, "The Consecration of an Egyptian Temple according to the Use of Edfu," *JEA* 32 (1946) 75-91.

H. J. Polostsky, "A passage in the short Ridīsīyah inscription," *ASAE* 45 (1947) 145-146.

*Labib Habachi, "A statue of Osiris made for Ankhefenamun, prophet of the house of Amun in Khapu and his daughter," *ASAE* 47 (1947) 261-282.

*William C. Hayes, "Horemkhaʻuef on Nekhen and his Trip to It-towe," *JEA* 33 (1947) 3-11.

H. W. Fairman and Bernhard Grdseloff, "Texts of Hatshepsut and Sethos I inside Speos Artemidos," *JEA* 33 (1947) 12-33.

*M. F. Laming Macadam, "On a Late Napatan or Early Meroitic King's Name," *JEA* 33 (1947) 93-94.

Miriam Lichtheim, "Oriental Institute Museum Notes. Situla No. 11395 and some Remarks on Egyptian Situlae," *JNES* 6 (1947) 169-179.

*William C. Hayes, "A Foundation Plaque of Ptolemy IV," *JEA* 34 (1948) 114-115.

Bernhard Grdseloff, "A New Middle Kingdom Letter from El-Lāhūn," *JEA* 35 (1949) 59-62.

*Rosalind Moss, "An Egyptian Statuette in Malta," *JEA* 35 (1949) 132-134.

*John D. Cooney, "A Souvenir of Napoleon's Trip to Egypt," *JEA* 35 (1949) 153-157.

Harold H. Nelson, "Certain Reliefs at Karnak and Medinet Habu and the Ritual of Amenophis I," *JNES* 8 (1949) 201-232, 310-345.

*William C. Hayes, "The Sarcophagus of Sennemūt," *JEA* 36 (1950) 19-23.

*A. J. Arkell, "Varia Sudanica," *JEA* 36 (1950) 24-40.

*Rosalind Moss, "The Ancient Name of Serra (Sudan)," *JEA* 36 (1950) 41-42.

Eberhard Otto, "An Ancient Egyptian Hunting Ritual," *JNES* 9 (1950) 164-177.

Charles F. Nims, "Egyptian Catalogues of Things," *JNES* 9 (1950) 253-262.

*Ahmed Fakhry, "The rock inscriptions of Gabal el-Teir at Kharag Oasis," *ASAE* 51 (1951) 404-434. *[Demotic]*

*Labib Habachi, "Clearance of the area to the east of Luxor Temple and discovery of some objects," *ASAE* 51 (1951) 447-468.

*Henri Wild, "A Bas-relief of Sekhemrē'-sewadjtowĕ Sebkḥotpe," *JEA* 37 (1951) 12-16.

William C. Hayes, "Inscriptions from the Palace of Amenhotep III," *JNES* 10 (1951) 35-56, 82-112, 156-183, 231-242.

Alan [H.]Gardiner, "Some Reflections on the Nauri Decree," *JEA* 38 (1952) 24-33.

Ricardo A. Caminos, "Gebel Es-Silsilah No. 100," *JEA* 38 (1952) 46-61.

Hermann Ranke, 'The Statue of a Ptolemaic Στρατηγος of the Mendesian Nome in the Cleveland Museum of Art," *JAOS* 73 (1953) 193-198.

*Alan [H.]Gardiner, "The Memphite Tomb of General Ḥaremḥab" *JEA* 39 (1953) 1-12.

Alan [H.]Gardiner, "The Harem at Miwĕr," *JNES* 12 (1953) 145-149.

John A. Wilson, "A Group of Sixth Dynasty Inscriptions," *JNES* 13 (1954) 243-264.

William Kelly Simpson, "The Pharaoh Taharqa," *Sumer* 10 (1954) 193-194.

*Labib Habachi, "Preliminary report on Komose Stela and other inscribed blocks found reused in the foundations of two statues at Karnak," *ASAE* 53 (1955) 195-202.

Alan [H.]Gardiner, "A Unique Funerary Liturgy," *JEA* 41 (1955) 9-17.

R. O. Faulkner, "The Installation of the Vizier," *JEA* 41 (1955) 18-29. *[Rekhmirē']*

*M. Cassirer, "A Granite Group of the Eighteenth Dynasty," *JEA* 41 (1955) 72-74.

Battiscombe Gunn, "The Decree of Amonrasonthēr for Neskhons," *JEA* 41 (1955) 83-95. (Appendix by I. E. S. Edwards, pp. 96-105)

Alan [H.]Gardiner, "An unexplained passage in the inscription of Weni," *JEA* 41 (1955) 121.

J. Vercoutter, "New Egyptian Texts from the Sudan," *Kush* 4 (1956) 66-82.

J. Leibovitch, "A Hieroglyphic Inscription from Qubeibeh," *BIES* 21 (1957) #3/4, IV.

H. M. Stewart, "A Possibly Contemporary Parallel to the Inscription of Suty and Hor," *JEA* 43 (1957) 3-5.

H. N. Chittick, "An Inscription on Gebel Barkal," *JEA* 43 (1957) 42-44. (Note by A. J. Arkell, p. 44)

*Labib Habachi, "A Statue of Bakennifi, Nomarch of Athribis during the Invasions of Egypt by Assurbanipal," *MDIÄA* 15 (1957) 68-77.

William C. Hayes, "Varia from the Time of Hatshepsut," *MDIÄA* 15 (1957) 78-90. [1. Dated Inscriptions of "Regnal Year 7"; 2. Sennemut behind the Doors at Deir el Bahri; 3. Sennemut Presents a Sistrum to Mût; 5. An Administrative Letter to Thuty]

Ricardo A. Caminos, "A Fragmentary Duplicate of Papyrus Anastasi I in the Turin Museum," *JEA* 44 (1958) 3-4.

Hans Goedicke, "A New Inscription from Hatnub," *ASAE* 56 (1959) 55-58.

Hans Goedicke, "A Puzzling Inscription," *JEA* 45 (1959) 98-99.

C. Aldred, "The Gayer Anderson Jubilee Relief of Amenophis IV," *JEA* 45 (1959) 104.

William Kelly Simpson, "Historical and Lexical Notes on the New Series of Hammamat Inscriptions," *JNES* 18 (1959) 20-37.

Henry G. Fischer, "Old Kingdom Inscriptions in the Yale Gallery," *MIO* 7 (1959-60) 299-315.

Helen K. Jacquet-Gordon, "The Inscriptions on the Philadelphia-Cairo Statue of Osorkon II (Membra Dispesa III)," *JEA* 46 (1960) 12-23.

H. W. Fairman, "A Block of Amenophis IV from Athribis," *JEA* 46 (1960) 80-82.

Henry G. Fischer, "The Inscription of *'in-it.f.* born of *tfi*," *JNES* 19 (1960) 258-268.

Hans Goedicke, "The Inscription of *dmi*," *JNES* 19 (1960) 288-291.

*Cyril Aldred, "The Tomb of Akhenaten at Thebes," *JEA* 47 (1961) 41-59. (Appendix by A. T. Sandison, pp. 60-65)

Labib Habachi, "Four Objects Belonging to Viceroys of Kush and Officials Associated with Them," *Kush* 9 (1961) 210-225.

Henry G. Fischer, "Three Old Kingdom Palimpsests in the Louvre," *ZÄS* 86 (1961) 21-31.

*Henry G. Fischer, "A Provincial Statue of the Egyptian Sixth Dynasty," *AJA* 66 (1962) 65-69. (Erratum, p. 226)

R. J. Williams, "Reflections on the *Lebensmüde,*" *JEA* 48 (1962) 49-56.

K. A. Kitchen, "Amenysonb in Liverpool and the Louvre," *JEA* 48 (1962) 159-160.

*Jean Vercoutter, "Preliminary Report of the Excavations at Aksha by the Franco-Argentine Archaeological Expedition, 1961," *Kush* 10 (1962) 109-117. [Notes relating to Inscriptions found at Aksha, by *A. Rosenvasser,* pp. 116-117]

Constant de Wit and Paul Mertens, "The Epigraphic Mission to Kumma and Semna (1961) Report and Results," *Kush* 10 (1962) 118-149.

Hans Goedicke, "The Inscription of *Ḥr-wr-r'* (Sinai no. 90)," *MDIÄ* 18 (1962) 14-25.

*Henry G. Fischer, "Varia Aegyptiaca," *JARCE* 2 (1963) 17-51. [3. Inscriptions on Old Kingdom Statues, pp. 24-28]

*T. G. H. James, "The Northampton Statue of Sekhemka," *JEA* 49 (1963) 5-12.

Fritz Hintze, "Preliminary Note on the Epigraphic Expedition to Sudanese Nubia, 1962," *Kush* 11 (1963) 93-95.

J[ean] Vercoutter, "Excavations at Aksha, September 1961-January 1962," *Kush* 11 (1963) 131-140. [Addenda (concerning inscriptions mentioned in this Report) by *A. Rosenvasser,* p. 140]

*Jaroslav Černý, "The Contribution of the Study of Unofficial and Private Documents to the History of Pharonic Egypt," *SSR* 7 (1963) 31-57.

W. Ward, "The Inscribed Offering-Table of Nefer-Seshem-Ra from Byblos," *BMB* 17 (1964) 37-46.

Henry G. Fischer, "A Group of Sixth Dynasty Titles Relating to Ptah and Sokar," *JARCE* 3 (1964) 25-29.

Fritz Hintze, "Preliminary Note on the Epigraphic Expedition to Sudanese Nubia, 1963," *Kush* 12 (1964) 40-42.

Richard A. Parker, "Hathor, Lady of the Acacia," *JARCE* 4 (1965) 151.

Labib Habachi, "A Family from Armant in Aswân and in Thebes," *JEA* 51 (1965) 123-136.

Frtiz Hintze, "Preliminary Note on the Epigraphic Expedition to Sudanese Nubia, 1963," *Kush* 13 (1965) 13-16.

Labib Habachi, "Varia from the Reign of King Akhenaten," *MDIÄA* 20 (1965) 70-92. [Libation Bowl from Karnak; Altars for Offerings from Karnak; A Pedestal Belonging to a Group of Statuary of the Royal Family from Fayum Province; The Graffito of Bak and Men at Aswan and a Second Graffito Close by Showing Akhenaten before the Hawk-headed Aten]

*Raphael Giveon, "Two Egyptian Documents Concerning Bashan from the Time of Ramses II," *RDSO* 40 (1965) 197-202. [1. The Job Stone, pp. 197-200; 2. The Stela of Benanzan, pp. 200-202]

Edward F. Wente, "The Suppression of the High Priest of Amenhotep," *JNES* 25 (1966) 73-87.

H. S. Smith, "Preliminary Report on the Rock Inscriptions in the Egypt Exploration Society's Concession at Buhen," *Kush* 14 (1966) 330-334.

K. A. Kitchen, "An unusual Egyptian text from Byblos," *BMB* 20 (1967) 149-153.

Christine Soghor, "Mendes 1965 and 1966. II. *Inscriptions from Tell el Rub'a,*" *JARCE* 6 (1967) 16-32.

*H. M. Stewart, "Stelophorous Statuettes in the British Museum," *JEA* 53 (1967) 34-38.

J. Gwyn Griffith, "*Lebensmüde* 83," *JEA* 53 (1967) 157-158.

*Labib Habachi, "An Embalming Bed of Amenhotep, Steward of Memphis under Amenophis III," *MDIÄA* 22 (1967) 42-47.

*Hassan S. K. Bakry, "Was there a Temple of Horus at Heliopolis?" *MDIÄA* 22 (1967) 53-59.

Mahmud Abd El-Razik, "Some Remarks on the Great Pylon of the Luxor Temple," *MDIÄA* 22 (1967) 68-70.

Jaroslav Černý, "A Stone with an Appeal to the Finder," *OA* 6 (1967) 47-50.

*Helen Jaquet-Gordon, "A Statuette of Ma'et and the Identity of the Divine Adoratress Karomama," *ZÄS* 94 (1967) 86-93.

L. Kákosy, "Imḥotep and Amenḥotep Son of Ḥapu as Patrons of the Dead," *AOASH* 21 (1968) 109-117.

*H. S. K. Bakry, "A Statue of Pedeamūn-nebnesuttaui," *ASAE* 60 (1968) 15-25.

T. G. H. James, "An Early Middle-kingdom Account," *JEA* 54 (1968) 51-56.

*Labib Habachi, "The Owner of Tomb no. 282 in the Theban Necropolis," *JEA* 54 (1968) 107-113.

I. E. S. Edwards, "Ḳenḥikhopshef's Prophylactic Charm," *JEA* 54 (1968) 155-160.

Geoffrey T. Martin, "A New Prince of Byblos," *JNES* 27 (1968) 141-142.

H. S. K. Bakry, "A Fragment of a Sphinx Found in the Mortuary Temple of Amenophis III," *MDIÄA* 23 (1968) 68.

H. S. K. Bakry, "A Family from Saîs," *MDIÄA* 23 (1968) 69-74.

*G. A. Gaballa, "Minor War Scenes of Ramesses II at Karnak," *JEA* 55 (1969) 82-88.

*Sh. Yeivin, "An Ostracon from Tel Arad exhibiting a Combination of Two Scripts," *JEA* 55 (1969) 98-102. *[Hieratic]*

Bengt Julius Peterson, "Some Reliefs from the Memphite Necropolis," *MB* 5 (1969) 3-15.

Ḥassan S. K. Bakry, "A Ramesside block statue from tell el-Bakleyyah," *SCO* 18 (1969) 229-237.

*H. C. Jelgersma, "A grammatical peculiarity in the tomb inscriptions of the sons of Ramses III in the Valley of the Queens in Thebes," *JEOL* #21 (1969-70) 169-174.

Jadwiga Lipinska, "Inscriptions of Amenemone from the Temple of Tuthmosis III at Deir el-Bahari," *ZÄS* 96 (1969-70) 28-30.

§847 *4.3.1.1.14 Egyptian Papyri - Unclassified [See also:
          Papyrology - General Studies §822 ←]*

*G. Seyffarth, "Three Lectures on Egyptian Antiquities, &c., delivered at the
Stuyvesant Institute, New York, May 1856," *ER* 8 (1856-57) 34-104. [I.
The Papyri, pp. 43-46]

*Daniel Hy. Haigh, "Note on the calendar in Mr. Smith's papyrus," *ZÄS* 9
(1871) 72-73. *[Pap. Ebers]*

*August Eisenlohr, "On the Political Condition of Egypt before the Reign of
Ramses III; *probably in connection with the establishment of the Jewish
Religion.* From the Great Harris Papyrus," *SBAT* 1 (1872) 355-384.

S[amuel] Birch, "Harris Papyrus," *ZÄS* 10 (1872) 119-120; 11 (1873) 9-12,
34-39, 65-72, 152-154.

Charles H. Brigham, "The Great Harris Papyrus," *PAPA* 5 (1873) 10.

C. W. Goodwin, "Notes from unpublished papyri," *ZÄS* 11 (1873) 15-16,
39-40.

C. W. Goodwin, "On Four Songs contained in an Egyptian Papyrus in the
British Museum," *SBAT* 3 (1874) 380-388.

C. W. Goodwin, "Notes on the Mayer Papyri," *ZÄS* 12 (1874) 61-65.
[A & B]

E. L. Lushington, "Fragment of the First Sallier Papyrus," *SBAT* 4 (1875)
263-266.

*Claude R. Conder, "The First Traveller in Palestine," *PEFQS* 8 (1876) 74-
88.

Giovanni Kminek-Szedlo, "The Papyrus of Bek-en-Amen preserved in the
Municipal Museum of Bologna," *SBAP* 2 (1879-80) 71-72.

Giovanni Kminek-Szedlo, "The Papyrus of Bek-en-Amen (written in
Hieratic Script), in the Municipal Museum of Bologna, No. 1,086,"
SBAT 7 (1880-82) 411-428.

†S. Birch, "Four Fragments of Papyrus, belonging to the Edinburgh Museum
of Science and Art," *SBAP* 7 (1884-85) 79-89.

S.   Birch,   "Roman   Papyri,"   *SBAP*   7   (1884-85)   204-210.

F. L. Griffith, "Notes on the Text of the d'Orbiney Papyrus," *SBAP* 11 (1888-89) 161-172, 414-416.

P. J. de Horrack, "Note on the D'Orbiney Papyrus," *SBAP* 12 (1889-90) 49-50.

W. Max Müller, "The Sign Papyrus of Tanis," *SBAP* 13 (1890-91) 445-446.

Wilhelm Spiegelberg, "The Verso of the Papyrus Abbott," *SBAP* 13 (1890-91) 576-582.

A. Eisenlohr, "Remarks on 'Un Papyrus Bilingue du Temple de Philopator'," *SBAP* 14 (1891-92) 340-342.

H. W. Mengedoht, "Egyptian Papyrus of Mu-tem-ua. The Book of the Tuat," *BOR* 6 (1892-93) 151-152.

F. Cope Whitehouse, "The Moeris Papyrus," *SBAP* 16 (1893-94) 20-24.

J. Hunt Cooke, "Exploration and Discovery: The Westcar Papyrus," *BW* 4 (1894) 49-53.

August Eisenlohr, "The Rollin Papyri and their Baking Calculations," *SBAP* 19 (1897) 91-104, 147-155, 252-265.

*Charles Warren, "Egyptian Weights and Measures Since the Eighteenth Dynasty and of the Rhind Mathematical Papyrus," *PEFQS* 32 (1900) 149-150.

M. Philippe Virey, "'The Oldest Book in the World'. Society, Ethics, Religion, in Egypt Before 2000 B.C.," *RP* 1 (1902) 306-320. *[Papyrus Prisse]*

W. Spiegelberg, "The Fragments of the Astarte Papyrus of the Amherst Collection," *SBAP* 24 (1902) 41-50.

Alan H. Gardiner, "The Hero of the Papyrus d'Orbiney," *SBAP* 27 (1905) 185-186.

Anonymous, "An Hieratic Papyrus," *RP* 5 (1906) 284-285.

E. Revillout, "The Burgh Papyrus. Transcribed, Translated, and Annotated," *SBAP* 28 (1906) 178-181.

Alan H. Gardiner, "Four papyri of the 18th Dynasty from Kahun," *ZÄS* 43 (1906) 27-45. [A. Berlin Pap. 9784; B. Gurob Pap. II 1 (*Griffith,* The Petrie Pap. 39, 1-13); C. Gurob Pap. II 2 (*Griffith,* The Petrie Pap. 39, 14-23); D. Berlin Pap. 9785]

*A. H. Sayce, "The Oldest Book in the World," *AAOJ* 29 (1907) 303-315.

F. Ll. Griffith, "Papyrus Dodgson," *SBAP* 31 (1909) 100-109.

F. Ll. Griffith, "Additional Notes on the Papyrus Dodgson, Etc.," *SBAP* 31 (1909) 289-291.

Anonymous, "Egyptian Papyri for University of Pennsylvania," *RP* 10 (1911) 116.

*E. J. Pilcher, "The Assuan Papyri and the Grave-Goods of Gezer," *PEFQS* 44 (1912) 30-35.

Joseph Offord, "The Great Peteesi Papyrus," *AAOJ* 35 (1913) 162-166.

[J. O. Kinnaman], "The Libby Papyrus," *AAOJ* 35 (1913) 241-243.

*W. Max Müller, "An Egyptian Document for the History of Palestine," *JQR, N.S.,* 4 (1913-14) 651-656. [Pap. 1116A]

T. Eric Peet, "The Great Tomb Robberies of the Ramesside Age: Papyri Mayer A and B.," *JEA* 2 (1915) 173-177.

T. Eric Peet, "The Great Tomb Robberies of the Ramesside Age. Papyri Mayer A and B. II. Papyrus Mayer B," *JEA* 2 (1915) 204-206.

*Warren R. Dawson, "Egyptological Notes," *IAQR* 16 (1920) 337-340, 520-522. [3. *(Hood Papyrus)* , pp. 520-521. *[no sub title]*

T. Eric Peet, "Fresh Light on the Tomb Robberies of the Twentieth Dynasty at Thebes. Some New Papyri in London and Turin," *JEA* 11 (1925) 37-55.

T. Eric Peet, "Fresh Light on the Tomb Robberies of the Twentieth Dynasty at Thebes. An Additional Note," *JEA* 11 (1925) 162-164. [Papyrus B.M. 10068]

T. Eric Peet, "The Legend of the Capture of Joppa and the Story of the Foredoomed Prince. Being a Translation of the Verso of Papyrus Harris 500," *JEA* 11 (1925) 225-229.

Aylward M. Blackman and T. Eric Peet, "Papyrus Lansing: A Translation with Notes," *JEA* 11 (1925) 284-298.

S. R. K. Granville, "A New Duplicate of the Hood Papyrus," *JEA* 12 (1926) 171-175.

S. R. K. Granville, "Note on the Nature and Date of the 'Papyri' of Nakht, B.M. 10471 and 10473," *JEA* 13 (1927) 50-56.

Warren R. Dawson, "The Papyrus Lansing," *ZÄS* 62 (1927) 64-65.

Jaroslav Černý, "Papyrus Salt 124 (Brit. Mus. 10055)," *JEA* 15 (1929) 243-258.

John A. Wilson, "On Papyrus Harris 78:8-10; 79:3," *ZÄS* 65 (1930) 60-61.

*Vladimir Vikentiev, "Nâr-Ba-Thai," *JEA* 17 (1931) 67-80. [II. The hero of Papyrus d'Orbiney and his relation to *n'r*-fish, pp. 71-74]

H. I. Bell, A. D. Nock, and Herbert Thompson, "Magical Texts from a Bilingual Papyrus in the British Museum Edited with Translations, Commentary, and Facsimiles," *PBA* 17 (1931) 235-287.

R. O. Faulkner, "The Bremner-Rhind Papyrus-I," *JEA* 22 (1936) 121-140. [A. The Songs of Isis and Nephthys]

Edward Ulback, "The Kerasher Papyrus," *OC* 50 (1936) 97-99.

R. O. Faulkner, "The Bremner-Rhind Papyrus-II," *JEA* 23 (1937) 10-16. [B. The 'Colophon'; C. The Ritual of Bringing in Sokar]

R. O. Faulkner, "The Bremner-Rhind Papyrus-III," *JEA* 23 (1937) 166-185. [D. The Book of Overthrowing 'Apep]

Alan W. Shorter, "The Papyrus of Khnememhab in University College, London," *JEA* 23 (1937) 34-38.

R. O. Faulkner, "The Bremner-Rhind Papyrus-IV," *JEA* 24 (1938) 41-53. [D. The Book of Overthrowing 'Apep *(concluded);* E. The names of 'Apep]

*Battiscombe Gunn, "P. Chester Beatty I, 6, 6," *JEA* 25 (1939) 101-102.

*Lynn H. Wood, "The Kahun Papyrus and the Date of the Twelfth Dynasty (with a chart)," *BASOR* #99 (1945) 5-9.

G. Posener, "One more Duplicate of the Hood Papyrus," *JEA* 31 (1945) 112.

John Barns, "Three Hieratic Papyri in the Duke of Northumberland's Collection," *JEA* 34 (1948) 35-46.

Alan [H.] Gardiner, "A Pharaonic Encomium," *JEA* 41 (1955) 30.

Alan [H.]Gardiner, "The Pharaonic Encomium (II)," *JEA* 42 (1956) 8-20.

Adhémar Massart, "The Egyptian Geneva Papyrus MAH 15274," *MDIÄA* 15 (1957) 172-185.

R. O. Faulkner, "Giessen University Library Papyrus No. 115," *JEA* 44 (1958) 66-74.

Ricardo A. Caminos, "Papyrus Berlin 10463," *JEA* 49 (1963) 29-37.

Claire Epstein, "A New Appraisal of Some Lines from a Long-known Papyrus," *JEA* 49 (1963) 49-56. [Papyrus Hermitage no. 1116A]

Shirley Alexander, "Notes on the Use of Gold-leaf in Egyptian Papyri," *JEA* 51 (1965) 48-51. (Addendum, by T. G. H. James, pp. 51-52)

George R. Hughes, "No Ramesses III funerary estate in Pap. Louvre E 7845A," *JEA* 52 (1966) 178-179.

A. F. Rainey, "The Soldier-Scribe in *Papyrus Anastasi I,*" *JNES* 26 (1966) 58-60.

Elzbieta Dabrowwska Smektala, "Fragment of Hieratic Papyrus of *'Ir·ty·rw-ṯзw,*" *BIFAO* 66 (1968) 183-189.

E. A. E. Raymond, "A Dispute in the Hawara Necropolis," *CdÉ* 43 (1968) 55-77. [P. Cairo 50127]

Hans Goedicke, "Papyrus Lansing 3,9-3,10," *JARCE* 7 (1968) 128-130.

Abd-el-Moḥsen Bakir, "The Middle-kingdom Cairo Letter. A Reconsideration (Papyrus 91061=CGC No. 58045)," *JEA* 54 (1968) 57-59.

Ricardo A. Caminos, "A Fragmentary Hieratic School-book in the British Museum (Pap. B.M. 10298)," *JEA* 54 (1968) 114-120.

*P. Ghalioungui, "The '*smr*' Animal of the Ebers Papyrus," *BIFAO* 68 (1969) 39-40.

§848　*4.3.1.1.14.1 Demotic Papyri - Unclassified*

*G. Seyffarth, "Three Lectures on Egyptian Antiquities, &c., delivered at the Stuyvesant Institute, New York, May 1856," *ER* 8 (1856-57) 34-104. [I. The Demotic Documents, p. 70]

*G. P. G. Sobhy, "Miscellanea," *JEA* 16 (1930) 3-5. [2. Demotica, pp. 3-5]

Nathaniel Julius Reich, "New Documents from the Serapeum of Memphis," *Miz* 1 (1933) 9-129.

P. A. A. Boeser, "Demotic Papyrus from the Roman Imperial Time," *EgR* 3 (1935) 27-63.

Nathaniel Julius Reich, "The Elkan Adler Papyrus No. 31," *JAOS* 56 (1936) 258-271.

N. J. Reich, "The Papyrus-Archive in the Philadelphia University Museum (The Papyri from Dira' abū 'l-Naga) I," *Miz* 7 (1938) 11-19.

N. J. Reich, "The Papyrus-Archive in the Philadelphia University Museum (The Papyri from Dira' abū 'l-Naga) II," *Miz* 8 (1938) 7-14.

N. J. Reich, "The Papyrus-Archive in the Philadelphia University Museum (The Papyri from Dira' abū 'l-Naga) III," *Miz* 9 (1938) 7-18.

George R. Hughes and Charles F. Nims, "Some Observations on the British Museum Demotic Theban Archive," *AJSL* 57 (1940) 244-261.

Herbert Thompson, "Two Demotic Self-Dedications," *JEA* 26 (1940) 68-78. [B.M. Eg. 10622; B.M. Eg. 10624]

Girgis Mattha, "Notes on a Demotic Papyrus from Thebes," *ASAE* 51 (1951) 265-267.

Aksel Volten, "An 'Alphabetical' Dictionary and Grammar in Demotic. (Pap. Carlesberg XII verso.)," *ArOr* 20 (1952) 496-508.

*Roland J. Williams, "Grammatical Notes on the Demotic of Papyrus Insinger," *JEA* 38 (1952) 62-64.

*J. J. Rabinowitz, "The Aramaic Papyri, the Demotic Papyri from Gebelen and Talmudic Sources," *B* 38 (1957) 269-274.

A. F. Shore and H. S. Smith, "Two Unpublished Demotic Documents from the Asyūt Archive," *JEA* 45 (1959) 52-60. [B.M. 10589; B.M.10601]

J. Gwyn Griffiths, "A Note on P. Demot. Mag. Lond. et Leid. XIII, 2," *ZÄS* 84 (1959) 156-157.

Mustafa El-Amir, "The Unpublished Demotic Papyri in the Turin Museum," *AO* 25 (1960) 203-228.

Charles F. Nims, "Demotic Papyrus Loeb 62: A Reconsideration," *AO* 25 (1960) 266-276.

§849   ***4.3.1.1.15 Egyptian Texts Bearing on Biblical Studies
[See also: Egyptian Backgrounds
§289; Egyptian Backgrounds to
the Pentateuch §300 ←]***

*August Eisenlohr, "On the Political Condition of Egypt before the Reign of Ramses III; *probably in connection with the establishment of the Jewish Religion.* From the Great Harris Papyrus," *SBAT* 1 (1872) 355-384.

*Max Müller, "The supposed Name of Judah in the List of Shoshenq," *SBAP* 10 (1887-88) 81-83. (Note by P. le Page Renouf, pp. 83-86)

P. le Page Renouf, "The Tablet of the Seven Years of Famine," *SBAP* 13 (1890-91) 443-444.

*James Henry Breasted, "Some Egyptian Names in Genesis—A New Inscription of the Oldest Period, etc.," *BW* 2 (1893) 285-288.

*P. le Page Renouf, "The Lay of the Threshers," *SBAP* 19 (1897) 121-122. *[Ref. Deut. 25:4]*

J. N. Fradenburg, "Notes on Literature in Egypt in the Time of Moses," *JTVI* 31 (1897-98) 169-192. (Discussion, pp. 192-193) (Remarks by C. R. Conder, pp. 193-194)

*E[douard] Naville, "Egyptian Writing in Foundation Walls and the Age of the Book of Deuteronomy," *SBAP* 29 (1907) 232-242.

*A. M. Skelly, "The Inscriptions of Sinai and Their Relation to Certain Facts of Scripture," *ACQR* 37 (1912) 678-692.

*Joseph Offord, "The Localities of the Exodus: and a New Egyptian Papyrus," *PEFQS* 44 (1912) 202-205.

*J. W. Jack, "Moses and the New Sinai Inscriptions," *ET* 37 (1925-26) 327-330.

*S. Yeivin, "A New Egyptian Source for the History of Palestine and Syria," *JPOS* 14 (1934) 194-239. *[Stela of Thothmes III]*

*A. Malamat, "Scales of Rationing in Pap. Anastasi I and the Bible," *BIES* 19 (1955) #3/4, ii.

*Jaroslav Černý, "Reference to Blood Brotherhood among Semites in an Egyptian Text of the Ramesside Period," *JNES* 14 (1955) 161-163.

*K. A. Kitchen, "A Recently Published Egyptian Papyrus and Its Bearing on the Joseph Story," *TB* #2 (1956-57) 1-2.

*J. J. Rabinowitz, "The Aramaic Papyri, the Demotic Papyri from Gebelen and Talmudic Sources," *B* 38 (1957) 269-274.

*Raphael Giveon, "A Ramesside 'Semitic' Letter," *RDSO* 37 (1962) 167-173. *[Ref. Judg. 3:31]*

*P. C. Craigie, "The Song of Deborah and the Epic of Tukulti-Ninurta," *JBL* 88 (1969) 253-265.

§850   **4.3.1.2 Coptic Texts (including Sahidic)**

Anonymous, "A Catalogue of the rev. H. Tattam's Coptic and Sahidic Manuscripts purchased or copied in Egypt," *ZDMG* 7 (1853) 94-97.

*C. W. Goodwin, "Topographical notes from Coptic papyri," *ZÄS* 7 (1869) 73-75.

*A. H. Sayce, "Gleanings from the land of Egypt," *RTR* 13 (1890) 62-67, 181-191. [§II.— An inscription from the tombs of Beni-Mohammed el-Kufûr, pp. 65-67]

W. E. Crum, "Another Fragment of the Story of Alexander," *SBAP* 14 (1891-92) 473-482. *[Coptic Text]*

*Cyrus Adler, "Notes on the Johns Hopkins and Abbott collections of Egyptian antiquities, with the translation of two Coptic inscriptions by Mr. W. Max Müller," *JAOS* 15 (1893) xxxi-xxxiv.

*A. H. Sayce, "Gleanings from the land of Egypt," *RTR* 15 (1893) 147-148. [§IV. Near the Cataract of Assouân] *[Coptic Text]*

*A. H. Sayce, "Gleanings from the land of Egypt," *RTR* 20 (1898) 111-112. [§VII *(untitled)* & §VIII *(untitled)*] *(Coptic stela)*

*A. H. Sayce, "Gleanings from the land of Egypt," *RTR* 20 (1898) 169-176. *(Coptic texts)*

M. A. Murray, "Coptic Stele of Apa Telemē," *AEE* 1 (1914) 156-158.

A. E. R. Boak, "A Coptic Syllabary at the University of Michigan," *Aeg* 4 (1923) 296-297.

N. Lewis, "Mummy-Tickets from Achmîm-Panopolis," *Miz* 2 (1936) 70-72. *[marked as continued, but never was]*

*R. Engelbach, "A Coptic Ostracon mentioning Iēb (Elephantine)," *ASAE* 38 (1938) 47-52.

Nathaniel Julius Reich, "Coptic Ostracon Merton 1," *JAOS* 58 (1938) 151-152.

W. E. Crum, "Coptic Documents in Greek Script," *PBA* 25 (1939) 249-271.

*Ahmed Fakhry, "The rock inscriptions of Gabal el-Teir at Kharag Oasis," *ASAE* 51 (1951) 401-434.

L. Kákosy, "Remarks on the Interpretation of a Coptic Magical Text," *AOASH* 13 (1961) 325-328.

A. Badawy, "The Funerary Stela with Coptic Cryptogram(?)," *BO* 18 (1961) 17-19.

§851 *4.4 Semitic Texts - General Studies*

Cyril C. Graham, "On the Inscriptions found in the region of El-Harrah, in the Great Desert South-east and East of the Hauran," *JRAS* (1860) 286-297.

S. S. Haldeman, "On the Occurrence of Semitic Consonants on the Western Continent," *JAOS* 10 (1880) ciii.

*George A. Barton, "On the Sacrifices כלל and כלל שלם in the Marseilles Inscription," *JAOS* 16 (1894-96) lxvii-lxix.

J. A. Montgomery, "Some Gleanings from Pognon's ZKR Inscription," *JBL* 28 (1909) 57-70.

*F. W. Green, "Notes on Some Inscriptions in the Etabi District. I.," *SBAP* 31 (1909) 247-254.

*F. W. Green, "Notes on Some Inscriptions in the Etabi District. II.," *SBAP* 31 (1909) 319-323.

Anonymous, "A New Collection of Ancient Texts," *MR* 92 (1910) 137-141. *(Review)*

*Joseph Offord, "On—Anu, Heliopolis in a Semitic Inscription; and the Gilgals and Massebahs of Palestine," *PEFQS* 51 (1919) 123-133.

*G. R. Driver, "Old and New Semitic Texts," *PEQ* 70 (1938) 188-192. [I. From the Late Rev. Prof. A. H. Sayce's Papers; II. In the Ashmolean Museum, Oxford; III. On Mr. J. L. Starkey's Two Seals from Tell ed-Duweir; IV. A New Phoenico-Aramaean Name]

Nelson Glueck, "Ostraca from Elath," *BASOR* #80 (1940) 3-10.

*H. L. Ginsberg, "Affinities between Semitic Inscriptions and Biblical Literature of Persian and Greek Periods," *JBL* 59 (1940) x.

Nelson Glueck, "Ostraca from Elath," *BASOR* #82 (1941) 3-11.

W[illiam] F[oxwell] Albright, "Ostracon No. 6043 from Ezion-Geber," *BASOR* #82 (1941) 11-15.

Charles C. Torrey, "On the Ostraca from Elath (Bulletin No. 80)," *BASOR* #82 (1941) 15-16.

Franz Rosenthal, "The Script of Ostracon No 6043 from Ezion-Geber," *BASOR* #85 (1942) 8-9.

P. Kahane, "Notes on the Sichem Plaque," *BIES* 12 (1946) II-III. *[Proto-Semitic]*

W[illiam] F[oxwell] Albright, "The So-called Enigmatic Inscription from Byblus," *BASOR* #116 (1949) 12-14.

*S. Yeivin, "Ostracon A1/382 from Hazor and its Implications," *EI* 9 (1969) 136. *[English Summary]*

§852 *4.4.1 Levantine (Northwest Semitic) Texts*

Stanley A. Cook, "Notes on Semitic Inscriptions. IV," *SBAP* 26 (1904) 221-223. [4. Errors in Inscriptions]

Hope W. Hogg, "North-Semitic Epigraphy," *AJSL* 18 (1901-02) 1-8.

Stanley A. Cook, "North-Semitic Epigraphy," *JQR* 16 (1903-04) 258-289.

*Charles C. Torrey, "New Notes on some Old Inscriptions," *ZA* 26 (1912) 77-92. [Byblos, Lines 10-13; Tabnīt; Ešmūn'azar; Bod-'Aštart; Siloam; Zenjīrlī. Bar-Rekeb; Nērab II; Guzneh; The Abydos Lion-weight (CIS II 108)]

D. D. Luckenbill, "A Messenger from Ibla," *AJSL* 39 (1922-23) 65-66.

Hartwig Hirschfield, "Gleanings in Semitic Epigraphy," *PEFQS* 59 (1927) 103-104.

*Julian Obermann, "Wind, Water and Light in an Archaic Inscription from Shechem," *JBL* 57 (1938) 239-254.

Cyrus H. Gordon, "Two Northwest-Semitic Inscriptions from Tarsus," *BASOR* #78 (1940) 9-11.

Jonas C. Greenfield, "Studies in Western Semitic Inscriptions, I. Stylistic Aspects of the Sefire Treaty Inscriptions," *AO* 29 (1965-66) 1-18.

Cyrus H. Gordon, "Northwest Semitic Texts in Latin and Greek Letters," *JAOS* 88 (1968) 285-289.

§853 *4.4.2 Sinai / Proto-Sinaitic Inscriptions*

*B. S., "The Voice of Israel from the Rocks of Sinai," *JSL, 2nd Ser.,* 1 (1851-52) 339-350. *(Review)*

Anonymous,"Forster's Primæval Language," *CTPR,3rd Ser.,* 9(1853) 33-48.

F. W. G., "The Sinaitic Inscriptions," *JSL, 2nd Ser.,* 4 (1853) 328-345.

John Hogg, "On the *Sinaic* Inscriptions; and on the Ancient Altar and Palm-Grove *Diodorus*," *JSL, 3rd Ser.,* 8 (1858-59) 162-168.

Q. E. D., "Sinaitic Inscriptions," *JSL, 4th Ser.,* 4 (1863-64) 178.

*F. de P. Castells, "The Earliest Hebrew Script," *ET* 20 (1908-09) 429-431.

J. M. Powis Smith, "A New Disclosure from Sinai," *JR* 6 (1926) 195-200.

Kirsopp Lake and Robert P. Blake, "The Serâbît Inscriptions, I. The Rediscovery of the Inscriptions," *HTR* 21 (1928) 1-8.

Romain F. Butin, "The Serâbît Inscriptions, II. The Decipherment and Significance of the Inscriptions," *HTR* 21 (1928) 9-67.

Charles Bruston, "Notes. The Serâbît Inscriptions," *HTR* 22 (1929) 175-180.

A. E. Cowley, "The Sinaitic Inscriptions," *JEA* 15 (1929) 200-218.

*Alan H. Gardiner, "The Sinai Script and the Origin of the Alphabet," *PEFQS* 61 (1929) 48-55.

Julius L. Siegel, "The Date and the Historical Background of the Sinaitic Inscriptions," *AJSL* 49 (1932-33) 46-52.

‡Romain F. Butin, "The Serabit Expedition of 1930: IV. The Protosinaitic Inscriptions," *HTR* 25 (1932) 130-203. [Bibliography, pp. 131-132]

*R[omain F.] Butin, "The Protosinaitic Inscriptions of Serabit and the Origin of the Alphabet," *AJA* 37 (1933) 115.

W[illiam] F[oxwell] Albright, "Some Suggestions for the Decipherment of the Proto-Sinaitic Inscriptions," *JPOS* 15 (1935) 334-340.

Harold Garner, "Sinai and Its Inscriptions," *LQHR* 161 (1936) 472-479.

*S. Yeivin, "The Palestino-Sinaitic Inscriptions," *PEQ* 69 (1937) 180-193. [II. The Chronology of the Palestinian Sinaitic Ostraca, pp. 184-193]

J. Leibovitch, "Recent discoveries and developments in protosinaïtic," *ASAE* 40 (1940-41) 101-131.

*Ruth B. Kallner, "Two Inscribed Sherds," *KSJA* 1 (1942) VII. [1. Palestino-"Proto-Sinaitic" characters].

*Herbert G. May, "Moses and the Sinai Inscriptions," *BA* 8 (1945) 93-99.

Alan [H.] Gardiner, "Once again the Proto-Sinaitic Inscriptions," *JEA* 48 (1962) 45-48.

J. Leibovitch, "The Date of the Proto-Sinaitic Inscriptions," *Muséon* 76 (1963) 201-203. (Additional note by W. F. Albright, pp. 203-205)

§854 *4.4.3 Canaanite Texts and Inscriptions - General Studies*

*W[illiam] H. Ward, "On the Pseudo-Phœnician Inscription of Brazil," *JAOS* 10 (1880) lxxxv-lxxxvi.

*Charles C. Torrey, "The Zakar and Kalamu Inscriptions," *JAOS* 35 (1915) 353-369.

*W[illiam] F[oxwell] Albright, "New Light on Early Canaanite Language and Literature," *BASOR* #46 (1932) 15-20.

*W[illiam] F[oxwell] Albright, "More Light on the Canaanite Epic of Alyân Baal and Môt," *BASOR* #50 (1933) 13-20.

George A. Barton, "Notes on the Ain Shems Tablet," *BASOR* #52 (1933) 5-6.

W[illiam] F[oxwell] Albright, "The Cuneiform Tablet from Beth-Shemesh," *BASOR* #53 (1934) 18-19.

*Theodor H[erzl] Gaster, "The Beth-Shemesh Tablet and the Origins of Ras-Shamra Culture," *PEFQS* 66 (1934) 94-96.

B. Maisler, "A Canaanite Inscription from Shechem," *BIES* 6 (1938-39) #1, V.

J. Philip Hyatt, "Early Canaanite Literature," *BA* 2 (1939) 2-3.

S. Yeivin, "Note on the Shechem Stele," *BIES* 8 (1940-41) #2, II.

*T. H. Gaster, "A Canaanite Magical Text," *Or, N.S.,* 11 (1942) 41-79.

W[illiam] F[oxwell] Albright, "A Prince of Taanach in the Fifteenth Century B.C.," *BASOR* #94 (1944) 12-27.

*J. T. Milik and Frank M. Cross Jr., "Inscribed Javelin-Heads from the Period of the Judges: A Recent Discovery in Palestine," *BASOR* #134 (1954) 5-15. *[Proto-Canaanite]*

*S. E. Loewenstamm, "Notes on the Alalakh Tablets. A Comparison of the Alalakh with the Ugaritic Documents," *IEJ* 6 (1956) 217-225.

*Matitiahu Tsevat, "Alalakhiana," *HUCA* 29 (1958) 109-134. [I. Comments and Notes on the Texts; II. The Alalakh Texts—The Language of Canaan—The Bible]

Yagael Yadin, "Note on a Proto-Canaanite Inscription from Lachish," *PEQ* 91 (1959) 130-131.

Harvey Sobelman, "The Proto-Byblian Inscriptions: A Fresh Approach," *JSS* 6 (1961) 226-245.

M. F. Martin, "A Twelfth Century Bronze Palimpsest," *RDSO* 37 (1962) 175-197.

*W[illiam] A. Ward and M. F. Martin, "The Balu'a Stele: A New Transcription with Palaeological and Historical Notes," *ADAJ* 8&9 (1964) 5-29.

W[illiam] F[oxwell] Albright, "The Beth-Shemesh Tablet in Alphabetic Cuneiform," *BASOR* #173 (1964) 51-53.

*Joseph Naveh, "Canaanite and Hebrew Inscriptions (1960—1964)," *Léš* 30 (1965-66) #1, n.p.n.

Frank Moore Cross Jr., "The Canaanite Cuneiform Tablet from Taanach," *BASOR* #190 (1968) 41-46.

B. Peckham, "Notes on a Fifth-Century Phoenician Inscription from Kition, Cyprus (CIS 86)," *Or, N.S.,* 37 (1968) 304-324.

*C[yrus] H. Gordon, "The Canaanite Text from Brazil," *Or, N.S.,* 37 (1968) 425-436.

Lawrence E. Stager, "An Inscribed Potsherd from the Eleventh Century B.C.," *BASOR* #194 (1969) 45-52.

§855 *4.4.4 Ammonite Literature*

Y. Aharoni, "A New Ammonite Inscription," *IEJ* 1 (1950-51) 219-222.

Yonah Yellin-Kallai, "Notes on the New Ammonite Inscription," *IEJ* 3 (1953) 123-126.

Rafik W[afa] Dajani, "The Amman Theatre Fragment," *ADAJ* 12&13 (1967-68) 65-67.

S[iegfried] H. Horn, "The Amman Citadel Inscription," *ADAJ* 12&13 (1967-68) 81-83.

Siegfried H. Horn, "The Ammān Citadel Inscription," *BASOR* #193 (1969) 2-13. [J9000]

Frank Moore Cross Jr., "Epigraphic Notes on the Ammān Citadel Inscription," *BASOR* #193 (1969) 13-19.

B. Oded, "The 'Amman Theater Inscription'," *RDSO* 44 (1969) 187-189.

(§856) *4.4.5 Edomite Literature*

§857 *4.4.6 Hebrew Texts - General Studies*
       (other than Biblical Texts)

Anonymous, "A Plea for the Study of Hebrew Literature," *SPR* 9 (1855-56)
    32-55.

*E. H. Palmer, "An Athenian bilingual inscription," *JP* 4 (1872) 48-50.
    (Additional remarks by J. E. Sandys, pp. 50-54)

*C. Clermont-Ganneau, "Letters from M. Clermont-Ganneau," *PEFQS* 6
    (1874) 3-10. [Hebrew Inscriptions, pp. 8-9]

C. R. Conder, "Hebrew Inscriptions," *PEFQS* 15 (1883) 170-174.

†Ch. Clermont-Ganneau, "Hebrew Epitaph of Youdan, son of Rabbi
    Tarphon, from the Necropolis of Joppa," *SBAP* 6 (1883-84) 123-125.

John P. Peters, "Two Fragments of Hebrew Popular Melodies," *JBL* 5
    (1885) 88-90.

*A. H. Sayce, "New Phœnician & Israelitish Inscriptions," *BOR* 1 (1886-87)
    193-194. (Note by W. M. F. Petrie, p. 194)

*C. Clermont-Ganneau, "Notes on Hebrew and Jewish Inscriptions,"
    PEFQS 23 (1891) 240-243. [I. The Hebrew Inscription from Tell el
    Hesy, p. 240. II. Jewish Inscriptions and Ossuaries *a.,* pp. 240-241]

*C. Clermont-Ganneau, "The Hebrew Phoenician Inscription of Tell el
    Hesy," *PEFQS* 24 (1892) 126-128.

Claude R. Conder, "Notes by Major Conder, R.E. II. The Tell el Hesy
    Text," *PEFQS* 24 (1892) 203-204.

*C. [Clermont-]Ganneau, "Note on Professor Theodore F. Wright's
    Inscribed Weight or Bead," *PEFQS* 25 (1893) 257.

*E. Davis, "The Siloam and Later Palestinian Inscriptions Considered in
    Relation to Sacred Textual Criticism," *PEFQS* 26 (1894) 269-277.

*Claude R. Conder, "Notes on Mr. Davis' Paper," *PEFQS* 26 (1894) 301-
    302. *[Ref. article by Davies (above)]*

C. Clermont-Ganneau, "Hebrew Inscription from near the Ash-Heaps at Jerusalem," *PEFQS* 27 (1895) 83.

*Charles Clermont-Ganneau, "A Newly Discovered Hebrew and Greek Inscription Relating to the Boundary of Gezer," *PEFQS* 31 (1899) 118-127.

*C. Clermont-Ganneau, "Note on the Inscribed Jar-Handle and Weight Found at Tell Zakariya. 1. The Handle of the Royal Jar of Hebron," *PEFQS* 31 (1899) 204-207, 355.

*A[ngus] C[rawford], "Notes—Archæological, Etc.," *PER* 13 (1899-1900) 48-50. [Jar Handle Inscriptions]

*C. Clermont-Ganneau, "Notes on Squeezes of Inscriptions in Baron Ustinow's Collection, Sent by the Rev. J. E. Hanauer," *PEFQS* 32 (1900) 110-123. (Note by J. E. Hanauer, and the Bishop of Salisbury, pp. 121-122)

*D. S. Margoliouth, "The Non-Biblical Literature of the Jews," *ET* 13 (1901-02) 190-192.

S[tanley] A. Cook, "Notes and Queries. *Hebrew Inscription at Fik,*" *PEFQS* 35 (1903) 185-186.

J. E. Hanauer, "*Hebrew Inscriptions at Fik (see* p. 185)," *PEFQS* 35 (1903) 274.

*A. Cowley, "Hebrew and Aramaic Papyri (with facsimiles)," *JQR* 16 (1903-04) 1-8.

*Stanley A. Cook, "Notes on Semitic Inscriptions. III," *SBAP* 26 (1904) 109-112, 164-167. [3. Personal Names on Hebrew Intaglios]

J. E. Hanauer, "Notes and Queries. 3. *Hebrew Inscription from Fik (Quarterly Statement,* 1903, p. 185)," *PEFQS* 36 (1904) 181.

*Hans H. Spoer, "Some Hebrew and Phoenician Inscriptions," *JAOS* 28 (1907) 355-359. [1. New Ossuaries from Jerusalem]

R. A. Stewart Macalister, "Notes and Queries. 3. *The Hebrew Graffito in the Golden Gate,*" *PEFQS* 40 (1908) 164-165.

A. Büchler, "Notes and Queries. 3. *The Hebrew Graffito in the Golden Gate,*" *PEFQS* 40 (1908) 261.

David G. Lyon, "Hebrew Ostraca from Samaria," *HTR* 4 (1911) 136-143.

M. Lidzbarski, "An Inscribed Jewish Ossuary," *PEFQS* 45 (1913) 84-85.

G. Buchanan Gray, "An Inscribed Jewish Ossuary: A Correction," *PEFQS* 46 (1914) 40-42.

[Hans Henry] Spoer, "An Inscribed Jewish Ossuary," *PEFQS* 46 (1914) 200-201. (Note by G. Buchanan Gray, p. 201.)

*J. E. Pilcher, "Signet with Old-Hebrew Inscription," *PEFQS* 51 (1919) 177-181.

A. Marmorstein, "The Jewish Inscription from 'Ain Duk," *PEFQS* 52 (1920) 139-141.

Stanley A. Cook, "The 'Ain Duk Mosaic," *PEFQS* 52 (1920) 142.

E. Burrows, "Note on the Hebrew inscription of 'Alma," *B* 3 (1922) 454-456.

*L. A. Mayer, "A Tomb in the Kedron Valley Containing Ossuaries with Hebrew Graffiti Names," *BSAJB* #5 (1924) 56-60.

*A. H. Sayce, "Unpublished Hebrew, Aramaic and Babylonian Inscriptions from Egypt, Jerusalem and Carchemish," *JEA* 10 (1924) 16-17.

E. L. Sukenik, "Notes on the Jewish Graffiti in Beth-phage," *JPOS* 4 (1924) 171-174.

Stanley A. Cook, "Inscribed Hebrew Objects from Ophel," *PEFQS* 56 (1924) 180-186.

W[illiam] F[oxwell] Albright, "The Hebrew Ostrakon," *PEFQS* 57 (1925) 219.

*W[illiam] F[oxwell] Albright, "Notes on Early Hebrew and Aramaic Epigraphy," *JPOS* 6 (1926) 75-102. [1. The End of the Sarcophagus Text of Aḥîrâm; 2. An Unexplained Word in the Kilamûwa Stele; 3. The Beginning of the Zakir Stele; 4. The New Hebrew Ostracon from Jerusalem; 5. The Seals of the Temple Treasury after the Exile]

Allen H. Godbey, "Notable Hebrew Inscriptions," *MQR, 3rd Ser.,* 52 (1926) 595-610.

J. Ory, "An Inscription Newly Found in the Synagogue of Kerazeh," *PEFQS* 59 (1927) 51-52.

A. Marmorstein, "About the Inscription of Judah Ben Ishmael," *PEFQS* 59 (1927) 101-102.

J. A. Montgomery, "Two Notes on the Kalamu Inscription," *JBL* 47 (1928) 196-197.

E. L. Sukenik, "A Jewish Hypogeum Near Jerusalem," *JPOS* 8 (1928) 113-121.

W[illiam] F[oxwell] Albright, "A Neglected Hebrew Inscription of the Thirteenth Century B.C.," *AfO* 5 (1928-29) 150-152.

E. L. Sukenik, "Additional Note on 'A Jewish Hypogeum Near Jerusalem'," *JPOS* 9 (1929) 45-49.

*Solomon Gandz, "The knot in Hebrew literature, or from the knot to the alphabet," *Isis* 14 (1930) 189-214.

B. Maisler, "A Hebrew Ossuary Inscription," *PEFQS* 63 (1931) 171-172.

E. L. Sukenik, "Funerary Tablet of Uzziah, King of Judah," *PEFQS* 63 (1931) 217-221.

E. L. Sukenik, "The Funerary Tablet of Uzziah," *PEFQS* 64 (1932) 106-107.

*E. L. Sukenik, "Inscribed Hebrew and Aramaic Potsherds from Samaria," *PEFQS* 65 (1933) 152-156. [I. Hebrew, pp. 152-155]

E. L. Sukenik, "Inscribed Potsherds with Biblical Names from Samaria," *PEFQS* 65 (1933) 200-204.

Theodor H. Gaster, "The Tell-Duweir Ewer Inscription," *PEFQS* 66 (1934) 176-178.

E. Burrows, "The Tell-Duweir Ewer Inscription," *PEFQS* 66 (1934) 179-180.

*S. Yeivin, "Note on the Duweir Ewer," *JPOS* 15 (1935) 98-100.

Theodor H. Gaster, "The Tell-Duweir Ewer Inscription. A Supplementary Note," *PEFQS* 67 (1935) 34-35.

Eric Burrows, "Further Note on the Tell-Duweir Ewer Inscription," *PEFQS* 67 (1935) 87-89.

Charles Marston, "Hebrew Potsherds from Tell Duweir," *PEFQS* 67 (1935) 91-92.

F. Melian Stawell, "The Inscriptions on the Tell Duweir Bowl and Ewer," *PEFQS* 68 (1936) 97-101.

E. L. Sukenick, "Note on a Fragment of an Israelite Stele Found at Samaria," *PEFQS* 68 (1936) 156.

W[illiam] F[oxwell] Albright, "Ostracon C-1101 of Samaria," *PEFQS* 68 (1936) 211-215.

W[illiam] F[oxwell] Albright, "A Hebrew Letter from the Twelfth Century B.C.," *BASOR* 73 (1939) 9-13.

W[illiam] F[oxwell] Albright, "An Aramaean Magical Text in Hebrew from the Seventh Century B.C.," *BASOR* #76 (1939) 5-11.

*H. Torczyner, "The Siloam Inscription, The Gezer Calendar and the Ophel Ostracon," *BIES* 7 (1939-40) #1, I.

A. Sperber, "Idiomatic Characteristics of the Hebrew Inscriptions," *JBL* 58 (1939) xv-xvi.

E. L. Sukenik, "Notes on the Sherd from Tell eṣ-Ṣarem," *KSJA* 1 (1942) VII.

*David Diringer, "The Palestinian Inscriptions and the Origin of the Alphabet," *JAOS* 63 (1943) 24-30.

S. A. Birnbaum, "On the Possibility of Dating Hebrew Inscriptions," *PEQ* 76 (1944) 213-217.

*G. R. Driver, "Brief Notes (II) Notes on Old Inscriptions," *PEQ* 77 (1945) 5-12. [(1) Hebrew, pp. 5-9]

D. Diringer, "Note by D. Diringer," *PEQ* 77 (1945) 53-54. *[Ref. article by Driver (above)]*

H. Torczyner, "A Hebrew Incantation of the Biblical Period against the Demons of the Night," *BIES* 12 (1946) (III?) IV-V. *[Some variance in page numbers as there appears to be more than one edition of English summaries]*

N. Avigad, "The Inscription in the Bene Ḥezir Tomb," *BIES* 12 (1946) V-VI.

A. Reifenberg, "Discovery of a New Hebrew Inscription of the Pre-Exilic Period," *BIES* 13 (1946-47) #3/4, II.

Yiga'el Sukenik, "The 'Ophel Ostracon'," *BIES* 13 (1946-47) #3/4 V-VI.

Theodor H. Gaster, "The Magical Inscription from Arslan Tash," *JNES* 6 (1947) 186-188.

Arthur Reifenberg, "A newly discovered Hebrew Inscription of the pre-exilic period," *JPOS* 21 (1948) 134-137.

*David Diringer, "The Early Hebrew Hand-Book," *PEQ* 82 (1950) 16-24.

B. Maisler, "Two Hebrew Ostraca from Tell Qasîle," *JNES* 10 (1951) 265-267.

P. A. H. de Boer, "Notes on an Oxyrhynchus Papyrus in Hebrew," *VT* 1 (1951) 49-57.

N. Zori, "A Hebrew Inscription from the Arabah," *BIES* 17 (1952-53) #1/2, IV.

N. Avigad, "A Hebrew Inscription from Tell en-Naṣbeh," *BIES* 17 (1952-53) #3/4 I.

*N. Avigad, "Another *Bat le-melekh* Inscription," *IEJ* 3 (1953) 121-122.

N. Avigad, "The Epitaph of a Royal Steward from Siloam Village," *IEJ* 3 (1953) 137-152.

H. H. Lehmann, "A legal certificate from Bar Kochba's Days," *VT* 3 (1953) 391-396.

B. Mazar, "A Hebrew Inscription from 'Illar," *BIES* 18 (1953-54) #3/4, IV-V.

J. J. Rabinowitz, "The Legal Document from Murabba'at," *B* 35 (1954) 198-206.

G. E. Wright, "Epitaph of a Judean Official," *BA* 17 (1954) 22-23.

M. H. Gottstein, "Hebrew Fragments in the Mingana Collection," *JJS* 5 (1954) 172-176.

S. Yeivin, "Some Notes on the Documents from Wadi Murabba'at dating from the days of Bar Kokh'ba," *'Atiqot* 1 (1955) 95-108.

N. Avigad, "The Second Tomb-Inscription of the Royal Steward," *IEJ* 5 (1955) 163-165.

S. A. Birnbaum, "The Beth Mashku Document," *PEQ* 87 (1955) 21-33.

*S. A. Birnbaum, "The Negeb Script," _VT_ 6 (1956) 337-371. [The Kephar Bebhayu Marriage Document]

*Jacob J. Rabinowitz, "A Legal Formula in Egyptian, Egyptian-Aramaic, and Murabba'at Documents," _BASOR_ #145 (1957) 33-34.

S. A. Birnbaum, "The Kephar Bebhayu Conveyance," _PEQ_ 89 (1957) 108-132.

*James B. Pritchard, "The Inscribed Jar-Handles from Gibeon," _AJA_ 62 (1958) 225.

N. Avigad, "Some Notes on the Hebrew Inscription from Gibeon (Review Article)," _IEJ_ 9 (1959) 130-133.

*N. Tsori, "A Spindle Whorl with Hebrew Inscription," _IEJ_ 9 (1959) 191-192.

*James B. Pritchard, "More Inscribed Jar Handles from el-Jîb," _BASOR_ #160 (1960) 2-6.

J. Neveh, "A Hebrew Letter from the Seventh Century B.C.," _IEJ_ 10 (1960) 129-139.

Anonymous, "New Moabite Inscription Found," _AT_ 5 (1960-61) #4, 15. _[Hebrew]_

*M. Dothan, "An Inscribed Jar from Azor," _'Atiqot_ 3 (1961) 181-184.

*A. M. Honeyman, "Two Semitic Inscriptions from Malta," _PEQ_ 93 (1961) 151-153.

Frank Moore Cross Jr., "Epigraphic Notes on Hebrew Documents of the Eighth-Sixth Centuries B.C.: I. A New Reading of a Place Name in the Samaria Ostraca," _BASOR_ #163 (1961) 12-14.

H. Neil Richardson, "A New Seventh Century Hebrew Ostracon," _JAAR_ 29 (1961) 3.

Joseph Naveh, "A Hebrew Letter from the Time of Jeremiah," _Arch_ 15 (1962) 108-111.

S. Yeivin, "The Judicial Petition from Meẓad Ḥashavyahu," _BO_ 19 (1962) 3-10.

Frank Moore Cross Jr., "Epigraphic Notes on Hebrew Documents of the Eighth-Sixth Centuries B.C.: II. The Murabba'ât Papyrus and the Letter from Near Yabneh-Yam," *BASOR* #165 (1962) 34-46.

*Frank Moore Cross Jr., "Epigraphic Notes on Hebrew Documents of the Eighth-Sixth Centuries B.C.: III. The Inscribed Jar Handles from Gibeon," *BASOR* #168 (1962) 18-23.

J. Naveh, "More Hebrew Inscriptions from Meṣad Ḥashavyahu," *IEJ* 12 (1962) 27-32.

M. Avi-Yonah, "A List of Priestly Courses from Caesarea," *IEJ* 12 (1962) 137-139.

*A[lan] R. Millard, "Alphabetic Inscriptions on Ivories from Nimrud," *Iraq* 24 (1962) 41-51. [ND. 10151; ND. 10359; ND. 8184; ND. 10304; ND. 10303]

D. Leslie, "Some notes on the Jewish Inscriptions of K'aifeng," *JAOS* 82 (1962) 346-361.

A[lan] R. Millard, "Recently Discovered Hebrew Inscriptions," *TB* #11 (1962) 4-10.

Frank Moore Cross Jr., "The Discovery of the Samaria Papyri," *CNI* 14 (1963) #3/4, 24-35.

J. Naveh, "Old Hebrew Inscriptions in a Burial Cave," *IEJ* 13 (1963) 74-92.

Shemaryahu Talmon, "The New Hebrew Letter from the Seventh Century B.C. in Historical Perspective," *BASOR* #176 (1964) 29-38.

J. D. Amusin and M. L. Heltzer, "The Inscription from Meṣad Ḥashavyahu. Complaint of a Reaper of the Seventh Century B.C.," *IEJ* 14 (1964) 148-157.

J. Naven, "Some Notes on the Reading of the Meṣad Ḥashavyahu Letter," *IEJ* 14 (1964) 158-159.

*T. Donald, "The Semantic Field of Rich and Poor in the Wisdom Literature of Hebrew and Accadian," *OA* 3 (1964) 27-41.

*Joseph Naveh, "Canaanite and Hebrew Inscriptions (1960—1964)," *Lěš* 30 (1965-66) #1, n.p.n.

*Yohanan Aharoni, "The Use of Hieratic Numerals in Hebrew Ostraca and the Shekel Weights," *BASOR* #184 (1966) 13-19.

Y[ohanan] Aharoni, "Hebrew Ostraca from Tel Arad," *IEJ* 16 (1966) 1-7.

*Yohanan Aharoni, "Arad: Its Inscriptions and Temple," *BA* 31 (1968) 2-32.

D[avid] Ussishkin, "On the Short Inscription from the Tomb of '...yahu Who Is Over the House'," *Lĕš* 33 (1968-69) #4, 3.

David Ussishkin, "On the Shorter Inscription from the 'Tomb of the Royal Steward'," *BASOR* #196 (1969) 16-22.

Y[ohanan] Aharoni, "Three Hebrew Ostraca from Arad," *EI* 9 (1969) 134. [English Summary]

B.A.Levine, "Notes on a Hebrew Ostracon from Arad,"*IEJ* 19 (1969) 49-51.

D[avid] N[oel] Freedman, "The Orthography of the Arad Ostraca," *IEJ* 19 (1969) 52-56.

*Sh. Yeivin, "An Ostracon from Tel Arad exhibiting a Combination of Two Scripts," *JEA* 55 (1969) 98-102.

§858 *4.4.6.1 Hebrew Inscriptions and Texts from Gezer*

*W. W. Moore, "Recent Discoveries in Palestine," *USR* 4 (1892-93) 177-192. [The Gezer Inscription, p. 185]

*Charles Clermont-Ganneau, "A Newly Discovered Hebrew and Greek Inscription Relating to the Boundary of Gezer," *PEFQS* 31 (1899) 118-127.

S[tanley] A. Cook, "Hebrew Inscription from Gezer," *PEFQS* 35 (1903) 275-276.

R. A. Stewart Macalister, "Three Ossuary Inscriptions from Gezer," *PEFQS* 38 (1906) 123-124.

*C[laude] R. Conder, "Notes and Queries. 1. *The Gezer Zodiacal Signs,*" *PEFQS* 40 (1908) 162-163.

S. Gobiet, "The Gezer Stone," *BW* 34 (1909) 57-59.

Anonymous, "A New Hebrew Inscription," *MR* 91 (1909) 807-808.

*Mark Lidzbarski, G. B. Gray, and E. J. Pilcher, "An Old Hebrew Calendar-Inscription from Gezer," *PEFQS* 41 (1909) 26-34.

Séb. Ronzevalle, "The Gezer Hebrew Inscription," *PEFQS* 41 (1909) 107-112.

Gustaf Dalman, "Notes on the Old Hebrew Calendar-Inscription from Gezer," *PEFQS* 41 (1909) 118-119.

G. B. Gray, "The Gezer Inscription," *PEFQS* 41 (1909) 189-193.

Mark Lidzbarski, "The Old Hebrew Calendar-Inscription from Gezer," *PEFQS* 41 (1909) 194-195.

Stanley A. Cook, "Notes and Queries. (4.) *Miscellanea,*" *PEFQS* 41 (1909) 232-233. *[Gezer Calendar]*

*Stanley A. Cook, "The Old Hebrew Alphabet and the Gezer Tablet," *PEFQS* 41 (1909) 284-309.

E. J. Pilcher, "The Handwriting of the Gezer Tablet," *PEFQS* 42 (1910) 32-39.

M. Lidzbarski, "Notes and Queries. *The Calendar Inscription from Gezer,*" *PEFQS* 42 (1910) 238.

G. B. Gray, "Notes and Queries. 1. *The Gezer Calendar Inscription: A Correction,*" *PEFQS* 43 (1911) 161.

*W. R. Taylor, "Recent Epigraphic Discoveries in Palestine," *JPOS* 10 (1930) 16-22. [A New Gezer Inscription, p. 17; A New Gezer Boundary Stone, pp. 19-21]

W. R. Taylor, "A New Gezer Inscription," *JPOS* 10 (1930) 79-81.

W. R. Taylor, "Some New Palestinian Inscriptions," *BASOR* #41 (1931) 27-29. *[New Gezer Boundary Stone]*

W[illiam] F[oxwell] Albright, "The Inscription from Gezer at the School in Jerusalem," *BASOR* #58 (1935) 28-29.

*H. Torczyner, "The Siloam Inscription, The Gezer Calendar and the Ophel Ostracon," *BIES* 7 (1939-40) #1, I.

*Julian Obermann, "A Revised Reading of the Tell el-Ḥesi Inscription Inscription. With a Note on the Gezer Sherd," *AJA* 44 (1940) 93-104.

*S. Birnbaum, "The Dates of the Gezer Tablet and of the Samaria Ostraca," *PEQ* 74 (1942) 104-108. [1. The Gezer Tablet, pp. 104-107]

*W[illiam] F[oxwell] Albright, "The Gezer Calendar," *BASOR* #92 (1943) 16-26.

*David Diringer, "The Dating of Early Hebrew Inscriptions (The Gezer Tablet and the Samaria Ostraca)," *PEQ* 75 (1943) 50-54.

*Louis Finkelstein, "A Talmudic Note on the Word for Cutting Flax in the Gezer Calendar," *BASOR* #94 (1944) 28-29.

*N. Avigad, "Epigraphical Gleanings from Gezer," *PEQ* 82 (1950) 43-49.

*Wolf Wirgin, "The Calendar Tablet from Gezer," *EI* 6 (1960) 9*-12*.

B. D. Rahtjen, "A Note Concerning the Form of the Gezer Tablet," *PEQ* 93 (1961) 70-72.

§859 *4.4.6.2 The Lachish Ostraca*

C[laude] R. Conder, "Notes by Major Conder. III. The Lachish Inscription," *PEFQS* 23 (1891) 70.

A. H. Sayce, "The Lachish Inscription," *PEFQS* 23 (1891) 158-159.

C[laude] R. Conder, "The Lachish Inscription," *PEFQS* 23 (1891) 250-251.

A. Neubauer, "The Lachish Inscription," *PEFQS* 23 (1891) 310.

C[laude] R. Conder, "Notes by Major Conder, R.E., I. The Lachish Text," *PEFQS* 23 (1891) 311.

*W. W. Moore, "Recent Discoveries in Palestine," *USR* 4 (1892-93) 177-192. [The Latest Discovery (the Lachish Letters), pp. 189-192]

*A[ngus] Crawford, "Palestinian Antiquities," *PER* 12 (1898-99) 392-398. [The Lachish Tablet, pp. 394-397]

A. H. Sayce, "Notes and Queries. 4. *The Cuneiform Tablet Discovered at Lachish,*" *PEFQS* 37 (1905) 167-169.

*C[laude] F. Conder, "Notes on Palestinian Archaeology. II.—The Lachish Tablet," *PEFQS* 38 (1906) 148-149.

Agnes Smith Lewis, "Canaan and the Babylonian Civilization," *ET* 25 (1913-14) 43. *[Lachish Letters]*

Charles Marston, "The Lachish Letters," *ET* 46 (1934-35) 502-504.

W[illiam] F[oxwell] Albright, "Two Great Discoveries Bearing on the Old and New Testaments," *BASOR* #58 (1935) 2-4. [The Ostraca from Lachish, pp. 2-3]

*J. W. Jack, "Nedabiah in the Lachish Letters," *ET* 47 (1935-36) 430-431.

*W[illiam] F[oxwell] Albright, "A Supplement to Jeremiah: The Lachish Ostraca," *BASOR* #61 (1936) 10-16.

Millar Burrows, "I Have Written on the Door (Lachish Letter IV)," *JAOS* 56 (1936) 491-493.

*David J. Gibson, "Correspondence," *PEFQS* 68 (1936) 102-103. *[Lachish Letters]*

Cyrus H. Gordon, "Lachish Letter IV," *BASOR* #67 (1937) 30-32.

Theodor H. Gaster, "An Archaic Inscription from Lachish," *PEQ* 69 (1937) 142-143.

*S. Yeivin, "The Palestino-Sinaitic Inscriptions," *PEQ* 69 (1937) 180-193. [I. A Palestinian Letter to the Dead? (A New Lachish Ostracon), pp. 180-184]

J. W. Jack, "The Lachish Letters," *ET* 49 (1937-38) 380-381.

Raymond S. Haupert, "The Lachish Letters," *BA* 1 (1938) 30-32.

W[illiam] F[oxwell] Albright, "The Oldest Hebrew Letters: The Lachish Ostraca," *BASOR* #70 (1938) 11-17. *[Includes translation of texts]*

Cyrus H. Gordon, "Notes on the Lachish Letters," *BASOR* #70 (1938) 17-18.

H. L. Ginsberg, "Lachish Notes," *BASOR* #71 (1938) 24-27. *(Review)*

*Julian Obermann, "The Archaic Inscriptions from Lachish. A Non-Phoenician System of the North Semitic Alphabet," *JAOSS* #2 (1938) 1-48.

J. W. Jack, "The Lachish Letters: Their Date and Import. An Examination of Professor Torczyner's View," *PEQ* 70 (1938) 165-187.

S. Yeivin, "The Historical Background of the Lachish Letters," *BIES* 6 (1938-39) #1, I-II.

Joseph Reider, "The Lachish Letters," *JQR, N.S.,* 29 (1938-39) 225-239.

W[illiam] F[oxwell] Albright, "A Reexamination of the Lachish Letters," *BASOR* #73 (1939) 16-21.

D. Winton Thomas, "The Lachish Letters," *JTS, N.S.,* 40 (1939) 1-15.

*Charles Marston, "How the Old Testament Stands To-day. The Lachish Discoveries," *JTVI* 71 (1939) 156-165. (Discussion, pp. 165-169)

S. Birnbaum, "The Lachish Ostraca I," *PEQ* 71 (1939) 20-28.

S. Birnbaum, "The Lachish Ostraca II," *PEQ* 71 (1939) 91-110.

H. L. Ginsberg, "Lachish Ostraca New and Old," *BASOR* #80 (1940) 10-13.

*D. Winton Thomas, "The Site of Ancient Lachish. *The Evidence of Ostrakon IV from Tell ed-Duweir,*" *PEQ* 72 (1940) 148-149.

W[illiam] F[oxwell] Albright, "The Lachish Letters after Five Years," *BASOR* #82 (1941) 18-24.

David Diringer, "On Ancient Hebrew Inscriptions Discovered at Tell Ed-Duweir (Lachish)-I," *PEQ* 73 (1941) 38-56.

David Diringer, "On Ancient Hebrew Inscriptions Discovered at Tell Ed-Duweir (Lachish)-II," *PEQ* 73 (1941) 89-109.

David Diringer, "On Ancient Hebrew Inscriptions Discovered at Tell Ed-Duweir (Lachish)-III," *PEQ* 75 (1943) 89-99.

Herbert Gordon May, "Lachish Letter IV: 7-10," *BASOR* #97 (1945) 22-25.

W[illiam] F[oxwell] Albright, "Postscript to Professor May's Article," *BASOR* #97 (1944) 26.

D. Winton Thomas, "The Lachish Ostraca: Professor Torczyner's Latest Views," *PEQ* 78 (1946) 38-42.

*D. Winton Thomas, "Jerusalem in the Lachish Ostraca," *PEQ* 78 (1946) 86-91.

D. Winton Thomas, "Ostracon III: 13-18 From Tell Ed-Duweir," *PEQ* 80 (1948) 131-136.

H. Tur-Sinai (Torczyner), "Lachish Letter IV," *JQR, N.S.*,39 (1948-49) 365-377.

D. Winton Thomas, "A Reply to Professor H. Tur-Sinai (Torczyner)," *JQR, N.S.*, 40 (1949-50) 192.

Frank M. Cross Jr., "Lachish Letter IV," *BASOR* #144 (1956) 24-26.

G. G. Garner, *Writing and the Bible:* Dispatches from Desperate Days," *AT* 2 (1957-58) #2, 2-4. *[The Lachish Letters]*

S. Yeivin, "The Judicial Petition from Meẓad Ḥashavyāhū," *BO* 19 (1962) 3-10.

N. R. Ganor, "The Lachish Letters," *PEQ* 99 (1967) 74-77.

§860 *4.4.6.3 The Siloam Inscription*

C. Schick, "Phoenician Inscription in the Pool of Siloam," *PEFQS* 12 (1880) 238-239.

A. H. Sayce, "The Inscription at the Pool of Siloam," *PEFQS* 13 (1881) 69-73.

A. H. Sayce, "The Ancient Hebrew Inscription Discovered at the Pool of Siloam in Jerusalem," *PEFQS* 13 (1881) 141-154.

Isaac Taylor, "The Date of the Siloam Inscription," *PEFQS* 13 (1881) 155-157.

A. H. Sayce, "The Ancient Hebrew Inscription in the Pool of Siloam. I," *PEFQS* 13 (1881) 282-285.

Claude R. Conder, "The Ancient Hebrew Inscription in the Pool of Siloam. II," *PEFQS* 13 (1881) 285-287.

Claude R. Conder, "The Ancient Hebrew Inscription in the Pool of Siloam. III," *PEFQS* 13 (1881) 288-292.

Isaac Taylor, "The Ancient Hebrew Inscription in the Pool of Siloam. IV," *PEFQS* 13 (1881) 292-293.

S. Beswick, "The Ancient Hebrew Inscription in the Pool of Siloam. V," *PEFQS* 13 (1881) 293-296.

Henry Sulley, "The Ancient Hebrew Inscription in the Pool of Siloam. VI," *PEFQS* 13 (1881) 296-297.

S[elah] M[errill], "The Siloam Inscription," *AAOJ* 4 (1881-82) 71-73. *(Editorial)*

William Wright, "Remarks on the Siloam Inscription," *SBAP* 4 (1881-82) 68-71.

H. B. Waterman, "The Siloam Inscription, with a Suggested Translation," *ONTS* 1 (1882) 52-53.

*W. F. Birch, "Varieties," *PEFQS* 14 (1882) 59-61. *[The Siloam Inscription]*

A. H. Sayce, "The Siloam Inscription," *PEFQS* 14 (1882) 62-63.

C[harles] A. Briggs, "The Recently Discovered Inscriptions at the Pool of Siloam," *PR* 3 (1882) 401-404.

A. H. Sayce, "The Siloam Inscription," *PEFQS* 15 (1883) 210-215.

W., F. Birch, "The Siloam Inscription," *PEFQS* 22 (1890) 208-210.

*W. W. Moore, "Recent Discoveries in Palestine," *USR* 4 (1892-93) 177-192. [The Siloam Inscription, pp. 177-182]

*E. Davis, "The Siloam and Later Palestinian Inscriptions Considered in Relation to Sacred Textual Criticism," *PEFQS* 26 (1894) 269-277.

*Claude R. Conder, "Notes on Mr. Davis' Paper," *PEFQS* 26 (1894) 301-302. *[Ref. article by E. Davis, above]*

C[laude] R. Conder, "Date of the Siloam Text," *PEFQS* 29 (1897) 204-208. (Note by C. Clermont-Ganneau, pp. 306-307)

*Ch. Clermont-Ganneau, "Notes on the Seal Found at Ophel, the Greek Inscriptions from Nazareth and Kefr esh Shems, the Siloam Text, and the Tombs of the Kings," *PEFQS* 29 (1897) 304-307. [(4) The Siloam Text, pp. 306-307]

E. J. Pilcher, "The Date of the Siloam Inscription," *SBAP* 19 (1897) 165-182.

A. B. Davidson, "The Siloam Inscription," *ET* 9 (1897-98) 384.

E. J. Pilcher, "On the Date of the Siloam Inscription. I.," *PEFQS* 30 (1898) 56-58. (Note by C. Clermont-Ganneau, p. 158)

*Ebenezer Davis, "On the Date of the Siloam Inscription. II.," *PEFQS* 30 (1898) 58-60.

*E. J. Pilcher, "Herodian Pottery and the Siloam Inscription," *SBAP* 20 (1898) 213-222.

*Frank R. Blake, "The Word זדה in the Siloam Inscription," *JAOS* 22 (1901) 55-60.

Anonymous, "The Siloam Inscription and Translation," *RP* 1 (1902) 31-32.

Paul Carus, "The Siloam Inscription," *OC* 17 (1903) 662-665.

W. A. Wordsworth, "The Siloam Inscription," *PEQ* 71 (1939) 41-43.

*H. Torczyner, "The Siloam Inscription, The Gezer Calendar and the Ophel Ostracon," *BIES* 7 (1939-40) #1, I.

§861 ***4.4.6.4 Hebrew Manuscripts - General Studies [See also: Biblical Manuscripts §234-§261 ←; for Studies on Qumran Texts see: Qumran Texts, relation to other Hebrew Manuscripts →]***

S. Schechter, "Hebrew Manuscripts in the University of Cambridge," *JQR* 4 (1891-92) 90-101; 245-255; 626-627. [1. (A) Responses of Isaiah of Trani; (B) Responses of the Geonim; 2. (A) The Commentary to the Prayers and Benedictions, by R. Judah Ben Jakar; and (B) The Commentary to the Haggadah for Passover Evening by the same author; 3. Commentary and Glosses to the Tractate Moed Katon of the Babylonian Talmud]

S. Schechter, "Notes on Hebrew MSS. in the University Library of Cambridge," *JQR* 5 (1892-93) 18-23, 244-245, 350-351. [4. The "Sepher Haminhagoth", pp. 18-23, 350-351; 5. Colophons of Moses ben Nathaniel and Joseph Chamiz, 244-245]

S. Schechter, "Notes on Hebrew MSS. in the University Library of Cambridge," *JQR* 6 (1893-94) 136-145. [Oo 1:3, 4, 5, 16, 19, 20, 23, 24, 30, 32, 33, 34, 35, 37, 38, 42, 45, 46, 47 48, 49, and Add. 271]

G. Margoliouth, "Persian Hebrew MSS. in the British Museum," *JQR* 7 (1894-95) 119-120.

S. Schechter, "The Lewis-Gibson Hebrew Collection," *JQR* 9 (1896-97) 115-127, 360.

Hartwig Hirschfeld, "Descriptive Catalogue of Hebrew MSS. of the Montefiore Library," *JQR* 14 (1901-02) 159-196, 379-412, 622-652, 768-796; 15 (1902-03) 135-166.

H[artwig] Hirschfeld, "Index to the Descriptive Catalogue of Hebrew MSS. of the Montefiore Library," *JQR* 15 (1902-03) 531-558.

*G. Margoliouth, "An Ancient Illuminated Hebrew MS. at the British Museum (with Plate)," *JQR* 17 (1904-05) 193-197.

A. Cohen, "Hebrew Incanabula in Cambridge," *JQR* 19 (1906-07) 744-750.

*G. Margoliouth, "Hebrew Illuminated Manuscripts," *JQR* 20 (1907-08) 118-144.

A. Cohen, "Hebrew Incanabula in Cambridge," *JQR* 20 (1907-08) 464-465.

J. L. Teicher, "Fragments of Unknown Hebrew Incunables," *JJS* 1 (1948-49) 105-110.

P. A. H. de Boer, "Notes on an Oxyrhynchus Papyrus in Hebrew. Brit. Mus. Or. 9180A," *VT* 1 (1951) 49-57.

§862 *4.4.6.5 Genizah Studies, especially Cairo Genizah*

*Charles Taylor, "The Geniza of Old Cairo," *ET* 9 (1897-98) 344-346.

S. Schechter, "Geniza Specimens," *JQR* 10 (1897-98) 654-659.

I. Abrahams, "The 'Fear of Sin'," *JQR* 10 (1897-98) 660-661.

Anonymous, "Biblical Research and Discovery. 'The Genizah of Old Cairo'," *CFL, O.S.,* 2 (1898) 141-143.

S. Schechter, "Geniza Fragments," *JQR* 16 (1903-04) 425-452, 776-777.

I. Abrahams, "An Eight-Century Genizah Document," *JQR* 17 (1904-05) 426-430.

*Herbert Loewe, "Some Talmudic Fragments from the Cairo Genizah, in the British Museum," *JQR* 17 (1904-05) 456-474.

Richard Gottheil, "Some Hebrew Manuscripts in Cairo," *JQR* 17 (1904-05) 609-655.

W. Bacher, "Notes on No. LXVIII of the J. Q. R.," *JQR* 18 (1905-06) 146-148. *[Ref. JQR* 17 (1904-05) pp. 609ff.]

N. Porges, "Notes on Gottheil's 'Some Hebrew MSS. in Cairo'," *JQR* 18 (1905-06) 149-150.

Alexander Marx, "Notes to *J.Q.R.* IV.," *JQR* 18 (1905-06) 567-570. *[Ref. JQR* 17 (1904-05) pp. 609ff.; and *JQR* 18 (1905-06) pp. 146-150]

A. Cowley, "Bodleian Geniza Fragments," *JQR* 18 (1905-06) 399-405.

Alexander Marx, "Notes to *J.Q.R., XVIII, 399ff.," *JQR* 18 (1905-06) 768-771.

Israel Davidson, "Poetic Fragments from the Genizah," *JQR., N.S.,* 1 (1910-11) 105-111, 231-247. *[Parts I and II]*

H. Brody, "Some Notes to Davidson's Poetic Fragments from Genizah II," *JQR, N.S.,* 2 (1911-12) 155-157.

Israel Davidson, "Poetic Fragments from the Genizah III," *JQR, N.S.,* 2 (1911-12) 221-239.

Israel Davidson, "Poetic Fragments from the Genizah IV-VIII," *JQR, N.S.,* 4 (1913-14) 53-95.

Israel Davidson, "Poetic Fragments from the Genizah IX," *JQR, N.S.,* 8 (1917-18) 425-454.

H. Brody, "Remarks on the Poetic Fragments, (JQR, N.S. IV, 53ff.)," *JQR, N.S.,* 5 (1914-15) 91-96.

*B. Halper, "Descriptive Catalogue of Genizah Fragments in Philadelphia," *JQR, N.S.,* 12 (1921-22) 397-433.

*B. Halper, "Descriptive Catalogue of Genizah Fragments in Philadelphia II Talmud, Midrash, and Halaka (Texts, Translations, Commentaries, and Dictionaries)," *JQR, N.S.,* 13 (1922-23) 9-52.

Abinoam Yellin, "Genizah Fragments in the Jewish National Library," *JPOS* 3 (1923) 200-202.

B. Halper, "Descriptive Catalogue of Genizah Fragments in Philadelphia III, Liturgy," *JQR, N.S.,* 14 (1923-24) 189-268.

B. Halper, "Descriptive Catalogue of Genizah Fragments in Philadelphia IV, Secular Poetry," *JQR, N.S.,* 14 (1923-24) 505-513.

B. Halper, "Descriptive Catalogue of Genizah Fragments in Philadelphia V, Documents and Letters," *JQR, N.S.,* 14 (1923-24) 514-546.

B. Halper, "Descriptive Catalogue of Genizah Fragments in Philadelphia VI, Philosophy and Kabbalah," *JQR, N.S.,* 14 (1923-24) 547-552.

B. Halper, "Descriptive Catalogue of Genizah Fragments in Philadelphia VII, Miscellaneous (Medicine, Folk-lore, etc.)," *JQR, N.S.,* 14 (1923-24) 553-565.

Abinoam Yellin, "Cairo Genizah Fragments in the Jewish National Library," *JPOS* 4 (1924) 122-130.

Jacob Mann, "Genizah Studies," *AJSL* 46 (1929-30) 263-283.

Richard J. H. Gottheil, "A Further Astronomic Fragment from the Genizah," *JQR, N.S.,* 21 (1930-31) 75-83.

Joseph Marcus, "Gleanings from the Genizah," *JQR, N.S.,* 21 (1930-31) 85-88.

Richard J. H. Gottheil, "Further Fragments on Medicine from Genizah," *JQR, N.S.,* 21 (1930-31) 419-438.

Solomon L. Skoss, "Corrections," *JQR, N.S.,* 22 (1931-32) 117. *[Ref. JQR, N.S.,* 21 (1930-31) p. 425, n. 73]

Richard Gottheil, "A Genizah Fragment of a Treatise on the Sciences in General," *JQR, N.S.,* 23 (1932-33) 163-180.

Richard Gottheil, "Fragments of a Short Medical Vocabulary from the Cairo Genizah," *JQR, N.S.,* 26 (1935-36) 7-27.

*J. Braslavski, "Geniza Fragments with Mentions of Dallāta, Kadesh, 'Ammāta and Baneas," *BIES* 5 (1937-38) #4, III.

J. Braslawski*[sic]*, "Genizah Fragments Concerning Beth-Gubrin, Hebron and el-'Arish," *BIES* 10 (1942-44) #2/3, III.

*S. Atlas and M. Perlmann, "Saadia on the Scroll of the Hasmonaeans," *PAAJR* 14 (1944) 1-23.

*Alexander Marx, "The Importance of the Geniza for Jewish History," *PAAJR* 16 (1946-47) 183-204.

*M. Wallenstein, "A Piyyuṭ from the Cairo Genizah (Bodley MS. 2716/6, fol. 16b 6-17a 6)," *JMUEOS* #25 (1947-53) 20-24.

M. Zulay, "A Plea for a 'Corpus of Genizah Piyyutim'," *JJS* 1 (1948-49) 111-115.

T. W. Manson, "The Cairo Geniza," *DS* 2 (1949) 183-192. *(Review)*

Tovia Wechsler, "The 'Hidden Geniza' Once More or Mr. Trever versus Mr. Trever," *JQR, N.S.*, 41 (1950-51) 247-250.

*M. Wallenstein, "A Folio from Some Unpublished Piyyuṭim of the Cairo Genizah," *VT* 3 (1953) 167-174.

Shelomo Dov Goitein, "What Would Jewish and General History Benefit by a Systematic Publication of the Documentary Geniza Papers?" *PAAJR* 23 (1954) 29-39.

Alexander Scheiber, "Unknown Leaves from שאלות עתיקות," *HUCA* 27 (1956) 291-303. *[MS Kaufmann No. 152]*

Norman Golb, "Sixty Years of Genizah Research," *Jud* 6 (1957) 3-16.

Meir Wallenstein, "A Unique *Kol-Nidrê* Piyyuṭ from the Cairo Genizah in the Gaster Collection in the John Rylands Library," *BJRL* 41 (1958-59) 488-500.

S. D. Goitein, "The Geniza Collection of University Museum of the University of Pennsylvania," *JQR, N.S.*, 49 (1958-59) 35-52.

S. D. Goitein, "Geniza Papers of a Documentary Character in the Gaster Collection of the British Museum," *JQR, N.S.*, 51 (1960-61) 34-46.

Philip C. Hammond, "A Divorce Document from the Cairo Geniza," *JQR, N.S.*, 52 (1961-62) 131-153.

*Israel Yevin, "A Palestinian Fragment of Hafṭaroth and Other MSS with Mixed Pointing," *Text* 3 (1963) 121-127. [I. MS Heb. T.-S. B 17, 25; II. *Eb* 10; III. *MS P*]

*N. Fried, "The Hafṭaroth of T.-S. B. 17, 25," *Text* 3 (1963) 128-129.

E. Ashtor, "Prices of Books from the Geniza," *Tarbiz* 33 (1963-64) #2, VIII.

*Meir Wallenstein, "Genizah Fragments in the Chetham's Library," *BJRL* 50 (1967-68) 159-177.

*Abraham I. Katsh, "Unpublished Geniza Talmudic Fragments from the Antonin Collection," *JQR, N.S.,* 58 (1967-68) 297-308.

E. Y. Kutscher, "Geniza (G) Fragments of the *Mēkilta* of Rabbit Yišmaʿel," *Lěš* 32 (1967-68) #1/2, VI.

*Naphtali Wieder, "Genizah-Studies in the Babylonian Liturgy," *Tarbiẓ* 37 (1967-68) #2, II, #3, II.

§863 *4.4.6.6 The "Shapira Manuscripts" [See also: Forgeries §954→]*

Anonymous, "Note on the Drawings and Copies of Inscriptions from the 'Shapira Collection' Sent Home by Lieut. Conder and Mr. Drake," *PEFQS* 5 (1873) 79-80.

C. Clermont-Ganneau, El Haj Abd el Baki, Noel Temple Moore, C. F. Tyrwhitt Drake, M. W. Shapira, "The Shapira Collection," *PEFQS* 6 (1874) 114-124.

C. Clermont-Ganneau, "The Shapira Collection," *PEFQS* 6 (1874) 201-207.

[Aloys] Sprenger, "The Shapira Pottery," *PEFQS* 8 (1876) 99-103.

Freiherr von Munchhausen, M. W. Shapira, and Ad. Neubauer, "The Moabite Pottery," *PEFQS* 10 (1878) 41-45.

M. W. Shapira, C. Clermont-Ganneau, C. W. Wilson, Freiherr von Munchhausen, William Hayes Ward, Salim Kari, Ad. Neubauer, "The Moabite Pottery," *PEFQS* 10 (1878) 88-102.

A. Neubauer, A. H. Sayce, C. Clermont-Ganneau, Claude R. Conder, and Christian D. Ginsburg, "The Shapira Manuscripts," *PEFQS* 15 (1883) 195-209.

Charles A. Aiken, "The Shapira Manuscript of Deuteronomy," *PR* 4 (1883) 820-821.

†A. Lowy, "Remarks on the Shapira MS.," *SBAP* 6 (1883-84) 5.

*Anonymous, "Shapira's MSS," *ONTS* 3 (1883-84) 23-25. *[Text and translation]*

Cyrus Adler, "Remarks on the Shapira Hebrew Roll," *PAPA* 16 (1884) xli.

I. H. Hall, "On a Shapira Roll in Philadelphia," *JAOS* 11 (1885) cxc-cxci.

John A. Maynard, "New Light on the Shapira Deuteronomy," *ATR* 3 (1920-21) 236-238.

*A. S. Yahuda, "The Story of a Forgery and the Mēša Inscription," *JQR, N.S.,* 35 (1944-45) 139-163.

*H. M. Goshen-Gottstein, "The Shapira Forgery and the Qumran Scrolls," *JJS* 7 (1956) 187-194.

Oskar K. Rabinowicz, "The Shapira Forgery Mystery," *JQR, N.S.,* 47 (1956-57) 170-182. (Postscript by Solomon Zeitlin, pp. 182-183)

Oskar K. Rabinowicz, "The Shapira Scroll: A Nineteenth-Century Forgery," *JQR, N.S.,* 56 (1965-66) 1-21.

*H. G. Jefferson, "The Shapira Manuscript and the Dead Sea Scrolls," *RdQ* 6 (1967-69) 391-399.

A. D. Crown, "The fate of the Shapira Scroll," *RdQ* 7 (1969-71) 421-423.

§864 *4.4.7 Moabite Inscriptions*

Wm.Hayes Ward, "On the Moabite Inscription of King Mesha," *JAOS* 9 (1869-71) lxxvii-lxxviii.

William Hayes Ward, "The Inscription of Mesha, King of Moab," *BS* 27 (1870) 625-646, 777-778.

G[eorge] Rawlinson, "The Moabite Stone," *ContR* 15 (1870) 97-112.

Charles Warren, "The Moabite Stone. Captain Warren's First Account of the Inscription from Moab," *PEFQS* 2 (1870) 169-170.

George Grove, "The Moabite Stone. *Letter I.* Mr. Grove's Letter to the 'Times'," *PEFQS* 2 (1870) 170-171.

E. Deutsch, "The Moabite Stone," *PEFQS* 2 (1870) 171-172. *[Reply to George Grove (above)]*

E. Deutsch, "The Moabite Stone. *Letter II.* Mr. Deutsch's Letter to the 'Times'," *PEFQS* 2 (1870) 172-175.

Charles Clermont-Ganneau, "The Moabite Stone. *Letter III.* M. Ganneau's Letter to the 'Times'," *PEFQS* 2 (1870) 175-177.

E. Deutsch, "The Moabite Stone. *Letter IV.* To the Editor of the 'Times'," *PEFQS* 2 (1870) 178-179.

George Grove, "The Moabite Stone. *Letter V.* To the Editor of the 'Times'," *PEFQS* 2 (1870) 179.

Charles Warren, "The Moabite Stone. Captain Warren's Fuller Account of the Moabite Stone, Received March 28, 1870," *PEFQS* 2 (1870) 180-182.

Count de Vogue, "Extract from the 'Times,' Feb. 22, 1870, on the Count de Vogue's Pamphlet," *PEFQS* 2 (1870) 182-183.

F. A. Klein, "The Original Discovery of the Moabite Stone," *PEFQS* 2 (1870) 281-283.

Anonymous, "The Moabite Inscription," *NBR* 53 (1870-71) 1-29.

*A. B. Davidson, "Palestine Exploration and the Moabite Stone," *BFER* 20 (1871) 136-163. *(Review)*

Anonymous, "The Moabite Stone," *CR* 23 (1871) 161-190.

H. Petermann, "The Moabite Stone," *PEFQS* 3 (1871) 135-139.

B. G. Jenkins, "The New Moabite Stone. *An Examination of Mr. Henry Lumley's Letter to the 'Times' on the Discovery of a New Moabite Stone,*" *SBAT* 1 (1872) 328-334.

*Dunbar I. Heath, "The Moabite Jars, with a Translation," *JRAI* 2 (1872-73) 331-341. (Discussion, p. 341)

F. Petrie, "On the Moabite Stone," *JTVI* 6 (1872-73) 125-127.

Anonymous, "Note on the New Moabite Stone," *SBAT* 2 (1873) 146.

Anonymous, "The Moabite Stone," *PEFQS* 6 (1874) 2.

Anonymous, "The Shape of the Moabite Stone,"*PEFQS* 8 (1876) 181-182.

Anonymous, "The Moabite Monument, Erected by King Mesha about 890, B.C.," *AAOJ* 3 (1880-81) 228-234.

Ch. Clermont-Ganneau, "The Moabite Stone," *ContR* 52 (1887) 169-183.

Albert Löwy, "The Apocryphal Character of the Moabite Stone," *SRL* 9 (1887) 215-245.

George St. Clair, "The Form of the Moabite Stone, and the Extent of the Missing Parts," *PEFQS* 21 (1889) 150-152.

C[laude] R. Conder, "The Moabite Stone," *PEFQS* 22 (1890) 307-308.

C[laude] R. Conder, "A Passage on the Moabite Stone," *PEFQS* 22 (1890) 309.

*John D. Davis, "The Moabite Stone and the Hebrew Records," *AJSL* 7 (1890-91) 178-182.

*John D. Davis, "The Moabite Stone and the Hebrew Records," *JAOS* 15 (1893) lxvi-lxvii.

R. F. Harper, "Exploration and Discovery. The Moabite Stone," *BW* 7 (1896) 60-64.

*William T. Sabine, "The Witness of the Moabite Stone," *HR* 39 (1900) 419-424.

*T. C. Foote, "The Two Unidentified Geographical Names in the Moabite Stone," *JAOS* 22 (1901) 61-63.

G. A. Cooke, "Qorḥah and Qir-heres in the Moabite Stone," *ET* 13 (1901-02) 186-187.

Henry Mason Baum, "The Moabite Stone," *RP* 1 (1902) 59-62. (Note by S. R. Driver, pp. 62-64)

*A. Fotheringham, "The Black Obelisk and the Moabite Stone," *SBAP* 32 (1910) 152-154.

*A. Cowley, "A Passage in the Mesha Inscription, and the Early Form of the Israelitish Divine Name," *JRAS* (1920) 175-184.

N. S. Doniach, "The Moabite Stone, Lines 28-31," *PEFQS* 64 (1932) 102-103.

*A. S. Yahuda, "The Story of a Forgery and the Mēša Inscription," *JQR, N.S.,* 35 (1944-45) 139-163.

W[illiam] F[oxwell] Albright, "Is the Mesha Inscription a Forgery?" *JQR, N.S.,* 35 (1944-45) 247-250.

W[illiam] F[oxwell] Albright, "A Note on the Name of the Forger of the Moabite Antiquities," *JQR, N.S.,*36 (1945-46) 177.

Roland E. Murphy, "A Fragment of an Early Moabite Inscription from Dibon," *BASOR* #125 (1952) 20-23.

Joan Gorell, "An Ancient Moabite Monument," *AT* 4 (1959-60) #1 3-4.

William L. Reed and Fred V. Winnett, "A Fragment of an Early Moabite Inscription from Kerak," *BASOR* #172 (1963) 1-9.

David Noel Freedman, "A Second Mesha Inscription," *BASOR* #175 (1964) 50-51.

Anonymous, "Centenary of the Finding of the Moabite Stone," *BH* 4 (1968) 99-101.

P. D. Miller Jr., "A Note on the Meša' Inscriptions," *Or, N.S.,* 38 (1969) 461-464.

§865 *4.4.8 Phoenician Inscriptions and Texts, including Carthaginian*

Grenville Temple, "On the Phœnician Inscriptions, in a Letter addressed to the Secretary of the Royal Asiatic Society," *JRAS* (1837) 135-136.

Grenville Temple, "Remarks on a Phoenician Inscription presented to the Royal Asiatic Society," *JRAS* (1837) 137.

James Yates, "Remarks on 'Paläographische Studien über phönizische und punische Schrift, herausgegeben von Wilhelm Gesenius'," *JRAS* (1837) 138-153.

William W. Turner, "On the Phenician*[sic]* Inscription of Sidon," *PAOS, October* (1859) 4.

*John Hogg, "Sidonian Sarcophagus and Inscriptions," *JSL, 3rd Ser.,* 2 (1855-56) 425-434.

William W. Turner, "Remarks on the Phœnician Inscription of Sidon," *JAOS* 7 (1862) 48-59.

*H. Rawlinson, "Bilingual Readings—Cuneiform and Phoenician. Notes on some Tablets in the British Museum, containing Bilingual Legends (Assyrian and Phoenician)," *JRAS* (1864-65) 187-246.

M. Neubauer, "On the Phœnician passage in the *Pœnulus of Plautus,* Act V Sc. 1," *JP* 2 (1869) 324-330.

Emanuel Deutsch, "Letter of Mr. Emanuel Deutsch on the Characters Found by Lieut. Warren at the S.E. Angle of the Haram Area," *PEFQS* 1 (1869) 33-37.

Anonymous, "Phoenician Inscription on Jar Handles," *PEFQS* 2 (1870) 372.

J. M. Rodwell, "The Phoenician Passage in the Poenulus of Plautus," *SBAT* 2 (1873) 235-242.

William Wright, "On the Phoenician Inscription generally known as the 'Melitensis Quinta'," *SBAT* 3 (1874) 389-399.

William Wright, "Note on the Phoenician Inscription Melitensis Quinta," *ZDMG* 28 (1874) 143-145.

J. P. Harrison, "Note on the Phœnician Characters from Sumatra," *JRAI* 4 (1874-75) 387-399.

(   ) de Vogue, "Inscription at el Gebal," *PEFQS* 7 (1875) 104. *[Phoenician]*

A. Van Name, "On some alleged Phenician[sic]* and Nabathean Inscriptions recently received from Palestine," *JAOS* 10 (1880) xlix.

W[illiam] H. Ward, "On the Phœnician Inscriptions in the Cyprus Collection of Di Cesnola," *JAOS* 10 (1880) lxxxv.

*W[illiam] H. Ward, "On the Pseudo-Phœnician Inscription of Brazil," *JAOS* 10 (1880) lxxxv-lxxxvi.

Isaac H. Hall, "On some Phœnician Inscriptions in the new Cesnola Collection," *JAOS* 10 (1880) clxviii.

†W[illia]m Wright, "On the Phoenician Inscription discovered by Mr. Cobham, at Larnaca," *SBAP* 3 (1880-81) 49-50.

*†W[illiam] Wright, "On three Gems bearing Phoenician Inscriptions," *SBAP* 4 (1881-82) 54.

†A. Lowy, "Phoenician Inscription discovered in Cyprus by Mr. Cobham," *SBAP* 3 (1880-81) 60-61.

†W[illiam] Wright, "The Phoenician Inscription discovered by Mr. Cobham," *SBAP* 3 (1880-81) 71.

†D. Pierdes, "Fragment of a Phoenician Inscription recently found in Larnaca," *SBAP* 3 (1880-81) 72. (Remarks by Wm. Wright, pp. 72-73)

W[illia]m Wright, "A Phoenician Inscription at Melrose," *SBAP* 3 (1880-81) 85-86.

†W[illiam] Wright, "Phoenician Inscriptions from Cyprus," *SBAP* 3 (1880-81) 102-104.

*W. St. Chad Boscawen, "A Phœnician Funeral Tablet," *PEFQS* 14 (1882) 38-47.

*†Henry C. Reichart, "Cylinder with Phoenician Inscription," *SBAP* 6 (1883-84) 16-17. (Remarks by W. H. Rylands, p. 17)

W[illia]m Wright, "*Ex-voto* from the Temple of Baal at Carthage," *SBAP* 7 (1884-85) 31.

Isaac H. Hall, "On the Phœnician Inscriptions of the di Cesnola Collection in New York," *JAOS* 11 (1885) clxvi.

Isaac H. Hall, "Some Phoenician Inscriptions in New York," *AJSL* 2 (1885-86) 7-8.

Isaac H. Hall, "More Phoenician Inscriptions in New York," *AJSL* 2 (1885-86) 240-243.

William Wright, "Note on Seven Punic Inscriptions in the British Museum," *SBAP* 8 (1885-86) 211-213.

*A. H. Sayce, "New Phœnician & Israelitish Inscriptions," *BOR* 1 (1886-87) 193-194. (Note by W. M. F. Petrie, p. 194)

*William Wright, "Two Bilingual Inscriptions, Phoenician and Cypriote," *SBAP* 9 (1886-87) 47-49. (Remarks by P. le Page Renouf, pp. 49-51)

Richard Gottheil, "The Inscription of Tabnit," *AJSL* 5 (1888-89) 197.

Edward Montet, "On the Conception of a Future Life among the Semitic Races: whence and when the Notion was received," *IAQR, 1st Ser.,* 10 (1890) 319-339. [Documents of Phenician*[sic]* Origin, pp. 333-339] *[Index shows author's first name as Édouard]*

*A. H. Sayce, "The Inscriptions of Saris and Mount Olivet," *PEFQS* 22 (1890) 44.

*W. Bacher, "The Supposed Inscription upon 'Joshua the Robber'," *JQR* 3 (1890-91) 354-357.

*C. Clermont-Ganneau, "The Hebrew Phoenician Inscription of Tell el Hesy," *PEFQS* 24 (1892) 126-128.

C[laude] R. Conder, "The Prayer of Ben Abdas on the Dedication of the Temple of Joppa," *PEFQS* 24 (1892) 170-174.

A. H. Sayce, "The Phoenician Inscriptions on the Vase Handles Found at Jerusalem," *PEFQS* 25 (1893) 240-242.

Joseph Offord, "Phoenician Inscription at Greenock," *SBAP* 22 (1900) 114-115.

Joseph Offord, "Note on the Geography of Phoenician Inscriptions," *SBAP* 22 (1900) 120-121.

E. J. Pilcher, "Phoenician Inscription at Greenock," *SBAP* 22 (1900) 273-274.

Charles C. Torrey, "A Phoenician Royal Inscription," *JAOS* 23 (1902) 156-173.

James Oscar Boyd, "Two New Phoenician Inscriptions," *CFL, N.S.,* 6 (1902) 298.

A. H. Sayce, "Recent Biblical and Oriental Archaeology. A New Inscription from Sidon," *ET* 14 (1902-03) 123-124.

*Charles C. Torrey, "Semitic Epigraphical Notes," *JAOS* 24 (1903) 205-226. [V. Additional notes on the Bod-'Aštart Inscriptions, 211-218; A New Inscription from the Temple of Esmun, pp. 218-226]

Charles C. Torrey, "Two Letters from Professor Porter in regard to the Bod-'Aštart stones in Beirut," *JAOS* 25 (1904) 324-331.

E. J. Pilcher, "The Temple-Inscription of Bod-'Aštart, King of the Sidonians," *SBAP* 25 (1903) 123-129.

*H. Porter, "Another Phoenician Inscription from the Temple of Ešmun at Sidon," *PEFQS* 35 (1903) 333-335.

Ghosu el Howie, "Ancient Inscriptions at Sidon," *AAOJ* 27 (1905) 313-315.

*Charles C. Torrey, "Epigraphic Notes," *JAOS* 28 (1907) 349-354. [2. A Votive Statuette with a Phoenician Inscription, pp. 351-354]

Anonymous, "Phœnician Inscriptions," *MR* 89 (1907) 817-820.

C. J. Ball, "A Phoenician Inscription of B.C. 1500," *SBAP* 30 (1908) 243-244.

*Charles C. Torrey, "Notes on a Few Inscriptions," *JAOS* 29 (1909) 192-202. [A. On "Ereṣ Rešûf" in the Bod-'Aštart Inscription, pp. 192-193]

E. J. Pilcher, "The Punic Calendar," *PEFQS* 49 (1917) 146-148.

*E. J. Pilcher, "Neo-Babylonian Signet with Phoenician Inscription," *PEFQS* 53 (1921) 16-19.

Charles C. Torrey, "The Aḫīrām Inscription of Byblos," *JAOS* 45 (1925) 269-279.

Stanley A. Cook, "The Inscription of Aḥiram, King of Byblus," *PEFQS* 57 (1925) 210-215.

Charles C. Torrey, "An Inscription of Eliba 'al, King of Byblos," *JAOS* 46 (1926) 237-240.

*W[illiam] F[oxwell] Albright, "Notes on Early Hebrew and Aramaic Epigraphy," *JPOS* 6 (1926) 75-102. [1. The End of the Sarcophagus Text of Aḫîrâm, pp. 76-84]

Eric Burrows, "Phoenician Inscription from Ur," *JRAS* (1927) 791-794.

W[illiam] F[oxwell] Albright, "The End of the Inscription of Aḥîrâm Sarcophagus," *JPOS* 7 (1927) 122-127.

W. B. Stevenson, "An Ancient Phœnician Poem Discovered at Ras Shamra," *GUOST* 6 (1929-33) 44-45.

A. M. Honeyman, "Larnax Tēs Lapēthou: A Third Phoenician Inscription," *Muséon* 51 (1938) 285-298.

A. M. Honeyman, "The Phoenician Inscriptions of the Cyprus Museum," *Iraq* 6 (1939) 104-108.

Julian Obermann, "An Early Phoenician Political Document," *JBL* 58 (1939) 229-242.

*Julian Obermann, "A Revised Reading of the Tell el-Ḥesi Inscription. With a Note on the Gezer Sherd," *AJA* 44 (1940) 93-104.

G. Levi Della Vida, "A Phoenician Fragment from Rhodes," *JAOS* 60 (1940) 260-264.

G. Levi Della Vida, "A Neopunic Inscription in England," *JAOS* 60 (1940) 578-579.

A. M. Honeyman, "Observations on a Phoenician Inscription of Ptolemaic Date," *JEA* 26 (1940) 57-67.

*Charles C. Torrey, "A Forged Phoenician Royal Inscription in the Louvre," *AJSL* 58 (1941) 135-138.

A. M. Honeyman, "Punic Literature," *GUOST* 11 (1942-44) 30-38.

*G. R. Driver, "Brief Notes (II). Notes on Old Inscriptions," *PEQ* 77 (1945) 5-12. [(2) Phoenician, pp. 9-10]

William F[oxwell] Albright, "The Phoenician Inscriptions of the Tenth Century B.C. from Byblus," *JAOS* 67 (1947) 153-160.

Otto Eissfeldt, "The Beginnings of Phoenician Epigraphy According to a Letter written by Wilhelm Gesenius in 1835," *PEQ* 79 (1947) 68-86.

R. D. Barnett, J. Leveen, and C. Moss, "A Phoenician Inscription from Eastern Cilicia," *Iraq* 10 (1948) 56-71.

Julius Obermann, "Discoveries at Karatepe. A Royal Inscription from Cilicia," *JAOSS* #9 (1948) 1-49.

Ralph Marcus and I. J. Gelb, "A Preliminary Study of the New Phoenician Inscription from Cilicia," *JNES* 7 (1948) 194-198.

A. M. Honeyman, "Phoenician Inscriptions from Karatepe," *Muséon* 61 (1948) 43-57.

Jacob Leveen and Cyril Moss, "Second Recension of the Phoenician Inscription from Karatepe," *JJS* 1 (1948-49) 189-193.

Cyrus H. Gordon, "Phoenician Inscriptions from Karatepe," *JQR, N.S.,* 39 (1948-49) 41-50.

*Julian Obermann, "New Discoveries at Karatepe. A Complete Text of The Phoenician Royal Inscription from Cilicia," *CAAST* 38 (1949) 1-50.

Roger T. O'Callaghan, "The Phoenician Inscription on the King's Statue at Karatepe," *CBQ* 11 (1949) 233-248.

*Cyrus H. Gordon, "Azitawadd's Phoenician Inscription," *JNES* 8 (1949) 108-115.

Ralph Marcus and I. J. Gelb, "The Phoenician Stele Inscription from Cilicia," *JNES* 8 (1949) 116-120.

R[oger] T. O'Callaghan, "The Great Phoenician Portal Inscription from Karatepe," *Or, N.S.,* 18 (1949) 173-205.

Helmer Ringgren, "A Note on the Karatepe Text," *Oriens* 2 (1949) 127-128.

A. M. Honeyman, "Epigraphic Discoveries at Karatepe," *PEQ* 81 (1949) 21-39.

A. Dupont-Sommer, "Note on a Phoenician Papyrus from Saqqara," *PEQ* 81 (1949) 52-57.

*G. Douglas Young, "The Significance of the Karatepe Inscriptions for Near Eastern Textual Criticism," *OTS* 8 (1950) 291-299.

*I. J. Gelb, "The Contribution of the New Cilician Bilinguals to the Decipherment of Hieroglyphic Hittite," *BO* 7 (1950) 129-141.

G. R. Driver, "Note on a Phoenician Inscription of Ptolemaic Date," *JEA* 36 (1950) 82.

Johs. Pedersen, "The Phoenician Inscription of Karatepe," *AO* 21 (1950-53) 33-56.

*Julian Obermann, "Does Amarna Bear on Karatepe?" *JCS* 5 (1951) 58-61.

*William L. Moran, "'Does Amarna Bear on Karatepe?'—An Answer," *JCS* 6 (1952) 76-80.

*Cyrus H. Gordon, "Marginal Notes on the Ancient Middle East," *JKF* 2 (1952-53) 50-61. [I. Hebrew Parallels to Linguistic Features in King Azitawad's Phoenician Inscriptions from Karatepe, p. 51]

F. Løkkegaard, "Some Comments on the Sanchuniaton Tradition," *ST* 8 (1954) 51-76.

*J. T. Milik, "An Unpublished Arrow-head with Phoenician Inscription of the 11th-10th Century B.C.," *BASOR* #143 (1956) 3-6.

*A. Goetze and S. Levy, "Fragment of the Gilgamesh Epic from Megiddo," *'Atiqot* 2 (1959) 121-128.

*G. Garbini, "The God 'Astar in an Inscription from Byblos," *Or, N.S.,* 29 (1960) 322.

*A. M. Honeyman, "Two Semitic Inscriptions from Malta," *PEQ* 93 (1961) 151-153.

M[itchell] Dahood, "Karatepe Notes," *B* 44 (1963) 70-73. *[Phoenician]*

J. Naveh, "Phoenician and Punic Inscriptions (1960-1964)," *Lĕš* 30 (1965-66) #3, n.p.n.

*Giovani Colonna, "The Sanctuary at Pyrgi In Etruria," *Arch* 19 (1966) 11-23. [Punic Text, pp. 22-23] *(Trans. by Lionel Casson)*

Joseph A. Fitzmyer, "The Phoenician Inscriptions from Pyrgi," *JAOS* 86 (1966) 285-297.

Y. Yadin, "A Note on the Nimrud Bronze Bowls," *EI* 8 (1967) 6*.

R. D. Barnett, "Layard's Nimrud Bronzes and Their Inscriptions," *EI* 8 (1967) 1*-7*.

*Stanley Gevirtz, "A Spindle Whorl with Phoenician Inscription," *JNES* 26 (1967) 13-16.

M. Heltzer, "Some Considerations about the Phoenician Inscription Hispania 14," *OA* 6 (1967) 265-268.

Frank M. Cross Jr., "Jar Inscriptions from Shiqmona," *IEJ* 18 (1968) 226-233.

*C[yrus] H. Gordon, "The Authenticity of the Phoenician Text from Parahyba," *Or, N.S.,* 37 (1968) 75-80.

*C[yrus] H. Gordon, "The Canaanite Text from Brazil," *Or, N. S.,* 37 (1968) 425-436.

*F[rank] M. Cross Jr., "The Phoenician Inscription from Brazil. A Nineteenth-Century Forgery," *Or, N.S.,* 37 (1968) 437-460. [Reply by C. H. Gordon, pp. 461-463]

*Sabatio Moscati, "Antas: A New Punic Site in Sardinia," *BASOR* #196 (1969) 23-36.

Stanislav Segert, "Phoenician Background of Hanno's Periplus," *MUSJ* 45 (1969) 501-519.

*G. M. Lee, "On a Phoenician Bilingual Inscription at Larnax, Lapethos," *PEQ* 101 (1969) 122.

§866 *4.4.9 Aramaic Texts - General Studies*

*Ad. Neubauer, "On some newly-discovered Temanite and Nabataean Inscriptions," *SBE* 1 (1885) 209-232.

J. E. Hanauer, "Notes on Dr. Pot's Palmyrene Inscriptions," *PEFQS* 23 (1891) 156-158.

I. Abrahams, "An Aramaic Text of the Scroll of Antiochus," *JQR* 11 (1898-99) 291-299.

*Joseph Offord, "Herodotus and Palmyrene Inscriptions," *AAOJ* 25 (1903) 178.

A. Cowley, "Some Egyptian Aramaic documents," *SBAP* 25 (1903) 202-208, 259-266, 311-314. (Note by A. H. Sayce, pp. 315-316)

*A. Cowley, "Hebrew and Aramaic Papyri (with facsimiles)," *JQR* 16 (1903-04) 1-8.

Enno Littmann, "The Stele of Teima in Arabia. A Welcome to the Gods," *Monist* 14 (1903-04) 510-515.

Joseph Offord, "Notes and Queries. 1. *A New Tell el-Amarna Tablet*," *PEFQS* 36 (1904) 180.

*Hermann Ranke, "Business House of Murashu Sons of Nippur," *RP* 3 (1904) 364-374.

Stanley A. Cook, "Notes on Semitic Inscriptions," *SBAP* 26 (1904) 32-35. [I. Egyptian Slab with Aramaic Lettering, pp. 34-35]

A. H. Sayce, "Aramaic Inscriptions from Egypt," *SBAP* 26 (1904) 207-208.

*C[laude] R. Conder, "Notes on Palestinian Archaeology. III. The Aramean Alphabet," *PEFQS* 38 (1906) 149-151.

*S[tanley] A. Cook, "The Jewish Temple of Yahu, God of the Heavens, at Syene," *Exp, 7th Ser.,* 4 (1907) 497-505.

Charles C. Torrey, "Notes on a Few Inscriptions," *JAOS* 29 (1909) 192-202. [C. On Some Palmyrene Inscriptions, pp. 194-197]

Hans H. Spoer, "Two Unpublished Palmyrene Inscriptions," *JAOS* 29 (1909) 203.

*A. H. Sayce, "The Passover Ostrakon from Elephantine," *SBAP* 34 (1912) 212.

James A. Montgomery, "Report on an Aramaic Boundary Inscription in Cilicia," *JAOS* 28 (1907) 164-167.

George F. Moore, "Aramaic Papyri recently found at Assuan," *PAPA* 39 (1907) xx-xxi.

A. H. Sayce and A. H. Cowley, "An Aramaic Papyrus of the Ptolemaic Age from Egypt," *SBAP* 29 (1907) 260-272.

N. Herz, "The New Aramaic Papyri," *ET* 19 (1907-08) 522.

Stanley A. Cook, "Supplementary Notes on the New Aramaic Papyri," *Exp, 7th Ser.,* 5 (1908) 87-96.

S. R. Driver, "The Aramaic Inscription from Syria," *Exp, 7th Ser.,* 5 (1908) 481-490.

Anonymous, "The Oldest Aramaic Inscription," *MR* 90 (1908) 972-974.

R. A. S. Macalister, "Notes and Queries. (4.) *A Tomb with Aramaic Inscriptions near Silwan,*" *PEFQS* 40 (1908) 341-342.

*Anonymous, "Inscription Referring to Ben-Hadad," *RP* 7 (1908) 211.

A. H. Sayce, "Notes on Assyrian and Egyptian History. An Aramaic Ostracon,"*SBAP* 30 (1908) 13-19. [VI. An Aramaic Ostracon, pp. 18-19]

*A. H. Sayce, "Karian, Aramaic, and Greek Graffiti from Heshan," *SBAP* 30 (1908) 28-29.

A. H. Sayce, "An Aramaic Ostracon from Elephantine," *SBAP* 30 (1908) 39-41.

Owen C. Whitehouse, "Some Problems Suggested by the Recent Discoveries of Aramaic Papyri at Syene (Assouan)," *ET* 20 (1908-09) 200-205.

N. Herz, "Aramaic Papyri Discovered at Assuan," *ET* 20 (1908-09) 232-233.

A. H. Sayce, "The Aramaic Papyri of Assuan; a Rectification," *ZA* 22 (1908-09) 210.

James A. Montgomery, "A New Aramaic Inscription of Biblical Interest," *BW* 33 (1909) 79-84.

Edgar J. Goodspeed, "The Teima Stone," *BW* 33 (1909) 424-425. *[Plate facing p. 363]*

*James A. Montgomery, "An Aramaic Ostrakon from Nippur and the Greek Obolos," *JAOS* 29 (1909) 204-209.

M. Lidzbarski, "Notes and Queries. (2.) *The Jewish Aramaic Inscription at the Tomb near Silwan,*" *PEFQS* 41 (1909) 73. (Note by Stanley A. Cook, p. 232)

A. H. Sayce, "An Aramaic Ostracon from Elephantine," *SBAP* 31 (1909) 154-155. [Cairo Mus. #35468a]

*H. C. Tolman, "Notes on the recently found Aramaic Papyrus Fragments of the Behistan Inscription," *PAPA* 43 (1911) l-liv.

A. H. Sayce, "An Aramaic Ostracon from Elephantine," *SBAP* 33 (1911) 183-184.

*Samuel Daiches, "The Aramaic Ostracon from Elephantinê and the Festival of Passover," *SBAP* 34 (1912) 17-23.

P. Boylan, "The New Aramaic Papyri from Elephantine," *ITQ* 7 (1912) 40-50.

James A. Montgomery, "A New Aramaic Inscription from Asia Minor," *AJA* 17 (1913) 86.

A. H. Sayce, "A New Aramaic Inscription," *SBAP* 35 (1913) 192.

William Cruickshank, "Aramaic Incantation Texts," *ET* 26 (1914-15) 522-523. *(Review)*

*Charles C. Torrey, "The Zakar and Kalamu Inscriptions," *JAOS* 35 (1915) 353-369.

Charles C. Torrey, "An Aramaic Inscription from Cilicia," *JAOS* 35 (1915) 370-373.

L. D. Barnett, "An Aramaic Inscription from Taxila," *JRAS* (1915) 340-342.

A. Cowley, "The First Aramaic Inscription from India," *JRAS* (1915) 342-347.

A. Cowley, "Another Aramaic Papyrus of the Ptolemaic Period," *SBAP* 37 (1915) 217-223.

*Joseph Offord, "Archaeological Notes. VII. *An Aramaic Inscription from Taxila,*" *PEFQS* 48 (1916) 40-41.

*Joseph Offord, "Archaeological Notes. XI. *Babylonian Contract Tablet, with Aramaic Text,*" *PEFQS* 48 (1916) 97.

Joseph Offord, "Further Illustrations of the Elephantine Aramaic Jewish Papyri," *PEFQS* 49 (1917) 125-129.

*Charles C. Torrey, "The Bilingual Inscription from Sardis," *AJSL* 34 (1917-18) 185-198.

*George W. Gilmore, "Aramaic Papyri and the Jewish Temple at Elephantine," *HR* 75 (1918) 56-57.

George William Brown, "Note on Angarôs, in Montgomery's 'Aramaic Incantation Texts from Nippur'," *JAOS* 41 (1921) 159-160.

*A. H. Sayce, "Unpublished Hebrew, Aramaic and Babylonian Inscriptions from Egypt, Jerusalem and Carchemish," *JEA* 10 (1924) 16-17.

A. E. Cowley, "A Jewish Tomb-stone," *PEFQS* 57 (1925) 207-209.

G. R. Driver, "An Aramaic Inscription in the Cuneiform Script," *AfO* 3 (1926) 47-53.

Charles C. Torrey, "A Specimen of Old Aramaic Verse," *JAOS* 46 (1926) 241-247.

*W[illiam] F[oxwell] Albright, "Notes on Early Hebrew and Aramaic Epigraphy," *JPOS* 6 (1926) 75-102. [1. The End of the Sarcophagus Text of Aḥîrâm; 2. An Unexplained Word in the Kalamûwa Stele; 3. The Beginning of the Zakir Stele; 4. The New Hebrew Ostracon from Jerusalem; 5. The Seals of the Temple Treasury after the Exile]

Samuel Daiches, "A Jewish Tomb-stone," *PEFQS* 58 (1926) 31-32.

Abinoam Yellin, "The Newly Discovered Jewish Ossuary in Inscriptions," *JPOS* 9 (1929) 41-44.

A. Cowley, "Two Aramaic Ostraka," *JRAS* (1929) 107-112.

Samuel Daiches, "Some Notes on Ostrakon A," *JRAS* (1929) 584-585.

E. L. Sukenik, "A Synagogue Inscription from Beit Jibrin," *JPOS* 10 (1930) 76-78.

*W. R. Taylor, "Recent Epigraphic Discoveries in Palestine," *JPOS* 10 (1930) 16-22. [The Palmyrene Funerary Bust. pp. 16-17; Rediscovery of a Samaritan Inscription, pp. 18-19]

E. L. Sukenik, "Note on the Aramaic Inscription at the Synagogue of Gerasa," *PEFQS* 62 (1930) 48-49.

*W[illiam] F[oxwell] Albright, "The Discovery of an Aramaic Inscription Relating to King Uzziah," *BASOR* #44 (1931) 8-10.

T. Fish, "A Cuneiform Tablet from Sippar(?)," *JMUEOS* #18 (1932) 48-53.

R. Campbell Thompson and R. W. Hamilton, "An Aramaic Inscription of a Piece Black-painted Ware from Nineveh," *JRAS* (1932) 29-31.

G. R. Driver, "Notes on the Aramaic Inscription from Soudschin," *AfO* 8 (1932-33) 203-206.

*S[tephen] Langdon, "Note on the Aramaic Treaty of Bar-ga'ya and Mati'el," *JRAS* (1933) 23-24.

A. Marmorstein, "The Inscription of Er-Rame," *PEFQS* 65 (1933) 100-101.

*E. L. Sukenik, "Inscribed Hebrew and Aramaic Potsherds from Samaria," *PEFQS* 65 (1933) 152-156. [II. Aramaic, pp. 155-156]

Cyrus H. Gordon, "Aramaic Magical Bowls in the Istanbul and Baghdad Museums," *ArOr* 6 (1934) 319-334.

Cyrus H. Gordon, "An Aramaic Exorcism," *ArOr* 6 (1934) 466-474.

Charles C. Torrey, "An Aramaic Inscription from the Jauf," *JAOS* 54 (1934) 29-33.

James A. Montgomery, "Notes on Early Aramaic Inscriptions," *JAOS* 54 (1934) 421-425.

J. J. Obermann, "An Aramaic Inscription from Dura," *JBL* 53 (1934) x.

*Cyrus H. Gordon, "Aramaic and Mandaic Magic Bowls," *ArOr* 9 (1937) 84-106.

*G. R. Driver, "A Babylonian Tablet with an Aramaic Endorsement," *Iraq* 4 (1937) 16-18.

Charles C. Torrey, "The Beginning of the Dura Synagogue Inscription," *JQR, N.S.,* 28 (1937-38) 295-299.

Cyrus H. Gordon, "The Aramaic Incantation in Cuneiform," *AfO* 12 (1937-39) 105-117.

Charles C. Torrey, "Notes on the Aramaic Contract Published by Bauer and Meissner," *JAOS* 58 (1938) 394-398.

Cyrus [H.] Gordon, "An Aramaic Incantation in Cuneiform and its Biblical Affinities," *JBL* 57 (1938) xviii.

Joseph Reider, "Note on the Dura Synagogue Inscription," *JQR, N.S.,* 29 (1938-39) 343-344.

H. L. Ginsberg, "A Further Note on the Aramaic Contract Published by Bauer and Meissner," *JAOS* 59 (1939) 105.

E. L. Sukenik, "On the Beginning of the Dura Synagogue Inscription," *JQR, N.S.,*30 (1939-40) 87.

*Julian Oberman, "Two Magic Bowls: New Incantation Texts from Mesopotamia," *AJSL* 57 (1940) 1-31.

C[yrus] H. Gordon, "The Cuneiform Aramaic Incantation," *Or, N.S.,* 9 (1940) 29-38.

Raymond A. Bowman, "An Aramaic Journal Page," *AJSL* 58 (1941) 302-313.

Raymond A. Bowman, "The Old Aramaic Alphabet at Tell Halaf: The Date of the 'Altar' Inscription," *AJSL* 58 (1941) 359-367.

*Cyrus H. Gordon, "Aramaic Incantation Bowls," *Or, N.S.,* 10 (1941) 116-141, 272-284, 339-360.

*W[illiam] F[oxwell] Albright, "A Votive Stele Erected by Ben-Hadad I of Damascus to the God Melcarth," *BASOR* #87 (1942) 23-29.

Julian Obermann, "Inscribed Tiles from the Synagogue of Dura," *Bery* 7 (1942) 89-138.

J. Kutsher, "An Aramaic Leather Scroll of the Fifth Century B.C.," *KSJA* 1 (1942) IX.

*G. Levi Della Vida, "Some Notes on the Stele of Ben-Hadad," *BASOR* #90 (1943) 30-32.

*W[illiam] F[oxwell] Albright, "Reply to 'Some Notes on the Stele of Ben-Hadad, by G. Levi Della Vida'," *BASOR* #90 (1943) 32-34.

Raymond A. Bowman, "An Aramaic Religious Text in Demotic Script," *JNES* 3 (1944) 219-231.

J. N. Epstein, "Notes on the Sujin Pact," *KSJA* 2 (1945) VI. *[Aramaic Stele]*

E. L. Sukenik and J. Kutscher, "A Passover Ostracon from Elephantine," *KSJA* 2 (1945) VII. [אמה]

*G. R. Driver, "Brief Notes (II) Notes on Old Inscriptions," *PEQ* 77 (1945) 5-12. [(3) Aramaic, pp. 11-12]

Z. Ben-Hayyim, "Palmyrene Inscriptions," *BIES* 13 (1946-47) #3/4, VII.

H. L. Ginsberg, "An Aramaic Contemporary of the Lachish Letters," *BASOR* #111 (1948) 24-27.

A. Dupont-Sommer, "On the Aramaic 'waw' Text," *BASOR* #111 (1948) 27.

John Bright, "A New Letter in Aramaic, Written to a Pharaoh of Egypt," *BA* 12 (1949) 46-52.

*M. Black, "The Aramaic Liturgial Poetry of the Jews," *JTS* 50 (1949) 179-182.

C[yrus] H. Gordon, "An Incantation in Estrangelo Script," *Or, N.S,* 18 (1949) 336-341.

A. Malamat, "The New Aramaic Saqqârah Papyrus from the Time of Jeremiah," *BIES* 15 (1949-50) #1/2, II-III.

W. B. Henning, "The Aramaic Inscription of Asoka found in Lampāka," *BSOAS* 13 (1949-51) 80-88.

G. R. Driver, "New Aramaic Documents," *ZAW* 62 (1949-50) 220-224.

*Cyrus H. Gordon, "Two Magic Bowls from Teheran," *Or, N.S.,* 20 (1951) 306-315.

Manfred Cassirer, "A Fragmentary Palmyrene Inscription," *PEQ* 84 (1952) 52.

S. A. Birnbaum, "A Fragment in an Unknown Script," *PEQ* 84 (1952) 118-120.

Fuad Safar, "Inscriptions of Hatra," *Sumer* 9 (1953) 7-20.

*M. Schwabe, "Recently Discovered Jewish Inscriptions," *BIES* 18 (1953-54) #3/4, V.

Jacob J. Rabinowitz, "Some Notes on an Aramaic Contract from the Dead Sea Region," *BASOR* #136 (1954) 15-16.

S. Abramson and H. L. Ginsberg, "On the Aramaic Deed of Sale of the Third Year of the Second Jewish Revolt," *BASOR* #136 (1954) 17-19.

H. L. Ginsberg, "The Brooklyn Museum Aramaic Papyri," *JAOS* 74 (1954) 153-162.

E. Y. Kutscher, "New Aramaic Texts," *JAOS* 74 (1954) 233-248.

*J. J. Rabinowitz, "A Legal Formula in the Susa Tablets, in an Egyptian Document of the Twelfth Dynasty, in the Aramaic Papyri, and in the Book of Daniel [4, 14]," *B* 36 (1955) 223-226.

*Jacob J. Rabinowitz, "The Meaning of the Phrase אחרן מחר או יום in the Aramaic Papyri," *JNES* 14 (1955) 59-60.

Isaac Rabinowitz, "Aramaic Inscriptions of the Fifth Century B.C.E. from a North-Arab Shrine in Egypt," *JNES* 15 (1956) 1-9.

*J. J. Rabinowitz, "The Aramaic Papyri, the Demotic Papyri from Gebelen and Talmudic Sources," *B* 38 (1957) 269-274.

*Jacob J. Rabinowitz, "A Legal Formula in Egyptian, Egyptian-Aramaic, and Murabba'at Documents," *BASOR* #145 (1957) 33-34.

*Reuven Yaron, "Two Greek Words in the Brooklyn Museum Aramaic Papyri," *HUCA* 28 (1957) 49-51.

J. B. Segal, "An Aramaic Ostracon from Nimrud," *Iraq* 19 (1957) 139-145.

Reuven Yaron, "The Schema of the Aramaic Legal Documents," *JSS* 2 (1957) 33-61.

*J. J. Rabinowitz, "Grecisms and Greek Terms in the Aramaic Papyri," *B* 39 (1958) 77-82.

R[euven] Yaron, "Identities in the Brooklyn Aramaic Papyri," *B* 39 (1958) 344-354.

Jacob J. Rabinowitz, "Some Notes on an Aramaic Deed of Sale from the Judean Desert," *B* 39 (1958) 486-487.

W[illiam] F[oxwell] Albright, "An Ostracon from Calah and the North-Israelite Diaspora," *BASOR* #149 (1958) 33-36.

Reuven Yaron, "Note on a Judaean Deed of Sale of a Field," *BASOR* #150 (1958) 26-28.

Joseph A. Fitzmyer, "The Aramaic Suzerainty Treaty from Sefire in the Museum of Beirut," *CBQ* 20 (1958) 444-476.

*Reuven Yaron, "Notes on Aramaic Papyri," *RIDA, 3rd Ser.*, 5 (1958) 299-310. [P. Brooklyn 1; P. Brooklyn 12]

Joseph A. Fitzmyer, "The Aramaic Qorbān Inscription from Jebel Ḥallet eṭ-Ṭûri and Mark 7 11 / Matt 15 5," *JBL* 78 (1959) 60-65.

*H. L. Ginsberg, "Notes on Some Old Aramaic Texts," *JNES* 18 (1959) 43-149.

*J. J. Rabinowitz, "More on Grecisms in Aramaic Documents," *B* 41 (1960) 72-74.

R[euven] Yaron, "Aramaic Deeds of Conveyance," *B* 41 (1960) 248-274, 379-394.

Franz Rosenthal, "Notes on the Third Aramaic Inscription from Sefîre Sûjîn," *BASOR* #158 (1960) 28-31.

*Reuven Yaron, "Aramaic Marriage Contracts: Corrigenda and Addenda," *JSS* 5 (1960) 66-70.

*S. Yeivin, "The Ancient Synagogue of Ma'on (Nirim). F. The Inscription," *RFEASB* 3 (1960) 36-40.

Ruth Hestrin, "Synagogue Inscriptions: A New Aramaic Inscription from 'Alma," *RFEASB* 3 (1960) 65-67.

Ruth Amiran, "Another Inscription from 'Alma," *RFEASB* 3 (1960) 68.

*A. D. H. Bivar, "A Rosette *Phialē* Inscribed in Aramaic," *BSOAS* 24 (1961) 189-199.

Joseph A. Fitzmyer, "The Aramaic Inscriptions of Sefire I and II," *JAOS* 81 (1961) 178-222.

Reuven Yaron, "Notes on Aramaic Papyri II," *JNES* 20 (1961) 127-130. [I. Pap. Brooklyn 11:9-11: The Clause Concerning Seizure of Pledges; II. Aegyptia; III. The Erasures in Pap. Brooklyn 2:11-12]

*J. J. Rabinowitz, "The Susa Tablets, the Bible and the Aramaic Papyri," *VT* 11 (1961) 55-76.

*A[lan] R. Millard, "Alphabetic Inscriptions on Ivories from Nimrud," *Iraq* 24 (1962) 41-51. [ND. 10151; ND. 10359; ND. 8184; ND. 10304; ND. 10303]

Joseph A. Fitzmyer, "The Padua Aramaic Papyrus Letters," *JNES* 21 (1962) 15-24.

K. R. Veenhof, "An Aramaic Curse with a Sumero-Akkadian Prototype," *BO* 20 (1963) 142-144.

W. L. Moran, "A Note on the Treaty Terminology of the Sefire Stelas," *JNES* 22 (1963) 173-176.

Chr. Brekelmans, "Sefire IA 29-30," *VT* 13 (1963) 225-228.

Frank Moore Cross Jr., "An Ostracon from Nebī Yūnis," *IEJ* 14 (1964) 185-186.

Baruch A. Levine, "Notes on an Aramaic Dream Text from Egypt," *JAOS* 84 (1964) 18-22.

J. A. Fitzmyer, "The Aramaic Letter of King Adon to the Egyptian Pharaoh," *B* 46 (1965) 41-55.

Robert D. Biggs, "A Chaldaean Inscription from Nippur," *BASOR* #179 (1965) 36-38.

Joseph Naveh, "Addenda to the Aramaic Inscriptions," *Lᵉš* 30 (1965-66) #2, n.p.n.

Joseph Naveh, "The Scripts of Two Ostraca from Elath," *BASOR* #183 (1966) 27-30.

Frank Moore Cross Jr., "An Aramaic Inscription from Daskyleion," *BASOR* #184 (1966) 7-10.

George M. A. Hanfmann, "The New Stelae from Daskylion," *BASOR* #184 (1966) 10-13.

E. J. Bickerman, "The Parthian Ostracon No. 1760 from Nisa," *BO* 23 (1966) 15-17.

Jonas C. Greenfield, "Three Notes on the Sefire Inscription," *JSS* 11 (1966) 98-105.

N. Avigad, "Aramaic Inscriptions in the Tomb of Jason," *IEJ* 17 (1967) 101-111.

J. Naveh, "The Date of the Deir Allā Inscription in Aramaic Script," *IEJ* 17 (1967) 256-258.

H. J. Franken, "Texts from the Persian Period from Tell Dier 'Alla," *VT* 17 (1967) 480-481.

Siegfried H. Horn, "Where and When was the Aramaic Saqqara Papyrus Written?" *AUSS* 6 (1968) 29-45.

Richard S. Hasson, "Aramaic Funerary and Boundary Inscriptions from Asia Minor," *BASOR* #192 (1968) 3-11.

Stephen J. Lieberman, "The Aramaic Argillary Script in the Seventh Century," *BASOR* #192 (1968) 25-31.

Joseph Naveh, "Aramaica Dubiosa," *JNES* 27 (1968) 317-325.

*N. Avigad, "An Inscribed Bowl from Dan," *PEQ* 100 (1968) 42-44.

E. Hammershaimb, "Some Remarks on the Aramaic Letters from Hermopolis," *VT* 18 (1968) 265-267.

Bezalel Porten and Jonas C. Greenfield, "The Aramaic Papyri from Hermopolis," *ZAW* 80 (1968) 216-231.

Frank M. Cross Jr., "An Ostracon from Heshbon," *AUSS* 7 (1969) 223-229.

Frank Moore Cross Jr., "Two Notes on Palestinian Inscriptions of the Persian Age," *BASOR* #193 (1969) 19-24.

J. B. Segal, "Miscellaneous Fragments in Aramaic," *Iraq* 31 (1969) 170-174.

Michael H. Silverman, "Onomastic Notes to 'Aramaica Dubiosa'," *JNES* 28 (1969) 192-196.

J. A. Fitzmyer, "A Further Note on the Aramaic Inscription Sefire III 22," *JSS* 14 (1969) 197-200.

E. Y. Kutscher, J. Naveh, S. Shaked, "The Aramaic Inscriptions of Aśoka," *Lĕš* 34 (1969-70) #1/2, 6-7. *[English supplement]*

§867 *4.4.9.1 Elephantine Papyri*

C. H. W. Johns, "Notes on the Aramaic Papyrus from Elephantine," *SBAP* 27 (1905) 187-188.

Anonymous, "The Assuan Papyri," *CQR* 63 (1906-07) 380-402. *(Review)*

R. H. Mode, "The Assuan Aramaic Papyri," *BW* 29 (1907) 305-309.

C. H. W. Johns, "The Assuan Aramaic Papyri," *Exp, 7th Ser.,* 3 (1907) 544-551.

D. S. Margoliouth, "The New Papyri of Elephantine," *Exp, 7th Ser.,* 4 (1907) 481-494.

F. Ll. Griffith, "Note on the Elephantine Papyri," *Exp, 7th Ser.,* 4 (1907) 494-496.

Anonymous, "Jewish Papyri Found in Egypt," *RP* 6 (1907) 219-220.

N. Herz, "The Elephantine Papyri," *ET* 19 (1907-08) 233.

George F. Moore, "Aramaic Papyri recently Found at Assuan," *AJA* 12 (1908) 70-71.

Anonymous, "The Recent Discoveries in Egypt," *CFL, 3rd Ser.,* 8 (1908) 116.

Anonymous, "The Elephantine Papyri," *CQR* 66 (1908) 158-172.

Lydia G. Robinson, "Yedonya's Letter Concerning the Yahu Temple," *OC* 22 (1908) 324-327.

Anonymous, "Jewish Petition Found on Island of Elephantine," *RP* 7 (1908) 150.

Eduard Sachau, "Three Aramaic Papyri from Elephantine, Egypt," *SIR* (1907) 650-611.

P. Boylan, "The New Aramaic Papyri from Egypt," *IER, 4th Ser.,* 23 (1908) 113-128.

Joseph Offord, "Aramaic Jewish Papyrus from Egypt," *AAOJ* 31 (1909) 14-16.

*James A. Kelso, "The Significance of the Elephantine Papyri for Old Testament Criticism," *BWTS* 2 (1909-10) #1, 21-32.

Willis J. Beecher, "Egyptian Papyri and Biblical Problems," *AAOJ* 32 (1910) 144-153.

*Martin Srengling, "Chronological Notes from the Aramaic Papyri. The Jewish Calendar. Dates of the Achaemenias (Cyrus-Darius II)," *AJSL* 27 (1910-11) 233-266.

William W. Everts, "The Aramaic Papyri Found at Elephantine," *BS* 68 (1911) 94-104.

A. H. Sayce, "The Jewish Papyri of Elephantine," *ET* 23 (1911-12) 92-93. *(Review)*

F[ritz] Hommel, "A Postscript," *ET* 23 (1911-12) 136. *[Elephantine Papyri #19 (Papyrus 18) Col. 7, lines 5 and 6]*

Max L. Margolis, "The Elephantine Documents," *JQR, N.S.,* 2 (1911-12) 419-443.

*Henry Preserved Smith, "Light on Some Ancient History," *MTSQB* 6 (1911-12) #2, 11-23.

Robert W. Rogers, "The New Papyri from Upper Egypt. First Paper," *BRec* 9 (1912) 329-338.

Robert W. Rogers, "The New Papyri from Upper Egypt. Second Paper," *BRec* 9 (1912) 379-384.

D. S. Margoliouth, "The Elephantine Papyri," *Exp, 8th Ser.,* 3 (1912) 69-85.

*C. F. Burney, "The Priestly Code and the New Aramaic Papyri from Elephantine," *Exp, 8th Ser.,* 3 (1912) 97-108.

*Stanley A. Cook, "The Elephantine Papyri and the Old Testament," *Exp, 8th Ser.,* 3 (1912) 193-207.

*Agnes Smith Lewis, "Achikar and the Elephantine Papyri," *Exp, 8th Ser.,* 3 (1912) 207-212.

D. S. Margoliouth, "Note on the Elephantine Papyri," *Exp, 8th Ser.,* 3 (1912) 351-354.

*C. F. Burney, "New Aramaic Papyri and Old Testament History," *CQR* 74 (1912) 392-409.

William R. Arnold, "The Passover Papyrus from Elephantine," *JBL* 31 (1912) 1-33.

H. J. Elhorst, "The Passover Papyrus from Elephantine," *JBL* 31 (1912) 147-149.

Anonymous, "Aramæan Papyri from Elephantine," *MR* 94 (1912) 635-639.

Anonymous, "Date of Papyri from Elephantinê," *RP* 11 (1912) 106.

*Samuel Daiches, "The Aramaic Ostracon from Elephantine and the Festival of Passover," *SBAP* 34 (1912) 17-23.

James A. Montgomery, "Some Correspondences Between the Elephantine Papyri and the Gospels," *ET* 24 (1912-13) 428-429.

J. K. Fotheringham, "Dates in the Elephantine Papyri," *JTS* 14 (1912-13) 570-575.

*C. H. W. Johns, "Letters of Hammurabi and Cuneiform Parallels to the Old Testament," *JTS* 14 (1912-13) 608-614. *(Review)*

W. B. Stevenson, "Jewish Papyri of the Fifth Century B.C.," *GUOST* 4 (1913-22) 15-17.

Robert W. Rogers, "The New Papyri from Upper Egypt. First Paper," *BM* 2 (1914) 427-441.

Robert W. Rogers, "The New Papyri from Upper Egypt. Second Paper," *BM* 2 (1914) 560-568.

Robert Dick Wilson, "The Papyrus of Elephantine," *PTR* 12 (1914) 411-426.

*Stanley A. Cook, "The Significance of the Elephantine Papyri for the History of Hebrew Religion," *AJT* 19 (1915) 346-382.

Anonymous, "The Elephantine Papyri and the Old Testament," *HR* 69 (1915) 368.

*Joseph Offord, "The Elephantine Papyri as Illustrative of the Old Testament," *PEFQS* 47 (1915) 72-80, 144-151.

M. Sprengling, "The Aramaic Papyri of Elephantine in English," *AJT* 21 (1917) 411-452; 22 (1918) 349-375.

*Joseph Offord, "Archaeological Notes on Jewish Antiquities. LXII. *Peniel and a Hebrew Name at Elephantine*," *PEFQS* 52 (1920) 77-78.

*Alfred Guillaume, "Isaiah XLIV. 5 in the Light of the Elephantine Papyri," *ET* 32 (1920-21) 377-378.

*W. St. Clair Tisdall, "Egypt and the Book of Daniel; or, What say the Papyri?" *Exp, 8th Ser.,* 22 (1921) 340-357.

G. R. Driver, "Aramaic Papyri of the Fifth Century B.C.," *JTS* 25 (1923-24) 293-303. (Corr, p. 405) *(Review)*

G. R. Driver, "The Aramaic *Papyri* from Egypt: Notes on Obscure Passages," *JRAS* (1932) 77-90.

*O. Neugebauer, "The Chronology of the Aramaic Papyri from Elephantine (Remarks about a new Chronology proposed by A. Kenney-Herbert)," *Isis* 33 (1941) 575-578.

Max Vogelstein, "Bakshish for Bagoas?" *JQR, N.S.,* 33 (1942-43) 89-92.

*Zeev W. Falk, "The Deeds of Manumission of Elephantine," *JJS* 5 (1954) 114-117.

C[harles] C. Torrey, "More Elephantine Papyri," *JNES* 13 (1954) 149-153.

E. Hammershaimb, "Some observations on the Aramaic Elephantine papyri," *VT* 7 (1957) 17-34.

*Reuven Yaron, "Aramaic Marriage Contracts from Elephantine," *JSS* 3 (1958) 1-39.

*H. L. Ginsberg, "Notes on Some Old Aramaic Texts," *JNES* 18 (1959) 143-149. [III. The Elephantine Papyrus, The Alleged Preposition b⁽c⁾d]

*J. Hoftijzer and P. W. Pestman, "Hereditary Rights as laid down in the Marriage Contract Krael. 2," *BO* 19 (1962) 216-219.

*Anonymous, "Nehemiah and Sanballat. Papyri Discoveries in Egypt and Palestine help to clarify and confirm the Biblical record of the days following the Exile," *BH* 1 (1964) #4, 3-7, 13.

*Michael H. Silverman, "Aramean Name-Types in the Elephantine Documents," *JAOS* 89 (1969) 691-709.

§868 *4.4.9.2 Samarian (Samaritan) Texts*

(   ) Pritchett, "Note on the Newly Discovered Samaritan Stone," *PEFQS* 5 (1873) 118.

J. G. Pickard, "The Samaritan Stone from Gaza," *PEFQS* 5 (1873) 157-158.

*Claude R. Conder, "Samaritan Topography," *PEFQS* 8 (1876) 182-197. [II. The Samaritan Chronicle, pp. 190-197]

†William Wright, "Samaritan Tablet at Leeds from Nablus," *SBAP* 6 (1883-84) 25-26.

H. H. Spoer, "Notes on Some New Samaritan Inscriptions," *SBAP* 30 (1908) 284-291.

Anonymous, "A Samaritan Tablet," *RP* 9 (1910) 286-287.

S. R. Driver, "The Discoveries at Samaria," *PEFQS* 43 (1911) 79-83.

I. F. Wood, "A Samaritan Passover Manuscript," *JBL* 40 (1921) 159-161.

E. W. G. Masterman, "The Harvard Expeditions at Samaria," *PEFQS* 57 (1925) 25-30. [(4) The Ostraka, p. 30]

*W. R. Taylor, "Recent Epigraphic Discoveries in Palestine," *JPOS* 10 (1930) 16-22. [Rediscovery of a Samaritan Inscription, pp. 18-19]

W. R. Taylor, "Samaritan Inscription from Gaza," *JPOS* 16 (1936) 131-137.

I. Ben-Zevi, "The Beit el-Má Samaritan Inscription," *BASOR* #84 (1941) 2-3. (Postscript by W. F. Albright, p. 4)

*S. Birnbaum, "The Dates of the Gezer Tablet and of the Samaria Ostraca," *PEQ* 74 (1942) 104-108. [2. The Samaria Ostraca, pp. 107-108]

*David Diringer, "The Dating of Early Hebrew Inscriptions (The Gezer Tablet and the Samaria Ostraca)," *PEQ* 75 (1943) 50-54.

J. Kaplan, "A Samaritan Synagogue Inscription from Yabne," *BIES* 13 (1946-47) #3/4 IX. [Notes on the Foregoing Inscription by I. Ben-Zevie*[sic]*, pp. IX-X]

B. Maisler (Mazar), "The Historical Background of the Samaria Ostraca," *JPOS* 21 (1948) 117-133.

George Vernadsky, "Anent the Epic Poetry of the Alans," *AIPHOS* 12 (1952) 517-538.

*Emil G. Kraeling, "New Light on the Elephantine Colony," *BA* 15 (1952) 50-67. [First Published Elephantine Discoveries; Preparation of the Wilbour Papyri; Contents of the Papyri; Nos. 9-13 and Their Historical Significance]

Eamonn O'Doherty, "The Date of the Ostraca of Samaria," *CBQ* 15 (1953) 24-29.

*John MacDonald, "The Tetragrammaton in Samaritan Liturgical Compositions," *GUOST* 17 (1957-58) 37-47.

*J. Bowman and S. Talmon, "Samaritan Decalogue Inscriptions," *BJRL* 33 (1950-51) 211-236.

Y. Yadin, "Recipients or Owners: A Note on the Samaria Ostraca," *IEJ* 9 (1959) 184-187.

John Bowman, "An Interesting Leningrad Samaritan Manuscript," *Abr-N* 1 (1959-60) 73-78.

*I. Ben-Zvi, "A Lamp with a Samaritan Inscription: *'There is none like unto the God of Jeshurun'*," *IEJ* 11 (1961) 139-142.

Y. Yadin, "A Further Note on the Samaria Ostraca," *IEJ* 12 (1962) 64-66.

Y[ohanan] Aharoni, "The Samaria Ostraca—An Additional Note," *IEJ* 12 (1962) 67-69.

Frank M. Cross Jr., "The Discovery of the Samaria Papyri," *BA* 26 (1963) 110-121.

*Ivan Tracy Kaufman, "A Note on the Place Name *SPR* and the Letter *Samek* in the Samaria Ostraca," *BASOR* #172 (1963) 60-61.

*Anonymous, "Nehemiah and Sanballat. Papyri Discoveries in Egypt and Palestine help to clarify and confirm the Biblical record of the days following the Exile," *BH* 1 (1964) #4, 3-7, 13.

A. F. Rainey, "The Samaria Ostraca in the Light of Fresh Evidence," *PEQ* 99 (1967) 32-41.

St. Yonick, "The Samaritan Inscription from Siyagha. A Reconstruction and Restudy," *SBFLA* 17 (1967) 162-221.

Y. Yadin, "A Further Note on the *Lamed* in the Samaria Ostraca," *IEJ* 18 (1968) 50-51.

*C. H. R. Martin, "Alexander and the High Priest," *GUOST* 23 (1969-70) 102-114. *[Samaritan Chronicle No. II [MS H2]]*

§869 *4.4.9.3 Syriac Texts*

Richard J. H. Gottheil, "A Syriac Fragment," *AJSL* 4 (1887-88) 206-215.

R. J. H. Gottheil, "A Syriac Lexicographical Tract," *AJSL* 5 (1888-89) 215-229.

*C. Winckworth, "On Heathen Deities in the *Doctrine of Addai*," *JTS* 25 (1923-24) 402-403. [Appendix to Mr. Winckworth's note, by F. C. Burkitt, p. 403]

J. B. Segal, "New Syriac Inscriptions from Edessa," *BSOAS* 22 (1959) 23-40.

§870 *4.4.10 Ugaritic - Ras Shamra Texts*

W. B. Stevenson, "An Ancient Phoenician Poem Discovered at Ras Shamra," *GUOST* 6 (1929-33) 44-45.

Theodor Herzl Gaster, "Egyptological Points from the Ras Shamra Texts," *AEE* 17 (1932) 104-107. [I. The Anointing of Kings; II. The Khepresh-Crown; III. Horus in a Ras-Shamra Text?]

*W[illiam] F[oxwell] Albright, "New Light on Early Canaanite Language and Literature," *BASOR* #46 (1932) 15-20.

George A. Barton, "A North Syrian Poem on the Conquest of Death," *JAOS* 52 (1932) 221-231.

*W[illiam] F[oxwell] Albright, "The North-Canaanite Epic of 'Al'êyân Ba'al and Môt," *JPOS* 12 (1932) 185-208.

A. H. Sayce, "Etruscan Affinities in a Ras Shamra Tablet," *JRAS* (1932) 43-46.

Theodor Herzl Gaster, "'The Combat of Death and the Most High': A Epic from Ras Shamra. Transcribed from the Cuneiform Original with Translation and Notes," *JRAS* (1932) 857-896.

J. P. Naish, "The Ras esh-Shamra Tablets," *PEQ* 64 (1932) 154-163.

Theodor Herzl Gaster, "The Ritual Pattern of a Ras-Šamra Epic," *ArOr* 5 (1933) 118-123.

*W[illiam] F[oxwell] Albright, "New Light on Early Canaanite Language and Literature," *BASOR* #46 (1932) 15-20.

*W[illiam] F[oxwell] Albright, "More Light on the Canaanite Epic of Alyân Baal and Môt," *BASOR* #50 (1933) 13-20.

James A. Montgomery, "Notes on the Mythological Epic Texts from Ras Shamra," *JAOS* 53 (1933) 97-123. (Additional Notes, pp. 283-284)

*T[heodor] H[erzl] Gaster, "Ras Shamra and Egypt," *AEE* 18 (1934) 33-38.

James A. Montgomery, "Rash Shamra Notes. II," *JAOS* 54 (1934) 60-66.

Z. S. Harris, "The Structure of Ras Shamra C," *JBL* 53 (1934) ii-iii.

George A. Barton, "A Liturgy for the Spring Festival at Jerusalem in the Age of Abraham and Melchizedek," *JBL* 53 (1934) 61-78.

*W[illiam] F[oxwell] Albright, "The North-Canaanite Poems of 'Al'êyân Ba'al and the 'Gracious Gods'," *JPOS* 14 (1934) 101-140. [A New Tablet of the Epic of 'Al'êyân Ba'al and Môt, pp. 115-133]

H. L. Ginsberg and B. Maisler, "Semitised Hurrians in Syria and Palestine," *JPOS* 14 (1934) 243-267. [R.S. 1932.4475]

Theodor Herzl Gaster, "The Combat of 'Aleyân-Ba'al and Môt. A Epic from Ras-Shamra: The Second Tablet," *JRAS* (1934) 677-714; (1935) 1-44.

H. L. Ginsberg and B. Maisler, "The Ewirižar. A Reply" *JPOS* 15 (1935) 181-184.

*Theodor H[erzl] Gaster, "The Beth-Shemesh Tablet and the Origins of Ras-Shamra Culture," *PEFQS* 66 (1934) 94-96.

*Theodor Herzl Gaster, "The Ras Shamra Texts and the Old Testament," *PEFQS* 66 (1934) 141-146.

Theodor Herzl Gaster, "An ancient semitic Mystery-Play from a cuneiform tablet discovered at Ras esh-Shamra," *SMSDR* 10 (1934) 156-164.

*Walter G. Williams, "The Ras Shamra Inscriptions and Their Significance for the History of Hebrew Religion," *AJSL* 51 (1934-35) 233-246.

Theodor [Herzl] Gaster, "An Egyptological Text from Ras Shamra (R.S. 1929: No. 6)," *EgR* 3 (1935) 95-110.

George A. Barton, "A Second Liturgical Poem from Ras Shamra," *JAOS* 55 (1935) 31-58.

James A. Montgomery, "Rash Shamra Notes III," *JAOS* 55 (1935) 89-94.

James A. Montgomery, "Rash Shamra Notes IV: The Conflict of Baal and the Waters," *JAOS* 55 (1935) 268-277.

H. L. Ginsberg and B. Maisler, "The Ewiriẑar Letter. A Reply," *JPOS* 15 (1935) 181-184.

H. L. Ginsberg, "Notes on 'The Birth of the Gracious and Beautiful Gods'," *JRAS* (1935) 45-72.

James A. Montgomery, "Rash Shamra Notes V. *A Myth of Springs*," *JAOS* 56 (1936) 226-231.

James A. Montgomery, "Rash Shamra Notes VI: The Danel Text," *JAOS* 56 (1936) 440-445.

Julian Obermann, "An Antiphonal Psalm from Ras Shamra (with Plate)," *JBL* 55 (1936) 21-44.

Theodor H[erzl] Gaster, "The Combat of 'Aleyân-Ba'al and Mot. Two missing portions," *JRAS* (1936) 225-235.

H. L. Ginsberg, "The Rebellion and Death of Ba'lu," *Or, N.S.*, 5 (1936) 161-198.

Theodor Herzl Gaster, "The story of Aqhat," *SMSDR* 12 (1936) 126-149; 13 (1937) 25-56.

*Cyrus H. Gordon, "A Marriage of the Gods in Canaanite Mythology," *BASOR* #65 (1937) 29-33.

*Theodor Herzl Gaster, "The Battle of the Rain and the Sea: An Ancient Semitic Nature-Myth," *Iraq* 4 (1937) 21-32.

*Theodor H. Gaster, "A Genealogical List from Ras Shamra," *JPOS* 17 (1937) 105-107.

Theodor [Herzl] Gaster, "The Harrowing of Baal. A Poem from Ras Shamra," *AO* 16 (1937-38) 41-48.

*H. L. Ginsberg, "Women Singers and Wailers Among the Northern Canaanites," *BASOR* #72 (1938) 13-15.

H. L. Ginsberg, "Two North-Canaanite Letters from Ugarit," *BASOR* #72 (1938) 18-19.

Theodor H. Gaster, "On a Poem from Ras Shamra," *JBL* 57 (1938) 81-88.

Theodor Herzl Gaster, "The 'Graces' in Semitic Folklore. A Wedding Song from Ras Shamra," *JRAS* (1938) 37-56.

*R[oland] De-Vaux, "The Geographical Location of the Poem of *Krt*," *BIES* 6 (1938-39) #1, IV.

J. Philip Hyatt, "An Early Daniel, and other Parallels," *BA* 2 (1939) 8.

Theodor [Herzl] Gaster, "'Ba'al is Risen...': An Ancient Hebrew Passion Play from Ras Shamra-Ugarit," *Iraq* 6 (1939) 109-143.

*H. L. Ginsberg, "Two Religious Borrowings in Ugaritic Literature. I. A Hurrian Myth in Semitic Dress," *Or, N.S.,* 8 (1939) 317-327.

J. J. Obermann, "Ugaritic Votive Inscriptions," *JBL* 59 (1949) xiii-xiv.

H. L. Ginsberg, "Two Religious Borrowings in Ugaritic Literature. II. The Egyptian God Ptaḥ in Ugaritic Mythology?" *Or, N.S.,* 9 (1940) 39-44.

*W[illiam] F[oxwell] Albright, "Two Letters from Ugarit (Ras Shamrah)," *BASOR* #82 (1941) 43-49. [An Accadian Letter from the King of Carchemish; A Canaanite Letter from Ugarit and Habakkuk 3:7]

Julian Obermann, "Votive Inscriptions from Ras Shamra," *JAOS* 61 (1941) 31-45.

*George A. Barton, "Danel, A Pre-Israelite Hero of Galilee," *JBL* 60 (1941) 213-225.

*Theodor H. Gaster, "Ezekiel and the Mysteries," *JBL* 60 (1941) 289-310. [II. A Canaanite Liturgy from Ras Shamra-Ugarit, pp. 290-297]

Albrecht Goetze, "The Nikkal Poem from Ras Shamra," *JBL* 60 (1941) 353-374.

U. Cassuto, "Ba'al and Mot in the Texts of Ugarit," *BIES* 9 (1941-42) #2/3, I-II.

*J. Philip Hyatt, "The Ras Shamra Discoveries and the Interpretation of the Old Testament," *JAAR* 10 (1942) 67-75.

James A. Montgomery, "Rash Shamra Notes VII. The Ugaritic *Fantasia* of the Gracious and Beautiful Gods," *JAOS* 62 (1942) 49-51.

*John Stensvaag, "The Ugaritic Texts and the Bible," *JTALC* 7 (1942) 801-819.

U. Cassuto, "The Reception of Baal in the Ugaritic Tablet V AB," *BIES* 10 (1942-44) #2/3, I-II.

S. Yeivin, "A New Ugaritic Inscription from Palestine (Preliminary Note)," *KSJA* 1 (1942) VIII.

W[illiam] F[oxwell] Albright, "Two Little Understood Amarna Letters from the Middle Jordan Valley," *BASOR* #89 (1943) 7-17.

*H. L. Ginsberg, "The Ugaritic Texts and Textual Criticism," *JBL* 62 (1943) 109-115.

Cyrus H. Gordon, "The Poetic Literature of Ugarit," *Or, N.S.,* 12 (1943) 31-75.

W[illiam] F[oxwell] Albright, "A Vow to Asherah in the Keret Epic," *BASOR* #94 (1944) 30-31.

W[illiam] F[oxwell] Albright, "An Unrecognized Amarna Letter from Ugarit," *BASOR* #95 (1944) 30-33.

*Endre A. D. Singer, "Ugaritic Gleanings," *BIES* 11 (1944-45) #1/2, I-II. [1. I AB; vi:20f & I AB; i:4f; 2. Jer. 9:20 // II AB, v-vii; 3. II AB, vii: 156f]

*William Foxwell Albright, "The Old Testament and Canaanite Language and Literature," *CBQ* 7 (1945) 5-31. [V. Ugaritic and Biblical Poetry, pp. 19-22; VII. Canaanite and Biblical Literature, pp. 27-31]

*Theodor Herzl Gaster, "A King without a Castle—Baal's Appeal to Asherat," *BASOR* #101 (1946) 21-30.

M. D. U. Cassuto, "An Appeal for Peace in the Ugaritic Tablet V AB," *BIES* 12 (1946) III.

*Theodor Herzl Gaster, "A Canaanite Ritual Drama. The Spring Festival at Ugarit," *JAOS* 66 (1946) 49-76.

*Julian Obermann, "How Daniel was Blessed with a Son. An Incubation Scene in Ugaritic," *JAOSS* #6 (1946) 1-30.

U. Cassuto, "The Innermost Chambers of El in the Ugaritic Epics," *BIES* 13 (1946-47) #3/4, I-II. [V. AB, col. 5, lines 16^b-35^a]

*G. R. Driver, "On a Passage in the Baal Epic (IV AB iii 24) and Proverbs XXXI 21," *BASOR* #105 (1947) 11.

*Julian Obermann, "How Baal Destroyed a Rival. *A Mythological Incantation Scene*," *JAOS* 67 (1947) 195-208. [3AB A]

H. Neil Richardson, "A Ugaritic Letter of a King to His Mother," *JBL* 66 (1947) 321-324.

Theodor [Herzl] Gaster, "The Ugaritic Text I AB, vi 18," *JAOS* 68 (1948) 150.

*A. D. Singer, "Philological Notes," *JPOS* 21 (1948) 104-109. [I. On an Ugaritic Crux (II AB 5:70-71)]

W[illiam] F[oxwell] Albright, "The So-called Enigmatic Inscription from Byblus," *BASOR* #116 (1949) 12-14.

U. Cassuto, "The Seven Wives of King Keret," *BASOR* #119 (1950) 18-20.

*S. K. Mirsky, "Allusions to Sabbath in the Ugaritic Texts in the Light of Midrashic Literature," *JBL* 69 (1950) viii.

G. Douglas Young, "Ugaritic Prosody," *JNES* 9 (1950) 124-133.

*Theodor [Herzl] Gaster, "The Egyptian 'Story of Astarte' and the Ugaritic Poem of Baal," *BO* 9 (1952) 82-85.

*C[yrus] H. Gordon, "Sabbatical Cycle or Seasonal Pattern? Reflections on a New Book," *Or, N.S.,* 22 (1953) 79-81. *(Review)*

*John Gray, "The *Goren* at the City Gate: Justice and the Royal Office in Ugaritic Text 'Aqht," *PEQ* 85 (1953) 118-123.

Anonymous, "The Diplomatic Archives of Ugarit," *Antiq* 28 (1954) 35-37.

*Claude F. A. Schaeffer, "More Tablets from Syria and Cyprus," *Antiq* 28 (1954) 38-39.

*William Foxwell Albright, "Dwarf-Craftsmen in the Keret Epic and Elsewhere in North-West Semitic Mythology," *IEJ* 4 (1954) 1-4.

Joshua Finkel, "The Expedition of the Ugaritan King Keret in the Light of Jewish and Kindred Traditions," *PAAJR* 23 (1954) 1-28.

*Cyrus H. Gordon, "Ugarit as Link between Greek and Hebrew Literatures," *RDSO* 29 (1954) 161-169.

John Gray, "The Ras Shamra Texts: A Critical Assessment," *HJ* 53 (1954-55) 115-126.

Joshua Finkel, "A Mathematical Conundrum in the Ugaritic Keret Poem," *HUCA* 26 (1955) 109-149.

*E[phraim] A. Speiser, "Akkadian Documents from Ras Shamra," *JAOS* 75 (1955) 154-165.

*S. E. Loewenstamm, "Notes on the Alalakh Tablets. A Comparison of the Alalakh with the Ugaritic Documents," *IEJ* 6 (1956) 217-225.

W[illiam] F[oxwell] Albright, "Specimens of Late Ugaritic Prose," *BASOR* #150 (1958) 36-38.

*Helen Genevieve Jefferson, "Canaanite Literature and the Psalms," *Person* 39 (1958) 356-360.

*F. Charles Fensham, "Thunder-Stones in Ugaritic," *JNES* 18 (1959) 273-274. [V AB.C 19-28]

*Otto Eissfeldt, "The Alphabetical Cuneiform Texts from Ras Shamra published in 'Le Palais Royal d'Ugarit' Vol. II, 1957," *JSS* 5 (1960) 1-49.

R. Yaron, "A Document of Redemption from Ugarit," *VT* 10 (1960) 83-90.

*A. F. Rainey, "Administration in Ugarit and the Samaria Ostraca," *IEJ* 12 (1962) 62-63. [Tab. 17.227]

*U. Cassuto, "Baal and Mot in the Ugaritic Texts," *IEJ* 12 (1962) 77-86.

A. S. Kapelrud, "Baal and Mot in the Ugaritic Texts," *IEJ* 13 (1963) 127-129.

Baruch Levine, "Ugaritic Descriptive Rituals," *JCS* 17 (1963) 105-111.

D. R. Hillers, "An Alphabetic Cuneiform Tablet from Taanach (TT 433)," *BASOR* #173 (1964) 45-50.

W[illiam] F[oxwell] Albright, "The Beth-Shemesh Tablet in Alphabetic Cuneiform," *BASOR* #173 (1964) 51-53.

J. F. A. Sawyer and J. Strange, "Notes on the Keret-Text," *IEJ* 14 (1964) 96-98.

Ruggero Stefanini, "KubXXI 33 *(Bo 487): Mursili's Sins,*" *JAOS* 84 (1964) 22-30.

*A. R. Campbell, "Homer and Ugaritic Literature," *Abr-N* 5 (1964-65) 29-56.

S. E. Loewenstamm, "The Seven Day-Unit in Ugaritic Epic Literature," *IEJ* 15 (1965) 121-133.

*Johannes C. de Moor, "Frustula Ugaritica," *JNES* 24 (1965) 355-364. [3. *UM* Text 77:40-45, pp. 356-357]

*J. Gray, "The legacy of Canaan. The Ras Shamra texts and their relevance to the Old Testament," *VTS* 5 (1965) i-x, 1-348. *(2nd edition)*

*S. E. Loewenstamm, "Remarks on Stylistic Patterns in Biblical and Ugaritic Literature," *Lĕš* 32 (1967-68) #1/2, I-II.

Michael C. Astour, "Two Ugaritic Serpent Charms," *JNES* 27 (1968) 13-36.

Arthur L. Merrill, "The House of Keret. A Study of the Keret Legend," *SEÅ* 33 (1968) 5-17.

*Murray Lichtenstein, "The Banquet Motif in Keret and in Proverbs 9," *JANES* 1 (1968-69) #1, 19-31.

Jonas C. Greenfield, "Some Glosses on the Keret Epic," *EI* 9 (1969) 60-65. *[Non-Hebrew Section]*

Loren R. Fisher and F. Brent Knutson, "An Enthronement Ritual at Ugarit," *JNES* 28 (1969) 157-167. [Text 603 (RS 24.245)]

Charles Krahmalkov, "A Letter in Ugaritic Dialect," *JNES* 28 (1969) 262-264. [*PRU* II No. 20 (Gordon 1020)]

*P. Walcot, "The Comparative Study of Ugaritic and Greek Literatures," *UF* 1 (1969) 111-118.

Johannes C. de Moor, "Studies in the New Alphabetic Texts from Ras Shamra I," *UF* 1 (1969) 167-188.

T. L. Fenton, "Passages in Ugaritic Discourse—Restorations and Observations," *UF* 1 (1969) 199-200. [I. cta. 4IV 33-34; cta. 3III D 33-IV 48]

Murray Lichtenstein, "A Note on the Text of I Keret," *JANES* 2 (1969-70) 94-100.

§871 *4.4.11 East Semitic / Akkadian - General Studies*

*†Anonymous, "The Monuments of Nineveh and the Cuneiform Characters," *DR* 24 (1848) 329-349. *(Review)*

W. [St. Chad] Boscawen, "On an Early Chaldean Inscription," *SBAT* 4 (1875) 132-171.

W. St. C[had] Boscawen, "Early Semitic Inscriptions from Babylonia," *SBAP* 1 (1878-79) 44-46.

*W. St. Chad Boscawen, "On some early Babylonian or Akkadian Inscriptions," *SBAT* 6 (1878-79) 275-283.

*†Geo. Bertin, "Notes on Akkadian Poetry," *SBAP* 3 (1880-81) 121-122.

†Theo[philus] G. Pinches, "Babylonian Art, illustrated by Mr. H. Rassam's latest discoveries," *SBAP* 6 (1883-84) 11-15.

*W. St. Chad Boscawen, "The Cuneiform Inscriptions and the Era of Jewish Captivity," *JTVI* 18 (1884-85) 99-134. (Discussion, pp. 135-139)

D. G. Lyon, "On the second Part of the fifth Volume of the Cuneiform Inscriptions of Western Asia," *JAOS* 11 (1885) ccxviii.

Theo. G. Pinches, "Singašid's Gift to the Temple Ê-ana," *BOR* 1 (1886-87) 8-11.

*Thomas Laurie, "The Name of God and the Cuneiform Inscriptions," *BS* 45 (1888) 515-518.

C. Bezold, "Some unpublished Cuneiform Syllabaries," *SBAT* 11 (1888-89) 44-54.

[William Hayes] Ward, "On two stone objects with Archaic Cuneiform Hieroglyphic writing," *JAOS* 13 (1889) lvii-lviii.

S. A[rthur] Strong, "Four Cuneiform Texts," *JRAS* (1892) 337-368.

Robert Francis Harper, "The Discovery and Decipherment of the Cuneiform Inscriptions," *ONTS* 14 (1892) 14-19, 93-97.

Theo. G. Pinches, "Rough Notes on some Texts of the Seleucidæ," *BOR* 6 (1892-93) 35-36. (Additional Notes, p. 42) [82-7-4, 137+88-4-19, 17]

Theo. G. Pinches, "Discoveries in Ašnunnak," *BOR* 6 (1892-93) 66-68.

T[errien] de L[acouperie], "Cuneiform inscriptions near the Pamir," *BOR* 6 (1892-93) 168.

A. H. Sayce, "The Cuneiform and other Inscriptions found at Lachish and elsewhere in the South of Palestine," *PEFQS* 25 (1893) 25-32. (Note by C. R. Conder, p. 178)

W. W. Moore, "How the Terra Cotta Books were Read," *USR* 5 (1893-94) 92-111.

W. W. Moore, "What the Terra Cotta Books Contained," *USR* 5 (1893-94) 166-178.

H. V. Hilprecht, "Note on Recently Found Nippur Tablets," *PEFQS* 30 (1898) 54-55.

*C. P. Tiele, "Akkadian and Sumerian," *JRAS* (1900) 343-344. [K. 14,013]

*H. Porter, "A Cuneiform Tablet, Sarcophagus, and Cippus with Inscription, in the Museum at Beirut," *PEFQS* 32 (1900) 123-124.

*Louis H. Gray, "Stylistic Parallels Between the Assyro-Babylonian and the Old Persian Inscriptions," *AJSL* 17 (1900-01) 151-159.

George A. Barton, "(2) The Haverford Library Collection of Cuneiform Tablets," *AJA* 6 (1902) 36-37.

L. W. King, "Studies of some Rock-Sculptures and Rock-Inscriptions of Western Asia," *SBAP* 35 (1913) 66-94.

*Stephen Langdon, "Miscellania Assyriaca III," *Baby* 7 (1913-23) 93-98. [Tablet I of *HAR-RA* = *ḫubullu;* K. 4369, Tablet(?) of HAR-RA = *ḫubullu*]

Walter Eugene Clark, "The Alleged Indo-Iranian Names in Cuneiform Inscriptions," *AJSL* 33 (1916-17) 261-282.

T[heophile] J. Meek, "Some explanatory lists and grammatical texts," *RAAO* 17 (1920) 117-206. [K. 945; K. 1913; K. 2015 + K. 4563 + K. 5435a; K. 2024 + K. 2951 + 2983; K. 2044; K. 2725 + K. 2726; K. 2740; K. 2907; K. 2918; K. 4147; K. 4160; K. 4161; K. 4165; K. 4167; K. 4171; K. 4189; K. 4199; K. 4229; K. 4242; K. 4246; K. 4428; K. 4578; K. 4593; K. 4596; 4599; 4605; 4853; K. 4527a + K. 7741; K.5433a; K.5443; K.5455a; K.5926; K.5974; K.7300; K.7604; K.7605; K.7606; K.7626 + K. 7627; K.5645; K.7654; K.7674; K.7696; K.7712; K.7743; K.7766; K.7780; K.8206; K.8209; K.8216; K.8305; K.8267; K.8220; K.8315; K.8317; K.8431; K.8781; K.8631; K.8799; K.8894; K.9092; K.9123; K.9133; K.9176; K.9180; K.9887; K.9922; K.9935; K.9936; K.98939; K.9947; K.9993; K.9998; K.10013; K.10047; K.10921; K.11154; K.11169; K.11193; K.11196; K.11206; K.11215; K.11221; K.11890 + K. 13584; K.13586; K.12848; K.13588; K.13619; K.13632; K.13637; K.13639; K.13643; K.13687; K.14330; K.14423; K.14428; K.14490; K.14491; K.14536; K.14726; K.14794; K.14793; K.14811; K.14812; K.14813; K.14817; K.14824; K.14836; K.14889; K.14908; K.14909; K.15153; K.15338; K.15368; Sm. 9; Sm. 10; Sm. 19; Sm. 20 + Rm. 164; Sm. 22; Sm. 305; Sm. 1038; Sm. 1544; Sm. 1670; Sm. 1701; Sm. 1711; DT. 103; Rm. 361; Rm. 930; Rm. II, 38; Rm. 417; Rm. II 465; Rm. II 478; Rm. II 556;81-2-4, 447; 81-2-4, 507; 82-3-23, 28; 82-3-23, 146; 82-3-23, 149; 82-3-23, 151;82-5-22, 572; 825-22, 575; 83-1-18, 462; 83-1-18, 899; Ki. 1902-5-10, 4; Ki. 1902-5-10, 9; Ki. 1904-10-9, 30; Ki. 1904-10-9, 61; Ki. 1904-10-9, 66; Ki. 1904-10-9, 83; Th. 1905-4-9, 1; Th. 1905-4-9, 4; Th. 1905-4-9, 7; Th. 1905-4-9, 18; Th. 1905-4-9, 26; Th. 1905-4-9, 31 + 32; Th. 1905-4-9, 36; Th. 1905-4-9, 51; Th. 1905-4-9, 74; Th. 1905-4-9, 96]

Thorkild Peter Jacobsen, "An Unrecognized Text of Ilu-mutabil," *AJSL* 44 (1927-28) 261-263.

*S[tephen] Langdon, "Philological Notes," *RAAO* 28 (1931) 13-22. [5] A Grammatical Text from Kish, pp. 18-20. (W. 1928-2)]

*Patrick Railton, "Some Remains of the Ancient Near East," *JMUEOS* #18 (1932) 55-59. [A. Mesopotamian I (Akkadian Inscription)]

*John Garstang, "Jericho: City and Necropolis. Fourth Report," *AAA* 21 (1934) 99-136. (Note on an Inscribed Tablet and Fig. 2 by Sidney Smith, pp. 116-117)

S[tephen] Langdon, "A Curious Drehem Tablet," *JRAS* (1935) 358-360.

C. J. Gadd, "Tablets from Chagar Bazar," *Iraq* 4 (1937) 178-185. [A. 379; A. 380; A. 381; A. 382; A. 385; A. 386; A. 387; A. 391; A. 393]

O. R. Gurney, "Temple Records from Umma," *JRAS* (1937) 470-473.

*S[tephen] Langdon, "Tablets from Kish and Umma," *RAAO* 34 (1937) 67-79. [I. Two Tablets from the series ḪURRA = *ḫubullu* (Kish, 1927-2118; Kish 1924-799); II. Four Tablets from Umma]

‡*G. Boyer, "Introduction bibliographique à l'historire du droit suméro-akkadien," *AHDO* 2 (1938) 63-110.

Sidney Smith, "A Preliminary Account of Tablets from Atchana," *AJ* 19 (1939) 38-48.

*P. E. van der Meer, "Tablets of the ḪAR-ra = *ḫubullu* Series in the Ashmolean Museum," *Iraq* 6 (1939) 144-179.

Samuel I. Feigin, "The Oldest Occurrence of Niqum," *JAOS* 59 (1939) 107-108. [Oriental Institute Museum (A 7162)]

*J. W. Jack, "Recent Biblical Archaeology," *ET* 51 (1939-40) 420-423. [The Arsenal and Official Archives, p. 421]

*J. W. Jack, "Recent Biblical Archaeology," *ET* 51 (1939-40) 544-548. [Tablets from Chagar Bazar (Syria), p. 547]

W[illiam] F[oxwell] Albright, "A Tablet of the Amarna Age from Gezer," *BASOR* #92 (1943) 28-31.

*Albrecht Goetze, "The Vocabulary of the Princeton Theological Seminary," *JAOS* 65 (1945) 223-237 [PTS 1]

*Samuel Noah Kramer, "The Tablet Collection of the University Museum," *JAOS* 67 (1947) 321-322. [Philadelphia University Cuneiform Texts]

Albrecht Goetze, "Two Old Akkadian Tablets in St. Louis," *JCS* 1 (1947) 345-348.

*Taha Baqir, "Report on the Collection of Unpublished Texts in the Iraq Museum," *Sumer* 3 (1947) 113-117. [Forward by S[amuel] N[oah] Kramer, p. 112]

A. Goetze, "Texts and Fragments," *JCS* 2 (1948) 305-308. [MLC 2639]

Selim J. Levy, "Supplement to Unpublished Texts in the Iraq Museum," *Sumer* 4 (1948) 55.

Selim [J.] Levy, "Small Texts," *Sumer* 4 (1948) 132-133. [IM 52912]

A. Goetze, Texts and Fragments," *JCS* 4 (1950) 73-76. [NBC 7832; YBC 7158]

C. J. Gadd, "EN-AN-E-DU," *Iraq* 13 (1951) 27-39. [BM 130729]

Edmond Sollberger, "The Cuneiform Collection in Geneva," *JCS* 5 (1951) 18-20.

*Julian Obermann, "Does Amarna Bear on Karatepe?" *JCS* 5 (1951) 58-61.

*O. R. Gurney, "The Sultantepe Tablets. *A Preliminary Note*," *AS* 2 (1952) 25-35.

A. Goetze, "Texts and Fragments," *JCS* 7 (1953) 28-29. [MLC 2638]

Jussi Aro, "Abnormal Plene Writings in Akkadian Texts," *SO* 19 (1953) #11, 1-19.

A[lbrecht] Goetze, "Texts and Fragments," *JCS* 8 (1954) 144-148. [Cath. Univ. 1+2+64; Brym Mawr College T 46, T 47; Williams College 3; Patterson Museum 13; Crozer Theol. Sem. 195; Brooklyn Museum 08.482]

*E[phraim] A. Speiser, "Akkadian Documents from Ras Shamra," *JAOS* 75 (1955) 154-165.

Albrecht Goetze, "A Drehem Tablet Dealing with Leather Objects," *JCS* 9 (1955) 19-21.

T. Fish, "Kuš Texts of the Isin Period," *MCS* 5 (1955) 115-124.

*Edmond Sollberger, "Selected Texts from American Collections," *JCS* 10 (1956) 11-31. [7-8. A Sumerian Tablet with an Akkadian Counterpart, pp. 20-21. (NBC 382, NBC 184)]

Erica Reiner, *"Lipšur* Litanies," *JNES* 15 (1956) 129-149.

‡*G. Boyer and E. Szlechter, "Introduction bibliographique à l'Historire du Droit Suméro-Akkadien II (1939-1955)," *RIDA, 3rd Ser.,* 3 (1956) 41-79.

Cyrus H. Gordon, "Observations on the Akkadian Tablets from Ugarit," *RAAO* 50 (1956) 127-133.

A[lbrecht] Goetze, "Texts and Fragments," *JCS* 11 (1957) 77-78. [HSM 109; *Unnumbered Text*]

*G. R. Driver, "Aramaic Names in Accadian Texts," *RDSO* 32 (1957) 41-57.

I. J. Gelb, "Old Akkadian Stone Tablet from Sippar," *RDSO* 32 (1957) 83-94.

*Benno Landsberger, "The Seventh Tablet of the Series e a-*nâqu*," *JCS* 13 (1959) 128-131.

*Albrecht Goetze, "The 38th Tablet of the Series á-A-*nāqu*," *JCS* 13 (1959) 120-127. *[Bilingual Tablet]*

E. Leichty, "Two New Fragments of *Ludlu Bēl Nēmeqi*," *Or, N.S.,* 28 (1959) 361-363.

Edmond Sollberger, "Notes on the Early Inscriptions from Ur and El-'Obēd," *Iraq* 22 (1960) 69-89.

*W. W. Hallo, "New Viewpoints on Cuneiform Literature," *IEJ* 12 (1962) 13-26.

T. Donald, "Old Akkadian Tablets in the Liverpool Museum," *MCS* 9 (1964) n.p.n. *[Text only]*

J. V. Kinnier Wilson, "Lugal ud melambi nirgal: new Texts and Fragments," *ZA* 54 (1961) 71-89. [1. 83-1-18, 488 and 83-1-18, 693; 2. Th. 1905-4-9, 10 + 12 + 13 + 2391; 3. ND 4388; 4. D.T. 106, 83-1-18, 516, K. 15178]

Samuel Noah Kramer, "CT XLII: A Review Article," *JCS* 18 (1964) 35-48. *(Review)*

Albrecht Goetze, "The Archive of Attā from Nippur," *JCS* 18 (1964) 102-113. [2N-T374, 375, 377; 378, 364, 766*, 767*, 768, 769, 770*, 771*, 772*, 773*, 774*, 775, 775a, 776*, 777, 778*, 778a, 779*, 780*, 782*, 783*, 788]

*S. Levy and P. Artzi, "Sumerian and Akkadian Documents from Public and Private Collections in Israel," *'Atiqot* 4 (1965) i-xii, 1-15.

E. Sollberger, "Three Ur-Dynasty Documents," *JCS* 19 (1965) 26-30.

W. F. Leemans, "Cuneiform Texts in the Collection of Dr. Ugo Sissa," *JCS* 20 (1966) 35-47.

R. F. G. Sweet, "A Pair of Double Acrostics in Akkadian," *Or, N.S.,* 38 (1969) 459-460.

§872 *4.4.11.1 Akkadian Didactic and Wisdom Literature*

E. Douglas Van Buren, "Akkadian Sidelights on a Fragmentary Epoch," *Or, N.S.,* 19 (1950) 159-174.

R. J. Williams, "Notes on Some Akkadian Wisdom Texts," *JCS* 6 (1952) 1-7.

E[phraim] A. Speiser, "The Case of the Obliging Servant," *JCS* 8 (1954) 98-105.

*Edmund I. Gordon, "A new Look at the Wisdom of Sumer and Akkad," *BO* 17 (1960) 122-152. [Some General Remarks on the Wisdom Literature of Mesopotamia; Classification of the Mesopotamian Wisdom Literature]

*T. Donald, "The Semantic Field of Rich and Poor in the Wisdom Literature of Hebrew and Accadian," *OA* 3 (1964) 27-41.

§873 *4.4.11.2 Akkadian Historical Texts*

*Theo. G. Pinches, "Notes on a New List of Early Babylonian Kings: being a continuation of a Paper read 7th December 1880," *SBAP* 3 (1880-81) 37-46.

W. H. Rylands, "The Inscription of Sargon of Agade," *SBAP* 6 (1883-84) 68.

†Theo. G. Pinches, "Reply to M. J. Menant, on the Inscription of Sargon of Agade," *SBAP* 6 (1883-84) 107-108. (Remarks by Julius Oppert, p. 109)

*Theo. G. Pinches, "The Name of the City and Country over which Tarkû-timme Ruled," *SBAP* 7 (1884-85) 124-127. *[Ermê]*

*†Theo[philus] G. Pinches, "Exhibition of Photograph of Inscription from Hamadan," *SBAP* 7 (1884-85) 132-133. *[Tri-lingual Inscription: Ancient Persian; Median; Semitic Babylonian]*

*A. H. Sayce, "Adam and Sargon in the Land of the Hittites: A New Tel el-Amarna Discovery," *SBAP* 37 (1915) 227-245.

*A. H. Sayce, "Additional Notes on the Sargon Texts," *SBAP* 40 (1918) 15.

Anonymous, "Notes and Comments. Babylonian and Assyrian Memorial Deposits," *ICMM* 1 (1905) 372-373.

L. W. King, "The Cruciform Monument of Manishtusu," *RAAO* 9 (1912) 91-105.

C. J. Gadd, "Samsuiluna's Sippar Inscription," *JRAS* (1925) 94-99.

*C. J. Gadd, "On Two Babylonian Kings," *SO* 1 (1925) 25-33. [B.M. 79503]

A.T. Olmstead, "The Text of Sargon's Annals," *AJSL* 47 (1930-31) 259-280.

*W[illiam] F[oxwell] Albright, "Some Important Recent Discoveries: Alphabetic Origins and the Idrimi Statue," *BASOR* #118 (1950) 11-20. [2. The Inscription of the Statue of Idrimi, pp. 14-20]

*Anne Draffkorn, "Was King Abba-AN of Yamḫad a Vizier for the King of Ḫattuša?" *JCS* 13 (1959) 94-97. [Alalaḫ Tablet *456]

*W. G. Lambert, "A Vizer of Ḫattuša? A Further Comment," *JCS* 13 (1959) 132. [Alalaḫ Tablet *456]

*Hans G. Gütervock, "Sargon of Akkad Mentioned by Ḫattušili I of Ḫatti," *JCS* 18 (1964) 1-6.

*Albrecht Goetze, "Date Formula of Iddin-Dagan of Isin," *JCS* 19 (1965) 56. [NBC 6418; rev. NBC 9180 rev.]

R. Caplice, "Namburbi Texts in the British Museum," *Or, N.S.,* 34 (1965) 105-131.

*E. I. Gordon, "The Meaning of the Ideogram ^{d}KASKAL.KUR = 'Underground Water-course' and Its Significance for Bronze Age Historical Geography," *JCS* 21 (1967) 70-88.

R. Caplice, "Namburbi Texts in the British Museum, II," *Or, N.S.,* 36 (1967) 1-38.

R. Caplice, "Namburbi Texts in the British Museum, III," *Or, N.S.,* 36 (1967) 273-298.

*M. Civil, "Remarks on 'Sumerian and Bilingual Texts'," *JNES* 26 (1967) 200-211.

*E[dmond] Sollberger, "Samsu-iluna's bilingual inscription B, text of the Akkadian version," *RAAO* 61 (1967) 39-44.

Edmond Sollberger, "The Cruciform Monument," *JEOL* #20 (1967-68) 50-70.

Albercht Goetze, "Akkad Dynasty Inscriptions from Nippur," *JAOS* 88 (1968) 54-59. [6N-128; 5N-T 567; GN-T1033a; 6N-T1033; 6N-T264; 6N-T658; 6N-T112; 6N-T662]

*Jørgen Laessøe, "The Quest for the Country of *Utûm," *JAOS* 88 (1968) 120-122. [SH 825]

*Edmond Sollberger, A Tankard for Atta-Ḫašu," *JCS* 22 (1968-69) 30-33.

§874 *4.4.11.3 Akkadian Business and Legal Texts*

E. Revillout and V. Revillout, "A Contract of Apprenticeship from Sippara," *BOR* 2 (1887-88) 119-127.

*William J. Hinke, "Legal and Commercial Transactions Chiefly from Nippur," *RP* 8 (1909) 11-19. *(Review)*

*Albert T. Clay, "Inscriptions of Nebuchadnezzar and Naram Sin," *RP* 13 (1914) 73-75.

S[tephen H.] Langdon, "Ten tablets from the archives of Adab," *RAAO* 19 (1922) 187-194.

Henry Frederick Lutz, "Legal and Economic Documents from Ashjâly," *UCPSP* 10 (1931-46) 1-184.

S[tephen H.] Langdon, "A Business Document of the Dungi Period," *JRAS* (1936) 87-92.

P. Peters, "Ancient Law Code Found," *AusTR* 19 (1948) 75. *[Eshnunna]*

Anonymous, "The Akkadian Law Code of Tell Ḥarmel," *JCS* 2 (1948) 72. [IM. 51059; IM. 52614]

Albrecht Goetze, "Another Law Tablet from Harmal," *Sumer* 4 (1948) 54.

Josef Klíma, "New Discoveries of Legal Documents from Pre-Hammurapian Times," *ArOr* 19 (1951) Parts 1&2, 37-59. [I. The Laws from Eshnunna]

John Miles and O. R. Gurney, "The Laws of Eshnunna," *ArOr* 17 (1949) Part 2, 174-188.

*†M. D. W. Jeffreys, "A remark concerning the Laws of Eshnunna," *Sumer* 6 (1950) 194-195.

*D[onald] J. Wiseman, "Texts and Fragments," *JCS* 7 (1953) 108-109. [S. O. 1. An unidentified economic text from Syria. Copy and Comments]

*Edmond Sollberger, "Selected Texts from American Collections," *JCS* 10 (1956) 11-31. [2. An Old-Akkadian Contract, pp.18-20]

*Reuven Yaron, "Matrimonial Mishaps at Eshnunna," *JSS* 8 (1963) 1-16. [I. Death of the Wife in the Absence of Issue: L.E. 17 + 18; II. Adultery: L.E. 27 + 28; III. Divorce: L.E. 59]

§875 *4.4.11.4 Akkadian Correspondence*

Anonymous, "Abdi-Hiba of Jerusalem to the King of Egypt," *RP* 1 (1902) 113-114.

Leroy Waterman, "Some Kouyunjik Letters and Related Texts," *AJSL* 29 (1912-13) 1-36.

Leroy Waterman, "Textual Notes on the Letters of the Sargon Period," *AJSL* 27 (1911-12) 134-143.

§876 *4.4.11.5 Akkadian Astronomical, Mathematical, Medical and "Scientific" Texts*

*Robert Brown Jr., "Euphratean Stellar Researches," *SBAP* 14 (1891-92) 280-304.

*Robert Brown Jr., "Euphratean Stellar Researches. Part II," *SBAP* 15 (1892-93) 317-342.

*Robert Brown Jr., "Euphratean Stellar Researches. Part III," *SBAP* 15 (1892-93) 456-470.

*Robert Brown Jr., "Euphratean Stellar Researches. Part IV," *SBAP* 17 (1895) 16-36.

*Robert Brown Jr., "Euphratean Stellar Researches. Part V," *SBAP* 17 (1895) 284-303.

*Robert Brown Jr., "Euphratean Stellar Researches. Part V (Continued)," *SBAP* 18 (1896) 25-44.

*Morris Jastrow Jr., "Sumerian glosses in astrological letters," *Baby* 3 (1909-10) 227-235.

*A. H. Sayce, "The Atlas of the Empire of Sargon of Akkad," *AEE* 9 (1924) 1-5. (Note by [W. M.] Flinders Petrie, p. 5)

*Paul Haupt, "Philological Studies. 7. The Cuneiform Prototype of *Cipher* and *Zero*," *AJP* 45 (1924) 57-59.

*L[eon] L[egrain], "Nippur Old Drugstore," *UMB* 8 (1939-40) #1, 25-27. [C.B.S. 14221]

*M. I. Hussey, "Anatomical Nomenclautre in an Akkadian Omen Text," *JCS* 2 (1948) 21-32.

*H. Lewy, "Studies in Assyro-Babylonian Mathematics and Metrology. A. A New Volume of Babylonian Mathematical Texts," *Or, N.S.,* 18 (1949) 40-67, 137-170.

*J. V. Kinnier Wilson, "Two Medical Texts from Nimrud," *Iraq* 18 (1956) 130-146; 19 (1957) 40-49. [ND. 4358; 4368]

J. V. Kinnier Wilson, "The Nimrud Catalogue of Medical and Physiognomical Omina," *Iraq* 24 (1962) 52-62. [ND. 4366]

§877 *4.4.11.6 Akkadian Religious, Mythological, and Omen Texts*

*C. J. Ball, "A Bilingual Hymn (4R. 46, 5-19)," *SBAP* 15 (1892-93) 51-54.

Theophile James Meek, "A Hymn to Ishtar, K. 1286," *AJSL* 26 (1909-10) 156-161.

*Th[eophile] J. Meek, "Cuneiform Bilingual Hymns, Prayers and Penitential Psalms. Autographed, transliterated and translated with notes from the original tablets in the British Museum," *BAVSS* 10 (1913) Heft 1, I-IV, 1-127. [K. 879; K. 2769; K. 3007; K. 3025 + K. 8917; K. 3251*; K. 3259*; K. 3311*; K 3431*; K. 3585*; K. 3658; K. 4815*; K. 5039a*; K. 5098*; K. 5117*; K. 5118*; K. 5147*; K. 5150*; K. 5160; K. 5162*; K. 5218*; K. 5303; K. 5338; K5359*; K. 5970; K. 5982; K. 6063; K. 6191*; K. 7598; K. 8447*; K. 8472; K. 8488; K. 8607*; K. 8706; K. 8898; K. 8899; K. 8917 + K. 3205; K. 8937*; K. 9154; K. 9312*; K. 9333*; K. 9475*; K. 10205*; K. 13380; K. 13937; K. 13955; S. 778; S. 1294; Rm. 272*; Rm. 373; Rm 385; Rm. 514; Rm. 603*; DT. 45*; 80-7-19, 127*; 81-7-27, 77*; 81-7-27, 203] *[* Indicates Assyrian]*

*S[tephen H.] Langdon, "A bilingual tablet from Erech of the first century B.C.," *RAAO* 12 (1915) 73-84. [Corr. *RAAO* 26 (1929) p. 143] [AO 6458]

*Morris Jastrow Jr., "Sumerian and Akkadian Views of Beginnings," *JAOS* 36 (1916) 274-299.

S[tephen] Langdon, "Hymn in Paragraphs to Ishtar as the Belit of Nippur," *AfO* 1 (1923) 12-18. [K 9555 + Rm 613]

Henry Frederick Lutz, "A Fragment of the Anu-Enlil Series," *UCPSP* 9 (1927-31) 391-399. [UCBC 1215]

*S[tephen H.] Langdon, "The Legend of the kiškanu, *JRAS* (1928) 843-848. [CT 16, 14, 183-204]

*E. Power, "The ancient gods and language of Cyprus revealed by the Accadian inscriptions of Amathus," *B* 10 (1929) 129-169.

*Oliver R. Gurney, "A Bilingual Text Concerning Etana," *JRAS* (1935) 459-466. [K. 5119; a duplicate of Ki 1904-10-9,87]

Selim Levy, "Small Texts. A Lipit-Ishtar Votive Text in Akkadian," *Sumer* 4 (1948) 56-59. [IM 51976]

W. G. Lambert, "An Address of Marduk to the Demons," *AfO* 17 (1954-56) 310-321. [K. 83275; S. 2013; K. 3307 + K. 6626; K. 7063; K. 6210; K. 3759 + K. 8640 + K. 11767; K. 6584; K. 13768; K. 15061; K. 12229]

G. Castellino, "Rituals and Prayers against 'Appearing Ghosts'," *Or, N.S.,* 24 (1955) 240-274. [CT XXIII 15-18, KAR 21 (VAT 8252)]

*Beatrice L. Goff, "The Rôle of Amulets in Mesopotamian Ritual Texts," *JWCI* 19 (1956) 1-39.

Erica Reiner, "Plague Amulets and House Blessings," *JNES* 19 (1960) 148-155.

L. J. Krušina-Černý, "The Akkadian epic of the Creation of the World," *NOP* 1 (1960) #6, 15-16.

*William W. Hallo, "Royal Hymns and Mesopotamian Unity," *JCS* 17 (1963) 112-118.

*F. Charles Fensham, "Common Trends in the Curses of Near Eastern Treaties and *Kudurr*—Inscriptions Compared with the Maledictions of Amos and Isaiah," *ZAW* 75 (1963) 155-175.

A. K. Grayson and W. G. Lambert, "Akkadian Prophecies," *JCS* 18 (1964) 7-30.

W. W. Hallo, "Akkadian Prophecies," *IEJ* 16 (1966) 231-242.

*E. Reiner and H. G. Güterbock, "The Great Prayer to Ishtar and Its Two Versions from Boğasköy," *JCS* 21 (1967) 255-266.

D[onald] J. Wiseman, "A Lipšur Litany from Nimrud," *Iraq* 31 (1969) 175-183. [N D 4387 + 4405/77]

G. R. Castellino, "Incantation to Utu," *OA* 8 (1969) 1-57.

§878 *4.4.11.7 Assyrian and Babylonian Backgrounds §286;
        Assyrian and Babylonian Backgrounds
        to the Pentateuch §299 ←]*

*E. H. Plumptre, "Assyrian and Babylonian Inscriptions Bearing on Old
Testament History," *Exp, 2nd Ser.,* 1 (1881) 113-125, 223-236, 275-
291, 443-457. [1. History of the Creation and Fall; 2. The Fall of
Angels; 3. The Deluge; 4. The Tower of Babel; 5. Nimrod; 6. Ur of the
Chaldees; 7. The Four Kings; 8. The Destruction of Sodom and
Gomorrah; 9. Balaam and the Son of Beor; 10. Achan and Chusan
Rishatham]

*E. H. Plumptre, "Assyrian and Babylonian Inscriptions Bearing on Old
Testament History," *Exp, 2nd Ser.,* 2 (1881) 48-64, 230-240, 316-320,
437-458. [11. Solomon and the Kings of the Hittites; 12. Hosea,
Shalman and King Jareb; 13. Menahem and Pul; 14. Israel, Judah,
Syria, and Tiglath-Pileser; 15. Hosea, Shalmanezer, and Sargon; 16.
Sennacherib and Hezekiah]

*W. W. Moore, "The Cuneiform Corroborations of the Early Narratives of
Genesis," *USR* 6 (1894-95) 38-48.

§879 *4.4.11.8 The Behistun Inscription [See also: Persian Texts, including the Behistun Inscription §952 →]*

*H[enry] C. Rawlinson, "The Persian Cuneiform Inscription at Behistun, decyphered and translated; with a Memoir on Persian Cuneiform Inscriptions in general, and on that of the Behistun in Particular," *JRAS* (1846) i-lxxi, 1-349; (1850) 1-192. [Note at end of Volume dated 1850, pages numbered separately as I-XXI]

*†Anonymous, "Persian and Assyrian Inscriptions—Monuments of Darius Hystaspes," *QRL* 79 (1946-47) 413-449. [Behistun Inscription, pp. 428-430] *(Review)*

Anonymous, "Some Passages in the Life of King Darius, the Son of Hystaspes, by Himself," *DUM* 29 (1847) 14-27. *[Behistun Inscription]*

Edwin Norris, "Memoir on the Scythic Version of the Behistun Inscription," *JRAS* (1855) 1-213.

E[dwin] N[orris], "Addenda to the Paper at the Beginning of this Volume, on the Scythic Version of the Behistun Inscription," *JRAS* (1855) 431-433.

*G. B., "The Inscriptions at Persepolis and Scripture Chronology," *JSL, 3rd Ser.,* 4 (1856-57) 138-161.

*G. B., "On Daniel and Ezra, compared with the Inscription at Behistun," *JSL, 3rd Ser.,* 5 (1857) 170-172.

Anonymous, "Biblical Research and Discovery. The Life of Sir Henry Creswicke Rawlinson," *CFL, O.S.,* 2 (1898) 286-287. *[The Discovery of the Behistun Inscription]*

Henry C. Rawlinson, "The Behistun Inscription," *RP* 1 (1902) 327-350.

A.V.Williams Jackson, "The Great Behistun Rock and Some Results of a Re-examination of the Old Persian Inscriptions on it," *JAOS* 24 (1903) 77-95.

*Lawrence Mills, "The Cyrus Vase Inscription and Behistūn," *IAQR, 3rd Ser.,* 17 (1904) 319-325.

H. C. Tolman, "A Critical Note to Col. 4, L. 76, of the Behistan Inscription," *AJP* 29 (1908) 212.

*L[awrence H.] Mills, "The Stone-Sculptured Texts and the Manuscripts of Old Persia: Their Harmony and Authority," *IAQR, 3rd Ser.,* 28 (1909) 330-334.

*H. C. Tolman, "Notes on the recently found Aramaic Papyrus Fragments of the Behistan Inscription," *PAPA* 43 (1911) l-liv.

*L.˙H. Gray, "Iranian Miscellanies," *JAOS* 33 (1913) 281-294. [a. On the Aramaic Version of the Behistān Inscriptions, pp. 281-284]

Roland G. Kent, "Addendum on a difficult Old Persian passage," *JAOS* 41 (1921) 74-75. *[Behistun Inscription]*

*Arno Poebel, "Chronology of Darius' First Year of Reign," *AJSL* 55 (1938) 142-165, 285-314.

*A. T. Olmstead, "Darius and His Behistun Inscription," *AJSL* 55 (1938) 392-416.

Roland G. Kent, "Addendum on Bh. 1.86," *JAOS* 63 (1943) 67.

Roland G. Kent, "Addendum on Bh. 4.44," *JAOS* 63 (1943) 67-68.

Wilhelm Eilers, "The End of the Behistan Inscription," *JNES* 7 (1948) 106-110.

George C. Cameron, "The Inscription and Relief of Darius at Bisitun," *AJA* 54 (1950) 264.

Roland G. Kent, "Cameron's Old Persian Readings at Bisitun. Restorations and Notes," *JCS* 5 (1951) 55-57.

Roland G. Kent, "Cameron's New Readings of the Old Persian at Behistan," *JAOS* 72 (1952) 9-20.

Julius Lewy, "The Problems Inherent in Section 70 of the Bisutun*[sic]* Inscription," *HUCA* 25 (1954) 169-298.

W. C. Benedict and Elizabeth von Voigtlander, "Darius' Bisitun Inscription, Babylonian Version, Lines 1-29," *JCS* 10 (1956) 1-10.

*George G. Cameron, "The Monument of King Darius at Bisitun," *Arch* 13 (1960) 162-171.

*George G. Cameron, "The Elamite Version of the Bistiun Inscriptions," *JCS* 14 (1960) 59-68.

*I. M. Diakonoff, "On the Interpretation of §70 of the Bisutūn Inscription (Elamite Version)," *AAASH* 17 (1969) 105-107.

§880 *4.4.11.9 Cappadocian Texts*

†Theo[philus] G. Pinches, "Cappadocian Tablets in the British Museum," *SBAP* 4 (1881-82) 11-18.

†A[rchibald] H. Sayce, "Kappadokian Inscriptions," *SBAP* 4 (1881-82) 19-20.

†George Bertin, "The Cappadocian Tablets published by Mr. Pinches," *SBAP* 4 (1881-82) 20-21.

†Theo[philus] G. Pinches, "Remarks on the Cappadocian Tablets preserved in the Bibliotheque Nationale, and that in the British Museum," *SBAP* 4 (1881-82) 28-32.

A[rchibald] H. Sayce, "The Kappadokian Cuneiform Inscription now at Kairsariyeh," *SBAP* 5 (1882-83) 41-44. (Letter by George Bertin, pp. 45-46)

A[rchibald] H. Sayce, "The Cuneiform Tablets of Kappadokia," *SBAP* 6 (1883-84) 17-25.

A. H. Sayce, "Kappadokian Inscriptions," *ZA* 1 (1886) 312-314.

A. H. Sayce, "Abstract of Three Papers Read at the Oriental Congress. So-Called Kappadokian Cuneiform Tablets," *AJSL* 6 (1889-90) 151-152.

*A. H. Sayce, "The Hittite inscriptions of Cappadocia and their decipherment," *RTR* 14 (1893) 43-53.

[William] Ramsay and [D. G.] Hogarth, "Pre-Hellenic Monuments of Cappadocia," *RTR* 14 (1893) 89-97.

*A. H. Sayce, "New Cuneiform Inscriptions," *ET* 10 (1898-99) 115-116.

A. H. Sayce, "The Cappadocian cuneiform tablets," *Baby* 2 (1907-08) 1-45.

Theophilus G. Pinches, "The Cappadocian Tablets belonging to the Liverpool Institute of Archaeology," *AAA* 1 (1908) 49-80.

Archibald H. Sayce, "Notes on Passages in the Cappadocian Tablets," *AAA* 1 (1908) 81-82.

A. H. Sayce, "Cappadocian cuneiform tablets from Kara-Eyuk," *Baby* 4 (1910-11) 65-80.

A. H. Sayce, "The Cappadocian cuneiform tablets of the University of Pennsylvania," *Baby* 6 (1912) 182-192.

*A. H. Sayce, "Hittite Hieroglyphs on a Cappadocian Cuneiform Tablet in the Royal Scottish Museum, Edinburgh," *SBAP* 35 (1913) 203-204.

A[rchibald] H. Sayce, "The Cuneiform Tablets of Cappadocia," *A&A* 5 (1917) 101-103.

A. H. Sayce, "The Museum Collection of Cappadocian Tablets," *MJ* 9 (1918) 148-151.

G. R. Driver, "Studies in Cappadocian Tablets," *Baby* 10 (1927) 69-136.

Ferris J. Stephens, "Studies of the Cuneiform Tablets of Cappadocia," *CSQC* 2 (1926) #2, 11-58.

Ferris J. Stephens, "The Cappadocian Tablets in the University of Pennsylvania Museum," *JSOR* 11 (1927) 101-136.

G. R. Driver, "Studies in Cappadocian Texts," *ZA* 38 (1928-29) 217-232.

*Theophile James Meek, "The Akkadian and Cappadocian Texts from Nuzi," *BASOR* #48 (1932) 2-5.

*D[onald] J. Wiseman, "Texts and Fragments," *JCS* 7 (1953) 1098-109. [BM 77810]

Albrecht Goetze, "Tuttul in a 'Cappadocian' Proper Name," *JCS* 7 (1953) 110.

Michel Civil, "Texts and Fragments," *JCS* 15 (1961) 127. *[Cappadocian]*

§881 *4.4.11.10 Mari Texts*

*W[illiam] F[oxwell] Albright, "Western Asia in the Twentieth Century B.C.: The Archives of Mari," *BASOR* #67 (1937) 26-30.

Cyrus H. Gordon, "Šamši-Adad's Military Texts from Mari," *ArOr* 18 (1950) Parts 1&2. 199-207.

A. Leo Oppenheim, "The Archives of the Palace of Mari," *JNES* 11 (1952) 129-139.

*Albrecht Goetze, "An Old Babylonian Itinerary," *JCS* 7 (1953) 51-72. [CIOM 2134; UIOM 2370]

A. Leo Oppenheim, "The Archives of the Palace of Mari II," *JNES* 13 (1954) 141-148.

Cyril J. Gadd, "The Mari Letters," *ET* 66 (1954-55) 174-177, 195-198.

*A. Malamat, "'Prophecy' in the Mari Documents," *EI* 4 (1956) VI-VII.

Martin Noth, "Remarks on the Sixth Volume of Mari Texts," *JSS* 1 (1956) 322-333.

H. Lewy, "The Historical Background of the Correspondence of Baḫdi-Lim," *Or, N.S.,* 25 (1956) 324-352.

I. J. Gelb, "On the Recently Published Economic Texts from Mari," *RAAO* 50 (1956) 1-10.

W. L. Moran, "Mari Notes on the Execration Texts," *Or, N.S.,* 26 (1957) 339-345.

*Albrecht Goetze, "Remarks on Some Names Occurring in the Execration Texts," *BASOR* #151 (1958) 28-33

*A. Malamat, "History and Prophetic Vision in a Mari Letter," *EI* 5 (1958) 86*-87*.

*A. Malamat, "Prophetic Revelations in the New Documents from Mari and the Bible," *EI* 8 (1967) 75*.

*Jimmy J. Roberts, "Antecedents to Biblical Prophecy from the Mari Archives," *RestQ* 10 (1967) 121-133.

*Herbert B. Huffmon, "Prophecy in the Mari Letters," *BA* 31 (1968) 101-124. [Prophecy Outside Israel; The "Answerer;" The Ecstatic; Private Persons; Hair and Hem; Mari and Israel; Appendix]

*A. Malamat, "Hazor and its Northern Neighbours in New Mari Documents," *EI* 9 (1969) 137. [English Summary]

*Martin J. Buss, "Mari Prophecy and Hosea," *JBL* 88 (1969) 338.

§882 *4.4.11.11 Nuzi Texts*

Edward Chiera and Ephraim A. Speiser, "Selected 'Kirkuk' Documents," *JAOS* 47 (1927) 36-60.

Henry Frederick Lutz, "A Legal Document from Nuzi," *UCPSP* 9 (1927-31) 405-412. [UCBC 1285]

E[phraim] A. Speiser, "A Letter of Saushshatar and the Date of the Kirkuk Tablets," *JAOS* 49 (1929) 269-275.

Edward Chiera, "A Legal Document from Nuzi," *AJSL* 47 (1930-31) 281-286.

*Theophile James Meek, "The Akkadian and Cappadocian Texts from Nuzi," *BASOR* #48 (1932) 2-5.

E[phraim] A. Speiser, "New Kirkuk Documents Relating to Security Transactions," *JAOS* 52 (1932) 350-367; 53 (1933) 24-46.

*S. I. Feigin, "The Captives in Cuneiform Inscriptions," *AJSL* 50 (1933-34) 217-245; 51 (1934-35) 22-29.

*A. Saarisalo, "New Kirkuk documents relating to slaves," *SO* 5 (1934) #3, i-viii, 1-101.

*E. R. Lacheman, "New Nuzi Texts and a New Method of Copying Cuneiform Tablets," *JAOS* 55 (1935) 429-431.

E[phraim] A. Speiser, "Notes to Recently Published Nuzi Texts," *JAOS* 55 (1935) 432-443.

C[yrus] H. Gordon, "Fifteen Nuzi Tablets Relating to Women," *Muséon* 48 (1935) 113-132. [N 18; N 26; N 31; N 57; N 68; N 139; N 158; N 160; N 164; N 174; N 168; N 197; N 218, N 298; N 303]

*Theophile James Meek, "The Iterative Names in the Old Akkadian Texts from Nuzi," *RAAO* 32 (1935) 51-55.

*Cyrus H. Gordon, "Nuzi Tablets Relating to Theft," *Or, N.S.,* 5 (1936) 305-330.

Ernest R. Lacheman, "An Omen Text from Nuzi," *RAAO* 34 (1937) 1-8.

Theophile James Meek, "Notes on Early Texts from Nuzi," *RAAO* 34 (1937) 59-66.

Julius Lewy, "Notes on Pre-Ḫurrian Texts from Nuzi," *JAOS* 58 (1938) 450-461.

*J. W. Jack, "Recent Biblical Archaeology. The Nuzi Tablets," *ET* 51 (1939-40) 422-423. [Marriage Customs; Shoes as Legal Symbols]

*Cyrus H. Gordon, "Biblical Customs and the Nuzu Tablets," *BA* 3 (1940) 1-12.

Julius Lewy, "A New Volume of Nuzi Texts," *BASOR* #79 (1940) 29-32. *(Review)*

Hildegard Lewy, "The *aḫḫûtû* Documents from Nuzi," *Or, N.S.,* 9 (1940) 362-373.

H[ildegard] Lewy, "Gleanings from a New Volume of Nuzi Texts," *Or, N.S.,* 10 (1941) 201-222.

Hildegard Lewy, "The *Titennûtu* Texts from Nuzi," *Or, N.S.,* 10 (1941) 313-336.

Pierre M. Purves, "New Documents from Nuzi," *BASOR* #88 (1942) 38-39.

*A. Leo Oppenheim, "Assyriological Gleanings II," *BASOR* #93 (1944) 14-17. [Part V - Nuzi Text, p. 16]

*H[ildegard] Lewy, "Studies in Assyro-Babylonian Mathematics and Metrology. B. On Some Metrological Peculiarities of Old Akkadian Texts from Nuzi," *Or, N.S.,* 20 (1951) 1-12.

A. Leo Oppenheim, "On an Operational Device in Mesopotamian Bureaucracy," *JNES* 18 (1959) 121-128.

H[ildegard] Lewy, "Miscellania Nuziana," *Or, N.S.,* 28 (1959) 1-25. [I. An Assyro-Nuzian Synchronism]

*M. Tsevat, "A Reference to Gudea of Lagash in an Old Mari Text," *OA* 1 (1962) 9-10.

E[phraim] A. Speiser, "A Significant New Will from Nuzi," *JCS* 17 (1963) 65-71.

Hildegard Lewy, "The *Titennûtu* Texts from Nuzi," *Or, N.S.,* 10 (1941) 313-336.

Pierre M. Purves, "New Documents from Nuzi," *BASOR* #88 (1942) 38-39.

*A. Leo Oppenheim, "Assyriological Gleanings II," *BASOR* #93 (1944) 14-17. [Part V - Nuzi Text, p. 16]

*H[ildegard] Lewy, "Studies in Assyro-Babylonian Mathematics and Metrology. B. On Some Metrological Peculiarities of Old Akkadian Texts from Nuzi," *Or, N.S.,* 20 (1951) 1-12.

A. Leo Oppenheim, "On an Operational Device in Mesopotamian Bureaucracy," *JNES* 18 (1959) 121-128.

H[ildegard] Lewy, "Miscellania Nuziana," *Or, N.S.,* 28 (1959) 1-25. [I. An Assyro-Nuzian Synchronism]

*M. Tsevat, "A Reference to Gudea of Lagash in an Old Mari Text," *OA* 1 (1962) 9-10.

E[phraim] A. Speiser, "A Significant New Will from Nuzi," *JCS* 17 (1963) 65-71.

*Anonymous, "Archaeology Sheds Light on A Marriage Contract," *BH* 3 (1967) #1, 18-21.

*Hildegard Lewy, "A Contribution to the Historical Geography of the Nuzi Texts," *JAOS* 88 (1968) 150-162.

*David Freedman, "A New Approach to the Nuzi Sistership Contract," *JNES* 2 (1969-70) 77-85.

§883 *4.4.11.12 Tel el Amarna Letters*

A. H. Sayce, "Babylonian Tablets from Tel el-Amarna, Upper Egypt," *SBAP* 10 (1887-88) 488-525.

E. A. Wallis Budge, "On Cuneiform Despatches from Tushratta, King of Mitanni, Burraburiyash, the son of Kuri-Galzu, and the King of Alashiya, to Amenophis III, King of Egypt, and on the Cuneiform Tablets from Tell el-Amarna," *SBAP* 10 (1887-88) 540-569.

Owen C. Whitehouse, "Brevia: Recent Discovery of Cuneiform Tablets at Tell el Amarna," *Exp, 3rd Ser.,* 8 (1888) 157-160.

Francis Brown, "Babylon and Egypt, B.C. 1500," *PR* 9 (1888) 476-481. *[Tel el Amarna Letters]*

W. St. Chad Boscawen, "The Tel-el-Amarna Tablets," *BOR* 3 (1888-89) 286-288.

A. H. Sayce, "The Cuneiform Tablets from Tel el-Amarna, now preserved in the Boulaq Museum," *SBAP* 11 (1888-89) 326-413.

[A. H.] Sayce, "Letters from Palestine Before the Age of Moses," *EN* 1 (1889) 328-329.

C[laude] R. Conder, "The Tell Amarna Tablets," *PEFQS* 21 (1889) 28-30.

*C[laude] R. Conder, "Monumental Notice of Hebrew Victories," *PEFQS* 22 (1890) 326-329. *[Tel el Armana Tablets]*

A. H. Sayce, "The Cuneiform Inscriptions of Tel el-Amarna," *JTVI* 24 (1890-91) 12-27. (Discussion, pp. 28-31)

W. St. C[had] Boscawen, "Southern Palestine and the Tel-el-Amarna Tablets," *BOR* 5 (1891) 114-119.

*Anonymous, "Judges 3:8-10 and the Cuneiform Tablets," *ONTS* 12 (1891) 237.

C[laude] R. Conder, "Altaic Letter from Tell Amarna," *PEFQS* 23 (1891) 245-250.

C[laude] R. Conder, "The Tell Amarna Tablets," *SRL* 17 (1891) 292-318.

Anonymous, "The Tablets of Tel-el-Amarna," *AAOJ* 14 (1892) 335.

Claude R. Conder, "Notes by Major Conder, R. F.," *PEFQS* 24 (1892) 200-207. [Amarna, pp. 205-206]

W. St. Chad Boscawen, "Tell el Amarna Tablets in the British Museum," *PEFQS* 24 (1892) 291-295.

Wm. Flinders Petrie, "Corrections," *PEFQS* 24 (1892) 334-335.

Morris Jastrow Jr., "The Letters of Abdiḫeba," *AJSL* 9 (1892-93) 24-46.

W. St. Chad Boscawen, "Tel El-Amarna Tablets in the British Museum," *BOR* 6 (1892-93) 25-35, 69-72.

W. St. C[had] B[oscawen], "Syllabaries from Tel el-Amarna," *BOR* 6 (1892-93) 120.

Henry Hayman, "The Testimony of the Tell-el-Amarna Tablets," *BS* 50 (1893) 696-716.

†Anonymous, "The Tell Amarna Tablets," *ERCJ* 178 (1893) 1-32. *(Review)*

Morris Jastrow Jr., "'Men of Judah' in the El-Amarna tablets," *JBL* 12 (1893) 61-72.

Claude R. Conder, "Notes on the 'Quarterly Statement'," *PEFQS* 25 (1893) 78-79. [Tel el Amarna Tablets, p. 78]

*Theo. G. Pinches, "Was ⌐┬ ⌂⌐ ⌐ The Most High God of Salem?" *SBAP* 16 (1893-94) 225-229.

Anonymous, "The Tel-el-Amarna Tablets," *MR* 76 (1894) 303-306.

W. W. Moore, "A Batch of Old Letters," *USR* 6 (1894-95) 101-117. *[Tell-el-Amarna Tablets]*

W. W. Moore, "Other Witnesses from the Dust," *USR* 6 (1894-95) 186-193. *[Tell-el-Amarna Tablets]*

John M. P. Metcalf, "The Tell-el-Amarna Letters," *BS* 54 (1897) 334-347, 413-435. [Corr. p. x]

W. W. Elwang, "An Interesting Example of the Necessity of Extreme Caution in the Valuation of Inscriptions," *CFL, O.S.,* 1 (1897) 71.

*Joseph Offord, "Pre-Mosaic Palestine," *SBAP* 19 (1897) 7-26. *[Tell-el-Amarna Tablets]*

Carl W. Belser, "The Tell-el-Amarna Tablets," *TQ* 1 (1897) 306-316.

*A. H. Sayce, "The Ionians in the Tel el-Amarna Tablets," *SBAP* 24 (1902) 10-13.

*Percy E. Newberry, "Extracts from my Notebooks. VI.," *SBAP* 25 (1903) 130-138. [47. Wine Jar Inscriptions from Tell el Amarna, pp. 137-138]

Joseph Offord, "Notes and Queries. 1. *A New Tell el-Amarna Tablet,*" *PEFQS* 36 (1904) 180.

Anonymous, "Translation of New Tell-el-Amarna Tablets," *RP* 3 (1904) 219-220.

Hewlett Johnson, "The Tell el Armana Tablets, and the Lessons They Teach," *ICMM* 1 (1905) 238-253.

C. H. W. Johns, "Two Tell el-Amarna Letters," *ET* 19 (1907-08) 13-14. *(Review)*

*Anonymous, "The Pyramid Texts and the Future Life," *AAOJ* 30 (1908) 346-348. [Tell-el-Amarna Tablets, pp. 347-348]

O. E. Ravn, "Review of Fr. Böhl, *die Sprache der Amarna-briefe,*" *Baby* 3 (1909-10) 223-226. *(Review)*

*George Hempl, "The Old Doric of the Tell el Amarna Texts," *TAPA* 44 (1913) 185-214.

D. D. Luckenbill and T. G. Allen, "The Murch Fragment of an el-Amarna Letter," *AJSL* 33 (1916-17) 1-8.

A. H. Sayce, "The Discovery of the Tel el-Amarna Tablets," *AJSL* 33 (1916-17) 89-90.

*William Wallace Everts, "The Bible and the Amarna Documents," *R&E* 15 (1918) 311-318.

E. W. Hollingworth, "The Date of the Tel Amarna Tablets," *SBAP* 40 (1918) 100-103.

D. D. Luckenbill, "A Difficult Passage in an Amarna Letter," *AJSL* 35 (1918-19) 158-159.

Joseph Offord, "New Tablets from Amarna," *PEFQS* 51 (1919) 47.

*Samuel A. B. Mercer, "The Hittites, Mitanni and Babylonia in the Tell el-Amarna Letters," *JSOR* 8 (1924) 13-28.

John A. Maynard, "Short Notes on the Amarna Letters," *JSOR* 8 (1924) 76.

*W[illiam] F[oxwell] Albright, "Canaanite Ḥofšî, 'Free', in the Amarna Tablets," *JPOS* 4 (1924) 169-170.

John A. Maynard, "Textual Notes on the Amarna Letters," *JSOR* 9 (1925) 129-130.

Samuel A. B. Mercer, "Studies in the Tell el-Amarna Letters," *JSOR* 9 (1925) 241-248.

John R. Towers, "An Ancient Patriotic Poem?" *JMUEOS* #16 (1931) 51-54. [W 190; W 214; W 239]

J[ohn] R. Towers, "The Aten Hymns," *JSOR* 15 (1931) 60-63. *[Tel el-Amarna Tablets]*

*N. D. Mironov, "Aryan Vestiges in the Near East of the Second Millenary B.C.," *AO* 11 (1932-33) 140-217. [III. Palestine and Syria (Amarna Letters), 171-185]

Cyrus H. Gordon, "Eight new Cuneiform Fragments from Tell el Amarna," *JEA* 20 (1934) 137-138.

*George A. Barton, "The Possible Mention of Joshua's Conquest in the el-Amarna Letters," *ET* 47 (1935-36) 380.

*George A. Barton, "Pella in the el-Amarna Tablets," *ET* 47 (1935-36) 476-477.

*W[illiam] F[oxwell] Albright, "The Egyptian Correspondence of Abimilki, Prince of Tyre," *JEA* 23 (1937) 190-203.

C[yrus] H. Gordon, "Notes on the Amarna Tablets," *JBL* 58 (1939) vii.

C. J. Gadd, "The Tell El-Amarna Tablets: A Review," *PEQ* 72 (1940) 116-123. *(Review)*

W[illiam] F[oxwell] Albright and W. L. Moran, "A Re-interpretation of an Amarna Letter from Byblos (EA 82)," *JCS* 2 (1948) 239-248.

W[illiam] F[oxwell] Albright, "A Teacher to a Man of Shechem about 1400 B.C.," *BASOR* #86 (1942) 28-31. *[Tel el-Amarna Tablets]*

W[illiam] F[oxwell] Albright, "An Archaic Hebrew Proverb in an Amarna Letter from Central Palestine," *BASOR* #89 (1943) 29-32.

Cyrus H. Gordon, "The New Amarna Tablets," *Or, N.S.,* 16 (1947) 1-21.

William L. Moran, "An Unexplained Passage in an Amarna Letter from Byblos," *JNES* 8 (1949) 124-125.

W[illiam] F[oxwell] Albright and W. L. Moran, "Rib-Adda of Byblos and the Affairs of Tyre (EA 89)," *JCS* 4 (1950) 163-168.

P. van der Meer, "The Chronological Determination of the Mesopotamian Letters in the el-Amarna Tablets," *JEOL* #15 (1957-58) 74-96.

*Edward F. Campbell Jr., "The Amarna Letters and the Amarna Period," *BA* 23 (1960) 2-22. [The Chronology of the Period; The Amarna Letters and the Israelite Conquest; Rib-Adda and the North; Yanhamu; Lab'ayu; Some General Considerations]

Ronald Youngblood, "Amorite Influence in a Canaanite Amarna Letter *(EA 96),*" *BASOR* #168 (1962) 24-27.

A[lan] R. Millard, "A Letter from the Ruler of Gezer," *PEQ* 97 (1965) 140-143. [BM. 50745 = E.A. 378]

Pinhas Artzi, "The Exact Number of the Published Amarna Documents," *Or, N.S.,* 36 (1967) 432.

Pinhas Artzi, "Some Unrecognized Syrian Amarna Letters (EA 260, 317, 318)," *JNES* 27 (1968) 163-171.

J. J. Finkelstein, "Three Amarna Notes," *EI* 9 (1969) 33-34. *[Non-Hebrew Section]*

William L. Moran, "The Death of 'Abdi-Asirta," *EI* 9 (1969) 94-99. [EA 101] *[Non-Hebrew Section]*

Ichiro Nakata, "Scribal Peculiarities in EA: 285-290," *JANES* 2 (1969-70) 19-24.

§884 *4.4.11.13 Assyrian - General Studies*

T. M., "The Nineveh Inscriptions," *JSL, 3rd Ser.,* 1 (1855) 365-381.

Edward E. Salisbury, "Remarks on Two Assyrian Cylinders Received from Mosûl," *JAOS* 5 (1855-56) 191-194.

Anonymous, "The Nineveh Inscriptions," *JSL, 3rd Ser.,* 2 (1855-56) 192-194.

H. F. Talbot, "On the Assyrian Inscriptions," *JSL, 3rd Ser.,* 2 (1855-56) 414-425.

H. F. Talbot, "On the Assyrian Inscriptions—No. II," *JSL, 3rd Ser.,* 3 (1856) 188-194.

H. F. Talbot, "On the Assyrian Inscriptions—No. III," *JSL, 3rd Ser.,* 3 (1856) 422-426.

H. F. Talbot, "On the Assyrian Inscriptions—No. IV," *JSL, 3rd Ser.,* 4 (1856-57) 164-170.

Wm. Henry Green, "Assyrian Cuneiform Inscriptions," *PQPR* 1 (1872)516-537. (Errata, p. 620)

*H[enry] C. Rawlinson, "On the Inscriptions of Assyria and Babylonia," *JRAS* (1850) 401-483.

*H[enry] C. Rawlinson, "Memoir on the Babylonian and Assyrian Inscriptions," *JRAS* (1851) i-civ, 1-16.

*Anonymous, "Babylonian and Assyrian Libraries," *NBR* 51 (1869-70) 305-324.

H. F. Talbot, "Assyrian Notes. No. I," *SBAT* 3 (1874) 430-445.

*W. St. Chad Boscawen, "Notes on an Ancient Assyrian Bronze Sword bearing a Cuneiform Inscription," *SBAT* 4 (1875) 347-348.

Theo. G. Pinches, "Notes upon the Assyrian Report Tablets, with Translations," *SBAT* 6 (1878-79) 209-243.

Wm. Hayes Ward, "On the Ninevitic Cuneiform Inscriptions in this country," *JAOS* 10 (1880) xxxv-xxxvi.

*†Theo. G. Pinches, "Babylonian Art, illustrated by Mr. H. Rassam's latest discoveries," *SBAP* 6 (1883-84) 11-15.

Theo. G. Pinches, "Additions and Corrections to the Fifth Volume of the Cuneiform Inscriptions of Western Asia," *ZK* 1 (1884) 342-349; 2 (1885) 72-86, 157-160, 263-266, 328-334.

Theo[philus] G. Pinches, "Glimpses of Babylonian and Assyrian Life," *BOR* 1 (1886-87) 119-120. [I. A Ninevite Tragedy (K. 819)]

*Theo[philus] G. Pinches, "Glimpses of Babylonian and Assyrian Life. II—A Babylonian Wedding," *BOR* 1 (1886-87) 137-139.

*Theo[philus] G. Pinches, "Glimpses of Babylonian and Assyrian Life. III—A Babylonian Wedding Ceremony," *BOR* 1 (1886-87) 145-147.

A. H. Sayce, "W. A. I. II. 28. Col. I. 13-15," *ZA* 2 (1887) 95-97.

Hugo Winckler, "The Cuneiform Inscription in the Tunnel of Negub," *AJSL* 4 (1887-88) 52-53.

T. Hayter Lewis, "An Assyrian Tablet from Jerusalem," *PEFQS* 22 (1890) 265-266.

S. Arthur Strong, "Three Cuneiform Texts," *BOR* 6 (1892-93) 1-9.

*S. Arthur Strong, "On Some Babylonian and Assyrian Alliterative Texts —I," *SBAP* 17 (1895) 131-151. [DT. 83; K. 9290; K. 3452]

L. W. King, "Some recent acquisitions of the British Museum," *ZA* 10 (1895-96) 95-98. [95-4-6, 4]

*Robert Francis Harper, "Assyriological Notes," *AJSL* 13 (1896-97) 209-212. [Part II] [[435.] B 4.89-4-26, 161]

A. H. Sayce, "Assyriological Notes. No. 1," *SBAP* 19 (1896) 170-186.

A. H. Sayce, "Assyriological Notes. No. 2," *SBAP* 19 (1897) 68-76.

A. H. Sayce, "Assyriological Notes. No. 3," *SBAP* 19 (1897) 280-292.

*Robert Francis Harper, "Assyriological Notes," *AJSL* 14 (1897-98) 1-16. [Part III] [K. 762; [382.] 81-7-27, 199; [383.] 81-7-27, 199A; [359.] 80-7-19, 20; [223.] K. 112; [364.] 83-1-18, 34; [375.] 83-1-18, 41; [140.] K. 518; [35.] K. 983; [193.] K. 542; [187.] K. 589; K. 1014]

C. H. W. Johns, "Note," *SBAP* 20 (1898) 234. [K. 6223; K. 6332]

A. H. Sayce, "Assyriological Notes. No. 4," *SBAP* 20 (1898) 250-262.

*Robert Francis Harper, "Assyriological Notes. V," *AJSL* 15 (1898-99) 129-144. [K. 898; K. 8402; K. 924; K. 8375; K. 1012; K. 1061; 83-1-18, 2; [H. 391.] R^M 67 (H. 348)]

*A. H. Sayce, "New Cuneiform Inscriptions," *ET* 10 (1898-99) 115-116.

C. H. W. Johns, "A New Patêsi of Ašur," *AJSL* 18 (1901-02) 174-177.

*Fritz Hommel, "עֲזֵקָה ('Azeḳa) in an Assyrian Inscription," *ET* 13 (1901-02) 95-96.

*Fritz Hommel, "'Azeḳa: A Supplementary Note," *ET* 13 (1901-02) 114.

*Robert Francis Harper, "Assyriological Notes, VI," *AJSL* 19 (1902-03) 228-232. [K. 1516 (Harper 635); K. 822 (Harper 858)]

*Anonymous, "The Marashu Sons of Nippur," *MQR, 3rd Ser.,* 31 (1905) 184-185.

Theophile G. Pinches, "The Tablet in Cuneiform Script from Yuzghat," *JRAS* (1907) 145-160.

St[ephen] Langdon, "Assyriological Notes," *ZA* 22 (1908-09) 201-205. [1. Fragment of a Cylinder from Barsippa; 2. K. 41 + K. 257]

S[tephen] Langdon, "Tablets from Kis," *SBAP* 33 (1911) 185-196, 232-242.

R. Campbell Thompson, "Til-Barsip and its Cuneiform Inscriptions," *SBAP* 34 (1912) 66-74.

E[djar[sic]*] J. Banks, "Archaeological Notes," *HR* 65 (1913) 464-465. [A New Assyrian Inscription, p. 464]

S[tephen] Langdon, "A Tablet from Umma; in the Ashmolean Museum," *SBAP* 35 (1913) 47-52.

Stephen Langdon, "Miscellania Assyriaca II," *Baby* 7 (1913-23) 67-80.

Stephen Langdon, "Miscellania Assyriaca V," *Baby* 7 (1913-23) 237-241. [The Stevenson Collection]

D. D. Luckenbill, "On the Opening Lines of the Legend of Sargon," *AJSL* 33 (1916-17) 145-146.

V. S. Sukthankar, "An Assyrian tablet found in Bombay," *JAOS* 40 (1920) 142-144.

*John A. Maynard, "Short Notes on the Text of Harper's Assyrian and Babylonian Letters," *JSOR* 10 (1926) 95-96.

M. Charles Virolleaud, "Cuneiform Inscription in Syria," *Antiq* 2 (1928) 87-88.

*George W. Morey, "The Mystery of Ancient Glassware," *A&A* 28 (1929) 199-205. [K. 203 + 4747 + 10493: K. 5839: K. 6246 + 8157: K. 7619]

E[phraim] A. Speiser, "The Cuneiform Tablets from Tell Billa," *BASOR* #71 (1938) 23-24.

*John Garstang, "Jericho: City and Necropolis. Fourth Report," *AAA* 21 (1934) 99-136. [And a Note on an Inscribed Tablet and Fig. 2, by Sidney Smith, pp. 116-117]

E[phraim] A. Speiser, "An Assyrian Document of the Ninth Century B.C. from Tell Billah," *BASOR* #54 (1934) 20-21.

Julius Lewy, "Old Assyrian Documents from Asia Minor (About 2000 B.C.) I. The Texts TC III 252-254 and WAG no. 48/1464," *AHDO* 1 (1937) 91-108.

*Thompson R. Campbell, "(II) Fragments of Stone Reliefs and Inscriptions found at Nineveh," *Iraq* 4 (1937) 43-46.

Julius Lewy, "Old Assyrian Documents from Asia Minor (About 2000 B.C.) II. The Texts TC III 214 and Gelb no. 49," *AHDO* 2 (1938) 111-142.

*J. W. Jack, "Recent Biblical Archaeology. Tablets from Chagar Bazar (Syria)," *ET* 51 (1939-40) 547. [Barley Food; The Name Jacob]

C. J. Gadd, "Tablets from Chagar Bazar and Tall Brak, 1937-38," *Iraq* 7 (1940) 22-66. [A. 920-A. 1001; F. 1153; F. 1154; F. 1156; F. 1159; F. 1162; F. 1163]

I. J. Gelb, "A Tablet of Unusual Type from Tell Asmar," *JNES* 1 (1942) 219-226.

*O. R. Gurney, "The Sultantepe Tablets. *A Preliminary Note,*" *AS* 2 (1952) 25-35.

Jacob J. Finkelstien, "Cuneiform Texts from Tell Billa," *JCS* 7 (1953) 111-176.

O. R. Gurney, "The Assyrian Tablets from Sultantepe," *PBA* 41 (1955) 21-41.

E[phraim] A. Speiser, "Sultantepe Tablet 38 73 and Enūma Elis III 69," *JCS* 11 (1957) 43-44.

Edmond Sollberger, "Texts and Fragments," *JCS* 11 (1957) 62. [Genève, Switzerland, Musée d'Art et d'Histoire. Inventory No. 16514]

B. Landsberger and O. R. Gurney, "igi-duḫ-a = *tamartu,* short version," *AfO* 18 (1957-58) 81-86.

C. J. Gadd, "A False Attribution," *AfO* 18 (1957-58) 313.

O. R. Gurney, "The Sultantepe Tablets I (*Occasional Publications No.* 3) Correngenda," *AS* 8 (1958) 245-246.

Anonymous, "New Assyrian Inscriptions from Harran," *AT* 3 (1958-59) #3, 8, 15.

*W. G. Lambert, "The Sultantepe Tablets. A Review Article," *RAAO* 53 (1959) 119-138. *(Review)*

Joergen Laessoee, "The Bazmusian Tablets," *Sumer* 15 (1959) 15-18.

*Warren C. Benedict, "The Urartian-Assyrian Inscription of Kelishin," *JAOS* 81 (1961) 359-385.

A. K. Grayson, "An Assyrian Bronze Relief in the Iraq Museum. IM. 62197," *Sumer* 19 (1963) 111-112.

D. O. Edzard, "A New Inscription of Adad Nirari I," *Sumer* 20 (1964) 49-51. [IM. 60819]

*O. R. Gurney, "The Sultantepe Tablets," *AS* 17 (1967) 195-196. [I. Addendum; II. Additional Corrigenda]

P. Hulin, "Inscribed Fragments of a Statue from Nimrud," *Iraq* 28 (1966) 84-88. [ND 5571 / IM 60497B]

Erica Reiner and M. Civil, "Another Volume of Sultantepe Tablets," *JNES* 26 (1967) 177-200, 211.

Hildegard Lewy, "Old Assyrian Texts," *HUCA* 38 (1967) 1-33.

Stephanie Page, "The Tablets from Tell al Rimah 1967: A Preliminary Report," *Iraq* 30 (1968) 87-97. [TR. 4024; 4034; 4046; 4208; 4251]

H. W. F. Saggs, "The Tell al Rimah Tablets, 1965," *Iraq* 30 (1968) 154-174. [TR 2001; 2006; 2008; 2014-2020; 2021 + 2051; 2022; 2024-2026; 2028-2031; 2032 + 2054; 2033; 2034; 2036 + 2040; 2037-2039; 2044-2046; 2048-2050; 2052; 2053; 2055-2061; 2062A; 2062B; 2063A; 2064-2066; 2069A + 2908; 2078; 2080B + 2085; 2081; 2083A; 2084A; 2084F; 2086; 2087; 2090; 2095A, B; 2096; 2903]

D[onald] J. Wiseman, "The Tell al Rimah Tablets, 1966," *Iraq* 30 (1968) 175-205. [TR 3001-3031; 3037]

W. G. Lambert, "An Inscribed Strip of Lead," *AfO* 22 (1968-69) 64. [K 12826]

Hildegard Lewy, "Old Assyrian Texts in the University Museum," *HUCA* 40 (1969) 45-85.

*W. G. Lambert, "An eye-stone of Esarhaddon's queen and other similar gems," *RAAO* 63 (1969) 65-71. [Ashmolean 1967; 1483; AO 22497; AO 21306; AO 22499]

§885 *4.4.11.13.1 Assyrian Correspondence*

S. A. Smith, "Assyrian Letters," *SBAP* 9 (1886-87) 240-256. [K. 582; 514; 533; 679; 686; 669; 11; 525; 183; 1249; 1252; 1229; 487; 549; 578; 96]

S. Alden Smith, "Assyrian Letters. II," *SBAP* 10 (1887-88) 60-72. [K. 21; K. 80; K. 89; K 481; K 493; K. 498; K. 522]

S. Alden Smith, "Assyrian Letters. III," *SBAP* 10 (1887-88) 155-177. [K. 113; K. 146; K. 174; K. 479; K 492; K 502;K. 504, K. 506; K. 507; K. 508; K. 511]

*Theo. G. Pinches, "On a Series of Specimens of the Familiar Correspondence of the Babylonians and Assyrians," *SBAP* 7 (1884-85) 170.

S. Alden Smith,"Assyrian Letters. IV,"*SBAP* 10 (1887-88) 305-315. [K. 154; K. 523; K. 572; K. 1122; 80-7-19, 17; Rm. 77; *[also plates of S. 1046; 82-7-4, 37]*]

S. Arthur Strong, "A Letter of Assurbanipal," *AJSL* 9 (1892-93) 1-3.

Christopher Johnston, "Two Assyrian Letters," *JAOS* 15 (1893) 311-316. [K. 828; K. 84]

Robert Francis Harper, "The Letters of the Rm. 2 Collection of the British Museum," *ZA* 8 (1893) 341-359.

George Ricker Berry, "The Letters of the R^M 2. Collection (ZA VIII. pp. 341-359)," *AJSL* 11 (1894-95) 174-202.

C. H. W. Johns, "Sennacherib's Letters to his Father Sargon," *SBAP* 17 (1895) 220-239. [K. 125; K. 181; K. 5464; K. 7434]

H. W. Mengedoht, "Letter of an Assyrian Physician," *BOR* 8 (1895-1900) 95-96.

*Christopher Johnston, "The Epistolary Literature of the Assyrians and Babylonians," *JAOS* 18 (1897) 125-175. [Part I. Selected Letters, Transliterated and Translated. K 524; K 13; K 528; K 79; K 824; K 469; K 629; K 547; K 589; K 551; K 565; K 1024; S 1064; K 519; K 504; K 660; K 515; K 1274; K 1239]

*Christopher Johnston, "The Epistolary Literature of the Assyrians and Babylonians," *JAOS* 19 (1898) 42-96. [Part II. Notes and Glossary to the Selected Letters]

Christopher Johnston, "A recent interpretation of the Letter of an Assyrian Princess," *JAOS* 20 (1899) 244-249.

Christopher Johnston, "A Letter of Šamaš-šum-ukîn to Sardanapalus," *AJSL* 17 (1900-01) 146-150.

*R. Campbell Thompson, "Robert Francis Harper's Assyrian and Babylonian Letters," *AJSL* 17 (1900-01) 160-167.

C. H. W. Johns, "Some Assyrian Letters," *SBAP* 24 (1902) 293-299.

*Maximilian Streck, "Glossen zu O. A. Toffteen's 'Geographical List to RFHarper's Assyrian and Babylonian Letters, Vols. I-VIII'," *AJSL* 22 (1905-06) 207-223.

Christopher Johnston, "A Letter of Esarhaddon (BU. 91-5-9, 210; RFHarper, 403)," *AJSL* 22 (1905-06) 242-246.

S[tephen] Langdon, "A Letter of Rim-Sin, King of Larsa," *SBAP* 33 (1911) 221-222.

*John A. Maynard, "Short Notes on the Text of Harper's Assyrian and Babylonian Letters," *JSOR* 10 (1926) 95-96.

*John A. Maynard, "Textual Notes on Harper's Assyrian and Babylonian Letters," *JSOR* 12 (1928) 155-156.

*A. Leo Oppenheim, "Assyriological Gleanings I," *BASOR* #91 (1943) 36-38. *[III. Neo-Assyrian Letter, Harper ABL 555, pp. 38-39]*

George B. Denton, "A New Interpretation of a Well-Known Assyrian Letter," *JNES* 2 (1943) 314-315.

*A. Leo Oppenheim, "Notes to the Harper-Letters," *JAOS* 64 (1944) 190-196. [Corrections, emendations, restorations, to: R. F. Harper, *Assyrian and Babylonian Letters* (Chicago, 1892-1914)]

Donald J. Wiseman, "A Preliminary Report on the Cuneiform tablets found at Nimrud in 1949," *Sumer* 6 (1950) 103.

D[onald] J. Wiseman, "The Nimrud Tablets, 1949," *Iraq* 12 (1950) 184-200. [ND 201-286]

D[onald] J. Wiseman and J. V. Kinnier Wilson, "The Nimrud Tablets, 1950," *Iraq* 13 (1951) 102-122. [ND 421; ND 424; ND 496; ND 411; ND 428; ND 437]

Donald J. Wiseman, "The Assyrian Tablets Found at Nimrud (Kulhu) in 1950," *Sumer* 7 (1951) 55-57.

D[onald] J. Wiseman, "The Nimrud Tablets, 1951," *Iraq* 14 (1952) 61-72. [ND 1103; ND 1107; ND 1112; ND 1108; ND 1110; ND 1111; ND 1113; ND 1116; ND 1123; ND 1120]

D[onald] J. Wiseman, "The Nimrud Tablets, 1953," *Iraq* 15 (1953) 135-160. [ND. 3407; 3410; 3418; 3414; 3413; 3416; 3419; 3419 (envelope); 3426; 3441; 3443; 3452; 3455; 3457; 3467; 3470; 3469; 3471; 3468; 3472; 3473; 3475; 3474; 2657; 3476; 3482; 3478; 3483; 3484; 3485; 3487; 3491; 3492; 3488; 3498; 3499]

*H. W. F. Saggs, "The Nimrud Letters, 1952—I," *Iraq* 17 (1955) 21-56. [The Ukin-zer Rebellion and Related Texts. ND. 2717; ND. 2700; ND. 2360; ND. 2603; ND. 2674; ND. 2636; ND. 2663; ND. 2779; ND. 2602; ND. 22365]

*H. W. F. Saggs, "The Nimrud Letters, 1952—Part II," *Iraq* 17 (1955) 126-160. [Relations in the West. ND. 2715; ND. 2686; ND. 2773; ND. 2696; ND. 2765; ND. 2647; ND. 2645; ND. 2381; ND. 2437; ND. 2430; ND. 2680; ND. 2644]

H. W. F. Saggs, "The Nimrud Letters, 1952—Part III," *Iraq* 18 (1956) 40-56. [Miscellaneous Letters. ND 2449; ND 2643; ND 2725; ND 2665; ND 2799; ND 2720; ND 2697; ND 2792; ND 2408; ND 2649; ND 2460; ND 2452; ND 2623; ND 2470; ND 2052]

E. E. Knudsen, "A Version of the Seventh Tablet of Shurpu from Nimrud," *Iraq* 19 (1957) 50-54. [ND 5435]

*H. W. F. Saggs, "Nimrud Letters, 1952—Part IV," *Iraq* 20 (1958) 182-212. [The Urartian Frontier. ND. 2795; 2656; 2734 + 2416 + 2457; 2655; 2635; 2677; 2673; 2608; 2463; 2453]

*H. W. F. Saggs, "Nimrud Letters, 1952—Part V," *Iraq* 21 (1959) 158-179. [Administration: ND. 2784; 2762; 2409; 2355; 2372; 2438; 2798; 2462; 2690; 2780; 2783; 2366; 2359; 2367; 2777; 2683]

*H. W. F. Saggs, "The Nimrud Letters, 1952—Part VI," *Iraq* 25 (1963) 70-80. [The Death of Ukin-zer; and Other Letters: ND. 2385; ND. 2494; ND. 2666; ND. 2486; ND. 2370; ND. 2766]

H. W. F. Saggs, "Nimrud Letters, 1952—Part VII," *Iraq* 27 (1965) 17-32. [Apologies, A Theft, and Other Matters] [ND 2771; 2387; 2357; 2648; 2448; 2628; 2701; 2379; 2671; 2380; 2703; 2478; 2681; 2407]

*H. W. F. Saggs, "Nimrud Letters, 1952—Part VIII," *Iraq* 28 (1966) 177-191. [Imperial Administration: ND. 2070; 2356; 2625; 2495; 2631; 2382; 2418; 2642; 2742; 2637; 2800]

§886 *4.4.11.13.2 Assyrian Didactic and Wisdom Literature*

*Theo. G. Pinches, "The Lament of the 'Daughter of Sin'," *SBAP* 17 (1895) 64-74.

C[laude] R. Conder, "Translations of an Assyrian Parable," *PEFQS* 34 (1902) 95-96.

*Christopher Johnston, "Assyrian and Babylonian Beast Fables," *AJSL* 28 (1911-12) 81-100.

S[tephen] Langdon, "An Assyrian Royal Inscription from a Series of Poems," *JRAS* (1932) 33-41. [K. 4874]

W. G. Lambert and O. R. Gurney, "The Sultantepe Tablets *(Continued),*" *AS* 4 (1954) 65-99. [III. The Poem of the Righteous Sufferer]

O. R. Gurney, "The Sultantepe Tablets *(Continued),*" *AS* 6 (1956) 145-164. [V. The Tale of the Poor Man of Nippur]

C. J. Gadd, "Fragments of Assyrian Scholastic Literature," *BSOAS* 20 (1957) 255-265. [K. 2459; D.T. 147; K. 9282; K. 8843 + 10230; D. T. 290; K. 5035; K. 4815; 79-7-8, 49; K. 11856]

§887 *4.4.11.13.3 Assyrian Historical Texts*

*†Anonymous, "Persian and Assyrian Inscriptions—Monuments of Darius Hystaspes," *QRL* 79 (1846-47) 413-449. *(Review)*

H. F. Talbot, "The Annals of Esarhaddon. Translated from Two Cylinders in the British Museum," *JSL, 3rd Ser.,* 9 (1859) 68-79.

H. Fox Talbot, "Translation of some Assyrian Inscriptions," *JRAS* (1861) 35-105.(Additional Notes, pp. 362-369) [I. The Birs Nimrud Inscription; II. The Inscription of Michaux; III. The Inscription of Bellino]

W. H. Fox Talbot, E. Hincks, [Julius] Oppert, Henry C. Rawlinson, "Comparative Translations of the Inscriptions of Tiglath-Pelezer I," *JRAS* (1861) 150-219. (Comments by W. H. Milman; Geo. Grote; J. Gardiner Wilkinson; and H. H. Wilson)

H. F. Talbot, "Assyrian Texts Translated," *JRAS* (1862) 124-133, 135-198. [No. I. Inscription from a Broken Obelisk of Ashurakhbal; No. II. Inscription of Sennacherib; No. III. Inscription of Pul; No. IV. The Inscription of Senkereh; No. V. The Inscription of Nabonidus]

H. F. Talbot, "Assyrian Texts Translated," *JRAS* (1862) 261-273. [The Nakshi Rustam Inscription of Darius; Appendix, Inscription of Ashurbani-pal]

Anonymous, "Assyrian Annals, B.C. 681-625," *NBR* 52 (1870) 323-365.

George Smith, "The Cyprus monolith," *ZÄS* 9 (1871) 68-72

*Daniel Hy. Haigh, "The annals of Assurbanipal considered in their relation to the contemporary chronology of Lydia, Egypt and Israel," *ZÄS* 10 (1872) 125-129.

*A. H. Sayce, "Nimrod and the Assyrian Inscriptions," *SBAT* 2 (1873) 243-249.

*George Smith, "On a New Fragment of the Assyrian Canon belonging to the reigns of Tiglath-Pileser and Shalmaneser," *SBAT* 2 (1873) 321-322.

*George Smith, "On Fragments of an Inscription giving part of the Chronology from which the Canon of Berosus was copied," *SBAT* 3 (1874) 361-379.

W. [St. Chad] Boscawen, "Historical Inscription of Esarhaddon," *SBAT* 4 (1875) 84-97.

P. A. Nordell, "The Assyrian Canon," *BQ* 10 (1876) 141-164.

Ernest A. Budge, "On a recently discovered text of Assur-nazir-pal, with Translation and Notes," *SBAP* 1 (1878-79) 28-29.

*†W. St. C[had] Boscawen, "The Monuments and Inscriptions on the Rocks on the Nahr-el-Kelb, Syria," *SBAP* 2 (1879-80) 27-28.

*A. H. Sayce, "The Bilingual Hittite and Cuneiform Inscription of Tarkondemos," *SBAP* 3 (1880-81) 4-6.

E[rnest] A. Budge, "On a Recently Discovered Text of Assur-natsir-pal, B.C. 885," *SBAT* 7 (1880-82) 59-82.

*A. H. Sayce, "The Bi-lingual Hittite and Cuneiform Inscription of Tarkondêmos," *SBAT* 7 (1880-82) 294-308.

W. St. C[had] Boscawen, "The Monuments and Inscriptions on the Rocks at Nahr-el-Kelb," *SBAT* 7 (1880-82) 331-352.

*Paul Haupt, "Wateh-ben-Hazael, Prince of the Kadarenes about 650 B.C.," *AJSL* 1 (1884-85) 217-231. [Assyrian Decagon Cylinder]

A. H. Sayce, "An Inscription of Assur-bani-pal from Tartûs," *SBAP* 7 (1884-85) 141-143.

*L. W. King, "Sinsariskun and his rule in Babylonia," *ZA* 9 (1884-85) 396-400. [94-6-11, 36]

D. G. Lyon, "On the new edition of the Cylinder Inscription of Assur-banipal," *JAOS* 11 (1885) cxxix-cxxx.

James A. Craig and Robert F. Harper, "Inscription of Ašurbanipal, from a Barrel-Cylinder Found at Aboo-Habba. V. Rawl. 62, No. 1," *AJSL* 2 (1885-86) 87-89.

Robert F. Harper, "Some Corrections to the Texts of Cylinders A and B of the Esarhaddon Inscriptions as Published in R., 45-47, and III R., 15, 16," *AJSL* 3 (1886-87) 177-185.

Robert F. Harper, "Some Unpublished Esarhaddon Inscriptions (Cylinder C; 80, 7-19, 15; P.S. and K. 1679.)," *AJSL* 4 (1887-88) 18-25.

Hugo Winckler, "The Cuneiform Inscription in the Tunnel of Negub," *AJSL* 4 (1887-88) 52-53.

Robert Francis Harper, "Transliteration and Translation of Cylinder A of the Esarhaddon Inscriptions (I R. 45-47)," *AJSL* 4 (1887-88) 99-117.

Robert Francis Harper, "Cylinder B of the Esarhaddon Inscriptions (11-$\frac{48}{315}$-4). British Museum: III R. 15-16) Transliterated and Translated," *AJSL* 4 (1887-88) 146-157.

Morris Jastrow Jr., "Some Notes on 'The Monolith Inscription of Salmaneser II'," *AJSL* 4 (1887-88) 244-246.

B. T. A. Evetts, "On five unpublished cylinders of Sennacherib," *ZA* 3 (1888) 311-331. [Sennacherib 80, 17-19, 1 [Extract]]

*Lester Bradner Jr., "A Classification of Sentences in the Sennacherib (Taylor) Inscription," *AJSL* 6 (1889-90) 303-308.

C. Bezold, "Some unpublished Assyrian 'Lists of Officials'," *SBAP* 11 (1888-89) 286-287.

Edgar P. Allen, "Some additions and corrections to Lotz's Tiglath-Pileser," *JAOS* 14 (1890) civ-cviii. *[Prism Inscription]*

Morris Jastrow Jr., "The Ashurnaṣirbal slabs belonging to the New York Historical Society," *JAOS* 14 (1890) cxxxviii-cxl.

W. Muss-Arnolt, "Notes on the Publications Contained in Vol. II. of Eberhard Schrader's Keilinschriftliche Bibliothek. I. The Inscriptions of Sennacherib," *AJSL* 7 (1890-91) 56-71.

W. Muss-Arnolt, "Notes on the Publications Contained in Vol. II. of Eberhard Schrader's Keilinschriftliche Bibliothek. II. The Inscriptions of Esarhaddon," *AJSL* 7 (1890-91) 81-103.

S. Arthur Strong, "On Some Cuneiform Inscriptions of Sennacherib and Assurnasipal," *JRAS* (1891) 145-160.

S. Arthur Strong, "Two Edicts of Assurbanipal," *JRAS* (1891) 457-475.

S. Arthur Strong, "On an Unpublished Cylinder of Esarhaddon," *AJSL* 8 (1891-92) 113-123.

S. A. Smith, "An unpublished text of Asurbanipal," *RAAO* 2 (1892) 20-22.

S. Arthur Strong, "Three Cuneiform Texts," *BOR* 6 (1892-93) 1-9. [K. 4541; K. 4445; K. 7861]

George A. Barton, "Esrahaddon's account of the restoration of Istar's temple at Erech," *JAOS* 15 (1893) cxxx-cxxxii. [BM. 81-6-7, 209]

Morris Jastrow Jr., "The Inscription of Rammân-nirari I," *AJSL* 12 (1895-96) 143-172.

Morris Jastrow Jr., "The two copies of Rammannirari's Inscription," *ZA* 10 (1895-96) 35-48.

C. H. W. Johns, "A New Eponym List. 82-5-22, 121," *SBAP* 18 (1896) 205-207. [82-5-22, 121]

James A. Craig, "The Pa-še (Išin) Dynasty," *AJSL* 13 (1896-97) 220-221. [80, 7-19,126; 80, 7-8,19; Sm. 289]

Stephen H. Langdon, "Notes on the Annals of Asurbanipal (V. Rawlinson, pp. 1-10)," *JAOS* 24 (1903) 96-102.

*Christopher Johnson, "Šamaš-šum-ukîn the eldest son of Esarhaddon," *JAOS* 25 (1904) 79-83.

A. H. Sayce, "A New Historical Fragment from Nineveh," *JRAS* (1904) 750-752.

C. H. W. Johns, "An overlooked Fragment of an Eponym List," *SBAP* 26 (1904) 260-261.

*Anonymous, "Notes and Comments. Babylonian and Assyrian Memorial Deposits," *ICMM* 1 (1905) 372-373.

Anonymous, "Notes and Comments. The Memorial Tablet of Tukulti-Ninib I," *ICMM* 1 (1905) 373-375.

Anonymous, "Nineveh and the Cylinder of Sennacherib," *CFL, 3rd Ser.,* 12 (1910) 333-335.

*Anonymous, "Sennacherib Building his Capital at Nineveh. From the New Octagonal Cylinder in the British Museum," *CFL, 3rd Ser.,* 12 (1910) 429-430.

*W. S[t] C[had] Boscawen, "The Making of Nineveh. The Great Gate Cylinder of Sennacherib," *IAQR, 3rd Ser.,* 30 (1910) 314-335.

D. D. Luckenbill, "Inscriptions of Early Assyrian Rulers," *AJSL* 28 (1911-12) 153-203.

*Stephen Langdon, "Pir-idri (Ben-Hadad) King of Syria," *ET* 23 (1911-12) 68-69. [Assyrian Text: Berlin Museum, No. 742, p. 69]

W. E. M. Aitken, "Notes on a Collation of some Unpublished Inscriptions of Ashurnazirpal," *JAOS* 32 (1912) 130-134.

Wm. J. Hinke, "An Alabaster Slab of Ashur-nasir-pal," *ASRec* 8 (1912-13) 21-27.

Anonymous, "Rock-Inscription of Sennacherib," *RP* 12 (1913) 51.

A. T. Olmstead, "The Assyrian Chronicle," *JAOS* 34 (1914) 344-368.

*Albert T. Clay, "Inscriptions of Nebuchadnezzar and Naram Sin," *RP* 13 (1914) 73-75.

S[tephen] Langdon, "A New Inscription of Extraordinary Importance for History and Philology,"*SBAP* 36 (1914) 24-34. *[Prism of Sennacherib]*

W[illiam] F[oxwell] Albright, "The Conclusion of Esarhaddon's Broken Prism," *JAOS* 35 (1915) 391-393.

C. H. W. Johns, "II. An Overlooked Fragment of the Dynastic Chronicle," *SBAP* 40 (1918) 125-130. [81-7-27, 117]

John D. Davis, "The Statue of Shalmaneser at Asshur who was Contemporary with Hadadeazer," *PTR* 17 (1919) 184-189.

Anonymous, "An Assyrian Code of Laws," *BASOR* #3 (1921) n.p.n.

Ira Maurice Price, "The Nabopolassar Chronicle," *JAOS* 44 (1924) 122-129.

John A. Maynard, "Inscriptions from Ashur," *JSOR* 8 (1924) 1-12.

D. D. Luckenbill, "The First Inscription of Shalmaneser V," *AJSL* 41 (1924-25) 162-164.

D. D. Luckenbill, "The Black Stone of Esarhaddon," *AJSL* 41 (1924-25) 165-173.

*Sidney Smith, "Assyriological Notes," *JRAS* (1925) 295-299. [Esarhaddon Chronicle, Obv. 5; Esarhaddon and the Babylonians; Ṣarīnu; Nabonidus Chronicle, iii, 26]

D. D. Luckenbill, "Notes on the Assyrian Historical Texts," *AJSL* 43 (1926-27) 208-225. [1. Ititi; 2. Shalim-ahum; 3. Ilu-shuma; 4. Irishum; 5. Shumshi-Adad; 6. Adad-nirari I; 7. Shalmaneser I; 8. Tukulti-Urta I; 9. Assur-resh-ishi; 10. Tiglath-pileser I; 11. Assur-bel-kala; 12. Assur-dan II; 13. Adad-nirari II]

Henry Frederick Lutz, "The Warka Cylinder of Ashurbanipal," *UCPSP* 9 (1927-31) 385-390. [UCBC 1206]

C. W. H. Johns, "Confirmation of Endowments to Priests and Officials by Samsi-Adad V and his son Adad-Nirari III and by Sargon in the Reign of Sennacherib," *JRAS* (1928) 519-554. (Foreword by S. Langdon, pp. 519-520) [K. 2800, Sm. 318; K. 2655]

S[tephen H.] Langdon, "A Phoenician Treaty of Assarhaddon, Collation of K. 3500," *RAAO* 26 (1929) 189-194.

*Sidney Smith, "An Egyptian in Babylonia," *JEA* 18 (1932) 28-32.

S[tephen] Langdon, "Miscellaneous Communications. Note on the Cuneiform Tablet found at Samaria," *JRAS* (1936) 501-502.

*R. Campbell Thompson, "(I) An Assyrian Parallel to an Incident in the Story of Semiramis," *Iraq* 4 (1937) 35-43.

Thorkild Jacobsen, "The Inscription of Takil-ili-su of Malgium," *AfO* 12 (1937-39) 363-366.

R. Campbell Thompson, "A Selection from the Cuneiform Historical Texts from Nineveh (1927-32)," *Iraq* 7 (1940) 86-131.

*S[amuel] N[oah] Kramer, "Langdon's *Historical and Religious Texts from the Temple Library of Nippur*—Additions and Corrections," *JAOS* 60 (1940) 234-257.

Tom Jones, "Two Inscriptions of Ashurnasirpal," *AJSL* 58 (1941) 326.

Francis Rue Steele, "Esarhaddon Building Inscription from Nippur," *JAOS* 70 (1950) 69-72.

George G. Cameron, "The Annals of Shalmaneser III, King of Assyria. A new Text," *Sumer* 6 (1950) 6-26. [IM 54669]

Fuad Safar, "Another Remarkable Text of Shalamaneser*[sic]* III," *Sumer* 6 (1950) 197.

D. J. Wiseman, "Two Historical Inscriptions from Nimrud," *Iraq* 13 (1951) 21-26. [I. Fragment of the Annals of Tiglath-pileser III (ND. 400); II. Fragment of Aššurbanipal Royal Annals (Prism-ND. 814)]

Francis Rue Steele, "The University Museum Esarhaddon Prism," *JAOS* 71 (1951) 1-12.

Fuad Safar, "A Further Text of Shalmaneser III from Assur," *Sumer* 7 (1951) 3-21. [IM 55644]

D. J. Wiseman, "A New Stele of Aššur-naṣir-pal II," *Iraq* 14 (1952) 24-44.

D. J. Wiseman, "An Esarhaddon Cylinder from Nimrud," *Iraq* 14 (1952) 54-60. [ND. 1126]

C. J. Gadd, "Inscribed Barrel Cylinder of Marduk-apla-iddina II," *Iraq* 15 (1953) 123-134. [ND. 2090]

*Ferris J. Stephens, "The Provenience of the Gold and Silver Tablets of Ashurnaṣipal," *JCS* 7 (1953) 73-74. [YBC 2398; YBC 2399]

Alexander Heidel, "The Octagonal Sennacherib Prism in the Iraq Museum," *Sumer* 9 (1953) 117-188. [IM 56578]

C. J. Gadd, "Inscribed Prisms of Sargon II from Nimrud," *Iraq* 16 (1954) 173-201. [ND. 3411]

*H. W. F. Saggs, "Nimrud Letters, 1952—Part I," *Iraq* 17 (1955) 21-56. [The Ukin-zer Rebellion and Related Texts: ND. 2632; ND. 2717; ND. 2700; ND. 2360; ND. 2603; ND. 2674; ND. 2636; ND. 2663; ND. 2779; ND. 2602; ND. 2365]

*H. W. F. Saggs, "Nimrud Letters, 1952—Part II," *Iraq* 17 (1955) 126-160. [Relations with the West. ND. 2715; ND. 2686; ND. 2773; ND. 2696; ND. 2765; ND. 2647; ND. 2645; ND. 2381; ND. 2437; ND. 2430; ND. 2680; ND. 2644]

D. J. Wiseman, "A Fragmentary Inscription of Tiglathpileser III from Nimrud," *Iraq* 18 (1956) 117-129. [ND. 4301 + 4305]

Alexander Heidel, "A New Hexagonal Prism of Esarhaddon (676 B.C.)," *Sumer* 12 (1956) 9-37.

H. G. Güterbock, "A Note on the Stela of Tukulti-ninurta II found near Tell Ashara," *JNES* 16 (1957) 123.

D. J. Wiseman, "The Vassal Treaties of Esarhaddon," *Iraq* 20 (1958) 1-100. [ND. 4327; 4328; 4329; 4330; 4331; 4332; 4334; 4335; 4336; 4337; 4338; 4339; 4343; 4344; 4345; 4346; 4347; 4348; 4349; 4350; 4351; (4451*[sic]* sb *4351?;* 4352; 4354; 4355; 4356?); X 1, 2, 5-22; 4408]

Ḥ. Tadmor, "'Azeqa in Judah in a Royal Assyrian Inscription," *BIES* 24 (1959) #1, III-IV.

J. Læssøe, "Building Inscriptions from Fort Shalmaneser, Nimrud," *Iraq* 21 (1959) 38-41.

*J. Læssøe, "A Statue of Shalmaneser III, from Nimrud," *Iraq* 21 (1959) 147-157.

Jorgen Laessoee, "The Bazmusian Tablets," *Sumer* 15 (1959) 15-18. [IM. 60240; IM. 60241; IM. 61025; IM. 61026; IM. 61027; IM. 61028]

Paul Thieme, "The 'Aryan' Gods of the Mitanni Treaties," *JAOS* 80 (1960) 301-317.

W. G. Lambert, "The Sultantepe Tablets *(continued)* VIII. Shalmaneser in Ararat," *AS* 11 (1961) 143-158.

A[lan] R. Millard, "Esarhaddon Cylinder Fragments from Fort Shalmaneser, Nimrud," *Iraq* 23 (1961) 176-178. [ND. 7100; ND. 7097; ND. 7098; ND. 7099]

*J. V. Kinnier Wilson, "The Kurba'il Statue of Shalmaneser III," *Iraq* 24 (1962) 90-115.

P. Hulin, "Another Esarhaddon Cylinder from Nimrud," *Iraq* 24 (1962) 116-118. [ND. 11308]

Louis F. Hartman, "The Date of the Cimmerian Threat Against Ashurbanipal According to *ABL* 1391," *JNES* 21 (1962) 25-37.

*Faraj Basmachi, "Miscellania in the Iraq Museum," *Sumer* 18 (1962) 48-50. [An Assyrian Bronze Relief (I.M. 62197)]

A. K. Grayson, "The Walters Art Gallery Sennacherib Inscription," *AfO* 20 (1963) 83-96. [# 41,109]

P. Hulin, "The Inscriptions on the Carved Throne-base of Shalmaneser III," *Iraq* 25 (1963) 48-69.

*H. W. F. Saggs, "The Nimrud Letters, 1952—Part VI," *Iraq* 25 (1963) 70-80. [The Death of Ukin-zer; and Other Letters: ND. 2385; ND. 2494; ND. 2666; ND. 2486; ND. 2370; ND. 2766]

Albrecht Goetze, "Esarhaddon's Inscription from the Inanna Temple in Nippur," *JCS* 17 (1963) 119-131.

D. J. Wiseman, "Fragments of Historical Texts from Nimrud," *Iraq* 26 (1964) 118-124. [ND. 4369; ND. 5417; ND. 5414; ND. 5404; ND. 5470]

R. Borger, "An Additional Remark on the Kurba'il Statue of Shalmaneser III," *Iraq* 26 (1964) 125.

*R. Frankena, "The Vassal-Treaties of Esarhaddon and the Dating of Deuteronomy," *OTS* 14 (1965) 122-154.

H. Tadmor, "Introductory Remarks to a New Edition of the Annals of Tiglath-Pileser III," *PIASH* 2 (1965-67) #9, 1-20.

H. Tadmor, "Fragments of a Stele of Sargon II from the Excavations of Ashdod," *EI* 8 (1967) 75*.

Ebbe E. Knudsen, "Fragments of Historical Texts from Nimrud—II," *Iraq* 29 (1967) 49-69. [ND. 4306; 4378; 4378A-C; 5405; 5410; 5406; 5408; 5407; 5409; 5412; 5527; 5413 + 5522; 5414; 5416; 5518 + 5524 + 5525; 5528; 5530 + 5549; 5529; 5531; 5533; 5534; 5536; 5537; 5543; 5546 + 5547; 5548; 6205A-E; 6206]

A[lan] R. Millard, "Fragments of Historical Texts from Nineveh: Ashurbanipal," *Iraq* 30 (1968) 98-111. [BM 128230; 128305; 127940; 134481; 128306; 134454; 127923; 127916; 134464; 128130 + 12867; 127840; 128117; 123425; 128302+; 127941; 83-1-18, 602; 127889; 134480; 127994; 127943; 123410; 127896; 134557; 80-7-19, 333; 122616 + 128073; 123414; 122613]

Stephanie Page, "A Stela of Adad-nirari III and Nergal-ereš from Tell al Rimah," *Iraq* 30 (1968) 139-153.

J. D. Hawkins, "The Babil Stele of Assurnasirpal," *AS* 19 (1969) 111-120.

*A. F. Campbell, "An Historical Prologue in a Seventh-Century Treaty," *B* 50 (1969) 534-535.

H. Tadmor, "A Note on the Saba'a Stele of Adad-nirari III," *IEJ* 19 (1969) 46-48.

*Stephanie Page, "Adad-nirair III and Semiramis: The Stelae of Saba'a and Rimah," *Or, N.S.,* 38 (1969) 457-458.

§888 *4.4.11.13.3.1 The Black Obelisk*

Edward Hincks, "The Nimrûd Obelisk," *DUM* 42 (1853) 420-426.

J[ames] A. Craig, "Throne-Inscription of Salmanassar II.*[sic],*" *AJSL* 2 (1885-86) 140-146.

James A. Craig, "The Monolith Inscription of Salmaneser II," *AJSL* 3 (1886-87) 201-232.

Morris Jastrow Jr., "Corrections to the Text of the Black Obelisks of Salmaneser II," *AJSL* 5 (1888-89) 230-242.

James A. Craig, "Corrections to the Text of the Monolith of Salmaneser as Given in 'Hebraica,' II., No. 3, April, 1886," *AJSL* 10 (1893-94) 106.

H. W. Mengedoht, "The Black Obelisk. Annals of Salmaneser II., King of Assyria. B.C. 858-854," *BOR* 8 (1895-1900) 111-120, 141-144, 145-158, 169-175.

*A. Fotheringham, "The Black Obelisk and the Moabite Stone," *SBAP* 32 (1910) 152-154.

*Joseph Offord, "Archaeological Notes. X. *Notes,*" *PEFQS* 48 (1916) 94-97. *[The Black Obelisk]*

§889 *4.4.11.13.4 Assyrian Legal and Commercial Texts,*
including Oaths

†J. Oppert, "On the Translation by Theo. G. Pinches of an Assyrian Tablet relating to the Sale of a Female Slave," *SBAP* 6 (1883-84) 34-35. (Reply to Dr. Oppert by Theo. G. Pinches, pp. 36-37)

[W. Pakenham] Walsh, "The Will of Sennacherib," *ONTS* 5 (1884-85) 277-279.

Theo. G. Pinches, "An Assyrian Record of Receipts of Taxes," *AJSL* 2 (1885-86) 221-222.

*E. A. Wallis Budge, "On a Babylonian weight with a trilingual inscription," *SBAP* 10 (1887-88) 464-466. *[Assyrian]*

Robert Francis Harper, "Three Contract Tablets of Asuritililani," *AJSL* 7 (1890-91) 79.

George A. Barton, "Some Contracts of the Persian Period from the KH^2 Collection of the University of Pennsylvania," *AJSL* 16 (1899-1900) 65-82.

A. H. Sayce, "Recent Biblical Archaeology. Assyrian Deeds and Contracts," *ET* 13 (1901-02) 465-466.

William Cruickshank, "Assyrian and Babylonian Contracts," *ET* 14 (1902-03) 520-521. *(Review)*

Theophilus G. Pinches, "The Fragment of an Assyrian Tablet Found at Gezer," *PEFQS* 36 (1904) 229-236. (Note by A. H. Sayce, pp. 236-237)

C. H. W. Johns, "Note on the Gezer Contract Tablet," *PEFQS* 36 (1904) 237-244.

C[laude] R. Conder, "Notes and Queries. 1. *Remarks on the Gezer Tablet,*" *PEFQS* 36 (1904) 400-401.

C. H. W. Johns, "Notes and Queries. 2. *Remarks on the Gezer Tablet,*" *PEFQS* 36 (1904) 401-402.

*Anonymous, "Excavations at Gezer," *MR* 87 (1905) 981. *[Assyrian Text]*

C[laude] R. Conder, "Note on the Gezer Tablet," *PEFQS* 37 (1905) 74.

C. H. W. Johns, "The New Cuneiform Tablet from Gezer," *PEFQS* 37 (1905) 206-210.

A. H. Sayce, "Notes and Queries. *The New Cuneiform Tablet from Gezer,*" *PEFQS* 37 (1905) 272.

*A. H. Sayce, "Recent Oriental Archaeology. Legal and Commercial," *ET* 19 (1907-08) 498-499. [Assyrian, Neo-Babylonian, and Persian Legal Documents] *(Review)*

*Samuel A. B. Mercer, "The Oath in Cuneiform Inscriptions: III. The Oath in the Inscriptions Since the Time of the Ḫammurabi Dynasty," *AJSL* 30 (1913-14) 196-211.

Anonymous, "An Assyrian Code of Laws," *BASOR* #3 (1921) n.p.n.

Morris Jastrow Jr., "An Assyrian Law Code," *JAOS* 41 (1921) 1-59.

Theophilus G. Pinches, "A Loan-Tablet dated in the Seventh Year of Saracos," *JRAS* (1921) 383-387. *[Harding Smith Collection. W. 67]*

*John A. Maynard, "The Assyrian Law Code," *JSOR* 6 (1922) 17-20.

C. H. W. Johns, "Assyrian Deeds and Documents," *AJSL* 42 (1925-26) 170-204. (Note by D. D. Lukenbill, p. 170) [Ki. 1902-5-10, 33; Ki. 1904-10-9, 13; Ki. 1904-10-9, 21; Ki. 1904-10-9, 29; Ki. 1904-10-9, 31; Ki. 1904-10-9, 43; Ki. 1904-10-9, 44; Ki. 1904-10-9, 46; Ki. 1904-10-9, 56; Ki. 1904-10-9, 57; Ki. 1904-10-9, Ki. 1904-10-9, 58; Ki. 1904-10-9, 62; Ki. 1904-10-9, 98; Ki. 1904-10-9, 104; Ki. 1904-10-9, 214; Ki. 1904-10-9, 133; Ki. 1904-10-9, 135; Ki. 1904-10-9, 136; Ki. 1904-10-9, 139+238+401; Ki. 1904-10-9, 140; Ki. 1904-10-9, 176; Ki. 1904-10-9, 143; Ki. 1904-10-9, 144; Ki. 1904-10-9, 147+ 150+230+236+240; Ki. 1904-10-9, 148; Ki. 1904-10-9, 149; Ki. 1904-10-9, 161; Ki. 1904-10-9, 162; Ki. 1904-10-9, 163+247 Ki. 1904-10-9, 164; Ki. 1904-10-9, 165 Ki. 1904-10-9, 166; Ki. 1904-10-9, 167+194+235+251+252+258 +264+294+309+312+313+348+394+396+398+399+400; Ki. 1904-10-9, 178; Ki. 1904 -10-9, 179; Ki. 1904-10-9, Ki. 1904-10-9, 180; Ki. 1904-10-9, 181; Ki. 1904-10-9, 182; Ki. 1904-10-9, 183; Ki. 1904-10-9, 187; Ki. 1904-10-9, 188; Ki. 1904-10-9, 189; Ki. 1904-10-9, 190; Ki. 1904-10-9, 192+299; Ki. 1904-10-9, 190; Ki. 1904-10-9, 195; Ki. 1904-10-9, 197; Ki. 1904-10-9, 198; Ki. 1904-10-9, 199; Ki. 1904-10-9, 200+265; Ki. 1904-10-9, 209; Ki. 1904-10-9, 218; Ki. 1904-10-9, 231+272+376; Ki. 1904-10-9, 253; Ki. 1904-10-9, 266; Ki. 1904-10-9, 267; Ki. 1904-10-9, 275; Ki. 1904-10-9, 278; Ki. 1904-10-9, 286; Ki. 1904-10-9, 293; Ki. 1904-10-9, 310; Ki. 1904-10-9, 311; Ki. 1904-10-9, 314; Ki. 1904-10-9, 316; Ki. 1904-10-9, 320; Ki. 1904-10-9, 322; Ki. 1904-10-9, 335; Ki. 1904-10-9, 354; Ki. 1904-10-9, 369; Ki. 1904-10-9, 373; Ki. 1904-10-9, 374; Ki. 1904-10-9, 375; Ki. 1904-10-9, 377; Ki. 1904-10-9, 379; Ki. 1904-10-9, 380; Ki. 1904-10-9, 381; Ki. 1904-10-9, 382; Ki. 1904-10-9, 378; Ki. 1904-10-9, 383; Ki. 1904-10-9, 385; Ki. 1904-10-9, 386; Ki. 1904-10-9, 387; Ki. 1904-10-9, 393+404; Ki. 1904-10-9, 395; Ki. 1904-10-9, 406; Ki. 1904-10-9, 402; Ki. 1904-10-9, 403; Th.1095-4-9, 43;Th.1095-4-9, 44; Th.1095-4-9, 45+232; Th.1095-4-9, 232; Th.1095 -4-9, 47; Th.1095-4-9, 48; Th.1095-4-9, 49; Th.1095-4-9, 70; Th.1095-4-9, 76; Th.1095-4-9, 152; Th.1095-4-9, 153; Th.1095-4-9, 353; Th.1095-4-9, 356; Th.1095-4-9, 403; Th.1095-4-9, K. 14383; K. 14567; K. 14554; K. 14597; K. 14992; K. 15050; K. 15052; K. 14973; K. 15071; K. 15073; K. 15075; K. 15094; K. 15182; K. 15206; K. 15183; K. 15265; K. 15308; K. 15332; K. 15420; K. 15421; K. 15424; K. 16058; K. 16627; K. 16628; K. 16629; K. 16629; K. 16632; K. 1904-10-9, 313] *(Revised by Godfrey R. Driver)*

S[tephen] Langdon, "Tablets found in Mound Z at Harsagkalamma (Kish) by Herbert Weld (for Oxford) and Field Museum Expedition," *RAAO* 24 (1927) 89-98. [Kish, 1927-1; Kish 1927-2. Case Tablet; Kish, 1927-2; 1927-3; Earliest Slave of Slaves, Barton, P.B.S. IX, No. 4]

Anonymous, "The Akkadian Law Code of Tell Harmel," *JCS* 2 (1948) 72. [IM. 51059; IM. 52614]

J. J. Finkelstein, "The Middle Assyrian Šulmānu-Texts," *JAOS* 72 (1952) 77-80.

Hillel A. Fine, "Two Middle-Assyrian Adoption Documents," *RAAO* 46 (1952) 205-211.

Barbara Parker, "The Nimrud Tablets 1952—Business Documents," *Iraq* 16 (1954) 29-58. [ND. 2079; 2080; 2091; 2094; 2093; 2095; 2307; 2031; 2308; 2309; 2318; 2316; 2320; 2331; 2332; 2334; 2335; 2337; 2338; 2339; 2342]

J. J. Finkelstein, "Assyrian Contracts from Sultantepe," *AS* 7 (1957) 137-145.

Barbara Parker, "The Nimrud Tablets 1956—Economic and Legal Texts from the Nabu Temple at Nimrud," *Iraq* 19 (1957) 125-138. [ND. 5447; 5457; 5458; 5448; 5459; 5469; 5450; 5461; 5449; 5451; 5460; 5453; 5475/7; 5475/8; 5465; 5456; 5454; 5464; 5463; 5452; 5468; 5550; 5455]

I. J. Gelb and E. Sollberger, "The First Legal Document from the Later Old Assyrian Period," *JNES* 16 (1957) 163-175.

*W. G. Lambert, "Two Texts from the Early Part of the Reign of Ashurbanipal," *AfO* 18 (1957-58) 382-387. [2. CBS 733 + 1757, pp. 385-387]

*H. W. F. Saggs, "Nimrud Letters, 1952—Part V," *Iraq* 21 (1959) 158-179. [Administration: ND. 2784; 2762; 2409; 2355; 2372; 2438; 2798; 2462; 2690; 2780; 2783; 2366; 2359; 2367; 2777; 2683]

Barbara Parker, "Administrative Tablets from the North-West Palace, Nimrud," *Iraq* 23 (1961) 15-67. [ND. 2084; 2086; ND. 2097; ND. 2098; ND. 2303; ND. 2304; ND. 2310; ND. 2311; ND. 2312; ND. 2371; ND. 2374; ND. 2393; ND. 2386 + ND. 2730; ND. 2314; ND. 2424; ND. 2431; ND. 2440; 2442; ND. 2443 (ND. 2621); ND. 2447; ND. 2451; ND. 2458; ND. 2461; ND. 2465; ND. 2476; ND. 2482; ND. 2485; ND. 2489; ND. 2490 + ND. 2609; ND. 2491; ND. 2496; ND. 2497; ND. 2498; ND. 2499; ND. 2605; ND. 2606; ND. 2607; ND. 2612; ND. 2618; ND. 2619; ND. 2620; ND. 2622; ND. 2629; ND. 2638; ND. 2640; ND. 2646; ND. 2650; ND. 2651; ND. 2652; ND. 2653; ND. 2657; ND. 2672; ND. 2659; ND. 2664; ND. 2679; ND. 2684; ND. 2687; ND. 2691; ND. 2694; ND. 2699; ND. 2705; ND. 2706; ND. 2707; ND. 2727; ND. 2728 + ND. 2739; ND. 2732; ND. 2744; ND. 2750; ND. 2754; ND. 2758; ND. 2764; ND. 2768; ND. 2774; ND. 2778; ND. 2782; ND. 2785; ND. 2788; ND. 2789; ND. 2790; ND. 2791; ND. 2803]

Barbara Parker, "Economic Tablets from the Temple of Mamu at Balawat," *Iraq* 25 (1963) 86-103. [BT. 100-109; 112-120; 123-128; 131; 136; 138-140]

R. Yaron, "The Rejected Bridegroom (LE 25)," *Or, N.S.,* 34 (1965) 23-29. *[Laws of Eshnannu]*

*H. W. F. Saggs, "Nimrud Letters, 1952—Part VIII," *Iraq* 28 (1966) 177-191. [Imperial Administration: ND. 2070; 2356; 2625; 2495; 2631; 2382; 2418; 2642; 2742; 2637; 2800]

Ninel B. Jankowska, "The Middle Assyrian Legal Document *VDI* 80, 71 Again," *Or, N.S.,* 36 (1967) 334-335.

§890 *4.4.11.13.5 Assyrian Astronomical, Geographical, Medical, Mathematical and "Scientific" Texts*

*A. H. Sayce, "Miscellaneous Notes," *ZA* 2 (1887) 331-340. [17. Agricultural Calendar (K. 98); 18. An Assyrian Augural Staff; 19. Table of Lunar Longitudes]

C. H. W. Johns, "On some Lists of Aromatic Woods and Spices," *SBAP* 27 (1905) 35-38. [Rm. 367/VR 26, No. 2; K. 4257]

*C. J. Ball, C. H. W. Johns, Theophilus G. Pinches, and A. H. Sayce, "Communications on the 'Zodiac-Tablet' from Gezer," *PEFQS* 40 (1908) 26-30.

*George St. Clair, "Notes and Queries. 5. *The Zodiac-Tablet,*" *PEFQS* 40 (1908) 78-79.

*Edward Wesson, "An Assyrian Solar Eclipse," *SBAP* 34 (1912) 53-66.

R. Thompson Campbell, "A New Record of an Assyrian Earthquake," *Iraq* 4 (1937) 186-189. [BM. 123358: TN 1932-12-10, 30 (provenance 5, 6']

*P. E. v[an der] Meer, "A Topography of Babylon," *Iraq* 5 (1938) 55-64. [Ashmolean 1924-846; 1924-810; 1924-849]

*B. R. Townend, "An Assyrian Dental Diagnosis," *Iraq* 5 (1938) 82-84. [K. 1102]

*A. Draffkorn Kilmer, "Two New Lists of Key Numbers for Mathematical Operations," *Or, N.S.,* 29 (1960) 273-308.

W. G. Lambert, "A Middle Assyrian Medical Text," *Iraq* 31 (1969) 28-39.

§891 *4.4.11.13.6 Assyrian Grammatical Texts*

*H. F. Talbot, "Four New Syllabaries and a Bilingual Tablet. Edited, with Notes and Remarks," *SBAT* 3 (1874) 496-529. [S 23; S 15; S 14; S 17; S 12]

Morris Jastrow Jr., "Assyrian Vocabularies," *ZA* 4 (1889) 153-162; 5 (1890) 31-46. [K. 2009; K 4150; K 5449; K 4239; K 4159; K 4309; K 4258; K 4200; K 5432; S. 1806; S. 896; K 4249]

Morris Jastrow Jr., "Assyrian Vocabularies," *ZA* 6 (1891) 73-89. [K. 4150; K 4449a; K 4239]

*Stephen Langdon, "An Assyrian Grammatical Treatise on an Omen Text; C. T. 20, pp. 39-42.," *JAOS* 27 (1906) 88-103.

*Stephen [H.] Langdon, "Grammatical treatises upon a religious text concerning the *ardat lilî*," *Baby* 4 (1910-11) 187-191.

S[tephen] Langdon, "Assyrian grammatical texts," *RAAO* 13 (1916) 27-34. [I. Rm. 122; II. K. 9182; 79-7-8, 188]

S[tephen] Langdon, "Assyrian grammatical texts," *RAAO* 13 (1916) 91-97. [III. 46537]

S[tephen] Langdon, "Assyrian grammatical texts," *RAAO* 13 (1916) 181-192. [IV. Sm. 5; V. K 2055 and Rm. 2, II, 29 + K 5433A]

S[tephen] Langdon, "Assyrian grammatical texts," *RAAO* 14 (1917) 1-24. [VI. K. 4342; *Ana it-ti-šu*. Tablet? = Rm. 609 obv. and K. 4316; *Ana it-ti-šu*. Tablet? K. 4342 = RM. 609, etc. reverse [RM. 485; 3591 — 80-11-12, 475; K. 4558]; VII. *Ana itti-šu*. K. 245; VIII. *Ana itti-šu*. K. 56 + 60; IX. Sm. 9; X. K. 260]

S[tephen] Langdon, "Assyrian grammatical texts," *RAAO* 14 (1917) 75-86. [XI. Tablet II or g̃ar-gud=imru=ballu; K. 152 + 4204; XII. K. 2045; XIII. K. 2051]

C. H. W. Johns, "Prince Ashurbanipal's Reading Book and Some Related Tablets," *AJSL* 34 (1917-18) 60-66.

S[tephen] Langdon, "An Assyrian Grammatical Text," *SBAP* 40 (1918) 131-134. [Rm. 363 + K. 4151]

*Theophile James Meek, "Explanatory List, RM. 2, 588," *AJSL* 36 (1919-20) 154-160.

S[tephen] Langdon, "Assyrian grammatical texts," *RAAO* 18 (1921) 37-42. [XIV. K. 4313 = K. 2030*a* + 2043 and K. 11190]

S[tephen] Langdon, "Assyrian Syllabaries and other Texts," *RAAO* 28 (1931) 117-141. [(1) K. 2057 + 2056; (2) K. 4547 and 4411; (3) K. 4320 Commentary on *Shurpu,* Sm. 306; Notes (on Sm. 28); *Texts of those mentioned above as well as:* Rm. 358; Sm. 947; K. 4555 + 11222 CT 18, 43; 19, 39; K. 9906; K. 3611; Sm. 922 + 1287; K. 8668; 98595 (Dup. of Sm. 703, CT 11, 34)]

E[phraim] A. Speiser, "New Assyrian Eponyms from the Tablets of Tell Billah," *BASOR* #49 (1933) 14-15.

O. R. Gurney, "The Sultantepe Tablets," *AS* 3 (1953) 15-25. [I. The Eponym Lists; II. The Tablet from Room M. 2]

*D. J. Wiseman, "Assyrian Writing Boards," *Iraq* 17 (1955) 1-13. [ND. 3557; ND. 3579]

B. Landsberger and O. R. Gurney, "Practical Vocabulary of Assur," *AfO* 18 (1957-58) 328-341.

Anne Draffkorn Kilmer, "The First Tablet of *malku = šarru* Together with its Explicit Version," *JAOS* 83 (1963) 421-446.

Anne Draffkorn Kilmer, "Additions and Corrections: 'The First Tablet of "*malku = šarru* '" (JAOS 83, 4)," *JAOS* 85 (1965) 208.

K. Deller, "The Neo-Assyrian Epigraphical Remains at Nimrud," *Or, N.S.,* 35 (1966) 179-194.

Benno Landsberger, "The Third Tablet of the Series Ea A Nâqu," *JAOS* 88 (1968) 133-147.

§892 *4.4.11.13.7 Assyrian Mythological, Religious and Omen Texts*

*H[enry] Rawlinson, "Bilingual Readings—Cuneiform and Phoenician. Notes on some Tablets in the British Museum, containing Bilingual Legends (Assyrian and Phoenician)," *JRAS* (1864-65) 187-246.

*H. F[ox] Talbot, "A Fragment of Ancient Assyrian Mythology," *SBAT* 1 (1872) 271-280.

H. F[ox] Talbot, "A Prayer and a Vision from the Annals of Assurbanipal, king of Assyria," *SBAT* 1 (1872) 346-348.

*Claude R. Conder, "The Collection of M. Péretié," *PEFQS* 13 (1881) 214-218. *[Assyrian Funeral Tablet]*

C[laude] R. Conder, "Notes. *The Funeral Tablet,*" *PEFQS* 14 (1882) 155-157.

W. [St. Chad] B[oscawen], "The Plague Legends of Chaldea," *BOR* 1 (1886-87) 11-14.

†C. Bezold, "Note on the God Addu of Daddu, &c.," *SBAP* 9 (1886-87) 377. [K. 2100]

*C. Bezold, Remarks on some unpublished cuneiform Syllabaries, with respect to Prayers and Incantations, written in interlinear form," *SBAP* 10 (1887-88) 418-423. [K. 4175 + Sm. 57; K. 4603; K. 8276; K. 8284; K. 4816]

B. T. A. Evetts, "An Assyrian Religions Text," *SBAP* 10 (1887-88) 478. [K.2518]

A. H. Sayce, "An Assyrian Talismanic Tablet belonging to M. Bouriant," *BOR* 3 (1888-89) 17-18.

A. Delattre, "The Oracles Given in Favor of Esarhaddon," *BOR* 3 (1888-89) 25-31.

C. Bezold, "A Cuneiform 'List of Gods'," *SBAP* 11 (1888-89) 173-174. [K. 2100]

R. E. Brünnow, "Assyrian Hymns," *ZA* 4 (1889) 1-40, 225-258; 5 (1890) 55-80. [K. 3474c.I; K. 3187; K. 8232; K. 3312; K. 3182; K. 3650; K. 8233; K. 3459; K. 8292; K. 8236; K. 9699; K. 9459; K. 3216; K. 3419; K. 8235 & K. 8234; K. 8235; K. 8717 + D.T. 363; K. 3199; K. 9594; K. 3183; K. 9430; K. 3186; K. 8237; K. 9117; K. 2361 (Column IV); K. 3193; K. 2361 (Column IV & III); S. 389; Hymn to Marduk K. 7592; K. 8717 + DT 363; Prayer of Asurnaṣirabal the son of Šamširammân to Istar of Niniveh 81, 2 4, 188]

*W. St. C[had] Boscawen, "The Kerubim in Eden," *BOR* 3 (1888-89) 145-149. [Gizdhubar Legends Tablet IX, Col II, 1-16]

James A. Craig, "Prayer of the Assyrian King Asurbanipal (cir. 650 B.C.)," *AJSL* 10 (1893-94) 75-87. [K. 1285]

S. A[rthur] Strong, "Note on a Fragment of the Adapa-Legend," *SBAP* 16 (1893-94) 274-279. [K. 8214]

S. Arthur Strong, "On some Oracles to Esarhaddon and Ašurbanipal," *BAVSS* 2 (1894) 627-645. [K. 2401; K. 883; K. 164]

James A. Craig, "An Assyrian Incantation to the God Sin (cir. 650 B.C.)," *AJSL* 11 (1894-95) 101-109.

L. W. King, "New fragments of the Dibbarra-legend on two Assyrian Plague-tablets," *ZA* 11 (1896-97) 50-62.

*Clifton Daggett Gray, "A Hymn to Šamaš," *AJSL* 17 (1900-01) 129-145. [K. 3182; K. 9356; K. 3474; K. 3650; S. 1033; 83-1-18, 427]

Clifton Daggett Gray, "Some Unpublished Religious Texts of Šamaš," *AJSL* 17 (1900-01) 222-243.

*Robert Francis Harper, "Assyrian and Babylonian Prayers," *BW* 23 (1904) 279-286.

*Robert Francis Harper, "Babylonian and Assyrian Imprecations," *BW* 24 (1904) 26-30.

*Joseph Offord, "The Omen and Portent Tablets of the Assyrian and Babylonians," *AAOJ* 27 (1905) 69-72.

*Kerr D. MacMillan, "Some Cuneiform Tablets bearing on the Religion of Babylonia and Assyria," *BAVSS* 5 (1906) 531-712. (Index to Tablets, pp. 615-616) [K. 1279; K. 1453; K. 2004; K. 2613; K. 2764; K. 2769; K. 2871; K. 2875; K. 2920; K. 3153; K. 3258; K. 3356; K. 3361; K. 3364; K. 3477; K. 3479; K. 3600 + D.T. 75; K. 3853; K. 4620; K. 4659; K. 5008; K. 5117; K. 5118; K. 5124; K. 5126; K. 5142; K. 5144; K. 5245; K. 5254; K. 5260; K. 5261; K. 5268 + K. 5333; K. 5315; K. 5333; K. 5930; K. 6160; K. 6317; K. 6400; K. 6465; K. 6497; K. 6849; K. 6898; K. 6981; K. 7065; K. 7226; K. 7271; K. 7816; K. 7897; K. 7924; K. 8399; K. 8862; K. 8917; K. 9270 + K. 9289; K. 9279; K. 9289; K. 9291; K. 9296; K. 9299; K. 9312; K. 9453; K. 9480; K. 11173; K. 11174; 33851; S. 2054; D.T. 46; D.T. 75; 80,7—19, 125; 80,7—19, 126; 81, 2—4, 247; 83,1—19, 691]

*Stephen Langdon, "An Assyrian Grammatical Treatise on an Omen Text; C. T. 20, pp. 39-42.," *JAOS* 27 (1906) 88-103.

*R. Campbell Thompson, "An Assyrian Incantation against Ghosts," *SBAP* 28 (1906) 219-227. [K. 2175]

*Joseph Offord, "Babylonian and Assyrian Dream Books," *AAOJ* 29 (1907) 17-21. *(Review)*

R. Campbell Thompson, "An Assyrian Incantation against Rheumatism," *SBAP* 30 (1908) 63-69, 145-152, 245-251. [K. 2432 + S. 1899; K. 2473; K. 2453 + 81-2-4, 194]

L. W. King, "Note on the Inscription on the Eastern Lion at Tell-Ahmar," *AAA* 2 (1909) 185-186.

*Stephen [H.] Langdon, "Grammatical treatises upon a religious text concerning the *ardat lilī,*" *Baby* 4 (1910-11) 187-191.

Stephen Langdon, "Miscellanea Assyriaca IV," *Baby* 7 (1913-23) 230-236. *[An Omen Tablet]*

*Th[eophile] J. Meek, "Cuneiform Bilingual Hymns, Prayers and Penitential Psalms. Autographed, transliterated and translated with notes from the original tablets in the British Museum," *BAVSS* 10 (1913) Heft 1, I-IV, 1-127. [K. 879; K. 2769; K. 3007; K. 3025 + K. 8917; K. 3251*; K. 3259*; K. 3311*; K 3431*; K. 3585*; K. 3658; K. 4815*; K. 5039a*; K. 5098*; K. 5117*; K. 5118*; K. 5147*; K. 5150*; K. 5160; K. 5162*; K. 5218*; K. 5303; K. 5338; K5359*; K. 5970; K. 5982; K. 6063; K. 6191*; K. 7598; K. 8447*; K. 8472; K. 8488; K. 8607*; K. 8706; K. 8898; K. 8899; K. 8917 + K. 3205; K. 8937*; K. 9154; K. 9312*; K. 9333*; K. 9475*; K. 10205*; K. 13380; K. 13937; K. 13955; S. 778; S. 1294; Rm. 272*; Rm. 373; Rm 385; Rm. 514; Rm. 603*; DT. 45*; 80-7-19, 127*; 81-7-27, 77*; 81-7-27, 203] *[* Indicates Assyrian]*

Anonymous, "Assyrian Omen Literature," *HR* 67 (1914) 197.

R. M. Gwynn, "An Omen Text Dealing with Houses," *SBAP* 36 (1914) 240-248.

S[tephen] Langdon, "Philological Comments on K. 45. An Omen Tablet in the British Museum," *SBAP* 37 (1915) 42-43.

Harri Holma, "Further notes on the Tablet K. 45 + 198," *SBAP* 37 (1915) 113-116.

Theophile James Meek, "A Votive Inscription of Ashurbanipal (Bu. 89-4-26, 209)," *JAOS* 38 (1918) 167-175.

*S[tephen H.] Langdon, "A Hymn to the Moon-god adapted for the use of Shamash-shum-ukîn, Viceroy of Babylon," *SBAP* 40 (1918) 104-110.

C. H. W. Johns, "I. A Religious Foundation of Ašurbanipal's," *SBAP* 40 (1918) 117-125.

*Theophile James Meek, "Some Bilingual Religious Texts," *AJSL* 35 (1918-19) 134-144. [K. 2856; K. 1905-5-10, 19; Ki. 1904-10-9, 64; K. 2856; K. 1904-10-9, 87; K. 1904-10-9, 96; K. 1904-10-9, 138; K. 1905-4-9 10+12; Th. 1905-4-9, 13; Th. 1905-4-9, 93; Th. 1905-4-9, 93; Th. 1905-4-9, 245; Th. 1905-4-9, 393; Th. 1905-4-9, 394]

M[ichael] Sidersky, "Tablet of Prayers for a King(?) (K. 2279)," *JRAS* (1920) 565-572.

S[tephen] Langdon, "The assyrian Catalogue of liturgical texts, a restoration of the tablet," *RAAO* 18 (1921) 157-159.

John A. Maynard, "A Penitential Litany from Ashur," *JSOR* 6 (1922) 60-62. [VAT 9939]

*Theophilus G. Pinches, "The Worship of Idols in Assyrian History in Relation to Bible References," *JTVI* 57 (1925) 10-29, 31-32. (Discussion, pp. 29-31) [Appendix pp. 27-29, *Text*]

S[tephen] Langdon, "Fragment of an Incantation Series DT. 57," *JRAS* (1927) 535-539.

*Henry Frederick Lutz, "Two Assyrian Apotropaic Figurines Complementing Kar. 298, Rev. 4-7," *UCPSP* 9 (1927-31) 383-384. [UCBC 1200]

*S[tephen H.] Langdon, "The Legend of the kiškanu, *JRAS* (1928) 843-848. [CT 16, 14, 183-204]

Cecil J. Mullo-Weir, "A *šu-il-la* Prayer to Mushtabarrû-mûtānu (=Nergal)," *RAAO* 25 (1928) 111-113.

Cecil J. Mullo-Weir, "The Return of Marduk to Babylon with Shamashshumukin," *JRAS* (1929) 553-555. [*KAR.* 360 (VAT. 10060)]

Cecil J. Mullo-Weir, "Fragments of Two Assyrian Prayers," *JRAS* (1929) 761-766. [IV R. 21* *c,* col. ii; K. 8601]

Michael Sidersky, "Assyrian Prayers," *JRAS* (1929) 767-789. [K. 8664; K. 1290; K. 3515; K. 3507]

R. Campbell Thompson, "Assyrian Prescriptions for the 'Hand of a Ghost'," *JRAS* (1929) 801-823.

M. Sidersky, "A Prayer to Ishtar as the Belit of Nippur," *RAAO* 26 (1929) 21-30. [K. 9955 + Rm. 613]

*Cecil J. Mullo-Weir, "Restorations of Assyrian Rituals," *JRAS* (1931) 259-264. [K. 9380 + 11768; K. 2625; K. 3231]

*S[amuel] N[oah] Kramer, "Langdon's *Historical and Religious Texts from the Temple Library of Nippur*—Additions and Corrections," *JAOS* 60 (1940) 234-257.

O. R. Gurney, "The Text of Enûma Elîš. New Additions and Variants," *AfO* 17 (1954-56) 353-356.

O. R. Gurney, "The Sultantepe Tablets *(Continued)*," *AS* 5 (1955) 93-113. [IV. The Cuthaean Legend of Naram-sin]

W. G. Lambert, "An Address of Marduk to the Demons," *AfO* 17 (1956) 310-321.

W. G. Lambert, "Three Fragments: Era Myth; ḪAR-ra = ḫubullu; and Text Related to the Epic of Creation," *JCS* 10 (1956) 99-100. [K. 4347b; K. 2755; D.T. 184]

*E[phraim] A. Speiser, "Word Plays on the Creation Epoch's Version of the Founding of Babylon," *Or, N.S.,* 25 (1956) 317-323.

*A. Leo Oppenheim, "The Interpretation of Dreams in the Ancient Near East. With a Translation of an Assyrian Dream-Book," *TAPS, N.S.* 46 (1956) 179-373. [(Part II. The Assyrian Dream Book, pp. 256-344) K. 3758; Sm 543; K. 8171 + K. 11041 + K. 11684 + K. 14058; K. 13330; 4103; Sm 1069; K. 8583; K. 3333; K. 5175 + K. 6001; 79-7-8,77; 81-2-4,233; 81-2-4,166; K. 3941 + K. 4017; K. 14216; K. 12638; K. 3980 + K. 6399; K. 9197; K. 6267; Sm 29; Babylon 36383; K. 2582 + K. 3820 + K. 6739; + Sm 251; K. 6663 + K 8300; K. 4570 + K. 7251; K. 2266 + K. 4575 + K. 9919 + K. 12319 + Sm 2073; Sm 1458; K. 6673; K. 10663; K. 11841; K. 6611; Sm 801 + Sm 952 + Sm 1024; K. 14884; K. 2018A + K. 12525 + Sm 477 + Sm 544 + Sm 1562; 82-5-22,538; K. 12842; VAT 14279; K. 12641; K. 10852; K. 25 + K. 2046 + K. 2216 + K. 8442; K. 9945 + K. 10456 + K. 12590; K. 7068; K. 25 + K. 2046 + K. 2216 + K. 8442; K. 7248 + K. 8339 + K. 11781; K. 2239; K. 273; K. 6075; K. 9812; K. 6824; K. 6768; K. 9038]

W. G. Lambert, "A Part of the Ritual for the Substitute King," *AfO* 18 (1957-58) 109-112. [K. 2600 + 9512 + 10216]

Cecil J. Mullo Weir, "The Prayer Cycle in the Assyrian Ritual *bît rimki,* Tablet IV," *AfO* 18 (1957-58) 371-372.

*P. Hulin, "A Hemerological Text from Nimrud," *Iraq* 21 (1959) 42-53. [ND. 5545]

E. E. Knudsen, "An Incantation Tablet from Nimrud," *Iraq* 21 (1959) 54-61. [ND. 5577]

W. G. Lambert, "The Sultantepe Tablets. A Review Article," *RAAO* 53 (1959) 119-138. [K.9141; Rm 287] *(Review)*

W. G. Lambert, "An Address of Marduk to the Demons. New Fragments," *AfO* 19 (1959-60) 114-119. [K. 3278; Sm 2013; K. 3307 + 6626 + 7035 + 8640 + 9148 + 11350 + 11767; K. 7063; K. 6210; K. 6584 + 7867; K. 13768; K. 15061; K. 3349]

W. G. Lambert, "The Ritual from the Substitute King—a New Fragment," *AfO* 19 (1959-60) 119. [K. 3239]

W. G. Lambert, "Two Notes on Šurpu," *AfO* 19 (1959-60) 122. [1. LKA 91 and Tablet I; 2. Tablet VIII 6-9]

O. R. Gurney, "The Sultantepe Tablets *(Concluded)*. VII. The Myth of Nergal and Ereshkigal" *AS* 10 (1960) 105-131.

R. Frankena, "New Materials for the Tākultu Ritual: Additions and Corrections," *BO* 18 (1961) 199-207.

*Leo A. Oppenheim, "Analysis of an Assyrian Ritual (KAR 139)," *HRel* 5 (1965-66) 250-265.

Leo A. Oppenheim, "New Fragments of the Assyrian Dream-Book," *Iraq* 31 (1969) 153-165. [K. 3608 + 9897; K. 5869 + 6768; K. 9169; K. 13642; Sm. 1423]

*D[onald] J. Wiseman, "A Lipšur Litany from Nimrud," *Iraq* 31 (1969) 175-183. [N.D. 4387 + 4405/77]

§893 *4.4.11.13.8 Assyrian Texts Bearing on Biblical Studies [See also: Assyrian and Babylonian Backgrounds §286; Assyrian and Babylonian Backgrounds to the Pentateuch §299 ←]*

*Thomas Laurie, "Testimony of Assyrian Inscriptions to the Truth of Scripture," *BS* 14 (1857) 147-165.

*E. H. Plumptre, "Assyrian and Babylonian Inscriptions in Their Bearing on Old Testament History. XVII. Esarhaddon," *Exp, 2nd Ser.,* 4 (1882) 448-461.

*W. St. C[had] Boscawen, "The Kerubim in Eden," *BOR* 3 (1888-89) 145-149. [Gizdhubar Legends Tablet IX, Col II, 1-16]

E., "Brevia: The Cuneiform Inscriptions and the Old Testament," *Exp, 3rd Ser.,* 10 (1889) 157-160. *(Review)*

*C. H. W. Johns, "The Lost Ten Tribes of Israel," *SBAP* 30 (1908) 107-115, 137-141.

*Theophilus G. Pinches, "The Worship of Idols in Assyrian History in Relation to Bible References," *JTVI* 57 (1925) 10-29, 31-32. (Discussion, pp. 29-31.)

*Robert H. Pfeiffer, "Three Assyriological Footnotes to the Old Testament," *JBL* 47 (1928) 184-187. [2. *Judah's tribute to Assyria,* (Harper's *Letters,* No. 632), pp. 185-186]

*John Gray, "The Period and Office of the Prophet Isaiah in the Light of a New Assyrian Tablet," *ET* 63 (1951-52) 263-265.

*Abraham Malamat, "Amos 1:5 in the Light of the Til Barsip Inscriptions," *BASOR* #129 (1953) 25-26.

R. Frankena, "New Materials for the Tākultu Ritual: Additions and Corrections," *BO* 18 (1961) 199-207. [K. 252 and VAT 10126]

*Stephanie Page, "Joash and Samaria in a New Stela Excavated at Tel al Rimah, Iraq," *VT* 19 (1969) 483-484.

§894 *4.4.11.14 Babylonian - General Studies*

Anonymous, "Concerning two Dialects of the Aramic[sic]* Language," *MMBR* 5 (1798) 245-246.

*H[enry] C. Rawlinson, "On the Inscriptions of Assyria and Babylonia," *JRAS* (1850) 401-483.

*H[enry] C. Rawlinson, "Memoir on the Babylonian and Assyrian Inscriptions," *JRAS* (1851) i-civ, 1-16.

*James Hadley, "On a Recent Memoir by Professor Chwolson of St. Petersburgh, entitled 'Remains of Ancient Babylonian Literature in Arabic Translations'," *JAOS* 7 (1862) vi-vii.

*James Hadley, "On Chwolson's 'Remains of Ancient Babylonian Literature in Arabic Translations'," *JAOS* 7 (1862) liv.

O. D. Miller, "Ancient Babylonian Literature," *UQGR, N.S.,* 6 (1869) 159-174. *(Review)*

*Anonymous, "Babylonian and Assyrian Libraries," *NBR* 51 (1869-70) 305-324.

H. F. Talbot, "Ishtar and Izdubar: being the Sixth Tablet of the Izdubar Series. Translated from the Cuneiform," *SBAT* 5 (1876-77) 97-121.

†J. Oppert, "Dr. J. Oppert on Babylonian Tablets," *SBAP* 1 (1878-79) 18-19. (Remarks by Theophilus G. Pinches, pp. 20, 24)

*W. St. C[had] Boscawen, "Early Semitic Inscriptions from Babylonia," *SBAP* 1 (1878-79) 44-46.

*W. St. Chad Boscawen, "On some early Babylonian or Akkadian Inscriptions," *SBAT* 6 (1878-79) 275-283.

†Theo. G. Pinches, "Remarks upon the Recent Discoveries of Mr. Rassam at Aboo-habba," *SBAP* 3 (1880-81) 109-111.

A. H. Sayce, "The newly-discovered Cuneiform Inscription on the Nahr-el-Kelb," *SBAP* 4 (1881-82) 9-11, 34-36.

*†Theo. G. Pinches, "Babylonian Art, illustrated by Mr. H. Rassam's latest discoveries," *SBAP* 6 (1883-84) 11-15.

†Samuel Birch, "Description of Hypocephali, No. 8445, 8445a, and 8445f, in the British Museum," *SBAP* 6 (1883-84) 185-187.

Theo. G. Pinches, "The State Barge of Darius," *SBAP* 7 (1884-85) 148-152. [B.M. 76-10-16, 24]

Eberhard Schrader, "A South-Babylonian Aramaic-Greek Bilingual," *AJSL* 2 (1885-86) 1-3.

S. A. Smith, "Two unedited Texts, K. 6 and K. 7," *ZA* 1 (1886) 422-427.

William Hayes Ward, "Some Babylonian Cylinders," *BOR* 1 (1886-87) 115-117.

Theo. G. Pinches, "A Babylonian Tablet," *SBAP* 10 (1887-88) 526-529.

William Hayes Ward, "Notes on Oriental Antiquities. VII. Two Stone Tablets with Hieroglyphic Babylonian Writing," *AJA, O.S.,* 4 (1888) 39-41.

E. A. Wallis Budge, "On some recently acquiried Babylonian tablets," *ZA* 3 (1888) 211-230. [1. Darius 14-12-2. (Bu 25. 88-5-12.); 2. Darius 25-12-8. (Bu. 27. 88-5-12.); 3. Darius 19-4-26. (Bu. 625. 88-5-12.); 4. Cyrus 5. 1. 10. (Bu. 59. 88-5-12.); 5. Samas-sum-ukin 14. 7. 14. (Bu. 343. 88-5-12.)]

D. G. Lyon, "On the Babylonian inscribed tablets at Harvard University," *JAOS* 13 (1889) ccxxxiv.

Theo. G. Pinches, "An Early Babylonian Inscription from Niffer," *AJSL* 6 (1889-90) 55-58.

Robert Francis Harper, "The KH. Collection of Babylonian Antiquities Belonging to the University of Pennsylvania," *AJSL* 6 (1889-90) 59-60.

J. N. Strassmaier, "Abstract of Three Papers Read at the Oriental Congress. On Some Later Babylonian Inscriptions," *AJSL* 6 (1889-90) 152.

W. St. C[had] Boscawen, "Notes on some Babylonian Tablets," *BOR* 4 (1889-90) 57-59.

Theo. G. Pinches, "A Babylonian Tablet dated in the reign of Aspasinē," *BOR* 4 (1889-90) 131-134. [note, p. 168]

D. G. Lyon, "On a lapislazuli disc bearing a cuneiform inscription," *JAOS* 14 (1890) cxxxiv-cxxxvii.

A[rchibald] H. Sayce, "Amardian or 'Protmedic' Tablets in the British Museum," *RTR* 13 (1890) 126-131. [K. 1325; S. 2144; S. 691; K. 4713; K. 4697]

B. T. A. Evetts, "Discovery of Babylonian Antiquities in the City of London," *SBAP* 13 (1890-91) 54-64.

*A[ngus] C[rawford], "Archæological Notes," *PER* 5 (1891-92) 363-365. [Interesting Tablet (Babylonian), pp. 363-365]

*S. Arthur Strong, "On Some Babylonian and Assyrian Alliterative Texts
—I," *SBAP* 17 (1895) 131-151. [DT. 83; K. 9290; K. 3452]

H. V. Hilprecht, "Old Babylonian Inscriptions Chiefly from Nippur," *TAPS,
N.S.,* 18 (1896) 5-53.

H. V. Hilprecht, "Old Babylonian Inscriptions Chiefly from Nippur. Part
II," *TAPS, N.S.,* 18 (1896) 221-282.

*[George H. Schodde], "Biblical Research Notes," *ColTM* 17 (1897) 117-
121. [The Character of the Tablets Lately Discovered in Babylon, pp.
119-120]

Robert J. Lau, "Two Old-Babylonian Tablets: edited, with a note," *JAOS* 18
(1897) 363-365.

Theophilus G. Pinches, "Some Late-Babylonian Texts in the British
Museum," *RTR* 19 (1897) 101-112. [83-1-18, 2434; 82-3-23, 271; 82-3-
23, 607; 82-3-23, 845; 82-3-23, 3363; 82-3-23, 646; 82-3-23, 1271; 89-
10-14, 224]

Theophilus G. Pinches, "Two Archaic and Three later Babylonian Tablets,"
SBAP 19 (1897) 132-143.

George A. Barton, "Note on Meissner's *Altbabylonisches Privatrecht, No.
7,*" *JAOS* 20 (1899) 326.

*A. H. Sayce, "An Early Babylonian Document relating to the Shuhites,"
SBAP 21 (1899) 24-25.

Henry H. Howorth, "On the Earliest Inscriptions from Chaldea," *SBAP* 21
(1899) 289-302.

Theophilus G. Pinches, "The Collection of Babylonian Tablets Belonging to
Joseph Offord, Esq.," *PEFQS* 32 (1900) 258-268, 378-379.

Theophilus G. Pinches, "The Babylonian Tablet in the College Museum,
Beirut," *PEFQS* 32 (1900) 269-273.

A. H. Sayce, "Notes on the December Number of the *Proceedings,*" *SBAP*
22 (1900) 86. *[Ref. Howorth, SBAP 21 (1899) above]*

*Theo. G. Pinches, "The Temples of Ancient Babylonia. Part I.," *SBAP* 22
(1900) 358-371. [K. 3089; 4374 + 8377; 4413 + 8376; 4714; S 278]
[Part II never published]

Theophilus G. Pinches, "Requests and Replies," *ET* 12 (1900-01) 47-48. *[The Egibi-tablets]*

George A. Barton, "Inscription of the Blau Monuments," *AJA* 5 (1901) 2-3.

George A. Barton, "Some Notes on the Blau Monuments," *JAOS* 22 (1901) 118-125.

George A. Barton, "Notes on an Archaic Inscription published by Father Scheil," *JAOS* 22 (1901) 126-128.

Ellen Seton Strong, "The Text of an Archaic Tablet in the E. A. Hoffman Collection," *JAOS* 23 (1902) 19-20.

George A. Barton, "Interpretation of the Archaic Tablet of the E. A. Hoffman Collection," *JAOS* 23 (1902) 21-28.

*T. G. Pinches, "Greek Transcriptions of Babylonian Tablets," *SBAP* 24 (1902) 108-119. [Sp. III. 245 + 81-7-6, 141 (35726) Sp. II. 290 + Sp. III. 247 (34797) Sp. II. 291 + Sp. III 311 (34798) VATh. 412; Sp. III 246 (35727)]

*A. H. Sayce, "The Greeks in Babylonia—Graeco-Cuneiform Texts," *SBAP* 24 (1902) 120-125.

*F. C. Burkitt, "Notes on 'Greek Transcriptions of Babylonian Tablets'," *SBAP* 24 (1902) 143-145.

George A. Barton, "A New Collation of the Blau Monuments," *JAOS* 24 (1903) 388-389.

Ira Maurice Price, "An Ancient Babylonian (Ax-Head) Inscription," *AJSL* 21 (1904-05) 173-178.

Stephen Langdon, "The Supposed Variant of AH. 82, 7-14, 1042. Where is it? Its Probable Contents," *JAOS* 26 (1905) 98-103.

*Theophilus G. Pinches, "Nina and Nineveh," *SBAP* 27 (1905) 69-79, 155. [Babylonian Tablet, 76-79, 155]

Stephen Langdon, "An early Babylonian Tablet of Warnings from the King," *JAOS* 28 (1906) 145-154.

Anonymous, "Babylonian Literature," *MQR, 3rd Ser.,* 32 (1906) 387.

*C. J. Ball, "A 'Kassite' Text; and a First Dynasty Tablet," *SBAP* 29 (1907) 273-276.

Morris Jastrow Jr., "Urumuš," *ZA* 21 (1908) 277-283.

S[tephen] Langdon, "Babylonian Miscellaneous Texts. I.," *SBAP* 31 (1909) 324-326. [I. Berlin, VA 3309, 3111; II. VA 3300]

Stephen Langdon, "A Letter concerning K. 69," *Baby* 3 (1909-10) 239-240.

Stephen Langdon, "Notes upon CT XV 7-30," *Baby* 3 (1909-10) 250-254.

Stephen Langdon, "Another *bit nûri* Text," *Baby* 3 (1909-10) 255-258.

R. Campbell Thompson, "The Third Tablet of the Series *Ludlul bel nimeḳi*," *SBAP* 32 (1910) 18-24. [S. 55]

*Stephen [H.] Langdon, "A Babylonian Nurû," *SBAP* 32 (1910) 255-256.

Ivan Lee Holt, "Tablets from the R. Campbell Thompson Collection in Haskell Oriental Museum, The University of Chicago," *AJSL* 27 (1910-11) 193-232.

Stephen Langdon, "Two tablets of the period of Lugalanda," *Baby* 4 (1910-11) 246-247.

*T[heophilus] G. Pinches, "Babylonian Inscriptions," *SBAP* 33 (1911) 155-161. [88-5-12, 91 (78905); 82-7-14, 796 (56424); S. +,375 (30648); 82-7-14, 418 (56058); K. 106; 56424, line 10]

*Ellen Seton Ogden, "A Conjectural Interpretation of Cuneiform Texts. *vol. V, 81-7-27, 49 and 50*," *JAOS* 32 (1912) 103-114.

George A. Barton, "Babylonian Section. One of the Oldest Babylonian Tablets in the World," *MJ* 3 (1912) 4-6.

George A. Barton, "The Babylonian Tablets in the Collection of George Vaux, Jr.," *AJSL* 29 (1912-13) 126-137.

Ellen Seton Ogden, "Some Notes on the So-called Hieroglypic-Tablet," *JAOS* 33 (1913) 16-23.

Frederick A. Vanderburgh, "Three Babylonian Tablets, Prince Collection, Columbia University," *JAOS* 33 (1913) 24-32.

C. H. W. Johns, "Some Babylonian Tablets in the Manchester Museum," *JMUEOS* #3 (1913-14) 67-72.

Albert T. Clay, "Ancient Babylonian Antiquities," *A&A* 1 (1914-15) 27-31.

D. D. Luckenbill, "Notes on Some Texts from the Cassite Period," *AJSL* 31 (1914-15) 79-87.

A. H. Sayce, "The Yale Babylonian Collection," *ET* 27 (1915-16) 522-523.

Elihu Grant, "A New Type of Document from Senkereh," *AJSL* 33 (1916-17) 200-202.

Theophilus G. Pinches, "The Semitic Inscriptions of the Harding Smith Collection," *JRAS* (1917) 723-734. [N. 15; Seal Impression; N. 16; N. 83]

Stephen Langdon, "Syllabary in the Metropolitan Museum," *JSOR* 1 (1917) 19-23. [BM 46537]

S[tephen] Langdon, "The Toledo Collection of Cuneiform Tablets," *AJSL* 34 (1917-18) 123-128.

*William F. Edgerton, "Lishanum, Patesi of Marad," *AJSL* 38 (1921-22) 141.

S[tephen] Langdon, "The Tablets of Uruk," *AJSL* 39 (1922-23) 282-287.

S[tephen] Langdon, "Selection of Inscriptions Excavated at Kish," *AJSL* 40 (1923-24) 225-230.

*A. H. Sayce, "Unpublished Hebrew, Aramaic and Babylonian Inscriptions from Egypt, Jerusalem and Carchemish," *JEA* 10 (1924) 16-17.

R. Campbell Thompson, "A Babylonian Explanatory Text," *JRAS* (1924) 452-457.

Samuel A. B. Mercer, "Some Babylonian Cones," *JSOR* 10 (1926) 281-286.

*Sidney Smith, "Archaeological Notes," *JRAS* (1926) 433-446. [The King's Share, pp. 436-440 (B.M. 117580)]

*C. Leonard Woolley, "Excavations at Ur, 1929-30," *AJ* 10 (1930) 315-341. [Appendix: Tablets and Seal-Impressions, by E. Burrows, pp. 341-343]

*C. Leonard Woolley, "Excavations at Ur, 1929-30," *MJ* 21 (1930) 81-105. [Appendix: Tablets and Seal-Impressions, by E. Burrows, pp. 106-107]

Henry Frederick Lutz, "An Uruk Document of the Time of Cambyses," *UCPSP* 10 (1931-46) 243-250. [UCBC 892]

T. Fish, "A Nippur Tablet of Ur III," *JAOS* 56 (1936) 494. [8291]

R. T. Hallock, "Restorations in the Syllabary Rm 2, 588," *AJSL* 53 (1936-37) 45-47.

*G. R. Driver, "A Babylonian Tablet with an Aramaic Endorsement," *Iraq* 4 (1937) 16-18.

*S[tephen] Langdon, "Tablets from Kish and Umma," *RAAO* 34 (1937) 67-79. [I. Two Tablets from the series ḪURRA = ḫubullu (Kish, 1927-2118; Kish 1924-799)]

Ferris J. Stephens, "A Cuneiform Tablet from Dura-Europas," *RAAO* 34 (1937) 183-190. [K. 575 = YBC 6518]

*J. W. Jack, "Recent Biblical Archaeology," *ET* 51 (1939-40) 544-548. [Neo-Babylonian Tablets, pp. 547-548]

H. Holma and A. Salonen, "Some Cuneiform Tablets from the Time of the Third Ur Dynasty (Holma Collection Nos. 11-39)," *SO* 9 (1940) #1, 9-60.

*A. Leo Oppenheim, "Assyriological Gleanings I," *BASOR* #91 (1943) 36-38. *[I-II; Neo-Babylonian Texts]*

*A. Leo Oppenheim, "Assyriological Gleanings II," *BASOR* #93 (1944) 14-17 *[IV-VI; Neo-Babylonian Texts]*

A. Leo Oppenheim, "Assyriological Gleanings III," *BASOR* #97 (1945) 26-27. *[Neo-Babylonian Text]*

*Charles T. Fritsch, "Three Thousand Babylonian Clay Tablets," *PSB* 38 (1945) #4, 8-9. *[Princeton University Collection]*

A. Leo Oppenheim, "Assyriological Gleanings IV*[sic]*," *BASOR* #107 (1947) 7-11. [The Shadow of the King]

*Taha Baqir, "Report on the Collection of Unpublished Texts in the Iraq Museum," *Sumer* 3 (1947) 113-117. [Forward by S[amuel] N[oah] Kramer, p. 112]

T. Fish, "Some Ur III Tablets from Lagash," *ArOr* 17 (1949) Part 1, 227-229.

O. R. Gurney, "Texts from Dur-Kurigalzu," *Iraq* 11 (1949) 131-149.

*A[lbrecht] Goetze, "Texts and Fragments," *JCS* 1 (1947) 349-352. [NCB 4848; Crozer 201]

T. Fish, "More *gá-dub-ba* Texts," *MCS* 1 (1951) 20-26. [C.B.S. 7393; H. 6246; H. 6247; H. 6248; H. 6249; H. 6250; H. 7907]

T. Fish, "Zabar (Bronze) on Ur III Texts," *MCS* 1 (1951) 37-44. *[Transliteration only]*

T. Fish, "New KUŠ Texts," *MCS* 1 (1951) 50-55. [Harvard 7782; 7921; 7944; 7963]

*T. Fish, "Miscellany," *MCS* 1 (1951) 56-57. [1. Harvard 7058]

*F[rancis] R. S[teele], "Writing and History: New Tablets from Nippur," *UMB* 16 (1951-52) #2, 21-27.

T. Fish, "Manchester Texts," *MCS* 2 (1952) 14-15. *[Texts only]*

W. von Soden and T. Fish, "Manchester Texts," *MCS* 2 (1952) 16-20. *[Transliteration and Translation of MCS 2 (1952) 14-15]*

T. Fish, "New Ammizaduga Texts," *MCS* 2 (1952) 27-30. *[Transliteration only]*

T. Fish, "New Ammiditana Texts," *MCS* 2 (1952) 38-43.

*T. Fish, "KI.SU$_7$ on Umma Texts," *MCS* 2 (1952) 54-58. *[Sumerogram in Babylonian Text]*

T. Fish, "Miscellany - Ur III," *MCS* 2 (1952) 69-76. [BM. 105442; 100418; 111749; 113132; 112943; 105596; 111794; 111802; Harvard 6671; 6328; 6262; 8065; 6382; 6761; 8069; 6289; 6291; 6743; 8084; 6329; 7991; BM 105517; 105360; 105377; 113075; 112952; 113031]

Albrecht Gœtze, "The Stela *AO* 2776 of the Louvre," *RAAO* 46 (1952) 155-157.

T. Fish, "Varia from Ur III," *RAAO* 46 (1952) 51-53, 160-161. *[BM 103417; BM 105443; BM 113010]*

*F[rancis R. S[teele], "Writing and History: The New Tablets from Nippur," *UMB* 16 (1952-53) #2, 21-27.

A. Haldar, "Five Cuneiform Inscriptions in the National Museum of Stockholm," *BO* 10 (1953) 13-14.

T. Fish, "Miscellany - Ur III," *MCS* 3 (1953) 1-15. [H. 6694; H. 9170; H. 7191; H. 6339; H. 6337; H. 6311; H. 6385; H. 6167; H. 6376; H. 6378; H. 6383; H. 6396; H. 6496; BM. 102105]

T. Fish, "Sukkal-mah at Lagash," *MCS* 3 (1953) 25-32.

T. Fish, "British Museum Texts," *MCS* 3 (1953) 84-93. [BM. 10450; 100494; 100611; 102963; 103030; 103032; 103053; 105420; 105425; 105428; 105446; 105447; 105450; 105453; 105454; 105455; 105470; 105482; 105483; 105484; 105486; 105494; 105504; 105507; 105514; 105516; 105523; 105525; 105530; 105534; 105541; 105560; 105562; 105568; 105596; 111745; 111751; 111755; 111761; 111772; 111774; 111784; 111789; 111794; 111797; 111800; 111802; 1112931; 112941; 112945; 112946; 112947; 112960; 112984; 112985; 112993; 113000; 113017; 113022; 113061; 113064; 113089; 113090; 113117; 1131122; 113132; 113136; 113141; 113144; 113147; 113154; 113155; 113162; 113170; 103437] *[Transliteration only]*

Oliver R. Gurney, "Further Texts from Dur-Kurigalzu," *Sumer* 9 (1953) 21-34. [IM. 50057; 50099; 50077; 50024; 50029; 50032; 50034; 50033; 50034; 50031; 50030; 50042; 50082; 50080; 50027; 50046; 50076; 50961; 50968; 50051; 50037; 50038; 50045; 50084; 50038 + 50087; 50047; 49976; 50964; 49981]

D[onald] J. Wiseman, "Supplementary Copies of Alalakh Tablets," *JCS* 8 (1954) 1-30.

T. Fish, "Miscellaneous Texts," *MCS* 4 (1954) 12-21. [Selection from the Nelson Collection of Cuneiform Texts, Liverpool City Museum]

T. Fish, "AOTc Tablets (unpublished),"*MCS* 4 (1954) 106-108; 5 (1955) i-ii.

A. L[eo] Oppenheim, "'Siege-Documents' from Nippur," *Iraq* 17 (1955) 69-89. [2NT 293; 295-302]

T. Fish, "Unpublished Lagash Texts," *MCS* 5 (1955) 27-32.

*T. Fish, "Lagash and Umma in Ur III," *MCS* 5 (1955) 56-58.

T. Fish, "A Tablet from Drehem," *MCS* 5 (1955) 59-60. [H. 7970]

*W. G. Lambert, "Three Fragments: Era Myth; ḪAR-ra = *ḫubullu;* and a Text Related to the Epic of Creation," *JCS* 10 (1956) 99-100. [K. 4347b *(Lexical text)*]

Beatrice L. Goff and Briggs Buchanan, "A Tablet of the Uruk Period in the Goucher College Collection," *JNES* 15 (1956) 231-235.

T. Fish, "Umma Tablets concerning KUŠ," *MCS* 6 (1956) 1-54. [a) New Texts, pp. 2-21; b) Chronological List, pp. 22-23; Word Index, pp. 34-43; Personal Names, pp. 44-52; Place Names, p. 53; Names of Deities, pp. 53-54]

T. Fish, "Lagash Tablets concerning KUŠ," *MCS* 6 (1956) 55-77. [a) New Texts, pp. 55-56; b) Chronological List of *kuš* texts from Lagash, p. 57; Word Index, pp. 58-72; Personal Names, pp. 73-77; Place Names, p. 77; Names of Deities, p. 77]

T. Fish, "Drehem Tablets concerning KUŠ," *MCS* 6 (1956) 85-103. [a) New Texts, p. 85; b) Chronological List, p. 86; Word Index, pp. 87-98; Personal Names, pp. 99-102; Place Names, p. 103]

T. Fish, "More Lagash Texts dated Šulgi 46(48)," *MCS* 6 (1956) 104-113.

*Edmond Sollberger, "Selected Texts from American Collections," *JCS* 10 (1956) 11-31. [9-12. Tablets concerning Gifts of Silver Rings, pp. 21-24 (HTS 143, HTS 144, HTS 145)]

Albrecht Goetze, "Old Babylonian Documents from Sippar in the Collection of the Catholic University of America," *JCS* 11 (1957) 15-40.

T. Fish, "A Rim-Anum tablet," *MCS* 7 (1957) 3. [Liverpool 51.63.11] *[Text only]*

T. Fish, "An Ammizaduga Text," *MCS* 7 (1957) 4.

T. Fish, "Ur III tablets from Nippur," *MCS* 7 (1957) 5-12. [CBS 7287; 7299; 7980; 7991; 8093; 8095; 8106; 8121; 8127; 8144; 8155; 8189; 8201; 8202; 8232; 8183; 9146; 9147; 9152; 9164; Liverpool 51.63.41]

T. Fish, "Two Tablets," *MCS* 7 (1957) 28. [Liverpool 51.63.125; 51.63.136]

T. Fish, "*a-šá* on Ur III Telloh Tablets," *MCS* 7 (1957) 49-105; 8 (1958-59) 1-49.

Henry W. F. Saggs, "A Cylinder from Tell al Lahm," *Sumer* 13 (1957) 190-195. [IM. 55296]

*Donald J. Wiseman, "Abban and Alalah," *JCS* 12 (1958) 124-129.

T. Fish, "Unpublished Telloh Texts," *MCS* 8 (1958-59) 50-82.

T. Fish, "A copy of the Umma tablet *BM 106055,* and copies of other tablets relating to its subject-matter," *MCS* 8 (1958-59) 83-97. *[Text only]*

Stephen D. Simmons, "Early Old Babylonian Tablets from Ḫarmal and Elsewhere," *JCS* 13 (1959) 71-93, 105-119.

*Albrecht Goetze, "Amurrite Names in Ur III and Early Isin Texts," *JSS* 4 (1959) 193-203.

*W. G. Lambert, "The Sultantepe Tablets. A Review Article," *RAAO* 53 (1959) 119-138. *(Review)* [K. 9141, pp. 122-123]

*H[enry] W. F. Saggs, "Pazuzu," *AfO* 19 (1959-60) 123-127.

Stephen D. Simmons, "Early Old Babylonian Tablets from Ḫarmal and Elsewhere (Continued)," *JCS* 14 (1960) 23-32, 49-55, 75-87, 117-125; 15 (1961) 49-58, 81-83.

*Edmond Sollberger, "Graeco-Babyloniaca," *Iraq* 24 (1962) 63-72. [B.M. 34781 = Sp. II 273; B.M. 34797 = Sp. II 290 + Sp. III 247; B.M. 35727 = Sp III 246; B.M. 34799 = Sp II 292 + 81-7-6, 142; B.M. 35726 = Sp III 245 + 81-7-6, 141; B.M. 34798 = Sp II 291 + Sp 311; B.M. 34816 = Sp. II 315 = 82-7-4, 139; V.A.T. 412; B.M. 33769 = RM IV 327; B.M. 35458; Sp II 1048; B.M. 35459 = Sp II 1049; B.M. 33778 = Rm IV 336; B.M. 35154 = Sp II 706]

*D. O. Edzard, "Texts and Fragments," *JCS* 16 (1962) 78-81. [HSM 3625]

S[tephen D.] Simmons, "Texts and Fragments," *JCS* 17 (1963) 32.

M. Civil, "Texts and Fragments," *JCS* 17 (1963) 58. [MM 841]

Albrecht Goetze, "Remarks on the Old Babylonian Itinerary," *JCS* 18 (1964) 114-119.

*Wilfred G. Lambert, "The Reading of a Seal Inscription from Thebes," *KZFE* 3 (1964) 182-183.

Wilfred G. Lambert and Peter Walcot, "A New Babylonian Theogony and Hesiod," *KZFE* 4 (1965) 64-72. [BM 74329]

*D. J. Wiseman, "Some Egyptians in Babylonia," *Iraq* 28 (1966) 154-158. [BM 57337; 56348; 49785]

J. A. Brinkman, "Neo-Babylonian Texts in the Archaeological Museum at Florence," *JNES* 25 (1966) 202-209.

I. J. Gelb, "An Old Babylonian List of Amorites," *JAOS* 88 (1968) 39-46. [TA 1930, 615]

*W. G. Lambert, "Three Inscribed Luristran Bronzes," *AfO* 22 (1968-69) 9-11.

Albrecht Goetze, "Texts and Fragments," *JCS* 22 (1968-69) 51-52. *[No registration number, private collection]*

H. W. F. Saggs, "Neo-Babylonian Fragments from Harran," *Iraq* 31 (1969) 166-169.

*Khalid Ahmad al-A'dami, "A New Lu.SHA Text," *Sumer* 25 (1969) 97-98. [IM. 67343]

§895 *4.4.11.14.1 Babylonian Correspondence*

*Theo. G. Pinches, "On a Series of Specimens of the Familiar Correspondence of the Babylonians and Assyrians," *SBAP* 7 (1884-85) 170.

Robert Francis Harper, "Babylonian Letter.—The Joseph Shemtob Collection of Babylonian Antiquities Recently Purchased for the University of Pennsylvania," *AJSL* 5 (1888-89) 74-76.

W. St. [Chad] Boscaswen, "The Letters of Khammurabi," *BOR* 8 (1895-1900) 193-201.

*Christopher Johnston, "The Epistolary Literature of the Assyrians and Babylonians," *JAOS* 18 (1897) 125-175. [Part I. Selected Letters, Transliterated and Translated. K 524; K 13; K 528; K 79; K 824; K 469; K 629; K 547; K 589; K 551; K 565; K 1024; S 1064; K 519; K 504; K 660; K 515; K 1274; K 1239]

*Christopher Johnston, "The Epistolary Literature of the Assyrians and Babylonians," *JAOS* 19 (1898) 42-96. [Part II. Notes and Glossary to the Selected Letters]

†Joseph Offord, "Letter from Hammurabi to Sinidina, King of Larsa," *SBAP* 20 (1898) 150-152.

*R. Campbell Thompson, "Robert Francis Harper's Assyrian and Babylonian Letters," *AJSL* 17 (1900-01) 160-167.

*Maximilian Streck, "Glossen zu O. A. Toffteen's 'Geographical List to RFHarper's Assyrian and Babylonian Letters, Vols. I-VIII'," *AJSL* 22 (1905-06) 207-223.

George A. Barton, "On an Old Babylonian Letter addressed to Lushtamar," *JAOS* 29 (1909) 220-223.

P. Dhorme, "A Note on the New Cuneiform Tablet from Gezer," *PEFQS* 41 (1909) 106.

R. Campbell Thompson, "A Late Babylonian Letter," *SBAP* 31 (1909) 169-171. [Imperial Ottoman Mus. #S. 54]

S[tephen H.] Langdon, "A Letter of Rim-Sin, King of Larsa," *SBAP* 33 (1911) 221-222.

D. D. Luckenbill, "A Letter of Rim-Sin," *AJSL* 32 (1915-16) 98-101.

D. D. Luckenbill, "Old Babylonian Letters from Bismya," *AJSL* 32 (1915-16) 270-292.

G. W. Gilmore, "Babylonian Letter from Larsa," *HR* 75 (1918) 432.

G. R. Driver, "Corrections in 'Letters of the First Babylonian Dynasty'," *Baby* 9 (1926) 38-40.

*John A. Maynard, "Short Notes on the Text of Harper's Assyrian and Babylonian Letters," *JSOR* 10 (1926) 95-96.

Henry Frederick Lutz, "Old Babylonian Letters," *UCPSP* 9 (1927-31) 279-365.

*John A. Maynard, "Textual Notes on Harper's Assyrian and Babylonian Letters," *JSOR* 12 (1928) 155-156.

T. Fish, "Letters of the First Babylonian Dynasty," *BJRL* 16 (1932) 507-528.

T. Fish, "Letters of the First Babylonian Dynasty. 2," *BJRL* 17 (1933) 106-120.

*A. Leo Oppenheim, "Notes to the Harper-Letters," *JAOS* 64 (1944) 190-196. [Corrections, emendations, restorations, to: R. F. Harper, *Assyrian and Babylonian Letters* (Chicago, 1892-1914)]

*Albrecht Goetze, "A New Letter from Ramesses to Ḫattušiliš," *JCS* 1 (1947) 241-251. [NBC 3934]

T. Fish, "Letters of Hammurabi to Šamaš-ḫaṣir. (BIN VII, nos. 1-9)," *MCS* 1 (1951) 1-8.

T. Fish, "Letters of the First Babylonian Dynasty. (BIN VII, nos. 10-29)," *MCS* 1 (1951) 12-19.

T. Fish, "Letters of the First Babylonian Dynasty. (BIN VII, nos. 30-44)," *MCS* 1 (1951) 27-34.

T. Fish, "A Letter of the First Babylonian Dynasty," *RAAO* 45 (1951) 1-2.

P. B. Cornwall, "Two Letters from Dilmun," *JCS* 6 (1952) 137-142.

Albrecht Goetze, "*Appendix:*. The Texts Ni 615 and Ni 641 of the Istanbul Museum," *JCS* 6 (1952) 142-145.

T. Fish, "Letters of the First Babylonian Dynasty. (BIN VII, nos. 45-58 and 220-223)," *MCS* 2 (1952) 4-13a.

*T. Fish, "Miscellany," *MCS* 2 (1952) 59-62. [3. A First Dynasty Letter, p. 62]

*Alfred Haldar, "Five Cuneiform Inscriptions in the National Museum of Stockholm," *BO* 10 (1953) 13-14. [National Museum No. 2090]

Albrecht Goetze, "Old Babylonian Letters in American Collections. I. Catholic University of America (Washington, D.C.)," *JCS* 11 (1957) 106-109.

‡R. F. G. Sweet, "Bibliography of Old Babylonian Letters," *MCS* 7 (1957) 29-48.

Albrecht Goetze, "Fifty Old Babylonian Letters from Harmal," *Sumer* 14 (1958) 3-78. [IM. 51503; 51305; 51311; 51312; 51251; 51365; 51184; 51186; 51189; 51192; 51197; 51226; 51310; 51234; 51235; 51198; 51237; 51238A; 51238B; 51240 51376; 51113; 51053; 51046; 51047; 51048; 51062; 51105; 51108; 51110; 51111; 51112; 51154; 51155; 51156; 51180; 51194; 51382; 51049; 51321; 51182; 51260 51193; 51294; 51229; 51114; 51585; 51270; 51490; 51272]

H. W. F. Saggs, "An Unaddressed Old Babylonian Letter," *JCS* 14 (1960) 56-58.

Albrecht Goetze, "Old Babylonian Letters in American Collections II-VI," *JCS* 17 (1963) 77-86. [Crozer Theol. Sem. 191, 192; Princeton Univ. Library 517, 199, 546, 947; Crozer Theol. Sem. 193; Columbia Univ. Library, (unnumbered); McCormick Theological Semin. 27; Univ. of Tex. 18]

J. Laessøe and E. E. Knudsen, "An Old Babylonian Letter from a Hurrian Environment," *ZA* 55 (1963) 131-137. [SH. 811]

*Robert D. Biggs, "A Letter from Kassite Nippur," *JCS* 19 (1965) 95-102.

Khalid Ahmed al-A'dami, "Old Babylonian Letters from ed-Der," *Sumer* 23 (1967) 151-165. [IM. 49341; 49233; 49253; 52251; 49219; 49274; 49240; 49222; 50501; 49225; 49226; 49537]

§896 *4.4.11.14.2 Babylonian Texts Dealing with Daily Life*

*W. St. C[had] Boscawen, "Early Semitic Inscriptions from Babylonia," *SBAP* 1 (1878-79) 44-46. *[Text of trade dispute before a judge, p. 46]*

*Theo[philus] G. Pinches, "Babylonian Tablets relating to Householding," *SBAP* 5 (1882-83) 67-71.

Theo[philus] G. Pinches and Ernest A. Budge, "Some New Texts in the Babylonian Character, relating principally to the Restoration of Temples," *SBAP* 6 (1883-84) 179-182.

*Theo[philus] G. Pinches, "Tablets Referring to the Apprenticeship of *Slaves at Babylon*," *BOR* 1 (1886-87) 81-85.

*Theo[philus] G. Pinches, "Water Rate in Ancient Babylonia," *SBAP* 17 (1895) 278-279. [82-9-18, 3812]

Theo[philus] G. Pinches, "Assyriological Gleanings," *SBAP* 18 (1896-97) 250-258. [81-11-3,478; 83-1-18. 1846; 83-1-18. 1847; 81-11-8,154; 82-3-23,4344 + 4773 and 4593]

Theophilus G. Pinches, "Major Mockler-Ferryman's Tablet giving the Names of Temple-Overseers," *SBAP* 21 (1899) 164-167.

Theo[philus] G. Pinches, "Assyriological Gleanings," *SBAP* 22 (1901) 188-210. [82-5-22. 946; Rm. IV., 97 (33,541); 82-5-22, 946 (54626); Rm. IV, 90 (33,534)]

C. E. Keiser, "Tags and Labels from Nippur," *MJ* 3 (1912) 29-31.

*T[heophilus] G. Pinches, "An Early Mention of the Nahr Malka," *JRAS* (1917) 735-740.

Elihu Grant, "Balmunamge, the Slave Dealer," *AJSL* 34 (1917-18) 199-204.

John A. Maynard, "A Neo-Babylonian Grammatical School Text," *JSOR* 3 (1919) 65-69.

A. Goetze, "Thirty Tablets from the Reigns of Abī-ešuḫ and Ammī-ditānā," *JCS* 2 (1948) 73-112. [I. Tablets dealing with Animals, Crozer #'s 183, 169, 174, 170, 171, 172, 175, 179; II. Tablets dealing with grain, Crozer #'s 157, 161, 160, 163, 159, 158, 164, 154, 162, 153, 151, 155; III. Tablets dealing with beer, Crozer #'s 615, 180, 167, 181; IV. Miscellaneous Tablets, Crozer #'s, 178, 168]

*Albrecht Goetze, "An Old Babylonian Itinerary," *JCS* 7 (1953) 51-72.

*Edmond Sollberger, "Selected Texts from American Collections," *JCS* 10 (1956) 11-31. [13. An Old Babylonian School Text, p. 24 (Emory 106)]

Albrecht Goetze, "Reports on Acts of Extispicy from Old Babylonian and Kassite Times," *JCS* 11 (1957) 89-105.

Donald J. Wiseman, "Ration Lists from Alalakh VII," *JCS* 13 (1959) 19-33, 50-62.

Albrecht Goetze, "Remarks on the Ration Lists from Alalakh VII," *JCS* 13 (1959) 34-38, 63-64.

Albrecht Goetze, "The Roster of Women AT 298," *JCS* 13 (1959) 98-103.

*C. J. Gadd, "Two Sketches from the Life at Ur," *Iraq* 25 (1963) 177-188. [U. 16900F; U. 7793]

D[onald] J. Wiseman, "A Late Babylonian Tribute List?" *BSOAS* 30 (1967) 495-504. [BM 82684; BM 82685]

*I. J. Gelb, "Growth of a Herd of Cattle in Ten Years," *JCS* 21 (1967) 64-69.

*Edmond Sollberger, "Ladies of the Ur-III Empire," *RAAO* 61 (1967) 69-70. [1. The Wife of Sur-Nammu [BM 134880 = 1953-4-11, 277] *seal impression,* p. 69; 2. The Wife of Ir-Nanna *[agate plaque],* pp. 69-70]

*O. R. Gurney, "An Old Babylonian Treatise on the Tuning of the Harp," *Iraq* 30 (1968) 229-233. [U. 7/80]

*Samuel Greengus, "The Old Babylonian Marriage Contract," *JAOS* 89 (1969) 505-532.

O. R. Gurney, "A List of Copper Objects," *Iraq* 31 (1969) 3-7. [Ashmolean Prism 1931.128]

§897 *4.4.11.14.3 Babylonian Didactic and Wisdom Literature*

†Theo[philus] G. Pinches, "An Early Babylonian Deed of Brotherhood," *SBAP* 8 (1885-86) 25-27, 42-56.

*Christopher Johnston, "Assyrian and Babylonian Beast Fables," *AJSL* 28 (1911-12) 81-100.

S[tephen] Langdon, "Babylonian Proverbs," *AJSL* 28 (1911-12) 217-243. [K 4347; Sm. 61; Bu 80-7-19,130; K 8358; K 13868; K 8315; K 43476]

*Stephen Langdon, "Babylonian Wisdom," *Baby* 7 (1913-23) 129-229. [Introduction; The Babylonian Poem of the Righteous Sufferer; The Babylonian Dialogue of Pessimism; The Bilingual Book of Proverbs; The Babylonian Book of Proverbs; The supposed Rules of Monthly Diet]

S[tephen] Langdon, "A Tablet of Babylonian Wisdom," *SBAP* 38 (1916) 105-116, 131-137. [IK. 8282 + 7897; K. 3364; K. 8231; BM 33,851]

W[illiam] F[oxwell] Albright, "The Babylonian Sage Ut-Napišti^{m} Ruqu," *JAOS* 38 (1918) 60-65.

*G. R. Driver, "Some Recent Discoveries in Babylonian Literature," *Theo* 8 (1924) 2-13, 67-79, 123-130, 190-197. [III. The Righteous Sufferer, pp. 123-130]

Samuel Daiches, "The Babylonian Dialogue of Pessimism: The Folly of Hunting," *JRAS* (1928) 615-618.

W. G. Lambert, "Divine Love Lyrics from Babylon," *JSS* 4 (1959) 1-15.

Moshe Held, "A Faithful Lover in an Old Babylonian Dialogue," *JCS* 15 (1961) 1-26.

Moshe Held, "A Faithful Lover in an Old Babylonian Dialogue (JCS XV, pp. 1-26) Addenda et Corrigenda," *JCS* 16 (1962) 37-39.

§898 *4.4.11.14.4 Babylonian Epics, Legends and Myths*

S. Arthur Strong, "Additional Note on a Fragment of the Adapa-Legend," *SBAP* 17 (1895) 44.

Morris Jastrow Jr., "A new fragment of the Babylonian Etana Legend," *BAVSS* 3 (1898) 363-383.

Christopher Johnston, "On a Passage in the Babylonian Nimrod Epic," *AJSL* 16 (1899-1900) 30-36.

Morris Jastrow Jr., "Another Fragment of the Etana Myth," *JAOS* 30 (1909-10) 101-131.

*T[heophilus] G. Pinches, "Enlil and Ninlil, the Older Bel and Beltis," *SBAP* 33 (1911) 77-95. [BM 80-11-12, 484]

*Anonymous, "Three Babylonian Documents," *HR* 69 (1915) 108-111. [Sumerian Epic of Paradise, the Flood, and the Fall of Man, p. 109]

A. H. Sayce, "Two Early Babylonian Historical Legends," *SBAP* 37 (1915) 195-200. [K. 2546; K. 4445]

Theophilus G. Pinches, "The Legend of Divine Lovers: Enlil and Ninlil," *JRAS* (1919) 1895-205, 575-580. [BM 80-11-12, 484]

Leon Legrain, "Nippur's Golden Treasure," *MJ* 11 (1920) 133-139.

D. D. Luckenbill, "An Early Version of the Atra-ḫasis Epic," *AJSL* 39 (1922-23) 153-160.

W[illiam] F[oxwell] Albright, "Some Notes on the Early Babylonian Text of the Atraḫasîs Epic," *AJSL* 40 (1923-24) 134-135.

*G. R. Driver, "Some Recent Discoveries in Babylonian Literature," *Theo* 8 (1924) 2-13, 67-79, 123-130, 190-197. [I. The Epic of Creation, pp. 2-13]

Stephen Langdon, "The Legend of Etana and the Eagle, or the Epical Poem 'The city they hated'," *Baby* 12 (1931) 1-56.

T. Fish, "The Zu Bird," *BJRL* 31 (1948) 162-171.

*Hildegard Lewy, "The Babylonian Background of the Kay Kâûs Legend," *ArOr* 17 (1949) Part 2, 28-109.

Jørgen Læssøe, "The Atraḫasīs Epic: a Babylonian History of Mankind," *BO* 13 (1956) 89-102.

*W. G. Lambert, "Three Fragments: Era Myth; ḪAR-ra = *ḫubullu;* and a Text Related to the Epic of Creation," *JCS* 10 (1956) 99-100. [K. 2755; D.T. 184]

J. J. Finkelstein, "The So-Called 'Old Babylonian Kutha Legend'," *JCS* 11 (1957) 83-88.

W. G. Lambert, "Three Unpublished Fragments of Tukulti-Ninurta Epic," *AfO* 18 (1957-58) 38-51. [BM. 121033; BM. 98730 (Th. 1905-4-9, 236); BM. 98731 (Th. 1905-4-9, 234); VAT. 9596 + 12960; VAT. 10358; Rm. 142]

Erica Reiner, "More Fragments of the Epic of Era. A Review Article," *JNES* 17 (1958) 41-48.

W. L. Moran, "A New Fragment of DIN.TIR.KI = *BĀBILU* and *ENŪMA ELIŠ* VI 61-66," *SBO* 3 (1959) 257-265. [K. 10924; K. 3089]

B. Landsberger and J. V. Kinnier Wilson, "The Fifth Tablet of *Enuma Eliš,*" *JNES* 20 (1961) 154-179.

W. G. Lambert, "The Fifth Tablet of the Era Epic," *Iraq* 24 (1962) 119-125.

J. V. Kinnier Wilson, "Some Contributions to the Legend of Etana," *Iraq* 31 (1969) 8-17. [K. 2606; Sm 1839; Sm 157 + 1134; 81-1-18, 489; K. 8572]

W. G. Lambert, "New Evidence for the First Line of *Atra-ḫasīs,*" *Or, N.S.,* 38 (1969) 535-538.

§899 *4.4.12.13.4.1 The Gilgamesh Epic and "Flood Stories"*

M. Bennett, "The Chaldean Legend of the Flood," *DUM* 81 (1873) 146-157.

George Smith, "The Chaldean Account of the Deluge," *SBAT* 2 (1873) 213-234.

*A. H. Sayce, "The Chaldean Account of the Deluge, and Its Relation to the Old Testament," *TRL* 10 (1873) 364-377.

G. Smith, "The Eleventh Tablet of the Izdubar Legends. *The Chaldean Account of the Deluge,*" *SBAT* 3 (1874) 530-596.

H. F[ox] Talbot, "Commentary on the Deluge Tablet," *SBAT* 4 (1875) 49-83.

H. Fox Talbot, "A Tablet in the British Museum, relating apparently to the Deluge," *SBAT* 4 (1875) 129-131.

*Paul Haupt, "The Cuneiform Account of the Flood," *ONTS* 3 (1883-84) 77-85.

Paul Haupt, "The Dimensions of the Babylonian Ark," *AJP* 9 (1888) 419-424.

*Maximilian Lindsay Kellner, "The Deluge in the Izdubar Epic and in the Old Testament," *CR* 53 (1889) 40-66.

Theo. G. Pinches, "Exit Guṣṭabar!" *BOR* 4 (1889-90) 264.

*John D. Davis, "The Babylonian Flood-Legend and the Hebrew Record of the Deluge," *PR* 10 (1889) 415-431.

Paul Haupt, "On the dimensions of the Babylonian Ark," *JAOS* 14 (1890) lxxxix-xc.

J. Oppert, "The Chaldean Perseus," *BOR* 5 (1891) 1-3.

Terrien de Lacouperie, "Ashnunnak and the Flood of Umliash," *BOR* 6 (1892-93) 73-78.

W. Muss-Arnolt, "Remarks introductory to a comparative study on the translation of the Deluge-tablets, with special reference to Dr. P. Jensen's *Kosmologie,*" *JAOS* 15 (1893) cxc-cxcv.

W. St. Chad Boscawen, "Hymn to Gilgames," *BOR* 7 (1893-94) 121-125.

W. W. Moore, "The Chaldean Story of the Flood," *USR* 5 (1893-94) 249-261.

W. Muss-Arnolt, "The Chaldean Account of the Deluge. A Revised Translation," *BW* 3 (1894) 109-118.

*Fritz Hommel, "A Supplement Note to Gibil-Gamish," *SBAP* 16 (1893-94) 13-15.

P[aul] Haupt, "On a modern reproduction of the eleventh tablet of the Babylonian Nimrod Epic and a new fragment of the Chaldean account of the Deluge," *JAOS* 16 (1894-96) ix-xii.

Paul Haupt, "On two passages in the Chaldean Flood-tablet," *JAOS* 16 (1894-96) cv-cxi, cxxxix.

Anonymous, "The Babylonian Flood Legend," *MR* 77 (1897) 476-479.

*A. H. Sayce, "Assyriaca," *ET* 9 (1897-98) 480. *[Flood Tablet]*

J. A. Selbie, "Professor Sayce and a Recently Discovered Deluge Tablet," *ET* 9 (1897-98) 377-378.

T. K. Cheyne, "A Communication on a Fresh Form of the Deluge-Story," *OSHTP* (1897-98) 39.

A. H. Sayce, "Recent Biblical Archaeology. The New Babylonian Version of the Story of the Deluge," *ET* 10 (1898-99) 201-202.

Joseph Bruneau, "Biblical Research. IV. A New Tablet of the Deluge (Twenty-Fourth Century B.C.)," *AER* 18 (1898) 56-57.

Joseph Bruneau, "Biblical Research. I. Archaeology and its Discoveries. *The New Babylonian Account of the Deluge*," *AER* 18 (1898) 272-274.

*Joseph Offord, "Two Texts Referred to in Report of the Oriental Congress," *SBAP* 20 (1898) 53-55. [A New Fragment of the Babylonian Deluge Story, pp. 53-54]

Morris Jastrow Jr., "Adraḫasis and Parnapištim," *ZA* 13 (1898) 288-301.

*J. A. Selbie, "Professor Sayce and Recent Archaeological Discoveries," *ET* 10 (1898-99) 278-279. *[Babylonian Deluge Story]*

A. H. Sayce, "Professor Sayce and Recent Archaeological Discoveries," *ET* 10 (1898-99) 332. *[Babylonian Deluge Story]*

J. N. Fradenburgh, "The Deluge Tablets," *AAOJ* 22 (1900) 295-300.

C. H. W. Johns, "The Babylonian Noah's Ark," *Exp, 6th Ser.,* 3 (1901) 214-219.

Paul Haupt, "The Beginning of the Babylonian Nimrod Epic," *JAOS* 22 (1901) 7-12.

George Smith, "The Chaldean Account of the Deluge," *RP* 1 (1902) 363-376.

†Paul Haupt, "Translation of the Deluge Tablet (XI) and Biblical References," *RP* 1 (1902) 376-380.

[Theophilus G. Pinches], "The Story of Gilgames," *AAOJ* 25 (1903) 185-188.

T[heophilus] G. Pinches, "Gilgames and the Hero of the Flood," *SBAP* 25 (1903) 113-122, 195-201.

Paul Haupt, "The Introductory Lines of the Cuneiform Account of the Deluge," *JAOS* 25 (1904) 68-75.

*Samuel Daiches, "Ezekiel and the Babylonian Account of the Deluge," *JQR* 17 (1904-05) 441-455.

John Deneley Prince and Frederick A. Vanderburgh, "The New Hilprecht Deluge Tablet," *AJSL* 26 (1909-10) 303-308.

Theophilus G. Pinches, "The Oldest Library in the World and the New Deluge Tablets. I.," *ET* 21 (1909-10) 364-368.

Fritz Hommel, "The Oldest Library in the World and the New Deluge Tablets. II.," *ET* 21 (1909-10) 368-369.

George A. Barton, "Another View of Professor Hilprecht's Fragment of a Deluge Tablet," *ET* 21 (1909-10) 504-507.

Anonymous, "Hilprecht's Deluge Tablet," *MR* 92 (1910) 647-650.

[Paul Carus], "A New Deluge Fragment," *OC* 24 (1910) 310-312. *[Hilprecht's Fragment]*

Frank H. Ridgley, "The Nippur Version of the Flood Narrative," *BWTS* 3 (1910-11) #3, 16-25.

A. H. Sayce, "The Earliest Version of the Babylonian Deluge Story," *ET* 22 (1910-11) 45.

T[heophilus] G. Pinches, "The Date of Professor Hilprecht's New Deluge Fragment," *ET* 22 (1910-11) 89.

George A. Barton, "The Twelfth Line of Hilprecht's Deluge Tablet," *ET* 22 (1910-11) 89-90.

George A. Barton, "Another Word as to the Date of Hilprecht's Deluge Tablet," *ET* 22 (1910-11) 278-279.

George A. Barton, "Hilprecht's Fragment of the Babylonian Deluge Story," *JAOS* 31 (1910-11) 30-48.

Paul Haupt, "Some Difficult Passages in the Cuneiform Account of the Deluge," *JAOS* 32 (1912) 1-16.

Theophilus G. Pinches, "The Newly-Discovered Version of the Story of the Flood," *JTVI* 43 (1911) 135-150. (Discussion, pp. 150-158)

L. W. King, "A New Fragment of the Gilgamesh Epic," *SBAP* 36 (1914) 64-68. [Ki 1904-10-9,19]

*Theophilus G. Pinches, "The Niffer Story of the Creation and the Flood," *ET* 26 (1914-15) 490-494.

*[Julian] Morgenstern, "On Gilgames-Epic XI, 274-320. A Contribution to the Study of the Role of the Serpent in Semitic Mythology," *ZA* 29 (1914-15) 284-300.

*Anonymous, "Three Babylonian Documents," *HR* 69 (1915) 108-111. [Sumerian Epic of Paradise, the Flood, and the Fall of Man, p. 109]

*Theophilus G. Pinches, "The Old and New Versions of the Babylonian Creation and Flood Stories," *JTVI* 47 (1915) 301-322, 327-328. (Discussion, pp. 322-327)

*Anonymous, "A New Version of the Flood and the Fall of Man," *MR* 97 (1915) 313-317.

Anonymous, "'The New Flood Tablet' (?)" *MR* 98 (1916) 630-635.

Stephen Langdon, "The Epic of Gilgamish," *MJ* 8 (1917) 29-38.

*A. H. Sayce, "The Hittite Version of the Epic of Gilgames," *JRAS* (1923) 559-571.

*Sidney Smith, "Assyriological Notes," *JRAS* (1926) 433-446. [The Face of Humbaba, pp. 440-442. [BM. 116737] *(mask)*]

*Sidney Smith, "The Face of Hambaba," *AAA* 11 (1924) 107-114. *[Gilgamesh Epic]*

W[illiam] F[oxwell] Albright, "Gilgamesh and Engidu, Mesopotamian Genii of Fecundity," *JAOS* 40 (1920) 307-335.

*Paul Haupt, "Philological and Linguistic Studies," *AJP* 46 (1925) 197-212. [6. Odyssey and Gilgames Epic, pp. 208-211]

S[tephen] Langdon, "Philological Note on the Epic of Gilgamish, Book XI, 88," *JRAS* (1925) 718-720 *[Line 46]*

Paul Haupt, "The Cuneiform Flood Tablet, Restoration of II. 48-80," *OOR* 1 (1926) #2, 8-9.

Paul Haupt, "The Ship of the Babylonian Noah," *BAVSS* 10 (1927) Heft 2, 1-30.

Paul Haupt, "A Cuneiform Description of a Volcanic Eruption," *BAVSS* 10 (1927) Heft 2, 133-136. *[Gilgamesh Epic]*

S[tephen] Langdon, "Notes on the Philadelphia and Yale Tablets of the Gilgamish Epic," *JRAS* (1929) 343-347.

*Thorkild Jacobsen, "How did Gilgameš oppress Uruk?" *AO* 8 (1930) 62-74.

*Stephen Langdon, "The Sumerian Edition of the Epic of Gilgamish," *A&A* 33 (1932) 295-296, 332.

*S[tephen] Langdon, "The Sumerian Epic of Gilgamish," *JRAS* (1932) 911-947. [Kish 1932, 155]

S[amuel] Noah Kramer, "Gilgamesh and the Willow Tree," *OC* 50 (1936) 100-106.

*S[amuel] N[oah] Kramer, "The Death of Gilgamesh," *BASOR* #94 (1944) 2-12. [UM 29-16-86]

*S[amuel] N[oah] Kramer, "Dilmun, the Land of the Living," *BASOR* #96 (1944) 18-28.

*S[amuel] N[oah] Kramer, "The Epic of Gilgameš and Its Sumerian Sources. A Study in Literary Evolution," *JAOS* 64 (1944) 7-23.

*S[amuel] N[oah] Kramer, "Corrections to "The Epic of Gilgameš and Its Sumerian Sources'," *JAOS* 64 (1944) 83.

Emil G. Kraeling, "Xisouthros, Deucalion and the Flood Traditions," *JAOS* 67 (1947) 177-183. *[Berossos account of the Flood]*

*Samuel Noah Kramer, "Gilgamesh in the Land of the Living," *JCS* 1 (1947) 3-46. [YBC 9857; UM 29-13-209 + 29-16-414; UM 29-13-473; UM 29-15-364; CBS 7914; U 29-16-84; UIOM 1057]

Samuel Noah Kramer, "Gilgamesh and Agga," *AJA* 53 (1949) 1-18. (With Comments by Thorkild Jacobsen, pp. 17-18)

Alexander Heidel, "A Neo-Babylonian Gilgamesh Fragment," *JNES* 11 (1952) 140-143. [A. 3444]

*Cyrus H. Gordon, "Marginal Notes on the Ancient Middle East," *JKF* 2 (1952-53) 50-61. [VI. Babyloniaca: c. Notes on the 11th tablet of the Gilgamesh Epic, pp. 56-57]

O. E. Ravn, "The Passage on Gilgamesh and the Wives of Uruk," *BO* 10 (1953) 12-13.

Anonymous, "Cuneiform Tablets," *IEJ* 5 (1955) 274. *[Gilgamesh Epic]*

O. R. Gurney, "Two Fragments of the Epic of Gilgamesh from Sultantepe," *JCS* 8 (1954) 87-95. [1. S.U. 51, 129A(+) 237. Tablet VII; 2. S.U. 51, 7 Tablet VIII]

G. G. Garner, "Writing in the Ancient World: Part II. An Important Tablet Discovery," *AT* 1 (1956-57) #2, 5-6, 16.

*Samuel Noah Kramer, "Gilgamesh and the First Dynasty of Ur: A New and Unexpected Synchronism in Third Millennium Chronology," *AJA* 61 (1957) 184.

O. R. Gurney, "The Sultantepe Tablets *(continued),*" *AS* 7 (1957) 127-136. [VI. A Letter of Gilgamesh]

E[phraim] A. Speiser, "Gilgamesh VI 40," *JCS* 12 (1958) 41-42.

*A. Goetze and S. Levy, "Fragment of the Gilgamesh Epic from Megiddo," *'Atiqot* 2 (1959) 121-128.

W. G. Lambert, "New Light on the Babylonian Flood," *JSS* 5 (1960) 113-123.

S. G. F. Brandon, "The Epic of Gilgamesh: A Mesopotamian History," *HT* 11 (1961) 18-27.

A[lan] R. Millard, "Gilgamesh X: New Fragments," *Iraq* 26 (1964) 99-105.

C. J. Gadd, "Some Contributions to the Gilgamesh Epic," *Iraq* 28 (1966) 105-121. [V.E.T. VI, 394 (restored)]

Samuel Noah Kramer, "Reflections on the Mesopotamian Flood: The Cuneiform Data New and Old," *Exped* 9 (1966-67) #4, 12-18.

Anonymous, "The Babylonian Record of The Flood," *BH* 4 (1968) 24-28.

Tomasz Marszewski, "The 'Cedar-Land' Motif in the Sumerian Poem about Gilgamesh: The Problem of its Origin," *FO* 11 (1969) 201-222.

Hope Nash Wolff, "Gilgamesh, Enkidu, and the Heroic Life," *JAOS* 88 (1969) 392-398.

*Ruggero Stefanini, "Enkidu's Dream in the Hittite 'Gilgamesh'," *JNES* 28 (1969) 40-47.

§900 *4.4.11.14.5 Babylonian Geographical Texts*

*W[illiam] F[oxwell] Albright, "A Babylonian Geographical Treatise on Sargon of Akkad's Empire," *JAOS* 45 (1925) 193-245.

P. E. Van der Meer, "Topographical Texts of Babylon," *AfO* 13 (1939-41) 124-127. [BM 34798 = Sp. II, 291 + Sp. III, 311; K. 4153; Rm 921; 79-7-8, 291; Rm. 350]

S[amuel] N[oah] Kramer, "Foreword to the Harmal Geographical List," *Sumer* 3 (1947) 48-49.

*Selim J. Levy, "Harmal Geographical List," *Sumer* 3 (1947) 50-83.

*William W. Hallo, "The Road to Emar," *JCS* 18 (1964) 57-88. [YBC 4499]

§901 *4.4.11.14.6 Babylonian Historical Texts*

H. F[ox] Talbot, "On the Inscription of Khammurabi," *JRAS* (1863) 445-451.

Theophilus G. Pinches, "A new fragment of the History of Nebuchadnezzar III," *SBAP* 1 (1878-79) 12-14.

*W. St. Chad Boscawen, "Babylonian Dated Tablets, and the Canon of Ptolemy," *SBAT* 6 (1878-79) 1-78. (Discussion, pp. 79-133)

H. F. Talbot, "The Defence of a Magistrate falsely accused. From a Tablet in the British Museum," *SBAT* 6 (1878-79) 289-304.

*O. D. Miller, "The Antiquity of Sacred Writings in the Valley of the Euphrates," *OBJ* 1 (1880) 75-80.

*Theo. G. Pinches, "On a Cuneiform Tablet relating to the Capture of Babylon by Cyrus, and the Events which preceded and led to it," *SBAT* 7 (1880-82) 139-176.

*Theo. G. Pinches, "A New Fragment of the History of Nebuchadnezzer III," *SBAT* 7 (1880-82) 210-225.

Francis Brown, "The New Cuneiform Inscriptions on the Nahr-el-Kelb," *PR* 3 (1882) 168.

*Theo. G. Pinches, "Some recent Discoveries bearing on the Ancient History and Chronology of Babylonia," *SBAP* 5 (1882-83) 6-12. (Remarks by J. Oppert, p. 12)

Theo. G. Pinches and Ernest A Budge, "An Edict of Nebuchadnazzar, I, *c.* B.C. 1150," *SBAP* 6 (1883-84) 144-170.

*John P. Peters, "Miscellaneous Notes," *AJSL* 1 (1884-85) 115-119. [Inscription of Nebuchadnezzar I, pp. 118-119]

J. F. X. O'Conor, "The Cylinder of Nebukadnezzar*[sic]* at New York," *AJSL* 1 (1884-85) 201-209.

Ernest A. Budge, "Nebuchadnezzar, King of Babylon—On Recently Discovered Inscriptions of this King," *JTVI* 18 (1884-85) 140-182. (Discussion, pp. 183-191)

*Theo. G. Pinches, "The Early Babylonian King-Lists," *SBAP* 7 (1884-85) 65-71.

*William Simpson, "Exhibition of Photograph of Inscription from Hamadan," *SBAP* 7 (1884-85) 132. (Remarks by Theo. G. Pinches, pp. 132-133) *[Semitic Babylonian]*

J. F. X. O'Conor, "Inscription of Nebuchadnezzar, Variants of an Unpublished Duplicate of the New York Cylinder," *AJSL* 3 (1886-87) 166-170.

S. Alden Smith, "The Borsippa Inscription of Nebuchadnezzar," *BOR* 1 (1886-87) 133-137.

Theo. G. Pinches, "The Babylonian Chronicle," *JRAS* (1887) 655-681.

W. St. Chad Boscawen, "Inscriptions relating to Belshazzar," *BOR* 2 (1887-88) 14-18. [S. + 329.76.11.17]

C. J. Ball, "Inscriptions of Nebuchadrezzar II. Part I. The India House Inscription," *SBAP* 10 (1887-88) 87-129.

E. A. Wallis Budge, "Cylinder of Neriglissar," *SBAP* 10 (1887-88) 146.

C. J. Ball, "Inscriptions of Nebuchadrezzar II. II. The Phillipps' Cylinder," *SBAP* 10 (1887-88) 215-230, 299-300.

C. J. Ball, "Inscriptions of Nebuchadrezzar II," *SBAP* 10 (1887-88) 290-299. [III. The Cylinder of Mr. Rich; IV. A Cylinder from Babylon; V. The Cylinder from Senkereh]

C. J. Ball, "Inscriptions of Nebuchadrezzar. VI. The Cylinder marked 68-7-9 I," *SBAP* 10 (1887-88) 359-368.

*C. J. Ball, "New readings of the Hieroglyphs from Northern Syria," *SBAP* 10 (1887-88) 437-449. [The Seal (?) of Tarcondemus, pp. 439-442]

Francis Brown, "The Babylonian 'List of Kings' and the 'Chronicle'," *PR* 9 (1888) 293-299.

Karl Bezold, "Two Inscriptions of Nabonidus," *SBAP* 11 (1888-89) 84-103.

C. J. Ball, "Inscriptions of Nebuchadrezzar the Great. VII. The Cylinders from Birs Nimrud. K. 1685; K. 1686; K. 1687 (a fragment)," *SBAP* 11 (1888-89) 116-123.

C. J. Ball, "Inscriptions of Nebuchadrezzar the Great. VIII. The Cylinders regisered A.H. 82, 7-14, 631, and A.H. 82, 7-14, 649," *SBAP* 11 (1888-89) 124-130.

C. J. Ball, "Inscriptions of Nebuchadrezzar the Great. Part IX. The Cylinder 85, 4-30, British Museum," *SBAP* 11 (1888-89) 159-160.

C. Bezold, "On Two Duplicates of the Babylonian Chronicle," *SBAP* 11 (1888-89) 131-138.

C. J. Ball, "Inscriptions of Nebuchadrezzar the Great. Part X. The Cylinder A.H. 82-7-14, 1042, British Museum," *SBAP* 11 (1888-89) 195-210.

C. J. Ball, "Notes on the Cylinders 68-7-9, I (5 R. 34) and A.H. 82-7-14, 1042 [(A) and (B)]," *SBAP* 11 (1888-89) 211-218.

C. J. Ball, "Inscriptions of Nebuchadrezzer the Great. XI. The Nin-Mag Cylinder," *SBAP* 11 (1888-89) 248-253. [RM. 676, 12042, and $8\frac{81}{1}$ 30]

C. J. Ball, "Inscriptions of Nebuchadrezzar the Great. Two Passages of Cylinder 85, 4-30, I," *SBAP* 11 (1888-89) 320-325.

C. Bezold, "Some Notes on the 'Nin-Mag' Inscription," *SBAP* 11 (1888-89) 426-430.

C. J. Ball, "Remarks on the Nin-Mag Inscription," *SBAP* 11 (1888-89) 431-433.

Morris Jastrow Jr., "A Cylinder of Marduktabikzirim," *ZA* 4 (1889) 301-323.

*Terrien de Lacouperie, "Hyspaosines, Kharacenian king, on a Babylonian Tablet dated 127. a.c. and the Arsacian era, 248 a.c.," *BOR* 4 (1889-90) 136-144.

[D. G.] Lyon, "On an unpublished Nebuchadnezzar cylinder," *JAOS* 14 (1890) cxxxvii.

*B. T. A. Evetts, "A trilingual inscription of Artaxerxes Mnemon," *ZA* 5 (1890) 410-417. *[Persian and Babylonian]*

B. T. A. Evetts, "Note on E-anna-du," *SBAP* 13 (1890-91) 150.

W. St. C. Boscawen, "Inscription of Neriglissar," *BOR* 5 (1891) 213-218.

J. N. Strassmair, "Inscription of Nebuchadnezzar, son of Nin-eb-nadin-šum," *AJSL* 9 (1892-93) 4-5.

Alfred B. Moldenke, "A Cylinder of Nebuchadnezzar," *JAOS* 16 (1894-96) 71-78.

W. St. C[had] Boscawen, "A New Babylonian Inscription," *BOR* 8 (1895-1900) 136-140. [The Coronation Decree of Nabonidus]

C. H. W. Johns, "A New Babylonian Find," *ET* 7 (1895-96) 360-361. *[Stele of Nabonidus]*

*Theophilus G. Pinches, "Certain Inscriptions and Records Referring to Babylonia and Elam and their Rulers, and Other Matters," *JTVI* 39 (1895-96) 43-89. (Note by A. H. Sayce, p. 90) [S^P. III, 2; S^P. II, 987; S^P. 158 & S^P. II, 962]

L. W. King, "The fragments of a Babylonian Chronicle rejoined," *ZA* 10 (1895-96) 395-396. [K. 8533 & K. 8534 with K 8532]

*J. A. Selbie, "Professor Sayce and Recent Archaeological Discoveries," *ET* 10 (1898-99) 278-279. *[Chedorlaomer in Hammurabi's Letters]*

*C. H. W. Johns, "The Chedorlaomer Tablets," *ET* 10 (1898-99) 523.

*A. H. Sayce, "The New Babylonian Chronological Tablet," *SBAP* 21 (1899) 10-22.

*Theophilus G. Pinches, "A New Babylonian King of the Period of the First Dynasty of Babylon; with Incidental References to Immerum and Anmanila," *SBAP* 21 (1899) 158-163. *[Manamaltel]*

*Theophilus G. Pinches, "The Temples of Ancient Babylonia, I," *SBAP* 22 (1900) 358-371. [K. 3089; K 4374 + 8377; K. 4714; S. 278] *[Part II never published]*

Preston P. Bruce, "Three Inscriptions of Nabopolassar, King of Babylon (B.C. 625-604)," *AJSL* 16 (1899-1900) 178-186.

H. W. Mengedoht, "Inscription of Nabu-pal-iddina, King of Babylon, B.C. 883-852," *BOR* 9 (1901) 16-20.

*W. St. Chad Boscawen, "Explorations at Susa," *IAQR, 3rd Ser.,* 12 (1901) 330-356. [K. 3,426, p. 355]

*Theophilus [G.] Pinches, "Babylonian Inscription referring to Belshazzar," *GUOST* 2 (1901-07) 14-15.

*C[laude] R. Conder, "The Alleged Mention of Chedarlaomer on a Babylonian Tablet," *PEFQS* 36 (1904) 80-83.

*Anonymous, "Notes and Comments. Babylonian and Assyrian Memorial Deposits," *ICMM* 1 (1905) 372-373.

Anonymous, "A Babylonian Inscription," *RP* 4 (1905) 223. *[Libbit-Ishtar]*

*A. V. Williams Jackson, "Textual Notes on the Old Persian Inscriptions," *JAOS* 27 (1906) 190-194. [7. Kerman inscription of Darius, pp. 193-194]

*A. H. Sayce, "The Chedor-laomer Tablets," *SBAP* 28 (1906) 193-200, 241-251. [A. Sp. 158 + Sp. II. 962; B. Sp. II. 987; C. Sp. III, 2]

A. H. Sayce, "The Chedor-laomer Tablets—(continued)*," *SBAP* 29 (1907) 7-17.

D. D. Luckenbill, "Documents from the Temple Archives of Nippur," *RP* 5 (1906) 213-224.

D. D. Luckenbill, "A Study of the Temple Documents from the Cassite Period," *AJSL* 23 (1906-07) 280-322.

C. H. W. Johns, "The Babylonian Chronicle of the First Dynasty of Babylon," *SBAP* 29 (1907) 107-111.

C. H. W. Johns, "Notes on the Chronicle of the First Dynasty of Babylon," *SBAP* 29 (1907) 308-310.

Stephen Langdon, "Review of L. W. King's *Babylonian Chronicles*," *Baby* 2 (1907-08) 126-133. *(Review)*

C. H. W. Johns, "Some Further Notes on the Babylonian Chronicle of the First Dynasty," *SBAP* 31 (1909) 14-19.

C. H. W. Johns, "Further Notes on the Chronicle of the First Dynasty of Babylon," *SBAP* 32 (1910) 272-282.

A. T. Clay, "Babylonian Section. An Ancient Antiquary," *MJ* 3 (1912) 23-25. *[Inscription of Sargon I]*

Wm. J. Hinke, "Temple Records of the Kings of Ur," *ASRec* 8 (1912-13) 27-32.

G. B. Gordon, "Important Historical Documents Found in the Museum's Collection of Ancient Babylonian Clay Tablets," *MJ* 4 (1913) 37-41.

D. D. Luckenbill, "Two Inscriptions of Mesilim, King of Kish," *AJSL* 30 (1913-14) 219-223.

Edgar J. Banks, "A Nebuchadnezzar Cylinder," *OC* 29 (1914) 746-751.

*Albert T. Clay, "Inscriptions of Nebuchadnezzar and Naram Sin," *RP* 13 (1914) 73-75.

J. Dyneley Prince, "A New Šamaš-šum-ukîn Series," *AJSL* 31 (1914-15) 256-270.

*Anonymous, "Three Babylonian Documents," *HR* 69 (1915) 108-111. [The Cylinder of Nebuchadnezzar, pp. 109-110; The Foundation Stone of Naram-Sin, p. 111]

George A. Barton, "Kings Before the Flood," *MJ* 6 (1915) 55-58.

L. W. King, "Foundation-Inscriptions from the Royal Palace at Erech," *SBAP* 37 (1915) 22-23.

*A. H. Sayce, "Adam and Sargon in the Land of the Hittites: A New Tel el-Amarna Discovery," *SBAP* 37 (1915) 227-245.

S[tephen] Langdon, "New Inscriptions of Nabuna'id," *AJSL* 32 (1915-16) 102-117.

James B. Nies, "A Net Cylinder of Entemena," *JAOS* 36 (1916) 136-139.

James B. Nies, "A Net Cylinder of Entemena," *A&A* 5 (1917) 105-106.

John A. Maynard, "Babylonian Patriotic Sayings," *JSOR* 1 (1917) 85-87.

*A. H. Sayce, "Additional Notes on the Sargon Texts," *SBAP* 40 (1918) 15.

*Leon Legrain, "Reconstructing Ancient History," *MJ* 11 (1920) 169-180. [II. A New List of Kings Who Reigned from 3500 to 3300 B.C., pp. 175-180]

W. J. Holland, "Archaeological Notes and Comments. A Recently Discovered Babylonian Cylinder upon which is Inscribed a Proclamation of Nebuchadnezzar, King of Babylon (Reigned 605-562 B.C.)," *A&A* 14 (1922) 104.

*Leon Legrain, "Darius and Pseudo Smerdis. A Green Jade Relief. C.B.S. 14543," *MJ* 14 (1923) 200-202.

*Leon Legrain, "King Nabonidus and the Great Walls of Babylon," *MJ* 14 (1923) 282-287. [C.B.S. 16108]

*W. F. Lofthouse, "Tablet B. M. No. 21,901 and Politics in Jerusalem," *ET* 35 (1923-24) 454-456.

S[tephen H.] Langdon, "Bilingual Inscription of Samsuiluna (B)," *RAAO* 21 (1924) 119-125.

*G. R. Driver, "Some Recent Discoveries in Babylonian Literature," *Theo* 8 (1924) 2-13, 67-79, 123-130, 190-197. [The Fall of Nineveh, pp. 67-79]

*C. F. Burney, "The Fall of Nineveh. The Newly Discovered Babylonian Chronicle, No. 21,901, in the British Museum," *JTS* 26 (1924-25) 443-444. *(Review)*

W. A. Irwin, "A Nebuchadnezzar Inscription in the Royal Ontario Museum," *CJRT* 2 (1925) 264-272.

C. J. Gadd, "The Nabopolassar Chronicle Again," *Exp, 9th Ser.,* 3 (1925) 85-93.

*Sidney Smith, "Miscellanea," *RAAO* 22 (1925) 57-70. [(3) Naobinidus' Restoration of E-MAŠ-DA-RI, pp. 57-66]

W[illiam] F[oxwell] Albright, "Ea-mummu and Anu-adapa in the Panegyric of Cyrus," *JRAS* (1926) 285-290.

*Sidney Smith, "Archaeological Notes," *JRAS* (1926) 433-446. [Inscription of Darius on Gold Tablet, pp. 435-436 *(Babylonian Text)*]

T. G. Pinches, "Tablets Belonging to the Lord Amherst of Hackney," *JRAS* (1926) 105-113. [227. Belshazzar's Captain and his Three Slaves. Nabonidus, 10th year, 545 B.C.]

C. J. Gadd, "Babylonian Foundation Texts," *JRAS* (1926) 679-688. [I. Limestone and Copper Tablets of a Wife of Rîm-Sin [BM 116662 + 116663]; II. Clay Cones of the Utu-ḫegal, King of Erech [BM 117836 + 117837]; III. Clay Cone of Nam-maḫ-ni, Governor of Lagash [117838]]

*Leon Legrain, "The Tragic History of Ibi-Sin, King of Ur," *MJ* 17 (1926) 372-392. [U. 6399; U. 6378; U. 6716; U. 6370; U. 6373; U. 6368; U. 6729; U. 2962; U. 6375; ; U. 6374; U. 6372; U. 6700; U. 2922; U. 6701; U. 6725; U. 6377; U. 6731; U. 2625; U. 2596; U. 2548; U. 2647; U. 2699; U. 2682; U. 6381; U. 2584; U. 6382; U. 6383; U. 6724; U. 6386; U. 6730; U. 6710; U. 6384; U. 6385; U. 6387; U. 6388; U. 6389; U. 6708; U. 6391; U. 6709; U. 6390; U. 6392; U. 6393; U. 6395; U. 6394; U. 6396; U. 6397; U. 6712; U. 6713; U. 6714; U. 6727; U. 6958; U. 6314; U. 4954; U. 6322; U. 6715; U. 2616; U. 2662; U. 2585]

Samuel A. B. Mercer, "Some Babylonian Temple Records," *JSOR* 12 (1928) 146-150.

George A. Barton, "A New Inscription of Entemena," *JAOS* 51 (1931) 262-265.

Ferris J. Stephens, "A Newly Discovered Inscription of Libit-Ishtar," *JAOS* 52 (1932) 182-185. [YBC 2190]

A. Poebel, "The Beginning of the Fourteenth Tablet of Harra Hubullu," *AJSL* 52 (1935-36) 111-114.

Judah J. Slotki, "A Suggested Emendation in L. W. King's Chronicles," *JMUEOS* #20 (1936) 45. [Vol. II., p. 4, line 6]

Albrecht Goetze, "A Cylinder of Nebuchadrezzar from Babylon," *CQ* 23 (1946) 65-78.

*Albrecht Goetze, "A New Letter from Ramesses to Hattušiliš," *JCS* 1 (1947) 241-251. [NBC 3934]

*Albrecht Goetze, "Historical Allusions in Old Babylonian Omen Texts," *JCS* 1 (1947) 253-265.

Ferris J. Stephens, "A New Inscription of Enlil-bāni," *JCS* 1 (1947) 267-273. [NBC 8955]

Selim J. Levy, "Two Cylinders of Nebuchadnezzer II in the Iraq Museum," *Sumer* 3 (1947) 4-18. [I.M. 51923; I.M. 51924]

Samuel Noah Kramer, "Fragments of a Diorite Statue of Kurigalzu in the Iraq Museum," *Sumer* 4 (1948) 1-3. *(Followed by 26 unnumbered pages of translations and notes)* [I.M. 50009; I.M. 50140; I.M. 50010; I.M. 50011]

*Albrecht Goetze, "Sin-iddinam of Larsa. New Tablets from his Reign," *JCS* 4 (1950) 83-118. [Cornell University Library 78; YBT V 38 (YBC 4832); YBC 10366; Grain Lists, UIOM 2040; YBC 3306; YBC 3328, 4311, 5198, 5223; A Seventh Date of Sin-iddinam; The Reign of Sin-iddinam]

Edmond Sollberger, "Thirty-Two Dated Tablets from the Reign of Abī-ešuh," *JCS* 5 (1951) 77-97.

*Barbara E. Morgan, "Dated Texts and the Date-Formulae of the Reign of Ammizaduga," *MCS* 2 (1952) 31-37. *[Text only]*

*Barbara E. Morgan, "Dated Texts and the Date-Formulae of the Reign of Ammiditana," *MCS* 2 (1952) 44-53.

T. Fish, "First Babylonian Dynasty Tablets (in Manchester Museum)," *MCS* 2 (1952) 77-82.

*Alfred Haldar, "Five Cuneiform Inscriptions in the National Museum of Stockholm," *BO* 10 (1953) 13-14. [National Museum No. 2089; 2091; 2092; 2090; 2088]

Albrecht Goetze, "Four Ur Dynasty Tablets Mentioning Foreigners," *JCS* 7 (1953) 103-107.

Albrecht Goetze, "Ḫulibar of Duddul," *JNES* 12 (1953) 114-123.

*Barbara E. Morgan, "Dated Texts and the Date-Formulae of some First Dynasty Kings," *MCS* 3 (1953) 16-22.

T. Fish, "Ist. Babylonian Dynasty Tablets," *MCS* 3 (1953) 23-24. *[Texts only]*

*Barbara E. Morgan, "Dated Texts and Date-Formulae of Sin-Muballit," *MCS* 3 (1953) 33-36.

Barbara E. Morgan, "Dated Texts of the Reign of Hammurabi," *MCS* 3 (1953) 36-41.

T. Fish, "A Cylinder Inscription of Neubchadrezzar II," *MCS* 3 (1953) 46. *[Text only]*

*Barbara E. Morgan, "Dated Texts and Date-Formulae of the Reign of Samsuiluna," *MCS* 3 (1953) 56-69.

*Barbara E. Morgan, "Dated Texts Reign of Abiešuḫ," *MCS* 3 (1953) 72-76.

*Barbara E. Morgan, "Dated Texts and Date-Formulae of the Reign of Samsuditana," *MCS* 3 (1953) 76-79.

*A. J. Sachs and D. J. Wiseman, "A Babylonian King List of the Hellenistic Period," *Iraq* 16 (1954) 202-212. [BM. 35603]

Faisal El-Wailly, "Synopsis of Royal Sources of the Kassite Period," *Sumer* 10 (1954) 43-54.

Rivkah Harris, "The Archive of the Sin Temple in Khafajah (Tutub)," *JCS* 9 (1955) 381-88; 91-120.

*Samuel I. Feigin, "The Date List of the Babylonian King Samsu-ditana," *JNES* 14 (1955) 137-160. [Or. Inst. A 7754]

Benno Landsberger, "Remarks on the Archive of the Soldier Ubarum," *JCS* 9 (1955) 121-131. [Additions and corrections, *JCS* 10 (1956) p. 39]

*David Noel Freedman, "The Babylonian Chronicle," *BA* 19 (1956) 50-60. [B.M. 25127; B.M. 21901; B.M. 22047; B.M. 21946; B.M. 25124]

W[illiam] F[oxwell] Albright, "The Nebuchadnezzar and Neriglissar Chronicles," *BASOR* #143 (1956) 28-33.

*Jack Finegan, "Nebuchadnezzar and Jerusalem," *JAAR* 25 (1957) 203-205. [B.M. 21946]

*Joergen Laessoe, "An Old-Babylonian Archive Discovered at Tell Shemshara," *Sumer* 13 (1957) 216-218.

C. J. Gadd, "The Harran Inscriptions of Nabonidus," *AS* 8 (1958) 35-92.

W. F. Leemans, "Tablets from Bad-tibira and Samsuiluna's Reconquest of the South," *JEOL* #15 (1958) 214-218.

Anonymous, "Recent Acquisitions by the Institute: Fragments of Clay Cylinders of Nebuchadnezzar," *AT* 3 (1958-59) #4, 2.

W. L. Moran, "Notes on the New Nabonidus Inscriptions," *Or, N.S.,* 28 (1959) 130-140.

F. Charles Fensham, "The Treaty Between Solomon and Hiram and the Alalakh Tablets," *JBL* 79 (1960) 59-60.

*J[oergen] Laessoe, "The Second Shemshara Archive," *Sumer* 16 (1960) 12-19.

‡W[illiam] W. Hallo, "Royal Inscriptions of the Early Old Babylonian Period: A Bibliography," *BO* 18 (1961) 4-14.

William W. Hallo, "The Royal Inscriptions of Ur: A Typology," *HUCA* 33 (1962) 1-43.

*A[lbrecht] Goetze, "Šakkanakkus of the Ur III Empire," *JCS* 17 (1963) 1-31. [AO 6041 = TCL V p. 31; AO 5504 = TCL II pl. 18]

J. J. Finkelstein, "The Antediluvian Kings: A University of California Tablet," *JCS* 17 (1963) 39-51. [UCBC 9-1819]

William W. Hallo, "Beginning and End of the Sumerian King List in Nippur Recension," *JCS* 17 (1963) 52-57. [CBS 13293 & 13484 (cf. N. 3368)]

*W. G. Lambert, "A Vizer of Ḫattuša? A Further Comment," *JCS* 13 (1959) 132. [Alalaḫ Tablet *456]

Anonymous, "Recent Acquisition by the Institute. A Cast of the Nabonidus Cylinder from the British Museum which refers to Belshazzar," *BH* 1 (1964) #4, 8-11.

A[lan] R. Millard, "Another Babylonian Chronicle Text," *Iraq* 26 (1964) 14-35. [B.M. 96273]

Shah As-Siwani, "A Prism from Ur," *Sumer* 20 (1964) 69-76. [IM. 63999; IM. 66147 + 66148]

W. G. Lambert, "Nebuchadnezzar King of Justice," *Iraq* 27 (1965) 1-11. [B.M. 45690]

Albrecht Goetze, "An Inscription of Simbar-šīḫu," *JCS* 19 (1965) 121-135. [Univer. of Ill., Urbana, Ill. 2499]

*J. J. Finkelstein, "The Genealogy of the Hammurapi Dynasty," *JCS* 20 (1966) 95-118. [BM 80328]

William W. Hallo, "The Coronation of Ur-Nammu," *JCS* 20 (1966) 133-141. [YBC 4617 and variants; UET VI/1: 76 & 77]

Philo H. J. Houwink ten Cate, "A New Fragment of the 'Deeds of Suppiluliuma as Told by his Son, Mursili II'," *JNES* 25 (1966) 27-31. [*KBo* XIV 42; *KUB* XIX 22]

Philo H. J. Houwink ten Cate, "Mursilis' Northwestern Campaigns—Additional Fragments in His Comprehensive Annals," *JNES* 25 (1966) 162-191.

Jimmy J. Roberts, "The Babylonian Chronicles," *RestQ* 9 (1966) 275-280.

M. Civil, "Šu-Šîn's Historical Inscriptions: Collection B.," *JCS* 21 (1967) 24-38. [UM 29-15-566+; Ni4394 (part of tablet A), Ni 9654 (text B) Ni 13221 (text D)]

William W. Hallo, "New Texts from the Reign of Sin-iddinam," *JCS* 21 (1967) 95-99. [YBC 10890; NBC 6427; NBC 8014; 8253; 7646; 5644: Now YBC 169 & 286-293]

W. G. Lambert, "Enmeduranki and Related Matters," *JCS* 21 (1967) 126-138. [Rm 255; K 4874; K 13307; K 2211 + 8636 + 9168; K 3357 + 9941; VAT 17051; BM 47805 + 48032 + 48035 + 48037 + 48046]

*J. A. Brinkman, "Remarks on two Kudurrus from the Second Dynasty of Isin," *RAAO* 61 (1967) 70-74. [BM 90898]

W. G. Lambert, "A New Source for the Reign of Nabonidus," *AfO* 22 (1968-69) 1-8. [BM 34167 + 34375 + 34896 -34995 (Sp. 281 + 492 + Sp. II 407 + 519]

S. J. Lieberman, "An Ur III Text from Drēhem Recording 'Booty from the land of Mardu'," *JCS* 22 (1968-69) 53-62.

J. J. Finkelstein, "The edict of Ammiṣaduqa: a new text," *RAAO* 63 (1969) 45-64, 189-190. [BM 80289]

§902 *4.4.11.14.6.1 The Code of Hammurabi*

James Millar, "Law Code of Hammurabi," *GUOST* 2 (1901-07) 35.

T. G. Pinches, "Hammurabi's Code of Laws—'The Lament of the Daughter of Sin'," *SBAP* 24 (1902) 301-308.

C. H. W. Johns, "Notes on the Code of Hammurabi," *AJSL* 19 (1902-03) 96-107, 171-174.

C. H. W. Johns, "The Code of Hammurabi. (B.C. 2285-2242)," *ET* 14 (1902-03) 257-258.

C. H. W. Johns, "The Code of Ḥammurabi, Fresh Material for Comparison with the Mosaic Code," *JTS* 4 (1902-03) 172-183.

*Hugh Pope, "The Code of Hammurabi and the Code of Moses," *AER* 28 (1903) 502-515.

Charles Foster Kent, "The Recently Discovered Civil Code of Hammurabi," *BW* 21 (1903) 175-190.

Kerr D. Macmillan, "The Codex of Hammurabi in Translation," *CFL, N.S.,* 8 (1903) 362-364.

George H. Schodde, "The Code of Hammurabi," *ColTM* 23 (1903) 85-92.

George H. Schodde, "The Code of Hammurabi," *HR* 44 (1903) 213-218.

*Theophilus G. Pinches, "The Laws of the Babylonians, as Recorded in the Code of Hammurabi," *JTVI* 35 (1903) 237-247. (Discussion, pp. 247-255)

Anonymous, "The Oldest Code of Laws Ever Discovered," *MQR, 3rd Ser.,* 29 (1903) 600-603. *[Code of Hammurabi]*

Anonymous, "The Code of Hammurabi," *MR* 85 (1903) 641-644.

Anonymous, "The Laws of Hammurabi, King of Babylonia," *RP* 2 (1903) 66-96. [Frontpiece, Hammurabi Receiving the Laws from the Sun-god of Sippara; Editorial Introduction to the Laws of Hammurabi, King of Babylonia; Hammurabi's Introduction to his Code of Laws; Hammurabi's Code of Laws; Hammurabi's Conclusion; Cuneiform Text of Hammurabi's Laws (Plates 1-6)]

Robert Francis Harper, "Text of the Code of Hammurabi, King of Babylon (about 2250 B.C.)," *AJSL* 20 (1903-04) 1-84.

Robert Francis Harper, "List of Signs, Numerals, Scribal Errors, and Erasures in the Text of the Code of Hammurabi," *AJSL* 20 (1903-04) 116-136.

A. H. Godbey, "The Chirography of the Hammurabi Code," *AJSL* 20 (1903-04) 137-148.

A. H. Sayce, "The Laws of Khammurabi," *ET* 15 (1903-04) 184-186. *(Review)*

C. H. W. Johns, "The Code of Hammurabi," *ET* 15 (1903-04) 208-209. *(Review)*

*George S. Duncan, "The Code of Moses and the Code of Hammurabi," *BW* 23 (1904) 188-193, 272-278.

David G. Lyon, "The Structure of the Hammurabi Code," *JAOS* 25 (1904) 248-269.

David G. Lyon, "Notes on the Hammurabi Monument," *JAOS* 25 (1904) 266-278.

Anonymous, "The Code of Hammurabi," *MQR, 3rd Ser.,* 30 (1904) 600-601.

Adolf Hult, "The Babylonian Law Code of Hammurabi," *LCR* 23 (1904) 425-436.

Anonymous, "The Code of Hammurabi, King of Babylon," *MQR, 3rd Ser.,* 30 (1904) 186-187.

*John R. Sampey, "The Code of Hammurabi and the Laws of Moses," *R&E* 1 (1904) 97-107, 233-243.

*A. H. Godbey, "Deuteronomy and the Hammurabi Code," *RChR, 4th Ser.,* 8 (1904) 469-494.

*A. S. Zerbe, "The Code of Hammurabi and the Mosaic Book of the Covenant. (First Paper)," *RChR, 4th Ser.,* 9 (1905) 17-38.

*A. S. Zerbe, "The Code of Hammurabi and the Mosaic Book of the Covenant. (Second Paper)," *RChR, 4th Ser.,* 9 (1905) 165-181.

Anonymous, "The Code of Hammurabi. King of Babylon about 2250 B.C.," *ICMM* 1 (1905) 53-65.

*Hewlett Johnson, "The Code of Hammurabi and the Laws of Israel," *ICMM* 1 (1905) 133-145.

*Anonymous, "Surgical Treatment of the Eye and Hammurabi's Code," *ICMM* 1 (1905) 163.

A. H. Godbey, "The Place of the Code of Hammurabi," *Monist* 15 (1905) 199-226.

*James A. Kelso, "The Code of Hammurabi and the Book of the Covenant," *PTR* 3 (1905) 399-412.

*George Macloskie, "New Light on the Old Testament," *PTR* 3 (1905) 595-617. [3. Code of Hammurabi, pp. 608-611]

Robert Francis Harper, "Notes on the Code of Hammurabi," *AJSL* 22 (1905-06) 1-28.

C. H. W. Johns, "Assyriological Notes," *AJSL* 22 (1905-06) 224-241. [I. Some Further Notes on the Code of Hammurabi, pp.224-228]

Gabriel Oussani, "The Code of Hammurabi," *NYR* 1 (1905-06) 178-197.

*Gabriel Oussani, "The Code of Hammurabi and the Mosaic Legislation," *NYR* 1 (1905-06) 488-510.

*Gabriel Oussani, "The Code of Hammurabi and the Mosaic Legislation. (II)," *NYR* 1 (1905-06) 616-639.

David Gordon Lyon, "When and where was the Code of Hammurabi promulgated?" *JAOS* 27 (1906) 123-134.

*Andrew Craig Robinson, "The Bearing of Recent Oriental Discoveries on Old Testament History," *JTVI* 38 (1906) 154-176. (Discussion, pp. 176-181.) [The Code of Hammurabi, pp. 173-174]

G. Macloskie, "The Code of Hammurabi," *LCR* 25 (1906) 334-337.

D. H. Müller, "The Mosaic Law and the Code of Hammurabi," *Monist* 16 (1906) 313.

*W. T. Pilter, "A Ḥammurabi Text from Ashurbanipal's Library," *SBAP* 29 (1907) 155-164, 222-231. [Bu. '91-5-9.221]

*J. Robertson Buchanan, "The Code of Hammurabi and Israelitish Legislation: A Comparison of the Civil Codes in Babylonia and Israel," *GUOST* 3 (1907-12) 25-27.

*Anonymous, "Editorial Notes," *ICMM* 5 (1908-09) 1-12. [The Growth of Laws; Babylon—the Earliest Home of Law; Hammurabi's Code; The Bridge Between Hammurabi's and Israel's Law; Hebrew "Torah"; The Divine Authority of Israel's Laws; Israelitish Laws were the subject of Growth; The Authors of the Israelitish Laws; The Different Decalogues Written on Sinai; The Same Argument Retold More Simply; The Value of this View of the Growth of Law; The Relation of the Law-giver to Prophet; The Study of the Prophets; Ezekiel; Jeremiah]

S[tephen] Langdon, "A Fragment of the Hammurapi Code," *SBAP* 36 (1914) 100-106.

*Anonymous, "Ancient Semitic Law," *MR* 97 (1915) 968-972. *[Code of Hammurabi]*

Morris Jastrow Jr., "Older and Later Elements in the Code of Hammurapi," *JAOS* 36 (1916) 1-33.

*D. D. Luckenbill, "The Temple Women of the Code of Hammurabi," *AJSL* 34 (1917-18) 1-12.

R. H. Pfeiffer, "An Analysis of the Hammurabi Code," *AJSL* 36 (1919-20) 310-315.

*S[tephen] Langdon, "The Sumerian Law Code compared with the Code of Hammurabi," *JRAS* (1920) 489-515.

*William Wallace Everts, "The Laws of Moses and of Hammurabi," *R&E* 17 (1920) 37-50.

*P. A. Mattson, "Sidelights on the Scriptures from the laws of Hammurabi," *AQ* 6 (1927) 23-38.

*G. R. Driver, "A Problem of River-traffic," *ZA* 40 (1931) 228-233. [C. H. §240]

Theophile James Meek, "The Asyndeton Clause in the Code of Hammurabi," *JNES* 5 (1946) 64-72.

Theophile J[ames] Meek, "A New Interpretation of the Code of Hammurabi §§117-19," *JNES* 7 (1948) 180-183.

Jørgen Laessøe, "On the Fragments of the Hammurabi Code," *JCS* 4 (1950) 173-187.

*M. David, "The Codex of Hammurabi and its Relation to the Provision of Law in Exodus," *OTS* 7 (1950) 149-178.

*J. J. Rabinowitz, "Section 7 of the Code of Hammurapi. Light of a Legal Preposition in the Talmud," *BIES* 16 (1951) #3/4, IV. *[Misprinted as p. VI]*

R. Harris, "The *nadītu* Laws of the Code of Hammurapi in Praxis," *Or, N.S.,* 30 (1961) 163-169.

D. J. Wiseman, "The Laws of Hammurabi Again," *JSS* 7 (1962) 161-172.

E. Sollberger, "A New Fragment of the Code of Hammurapi," *ZA* 56 (1964) 130-132. [BM 59776]

J. J. Finkelstein, "A Late Old Babylonian Copy of the Laws of Hammurapi," *JCS* 21 (1967) 39-48. [BM. 78944 + 78979]

J. J. Finkelstein, "The Hammurapi law tablet *BE* XXXI *22,*" *RAAO* 63 (1969) 11-27.

§903   ***4.4.11.14.6.2 The Cyrus Cylinder***

A. H. Sayce, "The Latest Cuneiform Discovery," *AAOJ* 2 (1879-80) 287-289. *[Cyrus Cylinder]*

H[enry] C. Rawlinson, "Notes on a newly-discovered Clay Cylinder of Cyrus the Great," *JRAS* (1880) 70-97.

A. H. Sayce, "The Latest Cuneiform Discovery," *OBJ* 1 (1880) 55-57. *[Cyrus Cylinder]*

*D. G. Lyon, "The Cyrus cylinder," *JBL* 6 (1886) part 1, 139.

William Wallace Martin, "Certain Cuneiform Groups for Babylon," *MQR, 3rd Ser.,* 48 (1922) 712-715.

§904 *4.4.11.14.7 Babylonian Business and Legal Texts*

Lady Tite, "Babylonian Contract Tablets," *SBAT* 4 (1875) 256.

J. N. Strassmaier, "A Contract Tablet of the 17th year of Nabonidus," *SBAP* 2 (1879-80) 78-79.

*Theo. G. Pinches, "Notes upon Babylonian Contract Tablets and the Canon of Ptolemy," *SBAT* 6 (1878-79) 484-493.

J. N. Strassmaier, "A Contract Tablet from the 17th year of Nabonidus," *SBAT* 7 (1880-82) 407-410.

†Theo. G. Pinches, "Contract Tablet from Babylon inscribed with Unknown Characters," *SBAP* 5 (1882-83) 103-107, 152-154.

J. Oppert, "Contract Tablet from Babylon, inscribed with Unknown Characters," *SBAP* 5 (1882-83) 122-124.

Geo. Bertin, "Notes on the Babylonian Contract Tablets," *SBAP* 6 (1883-84) 84-88.

†Theo. G. Pinches, "Tablet, recording the Sale of a Slave, marked on the left hand with the name of his Mistress," *SBAP* 6 (1883-84) 102-106.

*Theo. G. Pinches, "Babylonian Legal Documents referring to House Property, and the Law of Inheritance," *SBAT* 8 (1883-84) 271-298.

*Theo. G. Pinches, "Documents relating to Slave-dealing in Babylonia in Ancient Times," *SBAP* 7 (1884-85) 32-36. [S. + 431]

*E. A. Wallis Budge, "On a Babylonian weight with a trilingual inscription," *SBAP* 10 (1887-88) 464-466. *[Babylonian]*

*William Hayes Ward, "On an inscribed Babylonian Weight," *JAOS* 13 (1889) lvi-lxvii.

*†John P. Peters, "A Boundary Stone of Nebuchadnezzar I," *SBAP* 8 (1885-86) 72-74.

Theophilus G. Pinches, "Two Contract-tablets from Babylon," *ZA* 1 (1886) 198-205. [S + 806; S + 492, S. + 76]

W. St. Chad Boscawen, "A Babylonian Land Grant," *BOR* 1 (1886-87) 65-68.

*E. Revillout and V. Revillout, "*Sword Obligations* in Egyptian and Babylonian Law," *BOR* 1 (1886-87) 101-104.

V. Revillout, "A Settlement of Accounts in Nabopolassar's Time," *BOR* 1 (1886-87) 117-119.

Theo. G. Pinches, "A Babylonian Dower-Contract," *BOR* 2 (1887-88) 1-8. [81-6-25, 45]

E. Revillout and V. Revillout, "A Claim of Priority as to deeds relating to Belshazzar," *BOR* 2 (1887-88) 44-48. [Note by W. St. C. Boscawen, pp. 44-45]

E. A. Wallis Budge, "Sale of a Garden (in the 18th year of Šamaš-šum-ukîn," *SBAP* 10 (1887-88) 146.

A. H. Sayce, "Some Unpublished Contract Tablets," *BOR* 4 (1889-90) 1-6. [Pitt Rivers Mus., Oxford # 93, 48, 52 and 77]

A. H. Sayce, "Babylonian Contract-Tablet belonging to the Imperial Academy of Sciences at St. Petersburg," *ZA* 5 (1890) 276-280.

Theo. G. Pinches, "Old Persian Names in Babylonian Contracts," *AJSL* 8 (1891-92) 134-135.

C. J. Ball, "A Babylonian Deed of Sale," *SBAP* 14 (1891-92) 166-169.

W. St. C[had] Boscawen, "The Horses of Namar," *BOR* 6 (1892-93) 139-140.

W. St. C[had] B[oscawen], "The Nabonidus Contracts," *BOR* 8 (1895-1900) 192.

W. St. C[had] Boscawen, "Notes on Babylonian Legal and Commercial Inscriptions," *BOR* 8 (1895-1900) 217-221.

Theophilus G. Pinches, "Some Early Babylonian Contracts or Legal Documents," *JRAS* (1897) 589-613.

Theophilus G. Pinches, "Some Early Babylonian Contract-Tablets or Legal Documents II," *JRAS* (1899) 103-120.

A. H. Sayce, "Contract from the Country of Khana," *SBAP* 21 (1899) 22-24.

*W. St. Chad Boscawen, "Explorations at Susa," *IAQR, 3rd Ser.,* 12 (1901) 330-356. [Inscription of Meli-Sikhu, pp. 341-348]

George A. Barton, "(1) A Babylonian Deed of Gift from the Sixth pre-Christian Millennium," *AJA* 6 (1902) 35-36.

William Cruickshank, "Assyrian and Babylonian Contracts," *ET* 14 (1902-03) 520-521. *(Review)*

*Hermann Ranke, "Business House of Murashu Sons of Nippur," *RP* 3 (1904) 364-374.

*W. T. Pilter, "A Ḫammurabi Text from Ashurbanipal's Library," *SBAP* 29 (1907) 155-164, 222-231. [Bu. '91-5-9, 221]

*C. H. W. Johns, "A Marriage Contract from the Chabour," *SBAP* 29 (1907) 177-184.

*C. J. Ball, "A 'Kassite' Text; and a First Dynasty Tablet," *SBAP* 29 (1907) 273-276. [2. A First Dynasty Tablet, pp. 274-275 *[Sale of a House]*]

A. H. Sayce, "A Boundary Stone," *ET* 19 (1907-08) 497-498.

*A. H. Sayce, "Recent Oriental Archaeology. Legal and Commercial," *ET* 19 (1907-08) 498-499. [Assyrian, Neo-Babylonian, and Persian Legal Documents] *(Review)*

Wm. J. Hinke, "A New Boundary Stone of Nebuchadrezzar I. from Nippur. A Reply," *RChR, 4th Ser.,* 13 (1909) 402-415.

*Anonymous, "Babylonian Legal and Business Documents," *RP* 9 (1910) 84-88. *(Review)*

*W. T. Pilter, "A Legal Episode in Ancient Babylonian Family Life," *SBAP* 32 (1910) 81-92, 129-142. [Bu. 88-5-12, 11 and 120]

George A. Barton, "A Babylonian Ledger Account of Reeds and Wood," *AJSL* 27 (1910-11) 322-327.

George A. Barton, "Another Babylonian Ledger Account of Reeds and Wood," *AJSL* 28 (1911-12) 207-210.

*Samuel A. B. Mercer, "The Oath in Cuneiform Inscriptions: The Oath in the Babylonian Inscriptions of the Time of the Ḫammurabi Dynasty," *AJSL* 29 (1912-13) 65-94. [Part II]

George A. Barton, "Still Another Babylonian Ledger of Reeds and Wood," *AJSL* 29 (1912-13) 138-142.

Leroy Waterman, "Business Documents of the Hammurabi Period," *AJSL* 29 (1912-13) 145-204. [Bu. 91-5-9 Collection = Bu. 450; 608; 744; 748; 868; 780; 856; 864; 873; 907; 967; 1003; 2373; 2456; 2487; 402; 469; 694; 735; 781; 557; 857; 2189; 2189A; 2180; 2495; 308; 458; 373; 355; 906; 2184; 936; 474; 2483; 2483A; 2497; 2497A; 2493; 2515; 2448; 752; 2500; 2509; 2517]

Leroy Waterman, "Business Documents of the Hammurabi Period. II," *AJSL* 29 (1912-13) 288-303. [Bu. 91-5-9,594; 600; 602; 612; 613; 614; 615; 618; 628; 630; 631; 639; 674]

Leroy Waterman, "Business Documents of the Hammurabi Period. III," *AJSL* 30 (1913-14) 48-73. [Bu. 91-5-9, 958; 677; 700; 740; 731; 706; 699; 644; 757; 663; 692; 689; 697; 792; 810; 806; 788; 891; 828; 835; 910; 682]

George S. Duncan, "Babylonian Legal and Business Documents from the First Babylonian Dynasty, Transliterated, Translated, and Annotated," *AJSL* 30 (1913-14) 166-195.

*Samuel A. B. Mercer, "The Oath in Cuneiform Inscriptions: III. The Oath in the Inscriptions Since the Time of the Ḫammurabi Dynasty," *AJSL* 30 (1913-14) 196-211.

*Albert T. Clay, "Inscriptions of Nebuchadnezzar and Naram Sin," *RP* 13 (1914) 73-75.

William J. Hinke, "The Significance of the Symbols on Babylonian Boundary Stones," *AJA* 20 (1916) 76-77.

Mary Inda Hussey, "A conveyance of Land Dated in the Reign of Ellil-bani," *JAOS* 36 (1916) 34-36. [Harvard Semitic Museum no. 1421]

Frederick A. Vanderburgh, "A Business Letter of Anu-šar-uṣur," *JAOS* 36 (1916) 333-336.

Theophile James Meek, "Old Babylonian Business and Legal Documents (the RFH Collection)," *AJSL* 33 (1916-17) 203-244.

Elihu Grant, "A First-Dynasty Legal Settlement," *AJSL* 34 (1917-18) 135-137.

*V. Schiel, "The Oldest Written Code," *MJ* 11 (1920) 130-132.

*George A. Barton, "An Important Social Law of the Ancient Babylonians —a Text Hitherto Misunderstood," *AJSL* 37 (1920-21) 62-71. [B.M. K. 251]

*G. R. Driver, "The Sale of a Priesthood," *JRASCS* (1924) 41-48.

C. P. T. Winckworth, "A Seleucid Legal Text," *JRAS* (1925) 655-671.

Henry Frederick Lutz, "Neo-Babylonian Administrative Documents from Erech. Parts I and II," *UCPSP* 9 (1927-31) 1-115.

Henry Frederick Lutz, "An Agreement Between a Babylonian Feudal Lord and His Retainer in the Reign of Darius II," *UCPSP* 9 (1927-31) 269-277. [Museum of Anthropology No. 9-68]

Henry Frederick Lutz, "The Verdict of a Trial Judge in a Case of Assault and Battery," *UCPSP* 9 (1927-31) 379-381. [UCBC 756]

Henry Frederick Lutz, "A Slave Sale Document of the Time of Neriglissar," *UCPSP* 9 (1927-31) 413-418 [UCBC 1292]

Samuel A. B. Mercer, "Some Babylonian Contracts," *JSOR* 12 (1928) 35-42; 13 (1929) 175-180; 14 (1930) 45-50.

*S[tephen H.] Langdon, "A Contract with a New Date of Samsu-iluna," *RAAO* 27 (1930) 83-84.

*A. Poebel, "Note on the Date of Samsuiluna, *RA* XXVII, 83," *AJSL* 48 (1931-32) 54-55.

Henry F[rederick] Lutz, "A Neo-Babylonian Debenture," *UCPSP* 10 (1931-46) 251-256. [UCBC 893]

Henry Frederick Lutz, "A Recorded Deposition Concerning Presentment for Tax Payment," *UCPSP* 10 (1931-46) 257-264. [UCBC 894]

T. Fish, "A Cuneiform Tablet from Sippar(?)," *JMUEOS* #18 (1932) 49-53.

S[tephen] Langdon, "A Babylonian Contract for the Rent of a Garden," *JRAS* (1934) 556-559.

Samuel I. Feigin, "A Purchase Contract from the Time of Samsu-Iluna," *JAOS* 55 (1935) 284-293.

*G. V. Bobrinskoy, "The Line of Bārhmī(?) Script in a Babylonian Contract Tablet," *JAOS* 56 (1936) 86-88.

*W. F. Leemans, "Some aspects of theft and robbery in Old-Babylonian documents," *RDSO* 32 (1937) 661-666.

Albrecht Goetze, "Diverse Names in an Old-Babylonian Pay-List," *BASOR* #95 (1944) 18-24. [YBC 7088]

*Ferris J. Stephens, "A Tablet from the Reign of Šamaš-šum-ukin," *JCS* 1 (1947) 273-274. *[Corrections to G. R. Driver, "The Sale of a Priest-hood" JRAS 1924 (Centenary Sup) 41. ff.]*

*A[lbrecht] Goetze, "Texts and Fragments," *JCS* 1 (1947) 349-352. [Fragment of a Late Babylonian contract, [Columbia University 8x]; Fragment of a Late Babylonian contract mentioning the 3rd year of Artaxerxes [Crozer Theological Seminary 204; Crozer Th. Sem. 201 (work on canals)]] *[Texts only]*

Taha Biqir, "A New Law-Code from Tell Harmal," *Sumer* 4 (1948) 52-53.

Albrecht Goetze, "The Laws of Eshnunna Discovered at Tell Harmal," *Sumer* 4 (1948) 63-102. [IM 51059; IM 52614]

*Albrecht Goetze, "Sin-iddinam of Larsa. New Tablets from his Reign," *JCS* 4 (1950) 83-118. [Cornell University Library 78; YBT V 38 (YBC 4832); YBC 10366; Grain Lists, UIOM 2040; YBC 3306; YBC 3328, 4311, 5198, 5223; A Seventh Date of Sin-iddinam; The Reign of Sin-iddinam]

T. Fish, "A Lipit-Ištar Cone," *MCS* 2 (1952) 20.

T. Fish, "Texts from Umma about Reeds," *MCS* 3 (1953) 42-45.

*T. Fish, "Seasonal Labour according to GURUŠ Texts from Umma," *MCS* 4 (1954) 1-8.

T. Fish, "British Museum Texts (GURUŠ)," *MCS* 4 (1954) 9-11. [BM 105397; 105399; 105416; 105561; 111779; 111791; 112935; 113037; 103437; 105367; 105429; 105513; 105397; 105399; 105416; 105429; 105513] *[Transliteration only]*

W. F. Leemans, "The Old-Babylonian Business Documents from Ur," *BO* 12 (1955) 112-122. *(Review)*

John W. Snyder, "Babylonian Suretyship Litigation: A Case History," *JCS* 9 (1955) 25-28. [B878 - Davenport Public Museum Collection]

T. Fish, "Chronological List of Ur III Economic Texts from Lagash," *MCS* 5 (1955) 33-55.

T. Fish, "Chronological List of Ur III Economic Texts from Umma," *MCS* 5 (1955) 61-91.

*H[ildegard] Lewy, "Chronological Notes Relating to a New Volume of Old Babylonian Contracts," *Or, N.S.,* 24 (1955) 275-287.

T. Fish, "Purchase of half a wall," *MCS* 7 (1957) 1-2. [Liverpool Museum, 51.63.177]

*W. G. Lambert, "Two Texts from the Early Part of the Reign of Ashurbanipal," *AfO* 18 (1957-58) 382-387. [1. K. 4449, pp. 382-385]

Reuven Yaron, "On Defension Clauses of some Oriental deeds of sale and lease, from Mesopatamia*[sic]* and Egypt," *BO* 15 (1958) 15-22.

*Rivkah Harris, "Old Babylonian Temple Loans," *JCS* 14 (1960) 126-136.

*J. J. Finkelstein, "Ammiṣaduqa's Edict and the Babylonian 'Law Codes'," *JCS* 15 (1961) 91-104.

*Albrecht Goetze, "Two Ur-Dynasty Tablets Dealing with Labor," *JCS* 16 (1962) 13-16.

Mogens Weitemeyer, "Hiring of Workers. Dockets from the Old Babylonian Period," *AO* 29 (1965-66) 19-22 [Bu. 88-5-12]

*M. B. Rowton, "Watercourses and Water Rights in the Official Correspondence from Larasa and Isin," *JCS* 21 (1967) 267-274.

*J. A. Brinkman, "Remarks on Two Kudurrus from the Second Dynasty of Isin," *RAAO* 61 (1967) 70-74.

Stephanie Page, "A New Boundary Stone of Merodach-Baladan I," *Sumer* 23 (1967) 45-67. [IM. 67953]

*Samuel Greengus, "The Old Babylonian Marriage Contract," *JAOS* 89 (1969) 505-532.

§905 *4.4.11.14.8 Babylonian Literary Texts and Style*

A. H. Sayce, "The literary works of Ancient Babylonia," *ZK* 1 (1884) 187-194. (Additional Note, p. 353) [S. 669; K *unnumbered;* Rm. 618; Rm. 150]

*William Hayes Ward, "Light on Scriptural Texts from Recent Discoveries. Hebrew and Babylonian Poetry," *HR* 30 (1895) 408-411.

*Theo. G. Pinches, "The Lament of the 'Daughter of Sin'," *SBAP* 17 (1895) 64-74.

Morris Jastrow Jr., "The Text-Book Literature of the Babylonians," *BW* 9 (1897) 248-268.

*C[laude] R. Conder, "Hebrew and Babylonian Poetry," *PEFQS* 30 (1898) 170-176.

Stephen Langdon, "Babylonian Literary Redaction," *ET* 19 (1907-08) 254-257.

*A. C. Baird, "Hebrew and Babylonian Psalms: A Comparison," *GUOST* 3 (1907-12) 27-30.

*Stephen Langdon, "Methods of Theological Redactors in Babylonia," *ET* 25 (1913-14) 369-371.

W. G. Lambert, "Ancestors, Authors, and Canonicity," *JCS* 11 (1957) 1-14. [Additions and Corrections, p. 112]

*W. G. Lambert, "Two Texts from the Early Part of the Reign of Ashurbanipal," *AfO* 18 (1957-58) 382-387. [1. K. 4449, pp. 382-385]

Samuel Noah Kramer, "New Literary Catalogue from Ur," *RAAO* 55 (1961) 169-176.

W. G. Lambert, "A Catalogue of Texts and Authors," *JCS* 16 (1962) 59-77.

*W. G. Lambert, "Literary Style in the First Millennium Mesopotamia," *JAOS* 88 (1968) 123-132. [BM 33428 = Rm III 105 & Khorsabad 1932, 26]

§906 *4.4.11.14.9 Babylonian Medical, Astronomical, Geographical, Mathematical, and "Scientific" Texts*

A. H. Sayce, "Revised Translation of a Passage in the Great Astronomical Work of the Babylonians," *SBAT* 4 (1875) 36-37.

*H. Fox Talbot, "Notice of a very Ancient Comet. From a Chaldean Tablet," *SBAT* 4 (1875) 257-262.

C. Bozold, "A new Text concerning the Star Kak-si-di," *SBAP* 10 (1887-88) 265. [K. 2071; K. 2894; K. 2310]

*T[heophilus] G. Pinches, "An Astronomical or Astrological tablet from Babylon," *BOR* 2 (1887-88) 202-207. [78-1I-7, 4]

*A. H. Sayce, "An ancient Babylonian Work on Medicine," *ZK* 2 (1885) 1-14, 205-216.

Robert Brown Jr., "Remarks on the Tablet of Thirty Stars. Part I," *SBAP* 12 (1889-90) 137-152.

Robert Brown Jr., "Remarks on the Tablet of Thirty Stars. Part II," *SBAP* 12 (1889-90) 180-206.

*C. J. Ball, C. H. W. Johns, Theophilus G. Pinches and A. H. Sayce, "Communications on the 'Zodiac-Tablet' from Gezer," *PEFQS* 40 (1908) 26-30.

*Samuel Daiches, "Notes on the Gezer Calendar and Some Babylonian Parallels," *PEFQS* 41 (1909) 113-118.

*L. W. King, "A Neo-Babylonian Astronomical Treatise in the British Museum, and its bearing on the Age of Babylonian Astronomy," *SBAP* 35 (1913) 41-46.

H. F. Lutz, "A Mathematical Cuneiform Tablet," *AJSL* 36 (1919-20) 249-257. [CBS 8536]

*Anonymous, "Notes and Comments. Two Babylonian Multiplication Tablets in Ontario," *A&A* 26 (1928) 145-146.

*R. Campbell Thompson and C. J. Gadd, "A Middle-Babylonian Chemical Text," *Iraq* 3 (1936) 87-96. [BM 120960]

*G. V. Bobrinskoy, "The Line of Bārhmī (?) Script in a Babylonian Contract Tablet," *JAOS* 56 (1936) 86-88. *[Arabic Numerals(?)]*

*Charles C. Torrey, "Note on the Line of Bārhmī (?) Script on a Babylonian Tablet," *JAOS* 56 (1936) 490-491. *[Arabic Numerals(?)]*

*B. L. van der Waerden, "On Babylonian Astronomy I. The Venus Tablets of Ammiṣaduqa," *JEOL* #10 (1945-48) 414-424.

*Thorkild Jacobsen, "Mathematical Cuneiform Texts," *BASOR* #102 (1946) 17-19. *(Review)*

*A. Sachs, "Notes on Factional Expressions in Old Babylonian Mathematical Texts," *JNES* 5 (1946) 203-214.

*Hildegard Lewy, "Marginal Notes on a Recent Volume of Babylonian Mathematical Texts," *JAOS* 67 (1947) 305-320.

A. J. Sachs, "Two Neo-Babylonian Metrological Tablets from Nippur," *JCS* 1 (1947) 67-71.

O. Neugebauer, "Unusual Writings in Seleucid Astronomical Texts," *JCS* 1 (1947) 217-219.

A. J. Sachs, "Babylonian Mathematical Texts. I. Reciprocals of Regular Sexagesimal Numbers," *JCS* 1 (1947) 219-240. [N. 3958; N. 3891]

*A[lbrecht] Goetze, "Texts and Fragments," *JCS* 1 (1947) 349-352. [Fragment of an astronomical observation (Columbia University 6x)] *[Text only]*

*H. Lewy, "Studies in Assryo-Babylonian Mathematics and Metrology. A. A New Text of Babylonian Mathematical Texts," *Or, N.S.,* 18 (1949) 40-67, 137-170.

*O. Neugebauer, "Comments on Publications by Mrs. Hildegard Lewy on Mathematical Cuneiform Texts," *Or, N.S.,* 18 (1949) 423-426.

*Taha Baqir, "An Important Mathematical Problem Text from Tel Harmal (On the Euclidean Theorem)," *Sumer* 6 (1950) 39-54. [IM. 55357]

*Taha Baqir, "Another Important Mathematical Text from Tel Harmal," *Sumer* 6 (1950) 130-148. [IM. 52301]

*Friedrich Drenckhahn, "A Geometrical Contribution to the Study of the Mathematical Problem-Text from Tell Harmal (IM. 55357) in the Iraq Museum, Baghdad," *Sumer* 7 (1951) 22-27.

*Taha Baqir, "Some More Mathematical Texts from Harmal," *Sumer* 7 (1951) 28-45. [IM. 53953; IM. 54538; IM. 53961; IM. 53937; IM. 54010; IM. 53965; IM. 54559; IM. 54464]

*Albrecht Goetze, "A Mathematical Compendium from Tell Harmal," *Sumer* 7 (1951) 126-155. [IM. 52916; IM. 52685]

*E. M. Bruins, "Comments on the Mathematical Tablets of Tell Harmal," *Sumer* 7 (1951) 179-185.

A. [J.] Sachs, "Babylonian Mathematical Texts II-III," *JCS* 6 (1952) 151-156. [II. Approximations of Reciprocals of Irregular Numbers in an Old-Babylonian Text; III. The Problem of Finding the Cube Root of a Number] [YBC. 6295; VAT 8547]

*A. W. Hanson, "Field Plans," *MCS* 2 (1952) 21-26. *[Surveying]*

E. M. Bruins, "Revision of the Mathematical Texts from Tell Harmal," *Sumer* 9 (1953) 241-253. [IM. 54559; IM 53965; IM 53957; IM 54478; IM. 53961; IM. 54010; IM. 52301; IM. 53963; IM. 31247]

*E. M. Bruins, "Three Geometrical Problems," *Sumer* 9 (1953) 255-259. [IM. 43996]

*E. M. Bruins, "Some Mathematical Texts," *Sumer* 10 (1954) 55-61. [IM. 52001; IM. 54346; IM. 54216; IM. 54548]

A. Sachs and O. Neugebauer, "A Procedure Text concerning Solar and Lunar Motion: B.M. 36712," *JCS* 10 (1956) 131-136.

*H. W. F. Saggs, "A Babylonian geometrical text," *RAAO* 54 (1960) 131-146.

*A[sger] Aaboe, "A Seleucid Table of Daily Solar(?) Positions," *JCS* 18 (1964) 31-34. [B.M. 37089]

*Derek J. de Solla Price, "The Babylonian 'Pythagorean Triangle' Tablet," *Cent* 10 (1964-65) 1-13. [Plimpton 322]

*O. Neugebauer and A. Sacs, "Some Atypical Astronomical Cuneiform Texts. I," *JCS* 21 (1967) 183-218. [B.M. 36731 = 80-6-17,464; B.M. 36838 = 80-6-17,578; B.M. 36301 = 80-6-17,27; B.M. 37149 = 80-6-17,899; B.M. 41004 = 81,4-28,551; B.M. 37266 - 80-6-17,1022x]

Asger Aaboe, "Two Atypical Multiplication Tablets from Uruk," *JCS* 22 (1968-69) 89-91.

*O. Neugebauer and A. Sacs, "Some Atypical Astronomical Cuneiform Texts. II," *JCS* 22 (1968-69) 92-113. [MNB 1856; B.M. 36744 (= 80-6-17, 477) + 37031 (= 80-6-17,775); B.M. 36722 (= 80-6-17,455) and B.M. 40082 (= 81-2-1,47)]

*Asger Aaboe and Abraham Sachs, "Two Lunar Texts of the Achaemenid Period from Babylon," *Cent* 14 (1969) 1-22. [B.M. 36822 (=80-6-17,561) + B.M. 37022 (=80-6-17,766); B.M. 36599 (= 80-6-17,328 + 444) + B.M. 36941 (=80-6-17, 682); B.M. 36737 (=80-6-17,470); B.M. 47912 (=80-11-3,619)]

§907 *4.4.11.14.10 Babylonian Religious Texts, including Omen Texts*

Theo. G. Pinches, "Two Texts from Sippara of the Sungod," *ZK* 2 (1885) 324-328. [Additional Notes, pp. 414-416]

Theo. G. Pinches, "Fragment of a Babylonian Tithe-List," *BOR* 1 (1886-87) 76-78.

W. St. C[had] Boscawen, "A Royal Tithe of Nabonidus," *BOR* 1 (1886-87) 209-210.

E. Revillout and V. Revillout, "Istar Taribi," *BOR* 2 (1887-88) 57-59.

Theo. G. Pinches, "Gifts to a Babylonian Bit-ili or Bethel," *BOR* 2 (1887-88) 142-145. [82-7-4,13]

*C. Bezold, Remarks on some unpublished cuneiform Syllabaries, with respect to Prayers and Incantations, written in interlinear form," *SBAP* 10 (1887-88) 418-423. [K. 4175 + Sm. 57; K. 4603; K. 8276; K. 8284; K. 4816]

Francis Brown, "The Religious Poetry of Babylonia," *PR* 9 (1888) 69-86.

D. G. Lyon, "On a sacrificial Tablet from Sippar," *JAOS* 13 (1889) cxi.

C. J. Ball, "A Babylonian Ritual Text," *JRAS* (1892) 841-853.

Theo. G. Pinches, "A Babylonian Decree that a certain Rite should be performed," *SBAP* 15 (1892-93) 417-420.

*Theophilus G. Pinches, "Certain Inscriptions and Records Referring to Babylonia and Elam and their Rulers, and Other Matters," *JTVI* 39 (1895-96) 43-89. [Note by A. H. Sayce, p. 90]

A. H. Sayce, "Yehveh in Early Babylonia," *ET* 9 (1897-98) 522. [Bu. 88-5-12,329]

S. A. Strong, "A Hymn to Nebuchadnezzar," *SBAP* 20 (1898) 154-162.

W. St. Chad Boscawen, "A Babylonian Talisman," *BOR* 9 (1901) 67-68.

Louise Seymour Houghton, "The Cry of the Penitent. A Babylonian Prayer," *BW* 22 (1903) 49-51.

Robert Francis Harper, "Babylonian Penitential Psalms," *BW* 23 (1904) 358-365.

*Robert Francis Harper, "Assyrian and Babylonian Prayers," *BW* 23 (1904) 279-286.

Robert Francis Harper, "Prayers from the Neo-Babylonian Historical Inscriptions," *BW* 23 (1904) 428-434.

*Robert Francis Harper, "Babylonian and Assyrian Imprecations," *BW* 24 (1904) 26-30.

*Joseph Offord, "The Omen and Portent Tablets of the Assyrian and Babylonians," *AAOJ* 27 (1905) 69-72.

*Morris Jastrow Jr., "A Babylonian Parallel to the Story of Job," *JBL* 25 (1906) 135-191.

Anonymous, "Babylonian Incantation Tablet," *RP* 5 (1906) 352.

*Theophilus G. Pinches, "The Babylonian Gods of War and their Legends," *SBAP* 28 (1906) 203-218, 270-283. [K. 5268 & K. 5373]

Morris Jastrow Jr., "Notes on Omen Texts," *AJSL* 23 (1906-07) 97-115.

*Anonymous, "Job of the Cuneiform Inscriptions," *MR* 89 (1907) 307-310. *[Tabi-utul-Bel]*

Stephen Langdon, "Rythm*[sic]* in Babylonian psalms," *Baby* 2 (1907-08) 162-167.

*Theophilus G. Pinches, "The Goddess Istar in Assyro-Babylonian Literature," *SBAP* 31 (1909) 20-37, 57-69. [K. 2109; 81-7-6,102; 83-1-18,2348; K. 20 + K. 4385]

D. D. Lukenbill, "A Neo-Babylonian Catalogue of Hymns," *AJSL* 26 (1909-10) 27-32.

Stephen [H.] Langdon, "A fragment of Nippurian liturgy," *Baby* 3 (1909-10) 241-249.

*J. A. Montgomery, "Babylonian Section. A Love Charm on an Incantation Bowl," *MJ* 1 (1910) 48-49.

[Paul Carus], "Tabi-utul-Bel, the Pious Sufferer," *OC* 24 (1910) 505-509.

*Clara Bewick Colby, "The Story of Tabi-utul-Bel and Nebuchadnezzar," *OC* 24 (1910) 766-767. [Editorial Comment, pp. 767-768]

*J. Dyneley Prince, "A Hymn to Tammuz," *AJSL* 27(1910-11) 84-89. [*C.T.* XV. Plates 20, 21]

*Stephen [H.] Langdon, "Grammatical treatises upon a religious text concerning the *ardat lilī*," *Baby* 4 (1910-11) 187-191.

*Stephen Langdon, "Concerning 'Jahweh' in Lexicographical Babylonian Tablets," *ET* 22 (1910-11) 139-140.

S[tephen] Langdon, "A Tablet of Prayers from the Nippur Library," *SBAP* 34 (1912) 75-79.

S[tephen] Langdon, "The Originals of Two Religious Texts of the Asurbanipal Library," *SBAP* 34 (1912) 152-157.

J. Dyneley Prince, "A Political Hymn to Shamash," *JAOS* 33 (1913) 10-15.

J. Dyneley Prince, "A Tammuz Fragment," *JAOS* 33 (1913) 345-348. [K. 3356]

Stephen Langdon, "Babylonian Liturgies," *RP* 12 (1913) 171-180.

*Stephen Langdon, "Methods of Theological Redactors in Babylonia," *ET* 25 (1913-14) 369-371.

George W. Gilmore, "Ethnic Scriptures. II. Babylonia, Psalms and Incantations," *HR* 67 (1914) 191-196.

R. M. Gwynn, "An Omen Text dealing with Houses," *SBAP* 36 (1914) 240-248. [80-7-19,81; K. 45]

S[tephen] Langdon, "A hymn to Tammuz," *RAAO* 12 (1915) 33-45.

S[tephen] Langdon, "A fragment of a series of ritualistic prayers to astral deities in the ceremonies of divination," *RAAO* 12 (1915) 189-192. [B.M. No. 191 = Ki. 1904-10-9,157]

S[tephen] Langdon, "A Fragment of a Liturgy to Ninib (Ninurashā)," *SBAP* 37 (1915) 66-70. [K. 3026; K 5150]

*Theophilus T. Pinches, "Notes on the Deification of Kings and Ancestor Worship in Babylonia," *SBAP* 37 (1915) 87-95, 126-134. [J. 3, J. 15, J. 14, J. 7; J. 5, J. 9, J. 10, J. 16]

S[tephen] Langdon, "A ritual of atonement addressed to Tammuz and Ishtar," *RAAO* 13 (1916) 105-117.

George A. Barton, "Ancient Babylonian Expressions of the Religious Spirit," *JAOS* 37 (1917) 23-42.

Stephen Langdon, "A Ritual Atonement for a Babylonian King," *MJ* 8 (1917) 39-44. [#1519; 1203]

H. F. Lutz, "A Cassite Liver-Omen Text," *JAOS* 38 (1918) 77-96.

*Theophile James Meek, "Some Bilingual Religious Texts," *AJSL* 35 (1918-19) 134-144. [K. 2856; K. 1905-5-10, 19; Ki. 1904-10-9, 64; K. 2856; K. 1904-10-9, 87; K. 1904-10-9, 96; K. 1904-10-9, 138; K. 1905-4-9 10+12; Th. 1905-4-9, 13; Th. 1905-4-9, 93; Th. 1905-4-9, 93; Th. 1905-4-9, 245; Th. 1905-4-9, 393; Th. 1905-4-9, 394]

H. F. Lutz, "An Omen Text Referring to the Action of a Dreamer," *AJSL* 35 (1918-19) 145-157. [PUM 4501]

John A. Maynard, "A Lamentation to Aruru (Metropolitan Museum No. 112)," *JSOR* 3 (1919) 14-18.

*S[tephen] Langdon, "The religious interpretation of babylonian seals and a new prayer of Shamash-sum-ukîn (BM. 78219)," *RAAO* 16 (1919) 49-68. [BM. 78219 (88-5-12,70)]

*G. Buchanan Gray, "Job, Ecclesiastes, and a New Babylonian Literary Fragment," *ET* 31 (1919-20) 440-443.

Ira Maurice Price, "An Inscribed Eye of a Babylonian Idol," *JAOS* 43 (1923) 51-53.

Leon Legrain, "The Golden Boats of Marduk and Nabu in Babylon," *MJ* 14 (1923) 267-281. [CBS 9]

*Sidney Smith, "The Face of Humbaba," *AAA* 11 (1924) 107-114.

Eric Burrows, "Hymn to Ninurta as Sirius (K 128)," *JRASCS* (1924) 33-40.

*G. R. Driver, "The Sale of a Priesthood," *JRASCS* (1924) 41-48.

T. G. Pinches, "Hymns to Pap-due-garra," *JRASCS* (1924) 63-86.

*G. R. Driver, "Some Recent Discoveries in Babylonian Literature," *Theo* 8 (1924) 2-13, 67-79, 123-130, 190-197. [IV. The Death and Resurrection of Bel, pp. 190-197]

Sidney Smith, "Miscellanea," *RAAO* 21 (1924) 75-92. (*Addendum to p. 79,* p. 155) [(1) Samsu-iluna's Restoration at Sippar, Column I. (115039, Bole, Column II. (102404, Bole), Column III. 102404, Bole), pp. 75-78 [BM56620]]

S[tephen] Langdon, "An Incantation for Expelling Demons from a House," *ZA* 36 (1924-25) 209-214. [K. 2407]

*Theophilus G. Pinches, "The Worship of Idols in Assyrian History in Relation to Bible References," *JTVI* 57 (1925) 10-29, 31-32. (Discussion, pp. 29-31) [Appendix pp. 27-29] *[Babylonian Text]*

*Sidney Smith, "Miscellanea," *RAAO* 22 (1925) 57-70. [(3) Naobinidus' Restoration of E-MAŠ-DA-RI, pp. 57-66]

*Stephen Langdon, "Calendars of Liturgies and Prayers," *AJSL* 42 (1925-26) 110-127.

*Sidney Smith, "Archaeological Notes," *JRAS* (1926) 433-446. [The Seal before God (B.M. 117666), pp. 422-446]

F. W. Geers, "A Babylonian Omen Text," *AJSL* 43 (1926-27) 22-41.

Henry Frederick Lutz, "An Old-Babylonian Divination Text," *UCPSP* 9 (1927-31) 367-377. [UCBC 755]

*Theophilus G. Pinches, "The Influence of the Heathenism of the Canaanites upon the Hebrews," *JTVI* 60 (1928) 122-142, 145-147. (Discussion, pp. 143-145) *[Babylonian Text, pp. 132-134]*

*Cecil J. Mullo-Weir, "Four Hymns to Gula," *JRAS* (1929) 1-18. [(a) King, No. 6, 11. 71-95; (b) King, No. 4. 11. 24ff.; (c) Craig, *RT.* i, 18; (d) K. 232]

S[tephen] Langdon, "A Babylonian Ritual of Sympathetic Magic by Burning Images," *RAAO* 26 (1929) 39-42.

Cecil J. Mullo-Weir, "Restoration of a Hymn to Shamash," *JRAS* (1930) 41-42.

*S[tephen H.] Langdon, "Restoration of the 'Utukkê' limûti Series, Tablet C," *RAAO* 28 (1931) 159-163.

*T. Fish, "Miscellanea," *Iraq* 6 (1939) 184-186. [Unnumbered Tablet of the Ashmolean Museum, p. 184]

*S. L. Terrien, "The Babylonian Dialogue on Theodicy and the Book of Job," *JBL* 63 (1944) vi.

A. Leo Oppenheim, "Assyriological Gleanings IV," *BASOR* #103 (1946) 11-14. *[Mesopotamian Harvest Song]*

*Albrecht Goetze, "Historical Allusions in Old Babylonian Omen Texts," *JCS* 1 (1947) 253-265.

*Ferris J. Stephens, "A Tablet from the Reign of Šamaš-šum-ukin," *JCS* 1 (1947) 273-274. *[Corrections to G. R. Driver, "The Sale of a Priesthood" JRAS 1924 (Centenary Sup) 41ff.]*

*A[lbrecht] Goetze, "Texts and Fragments," *JCS* 1 (1947) 349-352. [Fragment of an astrological omen, Columbia University 7x]

*T. Fish, "Miscellany," *MCS* 1 (1951) 56-57. [2. (d)Ha-ni] *[Night sky deity of Ur III]*

*H. H. Figulla, "Accounts Concerning Allocations of Provisions for Offerings in the Ningal-Temple at Ur," *Iraq* 15 (1953) 88-122, 171-192.

*T. Fish, "Miscellany," *MCS* 2 (1952) 59-62. [2. Hymn to Marduk, pp. 61-62]

T. Fish, "Towards a Study of Lagash 'Mission' or 'Messenger' Texts," *MCS* 4 (1954) 78-105; 5 (1955) 1-26.

Albrecht Goetze, "An Incantation Against Diseases," *JCS* 9 (1955) 8-18. [UIOM 1059; HTS 2]

Benno Landsberger and Thorkild Jacobsen, "An Old Babylonian Charm against Merḫu," *JNES* 14 (1955) 14-21.

J[ørgen] Læssøe, "A Prayer to Ea, Shamash, and Marduk, from Hama," *Iraq* 18 (1956) 60-67. [6A 343]

*Franz Köcher and A. L. Oppenheim, "The Old Babylonian Omen Text VAT 7525," *AfO* 18 (1957-58) 62-77. [*Appendix.* A Hittite Parallel, by H. G. Güterbock, pp. 78-80. (KUB XXIX 9 and 10)]

W. G. Lambert, "An Incantation of the Maqiû Type," *AfO* 18 (1957-58) 288-299. [CBS. 334; CBS. 1203; K. 3379 and K. 2585; K. 3360 + 8019 + 14202 + Sm. 1143; Sm. 1115; VAT 13702; Bu. 91-5-9,143 + 176]

Benno Landsberger, "Corrections to the Article, '*An Old Babylonian Charm Against Merhu'*," *JNES* 17 (1958) 56-58.

A. L. Oppenheim, "A New Prayer to the 'Gods of the Night'," *SBO* 3 (1959) 282-301. [K. 2315 + K 3125 + 83-1-18, 469]

W. G. Lambert, "Three Literary Prayers of the Babylonians," *AfO* 19 (1959-60) 47-66.

O. R. Gurney, "A Tablet of Incantations Against Slander," *Iraq* 22 (1960) 221-227.

E. Reiner, "The Etiological Myth of the 'Seven Sages'," *Or, N.S.* 30 (1961) 1-11.

E. E. Knudsen, "Two Nimrud Incantations of the Utukku Type," *Iraq* 27 (1965) 160-170. [IM 67618 / ND 5576; IM 67619 / ND 5577]

Robert D. Biggs, "More Babylonian 'Prophecies'," *Iraq* 29 (1967) 117-132.

David B. Weisberg, "A Neo-Babylonian Temple Report," *JAOS* 87 (1967) 8-12.

C. J. Gadd, "Omens Expressed in Numbers," *JCS* 21 (1967) 52-63. [DT. 72 92684; DT 78 92685]

*E. Reiner and H. G. Güterbock, "The Great Prayer to Ishtar and Its Two Versions from Boğasköy," *JCS* 21 (1967) 255-266.

W. G. Lambert, "The Gula Hymn of Bulluṭsa-rabi," *Or, N.S.,* 36 (1967) 105-132.

D[onald] J. Wiseman, "The Nabu Temple Texts from Nimrud," *JNES* 27 (1968) 248-250.

Robert D. Biggs, "An Esoteric Babylonian Commentary," *RAAO* 62 (1968) 51-58. [*LBAT 1601* (=BM 34647)]

Albrecht Goetze, "An Old Babylonian Prayer of the Divination Priest," *JCS* 23 (1968-69) 25-29.

*D[onald] J. Wiseman, "A Lipšur Litany from Nimrud," *Iraq* 31 (1969) 175-183. [N.D. 4387 + 4405/77]

§908 *4.4.11.14.10.1 Babylonian "Creation" and Paradise Stories*[1]

George Smith, "On some Fragments of the Chaldean Account of the Creation," *SBAT* 4 (1875) 363-364.

H. F. Talbot, "Chaldean Account of the Creation," *SBAT* 5 (1876-77) 426-440.

†E. A. [Wallis] Budge, "The Fourth Tablet of the Creation series, relating to the fight between Marduk and Tiamat," *SBAP* 6 (1883-84) 5-9. (Remarks by Theo. G. Pinches, pp. 9-10; by Geo. Gertin, pp. 10-11)

E. A. Wallis Budge, "The fourth Tablet of the Creation Series," *SBAP* 10 (1887-88) 86.

Theo. G. Pinches, "A Babylonian Duplicate of Tablets I. and II. of the Creation Series," *BOR* 4 (1889-90) 25-33. [82-7-14,402]

W. St. C[had] Boscawen, "The Babylonian Legend of the Serpent-Tempter," *BOR* 4 (1889-90) 251-255.

*T. G. Pinches, "A New Version of the Creation-Story," *JRAS* (1891) 393-408.

W. Muss-Arnolt, "Comparative Study of the Translations of the Babylonian Creation Tablets with Special Reference to Jensen's Kosmologie and Barton's Tiamat," *AJSL* 9 (1892-93) 6-23.

William Hayes Ward, "Light on Scriptural Texts from Recent Discoveries. V. The Babylonian Creation Story," *HR* 26 (1893) 26-27.

W. Muss-Arnolt, "The Babylonian Account of Creation,"*BW* 3 (1894) 17-27.

---

1.   This subdivision may contain articles which by their nature are actually a discussion of Babylonian religious thought, and not directly related to text critical studies.

William Hayes Ward, "Light on Scriptural Texts from Recent Discoveries. The Babylonian Creation Story," *HR* 27 (1894) 221-223.

A. H. Sayce, "The Kuthaean Legend of the Creation," *SBAP* 20 (1898) 187-189.

*Morris Jastrow Jr., "Adam and Eve in Babylonian Literature," *AJSL* 15 (1898-99) 193-214.

*Morris Jastrow Jr., "The Hebrew and Babylonian Accounts of Creation," *JQR* 31 (1900-01) 620-654.

*T. G. P[inches], "Talmudische und midrashische Parallelen zum Babylonischen Weltschöpfungsepos," *JRAS* (1904) 369-370. *[English Text]*

Anonymous, "Creation Tablets a Misnomer," *RP* 4 (1905) 61.

*Andrew Craig Robinson, "The Bearing of Recent Oriental Discoveries on Old Testament History," *JTVI* 38 (1906) 154-176. (Discussion, pp. 176-181) [The Babylonian Creation Tablets, pp. 165-167; The Babylonian Flood Tablet, pp. 167-170]

S[tephen] H. Langdon, "The Edinburgh Fragment of the Epic of Creation," *ET* 22 (1910-11) 278.

A. H. Sayce, "A New Fragment of the Creation Legend," *SBAP* 33 (1911) 6-7.

Arno Poebel, "The Babylonian Story of the Creation and the Earliest History of the World," *MJ* 4 (1913) 41-50.

S[tephen] Langdon, "An Account of the Pre-Semitic Version of the Fall of Man," *SBAP* 36 (1914) 253-263.

*Theophilus G. Pinches, "The Niffer Story of the Creation and the Flood," *ET* 26 (1914-15) 490-494.

*[Julian] Morgenstern, "On Gilgames-Epic XI, 274-320. A Contribution the the Study of the Role of the Serpent in Semitic Mythology," *ZA* 29 (1914-15) 284-300.

S[tephen] Langdon, "Some Corrections to 'An Account of the Pre-Semitic Version of the Fall of Man.' *(See S.B.A. 'Proceedings', Vol XXXVI, 1914, pp. 253-264.),*" *SBAP* 37 (1915) 263.

*Theophilus G. Pinches, "The Old and New Versions of the Babylonian Creation and Flood Stories," *JTVI* 47 (1915) 301-322, 327-328. (Discussion, pp. 322-327)

*Anonymous, "A New Version of the Flood and the Fall of Man," *MR* 97 (1915) 313-317.

George A. Barton, "New Babylonian Material Concerning Creation and Paradise," *AJT* 21 (1917) 571-597.

George A. Barton, "A New Babylonian Account of the Creation of Man," *PAPS* 56 (1917) 275-280.

Anonymous, "A Babylonian Account of Paradise, the Fall and Redemption," *BASOR* #3 (1921) n.p.n.

G. B. Michell, "The So-called 'Babylonian Epic of Creation'," *JTVI* 64 (1932) 102-112, 117-119. (Discussion, pp. 112-115) (Communications by A. G. Shortt, pp. 115-116; G. Wilson Heath, pp. 116-117)

Ernst F. Weidner, "The Creation of Man and the Fixing of Anunnaki," *JTVI* 70 (1938) 286-291.

*Merrill F. Unger, "The Babylonian and Biblical Accounts of Creation," *BS* 109 (1952) 304-317.

*E[phraim] A. Speiser, "Word Plays on the Creation Epoch's Version of the Founding of Babylon," *Or, N.S.,* 25 (1956) 317-323.

*James Albertson, "Genesis 1 and the Babylonian Creation Myth," *TFUQ* 37 (1962) 226-244.

C[lifford] A. W[ilson], "The Babylonian Epic of Creation," *BH* 3 (1967) #4, 28-30.

*A[lan] R. Millard, "A New Babylonian 'Genesis' Story," *TB* #18 (1967) 3-28. [The Epic of Atrahasis, pp. 4-6]

Anonymous, "A New Babylonian Record of Creation," *BH* 4 (1968) 69-74.

§909 **4.4.11.14.11 Babylonian Texts Bearing on Biblical Studies [See also: Assyrian and Babylonian Backgrounds §286; Assyrian and Babylonian Backgrounds to the Pentateuch §299 ←]**

*William Hayes Ward, "Light on Scriptural Texts from Recent Discoveries. Hebrew and Babylonian Poetry," *HR* 30 (1895) 408-411.

Theophilus G. Pinches, "Certain Inscriptions and Records Referring to Babylonia and Elam and Their Rulers, and Other Matters," *JTVI* 29 (1895-96) 43-89. (Communication by A. H. Sayce, p. 90) [Sᴘ· III.,2; Sᴘ· II, 987; Sᴘ· 158 + Sᴘ· II, 962]

*C. H. W. Johns, "Note on 'Ancient Hebrew Tradition'," *Exp, 5th Ser.,* 8 (1898) 158-160. [K. 3500]

*A. C. Baird, "Hebrew and Babylonian Psalms: A Comparison," *GUOST* 3 (1907-12) 27-30.

*A. van Hoonacker, "Zech. I 8, 10 s.; VI 1 ss. and the *Dul-azag* of the Babylonians," *JTS* 16 (1914-15) 250-252.

*Theo. G. Pinches, "Two Late Tablets of Historical Interest," *SBAP* 38 (1916) 27-34. [H.S.W. 48; H.S.W. 49; BM. 57002]*[cf. Book of Daniel]*

*Stephen Langdon, "A Babylonian Tablet on the Interpretation of Dreams," *MJ* 8 (1917) 116-122. *[cf. Judges 7:13]*

*Theophilus G. Pinches, "Some Texts of the Relph Collection, with Notes on Babylonian Chronology and Genesis xiv," *SBAP* 39 (1917) 4-15, 55-72, 89-98.

*Walter T. McCree, "Josiah and Gadd's Babylonian Tablet," *CJRT* 1 (1924) 307-312.

*M. David, "The Codex of Hammurabi and its Relation to the Provision of Law in Exodus," *OTS* 7 (1950) 149-178.

*I. Mendelsohn, "The Disinheritance of Jephthah in the Light of Paragraph 27 of the Lipit-Ishtar Code," *IEJ* 4 (1954) 116-119.

*I. Mendelsohn, "Samuel's Denunciation of Kingship in the Light of the Akkadian Documents from Ugarit," *BASOR* #143 (1956) 17-22.

*David B. Weisberg, "Some Observations on Late Babylonian Texts and Rabbinic Literature," *HUCA* 39 (1968) 71-80.

§910 *4.4.11.15 Sumerian - General Studies*[1]

*H. F. Talbot, "Four New Syllabaries and a Bilingual Tablet. Edited, with Notes and Remarks," *SBAT* 3 (1874) 496-529. [S 23; S 15; S 14; S 17; S 12]

Ira M. Price, "The de Sarzec Inscriptions," *AJSL* 4 (1887-88) 54-56.

*C. J. Ball, "New readings of the Hieroglyphs from Northern Syria," *SBAP* 10 (1887-88) 437-449.

William Hayes Ward, "On two stone objects with Archaic Cuneiform Hieroglyphic Writing," *JAOS* 13 (1889) lvii-lviii.

Henry H. Howorth, "On the Earliest Inscriptions from Chaldea. Part I.," *SBAP* 21 (1899) 289-302. *[Part II not published]*

J. Dyneley Prince, "The Unilingual Inscriptions K. 138 and K. 3232," *JAOS* 21 (1900) 1-39.

T. G. Pinches, "Sumerian or Cryptography," *JRAS* (1900) 75-96.

*C. P. Tiele, "Akkadian and Sumerian," *JRAS* (1900) 343-344. [K. 14,013]

*H. Porter, "A Cuneiform Tablet, Sarcophagus, and Cippus with Inscription, in the Museum at Beirût," *PEFQS* 32 (1900) 123-124.

*T. G. Pinches, "Greek Transcriptions of Babylonian Tablets," *SBAP* 24 (1902) 108-119. [Sp. III. 245 + 81-7-6, 141 (35726); Sp. II. 290 + Sp. III. 247 (34797); Sp. II. 291 + Sp. III. 311 (34798); VATh. 412; Sp. III. 246 (35727)]

*A. H. Sayce, "The Greeks in Babylonian—Graeco-Cuneiform Texts," *SBAP* 24 (1902) 120-125.

J. Dyneley Prince and Frederick A Vanderburgh, "A Composite Bau-Text," *AJSL* 26 (1909-10) 137-150.

*Morris Jastrow Jr., "Sumerian glosses in astrological letters," *Baby* 3 (1909-10) 227-235.

George A. Barton, "The Inscription of Enkhegal, King of Lagash," *AJA* 17 (1913) 84-85.

---

1.   Listed here as a matter of convenience due to geographical distribution. Actual linguistic family has not been determined.

George A. Barton, "The Tablet of Enkhegal," *MJ* 4 (1913) 50-54.

Stephen Langdon, "Miscellania Assyriaca III," *Baby* 7 (1913-23) 93-98. [Tablet I of *HAR-RA* = *ḫubullu;* K. 4369, Tablet(?) of HAR-RA = *ḫubullu*]

D. D. Luckenbill, "The Chicago Syllabary," *AJSL* 33 (1916-17) 169-199.

*Theophile James Meek, "Explanatory List, RM. 2, 588," *AJSL* 36 (1919-20) 154-160.

R. M. Gwynn, "A Sumerian Tablet," *Herm* 19 (1920-22) 273-275.

George A. Barton, "The Archaic Inscription in Découvertes in Chaldeé, Plate 1bis," *JAOS* 42 (1922) 338-342.

T. Fish, "Some Sumerian Tablets in the John Rylands Library," *BJRL* 8 (1924) 406-411.

Sidney Smith, "Miscellanea," *RAAO* 21 (1924) 75-92. (*Addendum to p. 79,* p. 155) [(1) Samsu-iluna's Restoration at Nippur, Column I. (115039, Bole, Column II. (102404, Bole), Column III. 102404, Bole), pp. 75-78 [BM56620]]

T. Fish, "The 'Behrens Collection' of Sumerian Tablets in the Manchester Museum," *JMUEOS* #12 (1926) 29-46. [3309; 3464-3510; 3512]

G. R. Driver, "A Sumerian Tablet at Oxford," *AfO* 4 (1927) 26.

T. Fish, "Two Sumerian Records in the Manchester Museum," *JMUEOS* #15 (1930) 41-42.

S[tephen] Langdon, "New Texts from Jemdet Nasr," *JRAS* (1931) 837-844.

*S[tephen] Langdon, "Philological Notes," *RAAO* 28 (1931) 13-22. [5) A Grammatical Text from Kish, pp. 18-20. (W. 1928-2)]

G. R. Driver, "Two Sumerian Inscriptions at Oxford," *Or, N.S.,* 1 (1932) 86-88.

S[amuel] N[oah] Kramer, "Dr. Chiera's List of Duplicates to de Genouillac's *Textes Religieux Sumériens,*" *JAOS* 54 (1934) 407-420.

*S[tephen] Langdon, "Tablets from Kish and Umma," *RAAO* 34 (1937) 67-79. [I. Two Tablets from the series ḪURRA = *ḫubullu* (Kish, 1927-2118; Kish 1924-799); II. Four Tablets from Umma]

T. Fish, "KI.UD on Ur III Tablets," *AJSL* 55 (1938) 315-316.

*P. E. v[an] der] Meer, "A Topography of Babylon," *Iraq* 5 (1938) 55-64. [Ashmolean 1924-846; 1924-810; 1924-849]

*P. E. van der Meer, "Tablets of the ḪAR-ra = ḫubullu Series in the Ashmolean Museum," *Iraq* 6 (1939) 144-179.

*T. Fish, "Miscellanea," *Iraq* 6 (1939) 184-186. [II. BM. 105346, pp. 184-185; III. Sumerian Tablet, p. 186]

T. Fish, "Some Sumerian Tablets of the Third Dynasty of Ur," *JRAS* (1939) 29-39. [CBS. 8090; B.M. 105545; B.M. 106064; B.M. 113129; B.M. 105412]

*S[amuel] N[oah] Kramer, "Langdon's *Historical and Religious Texts from the Temple Library of Nippur*— Additions and Corrections," *JAOS* 60 (1940) 234-257.

*Thorkild Jacobsen, "Parerga Sumerologica," *JNES* 2 (1943) 117-121. [I. "Ur-Shanabi(k), Husband of Nanshe"; II. azu with value z u_x and Ur-Nanshe(k)'s Invocation to the Reed; III. The God Ig-Alima(k) (^{d}GÁL-ALIM); IV. The Presumed Deity ^{d}Diš-Dingir-Ra; V. Dugud, "Cloud"; VI. The Concept of Divine Parentage of the Ruler in the Stele of the Vultures; VII. "Tears of Joy"(?): Stele of the Vultures. Obv. XI 16-18]

*Albrecht Goetze, "The Vocabulary of the Princeton Theological Seminary," *JAOS* 65 (1945) 223-237. [PTS 1]

*Charles T. Fritsch, "Three Thousand Babylonian Clay Tablets," *PSB* 38 (1945) #4, 8-9. *[Princeton University Collection]*

Samuel N[oah] Kramer, "Interim Report of Work in the Museum at Istanbul (to October 16, 1946)," *BASOR* #104 (1946) 8-12.

*Samuel Noah Kramer, "The Tablet Collection of the University Museum," *JAOS* 67 (1947) 321-322. [Philadelphia University Cuneiform Texts]

Samuel N[oah] Kramer, "Second Interim Report on Work in the Museum at Istanbul," *BASOR* #105 (1947) 7-11.

*O. R. Gurney, "The Sultantepe Tablets. *A Preliminary Note*," *AS* 2 (1952) 25-35.

*F[rancis R. S[teele], "Writing and History: The New Tablets from Nippur," *UMB* 16 (1952-53) #2, 21-27.

Samuel Noah Kramer, "Four Firsts in Man's Recorded History: School/ Law/Taxes/Wisdom," *Arch* 7 (1954) 138-148.

Thorkild Jacobsen, "Texts and Fragments," *JCS* 8 (1954) 82-86. [10051; 10091; 10050; 10047; 10054; 10052; 10099] *[Texts only]*

*Edmond Sollberger, "Selected Texts from American Collections," *JCS* 10 (1956) 11-31. [1. An Inscribed Statuette from the Time of Gudea (HMS 8826); 2. An Old-Akkadian Contract (Metropolitan Museum of Art, 86.11.204); 3. A Sargonic Letter in Sumerian (OIM A.636.); 4-5. Texts Relating to Ibbī-Sīn's Coronation (Emory 38, Emory 55); 6. *gú* and *sa* as Measures (Emory 45); 7-8. A Sumerian Tablet with an Akkadian Counterpart (NBC 382, NBC 184); 9-12. Tablets concerning Gifts of Silver Rings (HTS 143; HTS 144; HTS 145; HTS 146.); 13. An Old Babylonian School Text (Emory 106)]

*T. Fish, "URÚ.ki," *JSS* 1 (1956) 206-215. *[Quarter of Lagash]*

L. J. Krušina-Černý, "Two Prague Collections of the Sumerian Tablets of the Third Dynasty of Ur," *ArOr* 25 (1957) 547-562.

J. Lœssøe, "A Cuneiform Inscription from the Island of Bahrain," *Kuml* (1957) 165-166.

Edmond Sollberger, "On Two Early Lagaš Inscriptions in the Iraq Museum," *Sumer* 13 (1957) 61- 64. [IM. 57010; IM. 55204]

Samuel Noah Kramer, "Corrections and Additions to SRT," *ZA* 52 (1957) 76-90.

William W. Hallo, "Contributions to Neo-Sumerian," *HUCA* 29 (1958) 69-108.

Samuel Noah Kramer, "A Sumerian Document with Microscopic Cuneiform," *Exped* 1 (1958-59) #3, 2-3.

L. J. Krušina-Černý, "Two Prague Collections of the Sumerian Tablets of the Third Dynasty of Ur (s.)," *ArOr* 27 (1959) 357-378.

*Benno Landsberger, "The Seventh Tablet of the Series e a-*nâqu*," *JCS* 13 (1959) 128-131.

*Albrecht Goetze, "The 38th Tablet of the Series á-A-*nāqu*," *JCS* 13 (1959) 120-127.

*Albrecht Goetze, "The Chronology of Šulgi Again," *Iraq* 22 (1960) 151-156. [5N-T 490; 6N-T 147; MLC 42; Smith Coll. 555; 6N-T 850; 6N-T382]

*Edmond Sollberger, "Graeco-Babyloniaca," *Iraq* 24 (1962) 63-72. [B.M. 34781 = Sp. II 273; B.M. 34798 = Sp II 291 + Sp III 311; B.M. 33769 = Rm IV 327]

*D. O. Edzard, "Texts and Fragments," *JCS* 16 (1962) 78-81. [HSM 3662; HSM 3625; HSM 7794; HSM 7522; HSM 7500; HSM 1659]

*Trevor Donald, "A Sumerian Plan in the John Rylands Library," *JSS* 7 (1962) 184-190. *[Architectural Plan]*

William W. Hallo, "On the Antiquity of Sumerian Literature," *JAOS* 83 (1963) 167-176.

*Peter Hulin, "A Table of Reciprocals with Sumerian Spellings," *JCS* 17 (1963) 72-76. [S.U. 52/5]

*S. Levy and P. Artzi, "Sumerian and Akkadian Documents from Public and Private Collections in Israel," *'Atiqot* 4 (1965) i-xii, 1-15.

Robert D. Biggs, "The Abū Ṣalābīkh Tablets. A Preliminary Survey," *JCS* 20 (1966) 73-88.

George G. Cameron, "A Lagash Mace Head Inscription," *JCS* 20 (1966) 125. [89538]

*M. Civil, "Remarks on 'Sumerian and Bilingual Texts'," *JNES* 26 (1967) 200-211.

*Edmond Sollberger, "A Tankard for Atta-Ḫušu," *JCS* 22 (1968) 30-33.

*Khalid Ahmad al-A'dami, "A New Lu.SHA Text," *Sumer* 25 (1969) 97-98. [IM. 67343]

S[amuel] N[oah] Kramer, "From the Sumer—Preview of a Supplement to *ANET*," *PIASH* 4 (1969-70) 14-28.

§911 *4.4.11.15.1 Sumerian Correspondence, Literary Texts and Wisdom Literature*

Theo. G. Pinches, "The Erechite's Lament Over the Desolation of His Fatherland," *BOR* 1 (1886-87) 21-22.

Theo. G. Pinches, "Lament over the Desolation of Ur *(Mukeyyer),*" *BOR* 2 (1887-88) 60-63. [K. 3931]

T. Fish, "Two Sumerian Letters in the British Museum," *JRAS* (1939) 615-620. [BM. 88140; BM. 105563]

Samuel N[oah] Kramer, "The Oldest Literary Catalogue: A Sumerian List of Literary Compositions Compiled About 2000 B.C.," *BASOR* #88 (1942) 10-19.

Samuel N[oah] Kramer, "Sumerian Literature; A Preliminary Survey of the Oldest Literature in the World," *PAPS* 85 (1942) 293-323.

Thorkild Jacobsen, "New Sumerian Literary Texts," *BASOR* #102 (1946) 12-17.

Samuel Noah Kramer, "Sumerian Wisdom Literature: A Preliminary Survey," *BASOR* #122 (1951) 28-30.

S[amuel] N[oah] K[ramer], "Mercy, Wisdom, and Justice: Some New Documents from Nippur," *UMB* 16 (1951-52) #2, 29-39.

S[amuel] N[oah] Kramer, "Preliminary Report on the Unpublished Sumerian Literary Tablets from Nippur in the Museum of the Ancient Orient (Istanbul)," *Or, N.S.,* 21 (1952) 249-251.

S[amuel] N[oah] Kramer, Muazzez Çiğ, and Hatice Kizilyay, "Five New Sumerian Literary Texts," *TTKB* 16 (1952) 355-365.

*Samuel Noah Kramer, "A 'Fulbright' in Turkey," *UMB* 17 (1952-53) #2, 5-56. [Law and Love, a Hymn, a Prayer, and a Word to the Wise, pp. 23-42; (The Shu-Sin Love poem [#2461], pp. 23-30); (A Word to the Wise: The "Book" of Proverbs, pp. 37-42)]

Samuel Noah Kramer, Hatrice Kizilyay (Bozkurt) and Muazzez Cig, "Selected Sumerian Literary Texts. Final Report of a 'Fulbright' Research Year in the Istanbul Museum of the Ancient Orient," *Or, N.S.,* 22 (1953) 190-193.

Edmund I. Gordon, "The Sumerian Proverb Collections: A Preliminary Report," *JAOS* 74 (1954) 82-85.

Samuel Noah Kramer, "'Man and his God.' A Sumerian variation on the 'Job' motif," *VTS* 3 (1955) 170-182. [CBS 13394; CBS 8321 + Ni 4137; Ni 4587; CBS 15205]

Edmund I. Gordon, "'Aesopic' Animal Fables from Sumer," *AJA* 61 (1957) 188.

Edmund I. Gordon, "Sumerian Proverbs: 'Collection Four',"*JAOS* 77 (1957) 67-79.

*Samuel Noah Kramer, "Love, Hate, and Fear. Psychological Aspects of Sumerian Culture," *EI* 5 (1958) 66*-74*.

Edmund I. Gordon, "Sumerian Animal Proverbs and Fables: 'Collection Five'," *JCS* 12 (1958) 1-21, 43-75.

Muazzez Çiğ, Hatice Kizilyay, and Samuel Noah Kramer, "New Sumerian Literary Fragments," *TAD* 8 (1958) #2, 37-38.

*Edmund I. Gordon, "A new Look at the Wisdom of Sumer and Akkad," *BO* 17 (1960) 121-152. [Some General Remarks on the Wisdom Literature of Mesopotamia; Classification of the Mesopotamian Wisdom Literature]

M[iguel] Civil, "The Home of the Fish. A New Sumerian Literary Composition," *Iraq* 23 (1961) 154-175. [Ni. 9668; Ni 4399]

Samuel Noah Kramer, "New Literary Catalogue from Ur," *RAAO* 55 (1961) 169-176.

Samuel Noah Kramer, "Literary Texts from Ur VI, Part II," *Iraq* 25 (1963) 171-176.

*Samuel Noah Kramer, "The Biblical 'Song of Songs' and the Sumerian Love Songs," *Exped* 5 (1962-63) #1, 25-31.

*Miguel Civil, "Sumerian Harvest Time," *Exped* 5 (1962-63) #4, 37-39.

*W. G. Lambert, "Celibacy in the World's Oldest Proverbs," *BASOR* #169 (1963) 63-64.

Fadhil A. Ali, "Two Collections of Sumerian Letters," *ArOr* 33 (1965) 529-540.

Edmond Sollberger, "The Rulers of Lagaš," *JCS* 21 (1967) 279-291. [BM 23103]

William W. Hallo, "The Lame and the Halt," *EI* 9 (1969) 66-70 *[Non-Hebrew Section]*

Samuel Noah Kramer, "Lamentation Over the Destruction of Nippur," *EI* 9 (1969) 89-93. *[Non-Hebrew Section]*

Samuel Noah Kramer, "Sumerian Similes: A Panoramic View of Some of Man's Oldest Literary Images," *JAOS* 89 (1969) 1-10.

Samuel Noah Kramer, "Sumerian Sacred Marriage Songs and the Biblical 'Song of Songs'," *MIO* 15 (1969) 262-274.

§912 *4.4.11.15.2 Sumerian Historical Texts*

Fritz Hommel, "Sumerological Notes. I. A Parallel Passage in the Gudi'a Inscriptions," *BOR* 1 (1886-87) 180-181.

Fritz Hommel, "Sumerological Notes. II. A Parallel Passage in the Gudi'a Inscriptions," *BOR* 1 (1886-87) 181.

*C. Leonard Woolley, "Excavations at Tel el Obeid," *AJ* 4 (1924) 329-346. [Foundation-tablet of A-an-ni-pad-da, pp. 343-344 *(plate XLV)*]

Hope W. Hogg, "Inscribed Nail of Ellil-Bani, Twelfth King of the Babylonian Dynasty of Isin," *JMUEOS* #1 (1911) 1-10.

Hope W. Hogg, "Clay 'Nail' of Ellil-Bani. Notes on the Text," *JMUEOS* #1 (1911) 11-20.

T[heophilus] G. Pinches, "Light Upon Early Babylonian History," *ET* 23 (1911-12) 305-309.

Theophilus G. Pinches, "Further Light Upon Early Babylonian History," *ET* 23 (1911-12) 567.

T[heophilus] G. Pinches, "Text Referring to the Stele of Me-Silim," *JTVI* 44 (1912) 296.

George A. Barton, "The Inscription of Enkhegel, King of Lagash," *AJA* 17 (1913) 84-85.

C. H. W. Johns, "A New Inscription of An-àm," *AJSL* 30 (1913-14) 290-291.

George S. Duncan, "The Sumerian Inscriptions of Sin-Gâšid, King of Erech, Transliterated, Translated, and Annotated,"*AJSL* 31 (1914-15) 215-221.

James B. Nies, "A Net Cylinder of Entemena," *JAOS* 36 (1916) 136-139.

James B. Nies, "A Net Cylinder of Entemena," *A&A* 5 (1917) 105-106.

*H. F. Lutz, "Brief Notes. On the Reading of the Date-formula of the Fourth Year of Gimil-Sin," *JAOS* 37 (1917) 330-331.

James B. Nies, "A Pre-Sargonic Inscription on Limestone from Warka," *JAOS* 38 (1918) 188-196.

Mary I. Hussey, "A Galet of Eannatu," *JAOS* 38 (1918) 264-266.

*Leon Legrain, "A New Fragment of Chronology: The Dynasty of Agade," *MJ* 12 (1921) 75-77.

*C. J. Gadd, "Notes on some Babylonian Rulers," *JRAS* (1922) 389-396. [Sumerian Inscription, p. 392]

*Ira Maurice Price, "The Topography of the Gudea Inscriptions," *JAOS* 43 (1923) 41-48.

Leon Legrain, "The Inscription of the Kings of Agade. The Missing Fragment of the Nippur Tablet. CBS. 13972," *MJ* 14 (1923) 203-220.

George A. Barton, "A new inscription of Libit-Ishtar," *JAOS* 45 (1925) 154-155.

*C. J. Gadd, "On Two Babylonian Kings," *SO* 1 (1925) 25-33. [B.M. 79503]

*Sidney Smith, "Assyriological Notes," *JRAS* (1926) 433-446. [The Kings' Share [BM 117580]]

*Leon Legrain, "The Tragic History of Ibi-Sin, King of Ur," *MJ* 17 (1926) 372-392. [U. 6399; U. 6378; U. 6716; U. 6370; U. 6373; U. 6368; U. 6729; U. 2962; U. 6375; ; U. 6374; U. 6372; U. 6700; U. 2922; U. 6701; U. 6725; U. 6377; U. 6731; U. 2625; U. 2596; U. 2548; U. 2647; U. 2699; U. 2682; U. 6381; U. 2584; U. 6382; U. 6383; U. 6724; U. 6386; U. 6730; U. 6710; U. 6384; U. 6385; U. 6387; U. 6388; U. 6389; U. 6708; U. 6391; U. 6709; U. 6390; U. 6392; U. 6393; U. 6395; U. 6394; U. 6396; U. 6397; U. 6712; U. 6713; U. 6714; U. 6727; U. 6958; U. 6314; U. 4954; U. 6322; U. 6715; U. 2616; U. 2662; U. 2585]

C. J. Gadd, "Another A-anni-padda Inscription," *JRAS* (1928) 626-628. [BM. 90951]

T. Fish, "A Sumerian Administration Tablet of the Third Ur-Dynasty," *JMUEOS* #14 (1929) 61-66.

*S[tephen H.] Langdon, "A Year Date of Ibi-Sin in an Historical Inscription," *RAAO* 31 (1934) 114.

T. Fish, "A Rylands Cuneiform Tablet Concerning the Conquest of Kish under Agga," *BJRL* 19 (1935) 362-372.

*Albrecht Goetze, "Sin-iddinam of Larsa. New Tablets from his Reign," *JCS* 4 (1950) 83-118. [Cornell University Library 78; YBT V 38 (YBC 4832); YBC 10366; Grain Lists, UIOM 2040; YBC 3306; YBC 3328, 4311, 5198, 5223; A Seventh Date of Sin-iddinam; The Reign of Sin-iddinam]

*A. Goetze, "Texts and Fragments," *JCS* 4 (1950) 137-140. [Crozer Theological Seminary No. 199. Kenrick Seminary No. 1]

Thorkild Jacobsen, "The Reign of Ibbī-Suen," *JCS* 7 (1953) 36-47.

Edmond Sollberger, "Remarks on Ibbīsīn's Reign," *JCS* 7 (1953) 48-50.

Edmond Sollberger, "New Lists of the Kings of Ur and Isin," *JCS* 8 (1954) 135-136.

*Edmond Sollberger, "Selected Texts from American Collections," *JCS* 10 (1956) 11-31. [4-5. Texts Relating to Ibbī-Sīn's Coronation, pp. 18-20. (Emory 38, Emory 55)]

*I. M. Diakonoff, "Some Remarks on the 'Reforms' of Urukagina," *RAAO* 52 (1958) 1-15.

C. J. Gadd, "Rim-Sin Approaches the Grand Entrance," *Iraq* 22 (1960) 157-165. [U. 7734]

*William W. Hallo, "A Sumerian Amphictyony," *JCS* 14 (1960) 88-114.

*M. B. Rowton, "The Date of the Sumerian King List," *JNES* 19 (1960) 156-162.

M[ichel] Civil, "Texts and Fragments," *JCS* 15 (1961) 79-80. [N 3368 + CBS 14223; N 1610; N 77 rev.; N 236 rev.; CBS 14226 + N 537; N 405 rev]

Edmond Sollberger, "The Tummal Inscription," *JCS* 16 (1962) 40-47.

William W. Hallo, "Beginning and End of the Sumerian King List in the Nippur Recension," *JCS* 17 (1963) 52-57.

*E. Sollberger, "Samsu-iluna's bilingual inscription B, text of the Akkadian version," *RAAO* 61 (1967) 39-44. *[Sumerian Text]*

Raphael Kutscher, "Apillaša, Governor of Kazallu," *JCS* 22 (1968-69) 63-65.

§913 *4.4.11.15.3 Sumerian Legal and Commercial Texts*

William Cruickshank, "Sumerian Administrative Documents," *ET* 22 (1910-11) 231-232.

St[ephen] Langdon, "Some Sumerian contracts," *ZA* 25 (1911) 205-214.

S[tephen H.] Langdon, "Contracts from Larsa," *SBAP* 34 (1912) 109-113. [Ashmolean Museum, 1911-282; 1911-288; 111-276; 1911-280; 1911-278; 1911-284; 1911-281; 1911-279; 1911-285; 1911-286]

*Samuel A. B. Mercer, "The Oath in Cuneiform Inscriptions," *JAOS* 33 (1913) 33-50. [Part I] *[Sumerian Inscriptions]*

Mary Inda Hussey, "Tablets from Dréhem in the Public Library of Cleveland, Ohio," *JAOS* 33 (1913) 167-179.

Anonymous, "An Early Babylonian Law Code," *HR* 69 (1915) 369.

T[heophilus] G. Pinches, "An Early Mention of Nahr Malka," *JRAS* (1917) 735-740.

*V. Schiel, "The Oldest Written Code," *MJ* 11 (1920) 130-132.

*S[tephen] Langdon, "Assyrian Lexicographical Notes," *JRAS* (1921) 573-582. [A Sumerian Contract from Ellasar, pp. 577-582]

*T. Fish, "Sumerian Wage List of the Ur Dynasty," *BJRL* 9 (1925) 241-247.

*S[tephen] Langdon, "Tablets found in Mound Z at Harsagkalamma (Kish) by the Herbert Weld (for Oxford) and Field Museum Expedition," *RAAO* 24 (1927) 89-98. [Kish, 1927, 1; Kish 1927-2. Case Tablet; Kish, 1927-2; 1927-3; Earliest Sale of Slaves, Barton P.B.S. IX, No. 4]

*S[tephen] Langdon, "A Contract with a New Date of Samsu-iluna," *RAAO* 27 (1930) 83-84.

*A. Poebel, "Note on the Date of Samsuiluna, *RA* , XXVII, 83," *AJSL* 48 (1931) 54-55.

Samuel N[oah] Kramer, "New Tablets from Fara," *JAOS* 52 (1932) 110-132. [F-13, F-4893; F-602; F-974; F-973]

Thorkild Jacobsen, "New Texts of the Third Ur Period," *AJSL* 55 (1938) 419-421.

Francis R[ue] Steele, "The Lipit-Ishtar Law Code," *AJA* 51 (1947) 158-164.

Francis Rue Steele, "The Code of Lipit-Ishtar," *AJA* 52 (1948) 425-450.

A[lbrecht] Goetze, "Umma Texts Concerning Reed Mats," *JCS* 2 (1948) 165-202.

Francis Rue Steele, "An Additional Fragment of the Lipit-Ishtar Code Tablet from Nippur," *ArOr* 18 (1950) Parts 1&2, 489-493. [UM 29—16—203]

Josef Klímar, "New Discoveries of Legal Documents from Pre-Hammurapian Times," *ArOr* 19 (1951) Parts 1&2, 37-59 [II. Laws of Lipit Ishtar]

Donald E. McCown, "An Agricultural Document from Nippur," *Sumer* 7 (1951) 77-78.

*Samuel Noah Kramer, "A 'Fulbright' in Turkey," *UMB* 17 (1952-53) #2, 5-56. [Law and Love, a Hymn, a Prayer, and a Word to the Wise, pp. 23-42; (The Ur-Nammu Law Code, pp. 23-30)]

Roger T. O'Callaghan, "A New Inheritance Contract from Nippur," *JCS* 8 (1954) 137-143. [NBC 8935]

*Ferris J. Stephens, "Notes on some Economic Texts of the Time of Urukagina," *RAAO* 49 (1955) 129-136. [1. Who was Urukagina's Predecessor? 2. Lexical Notes *(no subs)*; 3. Seizure of Property for Debt; 4. The Date of Urukagina's Reforms]

*Tom B. Jones, "Bookkeeping in Ancient Sumer," *Arch* 9 (1956) 16-21.

W. F. Leemans and A. Falkenstein, "Texts and Fragments," *JCS* 10 (1957) 41. *[Sumerian Contract]*

*Samuel Noah Kramer, "Cuneiform Studies and the History of Literature: The Sumerian Marriage Texts," *PAPS* 107 (1963) 485-527.

Fadhil A. Ali, "Blowing the Horn for Official Announcement," *Sumer* 20 (1964) 66-68.

*J. J. Finkelstein, "Sex Offenses in Sumerian Laws," *JAOS* 86 (1966) 355-372. [Lipit-Ishtar §33; U. 7739; *YBT* I 28; 3N-T403+T340; Sm 49+752]

Albrecht Goetze, "An Archaic Legal Document," *JCS* 20 (1966) 126-127. [Denver Art Museum, 0-164]

Elmer B. Smick, "A Business Document from the Time of Abraham," *GJ* 9 (1968) #1, 25-31.

William W. Hallo, "The Neo-Sumerian Letter-Orders," *BO* 26 (1969) 171-176. [BM 13441; AO (?); BM 18568; BM 130705; NBC 9268; NBC 8861; HSM 1800; NBC 8863; NBC 6429, *and other unnumbered texts*]

*Samuel Greengus, "A Textbook Case of Adultery in Ancient Mesopotamia," *HUCA* 40 (1969) 33-44.

§914 *4.4.11.15.3 Sumerian Epic Literature and Mythological Texts*

*A. H. Sayce, "Recent Biblical and Oriental Archaeology. The Sumerian Origin of the First Account of the Creation in Genesis," *ET* 14 (1902-03) 124-125.

Stephen Langdon, "A Sumerian legend concerning *Dul-Azag*," *Baby* 3 (1909-10) 79-80.

S[tephen] Langdon, "A Reconstruction of a part of the Sumerian Text of the Seventh Tablet of Creation, with the aid of Assyrian Commentaries," *SBAP* 32 (1910) 115-123, 159-167.

S[tephen H.] Langdon, "A new Sumerian Document," *MJ* 5 (1914) 141-144. [The Sumerian Epic of Paradise, the Flood and the Fall of Man]

S[tephen H.] Langdon, "A Preliminary Account of a Sumerian Legend of the Flood and the Fall of Man," *SBAP* 36 (1914) 188-198.

*Anonymous, "Three Babylonian Documents," *HR* 69 (1915) 108-111. [Sumerian Epic of Paradise, the Flood, and the Fall of Man, p. 109]

J. Dyneley Prince, "The So-called Epic of Paradise," *JAOS* 36 (1916) 90-114.

Morris Jastrow Jr., "The Sumerian View of the Beginnings," *JAOS* 36 (1916) 122-135.

*Morris Jastrow Jr., "Sumerian and Akkadian Views of Beginnings," *JAOS* 36 (1916) 274-299.

S[tephen] Langdon, "Critical Notes Upon the Epic of Paradise," *JAOS* 36 (1916) 140-145.

J. Dyneley Prince, "Further Notes on the So-Called Epic of Paradise," *JAOS* 36 (1916) 269-273.

S[tephen] H. L[angdon], "Ishtar's Journey to Hell," *MJ* 7 (1916) 178-181. [Ni. 11088 + 11064]

W. W. Martin, "'Sumerian Epic of Paradise, the Flood, and the Fall of Man'," *MQR, 3rd Ser.,* 42 (1916) 640-653.

*S[tephen] Langdon, "The Necessary Revisions of the Sumerian Epic of Paradise," *AJSL* 33 (1916-17) 245-249.

*W. W. Martin, "The Unhistoricity of the Higher Criticism. As Evidenced by the Poebel Flood Tablet," *MQR, 3rd Ser.,* 44 (1918) 209-220.

W[illiam] F[oxwell] Albright, "Some Cruces in the Langdon Epic," *JAOS* 39 (1919) 65-90.

Leroy Waterman, "The Curse in the 'Paradise Epic'," *JAOS* 39 (1919) 322-328.

Edward Chiera, "A New Creation Story," *JAOS* 41 (1921) 459-460.

D. D. Luckenbill, "The Ashur Version of the Seven Tablets of Creation," *AJSL* 38 (1921-22) 12-35.

S[tephen H.] Langdon, "Miscellaneous Communications. The Chaldean Kings before the Flood," *JRAS* (1923) 251-259. [Ashmolean Museum, W-B. 62]

P. E. Burrows, "Notes on the antediluvian kings," *Or* #7 (1923) 50-59.

*S[tephen] Langdon, "The Legend of kiškanu," *JRAS* (1928) 843-848. [CT. xvi, 46; CT. 16, 46, 183-204]

*Stephen Langdon, "The Sumerian Edition of the Epic of Gilgamish," *A&A* 33 (1932) 295-296, 332.

*S[tephen] Langdon, "The Sumerian Epic of Gilgamish," *JRAS* (1932) 911-947. [Kish 1932, 155]

Theophilus G. Pinches, "The Tablet of the Epic of the Golden Age," *JTVI* 64 (1932) 159-173, 176-177. (Discussion, pp. 173-176)

*Oliver R. Gurney, "A Bilingual Text Concerning Etana," *JRAS* (1935) 459-466. [K. 5119; a duplicate of Ki 1904-10-9,87]

*Samuel N[oah] Kramer, "Ishtar in the Nether World According to a New Sumerian Text," *BASOR* #79 (1940) 18-27.

*S[amuel] N[oah] Kramer, "Man's Golden Age: A Sumerian Parallel to Genesis XI. 1," *JAOS* 63 (1943) 191-194. [CBS 29.16.422]

*S[amuel] N[oah] Kramer, "Dilmun, the Land of the Living," *BASOR* #96 (1944) 18-28.

*S[amuel] N[oah] Kramer, "The Epic of Gilgameš and Its Sumerian Sources. A Study in Literary Evolution," *JAOS* 64 (1944) 7-23.

*S[amuel] N[oah] Kramer, "Corrections to 'The Epic of Gilgameš and Its Sumerian Sources," *JAOS* 64 (1944) 83.

Samuel Noah Kramer, "A Sumerian 'Paradise' Myth," *CQ* 22 (1945) 207-220.

Samuel Noah Kramer, "Heroes of Sumer: A New Heroic Age in World History and Literature," *PAPS* 90 (1946) 120-130.

*Samuel Noah Kramer, "Gilgamesh in the Land of the Living," *JCS* 1 (1947) 3-46. [YBC 9857; UM 29-13-209 + 29-16-414; UM 29-13-473; UM 29-15-364; CBS 7914; U 29-16-84; UIOM 1057]

Samuel Noah Kramer, "A Blood-Plague Motif in Sumerian Mythology," *ArOr* 17 (1949) Part 1, 399-405. [Ni 9721]

Samuel Noah Kramer, "'Inanna's Descent to the Nether World' Continued and Revised," *JCS* 4 (1950) 199-214; 5 (1951) 1-17 .[YBC 4621; Ni. 9685]

Samuel Noah Kramer, "Tales of Sumer: Man's Oldest Myths," *UMB* 19 (1955) #4, 3-29. *[Illustrations by Hellmuth Schubert]*

S[amuel] N[oah] Kramer, "The Death of Ur-Nammu and His Descent to the Netherworld," *JCS* 21 (1967) 104-122. [Ni. 4487; HS 1428 + 1560; HS 1450; HS 1549; HS 1581; HS 1570; HS 1529; HS 1440]

*Miguel Civil, "Isme-Dagan and Enlil's Chariot," *JAOS* 88 (1968) 3-14. [CBS 6136]

*Samuel Noah Kramer, "The 'Babel of Tongues': A Sumerian Version," *JAOS* 88 (1968) 108-111. [Ash. 1924.475]

§915 *4.4.11.15.4 Sumerian Religious and Liturgical Texts*

*O. D. Miller, "The Antiquity of Sacred Writings in the Valley of the Euphrates," *OBJ* 1 (1880) 75-80.

*C. J. Ball, "A Bilingual Hymn (4R. 46, 5-19)," *SBAP* 15 (1892-93) 51-54.

J. Dyneley Prince, "The Hymn to Bêlit, K. 257 (HT. 126-131)," *JAOS* 24 (1903) 103-128.

*Kerr D. MacMillan, "Some Cuneiform Tablets bearing on the Religion of Babylonia and Assyria," *BAVSS* 5 (1906) 531-712. (Index to Tablets, pp. 615-616) [K. 1279; K. 1453; K. 2004; K. 2613; K. 2764; K. 2769; K. 2871; K. 2875; K. 2920; K. 3153; K. 3258; K. 3356; K. 3361; K. 3364; K. 3477; K. 3479; K. 3600 + D.T. 75; K. 3853; K. 4620; K. 4659; K. 5008; K. 5117; K. 5118; K. 5124; K. 5126; K. 5142; K. 5144; K. 5245; K. 5254; K. 5260; K. 5261; K. 5268 + K. 5333; K. 5315; K. 5333; K. 5930; K. 6160; K. 6317; K. 6400; K. 6465; K. 6497; K. 6849; K. 6898; K. 6981; K. 7065; K. 7226; K. 7271; K. 7816; K. 7897; K. 7924; K. 8399; K. 8862; K. 8917; K. 9270 + K. 9289; K. 9279; K. 9289; K. 9291; K. 9296; K. 9299; K. 9312; K. 9453; K. 9480; K. 11173; K. 11174; 33851; S. 2054; D.T. 46; D.T. 75; 80,7—19, 125; 80,7—19, 126; 81, 2—4, 247; 83,1—19, 691]

Vincent Brummer, "An early Chaldean incantation of the 'temple not exorcised'," *RTR* 28 (1906) 214-227.

*Mary Inda Hussey, "Some Sumerian-Babylonian Hymns of the Berlin Collection," *AJSL* 23 (1906-07) 142-176.

J. Dyneley Prince, "A Hymn to Nergal," *JAOS* 28 (1907) 168-182.

Frederick A. Vanderburgh, "A Hymn to Bêl (Tablet 29644, CT. XV, Plates 11 and 12)," *JAOS* 29 (1909) 184-191.

Frederick A. Vanderburgh, "A Hymn to Bêl (Tablet 29623, CT. XV, Plates 12 and 13)," *JAOS* 30 (1909-10) 61-71.

J. Dyneley Prince, "A Hymn to Tammuz *(Cuneiform Texts from the British Museum, Tablet 15821, Plate 18),*" *JAOS* 30 (1909-10) 94-100.

Frederick A. Vanderburgh, "A Hymn to Mullil. Tablet 29615, CT. XV, Plates 7, 8 and 9," *JAOS* 30 (1909-10) 313-324.

J. Dyneley Prince, "A Hymn to the Goddess Kir-gí-lu (Cuneiform Texts from the British Museum, XV., Plate 23) with translation and commentary," *JAOS* 30 (1909-10) 325-335.

Stephen Langdon, "An ancient magical text," *Baby* 6 (1912) 106-108.

Stephen Langdon, "A classical liturgy to Innini," *RAAO* 9 (1912) 5-11. [BM 23117]

*Th[eophile] J. Meek, "Cuneiform Bilingual Hymns, Prayers and Penitential Psalms. Autographed, transliterated and translated with notes from the original tablets in the British Museum," *BAVSS* 10 (1913) Heft 1, I-IV, 1-127.

S[tephen] Langdon, "A Hymn to Enlil with a theological redaction," *RAAO* 12 (1915) 27-32.

*S[tephen H.] Langdon, "A bilingual tablet from Erech of the first century B.C.," *RAAO* 12 (1915) 73-84. [Corr. *RAAO* 26 (1929) p. 143] [AO 6458]

Stephen Langdon, "A New Tablet of the Cult of Deified Kings in Ancient Sumer," *MJ* 8 (1917) 165-179.

John A. Maynard, "Studies in the Religious Texts from Assur," *AJSL* 34 (1917-18) 21-59.

*Stephen Langdon, "A Sumerian Liturgy Containing an Ode to the Word," *MJ* 9 (1918) 158-163.

*Theophile James Meek, "Some Bilingual Religious Texts, *AJSL* 35 (1918-19) 134-144. [K. 2856; K. 1905-5-10, 19; Ki. 1904-10-9, 64; K. 2856; K. 1904-10-9, 87; K. 1904-10-9, 96; K. 1904-10-9, 138; K. 1905-4-9 10+12; Th. 1905-4-9, 13; Th. 1905-4-9, 93; Th. 1905-4-9, 93; Th. 1905-4-9, 245; Th. 1905-4-9, 393; Th. 1905-4-9, 394]

S[tephen H.] Langdon, "Three New Hymns in the Cults of the Deified Kings," *SBAP* 40 (1918) 30-40, 45-46, 69-85. [B.M. 78183; Bodleian 146; Bodleian 170; Bodleian 168]

S[tephen] Langdon, "Two sumerian liturgical texts," *RAAO* 16 (1919) 207-209. [Tablet Nies 1315; Ashmolean Prism]

Edward Chiera, "Corrections to Langdon's 'Sumerian Liturgical Texts'," *AJSL* 36 (1919-20) 233-244.

Stephen Langdon, "A Hymn of Eridu," *JSOR* 5 (1921) 63-69.

*Steph[en] Langdon, "Hymn concerning the Cohabitation of the Earth God and the Earth Goddess, the begetting of the Moon God," *RAAO* 19 (1922) 67-77. [Ni. 9205]

*S[tephen H.] Langdon, "Two Sumerian Hymns from Eridu and Nippur," *AJSL* 39 (1922-23) 161-186. [W-B. 1922, 161; BM. 96706]

*S[tephen H.] Langdon, "The Legend of the kiškanu," *JRAS* (1928) 843-848. [CT 16, 14, 183-204]

Samuel A. B. Mercer, "A New Interpretation of the Gudea Cylinder A and Some Observations," *JSOR* 7 (1923) 56-59.

Stephen Langdon, "The Eyes of Ningal," *RAAO* 20 (1923) 9-11.

S[tephen] Langdon, "A Hymn in Strophes to Ur-Ninurta. CT. 36, 28-30," *JRAS* (1925) 487-497.

S[tephen] Langdon, "A Hymn to Ishtar as the Planet Venus and to Idin-Dagan as Tammuz," *JRAS* (1926) 15-42.

S[tephen] Langdon, "A List of the known Titles of Sumerian Penitential Psalms. (Ersaghunga), arranged in alphabetical order," *RAAO* 22 (1925) 119-125.

Henry Frederick Lutz, "Sumerian Temple Records of the Late Ur Dynasty," *UCPSP* 9 (1927-31) 117-268.

C. J. Gadd, "Entemena: a new incident," *RAAO* 27 (1930) 125-126. [B.M. 121208]

S[tephen] Langdon, "A Sumerian Hymn to Ishtar (Innini) and the Deified Ishme-Dagan," *JRAS* (1931) 367-379.

*S[tephen H.] Langdon, "Restoration of the 'Utukkê' limûti Series, Tablet C," *RAAO* 28 (1931) 159-163.

*S[amuel] N[oah] Kramer, "Langdon's *Historical and Religious Texts from the Temple Library of Nippur*— Additions and Corrections," *JAOS* 60 (1940) 234-257.

*A. Goetze, "Texts and Fragments," *JCS* 4 (1950) 137-140. [Sumerian Hymn to Nusku]

*T. Fish, "Miscellany," *MCS* 2 (1952) 59-62. [1. A Sumerian Exorcism Text, pp. 59-60]

*Samuel Noah Kramer, "A 'Fulbright' in Turkey," *UMB* 17 (1952-53) #2, 5-56. [Law and Love, a Hymn, a Prayer, and a Word to the Wise, pp. 23-42; (Hymn to the Air-God Enlil [Ni 4150], pp. 33-36); (The Hymnal Prayer to the Storm-God Ninurta [Ni 9695], pp. 36-37)]

Samuel Noah Kramer, "Hymn to the Ekur," *RDSO* 32 (1957) 95-102.

*William W. Hallo, "Royal Hymns and Mesopotamian Unity," *JCS* 17 (1963) 112-118.

Fadhil A. Ali, "Dedication of a Dog to Nintinugga," *ArOr* 34 (1966) 289-293.

W. W. Hallo, "New Hymns to the Kings of Isin," *BO* 23 (1966) 239-247.

*Samuel Noah Kramer, "Shulgi of Ur: A Royal Hymn and Divine Blessing," *JQR, 75th,* (1967) 369-380.

W. W. Hallo, "Individual Prayer in Sumerian: The Continuity of a Tradition," *JAOS* 88 (1968) 71-89.

S[amuel] N[oah] Kramer, "Inanna and Šulgi: A Sumerian Fertility Song," *Iraq* 31 (1969) 18-23. [Ni 4171]

§916 *4.4.11.16 Urartian and "Vannic" Texts*

A. H. Sayce, "The Cuneiform Inscriptions of Van, deciphered and translated," *JRAS* (1882) 377-732. *[Parts 1-3]*

A. H. Sayce, "The Cuneiform Inscriptions of Van," *JRAS* (1888) 1-48.

A.H. Sayce, "The Cuneiform Inscriptions of Van. Part IV," *JRAS* (1893) 1-39.

A. H. Sayce, "The Cuneiform Inscriptions of Van. Part V," *JRAS* (1894) 691-732.

K. J. Basmadjian, "Note on the Van Inscriptions," *JRAS* (1897) 579-583.

A. H. Sayce, "The Cuneiform Inscriptions of Van: Lexicographical Note," *JRAS* (1900) 798-799.

A. H. Sayce, "Fresh Contributions to the Decipherment of the Vannic Inscriptions," *JRAS* (1901) 645-660.

A. H. Sayce, "The Cuneiform Inscriptions of Van. Part VII," *JRAS* (1906) 611-653.

A. H. Sayce, "The Cuneiform Inscriptions of Van. Part VIII," *JRAS* (1911) 49-63.

A. H. Sayce, "A New Vannic Inscription," *JRAS* (1912) 107-112.

A. H. Sayce, "A New Inscription of the Vannic King Menuas," *JRAS* (1914) 75-77.

A. H. Sayce, "Some new Vannic Inscriptions," *JRAS* (1929) 297-336.

Albrecht Götze, "Some Notes on the Corpus Inscriptionum Chaldicarum," *JAOS* 55 (1935) 294-302. *(Review)*

P. Hulin, "Urartian Stones in the Van Museum," *AS* 8 (1958) 235-244.

H. W. F. Saggs, "Nimrud Letters, 1952—Part IV," *Iraq* 20 (1958) 182-212. [The Urartian Frontier] [ND. 2795; 2656; 2734 + 2416 + 2457; 2655; 2635; 2677; 2673; 2608; 2463; 2453]

P. Hulin, "New Urartian Inscriptions from Adilcevas," *AS* 9 (1959) 189-195.

P. Hulin, "New Urartian Inscribed Stones at Anzaf," *AS* 10 (1960) 205-207.

*Warren C. Benedict, "The Urartian-Assyrian Inscription of Kelishin," *JAOS* 81 (1961) 359-385.

Hans G. Güterbock, "Urartian Inscriptions in the Museum of Van," *JNES* 22 (1963) 268-272.

Warren C. Benedict, "Two Urartian Inscriptions from Azerbaijan," *JCS* 19 (1965) 35-40.

§917 *4.4.12 South Semitic Texts - General Studies*

H. J. Franken, "Clay Tablets from Deir 'Alla, Jordan," *VT* 14 (1964) 377-379.

H. J. Franken, "A Note on How the Deir 'Alla Tablets were Written," *VT* 15 (1965) 150-152.

H. J. Franken, "A Reply," *VT* 15 (1965) 535-536.

§918   *4.4.12.1 Ethiopian Texts*

William Wright, "List of the Magdala Collection of Ethiopic manuscripts in the British Museum," *ZDMG* 24 (1870) 599-616.

George H. Schodde, "Remarks on the Ethiopic," *AJSL* 1 (1884-85) 123-127.

A[rchibald] H. Sayce, "Fifth Interim Report on the Excavations at Meroë. 3. The Great Stela," *AAA* 7 (1914-16) 23-24.

A[rchibald] H. Sayce, "The Stela of Amon-Renas," *AAA* 7 (1914-16) 67-80.

*Edward Ullendorff, "The 'Death of Moses' in the Literature of the Falashas," *BSOAS* 24 (1961) 419-443.

Max Wurmbrand, "Remarks on the Text of the Falasha 'Death of Moses'," *BSOAS* 25 (1962) 431-437.

§919   *4.4.12.2 Arabic Texts*

*James Hadley, "On a Recent Memoir by Professor Chwolson of St. Petersburgh, entitled 'Remains of Ancient Babylonian Literature in Arabic Translations'," *JAOS* 7 (1862) vi-vii.

*James Hadley, "On Chwolson's 'Remains of Ancient Babylonian Literature in Arabic Translations'," *JAOS* 7 (1862) liv.

John P. Brown, "The History of the Learned Haikar, Vizir[sic]* of Sennacherib the King, and of Nadan, son of Haikar's Sister, translated from the Arabic," *JAOS* 8 (1866) lvi.

H[artwig] Hirschfeld, "Jewish Arabic Liturgies," *JQR* 6 (1893-94) 119-135, 399. *[The Tale of Hannah and Her Sons]*

H[artwig] Hirschfeld, "Jewish Arabic Liturgies, II," *JQR* 7 (1894-95) 418-427.

M. Steinschneider, "An Introduction to the Arabic Literature of the Jews, I.," *JQR* 9 (1896-97) 224-239, 604-630.

M. Steinschneider, "An Introduction to the Arabic Literature of the Jews, I *(continued),*" *JQR* 10 (1897-98) 119-138, 513-540; 11 (1898-99) 115-149, 305-343, 480-489, 585-625;12 (1899-1900) 114-132, 195-212.

M. Steinschneider, "An Introduction to the Arabic Literature of the Jews, II.," *JQR* 12 (1899-1900) 481-501.

M. Steinschneider, "An Introduction to the Arabic Literature of the Jews II *(continued),*" *JQR* 12 (1899-1900) 602-617; 13 (1900-01) 92-110, 296-320.

M. Steinschneider, "An Introduction to Arabic Literature of the Jews *(continued),*" *JQR* 13 (1900-01) 446-487. *[Includes Table of Contents and Index]*

H[artwig] Hirschfeld, "Arabic Portion of the Cairo Genizah at Cambridge," *JQR* 15 (1902-03) 167-181, 677-697; 16 (1903-04) 98-112, 290-299, 573-578, 690-694; 17 (1904-05) 65-68, 198-202, 431-440, 712-725; 18 (1905-06) 113-119, 119-120, 317-325, 325-329. 600-620.

I. Goldziher, "The Arabic Portions of the Cairo Genizah," *JQR* 15 (1902-03) 526-528.

H[artwig] Hirschfeld, "Note on J. Q. R., XVII, 168," *JQR* 17 (1904-05) 389-390. [Ref. *JQR* 16 (1903-04) 690ff.]

H[artwig] Hirschfeld, "Note on Genizah Fragment XXVI (July, 1905)," *JQR* 18 (1905-06) 146.

W. Bacher, "Notes on No. LXVIII of the J. Q. R.," *JQR* 18 (1905-06) 146-148. [Ref. *JQR* 17 (1904-05) 712ff.]

*H[artwig] Hirschfeld, "Arabic Portion of the Cairo Genizah at Cambridge," *JQR* 19 (1906-07) 136-161. *[Sa'adyah's Commentary on Leviticus]*

*Richard J. H. Gottheil, "An Eleventh-Century Document Concerning a Cairo Synagogue," *JQR* 19 (1906-07) 467-539.

Henry Malter, "Personifications of Soul and Body, A Study in Judaeo-Arabic Literature," *JQR, N.S.,*2 (1911-12) 453-479.

R. A. Stewart Macalister, "A Cistern with Cufic Graffiti near Jerusalem," *PEFQS* 47 (1915) 81-85.

Max van Berchem, "Note on the Graffiti of the Cistern at Wady el-Joz," *PEFQS* 47 (1915) 85-90, 195-198.

B. Halpern, "Descriptive Catalogue of Genizah Fragments in Philadelphia V, Documents and Letters," *JQR, N.S.,* 14 (1923-24) 514-546.

H[artwig] Hirschfeld, "Some Judaeo-Arabic Legal Documents," *JQR, N.S.,* 16 (1925-26) 279-286.

Jacob Mann, "Note on 'Some Judaeo-Arabic Legal Documents'," *JQR, N.S.,* 17 (1926-27) 83-85.

Hartwig Hirschfeld, "A Hebraeo—Sufic Poem," *JAOS* 49 (1929) 168-169.

A. R. Nykl and Martin Sprengling, "A Hebraeo—Sufic Poem," *AJSL* 46 (1929-30) 203-204.

*Julian Obermann, "The Sepulchre of the Maccabean Martyrs," *JBL* 50 (1931) 250-265. *[Arabic Faraġ-Book of Nissîm Ibm Shâhîn of Ḳairowân]*

A. Saarisalo, "A *waqf*-document from Sinai," *SO* 5 (1934) #1, 1-8.

Franz Rosenthal, "Some Pythagorean Documents transmitted in Arabic," *Or, N.S.,* 10 (1941) 104-115, 383-395.

Dimitri Baramki, "Kufic Texts," *ADAJ* 1 (1951) 20-22.

Anonymous, "Archaeological News. Amman—Iron Age Arabic Inscriptions Discovered," *ADAJ* 11 (1966) 104.

A. M. Al-Dhubaib, "Ancient Arabic Proverbs: Some Critical and Comparative Observations," *ALOUS* 7 (1969-73) 32-49.

§920　　　*4.4.12.3 Ṣafãtic Texts*

W. H. Worrell, "Four Safaitic Graffiti," *AJSL* 58 (1941) 217-218.

G. L[ankester] Harding, "Safaitic Inscriptions in the Iraq Museum," *Sumer* 6 (1950) 124-129.

G. Lankester Harding, "New Safaitic Texts," *ADAJ* 1 (1951) 25-29.

*Henry Field, "Camel Brands and Graffiti from Iraq, Syria, Jordan, Iran, and Arabia," *JAOSS* #15 (1952) i-vi, 1-41. *[Ṣafātic Inscriptions]*

*G. Lankester Harding, "The Cairn of Hani'," *ADAJ* 2 (1953) 8-56. *[Ṣafātic Texts]*

G. Lankester Harding, "Hani' Text No. 73," *ADAJ* 3 (1956) 82.

A. Jamme, "A Safaitic Inscription from the Negev," *'Atiqot* 2 (1959) 150-151.

A. Jamme, "Safaitic Inscriptions from Saudi Arabia," *OA* 6 (1967) 189-213.

*G. Lankester Harding, "A Safaitic Drawing and Text," *L* 1 (1969) 68-72.

§921 *4.4.12.4 South Arabian Texts*

Anonymous, "South Arabian Inscriptions," *MR* 81 (1899) 473-476.

D. S. Margoliouth, "Two South Arabian Inscriptions Edited from Rubbings in the possession of Major-General Sir Neill Malcolm, K.C.B.," *PBA* 11 (1924-25) 177-185.

Eric Burrows, "A New Kind of Old Arabic Writing from Ur," *JRAS* (1927) 795-806. [U. 7815; U. 7819]

F. V. Winnett, "Notes on the Lihyanite and Thamudic Inscriptions," *Muséon* 51 (1938) 299-310.

A. F. L. Beeston, "The Philby Collection of Old-South-Arabian Inscriptions," *Muséon* 51 (1938) 311-333.

J. Walker, "A South Arabian Inscription in the Baroda State Museum," *Muséon* 59 (1946) 159-162.

W[illiam] F[oxwell] Albright, "The Chaldaean Inscriptions in Proto-Arabic Script," *BASOR* #128 (1952) 39-45.

G. Ryckmans, "On Some Problems of South Arabian Epigraphy and Archæology," *BSOAS* 14 (1952) 1-10.

W. E. N. Kensdale, "Three Thamudic Inscriptions from the Nile Delta," *Muséon* 65 (1952) 285-290.

A. F. L. Beeston, "Remarks on the Ḥaḍrami Inscription Jamme 402," *Or,* *N.S.,* 22 (1953) 416-417.

A. J. Drewes, "Some Hadrami Inscriptions," *BO* 11 (1954) 93-94.

A. J. Drewes, "The inscription from Dibdib in Eritrea," *BO* 11 (1954) 185-186.

A. Jamme, "An Archaic South-Arabiain Inscription in Vertical Columns," *BASOR* #137 (1955) 32-38.

A. Jamme, "South-Arabian Antiquities in the U.S.A.," *BO* 12 (1955) 152-154.

G. W. Van Beek and A. Jamme, "An Inscribed South Arabian Clay Stamp from Bethel," *BASOR* #151 (1958) 9-16.

*John Walker, "The Liḥyānite Inscription on South Arabian coins," *RDSO* 34 (1959) 77-81.

A. M. Honeyman, "Epigraphic South Arabian Antiquities," *JNES* 21 (1962) 38-43.

*A. Jamme, "Preliminary Report on Epigraphic Research in Northwestern Wâdî Ḥaḍramawt and at al-'Abar," *BASOR* #172 (1963) 41-54. (Note by W. F. Albright, p. 54) *[Sahidic; Sabatean; Qatabanian Texts]*

A. Jamme, "The South-Arabian Collection of the University Museum (Cambridge, England). Documentation sud-arabe, IV," *RDSO* 40 (1965) 43-55. *[Parts I & II, French Text; Part III apparently not published]*

A. Jamme, "Documentation sud-arabe, V," *RDSO* 40 (1965) 287-299.

A. Jamme, "Inscriptions Photographed at Qaryat al-Fa'w by Ambassador Parker T. Hart (Documentation sud-arabe IV)*[sic]*," *RDSO* 41 (1966) 289-301. *[Part VI]*

A. Jamme, "Two New Hadrami Inscriptions from Ẓôfar," *BO* 24 (1967) 145-148.

§922 *4.4.12.4 .1 Ḥimyaritic Texts*

Cyril C. Graham, "On the Inscriptions found in the region of El-Harrah, in the Great Desert South-east and East of Hauran," *JRAS* (1860) 286-297.

William Wright, "Himyaritic Sepulcharal monument," *ZDMG* 24 (1870) 638-639.

*W. F. Prideaux, "On some recent Discoveries in South-Western Arabia," *SBAT* 2 (1873) 1-28. *[Himyaritic]*

H. Fox Talbot, "Note on M. Lenormant's 'Lettre sur l'Inscription Dedicatoire Himyaritique du Temple du Dieu Yat'a a Abian'," *SBAT* 2 (1873) 333-345.

W. F. Prideaux, "Himyaritic Inscriptions lately discovered near San'a, in Arabia," *SBAT* 4 (1875) 196-201.

W. F. Prideaux, "Notes on the Himyartic Inscriptions contained in the Museum of the Bombay branch of the Royal Asiatic Society," *SBAT* 6 (1878-79) 305-315.

E. A. Budge, "Some new Himyartic Inscriptions," *SBAP* 5 (1882-83) 155-157.

*C[laude] R. Conder, "Supposed Nabathean and Himyaritic Texts from Medeba," *PEFQS* 15 (1883) 184-189.

Hartwig Derembourg, "The Himyaritic Inscription 32 of the British Museum," *BOR* 5 (1891) 193-196.

G. U. Yule, "A Rock-cut Himyaritic Inscription on Jabal Jehaf, in the Aden Hinterland," *SBAP* 27 (1905) 153-155.

D. H. Muller, "The Himyaritic Inscription from Jabal Jehaf." *SBAP* 28 (1906) 143-148.

*F. W. Green, "Notes on Some Inscriptions in the Etabi Distirct. II.," *SBAP* 31 (1909) 319-323. *[Himyaritic]*

F. V. Winnett, "A Himyaritic Inscription from the Persian Gulf Region," *BASOR* #102 (1946) 4-6.

F. V. Winnett, "A Himyarite Bronze Tablet," *BASOR* #110 (1948) 23-25.

*W. Idris Jones, "A Pre-Islamic Site and a Sabean/Himyarite Inscription," *GUOST* 14 (1950-52) 10-19.

§923 *4.4.12.4.2 Minaean Texts*

Fritz Hommel, "A Minaean Inscription of the Ptolemaic Period," *SBAP* 16 (1893-94) 145-149.

A. F. L. Beeston, "Two South-Arabian Inscriptions: Some Suggestions," *JRAS* (1937) 59-78. [The Sarcophagus Inscription of Gizeh (Minæan); Glaser 1210]

§924 *4.4.12.4.2 Nabataean Texts*

A. Van Name, "On some alleged Phenician[sic]* and Nabathean Inscriptions recently received from Palestine," *JAOS* 10 (1880) xlix.

*C[laude] R. Conder, "Supposed Nabathean and Himyaritic Texts from Medeba," *PEFQS* 15 (1883) 184-189.

*Ad. Neubauer, "On some newly-discovered Temanite and Nabataean Inscriptions," *SBE* 1 (1885) 209-232.

Hartwig Derenbourg, "Yemen Inscriptions—The Glaser Collection," *BOR* 1 (1886-87) 167-180, 195-206. *[Nabataean]*

Charles C. Torrey, "Notes on a Few Inscriptions," *JAOS* 29 (1909) 192-202. [D. A New Copy of the "High Place" Inscription in Petra, pp. 197-202]

*S[tephen] Langdon, "The 'Shalamians' of Arabia," *JRAS* (1927) 529-533. *[Nabataean]*

C[laude] R. Conder, "Notes by Major Conder, R.E. I. The Sinaitic Inscriptions," *PEFQS* 24 (1892) 42-44.

Stanley A. Cook, "Notes on Semitic Inscriptions II," *SBAP* 26 (1904) 72-74. [2. Nabataean Graffiti from Egypt]

*Charles C. Torrey, "Epigraphic Notes," *JAOS* 28 (1907) 349-354. [1. An Inscription from the 'High-Place of the Goddess Al-'Uzzā, in Petra, pp. 349-351]

*F. W. Green, "Notes on Some Inscriptions in the Etabi Distirct. II.," *SBAP* 31 (1909) 319-323. *[Nabataean]*

Joseph Offord, "A Nabataean Inscription concerning Philip, Tetrarch of Auranitis," *PEFQS* 51 (1919) 82-85.

Enno Littmann, "Nabataean Inscriptions from Egypt," *BSOAS* 15 (1953) 1-28. (Introduction and Classical Notes by David Meredith)

Enno Littmann, "Nabataean Inscriptions from Egypt—II," *BSOAS* 16 (1954) 211-246. (Introduction and Classical Notes by David Meredith)

Jacob J. Rabinowitz, "A Clue to the Nabatean Contract from the Dead Sea Region," *BASOR* #139 (1955) 11-14.

A. Negev, "Nabatean Inscriptions from 'Avdat (Oboda), I," *IEJ* 11 (1961) 127-138.

A. Negev, "Nabatean Inscriptions from 'Avdat (Oboda)—II," *IEJ* 13 (1963) 113-124.

J. Naveh, "Some Notes on Nabatean Inscriptions from 'Avdat," *IEJ* 17 (1967) 187-189.

A. Negev, "New Dated Nabatean Graffiti from the Sinai," *IEJ* 17 (1967) 250-255.

§925 *4.4.12.4.3 Qatabanian Texts*

A. F. L. Beeston, "Two Shabwa Inscriptions," *Muséon* 60 (1947) 51-55.

A. Jamme, "Some Qatabanian Inscriptions Dedicating 'Daughters of God'," *BASOR* #138 (1955) 39-47.

Mahmud 'Ali Ghul, "New Qatabāni Inscriptions," *BSOAS* 22 (1959) 1-22.

Mahmud 'Ali Ghul, "New Qatabāni Inscriptions—II," *BSOAS* 22 (1959) 419-438.

*A. F. L. Beeston, "Epigraphic and Archaeological Gleanings from South Arabia," *OA* 1 (1962) 41-52.

§926 *4.4.12.4.4 Sabaean Texts*

D. H. Muller, "Notes and Observations upon the Sabaean Inscriptions at Bombay," *SBAT* 6 (1878-79) 198-202.

*F. W. Green, "Notes on Some Inscriptions in the Etbai District. I.," *SBAP* 31 (1909) 247-254. *[Sebean]*

John Walker, "A Sabean Inscription," *Muséon* 51 (1938) 133-135.

A. F. L. Beeston, "East and West Sabæan Inscriptions," *JRAS* (1948) 177-180.

A. F. L. Beeston, "The Oracle Sanctuary of Jār al-Labbā," *Muséon* 62 (1949) 207-228.

*W. Idris Jones, "A Pre-Islamic Site and a Sabean/Himyarite Inscription," *GUOST* 14 (1950-52) 10-19.

A. F. L. Beeston, "Four Sabaean Texts in the Istanbul Archaeological Museum," *Muséon* 65 (1952) 271-283.

A. Jamme, "An Arabic Dextrograde Sabaean Inscription from Mâreb," *BASOR* #134 (1954) 25-26.

A. Jamme, "Sabaean Inscriptions on Two Bronze Statues from Marib (Yemen)," *JAOS* 77 (1957) 32-36.

A. F. L. Beeston, "Two middle Sabaean Votive Texts," *BO* 16 (1959) 17-18.

A. Jamme, "The late Sabaean Ja 856," *BO* 17 (1960) 1-5.

*A. F. L. Beeston, "Epigraphic and Archaeological Gleanings from South Arabia," *OA* 1 (1962) 41-52. *[Sabaean]*

*A. Jamme, "Sabaean and Ḥasaean Inscriptions from Saudi Arabia," *SSR* 23 (1966) 1-107.

*A. Jamme, "New Ḥasaean and Sabaean Inscriptions from Saudi Arabia," *OA* 6 (1967) 181-187.

A. Jamme, "The Sabaean Onomastic Lists from(?) Sirwah in 'Arhab (Second Half) (Documentation sud-arabe VII)," *RDSO* 42 (1967) 361-406.

(§927) *4.5 Caucasian Texts (Aryan Family) - General Studies*

§928 *4.5.1 Elamite Texts*

*Theophilus G. Pinches, "Certain Inscriptions and Records Referring to Babylonia and Elam and their Rulers, and Other Matters," *JTVI* 39 (1895-96) 43-89. (Note by A. H. Sayce, p. 90) [S^P. III, 2; S^P. II, 987; S^P. 158 & S^P. II, 962]

*C. H. W. Johns, "The Chedorlaomer Tablets," *ET* 10 (1898-99) 523.

A. H. Sayce, "Recent Biblical Archaeology. The Anzanite Inscriptions," *ET* 13 (1901-02) 466-467. *(Review)*

*A. V. Williams Jackson, "Textual Notes on the Old Persian Inscriptions," *JAOS* 27 (1906) 190-194. [7. Kerman inscription of Darius, pp. 193-194]

*A. H. Sayce, "The Chedor-laomer Tablets," *SBAP* 28 (1906) 193-200, 241-251. [A. Sp. 158 + Sp. II. 962; B. Sp. II. 987; C. Sp. III, 2]

A. H. Sayce, "The Chedor-laomer Tablets—(continued),*" *SBAP* 29 (1907) 7-17.

*Ellen Seton Ogden, "A Conjectural Interpretation of Cuneiform Texts. *Vol. V, 81-7-27, 49 and 50,*" *JAOS* 32 (1912) 103-114.

*Leon Legrain, "Darius and Pseudo Smerdis. A Green Jade Relief. CBS. 14543," *MJ* 14 (1923) 200-202.

*Sidney Smith, "Archaeological Notes," *JRAS* (1926) 433-446. [Inscription of Darius on Gold Tablet, p. 435 *(Elamite Text)*]

Arno Poebel, "The Acropolis of Susa in the Elamite Inscriptions," *AJSL* 49 (1932-33), 125-140.

*Richard T. Hallock, "Darius I, King of the Persepolis Tablets," *JNES* 1 (1942) 230-232.

Richard T. Hallock, "Two Elamite Texts of Syllabary A," *JNES* 8 (1949) 356-358.

Walther Hinz, "The Elamite Version of the Record of Darius's Palace at Susa," *JNES* 9 (1950) 1-7.

Richard T. Hallock, "New Light form Persepolis," *JNES* 9 (1950) 237-252.

George G. Cameron, "The 'Daiva' Inscription of Xerxes: in Elamite," *WO* 2 (1954-59) 470-476.

*J. J. Rabinowitz, "A Legal Formula in the Susa Tablets, in an Egyptian Document of the Twelfth Dynasty, in the Aramaic Papyri, and in the Book of Daniel [4, 14]," *B* 36 (1955) 223-226.

Herbert H. Paper, "Elamite Texts from Tchogha-Zambil, 1936-39," *JNES* 14 (1955) 42-48.

George G. Cameron, "Persepolis Treasury Tablets Old and New," *JNES* 17 (1958) 161-176.

*George G. Cameron, "The Elamite Version of the Bistiun Inscriptions," *JCS* 14 (1960) 59-68.

Richard T. Hallock, "A New Look at the Persepolis Treasury Tablets," *JNES* 19 (1960) 90-100.

*J. J. Rabinowitz, "The Susa Tablets, the Bible and the Aramaic Papyri," *VT* 11 (1961) 55-76.

*William C. Brice, "A Comparison of the Account Tables of Susa in the Proto-Elamite Script with those of Hagia Triada in Linear A," *KZFE* 2 (1963) 27-38.

Edmond Sollberger, "The New Inscription of Šilhak-Inšušinak," *JCS* 19 (1965) 31-32. [BM 113886]

George C. Cameron, "New Tablets from the Persepolis Treasury," *JNES* 24 (1965) 167-192.

Erica Reiner, "The Earliest Elamite Inscription?" *JNES* 24 (1965) 337-340.

Christopher L. Hamlin, "A Proto-Elamite Account Tablet from Susa," *Exped* 10 (1967-68) #4, 30.

Edmond Sollberger, "Two Kassite Votive Inscriptions," *JAOS* 88 (1968) 191-195. [1. BM 81-7-1,3395; 2. BM 92699 = 82-7-14,4460]

*I. M. Diakonoff, "On the Interpretation of §70 of the Bisutūn Inscription (Elamite Version)," *AAASH* 17 (1969) 105-107.

§929   *4.5.2 Hurrian Texts*

*F. R. Steele, "The Points of the Compass in Hurrian," *JAOS* 61 (1941) 286-287.

*Hans Gustav Güterbock, "The Hittite Version of the Hurrian Kamarbi Myths: Oriental Forerunners of Hesiod," *AJA* 52 (1948) 123-134.

*Hans Gustav Güterbock, "The Song of Ullikummi. Revised Text of the Hittite Version of a Hurrian Myth," *JCS* 5 (1951) 135-161; 6 (1952) 8-42.

D. J. Wiseman, "Supplementary Copies of Alalakh Tablets," *JCS* 8 (1954) 1-30.

E[phraim] A. Speiser, "The Alalakh Tablets," *JAOS* 74 (1954) 18-25.

§930 *4.5.3 Hittite Texts - General Studies*

W. Hayes Ward, "On the Hittite Inscriptions," *JAOS* 10 (1880) cxxxix-cxli.

Dunbar J.*[sic]* Heath, "History of the Hittite Inscriptions," *PEFQS* 12 (1880) 206-210.

*W. H. Rylands, "The Inscribed Stones from Jerabis, Hamath, Aleppo, &c.," *SBAT* 7 (1880-82) 429-442.

W. St. C[had] Boscawen, "The Hittites. Their Inscriptions, II," *PEFQS* 13 (1881) 221-223.

Dunbar Isadore Heath, "III. Note on Above," *PEFQS* 13 (1881) 221-223.

A. H. Sayce, "The Decipherment of the Hittite Inscriptions," *SBAP* 4 (1881-82) 102-104.

W. H. Rylands, "An Inscribed Stone Bowl," *SBAP* 7 (1884-85) 154-155.

Anonymous, "The New Hieroglyphs of Western Asia," *CQR* 20 (1885) 257-286.

W. Hayes Ward, "On recently discovered Hittite Inscriptions," *JAOS* 11 (1885) x.

W. H. Rylands, "The Inscribed Lion from Marash," *SBAP* 9 (1886-87) 374-376.

Wm. H[ayes] Ward, "Unpublished or Imperfectly Published Hittite Monuments," *AJA, O.S.,* 4 (1888) 172-174. [III. Reliefs at Darchemish-Jerablûs]

Claude R. Conder, "The Marash Lion," *PEFQS* 20 (1888) 41-42.

Claude R. Conder, "The Hittite Monuments," *PEFQS* 20 (1888) 150-159.

*Hyde Clarke, "Cypriote and Khita," *SBAP* 12 (1889-90) 462-470.

Charles C. Stearns, "The Monuments and Inscriptions called Hittite," *HSR* 2 (1891-92) 125-145, 165-186.

A. H. Sayce, "The New Bilingual Hittite Inscriptions," *JRAS* (1892) 369-370.

Claude R. Conder, "Notes by Major Conder, R.E. III. Recent Hittite Discoveries," *PEFQS* 24 (1892) 204.

Claude R. Conder, "Recent Hittite Literature," *PEFQS* 25 (1893) 247-253.

D. G. Hogarth, "Note on pre-Hellenic finds," *RTR* 17 (1895) 25-27.

P. Jensen, "The Undeciphered Hittite Inscriptions, in Reply to Professor Sayce," *ET* 10 (1898-99) 304-310.

Fritz Hommel, "The Still Undeciphered Hittite Inscriptions, in Reply to Professor Jensen," *ET* 10 (1898-99) 367-371.

W. M. Ramsay, "Hittite Decipherment, I," *ET* 10 (1898-99) 384.

A. H. Sayce, "Hittite Decipherment, II," *ET* 10 (1898-99) 384.

P. Jensen, "The Hittite Inscriptions, in Reply to Professor Hommel," *ET* 10 (1898-99) 405-411.

Fritz Hommel, "Hittite Decipherment, I," *ET* 10 (1898-99) 423-424.

P. Jensen, "Hittite Decipherment, II," *ET* 10 (1898-99) 424-425.

Fritz Hommel, "The Hittite Inscriptions," *ET* 10 (1898-99) 459-462.

P. Jensen, "The Hittite Inscriptions," *ET* 10 (1898-99) 501-505.

W. M. Ramsay, "The Hittite Inscriptions. I," *ET* 10 (1898-99) 527.

P. Jensen, "The Hittite Inscriptions. II," *ET* 10 (1898-99) 528.

J. A. Selbie, "The Hittite Inscriptions," *ET* 10 (1898-99) 559-560; 11 (1899-1900) 446.

P. Jensen, "Professor Ramsay and the Hittite Inscriptions," *ET* 10 (1898-99) 567.

W. H. Rylands, "Hittite Inscriptions," *SBAP* 20 (1898) 263-266.

C[laude] R. Conder, "New Hittite Texts," *PEFQS* 31 (1899) 163.

A. H. Sayce, "Notes on—(2) The Hittite Inscriptions," *SBAP* 23 (1901) 98.

J. A. Selbie, "The Hittite Inscriptions: A Correction," *ET* 14 (1902-03) 431.

A. H. Sayce, "The Decipherment of the Hittite Inscriptions," *SBAP* 26 (1904) 17-25, 235-250.

A. H. Sayce, "The Hittite Inscriptions," *BW* 26 (1905) 30-40.

A. H. Sayce, "The Discovery of Archaic Hittite Inscriptions in Asia Minor," *SBAP* 27 (1905) 21-31, 43-47.

A. H. Sayce, "The Hittite Inscriptions translated and annotated," *SBAP* 27 (1905) 191-254.

E. Sibree, "Note on a Hittite Inscription (J. II)," *SBAP* 28 (1906) 27-28.

A. H. Sayce, "Unpublished Hittite Inscriptions in the Museum of Constantinople," *SBAP* 28 (1906) 91-95.

A. H. Sayce, "A Hittite Cuneiform Tablet from Northern Syria," *SBAP* 29 (1907) 91-100.

A. H. Sayce, "Hittite Inscriptions. The Method, Verification, and Results of my Decipherment of them," *SBAP* 29 (1907) 207-213, 253-259.

*A. H. Sayce, "The Hittite Inscriptions of Emir Ghazi and Aleppo," *SBAP* 30 (1908) 182-191.

A. H. Sayce, "Hittite Inscriptions from Gurun and Emir Ghazi," *SBAP* 30 (1908) 211-220.

A. H. Sayce, "The Hittite Inscriptions discovered by Sir W. Ramsay and Miss Bell on the Kara Dagh," *SBAP* 31 (1909) 83-87.

A. H. Sayce, "The Hittite Inscriptions," *SBAP* 31 (1909) 259-268, 327-332.

*C[laude] R. Conder, "Recent Hittite Discoveries," *PEFQS* 42 (1910) 42-53. [I. The Aleppo Text; II. The Yuzgat Text; III. The Boghaz-Keui Texts]

Anonymous, "Hittite Inscription from Cilicia," *RP* 9 (1910) 83.

R. Campbell Thompson, "On Some 'Hittite' Clay Tablets from Asia Minor," *SBAP* 32 (1910) 191-192.

A. H. Sayce, "Notes and News," *ET* 25 (1913-14) 521. *[Hittite Texts]*

R. Campbell Thompson, "Some Notes on a New Hittite Inscription found at Carchemish," *SBAP* 36 (1914) 165-167.

A. H. Sayce, "Geographical Notes on the Hittite Hieroglyphic Inscriptions," *SBAP* 36 (1914) 233-239.

A. H. Sayce, "The Inscriptions of Carchemish," *SBAP* 37 (1915) 8-21.

A. Cowley, "Notes on Hittite Hieroglyphic Inscriptions," *JRAS* (1917) 561-585.

A. H. Sayce, "Proto-Hittite," *JRAS* (1924) 245-255.

A. Cameron, "A Hittite Inscription from Angora," *JRAS* (1927) 320-321.

A. H. Sayce, "The Moscho-Hittite Inscriptions," *JRAS* (1927) 699-715.

Edgar Howard Sturtevant, "A Hittite Tablet in the Yale Babylonian Collection," *TAPA* 58 (1927) 5-31. [YBC 2506]

A. E. Cowley, "The Date of the Hittite Hieroglyphic Inscriptions of Carchemish," *PBA* 14 (1928) 39-48.

Anonymous, "The Hittite Inscription Casts of the American Palestine Exploration Society," *BASOR* #34 (1929) 8.

Ignace Gelb, "A Few Remarks on the Hieroglyphic Inscription from Byblos," *AJSL* 47 (1930-31) 135-138.

*A. H. Sayce, "Hittite and Moscho-Hittite," *RHA* 1 (1930-32) 1-8.

B. Hrozný, "Oriental Institute in Praha: Research Department," *ArOr* 4 (1932) 373-375. *[Hittite Hieroglyphic Inscriptions]*

*Patrick Railton, "Some Remains of the Ancient Near East," *JMUEOS* #18 (1932) 55-59. [B. Hittite, p. 59]

W[illiam] F[oxwell] Albright, "Hittite Scripts," *Antiq* 8 (1934) 453-455.

Albrecht Goetze, "Remarks on the Epigraphic Material Found at Tarsus in 1936," *AJA* 41 (1937) 287-288.

Albrecht Goetze, "Cuneiform Inscriptions from Tarsus," *JAOS* 59 (1939) 1-16.

*I. J. Gelb, "The Contribution of the New Cilician Bilinguals to the Decipherment of Hieroglyphic Hittite," *BO* 7 (1950) 129-141.

*Machteld J. Mellink, "KARATEPE: More Light on the dark ages," *BO* 7 (1950) 141-150. [b. The Hittite texts, pp. 145-146]

*G. Douglas Young, "The Significance of the Karatepe Inscriptions for Near Eastern Textual Criticism," *OTS* 8 (1950) 291-299.

E. P. Hamp, "Hieroglyphic Hittite Laīnuha," *AAI* 1 (1955) 93-95. *[Phoenician-Hittite]*

Albrecht Goetze, "The Inventory IBoT I 31," *JCS* 10 (1956) 32-38. [(=Bo 10402)]

J. J. Finkelstein, "A Hittite *mandattu*-Text," *JCS* 10 (1956) 101-105.

H. G. Güterbock, "Notes on Luwain Studies (A propos B. Rosenkranz' Book *Beiträge zur Erforschung des Luvischen*)," *Or, N.S.,* 25 (1956) 113-140. *[Hittite Texts] (Review)*

Hans G. Güterbock, "A View of Hittite Literature," *JAOS* 84 (1964) 107-115.

H. G. Güterbock, "Texts and Fragments," *JCS* 19 (1965) 33-34. [HSM 3644; KBo X 7 + HSM 3645] *[Hittite]*

*Philip B. Harner, "Exodus, Sinai, and the Hittite Prologues," *JBL* 85 (1966) 233-236.

J. D. Hawkins, "A Hieroglyphic Hittite Inscription from Porsuk," *AS* 19 (1969) 99-109.

*G. G. Giorgadze, "Hittites and Hurrians in Old Hittite Texts," *VDI* (1969) #1, 85.

§931 *4.5.3.1 Hittite Correspondence, Literary Texts, and Wisdom Literature*

C[laude] R. Conder, "A Hittite Prince's Letter," *PEFQS* 22 (1890) 115-121.

C[laude R.] Conder, "The Hittite Prince's Letter," *PEFQS* 23 (1891) 186.

Claude R. Conder, "Notes by Major Conder, R.E. I. Dusratta's Hittite Letter," *PEFQS* 24 (1892) 200-203, 334-335.

C[laude] R. Conder, "Dusratta's Hittite Letter," *JRAS* (1892) 711-809.

A. H. Sayce, "Notes on—(3) The Arzawa Letters," *SBAP* 23 (1901) 99-113.

*D. D. Luckenbill, "Hittite Treaties and Letters," *AJSL* 37 (1920-21) 161-211.

A. H. Sayce, "The Hittite Correspondence with Tut-Ankh-Amon's Widow," *AEE* 12 (1927) 33-35 [2 BoTU 41, p. 69]

M. Civil, "The 'Message of Lú-dingir-ra to His Mother' and a Group of Akkado-Hittite 'Proverbs'," *JNES* 23 (1964) 1-11.

§932 *4.5.3.2 Hittite Historical Texts*

A. H. Sayce, "The Hittite Monuments," *SBAP* 2 (1879-80) 76-78.

*A. H. Sayce, "The Bilingual Hittite and Cuneiform Inscription of Tarkondemos," *SBAP* 3 (1880-81) 4-6.

*A. H. Sayce, "The Bi-lingual Hittite and Cuneiform Inscription of Tarkondemos," *SBAT* 7 (1880-82) 294-308.

A. H. Sayce, "The Inscription of Tarkondêmos," *SBAP* 7 (1884-85) 143-147.

A. H. Sayce, "The Hittite Boss of Tarkondemos," *ZA* 1 (1886) 380-385.

*C. J. Ball, "New readings of the Hieroglyphs from Northern Syria," *SBAP* 10 (1887-88) 437-449. [The Seal (?) of Tarcondemus, pp. 439-442; Inscriptions from Gerâbîs, pp. 442-449]

*A. H. Sayce, "The Ivriz Texts. The Ardistama Inscriptions. Some Hittite Seals," *SBAP* 28 (1906) 133-137.

E. Sibree, "Note on the Boss of Tarkutimme," *SBAP* 28 (1906) 187-188.

A. H. Sayce, "The Discovery of a Hittite Record Office," *AAOJ* 29 (1907) 137-139.

A. H. Sayce, "A Hittite Record Office," *CFL, 3rd Ser.,* 8 (1908) 138.

P. S. Ronzevalle, "Hittite Stele from the Environs of Restan," *RP* 9 (1910) 67-69. *(Trans. by Helen M. Wright)*

*A. H. Sayce, "Adam and Sargon in the Land of the Hittites: A New Tel el-Amarna Discovery," *SBAP* 37 (1915) 227-245.

A. H. Sayce, "Texts from the Hittite Capital Relating to Egypt," *AEE* 7 (1922) 65-70. [Note by W. M. F[linders] P[etrie], p. 70]

A. H. Sayce, "Early Hittite Records," *AEE* 8 (1923) 98-104.

A. H. Sayce, "Grant of Sovereignty over Carchemish to His Son Biyassilis by the Hittite King Subbi-luliuma," *AEE* 10 (1925) 97.

*A. H. Sayce, "What happened after the Death of Tut'ankhamūn," *JEA* 12 (1926) 168-170.

E. H. Sturtevant, "The Tawagalawaš Text," *AJSL* 44 (1927-28) 217-231.

A. H. Sayce, "The Hittite Monument of Karabel," *JRAS* (1931) 429-432.

*A. H. Sayce, "The hieroglyphic Inscription on the Seal of Subbiluliuma," *AfO* 7 (1931-32) 184-185.

Albrecht Goetze, "Philological Remarks on the Bilingual Bulla from Tarsus," *AJA* 40 (1936) 210-214.

*I. J. Gelb, "Queen Pudu-ḫepa," *AJA* 41 (1937) 289-290.

Sedat Alp, "Military Instructions of the Hittite King Tuthaliya IV.(?)," *TTKB* 11 (1947) 403-414.

O. R. Gurney, "Mita of Paḫḫuwa," *AAA* 28 (1948) 48-54.

*Cyrus H. Gordon, "Azitawadd's Phoenician Inscription," *JNES* 8 (1949) 108-115. *[Hittite]*

Hans Gustav Güterbock, "The Deeds of Suppiluliuma as Told by His Son, Mursilli II," *JCS* 10 (1956) 41-68, 75-98, 107-130.

*Albrecht Goetze, "The Beginning of the Hittite Instructions for the Commander of the Boarder Guards," *JCS* 14 (1960) 69-73.

*Walter Federn, "Daḫamunzu (KBo V6 iii 8)," *JCS* 14 (1960) 33.

*Hans G. Güterbock, "Sargon of Akkad Mentioned by Ḫattušili I of Ḫatti," *JCS* 18 (1964) 1-6.

O. R. Gurney, "VBot. Nos. 95 and 97," *JCS* 21 (1967) 94. [BM 103041; 103043]

*Albrecht Goetze, "The Predecessors of Šuppiluliumaš of Ḫatti and the Chronology of the Ancient Near East," *JCS* 22 (1968-69) 46-50.

§933 *4.5.3.3 Hittite Legal and Commercial Texts (includes Treaties)*

*S[tephen] Langdon and Alan H. Gardiner, "The Treaty of Alliance between Ḫattušili, King of the Hittites and the Pharaoh Ramesses II of Egypt," *JEA* 6 (1920) 179-205.

*D. D. Luckenbill, "Hittite Treaties and Letters," *AJSL* 37 (1920-21) 161-211.

*George A. Barton, "An Obscure Passage in the Hittite Laws," *JAOS* 53 (1933) 358-359.

*F. Charles Fensham, "Clauses of Protection in Hittite and Vassal-Treaties and the Old Testament," *VT* 13 (1963) 133-143.

*Albrecht Goetze, "On §§613, 164/5 and 176 of the Hittite Code," *JCS* 20 (1966) 128-132.

*G. G. Giorgadze, "The Order of Succession to the Throne in the Old Hittite Kingdom (On the interpretation of §28 in the 'Decree of Telipinu')," *VDI* (1969) #4, 83.

§934 *4.5.3.4 Hittite Epic Literature and Mythological Texts*

*A. H. Sayce, "Notes on the Hittite Inscriptions and Mythology: The Rock Sculptures of Boghaz Keui," *SBAP* 35 (1913) 55-62.

*A. H. Sayce, "The Hittite Version of the Epic of Gilgemes," *JRAS* (1923) 559-571.

*A. H. Sayce, "The Astarte Papyrus and the Legend of the Sea," *JEA* 19 (1933) 56-59.

*Hans Gustav Güterbock, "The Hittite Version of the Hurrian Kamarbi Myths: Oriental Forerunners of Hesiod," *AJA* 52 (1948) 123-134.

*Hans Gustav Güterbock, "The Song of Ullikummi. Revised Text of the Hittite Version of a Hurrian Myth," *JCS* 5 (1951) 135-161; 6(1952) 8-42.

Vladimír Souček, "The World of Gods and Heroes: The Search for the Lost God," *NOP* 1 (1960) #4, 6-7.

*I. McNeill, "The Metre of the Hittite Epic," *AS* 13 (1963) 137-242.

H[arry] A. Hoffner, "The Elkunirsa Myth Reconsidered," *RHA* 23 (1965) 5-16.

*Harry A. Hoffner Jr., "A Hittite Analogue to the David and Goliath Contest of Champions?" *CBQ* 30 (1968) 220-225. *[Apology of Hattusilis III]*

Harry A. Hoffner Jr., "A Hittite Text in Epic Style about Merchants," *JCS* 22 (1968-69) 34-45.

*Ruggero Stefanini, "Enkidu's Dream in the Hittite 'Gilgamesh'," *JNES* 28 (1969) 40-47.

§935 *4.5.3.5 Hittite Religious and Liturgical Texts*

A. H. Sayce, "The Names of Vedic Deities on a Hittite Tablet," *JRAS* (1909) 1106-1107.

*E. H. Sturtevant, "A Hittite Text on the Duties of Priests and Temple Servants," *JAOS* 54 (1934) 363-406.

Benjamin Schwartz, "The Hittite and Luwian Ritual of Zarpiya of Kezzuwatna," *JAOS* 58 (1938) 334-353. [KUB 9.31 & HT 1]

O. R. Gurney, "Hittite Prayers of Mursili II," *AAA* 27 (1940) 3-163.

*E. Laroche, "Hattic Deities and Their Epithets," *JCS* 1 (1947) 187-216.

B[enjamin] Schwartz, "A Hittite Ritual Text (KUB 29.1 = 1780/c)," *Or, N.S.,* 16 (1947) 23-55.

*Franz Köcher and A. L. Oppenheim, "The Old-Babylonian Omen Text VAT 7525," *AfO* 18 (1957-58) 62-77. [*Appendix.* A Hittite Parallel, by H. G. Güterbock, pp 78-80. (KUB XXIX 9 and 10)]

*Hans G. Güterbock, "The Composition of Hittite Prayers to the Sun," *JAOS* 78 (1958) 237-245.

*Hans G. Güterbock, "An Outline of the Hittite *AN.TAḪ.ŠUM* Festival," *JNES* 19 (1960) 80-89.

*E. Reiner and H. G. Güterbock, "The Great Prayer to Ishtar and Its Two Versions from Boğasköy," *JCS* 21 (1967) 255-266.

*Ph[ilo] H. J. Houwink ten Cate and F. Josephson, "Muwatallis' Prayer to the Storm-God of Kummanni (KBo XI 1)," *RHA* 25 (1967) 101-140.

Philo H. J. Houwink ten Cate, "Muwatallis' 'Prayer to be Spoken in an Emergency'," *JNES* 27 (1968) 204-208.

*Ph. H. J. Houwink ten Cate, "Hittite Royal Prayers,"*Numen* 16 (1969) 81-98.

§936 *4.5.3.6 The Aleppo Inscriptions*

*Ch. Clermont-Ganneau, "Ideographic Inscription Found at Aleppo, Akin to Those of Hamath," *PEFQS* 5 (1873) 72-73.

*W. H. Rylands, "The Inscribed Stones from Jerabis, Hamath, Aleppo, &c.," *SBAT* 7 (1880-82) 429-442.

W. H. Rylands, "The Aleppo Inscription," *SBAP* 5 (1882-83) 146-149; 6 (1883-84) 132-133.

*A. H. Sayce, "The Hittite Inscriptions of Emir Ghazi and Aleppo," *SBAP* 30 (1908) 182-191.

*C[laude] R. Conder, "Recent Hittite Discoveries," *PEFQS* 42 (1910) 42-53. [I. The Aleppo Text, pp. 42-46]

A. H. Sayce, "The Hittite Inscriptions at Aleppo," *SBAP* 33 (1911) 227-231.

R. D. Barnett, "Hittite Hieroglyphic Texts at Aleppo," *Iraq* 10 (1948) 122-139.

§937 *4.5.3.7 Boghaz Keui Tablets*

A. H. Sayce, "Two Hittite Tablets from Boghaz Keui," *JRAS* (1907) 913-921.

A. H. Sayce, "The Hittite Cuneiform Tablets from Boghaz Keui," *JRAS* (1908) 548-549.

A. H. Sayce, "A Hittite Cuneiform Tablet from Boghaz Keui," *JRAS* (1908) 985-993.

T. G. Pinches, "Notes upon the Fragments of Hittite Cuneiform Tablets from Yuzgat, Boghaz Keui," *AAA* 3 (1909) 99-106.

A. H. Sayce, "Fragments of Hittite Cuneiform Tablets from Boghaz Keui," *JRAS* (1909) 963-980.

*C[laude] R. Conder, "Recent Hittite Discoveries," *PEFQS* 42 (1910) 42-53. [II. The Yuzgat Text, pp 46-50; III. The Boghaz-Keui Texts, pp. 50-53]

A. H. Sayce, "A Cuneiform Tablet from the Boghaz Keui with Docket in Hittite Hieroglyphics," *JRAS* (1912) 1029-1038.

Meta E. Williams, "Hittite Archives from Boghaz Keui, translated from the German Transcripts of Dr. Winckler," *AAA* 4 (1911-12) 90-98.

*A. H. Sayce, "Notes on the Hittite Inscriptions and Mythology: The Rock Sculptures of Boghaz Keui," *SBAP* 35 (1913) 55-62.

*A. Goetze, "Texts and Fragments," *JCS* 4 (1950) 137-140. [Small fragment of a Boğazköy tablet, Part of a god list]

§938 *4.5.3.8 Hamath Inscriptions*

J. Augustus Johnson, "Inscriptions Discovered at Hamath in Northern Syria," *PEFQS* 3 (1871) 173-176.

Hyde Clarke, "Note on the Hamath Inscriptions," *PEFQS* 4 (1872) 74-75.

Dunbar Isidore Heath, "The Hamath Inscriptions," *PEFQS* 4 (1872) 199-200; 5 (1873) 35-36.

Richard F. Burton, "Anthropological Collections from the Holy Land. No. III. Notes on the Hamah Stones, with Reduced Transcripts," *JRAI* 2 (1872-73) 41-52.

C. Carter Blake, "Note on the Hamah Stones," *JRAI* 2 (1872-73) 129-130.

Hyde Clarke, "The Hamath Inscriptions," *JRAI* 2 (1872-73) 309-310.

C. Staniland Wake, "The Hamath Inscriptions," *JRAI* 2 (1872-73) 446-447.

*Ch. Clermont-Ganneau, "Ideographic Inscription Found at Aleppo, Akin to Those of Hamath," *PEFQS* 5 (1873) 72-73.

W. Wright, "The Hamah Inscriptions," *PEFQS* 5 (1873) 74-77.

*Roswell D. Hitchcock, "The American Palestine Exploration Society," *PEFQS* 5 (1873) 111-112. [The Hamath Inscriptions, p. 111]

Hyde Clarke, "Hamath Inscriptions," *PEFQS* 5 (1873) 115.

*Hyde Clarke, "The Hamath Inscriptions.—Alphabets," *JRAI* 3 (1873-74) 135-136.

William Wright, "The Hamah Inscriptions: Hittite Remains," *BFER* 23 (1874) 90-99.

E. J. Davis, "On a New Hamathite Inscription at Ibreez," *SBAT* 4 (1875) 336-346.

A. Sayce, "On the Hamathite Inscriptions," *SBAT* 5 (1876-77) 22-32.

Dunbar Heath, "Squeezes of the Hamath Inscriptions," *JRAI* 9 (1879-80) 369-373. [Discussion, pp. 373-375]

W[illiam] H[ayes] Ward, "On the Hamath Inscriptions," *JAOS* 10 (1880) lxxv-lxxvi.

*W. H. Rylands, "The Inscribed Stones from Jerabis, Hamath, Aleppo, &c.," *SBAT* 7 (1880-82) 429-442.

*Dunbar I. Heath, "The Orders for Musical Services at Hamath," *PEFQS* 13 (1881) 118-124.

C[laude] R. Conder, "Hamath Inscriptions," *PEFQS* 15 (1883) 133-134.

C[laude] R. Conder, "The Hamathite Inscriptions,"*PEFQS* 15 (1883) 189-193.

†C. J. Ball, "The Inscribed Stones of Hamath, &c.," *SBAP* 9 (1886-87) 67-77, 153.

William Hayes Ward, "The Inscribed Stones from Hamath," *SBAP* 21 (1899) 80-81.

§939 **4.5.4 Greek Texts - General Studies**

Anonymous, "Researches in Greece," *QRL* 11 (1814) 458-480. *(Review)*

(   ) Hawtrey, "On a Greek Inscription lately found in Corfu," *TPS* 1 (1842-44) 149-151.

*E. Robinson and G. B. Whiting, "Notes on Biblical Geography," *BS* 5 (1848) 79-97. [The Greak Inscription at Apamea, pp. 91-92]

*(   ) Newbold, "On the Site of Caranus, and the Island of Ar-Ruád (الرواد), the Arvad or Arpad of Scripture," *JRAS* (1856) 32-36. [Greek text, p. 35]

Homer B. Morgan, "On an Ancient Greek Inscription, found at the site of Daphne, near Antioch, and copied by Rev. Homer B. Morgan, Missionary at Antioch," *PAOS* (November, 1858) 7.

Howard Crosby, "Translation of a Tablet Recently Discovered in Greece," *BS* 16 (1859) 421-425.

James Hadley, "On a Greek Inscription from Daphne," *PAOS* (May, 1859) 7.

James Hadley, "A Greek Inscription from Daphne, near Antioch, in Syria," *JAOS* 6 (1860) 550-555.

James Hadley, "On the Greek Inscription-Stone from Daphne," *PAOS* (October, 1861) xliv.

James Hadley, "On the Greek Inscription-Stone from Daphne," *JAOS* 7 (1862) xliv.

Julius Y. Leonard, "Greek Inscriptions from the Vicinity of Amasia, in the Ancient Pontus," *JAOS* 9 (1871) xlvii.

W. E. Currey, "A Theban inscription at the fountain of Dirce," *JP* 3 (1871) 189-191.

Thomas Chaplin, "Greek Inscription on a Stone found at Samaria, now in Possession of Yakoob esh Shellaby," *PEFQS* 3 (1871) 134.

*E. H. Palmer, "An Athenian bilingual inscription," *JP* 4 (1872) 48-50. (additional remarks by J. E. Sandys, pp. 50-54)

*Roswell D. Hitchcock, "The American Palestine Exploration Society," *PEFQS* 5 (1873) 111-112. [The Greek Inscriptions at Dog River, pp. 111-112]

*E. B. Finlay, "Greek Inscription," *PEFQS* 7 (1875) 103.

C. T. Newton, "On Greek Inscriptions," *ContR* 29 (1876-77) 70-94.

F. J. A. Hort, "Two Ephesian inscriptions," *JP* 7 (1876-77) 140-147.

*H. H. K[itchener], "Note on Gaza," *PEFQS* 10 (1878) 199-200. *[Greek Inscription]*

A. Duncan Savage, "A Greek Inscription concerning Golgoi," *AJP* 2 (1881) 223-224.

Julius Sachs, "On a Greek Inscription from Larisa," *PAPA* 15 (1883) xvii-xviii.

R. B. Girdlestone, "The Inscriptions at Jerash," *PEFQS* 15 (1883) 107-108.

†Samuel Birch, "Greek Inscription from Zagazig," *SBAP* 6 (1883-84) 206.

F. P. Brewer, "On a copper stamp bearing a Greek inscription," *JAOS* 11 (1885) viii-ix.

Isaac H. Hall, "On the Bronze Crab Inscription of the New York Obelisk," *JAOS* 11 (1885) clxviii-clxx.

A. C. Merriam, "Two Ptolemaic Inscriptions," *AJA* 2 (1886) 149-152.

A. H. Sayce, "Greek Inscription from Asswan," *SBAP* 9 (1886-87) 202-205.

A. C. Merriam, "Greek Inscriptions Published in 1886-87," *AJA, O.S.,* 3 (1887) 303-321.

A. H. Sayce, "Some Greek Graffiti from Abydos," *SBAP* 10 (1887-88) 377-388.

Carl D. Buck, "Inscriptions Found upon the Akropolis," *AJA, O.S.,* 4 (1888) 149-164.

†Carl D. Buck, "Discoveries in the Attic Deme of Ikaria. 1888. I. Inscriptions from Ikaria," *AJA, O.S.,* 4 (1888) 421-426.

Mortimer Lamson Earle, "A New Sikyonian Inscription," *AJA, O.S.,* 4 (1888) 427-430.

G. Schumacher, "Recent Discoveries. *Lejjûn,*" *PEFQS* 20 (1888) 103-104. *[Greek Inscription]*

A. H. Sayce, "Greek Graffiti at Abydos," *SBAP* 11 (1888-89) 318, 319.

Carl D. Buck, "Discoveries in the Attic Deme of Ikaria, 1888. VII. Inscriptions from Ikaria," *AJA, O.S.,* 5 (1889) 304-319.

†F. B. Tarbell, "Inscriptions," *AJA, O.S.,* 5 (1889) 426-427.

C[arl] D. Buck and F. B. Tarbell, "Discoveries at Anthedon in 1889. I. Inscriptions from Anthedon," *AJA, O.S.,* 5 (1889) 443-460.

I. H. Hall, "On a Greek Inscription from Tartûs or Tartosa in Syria," *JAOS* 13 (1889) xxi-xxiii.

*C[onrad] Schick, "Discovery of Rock-Hewn Chapels at Silwân," *PEFQS* 22 (1890) 16-18. *[Greek Text, p. 17]*

G. Schumacher, "Notes from Galilee. *Khurbet Husheh,*" *PEFQS* 22 (1890) 24-25. *[Greek Inscription]*

A. H. Sayce, "The Inscriptions of Saris and Mount Olivet," *PEFQS* 22 (1890) 44.

W. M. Flinders Petrie, "Notes on Places Visited in Jerusalem. *Silwan,*" *PEFQS* 22 (1890) 157. *[Greek Inscription]*

Harold N. Fowler, "On Some Greek Inscribed Wax Tablets in the University at Leyden," *PAPA* 25 (1893) xliv.

*C[onrad] Schick, "Letters from Herr Baurath von Schick. III. Tabitha Ground at Jaffa," *PEFQS* 25 (1893) 286-293.

A. S. Murray, "Note on the Inscriptions Found at Tabitha, near Jaffa," *PEFQS* 25 (1893) 300.

C. Clermont-Ganneau, "Note on the Inscription of the Monument of Red Stone with Reclining Female Figure described by Mr. Schick at p. 296," *PEFQS* 25 (1893) 306.

J. R. Wheeler, "Some Inscriptions from the Argive Heraeum," *AJA, O.S.,* 9 (1894) 315-360.

F. J. Bliss, "Inscriptions Collected in Moab," *PEFQS* 27 (1895) 371-372. (With Notes by A. S. Murray)

Federica Halbherr, "Inscriptions from Various Cretan Cities," *AJA, O.S.,* 11 (1896) 539-601.

F[ederica] Halbherr, "Epigraphical Researches in Gortyna," *AJA* 1 (1897) 159-238.

H. Porter, "A Greek Inscription from Near Nazareth," *PEFQS* 29 (1897) 188-189.

*Ch. Clermont-Ganneau, "Notes on the Seal Found on Ophel, the Greek Inscriptions from Nazareth and Kefr esh Shems, the Siloam Text, and the Tombs of the Kings," *PEFQS* 29 (1897) 304-307. [(2) Greek Inscription, p. 306]

S. A. Xanthodudidis, "Inscriptions from Gortyna, Lyttos, and Lató pros Kamara," *AJA* 2 (1898) 71-78.

F[ederica] Halbherr, "Addenda to the Cretan Inscriptions," *AJA* 2 (1898) 79-94.

*C. Clermont-Ganneau, "Notes on Squeezes of Inscriptions in Baron Ustinow's Collection, Sent by the Rev. J. E. Hanauer," *PEFQS* 32 (1900) 110-123. (Notes by J. E. Hanauer, and the Bishop of Salisbury, pp. 121-122)

S. O. Dickerman, "An Archaic Inscription from Cleonae," *AJA* 4 (1900) 164.

Edward Capps, "The Dating of Some Didascalic Inscriptions," *AJA* 4 (1900) 74-91, 180-181.

A. H. Sayce, "Note on the Greek Inscriptions Found at Tell Sandahannah," *PEFQS* 32 (1900) 376.

C. Clermont-Ganneau, "Archaeological and Epigraphic Notes on Palestine. 3. *The Inscription from the Columbarium es-Suk at Tell Sandahannah,*" *PEFQS* 33 (1901) 116-118.

James Dennison Rogers, "Fragment of an Archaic Argive Inscription," *AJA* 5 (1901) 159-174.

A. H. Sayce, "Greek Ostraka from Egypt," *SBAP* 23 (1901) 211-217.

*George Adam Smith, "Notes on a Journey Through Hauran, with Inscriptions Found by the Way," *PEFQS* 33 (1901) 340-361. [Note by R. A. S. Macalister, *PEFQS* 34 (1902) p. 79]

Frank Cole Babbitt, "An Ancient Herm from Trachones," *AJA* 6 (1902) 24-25. *[Greek Text]*

Carroll N. Brown, "Fragment of a Treasure List found in the Acropolis Wall of Athens," *AJA* 6 (1902) 45-46.

*T. G. Pinches, "Greek Transcriptions of Babylonian Tablets," *SBAP* 24 (1902) 108-119. [Sp. III. 245 + 81-7-6, 141 (35726); Sp. II. 290 + Sp. III. 247 (34797); Sp. II. 291 + Sp. III. 311 (34798); VATh. 412; Sp. III. 246 (35727)]

*A. H. Sayce, "The Greeks in Babylonian—Graeco-Cuneiform Texts," *SBAP* 24 (1902) 120-125.

*F. C. Burkitt, "'Notes on 'Greek Transcriptions of Babylonian Tablets'," *SBAP* 24 (1902) 143-145.

R. A. Stewart Macalister, "Reports by R. A. Stewart Macalister, M.A., F.S.A., IV. A Greek Inscription from Nablus," *PEFQS* 34 (1902) 240-242.

Benjamin Powell, "Greek Inscriptions from Corinth," *AJA* 7 (1903) 26-71.

S. O. Dickerman, "Archaic Inscriptions from Cleonae and Corinth," *AJA* 7 (1903) 147-156.

*John P. Peters, "Palestinian Exploration. *Notes of a Vacation in Palestine in 1902*," *JBL* 22 (1903) Part 1, 15-31. [12. Palestine Exploration Fund Map (Greek Inscription), p. 30]

*Howard Carter and G. Legrain, "Report on Work done in Upper Egypt (1903-1904)," *ASAE* 6 (1905) 112-129. [IX. Medinet Habu, (Greek Text), pp. 121-122]

(Miss) Leila Clement Spaulding, "Sixth-century Attic Inscriptions," *AJA* 8 (1904) 73.

Edgar J. Goodspeed, "Greek Ostraca in America," *AJP* 25 (1904) 45-58.

T. F. Wright, "Notes and Queries. 2. *Inscription at Janiah*," *PEFQS* 36 (1904) 180-181.

R. A. Stewart Macalister, "Reports by R. A. Stewart Macalister, M.A., F.S.A. (3) An Unpublished Inscription in the Northern Necropolis of Jerusalem," *PEFQS* 36 (1904) 255-257.

A. H. Sayce, "Notes and Queries. 1. *Inscription at Janiah*," *PEFQS* 36 (1904) 285-286.

A. H. Sayce, "Greek Inscriptions from Egypt," *SBAP* 26 (1904) 90-92.

*David M. Robinson, "Greek and Latin Inscriptions from Sinope and Environs," *AJA* 9 (1905) 294-333.

*Charles Wilson, "Centurial Inscriptions on the Syphon of the High-level Aqueduct at Jerusalem," *PEFQS* 37 (1905) 75-77.

Anonymous, "The Oldest Greek Inscription in Asia Minor," *RP* 4 (1905) 126.

August Frickenhaus, "The Building Inscriptions of the Erechtheum," *AJA* 10 (1906) 1-15.

G. M. Whicher, "A Greek Inscription from the Hauran," *AJA* 10 (1906) 289-293.

*Albert W. Van Buren, "Notes on Dr. D. M. Robinson's *Inscriptions from Sinope*," *AJA* 10 (1906) 295-299.

Leila Clement Spaulding, "On Dating Early Attic Inscriptions," *AJA* 10 (1906) 394-404.

*David M. Robinson, "Mr. Van Buren's Notes on Inscriptions from Sinope," *AJA* 10 (1906) 429-433.

David M. Robinson, "New Inscriptions from Sinope," *AJP* 27 (1906) 447-450.

*G. Legrain, "The Inscriptions in the Quarries of El Hosh," *SBAP* 28 (1906) 17-26.

William N. Bates, "New Inscriptions from the Asclepieum at Athens," *AJA* 11 (1907) 307-314.

Edgar J. Goodspeed, "Greek Ostraca in the Haskell Museum," *AJA* 11 (1907) 441-444.

*C. C. Edgar, "Notes from the Delta," *ASAE* 8 (1907) 154-159. [II. Inscribed Potsherds from Naukratis, p. 157; IV. A Greek Inscription from Behera, pp. 158-159]

Theodore F. Wright, "The Isaiah Inscription," *BW* 29 (1907) 388-390.

William Scott Ferguson, "Researches in Athenian and Delian Documents. I.," *Klio* 7 (1907) 213-240.

*Enno Littmann, "Preliminary Report of the Princeton University Expedition to Abysinnia," *ZA* 20 (1907) 151-182 (Contributions by R. Sudström) [Greek Inscription, pp. 170-171]

T. Leslie Shear, "A New Rhodian Inscription," *AJP* 29 (1908) 461-466.

*Arthur E. P. Weigall, "Upper-Egyptian Notes," *ASAE* 9 (1908) 105-112. [2. A Greek Inscription from Kalâbsheh, p. 106; 4. A Greek Inscription from Edfu, p. 107]

William Scott Ferguson, "Researches in Athenian and Delian Documents. II.," *Klio* 8 (1908) 338-355.

E. W. G. Masterman, "Two Greek Inscriptions from Khurbet Harrawi," *PEFQS* 40 (1908) 155-157.

*A. H. Sayce, "Karian, Aramaic, and Greek Graffiti from Heshan," *SBAP* 30 (1908) 28-29.

*F. W. Green, "Notes on Some Inscriptions in the Etabi District. II.," *SBAP* 31 (1909) 319-323. *[Greek]*

A. M. Woodward, "Greek Inscriptions from Thessaly," *AAA* 3 (1910) 145-160.

*David M. Robinson, "Greek and Latin Inscriptions at Sardes," *AJA* 14 (1910) 414-416.

*A. H. Sayce, "Karian, Egyptian and Nubian-Greek Inscriptions from the Sudan," *SBAP* 32 (1910) 261-268.

William K Prentice, "The Mnesimachus Inscription at Sardes," *AJA* 16 (1912) 526-534.

David M. Robinson, "New Greek Inscriptions from Attica, Achaia, Lydia," *AJP* 31 (1910) 377-403.

*A. H. Sayce, "Karian, Egyptian and Nubian-Greek Inscriptions from the Sudan," *SBAP* 32 (1910) 261-268.

C. C. Edgar, "Greek inscriptions from the Delta," *ASAE* 11 (1911) 1-2.

D. Lee Pitcairn, "Greek Inscriptions from the Decapolis," *PEFQS* 43 (1911) 56-58; 45 (1913) 190-191.

R. E. Brunnow, "Notes and Queries. *The Inscriptions in Q.S., Jan., p. 56 seq.,*" *PEFQS* 43 (1911) 114.

W. H. Buckler and David M. Robinson, "Greek Inscriptions from Sardes I," *AJA* 16 (1912) 11-82.

*J. E. Hanauer, "Damascus Notes," *PEFQS* 44 (1912) 40-45. [Greek Inscription, p. 40]

D.Lee Pitcairn, "A Greek Inscription from Decapolis,"*PEFQS* 44 (1912) 85.

W. H. Buckler and David M. Robinson, "Greek Inscriptions from Sardes II," *AJA* 17 (1913) 29-52.

David M. Robinson, "Inscriptions from Cyrenaica," *AJA* 17 (1913) 157-200.

W. H. Buckler and David M. Robinson, "Greek Inscriptions from Sardes III," *AJA* 17 (1913) 353-370.

Theodore Leslie Shear, "Inscriptions from Loryma and Vicinity," *AJP* 34 (1913) 451-460.

H. A. Ormerod, "Greek Inscriptions in the Museum of the Liverpool Royal Institution," *AAA* 6 (1913-14) 99-108.

W. H. Buckler and David M. Robinson, "Greek Inscriptions from Sardes IV," *AJA* 18 (1914) 35-74.

W. H. Buckler and David M. Robinson, "Greek Inscriptions from Sardes V," *AJA* 18 (1914) 321-362.

‡Marcus N. Tod, "Bibliography of 1912-13: Greek Inscriptions from Egypt," *JEA* 1 (1914) 140-143.

*Joseph Offord, "Jewish Notes," *PEFQS* 46 (1914) 46-47. *[Greek Inscription]*

W.Sherwood Fox,"A Ptolemaic Inscription in Toronto,"*AJA* 19(1915)72-73.

W. A. Oldfather, "Inscriptions from Locris," *AJA* 19 (1915) 320-339.

‡Marcus N. Tod, "Bibliography: Graeco-Roman Egypt: B. Inscriptions (1914)," *JEA* 2 (1915) 108-112.

C. C. Edgar, "Some Greek Inscriptions," *ASAE* 15 (1915) 105-112.

*C. C. Edgar, "A Women's Club in Ancient Alexandria," *JEA* 4 (1916) 253-254.

E. J. Pilcher, "Notes and Queries. 2," *PEFQS* 48 (1916) 153-154. *[Greek Inscription]*

W. Sherwood Fox, "Greek Inscriptions in the Royal Ontario Museum. Part I," *AJP* 38 (1917) 304-311.

W. Sherwood Fox, "Greek Inscriptions in the Royal Ontario Museum," *AJP* 38 (1917) 411-424. [Part II]

‡Marcus N. Tod, "Bibliography: Graeco-Roman Egypt. B. Greek Inscriptions (1915-1919)," *JEA* 6 (1920) 214-218.

Douglas P. Blair, "Some Greek Inscriptions from Beersheba," *PEFQS* 52 (1920) 15-16.

F. C. Burkitt, "Notes on the Greek Inscriptions from Beersheba," *PEFQS* 52 (1920) 16-22.

M. E. Lange, "An Inscription from Maiumas," *PEFQS* 52 (1920) 47.

Anonymous, "A Greek Synagogue Inscription from Jerusalem," *BASOR* #4 (1921) 13-14.

‡Marcus N. Tod, "Bibliography: Graeco-Roman Egypt. B. Greek Inscriptions (1920)" *JEA* 7 (1921) 105-106.

David M. Robinson, "Notes on Two Inscriptions from Sinope," *AJP* 43 (1922) 71-73.

C. C. Edgar, "A note on two Greek epigrams," *ASAE* 22 (1922) 78-80.

D. G. Hogarth, "Greek Inscriptions from Askalon," *PEFQS* 54 (1922) 22-23.

William Bell Dinsmoor, "The Inscriptions of Athena Nike," *AJA* 27 (1923) 318-321.

‡Marcus N. Tod, "Bibliography 1921-1922: Graeco-Roman Egypt. B. Greek Inscriptions," *JEA* 9 (1923) 235-238.

Harry J. Leon, "A Jewish Inscription at Columbia University," *AJA* 28 (1924) 251-252. *[Greek]*

Albrecht Alt, "Some Notes on the New Greek Inscription from Ghōr eṣ-Ṣāfi," *PEFQS* 56 (1924) 191-192.

Benjamin D. Meritt, "A Restoration in *I.G.* I, 37," *AJA* 29 (1925) 26-28.

Allen B. West, "The Place of *I.G.* I, 256 in the *Lapis Secundus,*" *AJA* 29 (1925) 180-187.

Benjamin D. Meritt, "A Restoration in *I.G.* I^2, 213," *AJA* 29 (1925) 445-447.

Marcus N. Tod, "Notes on Some Greek Graffiiti," *JEA* 11 (1925) 256-258.

‡Marcus N. Tod, "Bibliography 1923-1924: Greek Inscriptions," *JEA* 11 (1925) 327-330.

Benjamin Dean Meritt and Allen Brown West, "The Reconstruction of I.G. I^2, 193, 194, and 201," *TAPA* 56 (1925) 252-267.

Benjamin D. Meritt, "A Restoration of *I.G.,* I^2, 201," *AJA* 30 (1926) 189-190.

Edith Hall Dohan and Roland G. Kent, "New Inscriptions from Cyprus," *AJA* 30 (1926) 249-258.

H. I. Bell*[sic]*, "Waxed Tablets of the Third Century B.C.," *AEE* 12 (1927) 65-74.

*David M. Robinson, "The Discovery of a Prehistoric Site at Sizma," *AJA* 31 (1927) 26-50. *[Greek Text]*

Benjamin D. Meritt, "A Revision of *I.G.,* I^2, 216," *AJA* 31 (1927) 180-185.

Benjamin D. Meritt and Allen B. West, "Correspondences in *I.G.,* I^2, 196 and 198," *AJA* 32 (1928) 281-297.

J. D. Beazley, "Some Inscriptions on Vases," *AJA* 31 (1927) 345-353.

T. Callander, "Inscriptions from Isauria," *AJP* 48 (1927) 235-246.

‡Marcus N. Tod, "Bibliography: Greek Inscriptions (1925-1926)," *JEA* 13 (1927) 247-250.

*G. M. FitzGerald, "Two Inscriptions from Beisan," *PEFQS* 59 (1927) 154.

Allen B. West and Barbara P. McCarthy, "A Revision of *I.G.*, I^2, 302," *AJA* 32 (1928) 346-352.

Martin Sprengling, "The Epigraphic Material of Aghaya Kaleh," *AJSL* 45 (1928-29) 279-280.

*M. Rostovtzeff, "Greek Sightseers in Egypt," *JEA* 14 (1928) 13-15.

A. B. West, "*I.G.*, I^2, 302, Lines 35-47," *AJA* 33 (1929) 37-40.

J. D. Beazley, "Some Inscriptions on Vases—II," *AJA* 33 (1929) 361-367.

Jotham Johnson, "A Note on the Corcyra Expedition," *AJA* 33 (1929) 398-400. *[Greek Text]*

H. Theodric Westbrook, "A Herm Dedicated by Herodes Atticus," *AJA* 33 (1929) 402-404.

‡Marcus N. Tod, "Bibliography: Greek Inscriptions (1927-1928)," *JEA* 15 (1929) 259-261.

Arthur S. Hunt, "A Greek Cryptogram," *PBA* 15 (1929) 127-134.

A. H. M. Jones, "Notes on Jewish Inscriptions," *PEFQS* 61 (1929) 110. *[Greek Text]*

*Philip H. Davis, "The Eleusinion in Athens and the Plutonion," *AJA* 34 (1930) 51. [*I.G.* II^2, 1672]

Jotham Johnson, "A Revision of I.G. I^2, 310," *AJA* 35 (1931) 31-43.

*A. Cameron, "Latin Words in the Greek Inscriptions of Asia Minor," *AJP* 52 (1931) 232-262.

*Helena Carus, "Galatea Comes Alive," *OC* 45 (1931) 725-736. [Greek Text, p. 726]

David Moore Robinson, "New Inscriptions from Olynthus and Environs," *TAPA* 62 (1931) 40-56.

‡Marcus N. Tod, "Bibliography: Greek inscriptions (1929-1930)," *JEA* 18 (1932) 105-107.

Marcus N. Tod, "A Greek Epigram from Gaza," *Aeg* 13 (1933) 152-158.

W. S. Ferguson and William Bell Dinsmoor, "The Last Inventory of the Pronaos of the Parthenon," *AJA* 37 (1933) 52-57.

David Moore Robinson, "A New Greek Inscription from Macedonia," *AJA* 37 (1933) 602-604.

Agnes Newhall Stillwell, "Eighth Century B.C. Inscriptions from Corinth," *AJA* 37 (1933) 605-610.

‡Marcus N. Tod, "Bibliography: Greek Inscriptions (1931-1932)," *JEA* 19 (1933) 185-188.

*Carl W. Blegen, "Inscriptions on Geometric Pottery from Hymettos," *AJA* 38 (1934) 10-28.

Benjamin D. Meritt, "Epigraphic Notes," *AJA* 38 (1934) 67-70.

*L. B. Holland and Philip Davis, "The Porch-Ceiling of the Temple of Apollo on Delos," *AJA* 38 (1934) 71-80. *[Greek Text]*

David Moore Robinson, "Inscriptions from Olynthus, 1934," *TAPA* 65 (1934) 103-137.

J. D. Beazley, "Some Inscriptions on Vases. III," *AJA* 39 (1935) 475-488.

John L. Caskey, "New Inscriptions from Troy," *AJA* 39 (1935) 588-592.

Rhys Carpenter, "Early Ionian Writing," *AJP* 56 (1935) 291-301.

Benjamin D. Meritt, "Inscriptions of Colophon," *AJP* 56 (1935) 358-397.

‡Marcus N. Tod, "Bibliography: Graeco-Roman Egypt. Part II: Greek Inscriptions (1933-1934)," *JEA* 21 (1935) 104-107.

Joseph E. Fontenrose, "Notes on Milesian Inscriptions," *AJP* 57 (1936) 55-57.

James H. Oliver, "Inscriptions from Athens," *AJA* 40 (1936) 460-465.

*T. C. Skeat, "A Forthcoming Catalogue of Nome Strategi," *Miz* 2 (1936) 30-35.

‡Marcus N. Tod, "Bibliography: Graeco-Roman Egypt. Part II: Greek Inscriptions (1935-1936)," *JEA* 23 (1937) 106-109.

Francis R. Walton, "Notes on Some Inscriptions of Delos," *AJA* 42 (1938) 77-81.

Herbert C. Youtie, "IG III (= CIA III), Appendix, 66," *AJP* 59 (1938) 346-348.

Martin P. Nilsson, "The New Inscription of the Salaminioi," *AJP* 59 (1938) 385-393.

David Moore Robinson, "Inscriptions from Macedonia, 1938," *TAPA* 69 (1938) 43-76.

M. Schwabe, "The Greek Inscriptions discovered at Beth Shearim during the Third Season," *BIES* 6 (1938-39) #2, IV.

M. Schwabe, "A Graeco-Jewish Epigram from Beth She'arim," *BIES* 6 (1938-39) #3, I-II.

‡Marcus N. Tod, "Bibliography: Graeco-Roman Egypt. Part II: Greek Inscriptions (1937-1938)," *JEA* 25 (1939) 89-93.

M. Schwabe, "A Greco-Jewish Epigram from Beth Shearim," *BIES* 7 (1939-40) #1, II.

Herbert Bloch, "L. Calpurnius Piso Caesoninus in Samothrace and Herculaneum," *AJA* 44 (1940) 485-493.

M. Rostovtzeff, "A Note on the New Inscription from Samothrace," *AJP* 61 (1940) 207-208. (Addendum by C. B. Welles, p. 208)

A. Cameron, "The Epigram of the Fifth Century B.C.," *HTR* 33 (1940) 97-130.

M. Schwabe, "A Jewish-Greek Inscription from Sicily," *BIES* 8 (1940-41) #3, II-III.

Benjamin D. Meritt, "Selected Inscriptions from the Agora," *AJA* 45 (1941) 92.

J. D. Beazley, "Some Inscriptions on Vases. IV," *AJA* 45 (1941) 593-602.

Marcus N. Tod, "A Greek Epigram from Egypt," *JEA* 27 (1941) 99-105.

‡Marcus N. Tod, "Bibliography: Graeco-Roman Egypt. Greek Inscriptions (1939-1940)," *JEA* 27 (1941) 153-156.

*Marcus N. Tod, "Big Game Hunters in Ptolemaic and Roman Libya," *JEA* 27 (1941) 159-160.

M. Avi-Yonah, "Abbreviations in Greek Inscriptions (The Near East, 200 B.C. - A. D. 1100)," *QDAP* 9 (1942) Supplement, 1-125. *[Bound with Volume 9, but paged separately]*

Herbert C. Youtie, "Parega Ostracologica," *TAPA* 73 (1942) 64-85.

R. O. Fink, *"Feriale Duranum* I, 1, and *Mater Castrorum,"* *AJA* 48 (1944) 17-18.

J. M. R. Cormack, "L. Calpurnius Piso," *AJA* 48 (1944) 76-77.

Hans Lewy, "A dream of Mandulis," *ASAE* 44 (1944) 227-234.

Herbert C. Youtie, "Sambathis," *HTR* 37 (1944) 209-218. *[Greek Ostraca]*

Benjamin D. Meritt, "Three Attic Inscriptions," *AJP* 66 (1945) 234-242.

*Oliver Davies, "Three Great Anatolian Authors: Homer, Hipponax and Herodotus," *IAQR* 41 (1945) 387-388.

‡Marcus N. Tod, "Bibliography: Graeco-Roman Egypt. Greek Inscriptions (1941-1945)," *JEA* 31 (1945) 101-104.

Oscar Broneer, "Notes on the Xanthippos Ostrakon," *AJA* 52 (1948) 341-343.

Philip H. Davis, "In the Workshop of the Erechtheion," *AJA* 52 (1948) 485-489. (Edited by Leicester B. Holland)

Benjamin D. Meritt, "Notes on Attic Inscriptions," *AJP* 69 (1948) 69-73.

‡Marcus N. Tod, "Bibliography: Graeco-Roman Egypt. Greek Inscriptions (1945-1947)," *JEA* 34 (1948) 109-113.

Eugene Schweigert, "The Xanthippos Ostracon," *AJA* 53 (1949) 266-268.

J. D. Beazley, "Some Inscriptions on Vases: V," *AJA* 54 (1950) 310-322.

‡Marcus N. Tod, "Bibliography: Graeco-Roman Egypt. Greek Inscriptions (1948-1949)," *JEA* 36 (1950) 106-109.

C. H. Roberts, "A Hellenistic Epigram Recovered," *JJP* 4 (1950) 215-217.

E. L. Sukenik, "The Mosaic Inscriptions in the Synagogue at Apamea on the Orontes," *HUCA* 23 (1950-51) Part 2, 541-551.

*Ahmed Fakhry, "The rock inscriptions of Gabal el-Teir at Kharag Oasis," *ASAE* 51 (1951) 401-434.

Francis W. Schehl, "On an Inscription from Phistyon in Aetolia," *AJA* 56 (1952) 9-19.

W. Kendrick Pritchett, "Epigraphical Honor and the Hesperia Index," *AJA* 56 (1952) 161-168.

*Anthony E. Raubitschek, "International Epigraphy," *Arch* 5 (1952) 119-120.

‡P. M. Fraser, "Bibliography: Graeco-Roman Egypt: Greek Inscriptions (1950-51)," *JEA* 38 (1952) 115-126.

E. G. Turner, "SB 5174, 5175: some corrections," *JEA* 38 (1952) 132-133.

M. Schwabe, "Two Jewish-Greek Inscriptions Recently Discovered at Caesarea," *IEJ* 3 (1953) 127-130, 233-238.

*M. Schwabe, "Recently Discovered Jewish Inscriptions," *BIES* #18 (1953-54) #3/4, V.

Francis W. Schehl, "On the Epinicus Inscriptions from Didyma (LBW 222; *Mélanges Henri Weil* p. 151)," *AJA* 58 (1954) 13-26.

John [D.] Beazley, "Some Inscriptions on Vases: VI," *AJA* 58 (1954) 187-190.

David Meredith, "Inscriptions from the Berenice Road," *CdÉ* 29 (1954) 281-287.

M. Schwabe, "Greek Inscriptions Found at Beth She'arim in the Fifth Excavation Season, 1953," *IEJ* 4 (1954) 249-261.

‡P. M. Fraser, "Bibliography: Graeco-Roman Egypt; Greek Inscriptions (1952-3)," *JEA* 40 (1954) 124-141.

‡P. M. Fraser, "Bibliography: Graeco-Roman Egypt; Greek Inscriptions (1954)," *JEA* 41 (1955) 131-140.

W. Kendrick Pritchett, "An Unfinished Inscription, *IG* II^2 2362," *TAPA* 85 (1954) 159-167.

M. Schwabe, "A Greek Ostrakon from Appolonia," *Tarbiz* 24 (1954-55) #1, III-IV.

*L. R. Lind, "Nine Inscriptions and a Roman Brick Stamp in Kansas," *AJA* 59 (1955) 159-162. *[Greek]*

G. G. Arnakis, "Two Inscriptions from Baltaliman (Phidaleia)," *AJA* 59 (1955) 176-177.

P. M. Fraser and P. Maas, "Three Hellenistic Epigrams from Egypt," *JEA* 41 (1955) 115-118.

Daphine Hereward, "Notes on an Inscription from 'Hesperia'," *AJA* 60 (1956) 172-174.

*George E. Bean, "Victory in the Pentathlon," *AJA* 60 (1956) 361-368.

M. Schwabe and B. Lifshitz, "A Graeco-Jewish Epigram from Beth She'arim," *IEJ* 6 (1956) 78-88.

‡P. M. Fraser, "Bibliography: Graeco-Roman Egypt: Greek Inscriptions (1955)," *JEA* 42 (1956) 105-115.

P. M. Fraser, "Inscriptions from Cyrene," *Bery* 12 (1956-58) 101-128.

John D. Beazley, "Some Inscriptions on Vases: VII," *AJA* 61 (1957) 5-8.

D. A. Amyx, "Inscribed Sherds from the Amyklaion," *AJA* 61 (1957) 168-169.

A. G. Woodhead, "IG II^2 43 and Jason of Pherae," *AJA* 61 (1957) 367-373.

‡P. M. Fraser, "Bibliography: Graeco-Roman Egypt: Greek Inscriptions (1956)," *JEA* 43 (1957) 101-109.

D. M. Lewis, "The First Greek Jew," *JSS* 2 (1957) 264-266.

B. Lifshitz, "Greek Inscriptions from Eretz-Israel," *BIES* 22 (1958) #1/2, V-VI.

P. M. Fraser, "A Ptolemaic Inscription from Thera," *JEA* 44 (1958) 99-106.

‡P. M. Fraser, "Bibliography: Graeco-Roman Egypt: Greek Inscriptions (1957)," *JEA* 44 (1958) 108-116.

G. E. Bean, "Inscriptions in the Antalya Museum," *TTKB* 22 (1958) 21-91.

Morton Smith, "On the New Inscription from Serra Orlando," *AJA* 63 (1959) 183-184.

*G. E. Bean, "Notes and Inscriptions from Pisidia. Part I," *AS* 9 (1959) 67-117.

‡P. M. Fraser, "Bibliography: Graeco-Roman Egypt: Greek Inscriptions (1958)," *JEA* 45 (1959) 88-97.

George E. Bean, "New Inscriptions from Marmaris (The Rhodian Peraea)," *TAD* 9 (1959) #2, 42-45.

P. M. Fraser, "Inscriptions from Ptolemaic Egypt," *Bery* 13 (1959-60) 123-161.

John [D.] Beazley, "Some Inscriptions on Vases: VIII," *AJA* 64 (1960) 219-225.

*G. E. Bean, "Notes and Inscriptions from Pisidia. Part II," *AS* 10 (1960) 43-82.

Sherman E. Johnson, "Epigraphic Report on the Inscriptions Found at Sardis in 1958," *BASOR* #158 (1960) 6-10.

P. M. Fraser, "Bibliography: Graeco-Roman Egypt: Greek Inscriptions (1959)," *JEA* 46 (1960) 95-103.

Mabel Lang, "Epigraphical Notes," *AJA* 65 (1961) 62.

T. B. Mitford, "Further Contributions to the Epigraphy of Cyprus," *AJA* 65 (1961) 93-151.

B. Lifshitz, "The Greek Documents from Naḥal Ṣeelim and Naḥal Mishmar," *IEJ* 11 (1961) 53-62.

Y. H. Landau, "A Greek Inscription from Acre," *IEJ* 11 (1961) 118-126.

‡P. M. Fraser, "Bibliography: Graeco-Roman Egypt: Greek Inscriptions (1960)," *JEA* 47 (1961) 139-149.

*Kevin Herbert, "Greek and Latin Inscriptions at Bowdoin," *AJA* 66 (1962) 381-387.

Alan L. Boegehold, "The Nessos Amphora—A Note on the Inscription," *AJA* 66 (1962) 405-406.

*B. Lifshitz, "The Expedition to the Judean Desert, 1961. The Greek Documents from the Cave of Horror," *IEJ* 12 (1962) 201-207.

*Edmond Sollberger, "Graeco-Babyloniaca," *Iraq* 24 (1962) 63-72. [B.M. 34781 = Sp. II 273; B.M. 34797 = Sp. II 290 + Sp. III 247; B.M. 35727 = Sp III 246; B.M. 34799 = Sp II 292 + 81-7-6, 142; B.M. 35726 = Sp III 245 + 81-7-6, 141; B.M. 34798 = Sp II 291 + Sp 311; B.M. 34816 = Sp. II 315 = 82-7-4, 139; V.A.T. 412; B.M. 33769 = RM IV 327; B.M. 35458; Sp II 1048; B.M. 35459 = Sp II 1049; B.M. 33778 = Rm IV 336; B.M. 35154 = Sp II 706]

‡P. M. Fraser, "Bibliography: Graeco-Roman Egypt: Greek Inscriptions (1961)," *JEA* 48 (1962) 141-157.

Daphne Hereward, "Inscriptions from Thrace," *AJA* 67 (1963) 71-75.

Sterling Dow, "Alphabetized Inscriptions from Smyrna in Bowdoin and Leyden," *AJA* 67 (1963) 257-268.

*Cyrus H. Gordon, "The Dreros Bilingual," *JSS* 8 (1963) 76-79.

Henri Wittmann, "The inscription from Hamath 4.4.2 and 4.6.4," *CJL* 9 (1963-64) #2, 115-116.

Wesley E. Thompson, "A Note on IG I^2 310," *AJA* 68 (1964) 66.

Carl H. Kraeling, "A New Greek Inscription from Antioch on the Orontes," *AJA* 68 (1964) 178-179.

W. Kendrick Pritchett, "An Open Question in List 9," *AJA* 68 (1964) 400-401.

W. Kendrick Pritchett, "Epigraphical Restituta," *AJP* 85 (1964) 40-55.

*Roland F. Willetts, "Observations on Leg. Gort. II. 16-20," *KZFE* 3 (1964) 170-176.

G. E. Bean, "Inscriptions from Selge," *AAI* 2 (1965) 55-61.

Dina Peppas Delmouzou, "Epigraphical Notes," *AJA* 69 (1965) 151-152.

Henry R. Immerwahr, "Inscriptions on the Anacreon Krater in Copenhagen," *AJA* 69 (1965) 152-154.

Sterling Dow, "The Greater Demarkhia at Erkhia," *AJA* 69 (1965) 167.

Donald R. Laing Jr., "A New Arrangement of the Fragments of *IG* II², " *AJA* 69 (1965) 170.

Wesley E. Thompson, "The Early Parthenon Inventories," *AJA* 69 (1965) 223-230.

Alan L. Boegehold, "An Archaic Corinthian Inscription," *AJA* 69 (1965) 259-262.

George Huxley, "An Inscription in Kythera," *GRBS* 6 (1965) 47-49.

*Jan Dus, "The Dreros Bilingual and the Tabernacle of Ancient Israelites," *JSS* 10 (1965) 54-57. [Comment by Professor C. H. Gordon, pp. 57-58]

John F. Oates, "Concordances to the Milan Vogliano Papyri (Vols. II & III)," *BASP* 3 (1965-66) 33-48.

Fordyce W. Mitchel, "*IG* II² 1493: Corrigenda," *AJA* 70 (1966) 66.

W. Kendrick Pritchett, "*IG* I², 220: Prepis or Menekles?" *AJA* 70 (1966) 173-175.

Alan L. Boegehold, "The Salamis Epigram,"*AJA* 70 (1966) 183. [*IG* 12 927]

Robert K. Sherk, "The Text of the *Senatus Consultum De Agro Pergameno,*" *GRBS* 7 (1966) 361-369.

Y. H. Landau, "A Greek Inscription Found Near Hefzibah," *IEJ* 16 (1966) 54-70.

G. E. Bean, "Two Inscriptions from Aeolis," *TTKB* 30 (1966) 525-537.

Kevin Herbert, "Three Ptolemaic Inscriptions in the Wilbour Collection of the Brooklyn Museum," *AJA* 71 (1967) 189.

Robert C. Ross, "An Ephebic Inscription from Thespiae," *AJA* 71 (1967) 194.

Altai Amanžolov, "An 'Ancient Greek' Inscription from the Region of Alma-Ata," *ArOr* 35 (1967) 89-94.

*Barbara Levick, "Unpublished Inscriptions from Pisidian Antioch," *AS* 17 (1967) 101-121.

N. S. Belova, "A New Inscription from Hermonassa," *VDI* (1967) #1, 69.

Sterling Dow, "The *Ephemeris,* and the Dates of Discovery Given by Pittakes," *AJA* 72 (1968) 154-156.

A. S. Hall, "Notes and Inscriptions from Eastern Pisidia," *AS* 18 (1968) 57-92.

*David Rokeah, "A New Onomasticon Fragment from Oxyrhynchus and Philo's Exegesis," *JTS, N.S.,* 19 (1968) 70-82.

W. Kendrick Pritchett, "Two Illustrated Epigraphical Notes," *AJA* 73 (1969) 367-370.

*G. M. Lee, "On a Phoenicial Bilingual Inscription at Larnax, Lapethos," *PEQ* 101 (1969) 122.

§940 *4.5.4.1 Greek Correspondence*

Samuel Sharpe, "Three Petitions to King Ptolemy Philometor, from a Monk in the Temple of Serapis," *JSL, 4th Ser.,* 1 (1862) 17-24.

H. I. Bell, "Some private letters of the Roman period from the London Collection," *RÉ, N.S.,* 1 (1919) 199-209.

Adolf Deissmann, "The Letter of Zoilos," *Exp, 8th Ser.,* 24 (1922) 420-429.

Robert Chrisolm Horn, "Interpretation of a Papyrus Letter," *PAPA* 57 (1926) xix-xx.

*A. T. Olmstead, "The Persian Letter in Thucydides," *AJSL* 49 (1932-33) 154-161.

P. M. Fraser and C. H. Roberts, "A New Letter of Apollonius," *CdÉ* 23 (1948) 289-294.

T. C. Skeat, "A Letter from Philonides to Kleon revised (P. Lond. 593 = Crönert, *Raccolta Lumbroso* 530 = *Sammelbuch* 7183)," *JEA* 34 (1948) 80-81.

Francis W. Schehl, "Darius' Letter to Gadatas," *AJA* 54 (1950) 265.

William G. Forrest, "Alexander's Second Letter to the Chians," *Klio* 51 (1969) 201-205.

§941 *4.5.4.2 Greek Epitaphs, Ossuary and Sepulchral Texts*

C. T. Newton, "Observations on an Inscription in an unknown Character, *Found on a Fragment of Base in the Temple of Diana at Ephesus,*" *SBAT* 4 (1875) 334-335.

C. Clermont-Ganneau, "Judaeo-Greek Epitaph from Jaffa," *PEFQS* 9 (1877) 106.

*C. Clermont-Ganneau, "Notes on Hebrew and Jewish Inscriptions," *PEFQS* 23 (1891) 240-243. [II. Jewish Inscriptions on Ossuaries. *b.*, pp. 242-243]

A. S. Murray, "Greek Inscription on a Altar in the Garden of Mentor Mott, Esq., Beyrouth, Found at Beit-Meri, Lebanon," *PEFQS* 30 (1898) 34-35.

Warren J. Moulton, "Twelve Mortuary Inscriptions from Sidon," *AJA* 8 (1904) 283-287.

R. A. Stewart Macalister, "The Erotic Graffito in the Tomb of Apollophanes of Marissa," *PEFQS* 38 (1906) 54-62.

C[laude] R. Conder, "Notes on Palestinian Archaeology. I. The Tomb of Apollophanes," *PEFQS* 38 (1906) 147-148.

R. A. S. Macalister, "Notes and Queries. 3. *The Apollophanes Inscription,*" *PEFQS* 38 (1906) 158-159.

C[laude] R. Conder, "Notes and Queries. 1. *The Apollophanes Text,*" *PEFQS* 38 (1906) 238.

*R. H. Hall, "The *Di-Hetep-suten* Formula. A Funerary Stela of a Man from Gabelen; and other Notes," *SBAP* 30 (1908) 5-12. [From Gebelen: "Kharakein and Kharazieu(?)"; Mōḥōn = Mehendi; A Greek Mummy Ticket]

Hamilton Ford Allen, "Two Mummy-Labels in the Carnegie Museum," *PAPA* 43 (1911) xvi.

H. F. Allen, "Five Greek Mummy-Labels in the Metropolitan Museum, New York," *AJP* 34 (1913) 194-197.

W. Sherwood Fox, "Mummy-Labels in the Royal Ontario Museum," *AJP* 34 (1913) 437-450.

Hamilton Ford Allen, "A Chip of Wood, or Egyptian Mummy Labels," *A&A* 5 (1917) 6-12.

Stephen B. Luce Jr.*[sic]*, "An Attic Grave Stele," *MJ* 8 (1917) 10-14.

Eleanor F. Rambo, "A Group of Funerary Stelae," *MJ* 10 (1919) 149-155.

C. C. Edgar, "More tomb-stones from Tell el Yahoudieh," *ASAE* 22 (1922) 7-16.

J. Garrow Duncan, "A New Greek Inscription from a Greek Cemetery near Safi'," *PEFQS* 56 (1924) 35-40.

J. Garrow Duncan, "The Greek Inscription, Q.S., p. 35 sq.," *PEFQS* 56 (1924) 95-96.

A. D. Nock, "Magical Notes," *JEA* 11 (1925) 154-158.

A. D. Nock, "A curse from Cyrene," *AfRW* 24 (1926-27) 172-173.

C. C. Edgar, "A Greek epitaph from Saqqarah," *ASAE* 27 (1927) 31-32.

E. L. Sukenik, "Gleanings from the Judaeo-Greek Cemetery, Jaffa," *PEFQS* 64 (1932) 83-84.

*M. A. Murray, "Sacred Stones in Ancient Malta," *AEE* 19 (1934) 29-31.

Marcus N. Tod, "A Greek Epitaph from Jaffa," *PEFQS* 67 (1935) 85-86.

*J. Wahrhaftig, "A Jewish Prayer in a Greek Papyrus," *JTS* 40 (1939) 376-381.

V. Tscherikower and F. M. Heichelheim, "Jewish Religious Influence in the Adler Papyri," *HTR* 35 (1942) 25-44.

T. C. Skeat, "An Epitaph from Hermopolis," *JEA* 28 (1942) 68-69.

Antony*[sic]* E. Raubitschek, "The Priestess of Pandrosus," *AJA* 49 (1945) 434-435.

Eugene W. Schweigert, "Some Preliminary Observations on a New Inscription Pertaining to the Eleusinian Mysteries," *AJA* 50 (1946) 287-288.

M. Schwabe, "Varia Epigraphica Judaica IV," *BIES* 13 (1946-47) #1/2, III-IV. *[Inscribed Ossuary]*

David M. Robinson, "Two New Grave Stelae from Deme of Demosthenes," *AJA* 51 (1947) 366-369.

M. Schwabe, "Varia Epigraphica Judaica V-VI," *BIES* 14 (1947-48) #1/2, II. *[Inscribed Ossuary]*

G. E. Bean, "Epitaphs at Alabanda," *AAI* 1 (1955) 52-55.

S. Applebaum, "Three Greek Epitaphs from Teucheria, Cyrenaica," *BIES* 22 (1958) #1/2, VI.

George M. A. Hanfmann and Kelma Ziya Polatkan, "A Sepulchral Stele from Sardis. The Inscription of the Sepulchral Stele," *AJA* 64 (1960) 49-52.

Ned Nabers, "Prayers or Curses? Some Lead Tabellae from Morgantina," *AJA* 69 (1965) 171-172.

Ned Nabers, "Lead *Tabellae* from Morgantina," *AJA* 70 (1966) 67-68.

Robert J. Bull, "A Roman Veteran's Epitaph from Azzun, Jordan," *PEQ* 98 (1966) 163-165.

T. C. Skeat and E. G. Turner, "An Oracle of Hermes Trismegistos at Saqqâra," *JEA* 54 (1968) 199-208.

§942 *4.5.4.3 Greek Historical Texts*

Anonymous, "Decree of the Egyptian Priests in Honour of Ptolemy V," *MMBR* 17 (1804) 410-413.

S. Y., "A Translation of a Greek Inscription, erected to the Honour of Crato, 150 years before Christ," *MMBR* 41 (1816) 102-103.

†Anonymous, "Herodotus—Rawlinson," *BQRL* 28 (1858) 446-485. *(Review)*

†Anonymous, "Rawlinson's *Herodotus*," *ERCJ* 111 (1860) 32-67. *(Review)*

*C. Clermont-Ganneau, "Discovery of a Tablet from Herod's Temple," *PEFQS* 3 (1871) 132-133.

*Thomas W. Ludlow, "The Athenian Naval Arsenal of Philon," *AJP* 3 (1882) 317-328.

†Anonymous, "Sayce's Herodotus," *ERCJ* 159 (1884) 524-560. *(Review)*

*Salomon Reinach and Michael Breal, "Inscribed Base of an Archaic Bronze Statue from Mount Ptous," *AJA* 1 (1885) 358-360.

Isaac H. Hall, "A Greek Inscription from over a city-gate in Beirût," *JAOS* 11 (1885) xli-xlii.

Isaac H. Hall, "An unpublished Introduction to Hesiod's Works and Days," *PAPA* 17 (1885) xxiv-xxvii.

Evelyn Abbott, "On the date of the composition of the History of Herodotus," *JP* 15 (1886) 86-97.

*Fritz Hommel, "The Ten Patriarchs of Berosus," *SBAP* 15 (1892-93) 243-246.

*W. W. Moore, "Recent Discoveries in Palestine," *USR* 4 (1892-93) 177-192. [The Temple Tablet, pp. 185]

Fitz Gerald Tisdall, "The Credibility of Xenophon's Anabasis," *AJA* 6 (1902) 47-48.

*Joseph Offord, "Herodotus and Palmyrene Inscriptions," *AAOJ* 25 (1903) 178.

*F. Ll. Griffith, "The Dodecarchy and the XIIth Dynasty," *ZÄS* 47 (1910) 162.

*Joseph Offord, "A New Inscription Concerning the Jews in Egypt," *PEFQS* 46 (1914) 45-46.

*Francis A. Cunningham, "Daonos and the Babylonian God Ea," *AJA* 19 (1915) 81. *[Berosus]*

*A Marmorstein, "The Inscription of Theodotos," *PEFQS* 53 (1921) 23-28.

Alexander Pogorelski, "The New Athenian Stele with Decree and Accounts," *AJA* 27 (1923) 314-317.

Benjamin D. Meritt, "An Athenian Naval Catalogue," *AJA* 31 (1927) 462-470.

H. J. M. Milne, "A New Speech of Lysias," *JEA* 15 (1929) 75-77.

Christine Alexander, "Abstract of the Articles on Bacchic Inscription in the Metropolitan Museum," *AJA* 37 (1933) 264-270.

Nathaniel Julius Reich, "The Τεεβήσιος υἱοί and their Quarrel with Apollonios," *Miz* 1 (1933) 147-177.

Benjamin D. Meritt and Gladys Davidson, "The Treaty between Athens and Haliai," *AJP* 56 (1935) 65-71.

James Henry Oliver, "The Athenian Decree Concerning Miletus in 450/49 B.C.," *TAPA* 66 (1935) 177-198.

*Philip H. Davis, "The Accounts of the Theatre on Delos," *AJA* 41 (1937) 109.

David M. Robinson, "A New Fragment of the Fifth-Century Athenian Naval Catalogues," *AJA* 41 (1937) 292-299.

C. Bradford Welles, "New Texts from the Chancery of Philip V of Macedonia and the Problem of the 'Diagramma'," *AJA* 42 (1938) 245-260.

A[nton] E. Raubitschek, "Two Monuments Erected after the Victory of Marathon," *AJA* 44 (1940) 53-59.

Anton E. Raubitschek, "The Inscription on the Base of the Athena Promachos Statue," *AJA* 44 (1940) 109.

Benjamin D. Meritt, "Athens and Carthage—A Fifth Century Inscription," *AJA* 44 (1940) 110.

An[ton] E. Raubitschek, "Note on a Study of the Acropolis Dedications," *AJA* 45 (1941) 70.

James H. Oliver, "A Roman Patron of Athens," *AJA* 45 (1941) 89. [IG ii^2 4216]

*Marcus N. Tod, "A Bilingual Dedication from Alexandria," *JEA* 28 (1942) 53-56.

*James H. Oliver, "C. Sulpicius Galba, Proconsul of Achaia," *AJA* 46 (1942) 380-388.

A[nton] E. Raubitschek, "The Ostracism of Xanthippos," *AJA* 51 (1947) 257-262.

Benjamin D. Meritt, "Athens and the Amphiktyonic League," *AJP* 69 (1948) 312-314.

James H. Oliver, "Three Attic Inscriptions Concerning the Emperor Commodus," *AJP* 71 (1950) 170-179.

Robert E. Carter, "A Terracotta Tetrapodiskos Dedication at Corinth," *AJA* 56 (1952) 172.

P. M. Fraser and A. Rumpf, "Two Ptolemaic Dedications," *JEA* 38 (1952) 65-78.

C. Bradford Welles and J. A. S. Evans, "The Archives of Leon," *JJP* 7&8 (1953-54) 29-70.

Haiim B. Rosén, "The Stele of Lemnos, its Texts and Alphabetic System," *SH* 1 (1954) 1-20.

*Alexander Fuks, "The 'Old Oligarch'," *SH* 1 (1954) 21-35.

*J. Gwyn Griffiths, "Three notes on Herodotus, Book II," *ASAE* 53 (1955) 139-152.

*A. E. Wardmann, "Tactics and the Tradition of the Persian Wars," *HJAH* 8 (1959) 49-60.

S. Usher, "Some Observations on Greek Historical Narrative from 400 to 1 B.C. A Study in the Effect of Outlook and Environment on Style," *AJP* 81 (1960) 358-372.

*T. B. Mitford, "Ptolemy son of Pelops," *JEA* 46 (1960) 109-111.

*T. C. Skeat, "Notes on the Ptolemaic Chronology," *JEA* 47 (1961) 107-109. [II. "The Twelfth Year which is also the First": The Invasion of Egypt by Antiochus Epiphanes - (P. Lond. Inv. 1974)]

Alan E. Samuel, "Alexander's 'Royal Journals'," *HJAH* 14 (1965) 1-12.

*Arthur Ferrill, "Herodotus and the Strategy and Tactics of the Invasion of Xerxes," *AHR* 72 (1966-67) 102-115.

*O. W. Reinmuth, "A Working List of the Prefects of Egypt: 30 B.C. - 299 A.D.," *BASP* 4 (1967) 75-128. [Addenda, *BSAP* 5 (1968) 105-106]

Richard P. Harper, "Tituli Comandorum Cappadociae," *AS* 18 (1968) 93-147.

James H. Oliver, "Notes on the Inscription at Teos in Honor of Antiochus III," *GRBS* 9 (1968) 321-322.

Richard P. Harper, "Inscriptiones Comanis Cappadociae in A. D. 1967 Effossae: Titulorum Loci Supplementum," *AS* 19 (1969) 27-40.

§943 *4.5.4.4 Greek Legal and Commercial Texts*

A. C. Merriam, "The Law Code of the Cretan Gortyna," *PAPA* 17 (1885) xxxiv-xxxv.

J. R. Wheeler, "An Attic Decree," *AJA, O.S.,* 3 (1887) 38-49.

F. B. Tarbell, "The Decrees of the Demotionidai. A Study of the Attic Phratry," *AJA, O.S.,* 5 (1889) 135-153.

Anonymous, "Exploration and Discovery. A Tablet of Warning from the Temple of Herod," *BW* 7 (1896) 140-141.

*Charles Clermont-Ganneau, "A Newly Discovered Hebrew and Greek Inscription, Relating to the Boundary of Gezer," *PEFQS* 31 (1899) 118-127.

W. Sherwood Fox, "Two Tabellae Defixionum in the Royal Ontario Museum," *AJA* 17 (1913) 81.

*William B[ell] Dinsmoor, "Attic Building Accounts," *AJA* 17 (1913) 53-80. [I. The Parthenon]

*William Bell Dinsmoor, "Attic Building Accounts," *AJA* 17 (1913) 242-265. [II. The Erechtheum]

*William Bell Dinsmoor, "Attic Building Accounts," *AJA* 17 (1913) 371-398. [III. The Propylaea]

*William Bell Dinsmoor, "Attic Building Accounts," *AJA* 25 (1921) 118-129. [IV. The Statue of Athena Promachos]

*William Bell Dinsmoor, "Attic Building Accounts," *AJA* 25 (1921) 233-247. [V. Supplementary Notes]

*Stanley A. Cook, "The Synagogue of Theodotos at Jerusalem," *PEFQS* 53 (1921) 22-23.

Gerald M. FitzGerald, "Notes on Recent Discoveries. I. *The Theodotus Inscription,*" *PEFQS* 53 (1921) 175-181.

Allen B. West, "Notes on Payments made by the Treasurers of Athena in 416-5 B.C.," *AJA* 29 (1925) 3-16.

Benjamin D. Meritt, "Tribute Assessments in the Athenian Empire from 454 to 440 B.C.," *AJA* 29 (1925) 247-273.

Benjamin D. Meritt, "The Reassessment of Tribute in 438/7," *AJA* 29 (1925) 292-298.

Benjamin D. Meritt, "Notes on the Tribute Lists," *AJA* 29 (1925) 321-324.

Allen B. West and Benjamin D. Meritt, "The Athenian Quota List *I.G.* I^2, 216," *AJA* 29 (1925) 434-439.

Allen B. West and Benjamin D. Meritt, "Fragments of the Attic Tribute Lists," *AJA* 30 (1926) 137-149.

Philip H. Davis, "Two Attic Decrees of the Fifth Century," *AJA* 30 (1926) 177-188. [I. The Cleruchy on Lesbos: *I.G.* I, 96; II. The Alliance of Athens with Perdikkas II of Macedon in 422 B.C.]

*W. L. Westermann, "Orchard and Vineyard Taxes in the Zenon Papyri," *JEA* 12 (1926) 38-51.

David Moore Robinson, "A Deed of Sale at Olynthus," *TAPA* 59 (1928) 225-232.

Benjamin D. Meritt, "The Reconstruction of the Tribute Lists," *AJA* 33 (1929) 376-384.

Benjamin D. Meritt, "The Departure of Alcihbiades for Sicily," *AJA* 34 (1930) 125-152.

W. L. Westermann, "Regarding Receipts in the Zenon Archive," *JEA* 16 (1930) 24-30.

Dorothy Kent Hill, "Some Boundary Stones from the Piraeus," *AJA* 36 (1932) 254-259.

Eugene Vanderpool, "An Athenian Dikast's Ticket," *AJA* 36 (1932) 293-294.

Benjamin D. Meritt, "Fragments of Attic Building Accounts," *AJA* 36 (1932) 472-476.

*Elizabeth Grier, "The Accounts of Wages Paid in Kind in the Zenon Papyri," *TAPA* 63 (1932) 230-244.

Sterling Dow, "Note on Three Decrees of 306-5 B.C.," *AJA* 37 (1933) 412-416.

Sterling Dow, "New Readings in the Archon Lists *I.G.* ^{2} II, 1713 and 1716," *AJA* 37 (1933) 578-588.

Allen B. West, "The Two Callias Decrees," *AJA* 38 (1934) 390-407.

Philip H. Davis, "Some Delian Building Accounts Reconstructed," *AJA* 39 (1935) 117. [*I.G.* XI. 156]

*Allen B. West, "Prosopographical Notes on the Treaty between Athens and Haliai," *AJP* 56 (1935) 72-76.

David M. Robinson, "A New Fragment of the Athenian Decree on Coinage," *AJP* 56 (1935) 149-154.

*Philip H. Davis, "Delian Building Contracts," *AJA* 40 (1936) 122.

*T. C. Skeat, "A Forthcoming Catalogue of Nome Strategi," *Miz* 2 (1936) 30-35.

Esther V. Hansen, "The Victory Monument of Attalus I," *AJA* 41 (1937) 52-55.

A. Billheimer, "Amendments in Athenian Decrees," *AJA* 42 (1938) 456-485.

*William Linn Westermann, "Enslaved Persons Who Are Free. Rainer Papyrus (PER) Inv. 24,552," *AJP* 59 (1938) 1-30.

J. H. Iliffe, "The ΘΑΝΤΟΣ Inscription from Herod's Temple. *Fragment of a second copy,*" *QDAP* 6 (1938) 1-3.

*A. Cameron, "Inscriptions Relating to Sacral Manumission and Confession," *HTR* 32 (1939) 143-179.

F. M. Heichelheim, "An Alexandrian Decree of 175/174 B.C.," *JEA* 26 (1940) 154-156.

Christine Hanson and Franklin P. Johnson, "On Certain Portrait Inscriptions," *AJA* 50 (1946) 389-400.

*Hans Wolff Julius, "Consensual contracts in the papyri?" *JJP* 1 (1946) 54-79.

Benjamin D. Meritt, "An Athenian Treaty with an Unknown State," *AJP* 68 (1947) 312-315.

Eric G. Runer, "A Ptolemaic Vineyard Lease," *BJRL* 31 (1948) 138-161.

*William C. Hayes, "A Foundation Plaque of Ptolemy IV," *JEA* 34 (1948) 114-115.

*Franklin F. Russell, "Note on a Recent Greek Work in Greek Legal History," *SAENJ* 6 (1948) 77-88.

*Leopold Wenger, "Observations concerning the Papyrus Baraize and the Right of Redemption in Hellenistic Law," *JJP* 3 (1949) 9-20.

*F. Pringsheim, "A suggestion on P. Columbia Inv. No 480 (198—197 B.C.)," *JJP* 5 (1951) 115-120. *[Slavery in Egypt]*

*T[ony] Reekmans and E Van't Dack, "A Bodleian Archive on Corn Transport," *CdÉ* 27 (1952) 149-195.

J. J. Rabinovitz, "The Legal Papyrus from 'Auja el-Ḥafir," *BIES* 17 (1952-53) #3/4 II-III.

W. Kendrick Pritchett, "Sales Taxes in Ancient Athens," *Arch* 7 (1954) 112-113.

T. C. Skeat, "A Receipt for *ENKYKLION*," *JEA* 45 (1959) 75-78.

*Kristian Jeppesen, "A Royal Message to Ikaros: The Hellenistic Temples of Failaka," *Kuml* (1960) 187-193. [Appendix: The Ikaros Inscription, pp. 194-198]

Sterling Dow, "The 'Axon' *Inscriptiones Graecae* I^2 2," *AJA* 65 (1961) 349-356.

*L. H. Jeffery, "The Pact of the First Settlers of Cyrene," *HJAH* 10 (1961) 139-147.

Sterling Dow, "The Purported Decree of Themistokles: Stele and Inscription. Notes on the Text by M. H. Jameson," *AJA* 66 (1962) 353-368. ["The Themistokles Decree: Notes on the Text" by Michael H. Jameson, p. 368]

Donald W. Bradeen, "The Fifth-Century Archon List," *AJA* 67 (1963) 208 .

William M. Calder III, "The Historical Occasion of *IG* XIV 268," *AJA* 67 (1963) 209.

*S. Safrai, "The Avoidance of Public Office in Papyrus Oxy. 1477 and in Talmudic Sources," *JJS* 14 (1963) 67-70.

*Richard H. Pierce, "A Note on Some Alleged Certificates of Registration from Ptolemaic Egypt," *Aeg* 44 (1964) 170-173.

Sterling Dow, "The Heading of the Purported Decree of Themistokles," *AJA* 70 (1966) 187.

*T. C. Skeat, "A fragment on the Ptolemaic perfume monopoly," *JEA* 52 (1966) 179-180. [P. Lond. inv. 2859A]

J. David Thomas, "The name lists in the papyrus of the Revenue Laws," *Aeg* 47 (1967) 217-221.

*H. S. Smith, "A Note on Amnesty," *JEA* 54 (1968) 209-214.

Donald R. Laing Jr., "A Newly Constituted Maritime Text," *AJA* 73 (1969) 240. [IG II^2, 1615, 1618. 1619, & 1617]

*Timothy Long, "*P. Hibeh* 154: Export of Wine," *BASP* 6 (1969) 41-43.

§944 *4.5.4.5 Greek Religious Texts*

Edward Capps, "Studies in Greek Agnostic Inscriptions," *TAPA* 31 (1900) 112-137.

[C.] Clermont-Ganneau, "Royal Ptolemaic Greek Inscriptions and Magic Lead Figures from Tell Sandahannah," *PEFQS* 33 (1901) 54-58. (Notes by A. Stuart Murray and C. R. Conder, p. 59; W. H. D. Rouse, p. 60; F. J. Birch, p. 307)

*M. Gaster, "The Logos Ebraikes in the Magical Papyri of Paris, and the Book of Enoch," *JRAS* (1901) 109-117.

George Adam Smith, "Further Notes on the Inscriptions Found at Tell el-'Ash'ari," *PEFQS* 34 (1902) 27-29.

J. R. Wheeler, "Heracles Alexicacus," *AJA* 7 (1903) 85.

C. Clermont-Ganneau, "Archaeological and Epigraphic Notes on Palestine. 24. *Mount Hermon and its God in an inedited Greek Inscription*," *PEFQS* 35 (1903) 135-140, 231-242.

*R. A. S. Macalister, "Notes and Queries. 3. *Note on Objects in the Government Museum at Jerusalem*," *PEFQS* 36 (1904) 402. [2. The Table of Oblations with Greek Inscription from Tell el-Hesy]

*F. Ll. Griffith and U. Wilcken, "A bilingual sale of liturgies in 136 B.C.," *ZÄS* 45 (1908) 103-110.

Gustav Holscher, "Remarks on a Greek Inscription from a Temple at Khurbet Harrawi," *PEFQS* 41 (1909) 149-150. (Note by Stanley A. Cook, p. 232)

*Joseph Offord, "Archaeological Notes. V. *A Memorial of a Citizen of Askalon found in Thessaly*," *PEFQS* 47 (1915) 203-205.

S. Eitrem, "Notes on the magical papyrus, pap. Leid V (Y. 384)," *Aeg* 4 (1923) 59-60.

H. J. M. Milne, "A Prayer for Charaxus," *Aeg* 13 (1933) 176-178.

*C. C. McCown, "A New Deity in a Jerash Inscription," *JAOS* 54 (1934) 178-185. *[Πακειδᾶ]*

Ernst Riess, "Notes, Critical and Explanatory, on the Greek Magical Papyri," *JEA* 26 (1940) 51-56.

Campbell Bonner, "Aeolus Figured on Colic Amulets," *HTR* 35 (1942) 87-93; 37 (1944) 333-334.

M. Schwabe, "Two Funerary Inscriptions from Ascalon and their Archaeological Significance," *BIES* 13 (1946-47) #3/4, VIII.

J. D. Beazley, "Hymn to Hermes," *AJA* 52 (1948) 336-340.

Campbell Bonner, "A Note on Method in the Treatment of Magical Inscriptions," *AJP* 75 (1954) 303-305.

Edward W. Bodnar, "The Isthmian Fortification in Oracular Prophecy," *AJA* 64 (1960) 165-171.

E. R. Dodds, "New Light on the 'Chaldean Oracles'," *HTR* 54 (1961) 263-273.

Naphtali Lewis, "Exemption of Physicians from Liturgy," *BSAP* 2 (1964-65) 87-92.

*Sterling Dow and David H. Gill, "The Greek Cult Table," *AJA* 69 (1965) 103-114.

*Robert F. Healey, "A Calendar of Sacrifices of Eleusis," *AJA* 69 (1965) 169. [*I.G.* II² 1363]

Richard P. Harper, "A Dedication to the Goddess Anaitis at Ortaköy, North of Aksaray, (Nitalis?)," *AS* 17 (1967) 193.

Dorothy Crawford, "A Ptolemaic Petition on Stone," *CdÉ* 42 (1967) 355-359.

§945 *4.5.4.7 Greek Literary Texts*

*†Anonymous, "Allwood's Literary Antiquities of Greece," *BCQTR* 15 (1800) 539-549, 608-618; 16 (1800) 65-77.

Anonymous, "Herculanesia; or Archaeological and Philological Dissertations: containing a Manuscript found among the Ruins of Herculanium," *QRL* 3 (1810) 1-20. [Fragment of a Treatise on Piety, according to Epicurus, pp. 8-15]

†Anonymous, "Stanley's *Æschylus*," *QRL* 3 (1810) 389-398.

†Anonymous, "Blomfield.—*Æsch. Prometheus Vinctus*," *QRL* 5 (1811) 203-229. *(Review)*

†Anonymous, "Translations of Pindar," *QRL* 5 (1811) 437-457. *(Review)*

†Anonymous, Markland's *Euripidis Supplices*, &c.," *QRL* 7 (1812) 441-464. *(Review)*

†Anonymous, "Monk's *Euripidis Hippolytus*," *QRL* 8 (1812) 215-230. *(Review)*

†Anonymous, "Elmsley's *Euripidis Heraclidae*," *QRL* 9 (1813) 348-366. *(Review)*

*†Anonymous, "Ambrosian Manuscripts," *QRL* 16 (1816-17) 321-337. *(Review)*

†Anonymous, "Blomfield—*Æschyli Agamemnon*," *QRL* 25 (1821) 505-529. *(Review)*

†Anonymous, "Panegyrical Oratory of Greece," *QRL* 27 (1822) 382-404. *(Review)*

†Anonymous, "Moore's *Pindar*," *QRL* 28 (1822-23) 410-430. *(Review)*

*†Anonymous, "Merivale's *Anthology*," *QRL* 49 (1833) 349-381. *(Review)*

†Anonymous, "Modern Criticism on Æschylus," *QRL* 64 (1839) 370-395. *(Review)*

†Anonymous, "The Orestea of Æschylus," *QRL* 70 (1842) 315-355. *(Review)*

O. Cockayne, "Suggestions on the Critical Arrangement of the Text of the Medea," *TPS* (1844-46) 21-29.

Samuel Sharpe, "Fragments of Orations in Accusation and Defence of Demoethenes respecting the Money of Harpalus," *TPS* (1848-50) 39-72.

*†Anonymous, "A Critical History of the Language and Literature of Ancient Greece," *CTPR, 3rd Ser.,* 6 (1850) 332-358. *(Review)*

*†Anonymous, "Mure's *Ancient Greek Language and Literature*," *ERCJ* 92 (1850) 398-435. *(Review)*

†Anonymous, "Colonel Mure *on the Literature of Ancient Greece*," *QRL* 87 (1850) 434-468. *(Review)*

†Anonymous, "Badhem's *Euripides*," *QRL* 89 (1851) 196-203. *(Review)*

†Anonymous, "Mure's History of Greek Literature," *BQR* 16 (1852) 418-443. *(Review)*

*†[W. E. Gladstone], "Homer and his Successors in Epic Poetry," *QRL* 101 (1857) 80-122. *(Review)*

†Anonymous, "Epigrams," *QRL* 117 (1865) 204-249. *(Review)*

William W. Goodwin, "Critique on the Text of Thucydides (i. 22)," *JAOS* 8 (1866) xxxi.

†Anonymous, "Grote's *Plato*," *QRL* 119 (1866) 108-153. *(Review)*

†Anonymous, "Jowett's Translation of Plato," *BQRL* 54 (1871) 155-187. *(Review)*

†Anonymous, "Jowett's *Plato*," *QRL* 131 (1871) 492-522. *(Review)*

F. A. Paley, "Pre-Homeric Legends of the Voyage of the Argonauts," *DR, 3rd Ser.,* 1 (1879) 164-182. *[Original numbers as Volume 84]*

Henry Hayman, "Early Greek written literature," *JP* 8 (1879) 133-153.

†Anonymous, "Pindar's Odes of Victory," *QRL* 162 (1886) 156-180. *(Review)*

*†Anonymous, "Aristotle's Theory of Poetry and Fine Art," *ERCJ* 188 91898) 60-77. *(Review)*

†Anonymous, "The Setting of a Greek Play," *QRL* 188 (1898) 360-380. *(Review)*

Walter Woodburn Hyde, "The 'Bacchanals' of Euripides," *RP* 11 (1912) 179-207.

H. J. M. Milne, "A fragment of Xenophon's Symposium viii, 6-9," *Aeg* 4 (1923) 41-42.

A. D. Nock, "A New Edition of the Hermetic Writings," *JEA* 11 (1925) 126-137.

*S. R. K. Glanville, "A Note on Herodotus II, 93," *JEA* 12 (1926) 75-76.

*L. A. Post, "Feminism in Greek Literature," *QRL* 248 (1927) 354-373. *(Review)*

Hetty Goldman, "A Metrical Inscription, from the Necropolis of Eutresis," *AJA* 32 (1928) 178-181.

L. A. Post, "The Genius of Menander," *QRL* 250 (1928) 353-367.

W. A. Oldfather, "An Aesopic Fable in a Schoolboy's Exercise," *Aeg* 10 (1929) 255-256.

Burton Scott Easton, "Pseudo-Phocylides," *ATR* 14 (1932) 222-228.

James Oliver, "Notes and Comments. The Epigram on the Fallen at Marathon," *A&A* 34 (1933) 103.

Campbell Bonner, "A Fragment of a Romance (University of Michigan Inv. N. 3378)," *Aeg* 13 (1933) 203-207.

F. C. S. Schiller, "The Evolution of Plato's Republic," *Person* 15 (1934) 327-340.

Sterling Dow, "New Kinds of Evidence of Dating Polyeuktos," *AJA* 40 (1936) 57-70.

W. B. Sedgwick, "Light Reading in Ancient Greece," *QRL* 270 (1938) 250-263. *(Review)*

*Solomon Gandz, "The dawn of literature. Prolegomena to a history of unwritten literature," *Osiris* 7 (1939) 261-522. [Chapter XV.—*The Greeks,* pp. 401-415]

Paul C. Smither, "The Tall Story of the Bull," *JEA* 27 (1941) 158-159.

Eduard Fraenkel, "Aeschylus: New Texts and Old Problems," *PBA* 28 (1942) 237-258.

Alexander Turyn, "The Manuscripts of Sophocles," *Tr* 2 (1944) 1-42.

Jacqueline Chittenden, "Diaktoros Argeiphontes," *AJA* 52 (1948) 24-33.

Joshua Whatmough, "ΩΣΠΕΡ ΟΜΗΡΟΣ ΦΗΣΙ," *AJA* 52 (1948) 45-50. [Corrections, *AJA* 54 (1950), p. 203]

*Moses Hadas, "Third Maccabees and Greek Romance," *RR* 13 (1948-49) 155-162.

*Thalia Phillies Howe, "Illustrations to Aeschylos' Tetralogy on the Terseus Theme," *AJA* 57 (1953) 109.

H. D. Westlake, "The Sicilian Books of Theopompus' *Philippica,*" *HJAH* 2 (1953-54) 288-307.

*Philip Merlan, "Isocrates, Aristotle and Alexander the Great," *HJAH* 3 (1954-55) 60-81.

*William M. Calder III, "An Unrecognized Metrical Text from Temple G at Selinus," *AJA* 61 (1957) 182. *[Greek Marching Song]*

*P. Walcot, "Hesiod and the Instructions of 'Onchsheshonqy," *JNES* 21 (1962) 215-219.

*Rhys Carpenter, "'Once We Dwelt in Well-Watered Corinth'," *AJA* 67 (1963) 209.

Alan E. Samuel, "P. Beinecke Inv. 4, A New Fragment of Demosthenes," *BASP* 2 (1964-65) 33-40.

William M. Calder III, "A New Verse Inscription from Selinus," *AJA* 69 (1965) 262-264.

Eugene Vanderpool, "Pan in Paiania.   A Note on Lines 407-409 of Meander's *Dyskolos*," *AJA* 71 (1967) 309-311.

Walton Morris, "Observations on Meander's: *Dyscolus* 95-102," *BSAP* 4 (1967) 55-57.

*Rosamond Kent Sprague, "Logic and Literary Form in Plato," *Person* 48 (1967) 560-572.

E. L. Burge, "The Irony of Socrates," *AASCS* 3 (1969) 5-17.

A. W. James, "Some Examples of Imitation in the Similes of Later Greek Epic," *AASCS* 3 (1969) 78-90.

*Sterling Dow, "Some Athenians in Aristophanes," *AJA* 73 (1969) 234-235. [IG II^2 2343]

*P. Walcot, "The Comparative Study of Ugaritic and Greek Literature," *UF* 1 (1969) 111-118.

Yu. G. Vinogradov, "Cyclic Poetry in Olbia," *VDI* (1969) #3, 150.

§946 *4.5.4.6.1 Studies on Homer and His Writings*

Anonymous, "The Lycæum of Ancient Literature—No. I.," *MMBR* 22 (1806-07) 552-555. [The Epopæa of Homer]

†Anonymous, "Origin of the Homeric Poems," *QRL* 44 (1831) 121-168. *(Review)*

†G. H. L., "The Homeric Poems," *WR* 46 (1846-47) 195-213. *(Review)*

*†[W. E. Gladstone], "Homer and his Successors in Epic Poetry," *QRL* 101 (1857) 80-122. *(Review)*

James Hadley, "On Bekker's Digammated Text of Homer," *JAOS* 8 (1866) x-xi.

†Anonymous, "Homer and his Translators," *BQRL* 41 (1865) 290-324. *(Review)*

†Anonymous, "Homer's Illiad," *QRL* 117 (1865) 93-113. *(Review)*

†Anonymous, "The Homeric Question," *QRL* 125 (1868) 440-473. *(Review)*

†F. A. P[aley] "The Odyssey of Homer," *BQRL* 58 (1873) 414-445. *(Review)*

†Anonymous, "On the Antiquity of Our Homer," *CQR* 11 (1880-81) 421-430.

*Anonymous, "Writing in Homer," *MR* 78 (1896) 139-140.

A. W. Verrall, "The First Homer," *QRL* 209 (1908) 53-77. *(Review)*

*Joseph Offord, "Notes and Queries. 1. *A MS. of Homer at Jerusalem,*" *PEFQS* 44 (1912) 158. [Oxyrhynchus (#412)]

Henry Balfour, "The Archer's Bow in the Homeric Poems. An Attempted Diagnosis. *The Huxley Memorial Lecture for* 1921," *JRAI* 51 (1921) 289-309.

*J. Penrose Harland, "Scripta Helladica and the Dates of Homer and the Hellenic Alphabet," *AJA* 38 (1934) 83-92.

*Oliver Davies, "Three Great Anatolian Authors: Homer, Hipponax and Herodotus," *IAQR* 41 (1945) 387-388.

*H. L. Lorimer, "Homer and the Art of Writing: A Sketch of Opinion between 1713 and 1939," *AJA* 52 (1948) 11-23. [Corrections, *AJA* 54 (1950) p. 203]

Albert B. Lord, "Homer, Parry, and Huso," *AJA* 52 (1948) 34-44.

Sterling Dow, "Forward to Homer Supplement," *AJA* 54 (1950) 161.

W[illiam] F[oxwell] Albright, "Some Oriental Glosses on the Homeric Problem," *AJA* 54 (1950) 162-176.

Rhys Carpenter, "Argeiphontes: A Suggestion," *AJA* 54 (1950) 177-183.

C. M. Bowra, "The Comparative Study of Homer," *AJA* 54 (1950) 184-192.

Cornelia Catlin Coulter, "'A Song for Men in Days to Come'," *AJA* 54 (1950) 193-202.

Carl Roebuck, "Homer: The Ionian Background," *AJA* 59 (1955) 175-176.

James A. Notopoulos, "Homeric Formulae and Originality," *AJA* 59 (1955) 176.

*T. B. L. Webster, "Homer and the Mycenaean Tablets," *Antiq* 29 (1955) 10-14.

*L. J. D. Richardson, "Further Observations on Homer and the Mycenaean Tablets," *Herm* #86 (1955) 50-65.

Francis R. Bliss, "Homer and the Critics: The Structural Unity of *Odyssey* Eight," *BUS* 16 (1968) #3, 53-73.

§947 *4.5.4.7 Greek Medical, Astronomical, Geographical, Mathematical and "Scientific" Texts*

*Edgar Johnson Goodspeed, "The Ayer Papyrus: A Mathematical Fragment," *AJP* 19 (1898) 25-39.

*Edgar J. Goodspeed, "A Medical Papyrus Fragment," *AJP* 24 (1903) 327-329.

W. H. S. Jones, "'Hippocrates' and the *Corpus Hippocraticum*," *PBA* 31 (1945) 103-125.

*Sterling Dow, "Greek Numerals," *AJA* 56 (1952) 21-23.

O. Neugebauer, "Melothesia and Dodecatemoria," *SBO* 3 (1959) 270-275.

*Otto Neugebauer, "The Greek Mathematical Ostracon Crum 480," *CdÉ* 41 (1966) 160.

§948 *4.5.4.8 Greek Papyri [See also: Papyrology - General Studies §822; Egyptian Papyri - Unclassified §847; Demotic Papyri - Unclassified §848 ←]*

†Anonymous, "The New Papyri," *QRL* 172 (1891) 320-350. *(Review)*

Anonymous, "More Papyri," *MR* 82 (1900) 809-812. *[Oxyrhynchus]*

George Melville Bolling, "An Epic Fragment from Oxyrhynchus," *AJP* 22 (1901) 63-69.

F. C. Burkitt, "Fragments of some Early Greek MSS. on Papyrus," *SBAP* 24 (1902) 290-292. [Odyssey XII, 279-304]

*F. G. Kenyon, "The Evidence of Greek Papyri with Regard to Textual Criticism," *PBA* 1 (1903-04) 141-168.

Edgar J. Goodspeed, "Biblical Texts from the Papyri," *BW* 36 (1910) 67-68. *[Oxyrhynchus]*

*Joseph Offord, "Notes and Queries. 1. *A MS. of Homer at Jerusalem*," *PEFQS* 44 (1912) 158. [Oxyrhynchus (#412)]

Anonymous, "Papyri of the Græco-Egyptian Period," *RP* 11 (1912) 283.

H. I. Bell, "Syene Papyri in the British Museum," *Klio* 13 (1913) 160-174.

*J. de M. Johnson, "Antionë and its Papyri. Excavation by the Graeco-Roman Branch, 1913-14," *JEA* 1 (1914) 168-181.

*C. C. Edgar, "On the dating of early Ptolemaic papyri," *ASAE* 17 (1917) 209-223.

C. C. Edgar, "Selected papyri from the archives of Zenon (nos. 1-10)," *ASAE* 18 (1918) 159-182.

C. C. Edgar, "Selected papyri from the archives of Zenon (nos. 11-21)," *ASAE* 18 (1918) 225-244.

B. P. Grenfell, "New Papyri from Oxyrhynchus," *JEA* 5 (1918) 16-23.

C. C. Edgar, "Selected papyri from the archives of Zenon (nos. 22-36)," *ASAE* 19 (1919) 13-36.

C. C. Edgar, "Selected papyri from the archives of Zenon (nos. 37-48)," *ASAE* 19 (1919) 81-104.

*Joseph Offord, "Archaeological Notes on Jewish Antiquities. LIX. *Newly-published Palestinian Papyri,*" *PEFQS* 51 (1919) 184-186.

C. C. Edgar, "Selected papyri from the archives of Zenon (nos. 49-54)," *ASAE* 20 (1920) 19-40.

C. C. Edgar, "Selected papyri from the archives of Zenon (nos. 55-64)," *ASAE* 20 (1920) 181-206.

*Warren R. Dawson, "Egyptological Notes," *IAQR* 16 (1920) 337-340, 520-522. [1. The Historical Value of Greek Papyri, pp. 331-338]

H. Idris Bell, "The Historical Value of Greek Papyri," *JEA* 6 (1920) 234-246.

C. C. Edgar, "Selected papyri from the archives of Zenon (nos. 65-66)," *ASAE* 21 (1921) 89-109.

A. E. R. Boak, "A Zenon Letter of 256 B.C.: Papyrus Michigan 45," *Aeg* 3 (1922) 284-286.

C. C. Edgar, "Selected papyri from the archives of Zenon (nos. 67-72)," *ASAE* 22 (1922) 209-231.

A. E. R. Boak, "The University of Michigan Collection of Papyri," *Aeg* 4 (1923) 38-40.

S. Eitrem, "Notes on Pap. Soc. It. I 28 and 29," *Aeg* 4 (1923) 61-62.

C. C. Edgar, "Selected papyri from the archives of Zenon (nos. 73-88)," *ASAE* 23 (1923) 73-98, 187-209.

W. L. Westermann and A. G. Laird, "A New Zenon Papyrus at the University of Wisconsin," *JEA* 9 (1923) 81-90.

C. C. Edgar, "Selected papyri from the archives of Zenon (nos. 89-111)," *ASAE* 24 (1924) 17-52.

*S. Eitrem, "Notes on the magical papyrus, pap. Leid. V (Y. 384)," *Aeg* 4 (1923) 59-60.

*S. Eitrem, "Additional remarks on the magical papyrus, P. Leid. V. (continued from Vol. IV p. 183)," *Aeg* 6 (1925) 117-120.

S. Eitrem, "Pap. Brit. Mus. CXXI, Verso Col. I," *JEA* 11 (1925) 80-83.

Shirley Howard Weber, "Two Papyri from the Princeton Collection," *PAPA* 56 (1925) xlii.

L. D. Barnett, "The Alleged Kanarese Speeches in P. Oxy. 413," *JEA* 12 (1926) 13-15.

A. S. Hunt, "A Zenon Papyrus at Corpus Christi College, Cambridge," *JEA* 12 (1926) 113-115.

G. M. Bolling, "The New Ptolemaic Papyrus containing Parts of *Iliad,* XII, 128-263," *JEA* 14 (1928) 78-81.

C. C. Edgar, "Three Ptolemaic Papyri," *JEA* 14 (1928) 288-293.

James H. Oliver, "The ΒΟΥΛΗ papyrus," *Aeg* 11 (1930-31) 161-168.

C. C. Edgar, "A New Group of Zenon Papyri," *BJRL* 18 (1934) 111-130.

Anonymous, "Notes and Comments. 'The Lighter Side of the Greek Papyri'," *A&A* 34 (1933) 273-274.

Gertrude Malz, "Another Zenon Papyrus at the University of Wisconsin," *AJA* 39 (1935) 373-377.

Stanley Casson, "Early Greek Inscriptions on Metal: Some Notes," *AJA* 39 (1935) 510-517.

C. C. Edgar, "On P. Lille I. 4," *JEA* 23 (1937) 261.

*V. Tscherikower, "Palestine under the Ptolemies (A Contribution to the Study of the Zenon Papyri)," *Miz* 4&5 (1937) 9-90.

G. E. Kirk, "Three Greek Inscriptions from the Southern Desert," *PEQ* 70 (1938) 234-237.

*J. Gwyn Griffiths, "P. Oslo. 1, 105-9 and Metternich Stela, 85-6," *JEA* 25 (1939) 101.

O. M. Pearl, "Varia Papyrologica," *TAPA* 71 (1940) 372-390.

H. G. Meecham, "Some Notes on P. Ryl. III," *JEA* 32 (1946) 102.

*Hans Wolff Julius, "Consensual contracts in the papyri?" *JJP* 1 (1946) 54-79.

*Herbert C. Youtie, "The *Kline* of Sarapis," *HTR* 41 (1948) 9-30. *[P. Mich. Inv. 4686]*

John Barns, "Three Fayûm Papyri," *CdÉ* 24 (1949) 295-305. [I. Letter of Heraclitus to Dorion. (195 or 171 B.C.); 2. Affidavit of a Legionary (A.D. 92); 3. Petition to an Eirenophylax (Late 2nd Century)]

Harold Bell, "A Note on P.S.I. 1160," *JEA* 35 (1949) 167-169.

Raphael Taubenschlag, "Papyri and Parchments from the Eastern Provinces of the Roman Empire outside Egypt," *JJP* 3 (1949) 49-61.

T. Reekmans and E. Van't Dack, "A 2nd Century B.C. Petition (Bodleian Ms. Gr. Class. c (87) P)," *RIDA, 1st Ser.,* 5 (1950) 417-427.

*F. Pringsheim, "A suggestion on P. Columbia Inv. No 480 (199—197 B.C.)," *JJP* 5 (1951) 115-120. *[Slavery in Egypt]*

T. B. L. Webster, "Note: Addendum to Rendel Harris Papyri No 56," *JJP* 5 (1951) 237.

C. H. Roberts and E. G. Turner, "The beginning and the date of P. Ryl. IV. 586 (Plate I)," *JEA* 39 (1953) 113-114.

*C. H. Roberts, "The Rylands Collection of Greek and Latin Papyri," *BJRL* 36 (1953-54) 97-110.

E. P. Wegener, "Miscellanea Papyrologica," *JJP* 9&10 (1955-56) 97-116.

C. H. Roberts, "A Papyrus of Isoctrates in Erlangen," *JJP* 9&10 (1955-56) 135-136.

*Jacob J. Rabinowitz, "Miscellanea Papyrologica," *JJP* 11&12 (1957-58) 167-183. [P. Lond. 1711 and Jewish Talmudic Sources: 1. The General Hypothec Formula; 2. The Husband's Undertaking to Maintain and Clothe the Wife; 3. The Husband's Undertaking Not to Divorce the Wife Except for Certain Causes; 4. Proof by Three or More Villagers or City-dwellers; 5. ἔργῳ καὶ δυνάμει; 6. Ἀξιόποστος and ἐλεύθερος; II. Aramaic Papyrus Brookly*[sic]* 7 and P. Freib. III 29; III. A Note on the ΠΡΑΚΤΩΡ ΞΕΝΙΚΩΝ; The Meaning of ΑΛΛΟΣΣΩ in Some Papyri from Karanis]

*E. K. Borthwick, "The Oxyrhynchus Musical Monody and Some Ancient Fertility Superstitions," *AJP* 84 (1963) 225-243. [Oxy. 2436]

S. G. Kapsomenos, "The Orphic Papyrus Roll of Thessalonica," *BSAP* 2 (1964-65) 3-12. (Discussion, pp. 13-32)

Willy Morel, "Notes on Two Literary Papyri," *BSAP* 2 (1964-65) 79-82. [P. Oxy 2335; P. Oxy 2454]

Linda Fay Kaufman, "Two Papyri at Wellesley College," *BASP* 3 (1965-66) 29-31. [P. Oxy 824; P. Oxy 1578]

Gerald M. Browne, "*P. Hibeh* 133: A Reconsideration," *BASP* 3 (1965-66) 85-88.

John Shelton, "Account," *BASP* 3 (1965-66) 89-92. [P. Hib. 135 McCormick Theological Seminary BH 88442.4]

Roger O. Pack, "A Concordance to Literary Papyri: Basic Publications and Pack[2]," *BASP* 3 (1965-66) 95-118.

R. A. Coles, "More Papyri from the British Museum," *JEA* 53 (1967) 121-130. [5.) P. Lond. inv. 2210]

Paul R. Swarney, "Two McCormick Papyri. Fragments of an Account," *BASP* 5 (1968) 114-117, 120. [BH 88442.4 (*P. Hib.* 135)]

William H. Willis, "A Census of the Literary Papyri from Egypt," *GRBS* 9 (1968) 205-241.

*Floyd V. Filson, "Ancient Greek Synagogue Inscriptions," *BA* 32 (1969) 41-46.

Donald F. Jackson, "The Papyri of Xenophon's Hellencia," *BASP* 6 (1969) 45-52.

Roger S. Bagnall, "Some Notes on P. Hib. 198," *BASP* 6 (1969) 73-118.

P. W. Pestman, "A Greek Testament from Pathyris (P. Lond. inv. 2850)," *JEA* 55 (1969) 129-160.

§949 *4.5.5 Cypriote Texts*

R. Hamilton Lang, "On the Discovery of some Cypriote Inscriptions," *SBAT* 1 (1872) 116-128.

G. Smith, "On the Reading of the Cypriote Inscriptions," *SBAT* 1 (1872) 129-144.

Samuel Birch, "Cypriote Inscriptions. On the Reading of the Inscription on the Bronze Plate of Dali [Idailum]," *SBAT* 1 (1872) 153-172.

D. Pierides, "On a Digraphic Inscription found in Larnaca," *SBAT* 4 (1875) 38-43.

H. F. Talbot, "On the Cypriote Inscriptions," *SBAT* 5 (1876-77) 447-455.

Paul Schroeder, "On a Cypriote Inscription, now in the Imperial Ottoman Museum at Constantinople," *SBAT* 6 (1878-79) 134-143.

Isaac H. Hall, "Notes on certain Cypriote Inscriptions," *SBAT* 6 (1878-79) 203-208.

Isaac H. Hall, "On Moriz Schmidt's 'Collection of Cypriote Inscriptions'," *JAOS* 10 (1880) clvii-clx.

Isaac H. Hall, "On the cypriote Inscriptions of the new Cesnola Collection," *JAOS* 10 (1880) clxiii-clxiv.

Isaac H. Hall, "The Cypriote Inscriptions of the Cesnola Collection in New York," *JAOS* 11 (1882-85) 209-238.

Isaac H. Hall, "On the Cesnola Cypriote Inscriptions in New York," *JAOS* 11 (1882-85) cc.

A. H. Sayce, "New Cypriote Inscriptions from Abydos and Thebes," *SBAP* 6 (1883-84) 209-222.

A. H. Sayce, "The Kypriote Graffiti of Abydos," *SBAP* 7 (1884-85) 36-41.

A. H. Sayce, "New Kypriote Inscriptions discovered by Dr. Max Ohnefalsh-Richter," *SBAP* 9 (1886-87) 5-10.

†A. H. Sayce, "Kypriote Inscriptions in Egypt," *SBAP* 8 (1885-86) 158-159.

*William Wright, "Two Bilingual Inscriptions, Phoenician and Cypriote," *SBAP* 9 (1886-87) 47-49. (Remarks by P. le Page Renouf, pp. 49-51)

*C. J. Ball, "New readings of the Hieroglyphs from Northern Syria," *SBAP* 10 (1887-88) 437-449. *[Cypriote syllabary, pp. 437-438]*

Isaac H. Hall, "Further Inscriptions from the Cesnola Collection in New York," *JAOS* 13 (1889) xlviii-l.

I[saac] H. Hall, "Further Inscriptions in the Metropolitan Museum of Art, New York," *JAOS* 13 (1889) xclv-xclvi.

*Hyde Clarke, "Cypriote and Khita," *SBAP* 12 (1889-90) 462-470.

*I[saac] H. Hall, "On a scarab seal with a Cypriote inscription in the Metropolitan Museum of Art, New York," *JAOS* 15 (1893) ccviii-ccix.

Anonymous, "Syllabaric Inscriptions Found on Cyprus," *RP* 9 (1910) 344.

E. Power, "The decipherment of the inscriptions of Amathus," *B* 11 (1930) 235-249.

*J. L. Myers, "A Cypro-Mycenæan Inscription from Enkomi, near Salamis in Cyprus," *Man* 34 (1934) #26.

*Arthur Evans, "Note on a Cypro-Mycenæan Inscription from Enkomi," *Man* 34 (1934) #27.

John Franklin Daniel, "The Inscribed Pithoi from Kourion," *AJA* 43 (1939) 102-103.

Stanley Casson, "The Cypriot Script of the Bronze Age," *Iraq* 6 (1939) 39-44.

Wm. T. M. Forbes, "The Inscription of the Eleusis Vase," *AJA* 53 (1949) 356-357.

Tom B. Jones, "Notes on the Eteocypriote Inscriptions," *AJP* 71 (1950) 401-407.

Tom B. Jones, "The Eleusis Vase," *AJA* 55 (1951) 67.

Porphyrios Dikaios, "An Inscribed Tablet from Enkomi, Cyprus," *Antiq* 27 (1953) 103-105.

Porphyrios Dikaios, "A Second Inscribed Clay Tablet from Enkomi," *Antiq* 27 (1953) 233-237.

*Claude F. A. Schaeffer, "More Tablets from Syria and Cyprus," *Antiq* 28 (1954) 38-39.

Jacqueline V. Karogeorghis, "Some Inscribed Iron-Age Vases from Cyprus. II. The Inscriptions," *AJA* 60 (1956) 354-359.

P[orphyrios] Dikaios, "A New Inscribed Clay Tablet from Enkomi," *Antiq* 30 (1956) 40-41.

M. Ventris, "Notes on the Enkomi 1955 Tablet," *Antiq* 30 (1956) 41-42.

J. L. Benson and Oliver Masson, "Cypro-Minoan Inscriptions from Bamboula, Kourion. General Remarks and New Documents," *AJA* 64 (1960) 145-151.

‡Mme Ino Michaelidou-Nicolaou, "Inscriptiones Cypriae Alphabeticae 1960-1961, I.," *Bery* 14 (1961-63) 129-141.

T. B. Mitford, "Unpublished Syllabic Inscriptions of the Cyprus Museum," *Minos* 7 (1961-63) 15-48.

Jacqueline [V.] Karageorghis and Vassos Karageorghis, "Syllabic Inscriptions from Cyprus 1959-1961," *KZFE* 1 (1962) 143-150.

Porphyrios Dikaios, "The Context of the Enkomi Tablets," *KZFE* 2 (1963) 39-52.

*Michael C. Astour, "Second Millennium B.C. Cypriot and Creatan Onomastica Reconsidered," *JAOS* 84 (1964) 240-254.

Roland F. Willetts, "The Birmingham Symposium on Aegean Writing," *KZFE* 7 (1968) 176-178.

§950 *4.5.6 "Myceanæan" / Minoan Texts*

Rudolf Herzog, "On the Survival of Pre-Hellenic Signs in the Island of Kos," *Man* 1 (1901) #52.

Anonymous, "The Written Documents of Minoan Crete," *RP* 8 (1909) 167.

*F. W. Read, "A New Interpretation of the Phaestos Disk: The Oldest Music in the World?" *PEFQS* 53 (1921) 29-54.

R. A. S. Macalister, "The Phaestos Disc," *PEFQS* 53 (1921) 141-145.

F. Melian Stawell, "Suggestions Towards an Interpretation of the Minoan Scripts," *AJA* 28 (1924) 120-141.

*J. L. Myers, "A Cypro-Mycenæan Inscription from Enkomi, near Salamis in Cyprus," *Man* 34 (1934) #26.

*Arthur Evans, "Note on a Cypro-Mycenæan Inscription from Enkomi," *Man* 34 (1934) #27.

*K. Kourouniotis and Carl W. Blegen, "Archaeological Notes: Excavations at Pylos, 1939," *AJA* 43 (1939) 557-576.

Emmett L. Bennett Jr., "The Syllabary of the Linear Script B at Pylos and Knossos," *AJA* 46 (1942) 124.

A[lice] E. Kober, "Some Comments on a Minoan Inscription (Linear Class B)," *AJA* 46 (1942) 124.

A[lice] E. Kober, "The 'Adze' Tablets from Knossos," *AJA* 48 (1944) 64-75.

Alice E. Kober, "The Minoan Scripts: Fact and Theory," *AJA* 52 (1948) 82-103. [Corrections, *AJA* 54 (1950) p. 203]

John L. Myers, "The Minoan Script, According to Professor Bedřich Hrozný," *AJA* 52 (1948) 104-106.

George E. Mylonas, "Prehistoric Greek Scripts," *Arch* 1 (1948) 210-220.

*Emmett L. Bennett Jr., "Fractional Quantities in Minoan Bookkeeping," *AJA* 54 (1950) 204-222.

Alice [E.] Kober, "A note on some 'cattle' tablets from Knossos," *JKF* 1 (1950-51) 142-150.

*Bedřich Hrozný, "New Contribution to Knowledge of the Religious, Social and Public Conditions on the Peloponnesus (E. L. Bennett, The Pylos Tablets, Preliminary Transcription)," *JJP* 6 (1952) 11-13.

A. J. B. Wace, "The Discovery of Inscribed Clay Tablets at Mycenae," *Antiq* 27 (1953) 84-86.

Emmett L. Bennett Jr., "The Mycenae Tablets," *PAPS* 97 (1953) 422-470. [Introduction by Alan J. B. Wace, pp. 422-426]

William F. Arndt, "Progress in Deciphering the Minoan Script," *CTM* 25 (1954) 230-231.

Emmett L. Bennett Jr., "Junctions of Fragments of Minoan Inscriptions in Iraklion Museum," *Minos* 3 (1954) 122-125. (Corrections, p. 168)

L. R. Palmer, "Mycenaean Greek Texts from Pylos," *TPS* (1954) 18-53.

*Emmett L. Bennett Jr., "The Landholders of Pylos," *AJA* 59 (1955) 176; 60 (1956) 103-133.

*T. B. L. Webster, "Homer and the Mycenaean Tablets," *Antiq* 29 (1955) 10-14.

*L. J. D. Richardson, "Further Observations on Homer and the Mycenaean Tablets," *Herm* #86 (1955) 50-65.

Emmett L. Bennett Jr., "A List of Corrections," *Minos* 4 (1956) 66-69.

Michael Ventris, "Miscelanea. Some Comments on *Minos* IV: 1," *Minos* 4 (1956) 167-168.

‡Martín S. Ruipérez, "Miscelanea. Chronique Bibliographique sur le Linéaire B.," *Minos* 4 (1956) 175-179.

‡Olivier Masson, "Bibliographie Chypro-Minoeene 1941-1956," *Minos* 4 (1956) 179-180.

J. K. Anderson, "Note on 'Landholders of Pylos'," *AJA* 61 (1957) 174-175.

T. B. L. Webster, "Mycenaean Records: A Review," *Antiq* 31 (1957) 4-8.

Cyrus H. Gordon, "Notes on Minoan Linear A," *Antiq* 31 (1957) 124-130.

Cyrus H. Gordon, "Akkadian Tablets in Minoan Dress," *Antiq* 31 (1957) 237-240.

L. R. Palmer, "A Mycenaean Tomb Inventory," *Minos* 5 (1957) 58-92.

Emmett L. Bennett Jr., "Notes on Two Broken Tablets from Pylos," *Minos* 5 (1957) 113-116.

F. J. Tritsch, "PY Ad 684," *Minos* 5 (1957) 154-162.

‡Martín S. Ruipérez, "Miscelanea. Chronique Bibliographique sur le Linéaire B.," *Minos* 5 (1957) 212-216.

*W. French Anderson, "Arithmetical Procedure in Minoan Linear A and in Minoan-Greek Linear B," *AJA* 62 (1958) 363-368.

Maurice Pope, "The Linear A Question," *Antiq* 32 (1958) 97-99.

Cyrus H. Gordon, "Minoan Linear A," *JNES* 17 (1958) 245-255.

A. J. Beattie, "A Plain Guide to the Ventris Decipherment of the Mycenaean Linear B Script," *MIO* 6 (1958) 33-104.

T. B. Mitford, "The Tsepis Stele and Some Others," *Minos* 6 (1958-60) 37-54.

‡Emilio Peruzzi, "Miscelanea. Chronique Bibliographique sur le Linéaire A," *Minos* 6 (1958-60) 67.

‡M[artín] S. Ruipérez, "Miscelanea. Chronique Bibliographique sur le Linéaire B.," *Minos* 6 (1958-60) 67-73, 165-178; 7 (1961-63) 171-191.

John Chadwick, "A Critical Appendix to the Pylos Tablets (1955)," *Minos* 6 (1958-60) 138-148.

Emmett L. Bennett Jr., (ed.), "The Mycenae Tablets II," *TAPS, N.S.,* 48 (1958) Part 1, 1-122. [Introduction by Alan J. B. Wace and Elizabeth B. Wace; Translations and Commentary by John Chadwick]

L. R. Palmer, "New Religious Texts from Pylos," *TPS* (1958) 1-35.

Francis T. Gignac, "The Decoding of Linear B," *TFUQ* 33 (1958-59) 255-271.

*Mabel Lang, "The Palace of Nestor Excavations of 1958 - Part II," *AJA* 63 (1959) 128-137. *[Minoan Texts]*

*Thalia Phillies Howe, "Linear B and Hesiod's Bread-winners," *AJA* 63 (1959) 189.

John Chadwick, "Minoan Linear A: A Provisional Balance Sheet," *Antiq* 33 (1959) 269-278.

Benjamin Schwartz, "The Phaistos Disk," *JNES* 18 (1959) 105-112.

Benjamin Schwartz, "The Phaistos Disk II," *JNES* 18 (1959) 222-226.

Benjamin Schwartz, "Notes and Afterthoughts on the Phaistos Disk Solution," *JNES* 18 (1959) 227-228.

E. Peruzzi, "Recent Interpretations of Minoan (Linear A)," *Word* 15 (1959) 313-324.

Carl W. Blegen, "A necessary corrective to Beattie's article in *MIO* VI, 33-104," *MIO* 7 (1959-60) 180-183.

Emmett L. Bennett Jr., "Anonymous Writers in Mycenaean Palaces," *Arch* 13 (1960) 26-32.

Cyrus H. Gordon, "The Language of the Hagia Triada Tablets," *Klio* 38 (1960) 63-68.

Sinclair Hood, "The Date of the Linear B Tablets from Knossos," *Antiq* 35 (1961) 4-7.

W. D. Taylour, "New Linear B Tablets from Mycenae," *Antiq* 35 (1961) 57-58.

L. R. Palmer, "The Find Places of the Knossos Tablets," *Antiq* 35 (1961) 135-141.

John Broadman, "The Knossos Tablets: an Answer," *Antiq* 35 (1961) 233-235.

L. R. Palmer, "The Knossos Tablets: Some Clarifications," *Antiq* 35 (1961) 308-311.

William F. Wyatt Jr., "The Ma Tablets from Pylos," *AJA* 66 (1962) 21-41.

Sinclair Hood, "The Knossos Tablets: A Complete View," *Antiq* 36 (1962) 38-40.

John Broadman, "The Knossos Tablets: Again," *Antiq* 36 (1962) 49-51.

Cyrus H. Gordon, "Minoica," *JNES* 21 (1962) 207-210.

*Victor E. G. Kenna, "Seals and Script with special reference to ancient Crete," *KZFE* 1 (1962) 1-15.

William C. Brice, "Some Observations on the Linear A inscriptions," *KZFE* 1 (1962) 42-48.

George E. Mylonas, "An Inscribed Sherd from Mycenae," *KZFE* 1 (1962) 95-97.

W[illiam] C. Brice, "Remarks on ILA II 7a," *KZFE* 1 (1962) 165-166.

Kristian Jeppesen, "Some Remarks on the Archaeological Placing of the Phaistos Disc," *Kuml* (1962) 180-189.

John Chadwick (ed.), "The Mycenae Tablets III," *TAPS, N.S.,* 52 (1962) Part 7, 3-76. [With contributions from Emmett L. Bennett Jr.; Elizabeth B. French; William Taylour; Nicholas M. Verdelis; Charles K. Williams]

*William C. Brice and Ernest Grumach, "Studies in the Structure of Some Ancient Scripts," *BJRL* 45 (1962-63) 15-57. [II. The Question of Ligatured Signs in the Cretan Linear Scripts, pp. 40-57]

Gregory Nagy, "Greek-like Elements in Linear A," *GRBS* 4 (1963) 181-211.

*Victor E. G. Kenna, "Seals and Script II," *KZFE* 2 (1963) 1-6.

*William C. Brice, "A Comparison of the Account Tablets of Susa in the Proto-Elamite Script with those of Hagia Triada in Linear A," *KZFE* 2 (1963) 27-38.

John Chadwick, "Note on an inscribed sherd from Mycenae," *KZFE* 2 (1963) 75-76.

Ernest Grumach, "Studies in the Structure of Some Ancient Scripts. III. The Structure of the Cretan Hieroglyphic Script," *BJRL* 46 (1963-64) 346-384.

J. Boardman and L. R. Palmer, "The Knossos Tablets," *Antiq* 38 (1964) 45-51.

*Michael C. Astour, "Second Millennium B.C. Cypriot and Cretan Onomastica Reconsidered," *JAOS* 84 (1964) 240-254.

*Victor E. G. Kenna, "Seals and Script III: Cretan Seal Use and the Dating of Linear Script B," *KZFE* 3 (1964) 29-57.

Sinclair Hood, "Inscribed Cup from a Late Minoan I B Deposit at Knossos," *KZFE* 3 (1964) 111-113.

James T. Hooker, "The 'Unity of the Archives' at Knossos," *KZFE* 3 (1964) 114-121.

Spyros Jakovidis, "An inscribed Mycenaean Amulet," *KZFE* 3 (1964) 149-155.

Mark A. S. Cameron, "Four Fragments of wall paintings with Linear A inscriptions," *KZFE* 4 (1965) 7-15.

*James T. Hooker, "Sets and Files within the Knossos Tablets," *KZFE* 4 (1965) 86-95.

Anthony M. Snodgrass, "The Linear B Arms and Armour Tablets—again," *KZFE* 4 (1965) 96-110.

Mark A. S. Cameron, "The Wall Paintings with linear signs from the 'House of the Frescoes'," *KZFE* 4 (1965) 170-171.

*Margaret A. V. Gill, "Seals and Sealings: some comments. The Knossos Sealings with Linear B Inscriptions," *KZFE* 5 (1966) 1-16.

John Chadwick, and John T. Killen, "On the Reading of the Knossos Tablets," *Klio* 46 (1966) 93-101.

Michael C. Astour, "The Problem of Semitic in Ancient Crete," *JAOS* 87 (1967) 290-295. *(Review)*

James T. Hooker, "Linear A inscriptions from Knossos," *KZFE* 6 (1967) 110-113.

Margaret A. V. Gill, "On the authenticity of the Middle Minoan half-cylinder Oxford 1938. 790," *KZFE* 6 (1967) 114-118.

Arthur J. Beattie, "Some notes on readings in the Pylian Ta tablets," *KZFE* 6 (1967) 119-122.

Ernst Grumach, "The Minoan libation formula–again," *KZFE* 7 (1968) 7-26.

Mark A. S. Cameron, "The painted signs on fresco fragments from the 'House of the Frescoes'," *KZFE* 7 (1968) 45-64.

George E. Mylonas, "A tablet from Mycenae," *KZFE* 7 (1968) 65-66.

Mark A. S. Cameron, "A graffito related to a myrtle composition on a Minoan fresco from Knossos," *KZFE* 7 (1968) 97-99.

Victor E. G. Kenna, "The authenticity of the half-cylinder AM 1938. 790," *KZFE* 7 (1968) 175-176.

William C. Brice, "Epigraphische Mitteilungen," *KZFE* 7 (1968) 180-181. [Linear A, p. 181]

M. L. Voskresensky and V. P. Mazarov, "An Experiment in Interpreting Eteocretan Inscriptions (A preliminary report)," *VDI* (1968) #2, 94.

Keith Branigan, "The earliest Minoan scripts—the pre-palatial background," *KZFE* 8 (1969) 1-22.

Mervyn Popham, "An LM III B inscription from Knossos," *KZFE* 8 (1969) 43-45.

William C. Brice, "The Linear A tablets IV 8 and IV 9 from Tylissos," *KZFE* 8 (1969) 120-130.

*William C. Brice, "Epigraphische Mitteilungen," *KZFE* 8 (1969) 164-167. [General; Early Elamite Inscriptions; Cretan Cave Art; The Minoan Hieroglyphic Script; Early Linear Inscriptions; Linear A; Two Decipherments; 'The Coming of the Greeks']

John Chadwick, "Linear B Tablets from Thebes," *Minos* 10 (1969) 115-137.

§951 *4.5.7 Latin Texts*

*†Anonymous, "Ambrosian Manuscripts," *QRL* 16 (1816-17) 321-337. *(Review)*

†Anonymous, "History of Roman Literature," *QRL* 52 (1834) 57-95. *(Review)*

†Anonymous, "Life and Writings of Horace," *QRL* 62 (1838) 287-332. *(Review)*

*E. Robinson and G. B. Whiting, "Notes on Biblical Geography," *BS* 5 (1848) 79-97. [The Inscriptions, pp. 86-91]

†Anonymous, "Horace and His Translators," *QRL* 104 (1858) 325-361. *(Review)*

†Anonymous, "The English Translators of Virgil," *QRL* 110 (1861) 73-114. *(Review)*

George M. Lane, "On the Composition of the Amphitruo of Plautus," *JAOS* 7 (1862) xiv.

Theodore D. Woolsey, "On Ritschl and Mommsen's New Corpus of Latin Manuscripts," *JAOS* 8 (1866) xix.

†Anonymous, "Lord Lython's *Horace*," *QRL* 127 (1869) 478-493. *(Review)*

*C. Clermont-Ganneau, "Notes on Certain New Discoveries at Jerusalem," *PEFQS* 3 (1871) 103-107. [2. Roman Inscription, pp. 103-104]

†Anonymous, "The Satires of Horace: Professor Conington and Mr. Theodore Martin," *QRL* 130 (1871) 513-534. *(Review)*

†Anonymous, "Horace," *QRL* 174 (1892) 127-157. *(Review)*

Anonymous, "A Bronze Medal from Jaulan," *PEFQS* 26 (1894) 152.

†Anonymous, "Horace and his Translators," *QRL* 180 (1895) 111-137. *(Review)*

Minton Warren, "On the Contributions of the Latin Inscriptions to the Study of the Latin Language and Literature," *TAPA* 26 (1895) 16-27.

A. H. Sayce, "Roman Inscriptions at Assuan," *SBAP* 18 (1896) 107-109.

Joseph Offord, "Roman Inscriptions relating to Hadrian's Jewish War," *SBAP* 20 (1898) 56-69, 189.

C. A. Hornstein, "Latin Inscription Found at Baalbeck," *PEFQS* 32 (1900) 74-75.

*H. Porter, "A Cuneiform Tablet, Sarcophagus, and Cippus with Inscription, in the Museum at Beirut," *PEFQS* 32 (1900) 123-124. *[Latin Inscription]*

Joseph Offord, "Inscriptions relating to the Jewish War of Vespasian and Titus," *SBAP* 24 (1902) 325-328.

*George Hempl, "The Duenos Inscription," *TAPA* 33 (1902) 150-169.

Joseph Offord, "Inscriptions relating to the Jewish War of Vespasian and Titus *(continued)*," *SBAP* 25 (1903) 30-33.

*David M. Robinson, "Greek and Latin Inscriptions from Sinope and Environs," *AJA* 9 (1905) 294-333.

*Albert W. Van Buren, "Notes on Dr. D. M. Robinson's *Inscriptions from Sinope*," *AJA* 10 (1906) 295-299.

*David M. Robinson, "Mr. Van Buren's Notes on Inscriptions from Sinope," *AJA* 10 (1906) 429-433.

Minton Warren, "On the Stele Inscription in the Roman Forum," *PAPA* 38 (1906) xxxiii-xxxiv.

C. R. Morey, "Inscriptions from Rome," *AJA* 10 (1906) 427-428.

George N. Olcott, "Latin Inscriptions—Inedited or Corrected," *AJA* 10 (1906) 154-158.

Henry H. Armstrong, "The Autobiographic Element in Latin Literature and Inscriptions. Part I," *RP* 6 (1907) 111-116.

Henry H. Armstrong, "The Autobiographic Element in Latin Literature and Inscriptions. Part II," *RP* 6 (1907) 141-145.

George N. Olcott, "Unpublished Latin Inscriptions," *AJA* 12 (1908) 39-46.

*David M. Robinson, "Greek and Latin Inscriptions at Sardes," *AJA* 14 (1910) 414-416.

(Miss) Florence M. Bennett, "The Duenos Inscription," *PAPA* 42 (1910) xxi-xxiv.

Mary Bradford Peaks, "The Date of the Duenos Inscription," *PAPA* 43 (1911) xxxix-xli.

Joseph Offord and H. H. Clifford Gibbon, "Recently Found Inscriptions Relating to Roman Campaigns in Palestine," *PEFQS* 43 (1911) 91-97.

H. H. Clifford Gibbons, "Further Note on Inscriptions Relating to Roman Campaigns in Palestine," *PEFQS* 43 (1911) 192-194.

*Joseph Offord, "Jewish Notes," *PEFQS* 46 (1914) 46-47.

James A. Montgomery, "A Latin Inscription and Some Other Antiquities in Southern Lebanon," *AJA* 20 (1916) 75.

John C. Rolfe, "Latin Inscriptions at the University of Pennsylvania," *AJA* 20 (1916) 173-174.

*Joseph Offord, "Archaeological Notes on Jewish Antiquities. XXIII. *Latin Inscriptions from Lebanon and Arabia*," *PEFQS* 48 (1916) 193-194.

R. V. D. M[agoffin], "A Fine Latin Inscription," *A&A* 6 (1917) 165.

*Asad Rustum, "New Traces of the Old Lebanon Forest," *PEFQS* 54 (1922) 68-71.

*Eric Burrows, "Ḫurrian Sala(s)," *JRAS* (1927) 318-320. *[Latin Text]*

Lily Ross Taylor and Allen B West, "Latin Elegiacs from Corinth," *AJA* 32 (1928) 9-22.

Henry A. Sanders, "The wax tablet, PSI. IX, 1027," *Aeg* 11 (1930-31) 185-189.

Louise Adams Holland, "Qui Terminum Exarasset," *AJA* 37 (1933) 549-553.

Paul Jacobstall, "On Livy XXXVI, 40 (Boiian Silver)," *AJA* 47 (1943) 306-312. [Errata, *AJA* 48 (1944) p. 350]

E. G. Turner, "P Aberdeen 133 and P. Berlin 6866," *JEA* 33 (1947) 92.

T. Robert S. Broughton, "The *Elogia* of Julius Caesar's Father," *AJA* 52 (1948) 323-330.

Howard Comfort, "An Insulting Latin Graffito," *AJA* 52 (1948) 321-322.

Herbert C. Youtie, "Records of a Roman Bath in Upper Egypt," *AJA* 53 (1949) 268-270.

Arthur E. Gordon, "A New Fragment of the *Laudatio Turiae*," *AJA* 54 (1950) 223-226.

*Anthony E. Raubitschek, "International Epigraphy," *Arch* 5 (1952) 119-120.

*C. H. Roberts, "The Rylands Collection of Greek and Latin Papyri," *BJRL* 36 (1953-54) 97-110.

*L. R. Lind, "Nine Inscriptions and a Roman Brick Stamp in Kansas," *AJA* 59 (1955) 159-162.

*R. MacMullen, "Inscriptions on Armor and the Supply of Arms in the Roman Empire," *AJA* 64 (1960) 23-40.

*Kevin Herbert, "Greek and Latin Inscriptions at Bowdoin," *AJA* 66 (1962) 381-387.

*W. M. Gordon, "Interruption of *Usucapio*," *RIDA, 3rd Ser.*, 9 (1962) 325-333.

*Barbara Levick, "Unpublished Inscriptions from Pisidian Antioch," *AS* 17 (1967) 101-121.

§952 **4.5.8 Persian Texts, including the Behistun Inscription**
[See also: The Behistun Inscription §879 ←]

*†Anonymous, "Persian and Assyrian Inscriptions—Monuments of Darius Hystapes," *QRL* 79 (1846-47) 413-449. *(Review)*

†(   ) C., "Persian Cuneiform Inscriptions," *WR* 52 (1850) 39-56.

J. W. Donaldson, "On the restoration of an ancient Persian Inscription, analogous to those at Behistun," *JRAS* (1856) 1-8.

*Wm. Henry Green, "The Persian Cuneiform Inscriptions the Key to the Assyrian," *PQPR* 2 (1873) 274-292.

*†Theo[philus] G. Pinches, "Exhibition of Photograph of Inscription from Hamadan," *SBAP* 7 (1884-85) 132-133. *[Ancient Persian]*

*E. A. Wallis Budge, "On a Babylonian weight with a trilingual inscription," *SBAP* 10 (1887-88) 464-466. *[Persian]*

A.-H. Sayce*[sic]*, "Amardian or 'Ptromedic' Tablets in the British Museum," *RTR* 13 (1890) 126-131. [K. 1325; S 2144; S. 691; K. 4697; K. 4713*b*]

*B. T. A. Evetts, "A trilingual inscription of Artaxerxes Mnemon," *ZA* 5 (1890) 410-417. *[Persian]*

E. Scneider, "A Pelasgic Inscription on 'the Tomb of Midas'," *IAQR, 2nd Ser.,*9 (1895) 220. (Remarks by H[erbert] de Reuter, p. 220)

E. Scneider, "The Eugubine Tablets and the Oscan Inscription," *IAQR, 3rd Ser.,* 1 (1896) 160-165. (Remarks by Herbert de Reuter, pp. 165-166)

*Louis H. Gray, "Stylistic Parallels Between the Assyro-Babylonian and the Old Persian Inscriptions," *AJSL* 17 (1900-01) 151-159.

Louis H. Gray, "Notes on the Old Persian Inscriptions of Behistun," *JAOS* 23 (1902) 56-64.

*Lawrence Mills, "The Cyrus Vase Inscription and Behistūn," *IAQR, 3rd Ser.,* 17 (1904) 319-325.

Lawrence Mills, "The Cyrus Vase Inscription: Ezra and Isaiah," *IAQR, 3rd Ser.,* 18 (1904) 83-86.

Lawrence Mills, "The Cyrus Vase Inscription: Ezra and Isaiah," *IAQR, 3rd Ser.,* 18 (1904) 83-86.

*A. V. Williams Jackson, "Textual Notes on the Old Persian Inscriptions," *JAOS* 27 (1906) 190-194. [1. OP. *patiyāvahyaiy* (sic) Bh. 1. 55; 2. Dar. Pers. c = Spiegal L.; 3. Dar. Pers. d. = Spiegal H.; 4. Dar. Pers. e. = Spiegel I.; 5. Xerx. Pers. a = Spiegal Xerx. D; 6. Xerx. Pers. b = Spiegel A (p. 62); 7. Kerman inscription of Darius]

*A. H. Sayce, "Recent Oriental Archaeology. Legal and Commercial," *ET* 19 (1907-08) 498-499. [Assyrian, Neo-Babylonian, and Persian Legal Documents] *(Review)*

*L[awrence H.] Mills, "The Stone-Sculptured Texts and the Manuscripts of Old Persia: Their Harmony and Authority," *IAQR, 3rd Ser.,* 28 (1909) 330-334.

*L. H. Gray, "Iranian Miscellanies," *JAOS* 33 (1913) 281-294. [b. A New Fragment of the Avesta, pp. 284-285; d. Parsī-Persian Omen Calendar, pp. 288-293]

James R. Ware and Roland G. Kent, "The Old Persian Cuneiform Inscriptions of Artaxerxes II and Artaxerxes III," *TAPA* 55 (1924) 52-61.

*Sidney Smith, "Archaeological Notes," *JRAS* (1926) 433-446. [Inscription of Darius on Gold Tablet, pp. 433-435] *(Persian Text)*

Samuel Feigin, *"Al-la Ilâni,"* *AJSL* 43 (1926-27) 304-305.

Louis H. Gray, "Persian Version of the Darius Gold Tablet," *JRAS* (1927) 97-101.

Carl D. Buck, "A New Darius Inscription," *Lang* 3 (1927) 1-5.

Roland G. Kent, "The Recently Published Old Persian Inscriptions," *JAOS* 51 (1931) 189-240.

A. W. Davis, "An Achæmenian Tomb-Inscription at Persepolis," *JRAS* (1932) 373-377. (Note by C. J. Gadd, p. 377)

A. H. Sayce, "Persian plaque with cuneiform inscription discovered at Saqqara," *AfO* 8 (1932-33) 225.

*A. T. Olmstead, "The Persian Letter in Thucydides," *AJSL* 49 (1932-33) 154-161.

Roland G. Kent, "A New Inscription of Xerxes," *Lang* 9 (1933) 35-46.

Roland G. Kent, "Another Inscription of Xerxes," *Lang* 9 (1933) 229-231.

E. Denison Ross, "Persia's Contribution to Literature," *OC* 47 (1933) 21-27.

Roland G. Kent, "More Old Persian Inscriptions," *JAOS* 54 (1934) 34-52.

Isidore Dyen, "A Dubious Old Persian Tablet in Philadelphia," *JAOS* 56 (1936) 91-93.

Roland G. Kent, "The Present Status of Old Persian Studies," *JAOS* 56 (1936) 208-225.

M. Sprengling, "A New Pahlavi Inscription," *AJSL* 53 (1936-37) 126-144.

Roland G. Kent, "The *Daiva*-Inscription of Xerxes," *Lang* 13 (1937) 292-305.

Roland G. Kent, "The Restoration of Order by Darius," *JAOS* 58 (1938) 112-121.

*Arno Poebel, "The King of the Persepolis Tablets: The Nineteenth Year of Artaxerxes I," *AJSL* 56 (1939) 301-304.

Roland G. Kent, "The Nakš-i Rustam Inscriptions of Darius," *Lang* 15 (1939) 160-177.

M. Sprengling, "Pahlavi Notes," *AJSL* 58 (1941) 169-176.

Roland G. Kent, "Old Persian Studies," *JAOS* 62 (1942) 266-277.

*Richard T. Hallock, "Darius I, King of the Persepolis Tablets," *JNES* 1 (1942) 230-232.

Roland G. Kent, "Old Persian Texts," *JNES* 1 (1942) 415-423. [I. The Darius Suez c Inscription; II. An Inscription of Darius II]

Roland G. Kent, "Old Persian Texts III: Darius' Behistan Inscription, Column V," *JNES* 2 (1943) 105-114.

Roland G. Kent, "Old Persian Texts. IV: The Lists of Provinces," *JNES* 2 (1943) 302-306.

George G. Cameron, "Darius, Egypt, and the 'Lands Beyond the Sea'," *JNES* 2 (1943) 307-313. [Persepolis e (DPe)]

Roland G. Kent, "Old Persian Texts: V. Darius's Behistan Inscription, Column V: A Correction," *JNES* 3 (1944) 232-233.

*W. B. Henning, "The Murder of the Magi," *JRAS* (1944) 133-144. [TM 393; M. 549]

Roland G. Kent, "Old Persian Texts: VI. Darius' Naqš-i-Rustam B Inscription," *JNES* 4 (1945) 39-52.

Roland G. Kent, "Old Persian Texts: VII. Artaxerxes I, Persepolis A," *JNES* 4 (1945) 228-232.

Roland G. Kent, "Old Persian Texts: VIII. Addenda on Naqš-i-Rustam B," *JNES* 4 (1945) 232.

Roland G. Kent, "Old Persian Texts: IX. Naqš-i-Rustam D," *JNES* 4 (1945) 233.

Roland G. Kent, "The Oldest Old Persian Inscriptions," *JAOS* 66 (1946) 206-212.

Roland G. Kent, "On Some Old Persian Inscriptions of Darius I," *JAOS* 67 (1947) 30-33.

Richard N. Frye, "An Epigraphical Journey in Iran, 1948," *Arch* 2 (1949) 186-192.

*Hildegard Lewy, "The Babylonian Background of the Kay Kâûs Legend," *ArOr* 17 (1949) Part 2, 28-109.

Herbert H. Paper, "An Old Persian Text of Darius II *(D2Ha)*," *JAOS* 72 (1952) 169-170.

J. Harmatta, "A Recently Discovered Old Persian Inscription," *AAASH* 2 (1953-54) 1-14.

*David Stronach, "Excavations at Pasargadae: Second Preliminary Report," *Iran* 2 (1964) 21-39. [The Zendan Inscription, pp. 38-39]

*J. Harmatta, "The Bisitun Inscription and the Introduction of the Old Persian Cuneiform Script," *AAASH* 14 (1966) 255-283.

George G. Cameron, "An Inscription of Darius from Pasargadae," *Iran* 5 (1967) 7-10.

Carl Nylander, "Who Wrote the Inscriptions at Pasagadae? Achaemenian Problems, III," *OrS* 16 (1967) 135-180.

B. Gharib, "A newly found Old Persian Inscription," *IA* 8 (1968) 54-69.

§953 *4.5.9 Other Literature and Inscriptions - General Studies*

Daniel Sharpe, "On certain Lycian Inscriptions copied by the Rev. E. T. Daniell, Edward Forbes, Esq. and Lieut. Spratt, R.N.," *TPS* (1842-44) 193-215.

E. Thomas, "Sassanian Inscriptions," *JRAS* (1868) 241-358.

*John P. Peters, "Miscellaneous Notes," *AJSL* 1 (1884-85) 115-199. [An Aramaean Inscription, pp. 115-116]

*†Theo[philus] G. Pinches, "Exhibition of Photograph of Inscription from Hamadan," *SBAP* 7 (1884-85) 132-133. *[Median(?)]*

*A. H. Sayce, "The Karian Language and Inscriptions," *SBAT* 9 (1886-93) 112-154.

*E. W. West, "Notes on Indo-Scytian Coin-Legends," *BOR* 2 (1887-88) 236-239.

Robert Brown Jr., "The Etruscan Inscription of Lemnos," *SBAP* 10 (1887-88) 316-328, 346-358.

*E. A. Wallis Budge, "On a Babylonian weight with a trilingual inscription," *SBAP* 10 (1887-88) 464-466. *[Susian]*

J. Imbert, "Notes on the writings of the Lycian Monuments," *BOR* 3 (1888-89) 252-259.

W. Arkwright, "On a Lycian Inscription," *BOR* 4 (1889-90) 176-181.

*B. T. A. Evetts, "A trilingual inscription of Artaxerxes Mnemon," *ZA* 5 (1890) 410-417. *[Median(?)]*

*A[ngus] C[rawford], "Archæological Notes," *PER* 5 (1891-92) 363-365. [Etruscan Inscription and Merenptah, p. 363]

A. H. Sayce, "Notes on an Aramaean Inscription from Egypt," *PEFQS* 24 (1892) 251.

J.. G. R. Forlong, "'The Sacred Books of the East' Series. Pahlavi Texts, Part IV, Translated by E. W. West, and the Chronology of the Zendavesta," *IAQR, 2nd Ser.,* 6 (1893) 410-421.

J. Imbert, "On Two Lycian Inscriptions," *BOR* 7 (1893-94) 87-92.

A. H. Sayce, "The Karian and Lydian Inscriptions," *SBAP* 17 (1895) 39-43, 207.

L[awrence] H. Mills, "Fourteenth Review of the 'Sacred Books of the East' Series. Clarendon Press, Oxford. The Zend Avesta. Part II. Translated by James Darmesteter. (Vol. XXII)," *IAQR, 3rd Ser.,* 3 (1897) 129-137.

L[awrence] H. Mills, "Fifteenth Review of the 'Sacred Books of the East' Series. Clarendon Press, Oxford. (Vol. XVIII.) Palhlavi Texts. Part II. The Dâdistân-î-dînîk and the Epistles of Mânûskîhar. Translated by E. W. West," *IAQR, 3rd Ser.,* 3 (1897) 375-380.

L[awrence] H. Mills, "Sixteenth Review of the 'Sacred Books of the East' Series. Clarendon Press, Oxford. (Vol. XXIV.) Pahlavi Texts. Part III. Dînâ-î-Maînog-î Khirad, Sikand-Gûmânîk Vigâr Sad Dar. Translated by E. W. West," *IAQR, 3rd Ser.,* 4 (1897) 103-110.

G. Legrain, "Inscriptions from Gebel Abou Gorab," *SBAP* 27 (1905) 129.

*A. H. Sayce, "An Inscription of S-ankh-ka-Ra; Karian and other Inscriptions," *SBAP* 28 (1906) 171-177.

John L. Myres, "Midas beyond the Halys: a further note on the Black Stone from Tyana," *AAA* 1 (1908) 13-16. *[Phrygian]*

*A. H. Sayce, "Karian, Aramaic, and Greek Graffiti from Heshan," *SBAP* 30 (1908) 28-29.

*A. H. Sayce, "Karian, Egyptian and Nubian-Greek Inscriptions from the Sudan," *SBAP* 32 (1910) 261-268. [Karian Inscriptions, pp. 261-262]

Albert Thumb, "Lydian Inscriptions from Sardes," *AJA* 15 (1911) 149-160. [Prefatory note by Howard Crosby Butler, pp. 149-152] *(Trans. by R. E. Brünnow)*

*Charles C. Torrey, "The Bilingual Inscription from Sardis," *AJSL* 34 (1917-18) 185-198. *[Lydian and Aramaic]*

A. Cowley, "The Pahlavi Document from Avroman," *JRAS* (1919) 147-154. *[Iranian]*

*A. Rowe, "An Egypto-Karian Bilingual Stele in the Nicholson Museum of the University of Sydney," *JRAS* (1920) 85-95.

George W. Elderkin, "The Lydian Bilingual Inscription," *AJA* 29 (1925) 87-89.

George W. Gilmore, "The Lydian Inscriptions," *HR* 89 (1925) 184-185.

C. W. M. Cox and A. Cameron, "A native inscription from the Myso-Phrygian Borderland," *Klio* 25 (1932) 34-49. *[Phrygian]*

George W. Elderkin, "The Twenty-Sixth Lydian Inscription," *AJA* 37 (1933) 387-396.

Eva Fiesel, "The Inscription on the Etruscan Bulla," *AJA* 39 (1935) 195-197.

H. M. Hoenigswald, "Campanian Inscriptions at Yale," *AJA* 45 (1941) 582-586. *[Etruscan]*

W. B. Henning, "A new Parthian Inscription," *JRAS* (1953) 132-136.

Ilya Gershevitch, "A Parthian Title in the Hymn of the Soul," *JRAS* (1954) 124-126. *[Iranian]*

W. B. Henning, "'Surkh Kotal'," *BSOAS* 18 (1956) 366-367. *[Bactrian]*

F. V. Winnett, "Thamudic Inscriptions from the Negev," *'Atiqot* 2 (1959) 146-149.

*John Walker, "The Liḥyānite Inscription on South Arabian coins," *RDSO* 34 (1959) 77-81.

W. B. Henning, "The Bactrian inscription," *BSOAS* 23 (1960) 47-55.

*W. B. Henning, "A Bactrian Seal-Inscription," *BSOAS* 25 (1962) 335.

Cyrus H. Gordon, "Eteocretan," *JNES* 21 (1962) 211-214.

*Cyrus H. Gordon, "The Dreros Bilingual," *JSS* 8 (1963) 76-79.

J. Harmatta, "The Great Bactrian Inscription," *AAASH* 12 (1964) 373-471.

J. Harmatta, "Minor Bactrian Inscriptions," *AAASH* 13 (1965) 149-205.

*Simon Pembroke, "Last of the Matriarchs: A Study in the Inscriptions of Lycia," *JESHO* 8 (1965) 217-247.

*Jan Dus, "The Dreros Bilingual and the Tabernacle of Ancient Israelites," *JSS* 10 (1965) 54-57. [Comment by Professor C. H. Gordon, pp. 57-58]

*Giovanni Colonna, "The Sanctuary at Pyrgi In Etruria," *Arch* 19 (1966) 11-23. [Etruscan Text, pp. 22-23] *(Trans. by Lionel Casson)*

*A. Jamme, "Sabaean and Ḥasaean Inscriptions from Saudi Arabia," *SSR* 23 (1966) 1-107.

M. S[inclair] F. Hood, "The Tartaria Tablets," *Antiq* 41 (1967) 99-113. *[Romainan]*

George M. A. Hanfmann and Olivier Masson, "Carian Inscriptions from Sardis and Stratonikeia," *KZFE* 6 (1967) 123-134. *[Karian] (Latter part of article in French)*

Eužen Neustupný, "The Tartaria Tablets: a Chronological Issue," *Antiq* 42 (1968) 32-35. *[Romanian]*

J. Mackay, "The Tartaria Tablets," *Or, N. S.,* 37 (1968) 272-289. *[Romanian]*

J. Hartmatta, "Late Bactrian Inscriptions," *AAASH* 17 (1969) 297-432.

§954 *4.5.10 Forgeries, includes Texts and Antiquities [See also: The "Shapira Manuscripts" §863 ←]*

M. B., "The Pretend Patriarchal Inscriptions of Arabia," *DUM* 24 (1844) 724-740. *(Review)*

A. Van Name, "On some alleged Phenician[sic]* and Nabathean Inscriptions recently received from Palestine," *JAOS* 10 (1880) xlix.

*W[illiam] H. Ward, "On the Pseudo-Phœnician Inscription of Brazil," *JAOS* 10 (1880) lxxxv-lxxxvi.

J. Ménant, "Forgeries of Assyrian and Babylonian Antiquities," *AJA, O.S.,* 3 (1887) 14-31.

William Hayes Ward, "Assryo-Babylonian Forgery," *AJA, O.S.,* 3 (1887) 383-384.

*Charles C. Torrey, "Semitic Epigraphical Notes," *JAOS* 24 (1903) 205-226. [IV. On a Palestinian 'Forgery', pp. 209-210]

(Miss) Margaret E. Pinney, "Modern Forgeries of Greek Terra-cottas," *AJA* 28 (1924) 79.

W. R. Taylor, "A Jerusalem Forgery of the Balustrade Inscription of Herod's Temple," *JPOS* 13 (1933) 137-139.

Edith Hall Dohan, "A Ziro Burial and a Forgery," *AJA* 38 (1934) 185.

*S. Yeivin, "Miscellanea Archæologica," *ASAE* 34 (1934) 114-124. [II. The Berlin Stele 22485, pp. 121-124]

W. R. Taylor, "A Second Forgery of the Balustrade Inscription of Herod's Temple," *JPOS* 16 (1936) 37-38.

Charles C. Torrey, "A Forged Phoenician Royal Inscription in the Louvre," *AJSL* 58 (1941) 135-138.

*J. Duncan M. Derrett, "Greece and India: the Milindapañha, the Alexander-romance and the Gospels," *ZfRG* 19 (1967) 33-64.

P. M. Fraser, "Some Alexandrian Forgeries," *PBA* 47 (1961) 243-248. *[Alexander Book]*

Richard Stillwell, "An Antique Theme with Variations: 'Etruscan' Sculpture of the Twentieth Century," *AJA* 67 (1963) 194-195.

John D. Cooney, "Assorted Errors in Art Collecting," *Exped* 6 (1963-64) #1, 20-27.

Ellen L. Kohler, "Ultimatum to Terracotta-Forgers," *Exped* 9 (1966-67) #2, 16-21.

P[eter] M. Fraser, "The 'Alexander-Book' of M. Komoutsos once more," *CdÉ* 42 (1967) 209-211.

*C[yrus] H. Gordon, "The Authenticity of the Phoenician Text from Parahyba," *Or, N.S.,* 37 (1968) 75-80.

*C[yrus] H. Gordon, "The Canaanite Text from Brazil," *Or, N. S.,* 37 (1968) 425-436.

*F[rank] M. Cross Jr., "The Phoenician Inscription from Brazil.   A Nineteenth-Century Forgery," *Or, N.S.,* 37 (1968) 437-460. [Reply by C. H. Gordon, pp. 461-463]

Erle Leichty, "A Remarkable Forger," *Exped* 12 (1969-70) #3, 17-21. [CBS 192-311]

About the Author

William G. Hupper studied at Florida Beacon College and Gordon College. He has continued scholarly pursuits in Ancient Near Eastern studies and biblical languages, as an avocation, studying Hebrew under a private tutor. Software developed by him for Macintosh™ computers to produce Egyptian hieroglyphics on screen and in print is available commercially. Articles by Mr. Hupper appear in theological journals, as well as official government documents related to his vocation. He has been a member of the Society of Biblical Literature for over twenty-five years. Presently residing in Torrance, CA, he is employed in the traffic department of a multi-national manufacturing firm.